SCANDERBEIDE

THE OTHER VOICE IN EARLY MODERN EUROPE

A Series Edited by Margaret L. King and Albert Rabil Jr.

RECENT BOOKS IN THE SERIES

Margherita Sarrocchi

SCANDERBEIDE

The Heroic Deeds of George Scanderbeg, King of Epirus

ॐ

Edited and Translated
by Rinaldina Russell

THE UNIVERSITY OF CHICAGO PRESS
Chicago & London

Margherita Sarrocchi, c. 1560–1617

Rinaldina Russell is professor emerita of European languages and literatures at the City University of New York, Queens College. Among her publications are *Sister Maria Celeste's Letters to Her Father, Galileo* (2001) and an edition of Tullia d'Aragona's *Dialogue on the Infinity of Love* (1997), the latter published by the University of Chicago Press.

The University of Chicago Press, Chicago 60637
The University of Chicago Press, Ltd., London
© 2006 by The University of Chicago
All rights reserved. Published 2006
Printed in the United States of America

15 14 13 12 11 10 09 08 07 06 1 2 3 4 5

ISBN-13: 978-0-226-73507-8 (cloth)
ISBN-13: 978-0-226-73508-5 (paper)

ISBN-10: 0-226-73507-9 (cloth)
ISBN-10: 0-226-73508-7 (paper)

The University of Chicago Press gratefully acknowledges the generous support of James E. Rabil, in memory of Scottie W. Rabil, toward the publication of this book.

Library of Congress Cataloging-in-Publication Data

Sarrocchi, Margherita, ca. 1560–1617.
   [Scanderbeide. English]
   Scanderbeide : the heroic deeds of George Scanderberg, King of Epirus / Margherita Sarrocchi ; edited and translated by Rinaldina Russell.
      p. cm. — (The other voice in early modern Europe)
   Includes bibliographical references and index.
   ISBN 0-226-73507-9 (cloth : alk. paper) —
   ISBN 0-226-73508-7 (pbk. : alk. paper)
   1. Scanderberg, 1405–1468—Poetry. I. Russell, Rinaldina. II. Title. III. Series.

PQ4634.S163S3313 2006
851'.5—dc22

                              2006010779

CONTENTS

ACKNOWLEDGMENTS

The prose translation of this epic poem on a "holy war" was done in the spirit of scholarship and of historical truth. I owe my gratitude to the editors of the series for their continued support and to the National Endowment for the Humanities for my share of a grant awarded to a collective project of which translating the *Scanderbeide* was a part. Special thanks are due to Albert Rabil for his thoughtful attention and for providing all the editorial competence any scholar would wish.

Rinaldina Russell

THE OTHER VOICE IN EARLY MODERN EUROPE: INTRODUCTION TO THE SERIES

Margaret L. King and Albert Rabil Jr.

THE OLD VOICE AND THE OTHER VOICE

In western Europe and the United States, women are nearing equality in the professions, in business, and in politics. Most enjoy access to education, reproductive rights, and autonomy in financial affairs. Issues vital to women are on the public agenda: equal pay, child care, domestic abuse, breast cancer research, and curricular revision with an eye to the inclusion of women.

These recent achievements have their origins in things women (and some male supporters) said for the first time about six hundred years ago. Theirs is the "other voice," in contradistinction to the "first voice," the voice of the educated men who created Western culture. Coincident with a general reshaping of European culture in the period 1300–1700 (called the Renaissance or early modern period), questions of female equality and opportunity were raised that still resound and are still unresolved.

The other voice emerged against the backdrop of a three-thousand-year history of the derogation of women rooted in the civilizations related to Western culture: Hebrew, Greek, Roman, and Christian. Negative attitudes toward women inherited from these traditions pervaded the intellectual, medical, legal, religious, and social systems that developed during the European Middle Ages.

The following pages describe the traditional, overwhelmingly male views of women's nature inherited by early modern Europeans and the new tradition that the "other voice" called into being to begin to challenge reigning assumptions. This review should serve as a framework for understanding the texts published in the series the Other Voice in Early Modern Europe. Introductions specific to each text and author follow this essay in all the volumes of the series.

TRADITIONAL VIEWS OF WOMEN, 500 B.C.E.–1500 C.E.

Embedded in the philosophical and medical theories of the ancient Greeks were perceptions of the female as inferior to the male in both mind and body. Similarly, the structure of civil legislation inherited from the ancient Romans was biased against women, and the views on women developed by Christian thinkers out of the Hebrew Bible and the Christian New Testament were negative and disabling. Literary works composed in the vernacular of ordinary people, and widely recited or read, conveyed these negative assumptions. The social networks within which most women lived—those of the family and the institutions of the Roman Catholic Church—were shaped by this negative tradition and sharply limited the areas in which women might act in and upon the world.

GREEK PHILOSOPHY AND FEMALE NATURE. Greek biology assumed that women were inferior to men and defined them as merely childbearers and housekeepers. This view was authoritatively expressed in the works of the philosopher Aristotle.

Aristotle thought in dualities. He considered action superior to inaction, form (the inner design or structure of any object) superior to matter, completion to incompletion, possession to deprivation. In each of these dualities, he associated the male principle with the superior quality and the female with the inferior. "The male principle in nature," he argued, "is associated with active, formative and perfected characteristics, while the female is passive, material and deprived, desiring the male in order to become complete."[1] Men are always identified with virile qualities, such as judgment, courage, and stamina, and women with their opposites—irrationality, cowardice, and weakness.

The masculine principle was considered superior even in the womb. The man's semen, Aristotle believed, created the form of a new human creature, while the female body contributed only matter. (The existence of the ovum, and with it the other facts of human embryology, was not established until the seventeenth century.) Although the later Greek physician Galen believed there was a female component in generation, contributed by "female semen," the followers of both Aristotle and Galen saw the male role in human generation as more active and more important.

In the Aristotelian view, the male principle sought always to reproduce itself. The creation of a female was always a mistake, therefore, resulting

---

1. Aristotle, *Physics* 1.9.192a20–24, in *The Complete Works of Aristotle,* ed. Jonathan Barnes, rev. Oxford trans., 2 vols. (Princeton, 1984), 1:328.

from an imperfect act of generation. Every female born was considered a "defective" or "mutilated" male (as Aristotle's terminology has variously been translated), a "monstrosity" of nature.[2]

For Greek theorists, the biology of males and females was the key to their psychology. The female was softer and more docile, more apt to be despondent, querulous, and deceitful. Being incomplete, moreover, she craved sexual fulfillment in intercourse with a male. The male was intellectual, active, and in control of his passions.

These psychological polarities derived from the theory that the universe consisted of four elements (earth, fire, air, and water), expressed in human bodies as four "humors" (black bile, yellow bile, blood, and phlegm) considered, respectively, dry, hot, damp, and cold and corresponding to mental states ("melancholic," "choleric," "sanguine," "phlegmatic"). In this scheme the male, sharing the principles of earth and fire, was dry and hot; the female, sharing the principles of air and water, was cold and damp.

Female psychology was further affected by her dominant organ, the uterus (womb), *hystera* in Greek. The passions generated by the womb made women lustful, deceitful, talkative, irrational, indeed—when these affects were in excess—"hysterical."

Aristotle's biology also had social and political consequences. If the male principle was superior and the female inferior, then in the household, as in the state, men should rule and women must be subordinate. That hierarchy did not rule out the companionship of husband and wife, whose cooperation was necessary for the welfare of children and the preservation of property. Such mutuality supported male preeminence.

Aristotle's teacher Plato suggested a different possibility: that men and women might possess the same virtues. The setting for this proposal is the imaginary and ideal Republic that Plato sketches in a dialogue of that name. Here, for a privileged elite capable of leading wisely, all distinctions of class and wealth dissolve, as, consequently, do those of gender. Without households or property, as Plato constructs his ideal society, there is no need for the subordination of women. Women may therefore be educated to the same level as men to assume leadership. Plato's Republic remained imaginary, however. In real societies, the subordination of women remained the norm and the prescription.

The views of women inherited from the Greek philosophical tradition became the basis for medieval thought. In the thirteenth century, the supreme Scholastic philosopher Thomas Aquinas, among others, still

---

2. Aristotle, *Generation of Animals* 2.3.737a27–28, in *The Complete Works*, 1: 1144.

echoed Aristotle's views of human reproduction, of male and female personalities, and of the preeminent male role in the social hierarchy.

ROMAN LAW AND THE FEMALE CONDITION. Roman law, like Greek
philosophy, underlay medieval thought and shaped medieval society. The
ancient belief that adult property-owning men should administer households and make decisions affecting the community at large is the very ful-
crum of Roman law.

About 450 B.C.E., during Rome's republican era, the community's customary law was recorded (legendarily) on twelve tablets erected in the city's
central forum. It was later elaborated by professional jurists whose activity
increased in the imperial era, when much new legislation was passed, especially on issues affecting family and inheritance. This growing, changing
body of laws was eventually codified in the *Corpus of Civil Law* under the
direction of the emperor Justinian, generations after the empire ceased to
be ruled from Rome. That *Corpus*, read and commented on by medieval
scholars from the eleventh century on, inspired the legal systems of most of
the cities and kingdoms of Europe.

Laws regarding dowries, divorce, and inheritance pertain primarily to
women. Since those laws aimed to maintain and preserve property, the
women concerned were those from the property-owning minority. Their
subordination to male family members points to the even greater subordination of lower-class and slave women, about whom the laws speak little.

In the early republic, the *paterfamilias*, or "father of the family," possessed
patria potestas, "paternal power." The term *pater*, "father," in both these cases
does not necessarily mean biological father but denotes the head of a
household. The father was the person who owned the household's property
and, indeed, its human members. The *paterfamilias* had absolute power—
including the power, rarely exercised, of life or death—over his wife, his
children, and his slaves, as much as his cattle.

Male children could be "emancipated," an act that granted legal autonomy and the right to own property. Those over fourteen could be emancipated by a special grant from the father or automatically by their father's
death. But females could never be emancipated; instead, they passed from
the authority of their father to that of a husband or, if widowed or orphaned
while still unmarried, to a guardian or tutor.

Marriage in its traditional form placed the woman under her husband's
authority, or *manus*. He could divorce her on grounds of adultery, drinking
wine, or stealing from the household, but she could not divorce him. She
could neither possess property in her own right nor bequeath any to her

children upon her death. When her husband died, the household property passed not to her but to his male heirs. And when her father died, she had no claim to any family inheritance, which was directed to her brothers or more remote male relatives. The effect of these laws was to exclude women from civil society, itself based on property ownership.

In the later republican and imperial periods, these rules were significantly modified. Women rarely married according to the traditional form. The practice of "free" marriage allowed a woman to remain under her father's authority, to possess property given her by her father (most frequently the "dowry," recoverable from the husband's household on his death), and to inherit from her father. She could also bequeath property to her own children and divorce her husband, just as he could divorce her.

Despite this greater freedom, women still suffered enormous disability under Roman law. Heirs could belong only to the father's side, never the mother's. Moreover, although she could bequeath her property to her children, she could not establish a line of succession in doing so. A woman was "the beginning and end of her own family," said the jurist Ulpian. Moreover, women could play no public role. They could not hold public office, represent anyone in a legal case, or even witness a will. Women had only a private existence and no public personality.

The dowry system, the guardian, women's limited ability to transmit wealth, and total political disability are all features of Roman law adopted by the medieval communities of western Europe, although modified according to local customary laws.

CHRISTIAN DOCTINE AND WOMEN'S PLACE. The Hebrew Bible and the Christian New Testament authorized later writers to limit women to the realm of the family and to burden them with the guilt of original sin. The passages most fruitful for this purpose were the creation narratives in Genesis and sentences from the Epistles defining women's role within the Christian family and community.

Each of the first two chapters of Genesis contains a creation narrative. In the first "God created man in his own image, in the image of God he created him; male and female he created them" (Gn 1:27). In the second, God created Eve from Adam's rib (2:21–23). Christian theologians relied principally on Genesis 2 for their understanding of the relation between man and woman, interpreting the creation of Eve from Adam as proof of her subordination to him.

The creation story in Genesis 2 leads to that of the temptations in Genesis 3: of Eve by the wily serpent and of Adam by Eve. As read by

Christian theologians from Tertullian to Thomas Aquinas, the narrative made Eve responsible for the Fall and its consequences. She instigated the act; she deceived her husband; she suffered the greater punishment. Her disobedience made it necessary for Jesus to be incarnated and to die on the cross. From the pulpit, moralists and preachers for centuries conveyed to women the guilt that they bore for original sin.

The Epistles offered advice to early Christians on building communities of the faithful. Among the matters to be regulated was the place of women. Paul offered views favorable to women in Galatians 3:28: "There is neither Jew nor Greek, there is neither slave nor free, there is neither male nor female; for you are all one in Christ Jesus." Paul also referred to women as his coworkers and placed them on a par with himself and his male coworkers (Phlm 4:2–3; Rom 16:1–3; 1 Cor 16:19). Elsewhere, Paul limited women's possibilities: "But I want you to understand that the head of every man is Christ, the head of a woman is her husband, and the head of Christ is God" (1 Cor 11:3).

Biblical passages by later writers (although attributed to Paul) enjoined women to forgo jewels, expensive clothes, and elaborate coiffures; and they forbade women to "teach or have authority over men," telling them to "learn in silence with all submissiveness" as is proper for one responsible for sin, consoling them, however, with the thought that they will be saved through childbearing (1 Tm 2:9–15). Other texts among the later Epistles defined women as the weaker sex and emphasized their subordination to their husbands (1 Pt 3:7; Col 3:18; Eph 5:22–23).

These passages from the New Testament became the arsenal employed by theologians of the early church to transmit negative attitudes toward women to medieval Christian culture—above all, Tertullian (*On the Apparel of Women*), Jerome (*Against Jovinian*), and Augustine (*The Literal Meaning of Genesis*).

THE IMAGE OF WOMEN IN MEDIEVAL LITERATURE. The philosophical, legal, and religious traditions born in antiquity formed the basis of the medieval intellectual synthesis wrought by trained thinkers, mostly clerics, writing in Latin and based largely in universities. The vernacular literary tradition that developed alongside the learned tradition also spoke about female nature and women's roles. Medieval stories, poems, and epics also portrayed women negatively—as lustful and deceitful—while praising good housekeepers and loyal wives as replicas of the Virgin Mary or the female saints and martyrs.

There is an exception in the movement of "courtly love" that evolved in southern France from the twelfth century. Courtly love was the erotic love between a nobleman and noblewoman, the latter usually superior in social rank. It was always adulterous. From the conventions of courtly love derive modern Western notions of romantic love. The tradition has had an impact disproportionate to its size, for it affected only a tiny elite, and very few women. The exaltation of the female lover probably does not reflect a higher evaluation of women or a step toward their sexual liberation. More likely it gives expression to the social and sexual tensions besetting the knightly class at a specific historical juncture.

The literary fashion of courtly love was on the wane by the thirteenth century, when the widely read *Romance of the Rose* was composed in French by two authors of significantly different dispositions. Guillaume de Lorris composed the initial four thousand verses about 1235, and Jean de Meun added about seventeen thousand verses—more than four times the original—about 1265.

The fragment composed by Guillaume de Lorris stands squarely in the tradition of courtly love. Here the poet, in a dream, is admitted into a walled garden where he finds a magic fountain in which a rosebush is reflected. He longs to pick one rose, but the thorns prevent his doing so, even as he is wounded by arrows from the god of love, whose commands he agrees to obey. The rest of this part of the poem recounts the poet's unsuccessful efforts to pluck the rose.

The longer part of the *Romance* by Jean de Meun also describes a dream. But here allegorical characters give long didactic speeches, providing a social satire on a variety of themes, some pertaining to women. Love is an anxious and tormented state, the poem explains: women are greedy and manipulative, marriage is miserable, beautiful women are lustful, ugly ones cease to please, and a chaste woman is as rare as a black swan.

Shortly after Jean de Meun completed *The Romance of the Rose*, Mathéolus penned his *Lamentations*, a long Latin diatribe against marriage translated into French about a century later. The *Lamentations* sum up medieval attitudes toward women and provoked the important response by Christine de Pizan in her *Book of the City of Ladies*.

In 1355, Giovanni Boccaccio wrote *Il Corbaccio*, another antifeminist manifesto, although ironically by an author whose other works pioneered new directions in Renaissance thought. The former husband of his lover appears to Boccaccio, condemning his unmoderated lust and detailing the defects of women. Boccaccio concedes at the end "how much men naturally surpass women in nobility" and is cured of his desires.[3]

---

3. Giovanni Boccaccio, *The Corbaccio, or The Labyrinth of Love*, trans. and ed. Anthony K. Cassell, rev. ed. (Binghamton, N.Y., 1993), 71.

WOMEN'S ROLES: THE FAMILY. The negative perceptions of women expressed in the intellectual tradition are also implicit in the actual roles that women played in European society. Assigned to subordinate positions in the household and the church, they were barred from significant participation in public life.

Medieval European households, like those in antiquity and in non-Western civilizations, were headed by males. It was the male serf (or peasant), feudal lord, town merchant, or citizen who was polled or taxed or succeeded to an inheritance or had any acknowledged public role, although his wife or widow could stand as a temporary surrogate. From about 1100, the position of property-holding males was further enhanced: inheritance was confined to the male, or agnate, line—with depressing consequences for women.

A wife never fully belonged to her husband's family, nor was she a daughter to her father's family. She left her father's house young to marry whomever her parents chose. Her dowry was managed by her husband, and at her death it normally passed to her children by him.

A married woman's life was occupied nearly constantly with cycles of pregnancy, childbearing, and lactation. Women bore children through all the years of their fertility, and many died in childbirth. They were also responsible for raising young children up to six or seven. In the propertied classes that responsibility was shared, since it was common for a wet nurse to take over breast-feeding and for servants to perform other chores.

Women trained their daughters in the household duties appropriate to their status, nearly always tasks associated with textiles: spinning, weaving, sewing, embroidering. Their sons were sent out of the house as apprentices or students, or their training was assumed by fathers in later childhood and adolescence. On the death of her husband, a woman's children became the responsibility of his family. She generally did not take "his" children with her to a new marriage or back to her father's house, except sometimes in the artisan classes.

Women also worked. Rural peasants performed farm chores, merchant wives often practiced their husbands' trades, the unmarried daughters of the urban poor worked as servants or prostitutes. All wives produced or embellished textiles and did the housekeeping, while wealthy ones managed servants. These labors were unpaid or poorly paid but often contributed substantially to family wealth.

WOMEN'S ROLES: THE CHURCH. Membership in a household, whether a father's or a husband's, meant for women a lifelong subordination to others.

In western Europe, the Roman Catholic Church offered an alternative to the career of wife and mother. A woman could enter a convent, parallel in function to the monasteries for men that evolved in the early Christian centuries.

In the convent, a woman pledged herself to a celibate life, lived according to strict community rules, and worshiped daily. Often the convent offered training in Latin, allowing some women to become considerable scholars and authors as well as scribes, artists, and musicians. For women who chose the conventual life, the benefits could be enormous, but for numerous others placed in convents by paternal choice, the life could be restrictive and burdensome.

The conventual life declined as an alternative for women as the modern age approached. Reformed monastic institutions resisted responsibility for related female orders. The church increasingly restricted female institutional life by insisting on closer male supervision.

Women often sought other options. Some joined the communities of laywomen that sprang up spontaneously in the thirteenth century in the urban zones of western Europe, especially in Flanders and Italy. Some joined the heretical movements that flourished in late medieval Christendom, whose anticlerical and often antifamily positions particularly appealed to women. In these communities, some women were acclaimed as "holy women" or "saints," whereas others often were condemned as frauds or heretics.

In all, although the options offered to women by the church were sometimes less than satisfactory, they were sometimes richly rewarding. After 1520, the convent remained an option only in Roman Catholic territories. Protestantism engendered an ideal of marriage as a heroic endeavor and appeared to place husband and wife on a more equal footing. Sermons and treatises, however, still called for female subordination and obedience.

THE OTHER VOICE, 1300–1700

When the modern era opened, European culture was so firmly structured by a framework of negative attitudes toward women that to dismantle it was a monumental labor. The process began as part of a larger cultural movement that entailed the critical reexamination of ideas inherited from the ancient and medieval past. The humanists launched that critical reexamination.

THE HUMANIST FOUNDATION.   Originating in Italy in the fourteenth century, humanism quickly became the dominant intellectual movement in Europe. Spreading in the sixteenth century from Italy to the rest of Europe, it fueled the literary, scientific, and philosophical movements of the era and laid the basis for the eighteenth-century Enlightenment.

Humanists regarded the Scholastic philosophy of medieval universities as out of touch with the realities of urban life. They found in the rhetorical discourse of classical Rome a language adapted to civic life and public speech. They learned to read, speak, and write classical Latin and, eventually, classical Greek. They founded schools to teach others to do so, establishing the pattern for elementary and secondary education for the next three hundred years.

In the service of complex government bureaucracies, humanists employed their skills to write eloquent letters, deliver public orations, and formulate public policy. They developed new scripts for copying manuscripts and used the new printing press to disseminate texts, for which they created methods of critical editing.

Humanism was a movement led by males who accepted the evaluation of women in ancient texts and generally shared the misogynist perceptions of their culture. (Female humanists, as we will see, did not.) Yet humanism also opened the door to a reevaluation of the nature and capacity of women. By calling authors, texts, and ideas into question, it made possible the fundamental rereading of the whole intellectual tradition that was required in order to free women from cultural prejudice and social subordination.

A DIFFERENT CITY. The other voice first appeared when, after so many centuries, the accumulation of misogynist concepts evoked a response from a capable female defender: Christine de Pizan (1365–1431). Introducing her *Book of the City of Ladies* (1405), she described how she was affected by reading Mathéolus's *Lamentations*: "Just the sight of this book . . . made me wonder how it happened that so many different men . . . are so inclined to express both in speaking and in their treatises and writings so many wicked insults about women and their behavior."[4] These statements impelled her to detest herself "and the entire feminine sex, as though we were monstrosities in nature."[5]

The rest of *The Book of the City of Ladies* presents a justification of the female sex and a vision of an ideal community of women. A pioneer, she has received the message of female inferiority and rejected it. From the fourteenth to the seventeenth century, a huge body of literature accumulated that responded to the dominant tradition.

4. Christine de Pizan, *The Book of the City of Ladies*, trans. Earl Jeffrey Richards, foreword by Marina Warner (New York, 1982), 1.1.1, pp. 3–4.

5. Ibid., 1.1.1–2, p. 5.

The result was a literary explosion consisting of works by both men and women, in Latin and in the vernaculars: works enumerating the achievements of notable women; works rebutting the main accusations made against women; works arguing for the equal education of men and women; works defining and redefining women's proper role in the family, at court, in public; works describing women's lives and experiences. Recent monographs and articles have begun to hint at the great range of this movement, involving probably several thousand titles. The protofeminism of these "other voices" constitutes a significant fraction of the literary product of the early modern era.

THE CATALOGS. About 1365, the same Boccaccio whose *Corbaccio* rehearses the usual charges against female nature wrote another work, *Concerning Famous Women*. A humanist treatise drawing on classical texts, it praised 106 notable women: ninety-eight of them from pagan Greek and Roman antiquity, one (Eve) from the Bible, and seven from the medieval religious and cultural tradition; his book helped make all readers aware of a sex normally condemned or forgotten. Boccaccio's outlook nevertheless was unfriendly to women, for it singled out for praise those women who possessed the traditional virtues of chastity, silence, and obedience. Women who were active in the public realm—for example, rulers and warriors— were depicted as usually being lascivious and as suffering terrible punishments for entering the masculine sphere. Women were his subject, but Boccaccio's standard remained male.

Christine de Pizan's *Book of the City of Ladies* contains a second catalog, one responding specifically to Boccaccio's. Whereas Boccaccio portrays female virtue as exceptional, she depicts it as universal. Many women in history were leaders, or remained chaste despite the lascivious approaches of men, or were visionaries and brave martyrs.

The work of Boccaccio inspired a series of catalogs of illustrious women of the biblical, classical, Christian, and local pasts, among them Filippo da Bergamo's *Of Illustrious Women*, Pierre de Brantôme's *Lives of Illustrious Women*, Pierre Le Moyne's *Gallerie of Heroic Women*, and Pietro Paolo de Ribera's *Immortal Triumphs and Heroic Enterprises of 845 Women*. Whatever their embedded prejudices, these works drove home to the public the possibility of female excellence.

THE DEBATE. At the same time, many questions remained: Could a woman be virtuous? Could she perform noteworthy deeds? Was she even, strictly speaking, of the same human species as men? These questions were

Series Editors' Introduction

debated over four centuries, in French, German, Italian, Spanish, and English, by authors male and female, among Catholics, Protestants, and Jews, in ponderous volumes and breezy pamphlets. The whole literary genre has been called the *querelle des femmes*, the "woman question."

The opening volley of this battle occurred in the first years of the fifteenth century, in a literary debate sparked by Christine de Pizan. She exchanged letters critical of Jean de Meun's contribution to *The Romance of the Rose* with two French royal secretaries, Jean de Montreuil and Gontier Col. When the matter became public, Jean Gerson, one of Europe's leading theologians, supported de Pizan's arguments against de Meun, for the moment silencing the opposition.

The debate resurfaced repeatedly over the next two hundred years. *The Triumph of Women* (1438) by Juan Rodríguez de la Camara (or Juan Rodríguez del Padron) struck a new note by presenting arguments for the superiority of women to men. *The Champion of Women* (1440–42) by Martin Le Franc addresses once again the negative views of women presented in *The Romance of the Rose* and offers counterevidence of female virtue and achievement.

A cameo of the debate on women is included in *The Courtier*, one of the most widely read books of the era, published by the Italian Baldassare Castiglione in 1528 and immediately translated into other European vernaculars. *The Courtier* depicts a series of evenings at the court of the duke of Urbino in which many men and some women of the highest social stratum amuse themselves by discussing a range of literary and social issues. The "woman question" is a pervasive theme throughout, and the third of its four books is devoted entirely to that issue.

In a verbal duel, Gasparo Pallavicino and Giuliano de' Medici present the main claims of the two traditions. Gasparo argues the innate inferiority of women and their inclination to vice. Only in bearing children do they profit the world. Giuliano counters that women share the same spiritual and mental capacities as men and may excel in wisdom and action. Men and women are of the same essence: just as no stone can be more perfectly a stone than another, so no human being can be more perfectly human than others, whether male or female. It was an astonishing assertion, boldly made to an audience as large as all Europe.

THE TREATISES. Humanism provided the materials for a positive counterconcept to the misogyny embedded in Scholastic philosophy and law and inherited from the Greek, Roman, and Christian pasts. A series of humanist treatises on marriage and family, on education and deportment, and on the nature of women helped construct these new perspectives.

The works by Francesco Barbaro and Leon Battista Alberti—*On Marriage* (1415) and *On the Family* (1434–37)—far from defending female equality, reasserted women's responsibility for rearing children and managing the housekeeping while being obedient, chaste, and silent. Nevertheless, they served the cause of reexamining the issue of women's nature by placing domestic issues at the center of scholarly concern and reopening the pertinent classical texts. In addition, Barbaro emphasized the companionate nature of marriage and the importance of a wife's spiritual and mental qualities for the well-being of the family.

These themes reappear in later humanist works on marriage and the education of women by Juan Luis Vives and Erasmus. Both were moderately sympathetic to the condition of women without reaching beyond the usual masculine prescriptions for female behavior.

An outlook more favorable to women characterizes the nearly unknown work *In Praise of Women* (ca. 1487) by the Italian humanist Bartolommeo Goggio. In addition to providing a catalog of illustrious women, Goggio argued that male and female are the same in essence, but that women (reworking the Adam and Eve narrative from quite a new angle) are actually superior. In the same vein, the Italian humanist Mario Equicola asserted the spiritual equality of men and women in *On Women* (1501). In 1525, Galeazzo Flavio Capra (or Capella) published his work *On the Excellence and Dignity of Women*. This humanist tradition of treatises defending the worthiness of women culminates in the work of Henricus Cornelius Agrippa *On the Nobility and Preeminence of the Female Sex*. No work by a male humanist more succinctly or explicitly presents the case for female dignity.

THE WITCH BOOKS. While humanists grappled with the issues pertaining to women and family, other learned men turned their attention to what they perceived as a very great problem: witches. Witch-hunting manuals, explorations of the witch phenomenon, and even defenses of witches are not at first glance pertinent to the tradition of the other voice. But they do relate in this way: most accused witches were women. The hostility aroused by supposed witch activity is comparable to the hostility aroused by women. The evil deeds the victims of the hunt were charged with were exaggerations of the vices to which, many believed, all women were prone.

The connection between the witch accusation and the hatred of women is explicit in the notorious witch-hunting manual *The Hammer of Witches* (1486) by two Dominican inquisitors, Heinrich Krämer and Jacob Sprenger. Here the inconstancy, deceitfulness, and lustfulness traditionally associated with women are depicted in exaggerated form as the core features of witch behavior. These traits inclined women to make a bargain with the devil—sealed by sexual intercourse—by which they acquired unholy powers. Such bizarre claims, far from being rejected by rational men, were broadcast by intellectuals. The German Ulrich Molitur, the Frenchman Nicolas Rémy, and the Italian Stefano Guazzo all coolly informed the public of sinister orgies and midnight pacts with the devil. The celebrated French jurist, historian, and political philosopher Jean Bodin argued that because women were especially prone to diabolism, regular legal procedures could properly be suspended in order to try those accused of this "exceptional crime."

A few experts such as the physician Johann Weyer, a student of Agrippa's, raised their voices in protest. In 1563, he explained the witch phenomenon thus, without discarding belief in diabolism: the devil deluded foolish old women afflicted by melancholia, causing them to believe they had magical powers. Weyer's rational skepticism, which had good credibility in the community of the learned, worked to revise the conventional views of women and witchcraft.

WOMEN'S WORKS. To the many categories of works produced on the question of women's worth must be added nearly all works written by women. A woman writing was in herself a statement of women's claim to dignity.

Only a few women wrote anything before the dawn of the modern era, for three reasons. First, they rarely received the education that would enable them to write. Second, they were not admitted to the public roles—as administrator, bureaucrat, lawyer or notary, or university professor—in which they might gain knowledge of the kinds of things the literate public thought worth writing about. Third, the culture imposed silence on women, considering speaking out a form of unchastity. Given these conditions, it is remarkable that any women wrote. Those who did before the fourteenth century were almost always nuns or religious women whose isolation made their pronouncements more acceptable.

From the fourteenth century on, the volume of women's writings rose. Women continued to write devotional literature, although not always as cloistered nuns. They also wrote diaries, often intended as keepsakes for their children; books of advice to their sons and daughters; letters to family members and friends; and family memoirs, in a few cases elaborate enough to be considered histories.

A few women wrote works directly concerning the "woman question," and some of these, such as the humanists Isotta Nogarola, Cassandra

Fedele, Laura Cereta, and Olympia Morata, were highly trained. A few were professional writers, living by the income of their pens; the very first among them was Christine de Pizan, noteworthy in this context as in so many others. In addition to *The Book of the City of Ladies* and her critiques of *The Romance of the Rose*, she wrote *The Treasure of the City of Ladies* (a guide to social decorum for women), an advice book for her son, much courtly verse, and a full-scale history of the reign of King Charles V of France.

WOMEN PATRONS. Women who did not themselves write but encouraged others to do so boosted the development of an alternative tradition. Highly placed women patrons supported authors, artists, musicians, poets, and learned men. Such patrons, drawn mostly from the Italian elites and the courts of northern Europe, figure disproportionately as the dedicatees of the important works of early feminism.

For a start, it might be noted that the catalogs of Boccaccio and Alvaro de Luna were dedicated to the Florentine noblewoman Andrea Acciaiuoli and to Doña María, first wife of King Juan II of Castile, while the French translation of Boccaccio's work was commissioned by Anne of Brittany, wife of King Charles VIII of France. The humanist treatises of Goggio, Equicola, Vives, and Agrippa were dedicated, respectively, to Eleanora of Aragon, wife of Ercole I d'Este, duke of Ferrara; to Margherita Cantelma of Mantua; to Catherine of Aragon, wife of King Henry VIII of England; and to Margaret, Duchess of Austria and regent of the Netherlands. As late as 1696, Mary Astell's *Serious Proposal to the Ladies, for the Advancement of Their True and Greatest Interest* was dedicated to Princess Anne of Denmark.

These authors presumed that their efforts would be welcome to female patrons, or they may have written at the bidding of those patrons. Silent themselves, perhaps even unresponsive, these loftily placed women helped shape the tradition of the other voice.

THE ISSUES. The literary forms and patterns in which the tradition of the other voice presented itself have now been sketched. It remains to highlight the major issues around which this tradition crystallizes. In brief, there are four problems to which our authors return again and again, in plays and catalogs, in verse and letters, in treatises and dialogues, in every language: the problem of chastity, the problem of power, the problem of speech, and the problem of knowledge. Of these the greatest, preconditioning the others, is the problem of chastity.

THE PROBLEM OF CHASTITY. In traditional European culture, as in those of antiquity and others around the globe, chastity was perceived as woman's quintessential virtue—in contrast to courage, or generosity, or leadership, or rationality, seen as virtues characteristic of men. Opponents of women charged them with insatiable lust. Women themselves and their defenders—without disputing the validity of the standard—responded that women were capable of chastity.

The requirement of chastity kept women at home, silenced them, isolated them, left them in ignorance. It was the source of all other impediments. Why was it so important to the society of men, of whom chastity was not required, and who more often than not considered it their right to violate the chastity of any woman they encountered?

Female chastity ensured the continuity of the male-headed household. If a man's wife was not chaste, he could not be sure of the legitimacy of his offspring. If they were not his and they acquired his property, it was not his household, but some other man's, that had endured. If his daughter was not chaste, she could not be transferred to another man's household as his wife, and he was dishonored.

The whole system of the integrity of the household and the transmission of property was bound up in female chastity. Such a requirement pertained only to property-owning classes, of course. Poor women could not expect to maintain their chastity, least of all if they were in contact with high-status men to whom all women but those of their own household were prey.

In Catholic Europe, the requirement of chastity was further buttressed by moral and religious imperatives. Original sin was inextricably linked with the sexual act. Virginity was seen as heroic virtue, far more impressive than, say, the avoidance of idleness or greed. Monasticism, the cultural institution that dominated medieval Europe for centuries, was grounded in the renunciation of the flesh. The Catholic reform of the eleventh century imposed a similar standard on all the clergy and a heightened awareness of sexual requirements on all the laity. Although men were asked to be chaste, female unchastity was much worse: it led to the devil, as Eve had led mankind to sin.

To such requirements, women and their defenders protested their innocence. Furthermore, following the example of holy women who had escaped the requirements of family and sought the religious life, some women began to conceive of female communities as alternatives both to family and to the cloister. Christine de Pizan's city of ladies was such a community. Moderata Fonte and Mary Astell envisioned others. The luxurious salons of the French *précieuses* of the seventeenth century, or the comfortable English drawing rooms of the next, may have been born of the same impulse. Here women not only might escape, if briefly, the subordinate position that life in the family entailed but might also make claims to power, exercise their capacity for speech, and display their knowledge.

THE PROBLEM OF POWER. Women were excluded from power: the whole cultural tradition insisted on it. Only men were citizens, only men bore arms, only men could be chiefs or lords or kings. There were exceptions that did not disprove the rule, when wives or widows or mothers took the place of men, awaiting their return or the maturation of a male heir. A woman who attempted to rule in her own right was perceived as an anomaly, a monster, at once a deformed woman and an insufficient male, sexually confused and consequently unsafe.

The association of such images with women who held or sought power explains some otherwise odd features of early modern culture. Queen Elizabeth I of England, one of the few women to hold full regal authority in European history, played with such male/female images—positive ones, of course—in representing herself to her subjects. She was a prince, and manly, even though she was female. She was also (she claimed) virginal, a condition absolutely essential if she was to avoid the attacks of her opponents. Catherine de' Medici, who ruled France as widow and regent for her sons, also adopted such imagery in defining her position. She chose as one symbol the figure of Artemisia, an androgynous ancient warrior-heroine who combined a female persona with masculine powers.

Power in a woman, without such sexual imagery, seems to have been indigestible by the culture. A rare note was struck by the Englishman Sir Thomas Elyot in his *Defence of Good Women* (1540), justifying both women's participation in civic life and their prowess in arms. The old tune was sung by the Scots reformer John Knox in his *First Blast of the Trumpet against the Monstrous Regiment of Women* (1558); for him rule by women, defects in nature, was a hideous contradiction in terms.

The confused sexuality of the imagery of female potency was not reserved for rulers. Any woman who excelled was likely to be called an Amazon, recalling the self-mutilated warrior women of antiquity who repudiated all men, gave up their sons, and raised only their daughters. She was often said to have "exceeded her sex" or to have possessed "masculine virtue"—as the very fact of conspicuous excellence conferred masculinity even on the female subject. The catalogs of notable women often showed those female heroes dressed in armor, armed to the teeth, like men. Amazonian heroines romp through the epics of the age—Ariosto's *Orlando Furioso* (1532) and Spenser's *Faerie Queene* (1590–1609). Excellence in a woman was perceived as a claim for power, and power was reserved for the masculine realm. A woman who possessed either one was masculinized and lost title to her own female identity.

THE PROBLEM OF SPEECH. Just as power had a sexual dimension when it was claimed by women, so did speech. A good woman spoke little. Excessive speech was an indication of unchastity. By speech, women seduced men. Eve had lured Adam into sin by her speech. Accused witches were commonly accused of having spoken abusively, or irrationally, or simply too much. As enlightened a figure as Francesco Barbaro insisted on silence in a woman, which he linked to her perfect unanimity with her husband's will and her unblemished virtue (her chastity). Another Italian humanist, Leonardo Bruni, in advising a noblewoman on her studies, barred her not from speech but from public speaking. That was reserved for men.

Related to the problem of speech was that of costume—another, if silent, form of self-expression. Assigned the task of pleasing men as their primary occupation, elite women often tended toward elaborate costume, hairdressing, and the use of cosmetics. Clergy and secular moralists alike condemned these practices. The appropriate function of costume and adornment was to announce the status of a woman's husband or father. Any further indulgence in adornment was akin to unchastity.

THE PROBLEM OF KNOWLEDGE. When the Italian noblewoman Isotta Nogarola had begun to attain a reputation as a humanist, she was accused of incest—a telling instance of the association of learning in women with unchastity. That chilling association inclined any woman who was educated to deny that she was or to make exaggerated claims of heroic chastity.

If educated women were pursued with suspicions of sexual misconduct, women seeking an education faced an even more daunting obstacle: the assumption that women were by nature incapable of learning, that reasoning was a particularly masculine ability. Just as they proclaimed their chastity, women and their defenders insisted on their capacity for learning. The major work by a male writer on female education—that by Juan Luis Vives, *On the Education of a Christian Woman* (1523)—granted female capacity for intellection but still argued that a woman's whole education was to be shaped around the requirement of chastity and a future within the household. Female writers of the following generations—Marie de Gournay in France, Anna Maria van Schurman in Holland, and Mary Astell in England—began to envision other possibilities.

The pioneers of female education were the Italian women humanists who managed to attain a literacy in Latin and a knowledge of classical and Christian literature equivalent to that of prominent men. Their works implicitly and explicitly raise questions about women's social roles, defining problems that beset women attempting to break out of the cultural limits that had bound them. Like Christine de Pizan, who achieved an advanced education through her father's tutoring and her own devices, their bold questioning makes clear the importance of training. Only when women were educated to the same standard as male leaders would they be able to raise that other voice and insist on their dignity as human beings morally, intellectually, and legally equal to men.

THE OTHER VOICE. The other voice, a voice of protest, was mostly female, but it was also male. It spoke in the vernaculars and in Latin, in treatises and dialogues, in plays and poetry, in letters and diaries, and in pamphlets. It battered at the wall of prejudice that encircled women and raised a banner announcing its claims. The female was equal (or even superior) to the male in essential nature—moral, spiritual, and intellectual. Women were capable of higher education, of holding positions of power and influence in the public realm, and of speaking and writing persuasively. The last bastion of masculine supremacy, centered on the notions of a woman's primary domestic responsibility and the requirement of female chastity, was not as yet assaulted—although visions of productive female communities as alternatives to the family indicated an awareness of the problem.

During the period 1300–1700, the other voice remained only a voice, and one only dimly heard. It did not result—yet—in an alteration of social patterns. Indeed, to this day they have not entirely been altered. Yet the call for justice issued as long as six centuries ago by those writing in the tradition of the other voice must be recognized as the source and origin of the mature feminist tradition and of the realignment of social institutions accomplished in the modern age.

We thank the volume editors in this series, who responded with many suggestions to an earlier draft of this introduction, making it a collaborative enterprise. Many of their suggestions and criticisms have resulted in revisions of this introduction, although we remain responsible for the final product.

PROJECTED TITLES IN THE SERIES

Isabella Andreini, *Mirtilla*, edited and translated by Laura Stortoni

Tullia d'Aragona, *Complete Poems and Letters*, edited and translated by Julia Hairston

Tullia d'Aragona, *The Wretch, Otherwise Known as Guerrino*, edited and translated by Julia Hairston and John McLucas

Francesco Barbaro et al., *On Marriage and the Family*, edited and translated by Margaret L. King

Francesco Buoninsegni and Arcangela Tarabotti, *Menippean Satire: "Against Feminine Extravagance" and "Antisatire,"* edited and translated by Elissa Weaver

Rosalba Carriera, *Letters, Diaries, and Art*, edited and translated by Catherine M. Sama

Madame du Chatelet, *Selected Works*, edited by Judith Zinsser

Vittoria Colonna, Chiara Matraini, and Lucrezia Marinella, *Marian Writings*, edited and translated by Susan Haskins

Princess Elizabeth of Bohemia, *Correspondence with Descartes*, edited and translated by Lisa Shapiro

Isabella d'Este, *Selected Letters*, edited and translated by Deanna Shemek

Fairy-Tales by Seventeenth-Century French Women Writers, edited and translated by Lewis Seifert and Domna C. Stanton

Moderata Fonte and Lucrezia Marinella, *Religious Narratives*, edited and translated by Virginia Cox

Catharina Regina von Greiffenberg, *Meditations on the Life of Christ*, edited and translated by Lynne Tatlock

In Praise of Women: Italian Fifteenth-Century Defenses of Women, edited and translated by Daniel Bornstein

Lucrezia Marinella, *L'Enrico, or Byzantium Conquered*, edited and translated by Virginia Cox

Lucrezia Marinella, *Happy Arcadia*, edited and translated by Susan Haskins and Letizia Panizza

Chiara Matraini, *Selected Poetry and Prose*, edited and translated by Elaine MacLachlan

Alessandro Piccolomini, *Rethinking Marriage in Sixteenth-Century Italy*, edited and translated by Letizia Panizza

Christine de Pizan, *Debate over the "Romance of the Rose,"* edited and translated by David F. Hult

Christine de Pizan, *Life of Charles V*, edited and translated by Nadia Margolis

Christine de Pizan, *The Long Road of Learning*, edited and translated by Andrea Tarnowski

Oliva Sabuco, *The New Philosophy: True Medicine*, edited and translated by Gianna Pomata

Gabrielle Suchon, *"On Philosophy" and "On Morality,"* edited and translated by Domna Stanton with Rebecca Wilkin

Sara Copio Sullam, *Sara Copio Sullam: Jewish Poet and Intellectual in Early Seventeenth-Century Venice*, edited and translated by Don Harrán

Arcangela Tarabotti, *Convent Life as Inferno: A Report*, introduction and notes by Francesca Medioli, translated by Letizia Panizza

Laura Terracina, *Works*, edited and translated by Michael Sherberg

MARGHERITA SARROCCHI AND THE
WRITING OF THE *SCANDERBEIDE*

THE OTHER VOICE

Margherita Sarrocchi's *La Scanderbeide* is a poem on the war of resistance that George Scanderbeg, the Albanian prince, led against the Ottoman sultans from 1443 to 1468. Its claim to fame in literary history, it can now be reasonably assumed, will rest on its original and significant contribution to the poetry of warfare and to the representation of political conflicts. The first historical heroic epic authored by a woman, it appeared in a partial draft in 1606 and was published in its complete form posthumously in 1623. In selecting a military campaign that current events kept relevant to contemporary politics, Sarrocchi not only tackled a genre that more than any other seemed to be the purview of men but also dared to choose a subject matter potentially impervious to being shaped into poetic form. The decades preceding the publication of the *Scanderbeide* had been a period of great theoretical interest in poetics, one in which the scope and legitimacy of all literary genres, heroic poetry in particular, were exactingly weighed and passionately argued about. Torquato Tasso's *Jerusalem Delivered*, which first appeared in1581, had been accepted by most critics as the epic that best adhered to the literary and moral principles of the age, and it had consequently become the model for a spate of imitations that were competitively written and attentively scrutinized. When it first appeared, Sarrocchi's poem attracted a great deal of attention, but after a few decades its intrinsic and circumstantial merits were forgotten, and the name of its author has ever since been relegated to a few negligible footnotes in literary histories. Starting from the inception of Italian national history, furthermore, the Italian seventeenth century has been viewed by literati and by historians alike as a period of literary and political decadence. Dismissed as a product of that century, and written by a woman to boot, the *Scanderbeide* was left to lie buried among the myriad imitations of Tasso's masterpiece, seemingly doomed to be forever ignored.

1

Sarrocchi was a celebrity in her time and remains today an exception in the history of early modern women writers for the level of competency she achieved and for the ease with which her personal merits allowed her to move in Roman literary and social circles. Many prominent men who could observe her closely expressed astonishment at the extent of her knowledge, the quality of her poetic talent, and the deft expertise with which she stood the test of critical scrutiny in reunions of literati and in the gatherings of academicians. Gian Vittorio Rossi, a writer and critic of prestige, who proved to be an implacable satirist of all contemporary poets and intellectuals, in 1645 wrote praising her in unequivocal terms as a woman of outstanding capacities and as the only one to have completed a lengthy heroic poem, and to have done so with the favor of Apollo and the Muses.[1] In view of the increased restraints imposed on women in the post-Tridentine era, Sarrocchi's success is puzzling, but it can be explained in the context of the revival of Roman life at the turn of the century.

HISTORICAL CONTEXT

From the start of the Council of Trent (1542–63) and for several decades thereafter, the Catholic Church reorganized clergy and liturgy, reformulated theological dogma, and imposed tight control over the lives and minds of Italians by means of the Inquisition and the Index of Forbidden Books. At the same time a new educational program was devised and set in place for the preparation of clergymen and the edification of society.[2] The plan was part of a concerted strategy aiming to appropriate the educated classes and subject the entire artistic and literary production to the glory of God and the goals of the church. Toward the end of the century, however, the tight control imposed on the population yielded to a more liberal attitude. The cultural and artistic activities of the city of Rome came to life

---

1. "Nullam ego mulierem, quod quidem meminerim, legi vel audivi, vel ex veteribus vel ex recentibus quae ausa sit heroico carmini manus admovere, illudque perficere. . . . Nostra vero Sarrocchia, virile plane audacia, Etrusco heroico carmine, rhythmis adstricto, Scanderbegi Epirotarum longe fortissimi res gestas, Phoebo Musisque faventibus, multis libris prosecuta est" (I never heard nor read, as far as I can remember, of any woman among either the ancients or the moderns, who dared to handle a heroic poem, let alone complete it. . . . Our Sarrocchi indeed did complete in many cantos a heroic poem in verse in the Tuscan language about the deeds of the most valorous Scanderbeg of Epirus, and she did so with the favor of Apollo and the Muses). *Pinacotheca imaginum illustrium doctrinae vel ingenii laude virorum, qui auctore superstite diem suum obierunt,* new ed. (Wolfenbüttel: Jo. Christoph. Meisner, 1729), 259–60. The first edition came out in Cologne in 1645. On Gian Vittorio Rossi, see below, note 30.

2. About the educational policy promoted by the Church of Rome, see below, note 9.

again. Not only did liberal men appear among the religious authorities, but freethinkers and rebellious artists who were eager to try untested ways of expression and wished to be free of ideological restraints began to circulate as well. Historical and literary studies of recent decades have brought to light the ferment of ideas, of cultural programs, and of mental and moral attitudes that distinguished Rome between the papacy of Clement VIII (1592–1605) and that of Urban VIII (1623–44).[3]

At the beginning of the seventeenth century, Rome was still an economic and political force to be reckoned with, and the Roman court was again a powerful sponsor capable of influencing all Italian culture. New educational institutions and academies were organized; their members initiated or attended gatherings of friends in the palaces of the nobility and high prelates. Some institutions, such as the Accademia degli Umoristi and the Accademia dei Lincei, embraced the baroque avant-garde and the new scientific discoveries; others promoted more conservative trends in art, literature, and thought. The Curia itself became a center of patronage that encouraged, admonished, and imposed constraint.[4] By and large, the liberal arts, art, and architecture became efficient purveyors of ideology and transmitters of suggestions that played on the eyes, minds, and imagination of believers. These were the years of the great baroque churches and palaces, of the gardens, the fountains, the popular festivals of Rome. It was the time of Bernini and Caravaggio, of sacred music and opera.

3. Alberto Asor Rosa, *La cultura della controriforma* (Rome and Bari: Laterza,1979), 11. In the last decades critics, following the lead of Carlo Dionisotti, have given a perceptive view of various aspects of Counter-Reformation culture and of the relations between intellectuals and authorities. See Carlo Dionisotti, "La letteratura italiana nell'età del concilio di Trento," in *Geografia e storia della letteratura italiana* (Turin: Einaudi, 1967), 227–54; Alberto Asor Rosa, "La Nuova Scienza, il Barocco e la crisi della Controriforma," in *La letteratura italiana*, ed. Carlo Muscetta, vol. 5: *Il Seicento* (Rome and Bari: Laterza, 1974), 3–47; Marco Cuaz, *Intellettuali, potere e circolazione delle idee nell'Italia moderna (1500–1700)* (Turin: Loescher, 1982), 93–112; Mario Rosa, "La chiesa e gli stati regionali nell'età dell'assolutismo," in *Letteratura italiana*, ed. Alberto Asor Rosa, vol. 1: *Il letterato e le istituzioni* (Turin: Einaudi 1982), 257–389; Riccardo Merolla, "Lo stato della Chiesa," in *Letteratura italiana*, ed. Alberto Asor Rosa, vol. 2: *L'Età moderna* (Turin: Einaudi, 1988), 1019–1109; and Gregory Hanlon, "The Tridentine Church" and "The Rebirth of Rome," in *Early Modern Italy, 1550–1800: Three Seasons in European History* (New York: St. Martin's, 2000), 120–25 and 136–46.

4. Among contemporary popular texts describing functions and merits of ecclesiastical sponsors were Fabio Albergati's *Il cardinale* (Rome: Dragonelli, 1664; written in 1591) and Giovanni Botero's *Dell'uffitio del Cardinale*, libri 2 (Rome: Mutj, 1599). As recent scholars have remarked, and as these works indicate, the relationship between intellectuals and ecclesiastical authorities, which in the decades of the high Renaissance was one of subordination of the latter to the former, at the end of the sixteenth century underwent a reversal. Cf. Asor Rosa, "La Nuova Scienza," 34; Cuaz, *Intellettuali*, 96–97, 247–49.

Once again a center of artistic activity, whose splendor crossed the frontiers of the Papal States, Rome attracted artists and writers from the rest of Italy and Europe. And while outside its territory the church maintained a policy of strong ideological control, in Rome itself, notwithstanding a continued climate of alertness, an unexpected measure of freedom was bestowed on artists, musicians, and writers who concurred with official policies. Sarrocchi was part of that consensus, and as a successful product (and an exceptional one, being a woman) of the approved system of education, she was allowed the freedom to move pretty much unimpeded in cultural circles. The praise bestowed on her, at first most probably as an adolescent and then as an adult, must have strengthened in her that great sense of her own value that distinguished her, as well as her determination to outshine all others. And being a learned woman who strongly identified with the ideals of her society, she was consistently promoted by the people and the authorities who had educated and nurtured her. Her character and the prestige she enjoyed explain Sarrocchi's daring decision to prove her artistic mettle in heroic poetry, a field that at the time ranked highest in the literary categorization of genres. Those same circumstances of life conferred added interest on Sarrocchi's work, for in the context of contemporary social regulations, and indeed thanks to Sarrocchi's basic acceptance of them, the profeminist discourse that can be elicited from her poem appears realistically relevant to the status of the women of Sarrocchi's age.

SARROCCHI'S LIFE AND LITERARY ACTIVITY

Very few facts are known about Sarrocchi's family and early life. She was born in Naples around 1560 into a middle-class family of comfortable means that had originated in Gragnano, a small town near Castellamare di Stabia. Her father, Giovanni Sarrocchi, died prematurely, and the responsibility for Margherita's education was assumed by Cardinal Guglielmo Sirleto, a prominent scholar of Counter-Reformation theology, custodian and overseer of the Vatican Library, and a man keenly interested in the education of Catholic youth.[5] After placing her in the monastery of Santa Cecilia in Trastevere, Sirleto saw to it that Margherita would receive first-

---

5. We learn that Cardinal Sirleto was a close friend of Sarrocchi's father ("eiusdem Joannis familiarissuimus amicus erat") from Bartolomeo Chioccarelli, *De illustribus scriptoribus qui in civitate et regno Neapolis ab orbe condito ad annum usque 1646 floruerunt*, MS XIV.A.28.Biblioteca Nazionale di Napoli, 67. Cardinal Guglielmo Sirleto, or Sirleti (1514–85), was the main researcher on theological questions discussed at the Council of Trent and the central figure in editing its publications. Among the many important positions he occupied in the Roman bureaucracy were

class instruction in the liberal arts and sciences. Her teacher in Latin and Italian poetry was Rinaldo Corso, a tutor of repute and a prolific author of books on literature, dance, theology, and the law, who had also written a very successful text of Italian grammar.[6] Credit for Sarrocchi's enduring interest in the sciences goes to Luca Valerio, a distinguished mathematician and teacher, much respected in intellectual circles and in the bureaucracy of the Roman Curia. He taught mathematics, in addition to other disciplines such as rhetoric and Greek, first at the Collegio Romano, then, from about 1600, at the University "La Sapienza" of Rome. In 1611, by recommendation of Cardinal Marcantonio Colonna, he became Greek consultant at the Biblioteca Vaticana.[7] Among his young pupils was Ippolito Aldobrandini, who later became pope and reigned from 1592 to 1605 as Clement VIII. No doubt Sarrocchi's teachers exemplified the best there

---

those of secretary of state of Pius IV and of custodian of the Vatican Library. For a brief presentation of this figure, see his entry in *New Catholic Encyclopedia*, ed. Thomas Carson and Joann Cerrito, vol. 13 (Washington, DC: Gale, 2003), 167. For the part he played in reviving theological studies on a scientific basis and his interest in promoting an educational program that would combine the humanistic disciplines and religious principles, see Charles Dejob, *De l'influence du Concile de Trente sur la littérature et les beaux-arts chez les peuples catholiques* (Paris: F. Thorin, 1884), 5–8, 17–20, 353–66, and Georg Denzler, *Kardinal Guglielmo Sirleto (1514–1585): Leben und Werk. Ein Beitrag zur nachtridentinischen Reform* (Munich: M. Hueber, 1964).

6. This grammar, which went through several reprints before the end of the century, had the title of *Fondamenti del Parlar toscano* (Venice: Comin da Trino, 1549). Rinaldo Corso (1525–80?) had been at the service of Ferrante d'Avalos, the adopted son of Vittoria Colonna, and of Cardinal Girolamo da Correggio. After being for some years the high judge in the civil court of law at Correggio, he embraced an ecclesiastical career and became apostolic inquisitor. About him, his works, and his poetics, see Bernard Weinberg, *A History of Literary Criticism in the Italian Renaissance* (Chicago: University of Chicago Press, 1961), 904–5; Amedeo Quondam, *La parola nel labirinto. Società e scrittura del Manierismo a Napoli* (Rome and Bari: Laterza, 1975), 111–15; and the entry by Giovanna Romei in *Dizionario biografico degli Italiani*, ed. Alberto M. Ghisalberti (hereafter referred to as *DBI*), vol. 29 (Rome: Istituto della Enciclopedia Italiana Treccani, 1983), 687–90. For his commentaries on the poems of Vittoria Colonna and for his life of Veronica Gàmbara, see note 14 of this introduction.

7. Luca Valerio (1552–1618) was known in scientific circles for his application of Archimedean principles to problems of volume and gravity of solids and is still remembered in the history of physics for two books: *De centro gravitatis solidorum* (Bologna, 1604) and *Quadratura parabolae per simplex falsum* (Rome, 1606). In his *Dialogues concerning Two New Sciences*, published in 1638, Galileo refers to Valerio as the Archimedes of the modern age. On Valerio's career and teaching positions, see Filippo Maria Renazzi's *Storia dell'Università degli Studi di Roma detta comunemente "La Sapienza,"* vol. 3 (Rome: Stamperia Pagliarini, 1805), 36, 48; and Nunzio Federico Faraglia, "Fabio Colonna Linceo Napolitano," *Archivio per le province napoletane* (1885): 39–40. For an assessment of Valerio's contribution to physics, see Giulio Giorello, "Gli 'oscuri labirinti': calcolo e geometria nel Cinque e Seicento," in *Storia d'Italia. Annali 3: Scienza e tecnica nella cultura e nella società dal Rinascimento a oggi*, ed. Gianni Micheli (Turin: Einaudi, 1980), 261–380, especially 293–99, 321, 329, 446.

was in the educational program sponsored by Rome, which combined the humanistic curriculum with an innovative interest in the sciences, all made consonant with the theological and political directives of the post-Tridentine church. The biographical notes left by several of her contemporaries attest, in fact, that Sarrocchi was exemplary not only in the humanities, which implied a thorough grounding in the classics and in the disciplines of the trivium and quadrivium,[8] but also in mathematics,

---

8. An idea of what a humanistic education might have been for women of the upper classes since the second half of the fifteenth century is given by the letter that Leonardo Bruni sent to Battista da Montefeltro in 1424. To "the woman who enjoys secular literature" and "wants to perfect her Latin," he suggests reading Cicero, Virgil, Livy, and Sallust. To attain a good knowledge of history, because "the knowledge of the past gives guidance to our counsels and our practical judgment," he advises reading Livy and Sallust again, together with Tacitus, Curtius, and Julius Caesar. From there he goes on to recommend the orators, for they know, he explains, even better than the philosophers how to praise virtue and condemn vice. Among the poets he recommends Hesiod, Pindar, Euripides, Seneca, and Statius; but his greatest and longest praises go to Homer and Virgil, whom he valiantly defends against accusations of pagan immorality and falsity. All these readings must be, in Bruni's estimation, secondary to the study of divinity and moral philosophy, which remain the backbone of a woman's education. Leonardo Bruni, "On the Study of Literature (1524) to Lady Battista Malatesta of Montefeltro," in *The Humanism of Leonardo Bruni: Selected Texts*, trans. and with an introduction by Gordon Griffiths, James Hankins, and David Thompson (Binghamton, NY: Medieval and Renaissance Texts and Studies, 1987), 240–51; the quotations are from 243 and 245. For an evaluation of the program of studies proposed by Bruni, see Margaret L. King and Albert Rabil Jr., *Her Immaculate Hand: Selected Works by and about the Women Humanists of Quattrocento Italy* (Binghamton, NY: Center for Medieval and Early Renaissance Studies, 1983), 13–16.

On humanism in Italy and beyond, see Albert Rabil Jr., ed., *Renaissance Humanism: Foundations, Forms, and Legacy*, 3 vols. (Philadelphia: University of Pennsylvania Press, 1988). On the three most prominent women humanists, Isotta Nogarola (1418–66), Laura Cereta (1469–99), and Cassandra Fedele (1465–1558), see the following: Isotta Nogarola, *Complete Writings: Letterbook, Dialogue on Adam and Eve, Orations*, ed. and trans. Margaret L. King and Diana Robin (Chicago: University of Chicago Press, 2004); Albert Rabil Jr., *Laura Cereta, Quattrocento Humanist* (Binghamton, NY: Center for Medieval and Early Renaissance Studies, 1981); Laura Cereta, *Collected Letters of a Renaissance Feminist*, ed. and trans. Diana Robin (Chicago: University of Chicago Press, 1997); Cassandra Fedele, *Letters and Orations*, ed. and trans. Diana Robin (Chicago: University of Chicago Press, 2000). On the social status of learned women in the early Renaissance and on the reception given them by both men and women, see Margaret L. King, "Book-Lined Cells: Women and Humanism in the Early Italian Renaissance," in *Beyond Their Sex: Learned Women of the European Past*, ed. Patricia H. Labalme (New York: New York University Press, 1980), 66–90.

On women's education in the Renaissance and after, see also Ginevra Conti Odorisio, *Donna e società nel Seicento*, with an introduction by Ida Magli (Rome: Bulzoni, 1979); Gian Ludovico Masetti Zannini, *Motivi storici della educazione femminile. Scienza lavoro giuochi* (Naples: M. D'Auria, 1981); Maria Ludovica Lenzi, *Donne e Madonne. L'educazione femminile nel primo Rinascimento italiano.* (Turin: Loescher, 1982); and Margaret L. King, "The Schooling of Women," in her *Women of the Renaissance* (Chicago: University of Chicago Press, 1991), 164–72. On the problem of knowledge for women, see pp. xxvi–xxvii in the series editors' introduction to this volume.

which was part of the newly formed *Ratio studiorum* in all Jesuit colleges. Significantly, Valerio had himself been a pupil of Christopher Clavius, mathematician of the Collegio Romano, who was a strong proponent of mathematics as preliminary to the study of physics.[9]

The men who praised Sarrocchi's accomplishments were well-known literati who empathized with the cultural and political trends of their times.[10] Bartolomeo Chioccarelli, a Neapolitan scholar, reports that Sarrocchi excelled in rhetoric, Latin, Greek, geometry, philosophy, and theology.[11] Cristofano Bronzini, a writer then employed in the bureaucracy of the Vatican, adds that she was also versed in logic, astrology, and in other sciences. He could testify to Sarrocchi's learning and dialectical skill, he says, "having seen and heard her often. . . . in fact almost continuously."[12] Giulio Cesare Capaccio, a polygraph in the service of the Neapolitan king, states that Sarrocchi's achievements in poetry and her knowledge in many other disciplines were so astonishing that she could deservedly be considered the

9. The Collegio Romano was the Jesuit school of higher learning in Rome. The educational program, promoted by the Jesuits and endorsed by the church, combined the pursuit of knowledge in humanistic subjects and in the sciences with a concern for the theological principles and the goals of the church. On the curriculum of studies in Jesuit colleges, as exemplified by the *Ratio studiorum* (system of studies), see Gian Paolo Brizzi, ed., *La "ratio studiorum." Modelli culturali e pratiche educative dei Gesuiti in Italia tra Cinque e Seicento* (Rome: Bulzoni, c.1981); Allan P. Farrell, *The Jesuit Code of Liberal Education* (Milwaukee: Bruce, 1938); Aldo Scaglione, *The Liberal Arts and the Jesuit College System* (Amsterdam and Philadelphia: John Benjamins, 1986), 1–5, 51–52, 86–90; Giuseppe Cosentino, "Mathematics in the Jesuit Ratio Studiorum," in *Church, Culture, and Curriculum: Theology and Mathematics in the Jesuit Ratio Studiorum*, by Ladislaus Lukacs and Giuseppe Cosentino, trans., ed., and intro. by Frederick A. Homann (Philadelphia: Saint Joseph's University Press, 1999), 47–67.

10. Those who criticized Sarrocchi acerbically and made fun of her tended toward the bohemian fringes of society, such as the up-and-coming writers Giambattista Marino and Tommaso Stigliani and the artist Lodovico Cardi, or men who, like Gian Vittorio Rossi, were freethinkers and obviously inclined to be skeptical toward people among whom they lived. According to Mario Rosa, the discontent of at least some of these men, who had studied in seminaries and universities with a view to employment, is to be attributed to their difficulty in finding work in the bureaucracy of the church and other Italian states. See Rosa, "La chiesa e gli stati regionali," 306–7; Hanlon, "Roman Society," in *Early Modern Italy*, 143–46. See also this introduction, pp. 13–15, and notes 27, 29, 30, 31, and 52.

11. Chioccarelli, *De illustribus scriptoribus*, 67. Chioccarelli (1580–1646) is the only biographer who gives us the names of Sarrocchi's teachers and a complete list of her works (67–68). His *De illustribus scriptoribus* is the source of Angelo Borzelli in *Note intorno a Margherita Sarrocchi ed al suo poema La Scanderbeide* (Naples: Tipografia degli Artigianelli, 1935), 4–5, 8–9. I am grateful to Dott. Piera Russo of the Biblioteca Nazionale di Napoli for sending me a copy of Borzelli's monograph. On Chioccarelli, see *Dizionario enciclopedico della letteratura italiana*, ed. Giuseppe Petronio, vol. 5 (Palermo: Laterza UNEDI, 1966–70), 53–54.

12. Cristofano Bronzini, *Della dignità e nobiltà delle donne* (Florence: Zanobi Pignone, 1622), 130. On Bronzini (1580–1640), who was master of ceremony at the Vatican and secretary of Cardinal Carlo de' Medici, see *DBI*, vol. 14 (1972), 463.

Aspasia, the Ippatia, the Cornificia, the Cornelia, and the Proba of both Naples and Rome.[13] These praises will sound less hyperbolic when we consider that, in addition to the *Scanderbeide*, and to writing sundry Latin and Italian verse, reportedly in excellent style, Sarrocchi was the author of works, lost to us, whose titles bespeak a considerable range of interests and a very keen participation in the questions that were debated by her contemporaries. She wrote a commentary on the poetry of Giovanni della Casa, a favorite topic of academic lecturers; a translation from the Greek of Musaeus's *Hero and Leander*, and an essay on geometry, "Ex geometria habentur aliquot eius demontrationes allata ab eodem Luca Valerio in suo Commentatio ad Euclidem," which was a lesson on Valerio's Archimedean methods for dealing with problems of volume and gravity of solids. We also know that she wrote a theological treatise in Latin entitled *De praedestinatione*, choosing to deal with the question of grace and free will that had caused a long-standing controversy between Dominicans and Jesuits and that was debated by those orders in the presence of the pope from 1595 to 1602.[14]

Praised as a prodigy, young Margherita was introduced to members of the powerful Colonna family, whose palace, like those of many other aristocrats, had become a meeting place for artists and writers. Her association

---

13. Giulio Cesare Capaccio, *Illustrium mulierum et illustrium litteris vivorum elogia* (Naples: apud F. Iacobum Carlinum et Constantinum Vitalem, 1608), 203–4. Capaccio was the secretary of the city of Naples and the author of many erudite books on that town and its illustrious citizens. For his adherence to the aims of the Neapolitan king and to Counter-Reformation ideals, see Amedeo Quondam, "L'ideologia cortigiana di Giulio Cesare Capaccio," in *La parola nel labirinto*, 63, 187–225; and Mario Rosa, "Coscienza di ceto e problema dello Stato negli intellettuali napoletani del Seicento," *Letteratura italiana*, vol. 1: *Il letterato e le istituzioni*, 260. Capaccio's numerous writings are listed by Nicolò Toppi in his *Biblioteca napoletana, et apparato a gli huomini illustri in lettere di Napoli . . . Dalle loro origini, per tutto l'anno 1678* (Naples: Antonio Bulifon, 1678), 165–66.

14. In addition to Chioccarelli's biography (see note 11), references to Sarrocchi's commentary on Giovanni della Casa are found in Giulio Cesare Capaccio's *Illustrium mulierum*, 203, and in Nicolò Toppi's *Biblioteca napoletana*, 206. The translation from the Greek of Musaeus's *Hero and Leander* is mentioned by Aldo Manuzio in a letter he wrote to Margherita on December 18, 1585, from Bologna, where he was teaching at the university. Aldo Manuzio, *Lettere volgari . . . al molto ill. Sign. Lodovico Riccio* (Rome: Santi, 1592), 26–28. See below, note 20. Sarrocchi's essay on predestination and her lesson on Valerio's Archimedean applications are mentioned only by Chioccarelli, *De illustribus scriptoribus*, 67. Before dying, Sarrocchi entrusted her work on predestination to a Father Cartesio so that he would see to its publication. The essay was never published and is now lost. This being the situation, we cannot begin to speculate what that work may have revealed of Sarrocchi's ideas on free will and predestination, a very controversial subject at the time. Her tutor, Rinaldo Corso, may in his youth have sympathized with the Lutheran cause Corso. The dedicatory letter he wrote in 1545 for a tract ostensibly written by Cardinal Fregoso, entitled *Prefatione del reverentiss. Cardinal di Santa Chiesa m. Federico Fregoso nella Pistola di San Paolo ai Romani*, published in Venice in that year, was in fact the translation of a work by Martin Luther. See "Federico Fregoso," in *DBI*, vol. 50 (1998), 396–99.

with this group may explain the contacts she soon was able to establish with other nobles and men of consequence. At fifteen she was asked for a poem to be included in the verse anthology that Muzio Manfredi was editing to honor the ladies of Roman high society: the sonnet contributed by Sarrocchi celebrates Felice Orsini, who with her husband, Marcantonio Colonna, hosted the reunions she attended.[15] Two sonnets singing the praises of Costanza Colonna, Felice's sister-in-law, accompanied the dedication to the same lady in the 1606 edition of the *Scanderbeide*. Another sonnet, memorializing Margaret of Austria, queen of Spain, can be found in an anthology of poems gathered together in honor of their sovereign by some Spaniards living in Rome.[16] We know of Sarrocchi's correspondence with both established and up-and-coming men of letters,[17] but the most famous is the one she herself initiated with Torquato Tasso. The sonnets she sent him are now lost, but judging from the ones forwarded to her in return, which deal with ideas of repentance, withdrawal from the world, and the search for God, Margherita's poems must have proposed the theme of a

---

15. Borzelli (*Note intorno*, 15 n. 2) believes Sarrocchi to have become a member of the Colonna household. His assumption is based on Bartolomeo Sereno's observation, which he quotes from *Trattato de l'uso della lancia* (Naples: Gargano Nucci, 1610), that "in the residence of Signori Colonna shines the delightful intelligence of Margherita Sarrocchi." Sereno's expression, however, may simply mean that Sarrocchi was frequently present at the gatherings in the Colonna palace.

16. Muzio Manfredi's anthology is *Per donne romane. Rime di diversi raccolte e dedicate al Signor Giacomo Buoncompagni* (Bologna: Alessandro Benaco, 1575). Manfredi was a well-thought-of madrigalist and playwright from Cesena, in the Marche region. Donna Costanza Colonna was the daughter of Marcantonio Colonna Senior, hence the sister-in-law of the above-mentioned Felice Orsini. In 1567, she had married Francesco Sforza, marquis of Caravaggio. Among the poets featured in this anthology is Rinaldo Corso: he may in fact have been the person who suggested Margherita's contribution. The three sonnets by Sarrocchi appear in the collection of women poets edited by the Venetian playwright Luisa Bergalli, *Componimenti poetici delle più illustri rimatrici d'ogni secolo* (Venice: Antonio Mora, 1726), 111–12. The collection dedicated to the Spanish queen is *Poesias diversas compuestas en deferentes lenguas en las honras que hizo a Roma la Nacion de los Españoles. A la Magestad Catolica de la Reyna Margarita de Austria nuestra señora* (Rome: Iacopo Mascardo, 1612). Sarrocchi's poem can be read in Borzelli, *Note intorno*, 55.

17. We know of Sarrocchi's literary correspondence with Pietro Strozzi, Roberto Ubaldini, and Luigi de Heredia, among others. A sonnet by Strozzi addressed to Sarrocchi can be read in Borzelli, *Note intorno*, 55. Luigi de Heredia was a Sicilian soldier and a poet of Spanish descent who had resided in the Colonna household. Sarrocchi's sonnets to him are found in his collection of *Rime* edited by Salvatore Salomone Marino (Bologna: Gaetano Romagnoli, 1875). Roberto Ubaldini, a nephew of the future Pope Leo XI, was then a young man about town; later he was made a bishop, then pontifical nuncio to France, and finally a cardinal. His sonnet to Sarrocchi and her reply to him are in Borzelli 1935, 54. For other such exchanges and for Sarrocchi's contacts with men well known in literary and aristocratic circles of Rome and elsewhere, see again Borzelli, *Note intorno*, 11–12, 18–25.

spiritual journey, a favorite topic in those days and one considered proper for a woman corresponding in verse with a man.[18]

From a 1588 book by Giuliano Giasolino on the beneficial effects of the baths of Ischia, which mentions her as Sarrocchi Biraga, we learn for the first time that Margherita had married a Birago, a man not otherwise identified but assumed by most scholars to be from the region of Piemonte.[19] By that time she had made her Roman home a gathering place for literati and intellectuals of repute and of all social extractions. These reunions are described enthusiastically by Aldo Manuzio in a letter he sent to her on December 18, 1585.[20] According to Gian Vittorio Rossi, Margherita "wanted her house to be not only an altar to all fine arts, but also an oracle of philosophy, theology, all the beautiful disciplines, and even all virtues." And he adds rather caustically: "She participated in [other people's] discussions, she mediated their disagreements, and she maintained that whatever she had said was to be taken as a response of the oracle of Delphi."[21] The doors of prestigious academies were soon opened to her. At the dawn of the century, the academy enjoying the greatest favor among the Roman avantgarde was the Accademia degli Umoristi.[22] Sarrocchi was one of the early members—she joined around 1602—and remained active in it for several

18. At this time Torquato Tasso (1544–95) was in Ferrara and very ill. His sonnets to young Margherita are "Luce d'onor ch'abbaglia e par ch'offende," "Quasi per laberinto o per deserto," and "Qui bellezza e valor di nobil alma," all in Torquato Tasso, *Le Rime*, ed. Bruno Basile (Rome: Salerno, 1994), 1:899 and 900, 2:1846. In a letter Tasso addressed on August 24, 1583, to Maurizio Cattaneo in Rome, we read: "I have answered Signora Margherita Sarrocchi's sonnets but not with many flourishes, although I like them myself a lot, but as I was able to and as it seemed appropriate to my present condition." In October of 1585, he wrote to the same friend in answer to his praises of her: "About Signora Margherita Sarrocchi I believe everything that is being written to me; and I think one can gather as much from her writings themselves." I have translated from *Lettere di Torquato Tasso*, vol. 4 (Pisa: N. Capurro, 1826), 180, for the first letter, and from Tasso's *Prose*, ed. Ettore Mazzali (Milan and Naples: Ricciardi, 1959), 952, for the second letter.

19. In a note addressed to the duke of Mantua in 1613 (see below, note 38), Sarrocchi signed herself as Margherita Sarrocchi ne' Biraghi. Borzelli (*Note intorno*, 13) believed her husband to have been a literary man and an academician, perhaps related to Francesco Birago. I find that this Francesco is mentioned by Francesco Saverio Quadrio, in his *Della storia e della ragione d'ogni poesia*, vol. 4 (Bologna: F. Pisarri, 1739), 675, for having dedicated to Tasso's *Gerusalemme conquistata* of 1593 a voluminous work entitled *Avvertimenti Poetici, Istorici, Politici, Cavallereschi, e Morali* (Milan: Benedetto Somasco, 1616).

20. Aldo Manuzio the Younger (1547–97) was a grandchild of Aldo Manuzio (1449–1515), the star of the Renaissance printing industry, and himself a printer and a polygraph of consequence. For his letter to Sarrocchi, see above, note 14.

21. Rossi, *Pinacotheca*, 261.

22. The famed Accademia degli Umoristi had its beginning in the meetings of a few friends, who wrote comedies for their own amusement and met to perform them in the house of Paolo

years. Rossi writes: "I saw her often as she recited very elegant poems with witty epigrammatic endings to the general admiration of the entire audience."[23] From Piemonte, Agostino della Chiesa, present at several of Sarrocchi's lectures during his visits to Rome, also testified to her exceptional learning and skills.[24] According to Nicolò Toppi, she also astonished the best academicians in Naples, reciting her own learned poetic compositions and, at other times, discussing philosophical questions.[25] Sarrocchi was the first woman to be a regular member of an academy and, understandably, took great pride in her ability to shine in the assemblies of learned men, as no one of her sex had had the opportunity to do so earlier.[26] We also know that she was prone to criticize her fellow literati in public. "Far greater than her merits were her pride and vanity," Rossi tells us. "She

---

Mancini. As their reunions were attended by an increasingly larger number of writers, artists, and musicians, the initiators extended their activities to other fields of literature and established an academy that, from the label of "begli umori" (good humors) given them by friends, took the name of Umoristi. About the great success of the academy, seen in the context of the cultural policy pursued by the church, see Piera Russo, "L'Accademia degli Umoristi. Fondazione, struttura, leggi: il primo decennio di attività" in *Esperienze letterarie* 4, no. 4 (1979): 47–61. Among the early notes on the academy, see those by Quadrio, in *Della storia e della ragione d'ogni poesia*, 1:99; Girolamo Tiraboschi, in *Storia della letteratura italiana*, vol. 8, pt. 1 (Florence: Molini Landi, 1812; but written 1772–82), 41–48. Among the modern studies, see Michele Maylender's in *Storia delle Accademie d'Italia*, with preface by S. E. Luigi Rava, vol. 5 (Bologna: Forni, 1976), 370–81; F. W. Gravit, "The Accademia degli Umoristi and Its French Relationships," *Papers of the Michigan Academy* 29 (1935): 505–21; Giuseppe Gabrieli, "Accademie romane. Gli Umoristi," *Roma* 12, no. 4 (1935): 173–84.

23. Rossi, *Pinacotheca*, 260.

24. Francesco Agostino della Chiesa was custodian of archives at the court of Savoy in Turin; later he became a bishop. He wrote a note on Margherita Sarrocchi in his *Theatro delle donne letterate* (Mondovì: G. Gislandi and G. T. Rossi, 1620), 253–54. From Alessandro Tassoni, famous author of the first modern mock epic, *La secchia rapita* (1622; The Rape of the Bucket, 1715), who was a member of the Accademia degli Umoristi and its director for the period 1607–8, we learn that during an academic discussion on Petrarch's *Canzoniere*, Sarrocchi offered a comment on line 49 of the song "Standomi un giorno solo a la fenestra," which, in his view, was a better explanation than the one proposed by Castelvetro. See A. Tassoni, *Considerazioni sopra le rime del Petrarca* (Modena: Giulian Cassani, 1609), 407.

25. Toppi, *Biblioteca napoletana*, 206.

26. Not even in the high Renaissance had women been allowed in the academies as members. Sarrocchi remained the only woman academician until, well into the eighteenth century, a few other ladies became regular members. Lucrezia Marinella, for instance, who in the early 1600s enjoyed in Venice a kind of prestige, if not freedom, comparable to that in which Sarrocchi basked in Rome, never participated in the meetings of the Accademia Veneziana. About women's presence in academic gatherings and on their actual enrollment, see Elisabetta Graziosi, "Arcadia femminile: presenze e modelli," *Filologia e critica* 17, no. 3 (1992): 321–58, and Conor Fahy, "Women and Italian Cinquecento Literary Academies," in *Women in Italian Renaissance Culture and Society*, ed. Letizia Panizza (Oxford: European Humanities Research Center, 2000), 438–52.

considered herself better than anyone. . . . she would pursue with relentless hostility anyone who, during discussions, would not give preference to her assertions or would dare to criticize them. For that reason she made enemies of many men of letters."[27]

Because of her biting criticism Sarrocchi's name has remained tied in literary histories to that of Giambattista Marino, then a rising star just arrived from Naples but destined to become the most celebrated poet of his age. When in Rome in the years 1600–1606, Marino attended the gatherings of the Umoristi and was a welcome guest in Sarrocchi's home. Signs of their friendship appear in Marino's book of verse published in Venice in 1602. In the sonnet "Or qual nome, or qual loda, ond'io t'onori" (With what name, with what praise may I honor you?), he pretends to be at a loss as to how to celebrate her; comparing her to any famed woman of antiquity would be inadequate, because in the presence of her splendor even the rays of the sun go dark. In her return sonnet, "Cingati omai de' suoi più verdi allori Apollo" (May Apollo crown you with his greenest laurels), Margherita answers with matching fervor. With the rays of lofty genius, he will turn this iron age into gold. Undeserving of the praises he has bestowed on her, she will console herself to see how from her sweet nest a swan has flown that will rise so high.[28] Their relationship, however, broke up abruptly when Sarrocchi criticized Marino's work with a vivacity he did not relish. In a programmatic letter addressed to Claudio Achillini, which is the fourth

27. Rossi, *Pinacotheca*, 260. An idea of the off-the-record exchanges between academicians can be had from Rossi's amused description of a disagreement Sarrocchi had with Ottavio Tronsarelli about what emblem was to be adopted for a new academy, the Ordinati. See pp. 14–15. By custom, the emblem symbolized the program and directives of an institution and suggested a pertinent name for its members. Tronsarelli objected to Sarrocchi's idea of a saltcellar— the salt, obtained by drying the insipid element out of seawater, would represent the wisdom of the Ordinati—because it was too obvious a disparagement of the Umoristi, whose chosen symbol was a cloud rising from the sea and letting its vivifying rain fall on earth. Tronsarelli tried to dissuade Sarrocchi by saying that from such an emblem it would be difficult to derive a name worthy of an international institution. At that point, the actor Felice Cima—who, Rossi interjects, used to play in comedies the roles of French characters with a French accent—intervened to say that he had just thought of one. "What is it?" asked Sarrocchi. "Since you sentence us to labor in the saltworks [the word *salino* means both "saltcellar" and "saltwork"]—replied Cima— 'Academy of the Vagrants' makes a very fitting name." In those days vagrants, when arrested, were usually sentenced to work in saltworks. *Pinacotheca*, 694. Ottavio Tronsarelli, then a celebrated poet and a successful librettist, was used to dealing with prima donnas. Among other works, he adapted two cantos of Giambattista Marino's *Adone* for an opera by Domenico Mazzocchi. It was supposed to be sung by Margherita Costa and Cecca del Padule, singers who were at the time in stiff competition for the favor of Roman audiences. See note 46.

28. Both sonnets first appeared in Marino's *Rime* (Venice: G. B. Ciotti, 1602), 225. Now they can be read in Angelo Colombo's article "Il principe celebrato. Autografi poetici di Tomaso Stigliani e Margherita Sarrocchi," *Philologica* 1, no. 1 (1992): 13.

of five letters opening *La Sampogna,* Marino avows that he is far more pleased with the regard shown by those praiseworthy literati who have immortalized him in their writings than "he is saddened by the sharp criticism of scribblers of such poems as the *Scanderbeide.*"[29] Marino further retaliated against Sarrocchi's criticism by ridiculing her literary efforts in his masterwork *Adone* (9.187.5), where he refers to her as a chattering magpie who has the impudence to challenge poets by shrieking and croaking uncouth lines about wars and love. Rossi casually reports the gossip that Marino and Sarrocchi were lovers.[30] His offhand remark has led literary historians to presume that Marino's abandonment of her was the motivation of Sarrocchi's attack, even though their conflicting poetic taste and Sarrocchi's

29. Giambattista Marino, *La Sampogna,* ed. Vania de Maldé (Padua: Guanda, 1993), 27–28. In her remarks, Sarrocchi may have thrown doubts on Marino's poetic talent, for in a further reference to her in the forty-eighth stanza of "I sospiri d'Ergasto," the last idyll of the same collection, he writes that "I would like to praise my Muse, who perhaps equals that of any other poet. . . . but *whatever my abilities may be,* they have forced a new Magpie to keep her silence" (my italics). It may be fair at this point to remember that Marino's attempts at heroic poetry were failures: both his *Gerusalemme distrutta* (1633) and his *L'Anversa liberata* (published only in 1956 in Antwerp) remained unfinished. Another scathing enemy of Sarrocchi—we do not know for what reason—was Tommaso Stigliani, a fellow poet who had been a friend of both her and Marino. His acerbic wit led him to say that having been published when Libra and Pisces were in the ascendant, the *Scanderbeide* was destined to be bought by weight and its pages used to wrap up fish. T. Stigliani, *Canzoniero* (Rome: Giovanni Mannelli, 1625), 445. And following a line of thought advanced in note 10, I may add that both Marino and Stigliani had their lyric verse censored by the religious authorities for licentiousness.

30. Rossi writes exactly: "Baptistam Marinum, quem illa, ut fama erat, alio amore dilexerat, atque Platonico" (the rumor was that she had favored Battista Marino with a love other than platonic) (*Pinacotheca,* 260). In closing his biographical sketch, Rossi appears to throw at Margherita the accusation traditionally leveled against literary women: "As to moral conduct, her reputation was the same as that of women poets, singers, and musicians, and of all those whom the art of painting and acting has taken away from the spindle and the distaff." However, in the next sentence he admits he cannot vouch for the rumor, for he does not have the opportunity to ascertain its truthfulness (261). Modern literary historians, however, have taken as fact what was unsubstantiated gossip, and repeated it from one notice to the next. Rossi, for his part, was wont to castigate all the subjects of his biographies indiscriminately. His caustic wit caused the historian Crescimbeni to lament a century later that while immortalizing many authors by including them in his *Pinacotheca,* he made them pay very dearly for the honor. See Giovanni Mario Crescimbeni, *De' Commentarii intorno all'Istoria della volgar poesia* (Venice: Lorenzo Basegio, 1730), 169. Gian Vittorio Rossi (1577–1647), who used the pen name of Janus Nicius Erythraeus, was a prolific writer of European renown. After many years spent as secretary to Cardinal Andrea Peretti (1610–28), he withdrew to a villa on Monte Mario, which was then outside Rome, and there he wrote many Latin works which were later published in Amsterdam with the spurious location of Cologne or Wolfenbüttel. Both his *Pinacotheca imaginum,* a collection of three hundred short biographies of contemporary men and women, and the roman à clef *Eudemia* (1637) are biting satires of the courtly and literary societies of Rome. On this still important author, see the monograph by Luigi Gerboni, *Un umanista del Seicento, G. N. Eritreo* (Città di Castello, 1899). See also Benedetto Croce, "La Pinacotheca

assertive character would be sufficient explanation. As far as we can judge from her phrasing and her restrained poetic style, Sarrocchi may be considered a late practitioner of sixteenth-century Petrarchism; alternatively, she may be classed among the "moderate" or the "classicist" poets of her time.[31] We can assume her literary preferences had been influenced by the training she received from Rinaldo Corso, who was a devotee of both Vittoria Colonna (1490–1547), on whose lyrics he had written an erudite exegesis in 1542, and of Veronica Gàmbara (1485–1550), whose biography he had penned in 1566.[32] Sarrocchi's poetic taste may therefore have determined a dislike for the rhetorical exuberance of the new avant-garde poetry, of which Marino was to be heralded in the years to come as the leader. That Sarrocchi's preferences harked back to earlier times is also indicated by her commentary on Giovanni della Casa (1503–56), a favorite topic of discussion in sixteenth-century academic reunions. Perhaps because the Accademia degli Umoristi had began to be dominated by admirers of Marino, Margherita left it around 1608. By this time, she had joined a group of other disaffected members who met in the home of Cardinal Giovanni Battista Deti. Here they founded the Accademia degli Ordinati, which very

---

dell'Eritreo," in *Nuovi saggi sulla letteratura italiana del Seicento* (Bari: Laterza, 1931), 124–33; and *Dizionario enciclopedico della letteratura italiana*, ed. Giuseppe Petronio, 4:607–8. Rossi is seen by more modern scholars as a freethinker: his skeptical moralistic vein is viewed in the context of early seventeenth-century Roman circles that favored a secularization of private and public life, and in relation to his friendship with the libertine circle of Gabriel Naudé. See René Pintard, *Le libertinage érudit dans la première moitié du XVIIe siècle* (Paris: Boisin, 1943; Geneva: Slatkine, 1983), 109–16, 259–60; Mario Rosa, *Il letterato e le istituzioni*, 342–44; and Claudio Varese, "Momenti e implicazioni del romanzo libertino nel Seicento italiano," in *Il libertinismo in Europa*, ed. Sergio Bertelli (Milan and Naples: Ricciardi 1980), 265–70.

31. Giambattista Marino probably had Sarrocchi's manner in mind when, in the idyl "La ninfa avara," he acerbically criticized the poets who, harking back to the sixteenth century, sported a style that in his opinion was "pretty and erudite, but trite, common, and very stale," while in fact the time had come for Italian bards to "abandon the trodden path and move on to new ways and concepts." Marino, *La Sampogna*, 505. For the historical background of seventeenth-century poetry, see Anthony Oldcorn's "Lyric Poetry" and Paolo Cherchi's "Seicento: Poetry, Philosophy, and Science," in *The Cambridge History of Italian Literature*, ed. Peter Brand and Lino Pertile (Cambridge: Cambridge University Press, 1996), 251–76 and 301–17.

32. Rinaldo Corso wrote *Dichiaratione sopra la Prima Parte delle Rime della divina Vittoria Colonna* in 1542; its date of publication is not known. His *Dichiaratione sopra la Seconda Parte* was published in 1543 with a dedication to Veronica Gàmbara. The commentary on the poetry of Vittoria Colonna was edited several years later by Girolamo Ruscelli in the volume *Tutte le rime della illustris. Et eccellentiss. Signora Vittoria Colonna Marchesana di Pescara, con la esposizione del signor Rinaldo Corso* (Venice: G. B. e M. Sessa, 1558). The biography of Veronica Gàmbara is included in Corso's *Vita di Giberto terzo di Correggio detto il Difensore, colla vita di Veronica Gàmbara, apologia della casa di Correggio* (Ancona: A. de Grandi, 1566). See notes 6 and 14.

soon made clear its anti-Marinist tendencies.[33] Notwithstanding an impressive patronage of noblemen and prelates, however, the new group dissolved a few years later, and Sarrocchi, now outside all academies, fell back on her own personal resources and on the companionship and faithful assistance of her former tutor, Luca Valerio, who had taken up residence in her home.[34]

Sarrocchi's interest in the sciences continued. Cristofano Bronzini reports that in discussing questions of natural philosophy and the movements of the heavens, she showed such expertise as to make many men from the world of science seek her opinion and regard it highly.[35] Evidence of this assertion is the letters exchanged in 1611 between Sarrocchi, Galileo, and Guido Bettoli of the University of Perugia, when the latter asked Margherita to give him her views on Galileo's discoveries with the telescope.[36] The correspondence with Galileo began after Margherita had met him in February of 1611, when he was in Rome to receive the endorsement of the Accademia dei Lincei. Of this epistolary exchange seven of her letters remain; they are preserved, still unpublished, among Galileo's manuscripts at the Biblioteca

33. On the Accademia degli Ordinati, see Quadrio, *Della storia e della ragione d'ogni poesia,* 1:98; Tiraboschi, *Storia della letteratura italiana,* 8:48–50; and Maylender, *Storia delle Accademie d'Italia,* 4:140–41.

34. As the Academy of the Ordinati dissolved, the Accademia degli Umoristi entered a period of great popularity. Its membership list reads as a "Who's Who in Rome." Besides Giambattista Marino and Alessandro Tassoni, we find the names of Battista Guarini, son of the author of the pastoral drama *Pastor Fido* (1589); Francesco Bracciolini, a polygraph writer who, as the author of *Lo Scherno degli dei* (1618, The Scorn of the Gods), credited himself with the invention of the heroic-comic genre; Girolamo Preti, friend and follower of Marino's; Gabriello Chiabrera and Giovanni Ciampoli, who were anti-Marinists, the latter a friend and defender of Galileo; Virginio Cesarini, an aristocrat and writer of moral poetry, as well as a scientist and member of the Accademia dei Lincei; Ottavio Rinuccini, librettist of the Camerata Fiorentina and author, among other operas, of *Dafne* (1598) and of *Arianna* (1608). Better-known prelates among the members were Cardinal Giulio Mazzarini, known to the world as Jules Mazarin, Cardinal Sforza Pallavicino, theologian, literary critic, and future historian of the Council of Trent, and two popes: Clement VIII Aldobrandini and Urban VIII Barberini. See a more complete list in Maylender, *Storia delle Accademie d'Italia,* 4:375–80. In 1612 membership was open to French writers. A spin-off of this academy was that of the Malinconici, established by those who had been refused admission by the Umoristi because their membership had expanded beyond measure.

35. Bronzini, *Della dignità e nobiltà delle donne,* 135. According to Bronzini, Sarrocchi was asked by a Camillo Paleotti of Bologna if she would be willing to teach at the university of that city either geometry and logic or any other subject of (natural) philosophy she preferred (136).

36. Bettoli's colleagues in Perugia had raised disconcerting suspicions about Galileo's claims, for his new description of Jupiter and its satellites challenged the traditional Aristotelian view of the universe. In answer to these objections Sarrocchi wrote to Bettoli: "Everything that is being said about Signor Galileo's discoveries is true. That is, together with Jupiter are four stars that move of their own motion and keep always at equal distance from it but not from one another. I saw this with my own eyes through the telescope, and I showed it to several friends, and all

Nazionale Centrale of Florence.[37] They are mostly notes of acknowledgment and thanks for copies of his books or for mathematical theorems he had sent of some astronomical discoveries.[38] Some passages allow an insight into the problems Sarrocchi faced during the revision of her manuscript and will be considered later in the analysis of the poem.

The first *Scanderbeide* was published by Lepido Facij in Rome in 1606. It consisted of 946 octaves, or 7,568 lines, of poetry, in eleven cantos and three very brief summaries. The abrupt interruption at the end of canto 14 shows it to be a narrative still in the making. This version differs from the one that finally appeared in 1623, not only in length—the latter consisting of 2,251 stanzas or 18,008 lines, in twenty-three cantos—but also in content and organization. How subject and structure vary from one publication to the next will be discussed below. The incomplete state of the early poem seems not to be due to its going to press without the author's knowledge, as

the world knows about it. With Saturn are two stars, very close to it, one at one side and the second at the other. Venus, when meeting with the Sun, can be seen to light up and turn crescent like the moon. It remains so until it is full again, and while it is on the increase, it seems to be getting smaller. This is a clear sign, it is in fact a geometric proof, that Venus moves around the Sun. . . . Many great mathematicians, Father Clavius and Father Grienberger in particular, first denied this phenomenon, but later, after making certain of it, retracted and gave public lectures about it." This letter was published by Antonio Favaro in *Amici e corrispondenti di Galileo*, vol. 1 (Florence: Salimbeni, 1983), 29–30. Galileo kept the copy sent to him among other papers he considered proofs, vis-a-vis the authorities, of the recognition with which his scientific claims were being greeted. Bettoli had made the same request to Father Grienberger. Christopher Grienberger was the chief mathematician of the Collegio Romano. In subsequent years, Clavius and Grienberger adhered to Tycho Brahe's theory, because Brahe, by maintaining that the sun and its planets—as seen by Galileo—orbited the earth, did not contradict the scriptural geocentric view of the universe, while the Copernican theory did. Sarrocchi's support of Galileo at this point does not pertain to the heliocentric question. When, on March 5, 1616, Roberto Bellarmino, the chief Roman theologian, condemned Kepler's view of the universe, Luca Valerio sided with church authorities. May we assume Margherita did too? Sarrocchi's and Valerio's correspondence with Galileo came to an end then. It had started with a note, dated April 4, 1609, in which Valerio thanked Galileo for a theorem he had just received, adding that he had studied it in the company of his former pupil, Margherita Sarrocchi, "a woman very knowledgeable in all the sciences, and of very sharp intellect." *Opere di Galileo Galilei*, vol. 8 (Florence: Società Editrice Fiorentina, 1851), 38–41.

37. Manoscritti Galileiani, pt. 1, vol. 13, carte 10, 12, 14, 16, 18. Only one letter of Galileo to Sarrocchi remains. It was found in the Archivio Storico Gonzaga of Mantua and can be read in *Tre lettere di Galileo Galilei*, ed. Gilberto Govi (Rome: Tipografia delle scienze matematiche e fisiche, 1870), 9–10. It is dated January 21, 1612, and in it Galileo thanks Margherita for sending him her poem and adds that, made very weak in body and mind by a long debilitating disease, he is not in a condition to apply himself to reading it.

38. In a note sent to Galileo in 1612, Sarrocchi thanks him for a copy of *Discourse on Floating Bodies*, a work of his that had just come off the press (Favaro, *Amici e corrispondenti di Galileo*, 1:20).

its dedicatory letter states, for on April 4, 1609, Valerio wrote to Galileo that many errors remained in the printed *Scanderbeide* because Sarrocchi had not had a chance to review it.[39] However that may be, the criticism encountered in 1606 unsettled Sarrocchi, who busied herself adding to and subtracting from her work at least until 1613.[40]

By that time, Margherita had became a widow.[41] She herself died in Rome on October 27, 1617. Her body, crowned by laurel, was taken to the church of Santa Maria della Minerva and was buried there after a stately ceremony accompanied by music and poetic recitals. Valerio followed her in death a year later. *La Scanderbeide, Poema Heroico della Sig.ra Margherita Sarrocchi,* edited by Giovanni Latini, was published in Rome by Andrea Fei in 1623. The same edition was issued by Lepido Facii in 1626 and again in 1723.[42]

HEROIC POETRY AND SARROCCHI'S CHOICE OF SUBJECT

By the end of the sixteenth century, the epic genre in Italy had produced two masterpieces: Ludovico Ariosto's *Orlando Furioso* (1532) and Torquato Tasso's *Jerusalem Delivered* (1574). As the final achievements of two divergent manners of processing literary traditions, they stood for the alternative

---

Besides the seven sent to Galileo and one to Bettoli, two more letters of Sarrocchi are extant. One was addressed to Ferdinando Gonzaga, duke of Mantua, on January 19, 1613. In it Margherita asks for a recommendation to be presented to the pope and to Cardinal Borghese in connection with a litigation against Filippo Colonna. See Borzelli, *Note intorno,* 56–57. The second letter, which is in Latin, is addressed to Marco Antonio Bonciario, a professor of Latin living in Perugia, whom Sarrocchi praises for his accomplishments, virtues, and his forbearance in his state of blindness. It is found in *Lettere di uomini illustri scritte a M. Antonio Bonciario perugino* (Venice: G. B. Merlo, 1839), 33–34. A copy of this letter was kindly provided to me by Dott. Paolo Renzi, of the Biblioteca Comunale Augusta of Perugia, Italy.

39. Valerio adds that the "many errors in it are due to the hurry of those who printed it." See Favaro, *Amici e corrispondenti di Galileo,* 1:13–14. It is reasonable to assume that this publication came out with the author's knowledge, that it was also all of the poem Sarrocchi had written at that point, and that it remained so for a few years to come, for in a letter to Galileo dated May 21, 1609, Valerio still referred to "the eleven cantos" that would be sent to him for his opinion. Favaro, 1:7.

40. This we also know from Valerio, who, writing to Galileo on August 31, 1613, stated that all revisions had then been completed and publication was expected to take place soon. Ibid., 1:21.

41. Valerio refers to Margherita as a widow in the same letter of August 31. See previous note.

42. In 1701 Antonio Bulifon of Naples brought out a partial version of the *Scanderbeide.* It is divided into two parts, the first containing cantos 1–7, and the second containing cantos 8 and 9 and the summaries of 12 and 14. According to Canonici Fachini, the Bulifon version saw the light again in Rome in 1726. See Ginevra Canonici Fachini, *Prospetto biografico delle donne italiane rinomate in letteratura* (Venice: Alvisopoli, 1824), 161.

directions the epic writer could choose and became the paradigms by which any epic work would subsequently be judged. In a carefully designed pattern of many narrative strands, Ariosto's poem alternated the two main subjects of the Italian chivalric tradition: the deeds of Charlemagne's paladins, which had long been given a comic slant for the enjoyment of the masses, and the romantic adventures of the Arthurian knights, which greatly appealed to courtly audiences. With Torquato Tasso's *Jerusalem Delivered*, narrative poetry underwent a fundamental change and took the fitting name of "heroic." In his poem, and as theorized by Tasso himself in *Discorsi dell'arte poetica, et in particolare del poema heroico* (1567–70), the subject matter conjoined historical credibility with the Christian marvelous—consisting in miracles, visions, and interventions of angels and demons—and was intermingled with enough romantic episodes to divert the reader periodically from the earnest account of heroic deeds. There were no imaginary, entertaining characters embroiled in events leading to continuous and unexpected transformation, as found in chivalric poetry. In Tasso's heroic poem characters and their vicissitudes were treated with moral and religious seriousness; their concerns were dramatically poised between the pursuit of heroic and ascetic ideals and the mystifying lure of pleasure. All was brought within the boundary of one single action: the divinely inspired struggle for the possession of Jerusalem. Tasso's work was hailed in many theoretical writings as the prototype of a genre that in didactic intent and literary decorum was considered superior to any previous example of narrative poetry.[43] In spirit and intent, furthermore, the heroic poem suited an age experiencing renewal in its religious and moral concerns and entertained a readership keenly interested in the wars fought by major powers, whose consequences the Italian states had suffered in the past and in which many of them now participated. In the climate of conformity that had set in after the Council of Trent, and in the atmosphere of diminished freedom

---

43. For a succinct exposition of Tasso's vision of the heroic poem, I refer readers to Ernest Hatch Wilkins's *A History of Italian Literature* (Cambridge: Harvard University Press, 1954), 270–71. For the arguments in favor of and against the chivalric romance and the classicizing historical poem, fundamental remains Bernard Weinberg's "The Quarrel between Ariosto and Tasso," in *A History of Literary Criticism in the Italian Renaissance*, 954–1073. Not all contemporary theorists saw the features distinctive of the two genres very lucidly. The differences were clearly put forward by Giambattista Giraldi Cintio in *Discorsi intorno al comporre dei romanzi, delle comedie, e delle tragedie* (1554). Two centuries later, however, Quadrio still felt the need to dedicate well over three hundred pages to the distinction between the two categories: see his *Della storia e della ragione d'ogni poesia*, 4:287–643. For an excellent overview of narrative poetry in the period preceding the writing of the *Scanderbeide*, see Peter Marinelli, "Narrative Poetry," in Brand and Pertile, *Cambridge History of Italian Literature*, 233–50.

prevailing everywhere, the heroic poem became the most prestigious genre, the one most apt to celebrate religious piety and promote state policies.[44] Given Sarrocchi's literary aptitudes, her empathy with the ideological aims of her class, and her competitive spirit, the choice of a genre so congenial to men and so far never attempted by a woman comes as no surprise.

At the turn of the century, when Sarrocchi began working on her narrative, and for some time to come, there was no historical complete epic poem from the pen of a woman. The adaptation in octaves of a medieval picaresque fiction, *Il Meschino altramente detto il Guerino*, had been published in 1560 under the name of Tullia d'Aragona, and an unfinished chivalric poem by the title of *Tredici canti del Floridoro*, written by Moderata Fonte, had come to light in 1581.[45] Sarrocchi may have known both works, but the differences in the subject matter, tone, and structure are so great as to allow no meaningful comparison between them and the *Scanderbeide*. Those two romances aside, women writers of heroic poetry had given their preference

---

44. According to Antonio Belloni, in the seventeenth century alone, Italian poets produced at least ninety-eight poems in imitation of Tasso's *Jerusalem*. See his *Storia della letteratura d'Italia, Il Seicento* (Milan: Vallardi, 1929), 181. On Italy as the main producer of tracts on warfare, see John Rigby Hale, *War and Society in Renaissance Europe, 1450–1620* (London: Methuen, 1985), 57. On the ways in which epic poets in Italy and elsewhere adapted their descriptions of warfare to the changes brought about by the gunpowder revolution and by the new technologies of war, see Michael Murrin, *History and Warfare in Renaissance Epic* (Chicago: University of Chicago Press, 1994). See also canto 14.86n. On the political ideology of *Jerusalem Delivered*, see David Quint, "Political Allegory in the *Gerusalemme liberata*," in *Epic and Empire: Politics and Generic Form from Virgil to Milton* (Princeton: Princeton University Press, 1993), 213–47.

45. Moderata Fonte, *Tredici canti del Floridoro*, ed. Valeria Finucci (Modena: Mucchi, 1995). An English translation of this work is in preparation for this series. The attribution of *Il Meschino* to Tullia d'Aragona (1510–56) remains dubious, above all because there is no mention of it anywhere, before the Sessa brothers of Venice published it under the name of the famous courtesan. Gloria Allaire has argued in favor of the attribution in "Tullia d'Aragona's 'Il Meschino altramente detto il Guerino' as Key to a Reappraisal of Her Work," *Quaderni d'Italianistica* 16, no. 1 (1995): 33–50. *Il Meschino* is a rendition of a tale by Andrea da Barberino (1370–1431) by way of a Castilian translation by Hernández Alemán. It relates the fictional story of Guerin, the dispossessed lord of Durazzo, who is sold into slavery as a child and after many adventures finds his parents and repossesses his kingdom. Notwithstanding Crescimbeni's argument that the quest for Guerino's father confers on the *Meschino* a unity of action that almost qualifies it as a heroic poem (*De' Commentarii intorno all'Istoria della volgar poesia*, 67), the style, the tone, as well as the rambling fantastic adventures padding the quest, decidedly place that work in the area of medieval romances. Laura Terracina, *Discorso sopra il governo di tutti i canti d'Orlando Furioso* (Venice: Giolito, 1559), is a serious reworking of Ariosto's wittily sententious stanzas found at the beginning of each canto of his poem. On the work of Terracina, see Nancy Dersofi, "Laura Terracina," in *Italian Women Writers*, ed. Rinaldina Russell (Westport, CT: Greenwood Press, 1994), 423–50, and Daniel Javitch, *Proclaiming a Classic: The Canonization of "Orlando Furioso"* (Princeton: Princeton University Press, 1991), 173. An edition of Terracina's works is being prepared for this series by Michael Sherberg.

to the trials and tortures suffered by martyrs and virgin saints. Fonte was inspired by the life of Christ in two poems she published in 1581 and 1592. Between 1596 and 1606, Lucrezia Marinella had published four poetic writings based on the lives of virgin martyrs, the Virgin Mary, and Saint Francis. The three cantos of *Davide perseguitato* (1611) by Maddalena Salvetti Acciajuoli were inspired by the biblical story, and *Cecilia martire*, a poem published in Rome by Margherita Costa in 1644, also dealt with a sacred subject.[46] In 1635 Lucrezia Marinella would publish *L'Enrico, ovvero Bizantio acquistato* (The Enrico, or Byzantium Conquered), the only other historical poem written by a woman.[47] Five years later, Barbara degli Albizzi Tagliamochi, a renowned opera singer, published *Ascanio errante*.[48] Her

46. Maddalena Salvetti Acciajuoli was Florentine. In 1590 she had published a collection of poetry in praise of the Grand Duke Ferdinando de' Medici and his wife, Catherine of Lorraine. Of her poem, *Davide perseguitato*, which she left incomplete at her death, three cantos were published in Florence by Landini in 1611. There is no way of guessing where her narrative would have ended, considering that it starts from Adam and Eve and the creation of the angels. See Ambrogio Levati, *Dizionario biografico-cronologico*, vol. 5: *Donne illustri* (Milan: Nicolò Tosi, 1822), 71. The Roman Margherita Costa was a singer of renown and a prolific writer, if not one of great literary merit. She performed in Rome, Florence, Turin, and even in Paris, where she was summoned by Cardinal Mazarin in 1646. For her Domenico Mazzocchi composed *La catena d'amore*, an opera with libretto by Ottavio Tronsarelli. On Tronsarelli, see above, note 27. On Costa's career see *DBI*, vol. 30 (1980), 232–35. The sacred poems by the two Venetian writers are: Moderata Fonte, *La passione di Christo* (Venice: Guerra, 1581) and *La resurrezione di Gesù nostro Signore* (Venice: Imberti, 1592); Lucrezia Marinella, *La colomba sacra* (Venice: Ciotti, 1595), *Vita del serafico et glorioso San Francesco* (Venice: Bertano, 1597), *La vita di Maria Vergine imperatrice dell'universo* (Venice: Barezzi, 1602), and *Vita di Santa Giustina* (Florence, 1606). Marinella wrote on religious subjects in prose as well: *Dei gesti heroici e della vita meravigliosa della serafica Santa Caterina da Siena* (Venice: Barezzi, 1624), *Le vittorie di Francesco il serafico. I passi gloriosi della diva Chiara* (Padua: Crivellari, 1647), and *Holocausto d'amore della vergine Santa Giustina* (Venice: Leni, 1648). For an introduction to the works of Moderata Fonte, see Paola Malpezzi Price, "Moderata Fonte," in Russell, *Italian Women Writers*, 129–37, and Virginia Cox's introduction to her edition of Fonte's *The Worth of Women* (Chicago: University of Chicago Press, 1997). For a survey of Marinella's works and the circles in which she moved, see the introduction by Françoise Lavocat to her edition of Marinella's *Arcadia felice* (Florence: Olschki, 1998), especially ix–xxv, and Letizia Panizza's introductory pages to Lucrezia Marinella, *The Nobility and Excellence of Women*, ed. and trans. Anne Dunhill (Chicago: University of Chicago Press, 1999), 8–11. For an overview of seventeenth-century religious epic poetry, see Belloni, *Il Seicento*, 229–34.

47. Lucrezia Marinella's *L'Enrico, ovvero Bisantio acquistato* (Venice: Ghirardo Imberti, 1635). An English translation of this epic is forthcoming in this series. A reasoned census of epic poems by women is found in Valeria Finucci's introduction to her edition of *Tredici canti del Floridoro*, x–xii, and in two articles by Virginia Cox: "Fiction, 1560-1650," in *A History of Women Writing in Italy*, ed. Letizia Panizza and Sharon Woods (Cambridge: Cambridge University Press, 2000), 57–61, and "Women as Readers and Writers of Chivalric Poetry in Early Modern Italy," in *Sguardi sull'Italia. Miscellanea dedicata a Francesco Villari*, ed. Gino Bedoni, Sygmunt Baranski, Anna Laura Lepschy, and Brian Richardson (Leeds: Society for Italian Studies, 1997), 134–45.

48. *Ascanio errante* (Florence: Stamperia dei Landini, 1640).

subject, present in the "matter of Rome" cycle of medieval *cantari*, seems to be influenced by the theatrical treatment that such mythological themes received in early opera.[49] Because narrative poems by women are few and obey different sets of generic norms and expectations from those of poems written by men, criticism has generally focused on the difficulties the authors had to face in adapting to a man's mode of conceptualizing experiences and on judging female characters as embodiments of feminist claims. On this latter subject and on Marinella's *L'Enrico*, more will be said in the appropriate sections.

In Sarrocchi's time and specifically for her, the choice of Scanderbeg's war against the Turks as the subject of a heroic poem may have seemed obvious. For the Roman church the greatest threat to Christianity continued to be the Ottoman Empire. By the end of the fifteenth century, the sultans, who in 1453 had established their capital at Istanbul, formerly Byzantium, completed their conquest of the Balkans and advanced as far north as Vienna. Notwithstanding the victory of the Christian League at Lepanto in 1571, the coastal towns of southern Italy were constantly pillaged by Turkish ships and by pirate vessels from Africa, whose coastal regions were becoming part of the Turkish domain. In 1580, a fleet of Mehmet the Conqueror crossed the Adriatic from the port of Valona and laid siege to the Italian town of Otranto. In 1599 the city of Reggio was burned down by the Ottoman fleet under the command of Scipione Cicala, an Italian slave converted to Islam. The old plan of the liberation of Europe from the Turkish menace, a major concern for the popes who supported the Albanian leader, had been revived with great persistence by Ippolito Aldobrandini, Luca Valerio's former student and now Pope Clement VIII.[50] Besides the Church of Rome, the Aragonese kings of Naples had been involved in Scanderbeg's campaign. Their interest in Epirus could be traced to the eleventh century when, during the Third Crusade, the Norman Robert Guiscard of Sicily occupied part of the country. In 1258, Manfred, son of Frederick Hohenstaufen, German emperor and king of Sicily, married

---

49. On Barbara Albizzi Tagliamochi, see Ambrogio Levati, *Dizionario biografico-cronologico*, 5:78.

50. During his pontificate, Pope Clement VIII organized and financed contingents to participate in campaigns of Christian princes against the Turks led by the houses of Spain and Austria. About the papal backing of this off-and-on war, see Domenico Caccamo, "La diplomazia della Contro Riforma e la crociata: dai piani del Possevino alla lunga guerra di Clemente VIII," in *Archivio storico italiano* 128, no. 2 (1970): 255–81, especially 270–75. See also Angelo Tamborra, "La lotta contro il turco e l'intervento degli stati italiani alla fine del '500," in *Ungheria oggi* 5 (1965): 20–29, and Agostino Borromeo, "Clemente VIII," in *DBI*, vol. 26 (1982), 259–82.

Helen, the daughter of Michael II, despot of Epirus. After Manfred's death in 1266, the Albanian territories were claimed by the new dynasties of southern Italy: first by the Anjou, who, negotiating with the Albanian lords, created a kingdom of central Albania, and later by the Aragonese.[51] It was to Alfonso Aragona of Naples that Scanderbeg turned for military and financial support in 1450. In virtue of a treaty signed with that king the following year, he became a Neapolitan vassal and captain general of the Crown of Aragon. It is not surprising, therefore, that Sarrocchi, a citizen of Rome, sprung from the Neapolitan bourgeoisie that boasted a long tradition of support for the monarchy, should choose as her subject the resistance mounted against the Ottomans by Scanderbeg, the Neapolitan Aragonese vassal, who had been hailed in Rome and in Europe as the champion of Christianity. Sarrocchi may also have been encouraged to choose those events by Luca Valerio himself. His mother, whose Italianized name was Giovanna Rodomani, had arrived from Corcyra, and it is reasonable to infer that she belonged to one of the many Albanian families that had moved to Italy at the end of Scanderbeg's conflict.[52]

THE *SCANDERBEIDE*

Scanderbeide means poem on Scanderbeg, just as *Iliade* (Italian for *Iliad*) is a poem on Ilium, i.e., Troy. Scanderbeg was born George (Gjergj) Castrioti, or Kastrioti, in 1405, to Gjon Castrioti, a chieftain who had lost his territory in the region of Matia to the advancing Turks. After the battle of Niš in Serbia, where the Ottomans were defeated by the Hungarians in 1443— a war in which the Castrioti are likely to have participated as vassals of the sultan—Scanderbeg defected with his nephew, Hamza Castrioti, and took

51. For a more extensive explanation of the claims made through the centuries by the dynasties of the southern kingdom of Italy—the Hohenstaufen, the Angevins, and the Aragonas— see Athanas Gegaj, "L'Albanie sous l'Empire de Byzance et sous l'influence occidentale jusqu'au XVe siècle," in his *L'Albanie et l'invasion turque au XVe siècle* (Louvain: Bureaux du Recueil, Bibliothèque de l'Université, 1937), 3–7; Edwin E. Jacques, *The Albanians: An Ethnic History from Prehistoric Times to the Present* (Jefferson, NC: McFarland, 1995), 178–89, 165–66.

52. In his last will and testament dated March 26, 1618—in which he leaves his possessions to Giovanni Latini, who in 1623 will publish the *Scanderbeide* (Favaro, *Amici e corrispondenti di Galileo*, 1:22)—one reads that Valerio's mother was born on the island of Corcyra. Corcyra had been part of the Despotate of Epirus, and Epirus was the name Italians used interchangeably with that of Macedonia to indicate Albania. Valerio's great loyalty and attachment to Sarrocchi could therefore have been due not to "his teaching her," as a common friend, the painter Lodovico Cardi da Cingoli, who at the time was working in the Medici palace at Campo Marzio, sarcastically reported to Galileo (Favaro, 1:20–21; *Opere di Galileo Galilei*, 226–28), but, to a great extent, to her writing a poem that celebrated a cause dear to his heart.

possession of Kruja and other fortresses. He then abjured Islam and tried for many years to keep alive an alliance of Albanian chieftains while fighting first against Murad II—until this sultan died in 1451—and then against his successor, Mehmet the Conqueror. In 1468 Scanderbeg died of malaria in Alessio where he was bargaining for Venetian reinforcements and further financial support. His resistance to the Turks, an unremitting war of attrition, sieges, and major pitched battles, now stands in Albanian history as the first struggle for the independence of the country, which was eventually achieved in 1912.

The history of Scanderbeg's campaign concerns a complex web of diverging interests among the Albanian lords, for each one of them pursued alliances consistent with his specific territorial situation. Some of them, such as the Dukagins, never joined what in time was called the League of the Albanian People and always acted independently of it. Other nobles switched alliances back and forth: either to the Venetians, as the Spanis, the Dushmanis, the Altisferis, and the Arjanits did, or to a militancy under the sultan, as did Gjergi Stresi Balsha, Moisi Golemi of Dibra, and Hanza Castrioti.[53] In the face of these complications, Scanderbeg showed an outstanding diplomatic shrewdness, a great ability for political organization, and a military adroitness that allowed him to keep the enemy constantly at bay by taking advantage of the rugged Albanian terrain and using guerrilla tactics of ambushes and swift, unexpected attacks. Scanderbeg's successes aroused the lively interest of the popes, but their repeated attempts to organize a crusade against the Ottomans broke down each time in the face of political-ecclesiastical problems confronting the church at home and the lukewarm interest of European princes who were more urgently concerned with fending off one another. Eugenius IV (1431–47) tried in vain to persuade the reluctant Christian potentates to concerted action. Nicholas V (1447–55) named Scanderbeg "Champion of Christendom." Callixtus III (1455–58) made him captain general of the Holy See, while calling, still ineffectually, for a new campaign. His successor, Pius II, died suddenly at Ancona in 1464 while trying to assemble a fleet with the intention of sailing with it himself for Albania. And finally, Paul II (1464–71) gave the Albanian warrior yet a new but unhelpful title of *Athleta Christi*. A strong military operation against the Turks was mounted only by Poles and

---

53. On these defections, see Harry Hodgkinson, *Skanderbeg*, ed. Bejtullah Destani and Westrow Cooper, intro. David Abulafia (London: Center for Albanian Studies, 1999), 136, 144; Gegaj, *L'Albanie et l'invasion turque*, 57, 93; Jacques, *Albanians*, 185. A detailed presentation of the Albanian lords and their families is found in Gegaj, 7–30.

Hungarians, who were defeated by the Ottomans at Varna in 1444 and at Kosovo in 1448.

Before Scanderbeg died, his war had already taken a turn for the worse. At his death, his wife, Andronika, and their son, Gjon Castrioti, whose reception he had already negotiated with the Italians, moved to Italy on a Neapolitan ship sent to fetch them. Kruja (in the poem Croia) was captured in 1478. The Venetians lost most of their enclaves in the Balkans—Scutari and Durazzo fell in 1479 and 1501, respectively—and Albania became part of a Turkish empire now extending from the Euphrates into the center of Europe. Further agreements with the Venetians in the 1400s and a formal alliance with France against the house of Hapsburg in 1536 brought the Ottomans well into the European theater of politics and conflicts.

In Sarrocchi's time, the standard source for the Albanian wars was the chronicle of a Catholic priest of Scutari, whose Latinized name was Marinus Barletius (c. 1460–c. 1512). His *Historia de vita et gestis Scanderbegi* was published to great acclaim around 1506 or 1508 and was translated into Italian and many other European languages. Several Italian histories saw the light soon thereafter, but since they were all dependent on Barletius's work it is not possible to ascertain which and how many of them Sarrocchi consulted.[54] In the principal actions and in some specific episodes, indicated here in the footnotes to the poem, Sarrocchi follows the representation of events established by Barletius. The story, for instance, that Gjon Castrioti was impelled to relinquish his children to the sultan as hostages and that all but one were poisoned when adults is unfounded. It was believed, nonethe-

---

54. Some of the Italian works dependent on Barletius are *Vita dello Scanderbeg* by Luigi Groto (1541–1585), *Commentario de le cose de Scanderbeg* published in 1539 by an unknown author in Venice, *Commentarii de le cose de' Turchi, con gli fatti et la vita di Scanderbeg* by Paolo Giovio (1483–1552), and *Commentario delle cose dei Turchi e del Signor Giorgio Scanderbeg* by Demetrio Franco (Dimiter Frengu), also published in Venice in 1545, and again in 1584 and 1591 as *Gli illustri e gloriosi gesti . . . del signor Don Giorgio Castriott*. A chronicle more reliable than Barletius's was authored by the so-called Anonymous of Antivari, referred to as the Antibarensis. His *Historia Scanderbegi* contains facts related by his brother, who had been Scanderbeg's officer of the guards. We know of it and of its contents thanks to G. M. Biemmi, who drew from it in his *Historia di Giorgio Castrioto, detto Scander-Begh*, published in Brescia in 1742. The work of the Antibarensis had been published in 1480 and had been totally ignored. For a rich bibliography on Scanderbeg, see Gegaj, *L'Albanie et l'invasion turque*, vii–xx. While chronicles of the Albanian wars abounded when Sarrocchi began to write her poem, very little existed on the subject in poetic form. In 1585 in Carmagnola Baldassarre Scaramelli had published two undistinguished cantos on Scanderbeg. We know from Quadrio (*Della storia e della ragione d'ogni poesia*, 6:260) that, in his time, a manuscript of twelve cantos, penned by a Francesco Bardi and entitled *Giorgio Castriotto detto Scanderbeg*, was kept in the study of a Signor Adami. Today these cantos are nowhere to be found, and we cannot guess what effect they might have had on Sarrocchi if, in fact, she was acquainted with them.

less, that Gjergi, once taken to the Ottoman court in Edirne (Adrianople), was brought up as a Muslim with the name of Alexander (in Turkish, Iskander), that he was made an officer of the Janissaries and distinguished himself, winning rewards from the sultan, who also gave him the title of Beg (hence Scanderbeg).[55]

Given Sarrocchi's knowledge of history and epics, both classical and modern, she had no difficulty in turning a relatively recent military campaign into poetry. Her concerns about the *Scanderbeide* were primarily of a structural nature. This can be easily inferred from her correspondence with Galileo. In her letter to him, dated January 13, 1612, which accompanied a copy of her manuscript, she pressingly writes: "I beg Your Lordship to give me your sincere opinion and to be so severe a judge as to change and transpose lines the way you think best. . . . I would also like you to divide this poem into several cantos and give me your thoughts about it, because the cantos seem too long to me the way they are now."[56] The nature of her worries is confirmed by the type of revisions made to the draft of 1606.[57]

Scanderbeg's escape to Buda, his tarrying in the countryside in different locations, his chance encounters with enemy envoys, and Serrano's canny errand to negotiate with the Turks in charge of the fortress were episodes that delayed the start of the military action and were therefore duly excised. Structural as well as moral considerations no doubt led to the omission of the adulterous story of Serrano and Calidora, which in the first version intertwined in an improbable sequence of reprises with that of Alexander's fortunes. Serrano is the perfidious seducer who, aware of the effect his manly allure has on Calidora, the wife of a Turkish guard, decides to make political use of it. When scruples overtake him, he abandons her; later he is ready to consider matrimony but is held back by Alexander's objections. We see him at his end sleepless in bed, torn apart by bouts of

55. For an appraisal of this story, see Hodgkinson, *Skanderbeg*, 52–64, and Gegaj, *L'Albanie et l'invasion turque*, 42.

56. The letter is quoted by Favaro, *Amici e corrispondenti di Galileo*, 1:18. Once back in Florence, Galileo fell ill and did not keep his promise to examine Margherita's poem, an assurance he may have given her when he was in Rome. In a letter written at the end of the same year, Sarrocchi asks for her manuscript back and tactfully explains to Galileo that since she has by now made many changes in her work, it would be a waste of time for him to read the pages he has on hand. It is not surprising that Sarrocchi should turn to the celebrated scientist for a detailed critique of her work. Galileo was an enthusiastic litterateur and critic. In 1589 he had entered the national dispute about the relative merits of Ariosto's and Tasso's poems by making known his views in *Considerazioni al Tasso* and in *Postille all'Ariosto*. Both writings are now in G. Galilei, *Scritti letterari*, ed. Alberto Chiari (Florence: Le Monnier, 1970), 362–486, 487–635.

57. A similar opinion regarding Sarrocchi's concerns for structure and at least some of her revisions has been put forward by Virginia Cox in "Fiction, 1560–1650," 61–62.

carnal desire and guilty conscience. Calidora, on the other hand, who at first appears to be a woman of a modern turn of mind, in later sections changes into a sorceress who concocts a brew in the deep of the forest and casts a spell on her irresolute lover.[58] Two other stories of illicit love were also excised: those of Osman and the young wife of the old king of Bithynia, and of Ernesto and the queen's lady-in-waiting. A clean sweep was made of any allusion to wayward sexual attraction: to Dory's seductive beauty and its effect on Alexander (1.13 and 1.44–46); to the great Roman who "who lasciviously dreamed of lying in bed with his own mother" (1.70); as well as a stanza chastising men who in the name of love justify the pleasure taken in raping women (14.1). In canto 4, a soldier's catamite has become his camp-following spouse, while in canto 9 the suggestion of the homosexual bond tying Pallante's father to his friend Saladin, and the disclosure of the incestuous nature of Pallante's love for Flora, have been deleted. In omitting these details of deviant love, Sarrocchi has also eliminated much that would have detracted interest from the war. On the other hand, new episodes have been inserted. A vivid description of the maneuver executed by Attravante's war carriages, a deadly clash between Christians and Muslims over the armor of Agrismeta, the siege of Amantia, and Mauro's repeated betrayals all add variety and suspense to the main action, without detracting from its compactness. Another change that considerably improves the pace of the narrative was to opt for a beginning in medias res: what in the version of 1606 was told in direct narrative in four cantos is now abridged and narrated retrospectively in two. Overall, the many and substantial revisions moved away from a poem alternating two main narrative strands—those concerning Serrano and Calidora, and those relating to Scanderbeg's advance into his ancestral territory—toward a poem securely centered on the war between Albanians and Turks. To appreciate fully how the complex history of that prolonged campaign was made to conform to a unity of action, a summary is useful at this point.

In cantos 1–6, Scanderbeg's defection from the Ottoman army and his repossession of the ancestral territories are told in flashback by his envoy at the Neapolitan court of Alfonso of Aragon. An army of Italian troops is organized to go to his aid and soon arrives in Croia. Not everyone in town

58. Calidora, a *maga* first reluctant to succumb to sexual attraction, then seduced and abandoned, deviates from many aspects in which the traditional witch was conceived by male writers: on this topic see Virginia Cox's "Women as Readers and Writers," 143–44. For a brief sketch of the figure of the enchantress/sorceress in the epic, see Marilyn Migiel's entry "Enchantress" in *Feminist Encyclopedia of Italian Literature*, ed. Rinaldina Russell (Westport, CT: Greenwood Press, 1997), 76–77.

is happy: Selim, a devout Muslim and a friend of the dispossessed Ottoman governor, travels to the Turkish capital to report on Scanderbeg's treason. An impressive army made up of contingents from the many regions of the empire is assembled and reviewed; then, under the sultan's command, it marches to the plain of Presa and lays siege to the rebel town of Croia. Looking down from the walls at dusk, Alexander spots Ferratte, captain of the Janissaries, as he surreptitiously climbs the steep path to the citadel. Alexander, accompanied by a select group, comes upon Ferratte and slays him and his followers. Camouflaged in the armor of the dead, the Albanians effect an incursion by night into the Ottoman camp, causing confusion and wreaking havoc among the sleeping soldiers. When they withdraw, Alexander is separated from his men and takes refuge on a nearby mountain. Meanwhile Ferratte's corpse is recovered by the Turks and flayed, his skin filled with straw and set up to look like Scanderbeg's body: their intention is to demoralize the besieged Albanians into surrender by making them believe that their leader is dead. Instead, a second powerful attack is mounted by Alexander, who has come down the mountain and is now strengthened by new armed supporters from Buda. The Albanians and their allies, however, are blocked by a maneuver effected by the Scythian carriages and are forced to withdraw into Croia.

In cantos 7–12, Pallante and Flora are young Turkish lovers separated by the war. One day, while galloping toward Flora's home, Pallante is captured by Scanderbeg's ally, Vran, and is taken prisoner to Amantia. In admiration for the young man's valor and faithfulness in love, Vran allows Pallante to be reunited with his beloved. He also requests a ransom for the release of the young man and donates it to the couple. Scanderbeg, meanwhile, has sent an ambassador to the Ottoman court to ask for an exchange of prisoners. Offended by the religious slurs of Romidon, one of the envoy's servants, the sultan halts the ongoing negotiations and demands that their respective faiths be championed in single combat. The seemingly invincible Agrismeta, chosen to be the champion of the Islamic faith, is slain by the very young and beautiful Christian warrior Vaconte. The spectators rush into the enclosure where the duel has been fought and a bloody melee follows. Embittered by his champion's defeat, and enraged by the defection of Pallante and Flora, the emperor decides to punish Vran by conquering his town. Corcutte is the Ottoman general in charge of the expedition. The siege, described in detail in canto 10, is lifted when Scanderbeg, coming from Croia to the aid of his friend, takes Corcutte's army by surprise.

In cantos 13–17, Rosmonda, Murad's warrior daughter, is marching with an army to the aid of her father. On the slopes of Mount Olympus she meets Silveria, an alluring maiden huntress, and persuades her to seek fame and glory in the military. A commotion occurs in the Turkish camp when Vaconte, on a spying mission, is caught by the guards. Rosmonda, disobeying her father's order that no prisoners are to be taken, decides to save Vaconte's life, while the young hero falls instantly and helplessly in love with her. The time has come for Rosmonda, at the head of the Ottoman army, to mount an attack on the walls of Croia. Acts of valor are performed on both sides. Standing in the breach opened in the city walls, Alexander throws back the enemy almost single-handedly. From below, Silveria surpasses the most able Turkish warriors in inflicting casualties among the town's defenders. The insistent rain, however, making the terrain slippery and further climbing impossible, forces Rosmonda to give the sign of retreat. The sultan attributes Scanderbeg's invincibility to his sword and sends ambassadors to ask for it. Alexander is glad to relinquish it, convinced that it will cause new discord among the Turkish soldiers. A game is organized in the camp and the warriors compete for the weapon. Silveria wins the contest, is awarded the sword, and is also allowed to name the new captains of the Janissaries and the Spahis. This infuriates her male competitors, and a violent quarrel breaks out among them; some are killed and the maiden is wounded in the neck. Presently, Murad's surreptitious plans to kill his daughter's sheltered captive and to possess Silveria alienate Rosmonda. Aided by Marcello Benci, who has arrived from Italy to rescue Vaconte, the two women liberate the prisoner and all together flee to Croia. Shortly after, Rosmonda converts to Christianity and weds Vaconte with Scanderbeg's blessing.

In cantos 18–23, an army is assembled at Ancona, Italy, by Pope Pius II in support of the Albanian leader. His fleet is dispersed all over the eastern Mediterranean by a violent storm, only to be partially reassembled with the help of the king of Cyprus. As the Italian galleons navigate westward around the Cyclades, they are overtaken by a vast Persian fleet sailing to the aid of the emperor. The two fleets face each other and a ferocious battle ensues. The Italians are almost overwhelmed but manage to destroy the Persian vessels by throwing into them incendiary missiles and vases filled with poisonous snakes. By and by, the survivors among them reach Croia. Strengthened by these reinforcements, Scanderbeg resolves to provoke the enemy to a decisive encounter in the plain between Croia and Presa. The Turks fall into the trap and give battle. After varied and relentless action, the Ottoman army is on the run, and the sultan, deeply chagrined by the defeat of his army, collapses on the field and must be carried away. He dies in a last attempt to rejoin his men and to keep on fighting.

In obedience to the canons of literary theory, Sarrocchi organized the elements prescribed for the heroic epic into one main narrative strand. This was done first by a judicious selection of the historical events. The repetitive account of military encounters found in Barletius's and Demetrio Franco's texts—the chronicles Sarrocchi most likely consulted—is reduced to the early resistance mounted by Scanderbeg against Murad II. The first twelve cantos describe the siege of Croia, with sorties, penetration of the enemy camp, and incidents occurring in the fortress or directly relating to it. The siege of Amantia in canto 10 is the pivotal event that shifts the theater of war toward Turkish territory. From then on, most actions occur around Presa, center of operations for the Turks, in the vicinity of which their army is encamped. A symmetrical structure thus comes into being, and the narrative reaches closure with Scanderbeg's victory and the death of his opponent.[59] All together, even though some episodes take place in the Turkish capital of Elia or with the Italian fleet at sea, the attention remains focused on the Albanian land between the fortresses of Croia, Amantia, and Presa. This military triangle corresponds to the strategic points of Scanderbeg's real war: Kruja, Svetigrad, and Albesan.

This well-structured narrative is enlivened by minor episodes inspired by incidents that occurred later in Scanderbeg's campaign and by stories that were part of his legend. The sultan's promise to spare the people of Belgrade, Alexander hiding on the wooded mountain, his being given up for dead, the Albanian refusal to surrender in his absence, his being unsaddled in the fight and accepting a horse from a minor officer, the awe produced among the enemy by his seemingly miraculous sword are all suspenseful episodes skillfully plotted into the narrative.[60] Further interest is added for the Italian readership by the inclusion of an imaginary crusade by Pius II. The actual armed intervention organized by that pope aborted at Ancona, the port where the fleet gathered and where the pontiff, who was leading the expedition, died in 1464. In canto 19, however, the papal fleet takes off without delays and arrives at its destination, but not before providing the opportunity to describe, in canto 20, a spectacular sea battle reminiscent of the

---

59. In the poem the sultan collapses on the battlefield and dies soon after, while Murad II died of apoplexy in Edirne in 1451. See canto 23.59–60, 23.73–76n. For an overview of Murad's campaigns in the Balkans, I refer to Halil İnalcik, "The Interregnum and Recovery," in *The Ottoman Empire: The Classical Age, 1300–1600*, trans. Norman Itzkowitz and Colin Imber (New Rochelle, NY: Aristide D. Caratzas, 1973), 17–22.

60. The historical incidents and the legends that may have inspired Sarrocchi's narrative are mentioned by Franco, *Commentario delle cose dei Turchi*, 67; Gegaj, *L'Albanie et l'invasion turque*, 32, 76–78, 139; and by Hodgkinson, Skanderbeg, 81, 99.

victory of Lepanto of 1571.[61] The desire to celebrate the men in the service of Rome led Sarrocchi to include some characters named after real men who were not in the Albanian wars but who either participated in other military expeditions to the Balkans or were descendants of men who did. The Borso d'Este that appears in canto 18 is inspired by the real Borso d'Este (1413–71), an avowed ally of the church who pledged two galleons for the thwarted crusade of Pius II. Borso was also the ancestor of Giulia d'Este, to whom the *Scanderbeide* is dedicated. Cosimo, twice described in the poem as "the great Tuscan," is presumably Cosimo de' Medici the Elder (1389–1464), another supporter of Pius II, whose descendant and namesake, Cosimo I, grand duke of Tuscany (1519–74), contributed twelve galleys to the papal fleet that fought at Lepanto. The character of Giuliano Cesarini, who makes an appearance in cantos 18 and 19, is named after the legate of Pope Eugenius IV in Budapest, who died in the battle of Varna in 1444, but he also stands in commemoration of the recent mission and death of Gian Francesco Aldobrandini, nephew of Clement VIII and captain of the papal contingent sent by him into the renewed Balkan conflict.[62] Another personage who could not have embarked on any crusade in 1464, being at the time ten years of age, is the explorer Amerigo Vespucci (1454–1532). A character by the name of Americo appears in canto 19.32 and 19.62–64, and his travels are mentioned in canto 19.33.

The action of the war is relieved by romantic adventures that do not disturb its unity because they account for the part the characters play in the main narrative. The attempted kidnapping of Dori in canto 1 is an

---

61. Political considerations, we may assume, led to the omission of any mention of Venice, which had major interests in the Balkans and played an important part in the Albanian conflict. For the traces left in Venetian literature by the wars against the Turks, see Carlo Dionisotti, "La guerra d'Oriente nella letteratura veneziana del Cinquecento," in *Geografia e storia della letteratura italiana*, 201–26. Sarrocchi's disregard of Venice was due to the ongoing conflict between the Serenissima and the Roman church over a matter of jurisdictional prerogatives. The controversy, caused by the Venetian refusal to hand over to the ecclesiastic authorities two friars guilty of common crimes, went on from 1605 to 1607. During the confrontation, all religious ceremonies were barred in the territories of the republic by papal interdict. The controversy assumed great political consequences as two expert polemicists, Roberto Bellarmino for Rome and Paolo Sarpi for the Venetian Republic, battled in their writings on the relation between church and state.

62. On Borso and Cosimo, see Pope Pius, *Commentaries of Pius II*, Smith College Studies in History (Northampton, MA, 1936–57), 22:106, 43:848. At 25:213–16, one can read what Pius II had to say about the European sovereigns' reluctance to go to war against the Turks and about his own reason for a crusade. On the campaign promoted by Clement VIII, see note 50 in this introduction. On the effect of the battle of Lepanto on Italian letters in general, see Carlo Dionisotti, "Lepanto nella cultura italiana del tempo," *Lettere italiane* 23, no. 4 (1971): 473–92. On Giulia d'Este, see canto 1.2n.

entertaining interlude in the account of Scanderbeg's defection and also provides a justification for it. Felina's dramatic presence in canto 3—a transference into Islamic territory of the medieval anecdote of Emperor Justinian and the grieving widow—serves the function of setting the sultan's campaign in motion. The fortunes and misfortunes of Pallante and Flora in cantos 7 to 10 are made relevant to the main story by the military events they trigger. The sultan's courtship of his consort in canto 18 leads to the Persian army's entrance into the conflict. Finally, the adventure of Romidon, who in canto 7 brings about the ire of the sultan after barely escaping lynching by an enraged crowd of Turkish soldiers—a felicitous variation of the novella of Martellino in *Decameron* 2.1—contributes to the narrative of diplomatic negotiations an interlude full of life and historical relevance and also accounts for the resumption of the war. The result is a vast structure, made coherent by consistency of intent and evenness of tone throughout.

At the center of the narrative remains the protagonist. He holds together the various threads of the events, directly or indirectly. Like Aeneas in Virgil's *Aeneid*, Scipio in Petrarch's *Africa*, Godfrey in Tasso's *Jerusalem Delivered*—the masterpieces on which this poem incessantly but not exclusively draws—Alexander is pious, loyal to allies, invincible in battle, compassionate toward the vanquished, and exemplary in private life. Sarrocchi never forgets to show her hero displaying these typical qualities in action. Dynamism is conferred on the moves of Scanderbeg by the political and strategic aims he expresses in his speeches and puts to the test in his decisions. He also benefits from the group of warriors around him— Vran, Vaconte, Thopia, Pyrrhus—for these loyal followers keep their attention turned toward their leader, thus contributing to keeping the readers' interest focused on him. Vaconte, the other warrior with a leading narrative function, exhibits in turn the qualities of Ariosto's Rinaldo, Tasso's Tancred, and even the biblical David. He is the beautiful, valorous youth who falls prey to his own prowess and is taken prisoner by the warrior princess. Once in love with her, he must struggle with the conflict between duty and passion, between military glory and personal happiness—a struggle that Virgil dramatized for his hero in *Aeneid* 4.280–89 and Tasso recreated for Rinaldo in *Jerusalem* 16.30–35. The sultan, on the other hand, is the counterpart of many an epic villain. He is spoken of as a bloodthirsty tyrant, arrogant and evil, suspicious and deceptive. Life and death matter to him only in relation to victory, and he is ready to sacrifice the life of thousands of his subjects for the sake of his power and dominion (6.124). While retaining the stereotypical negative traits of the enemy, the passions and hatreds that motivate his behavior, his reactions to setbacks, both political and private, nonetheless make him a personable character that stands up vividly against his idealized antagonist. And when, at the end of the poem, Murad is vanquished but still unreconciled to defeat, he is allowed to tower above all around him, an undaunted hero with the political single-mindedness of Dante's Farinata and the tragic overtones of the biblical Saul (23.70).

Between the world of warfare and that of romantic fantasy a passage is opened through which two women warriors pass at ease. They are Rosmonda, the sultan's warrior daughter, and Silveria, a creature raised in the wilds of nature, lured into the army by a promise of glory. While providing a connection between the two sides of epic poetry, these creatures of imagination may be taken to symbolize, respectively, the possible harmony and the clash between dream and reality. Rosmonda embodies both power and feminine submission. In alien land, she is regent of the empire and leader of armies; she is seen leading the troops and directing the phases of the assault on the enemy fortress. As soon as she enters Christian territory, however, stricter social standards prevail and she converts, marries Vaconte, and serves the king under her husband's leadership. The similarity in the gender role embodied by Sarrocchi's Rosmonda and by Ariosto's Bradamante is indeed striking. But there are far more layers of meaning in the depiction of Rosmonda.

In contrast to earlier interpreters, who saw the representation of the woman warrior as a sign of the greater visibility of women in Renaissance society,[63] feminist scholars have argued that male authors manipulated their narratives in such a way as to counterbalance a potentially subversive representation of women, thus strengthening the traditional gender roles they seemed to contest. Ariosto's Bradamante has been put forward as a good

---

63. The character of the woman warrior had undergone a significant transformation under the pen of Ariosto. In the works of earlier romancers, intent on diverting the public with comical exaggerations, maidens-at-arms were represented as women with grotesque masculine attributes, who, on the model of Penthesilea, queen of the Amazons, abstained from all sexual and sentimental ties with men. Boiardo's Marfisa retains many aspects of the earlier type: not unattractive and more daring than anyone else on earth, she is so confident of her prowess that she will measure herself only against kings. In Ariosto's *Orlando Furioso*, a milder and far more socialized version of the female warrior appears: her aggressive proclivities are mitigated significantly, and her feminine features are enhanced in conformity to courtly expectations. This new type of female knight and her prominence in the *Furioso* seemed to some scholars a reflection of the new status women enjoyed during the Renaissance. An example of this interpretation is the one offered by Mario Santoro in his *Letture ariostesche* (Naples: Liguori, 1973), 81–134. Pio Rajna is much on target about the transformation of the type in *Le fonti dell'Orlando Furioso*, ed. F. Mazzoni (Florence: Sansoni, 1975), 47–55. A comprehensive survey of the maiden-at-arms as a gauge of women's position in contemporary society is Margaret Tomalin, *The Fortunes of the Warrior Heroine in Italian Literature: An Index of Emancipation* (Ravenna: Longo, 1982).

example of this manipulation. Notwithstanding her many proofs of power and valor, she must in the end abjure her autonomy, because the established hierarchical relationship between the sexes required that women submit to men's authority.[64] At the outset, Rosmonda seems a version of Bradamante transposed into a context that is historical and militarily more modern. But even though, in conformity with current principles of propriety, Sarrocchi makes use of a model of the woman warrior inherited from her male epic predecessors, her awareness of gender implications in this fictional type should not be underestimated. While Ariosto must in turn adopt, for his kaleidoscopic landscape of humanity, all positions made known by the current debate on women,[65] Sarrocchi's views on the subject are complex but coherently balanced. We may well ask, then, at precisely what distance from the line separating the man's figure of the woman warrior and the one fantasized by women authors her character should be placed.

The maidens-at-arms envisioned in the poems of Moderata Fonte and Lucrezia Marinella are stronger and more self-reliant than the ones created by men. The empowerment these fictional creatures enjoy makes them clear projections of their authors' utopian hopes and of the claims they advance in their profeminist tracts.[66] At the same time, however, the strong proclamations of self-sufficiency Fonte and Marinella give voice to in both genres, and the insistent resistance to love and marriage of some of their

64. For a probing study of Bradamante in *Orlando Furioso* in the context of the contemporary debate on women, see Pamela Joseph Benson, *The Invention of the Renaissance Woman: The Challenge of Female Independence in the Literature and Thought of Italy and England* (University Park: Pennsylvania State University Press, 1992), 91–122. On the debate on women, see Diana Robin, "Querelle des femmes: The Renaissance," in Russell, *Feminist Encyclopedia*, 270–73; and, in this volume, pp. xix–xx of the series editors' introduction. Good insights on how men's epics defined roles for women are found also in the studies of Gloria Allaire, Valeria Finucci, Maggie Günsberg, John C. McLucas, Marilyn Migiel, and Deanna Shemek, all listed in my bibliography.

65. About what Deanna Shemek calls the undecidability of Ariosto's version of the controversy, see her "Of Women, Knights, Arms, and Love: The 'querelle des femmes' in Ariosto's Poem," *Modern Language Notes* 104 (1989): 68–97. See also Benson, *Invention of the Renaissance Woman*, 91–122.

66. On Fonte's and Marinella's poems, see pp. 19–20 of this introduction. On the character of the female knight in epic poems authored by women, see Valeria Finucci's introduction to Fonte's *Tredici canti del Floridoro*, especially pp. xxvi–xxvii; and Stephen Kolsky's "Moderata Fonte's *Tredici Canti del Floridoro*: Women in a Man's Genre," *Rivista di studi italiani* 17 (1999): 165–84. See also Paola Malpezzi Price, "Lucrezia Marinella," in Russell, *Italian Women Writers*, 237–39; "Woman Warrior," in Russell, *Feminist Encyclopedia*, 357–59; and *Moderata Fonte: Women and Life in Sixteenth-Century Venice* (Madison: Fairleigh Dickinson University Press, 2003), 101–12. Both Fonte and Marinella back up their representations of the female warrior with statements about women's potential in the military field. See Fonte, *Worth of Women*, 100; Marinella, *Nobility and Excellence of Women*, 80.

creations, suggest a sense of exclusion and separateness, and a matching need for self-affirmation consistent with the reality of their daily lives, confined as they were to milieus in which distinctions of gender and social class were most rigidly respected.[67] No suggestions of alienation may be derived from Sarrocchi's depiction of female warriors. Sarrocchi lived in circles where men of the cloth and aristocrats, females and males, artists and intellectuals of various social classes mingled, and, as exceptional as that may have been, the very authorities that had sponsored Margherita's education allowed her a degree of freedom denied to her Venetian counterparts. In a way that reflects the author's status in life, Rosmonda and Silveria move confidently among men; they behave with comradery toward their fellow soldiers and act with resentment and hostility when provoked or wronged.

Rosmonda is at the same time a figure of self-assertiveness and of femininity.[68] Her intrepid martial spirit does not make her averse to love and marriage, and she finds no contradiction between loyalty to her husband and her continued soldiering. Her soldier's might is displayed again at the end of the poem, where she is chosen by the author, with some narrative incongruence, to be the slayer of Attravante, the contemptuous commander-in-chief of the enemy army.[69] Most singularly, this figure of warrior-wife is made to be the promoter of specific legal rights for women. When Rosmonda condones, in fact praises, Silveria for killing her assailants, the author is condemning the leniency with which cases of rape were adjudicated. The episode of the attempted rape in canto 13 is framed in terms of justice. The mother who wants the death of her sons to be vindicated asks Rosmonda for justice in the name of the "just compassion of the great Allah." Rosmonda declares herself to be a "just" sovereign, who does not "tolerate unjust behavior." In her self-defense, Silveria maintains she is not "eager to impart a death that is not deserved."[70] A demand for mutual recognition and parity in the relation between man and woman is implied in all

---

67. Virginia Cox attributes Fonte's and Marinella's celebration of celibate life to the collapse of the marriage market at the time of their writing: see "The Single Self: Feminist Thought and the Marriage Market in Early Modern Venice," *Renaissance Quarterly* 48 (1995): 513–81.

68. Rossi reports that some literati, unwilling to praise Sarrocchi wholeheartedly, repeated with considerable spite that she was a man among women and a woman among men ("nec sicut quidam, qui maligne eam laudabant, soliti erant dicere, fuit inter mulieres vir, et inter viros mulier"). *Pinacotheca*, 260.

69. See canto 23.67–68 and notes.

70. Canto 13.3, 13.21 and 13.24. The episode of the would-be rapists may bear a sign of how much the execution of Beatrice Cenci had distressed Sarrocchi. See my note to canto 13.25. For attitudes toward rape and the legislation against it in Italy, see Daniela Lombardi, "Intervention by Church and State in Marriage Disputes in Sixteenth- and Seventeenth-Century Florence,"

the love stories in the poem: in those of Pallante and Flora in canto 7, and of the sultan and his consort Hypsipyle in canto 18. In canto 17.68, Silveria openly voices a woman's right to consent to a man or refuse him when she tells the sultan that "not force, but only accord and pleasure, could induce her heart to acquiesce." But it is Rosmonda who highlights Sarrocchi's call for mutual acceptance between the sexes; and she does it at a significant point in the traditional epic plot. It is the moment when the woman warrior is seen by the hero with her helmet off for the first time and becomes the remote and quiet object of his gaze (see Clorinda and Tancred in *Jerusalem Delivered* 1.47). Rosmonda does not remain silent; after revealing herself to Vaconte, she speaks imperiously to him—who in this reversal of traditional roles stands awestruck before her—and, reminding him of the powers she possesses, requests a response and an offer of peace equal to the one she is making (13.86–94). Whenever female characters in the poem insist on their right to consent or refuse, we may detect Sarrocchi's personal claim and her championship of women's freedom and dignity which, in her time, the Council of Trent was trying to protect by requiring consensual agreement for marriages.[71]

in *Crime, Society, and the Law in Renaissance Italy*, ed. Trevor Dean and K. J. P. Lowe (Cambridge: Cambridge University Press, 1994), 142–56; John Bracket, *Criminal Justice and Crime in Late Renaissance Florence, 1537–1609* (Cambridge: Cambridge University Press, 1992); Constance Jordan, *Renaissance Feminism: Literary Texts and Political Models* (Ithaca, NY: Cornell University Press, 1990), 112–13; King, *Women of the Renaissance*, 29–31. Sarrocchi's episode and her attitude toward rape will seem more striking if we consider them in relation to the many stories and exempla of rape that appeared in literature mostly with the intent of extolling the chastity of women. In them, legal considerations were necessarily bypassed. The best known of these commonplace presentations is perhaps the exemplum featuring the Roman matron Lucretia, who was sexually assaulted by Sextus Tarquinius in the sixth century BCE. She is mentioned as a model of female virtue, for example, in Cornelius Agrippa's declamation in praise of women and in the Italian tracts influenced by it, as well as in the treatises authored by Fonte and Marinella. See Henricus Cornelius Agrippa, *Declamation of the Nobility and Preeminence of the Female Sex*, ed. and trans. Albert Rabil Jr. (Chicago: University of Chicago Press, 1996), 74; Moderata Fonte, *Worth of Women*, 112; Marinella, *Nobility and Excellence of Women*, 94. The application of commendable examples to the evaluation and encouragement of women's virtues is studied by Martha Ajmar in "Exemplary women in Renaissance Italy: Ambivalent Models of Behaviour?" in Panizza, *Women in Italian Renaissance Culture*, 244–64. On the revival of the Lucretia story by Florentine humanists, see Albert Rabil Jr., ed., *Knowledge, Goodness, and Power: The Debate over Nobility among Quattrocento Italian Humanists* (Binghamton, NY: Medieval and Renaissance Texts and Studies, 1991), 28–29. A general acceptance of violence to women is linked by Stephanie H. Jed to the birth of Renaissance humanism: see her *Chaste Thinking: The Rape of Lucretia and the Birth of Humanism* (Bloomington: Indiana University Press, 1988).

71. For women's right to consent and men's rule over women, see Jordan, *Renaissance Feminism*, 27–28 and 32–33. For the increasing positive evaluation of marriage in Italian texts of the second half of the sixteenth century, see Brian Richardson, "`Amore maritale`: Advice on Love and

While Rosmonda imposes and also accepts regulations, Silveria, a creature who has always been devoted to hunting and celibate living, does not compromise with the customs that society imposes. Her first encounter with Rosmonda takes place on top of Mount Olympus, the mythical residence of the gods. Their meeting becomes a symbolic confrontation between the author and her alter ego, and their mutual attraction can be read as a call for blissful isolation on one side and a life of challenges and struggle for self-assertion on the other. Silveria springs out of her natural habitat, lured by the prospect of glory: alerted to her attractiveness, we follow her as she moves in the Turkish camp with the agility of a primeval animal, under the admiring and resentful gaze of the soldiers. Are we to take the military life here as a metaphor for the public literary arena? Is war a symbol for the fight in which Sarrocchi had to engage in order to achieve recognition in a field reserved for men?[72] In the middle of the battle Silveria will die crushed by an elephant: that is, she will be eliminated by the same forces of nature that created her. Silveria's death may symbolize the renunciations that a woman must be ready to make in order to succeed in the real world, and Rosmonda and Silveria together could be read as embodying Sarrocchi's complex discourse on life and gender.

Sarrocchi's major merit as a woman writer, however, transcends any explicit or implied feminist message. The claim of her epic to fame rests on its original contribution to the representation and poetry of war, and on its demonstration, by that achievement, of a woman's capacity to compete successfully in such manly subjects as political and military strategy, man-to-man combat, and open-field battles.

The *Scanderbeide* is far from simply presenting a series of individual encounters in close succession, as is generally the case in epic poems. Even

---

Marriage in the Second Half of the Cinquecento," in Panizza, *Women in Italian Renaissance Culture*, 194–206, with ample bibliography; see also p. 204 for the edict of Trent and its view of matrimony as a bond between two consenting individuals.

72. In the mind of contemporaries, conspicuous excellence in any field conferred manly power on a woman, for she was seen as exceeding the capacities of her sex and being now endowed with those typical of men. Conversely, the female warrior, supreme "virago," could symbolize a claim to superior knowledge and authority. The conflation of military power and knowledge is suggested by the frequent juxtaposition of letters and warfare. Canto 20 of *Orlando Furioso*, for instance, opens with the observation that "ancient women have done marvelous deeds in the fields of arms and of the sacred Muses." Agrippa mentions the military life and the life of letters contiguously, when listing in his *Declamation* the activities in which women excelled in antiquity (94). The proximity of the two fields is also found in Fonte's *Tredici canti del Floridoro* 4.2 (261) and *Worth of Women* (100–101), and in Marinella's *Nobility and Excellence of Women* (79–80).

the individual fights deviate from the usual mode of describing combat. They involve known warriors and others who have never appeared before, the soldiers being separated and then united with the same or with other opponents later on. The result is a captivating study in aggression and response, which grows in suspense also because of the part given to chance. But it is in the description of intense skirmishes and extended melees that the poem displays its greatest originality. Battles take place over large stretches of terrain, following a tactical plan ordained in advance, and moving forward in response to the shifting of forces shown to occur during the action. In cantos 5 and 6, the reader is told how the two sorties are planned and how they are executed from stage to stage, the second fight being brought to a close by a concerted maneuver that involves many men and carriages. The attack on the walls of Croia, in canto 14, is impressed upon the reader with a constant coordination between details and overall tactical plan. We witness two waves of attack, the advancing and the backsliding of the soldiers who attempt to scale the walls, and, in the end, we are shown the effects of the rain on the ground, which make further climbing impossible. A complex tactical plan is carried out by the army besieging the fortress of Amantia, which involves both a frontal attack and an enveloping maneuver that entails crossing the river and scaling the walls on the opposite side. The battle of the last two cantos is even more skillfully orchestrated. After the topography, the condition of the river, its currents, and its banks are assessed; the armies are seen coming into view of each other, throwing darts, lances, and spears in successive waves. A major frontal battle follows; the war elephants come forward and then are forced to turn around, spreading devastation and carnage among the soldiers who led them to the attack. The narrative, vibrant with tension, creates a vision that we can call cinematic, for long shots of the war theater alternate with the close-ups of individual engagements. The readers are plunged into the middle of the action but retain a clear impression of the entire event and of the skirmishes occurring here and there simultaneously.

The episodes of war are tied together by a sustained interest in statecraft and in military strategy. Scattered throughout the text are considerations derived from political and military treatises current at the turn of the century, such as Giovanni Botero's *Reason of State*, Scipione Ammirato's *Discorsi*, and, by way of those tracts or directly, Machiavelli's *The Prince*, on how to maintain a state and overcome internal and external enemies.[73] Each

---

73. Giovanni Botero (1544–1617) and Scipione Ammirato (1531–1601), together with Antonio Possevino (1533–1611), were important church ideologues. They formulated its political policy and were the principal theorists of the papal principle of the superiority of religious

event is planned strategically, and the readers' interest, aroused from the start, is sustained throughout. The psychology and the conduct of the generals and captains are presented in conformity with their political aims. Opinions are put forward, and hidden intentions revealed, in the speeches they make.[74] Whether factual or formal, i.e., delivered in assemblies to decide policy or on the battlefield to rally the troops, the statements the warriors pronounce are tailored to their roles in the story and never fail to impress on the reader the motivations and aims of their behavior. Political and strategic concerns are kept alive even in the romantic interludes.

As the focus is maintained on the reasons for men's successes and failures, divine interventions become redundant and the religious motivation for the war is diffused. When pious zeal is mentioned by the author or voiced by a character, the impression is that these are programmatic reminders. Stereotypical is also the demarcation between the courageous and self-controlled Faithful on one side and the cruel and unruly Infidels on the other. The epithets thrown at the enemy are also formulaic and do not go beyond the limits of the execration of the pagans and Saracens already found in medieval and Renaissance romances.[75] Confirmation of the perfunctoriness of the endorsement of the holy war may perhaps be drawn from the fact that among the revisions to the early draft of the poem only two corrections can be imputed to religious ideological drive. In the 1606

---

authority over secular power. In the wake of their works, and of Botero's stated principle that the practical needs of state may justify its authoritarian rule, other tracts appeared: Ludovico Zuccolo, *Ragion di stato* (1621), Ludovico Settala, *Ragion di stato* (1627), and Virgilio Malvezzi, *Discorsi sopra Cornelio Tacito* (1622). On this subject, see Asor Rosa, *La cultura della controriforma*, 54–55; Rosa, *Il letterato e le istituzioni*, 312. On the political treatises of this period, see Giuseppe Toffanin, *Machiavelli e il tacitismo* (Padua: A. Draghi, 1921); Benedetto Croce, *Poeti e scrittori del pieno e tardo Rinascimento* II (Bari: Laterza, 1945); Benedetto Croce and Santino Caramella, eds., *Politici e moralisti del Seicento* (Bari: Laterza, 1930); Bruno Widmar, ed., *Scritti politici del Cinquecento e del Seicento* (Milan: Rizzoli, 1954); Friedrich Meinecke, *Machiavelism: The Doctrine of Raison d'État and Its Place in Modern History*, trans. from the German by Douglas Scott, with a general introduction by W. Stark (New Haven: Yale University Press, 1957); Rodolfo De Mattei, *Il problema della ragion di stato nell'età della Controriforma* (Milan and Naples: Ricciardi, 1979), and, by the same author, *Il pensiero politico italiano della Controriforma* (Naples: Ricciardi, 1982).

74. See Alexander's speech to Lagnete (1.40–47), Artecin's speech to the sultan (7.89–93), and those delivered at war councils in cantos 20.2–7 and 21.2–40.

75. One example may suffice. Sarrocchi's "la turca bugiarda fede," which I translated as "the false Turkish faith" (canto 3.3), is reminiscent of Ariosto's "la legge falsa di Babelle" (*Orlando furioso* 14.71.3), where "legge di Babelle" (law of Babylon) stands for "religion of the infidels." See a few lines below in this introduction. For the image of the enemy in Italian epics, see Gloria Allaire and her bibliography in "Noble Saracen or Muslim Enemy? The Changing Image of the Saracen in Late Medieval Italian Literature," in *Western Views of Islam in Medieval and Early Modern Europe: Perception of Other*, ed. David R. Blanks and Michael Frassetto (New York: St. Martin's, 1999), 173–84.

version, Polidor, a man of the Islamic faith, is simply described as having a "religious piety" for his God; in the corresponding episode of 1626, he is called "foolish" for it, and, soon after, "false" is added to "Turkish faith" (3.2 and 3.3). Perhaps counterbalancing this last disparagement, however, is the description of the Christian Romidon as an impetuous and thoughtless man, who is also "driven by a foolish zeal for his religion" (7.97).

Rather than religious inspiration, what gives uniformity of tone to the narrative, what holds the varied plot strongly together is a sense of destiny, a feeling for a people united to fight for a common cause. Significantly, the models that have left most obvious traces in the *Scanderbeide* are classic ones: namely, Virgil's *Aeneid*, Lucan's *Civil War*, Ovid's *Metamorphoses*, Livy's *Histories*; to a lesser degree, Plutarch's *Lives*, Herodotus's *Histories*, Thucydides' *Peloponnesian War*, and Petrarch's classical epic *Africa*. As the footnotes to the translation point out, recent historical events are conflated with ancient happenings; some details are transposed directly from their classic sources and fitted into the poem with minimal changes. A classical flavor is also created by the abundance of similes, by the persistent scansion of time, of the seasons, and of weather changes; by repeated mentions of the sun, the moon, and constellations in their natural and their mythical forms; and by the frequent references to Greek and Roman legends.

Virgil's *Aeneid* is the epic whose values have left the most obvious traces on the *Scanderbeide*. In both narratives the spirit is one of personal valor and magnanimity. Sarrocchi's invocation to the Muse—"Sing, O Muse, the king of Epirus,[76] tell how strongly he endured and how valorously he fought, when the Turkish emperor led Scythian, Persian, and Arabian armies to Croia to fight against him—is reminiscent of Virgil's pagan goddess rather than of Tasso's Christianized muse who "inhabits the heaven among the choirs of the blessed."[77] Scanderbeg, like Aeneas, is the predestined hero intent on fulfilling an earthly national mission. The sultan, like Turnus, Virgil's counterhero, is imperious and violent. Together they represent the contrast, dramatized in the *Aeneid*, between rationality and violence, reason and emotions. Both have the aura of ancient warriors. There are parallels between Virgil's women warriors and Sarrocchi's maiden-at-arms. The

---

76. This is Scanderbeg. On the title of king, see canto 1.1n.

77. *Jerusalem Delivered* 1.2. Much closer to Tasso's prelude, and to the cosmology of Dante's *Paradiso*, will be Marinella's invocation to the Muse: "Musa, che su nel ciel detti ed inspiri / Alle angeliche squadre eccelse lodi, / Che l'auree gemme oltre a gli eterni giri / D'alto diadema adorna immortal godi; / L'alma m'infiamma . . ." (O Muse, you who in the heavens dictate and inspire the angelic choirs with high praises, you who, adorned with a high diadem, perennially enjoy the golden gems that are beyond the eternal circles, do inflame my soul . . .), *L'Enrico* 1.2.1–5.

friendship between Rosmonda and Silveria may also have been suggested by the one existing between Camilla and Acca. Stemming directly from the *Aeneid* are the footrace, the archery competition, and the penetration of the enemy camp by night. Finally, the very structure of the *Scanderbeide* follows the blueprint of the Roman epic. Like the *Aeneid*, the Albanian story begins in medias res. When the decisive battle is under way, in the penultimate canto of both poems a woman warrior dies, after volunteering for a dangerous exploit. And in both epics, the story comes to an end with the death of the protagonist's major adversary. Most significantly, there is a sign in the poem indicating Sarrocchi's appropriation of her Virgilian inheritance. The fantastic transference of arms, in canto 9, from Aeneas to Vaconte, is intentionally made to recall to mind the gift of helmet and cuirass, once the property of Achilles' son, which is offered to Aeneas in canto 3 of the *Aeneid*.[78] This parallel clearly inscribes the early modern poem in the line of classical epic, just as Virgil had done, wishing, with his transference of armor, to establish a continuity between his poem and the Roman world whose origin it celebrated, and the world and the literature of the Trojans and the Greeks.

INFLUENCES AND CRITICAL HISTORY

About the 1606 publication, we know that it attracted a great deal of attention, acclaim, and criticism.[79] About the reception given to the publication of 1623, we know nothing. Nor is it possible to state demonstrably what influence the *Scanderbeide* may have had on the work of Sarrocchi's contemporaries or on subsequent Italian writers. For this to be done, some inroads ought first to be made into the study of seventeenth- and eighteenth-century epics, which, except for a listing and brief descriptions made by Antonio Belloni in 1893 about seventeenth-century heroic poetry, rest in total oblivion. It should also be kept in mind that the *Scanderbeide*, like most works published during the Renaissance and after, may have been known outside Italy and may have contributed to the construction of the Scanderbeg character appearing in several works published later in different countries. One such work is a poem by Henry Wadsworth Longfellow.

There is, however, one demonstrable case of emulation. The *Scanderbeide* exercised considerable influence on Lucrezia Marinella's *L'Enrico* (1635), the only other historical heroic poem written by a woman, notwithstanding the

---

78. Canto 9.18 and note; *Aeneid* 3.499–501.
79. See pp. 13, 16–17 of this introduction.

claim Marinella makes in her preface to have drawn her inspiration entirely from classic writings and from Aristotle's theory and to owe nothing to modern poets. This is indeed a surprising statement on the part of Marinella, for it would also include Tasso's *Jerusalem Delivered*, which is her primary model. In *L'Enrico* there are characters, episodes, segments, details of battles, comparisons, and descriptions that, notwithstanding the existence of previous models for both writers, show themselves to be closely patterned on similar ones in Sarrocchi's poem. Some of these passages are elaborately extended—this is especially discernable in the enlargement of parallel similes—with the obvious intention to surpass a predecessor.[80] The character of Erina in canto 8 of *L'Enrico*, a prophetess knowledgeable in the sciences and disposing of an astrological observatory, is a spawn from both Fonte's Risamante and Sarrocchi's Calidora, if not an appropriation of Sarrocchi's very persona. Finally, the strong emphasis Marinella places, again in her preface, on the qualifications of Enrico Dandolo to be the protagonist of a heroic epic suggests a wish to equal, if not to eclipse, Sarrocchi's choice of Scanderbeg, who in Italy and in Europe enjoyed at the time the unrivaled fame of champion of Christianity.

Interest in Sarrocchi waned after her death but rebounded at the end of the century thanks to Giovan Mario Crescimbeni. An adversary of baroque style and advocate for classical standards of poetry, Crescimbeni praised Sarrocchi as a judicious woman who "had the courage to oppose the new poetic fashion, and hated it to such an extent that she would not tolerate its being mentioned by wise men of letters, not even with the intent to criticize it. For this reason she incurred the angry resentment of both Marino and Stigliani." Crescimbeni's puff was perhaps what encouraged Antonio Bulifon, the publisher of many new editions of works by women, to come out in 1701 with a new edition of the early version of the *Scanderbeide*.[81] In the following century Francesco Saverio Quadrio gave

---

80. See, for example, Marinella's imitations in the following sections of *L'Enrico*: canto 1.1–18, where many geographical features on both sides of the Adriatic are described in a manner and progression similar to the ones followed by Sarrocchi in the first canto of her work; canto 2.3–35, for the review of the forces under Enrico's command, with digressive descriptions of warriors, weaponry, country of origin, and captain's exploits; canto 3.1–8, 9–13, 16–17, for the disposition of the troops and the captains' speeches; cantos 2.29–31 and 8.89–90, for the introductory description of Emilia and Claudia, both modeled on Rosmonda and Silveria; canto 15 for the sortie of the Byzantine captains—among them the female warrior Meandra—and their ruinous foray into the Latin camp; cantos 14.119–20 and 19.38–55, for the assault on the walls of Byzantium, during which Claudia gives as good a demonstration of infallible marksmanship as Silveria does during the attack on Croia.

81. Giovan Mario Crescimbeni, *De' Commentarii intorno all'Istoria della volgar poesia*, 146. For Bulifon's edition, see above, note 42.

Sarrocchi short shrift, mentioning her poem by title only and citing Gragnano as her town of origin.[82] In his monumental and much valued history of Italian literature, the abbot Girolamo Tiraboschi repeated the information given by Quadrio and, taking his cue from Gian Vittorio Rossi's gossipy surmises, went on to stigmatize Sarrocchi for sexual licentiousness.[83] As is the case for most women writers, we have repetitive notices of Sarrocchi in directories, dedicated to accomplished ladies of all categories, who have appeared in Italy throughout the centuries: a complete list of them can be found in Bandini Buti's encyclopedia of women poets and writers.[84]

Tommaso Vallauri praised Sarrocchi for the perfect finish of her versification, for the precision of her concepts, and for her rhetorical restraint, all of which he found lacking in her contemporaries.[85] The same qualities appealed to Antonio Belloni. In *Gli epigoni della Gerusalemme Liberata*, which appeared in 1893, he values the variety and realism of Sarrocchi's scenes, pointing out the care with which natural phenomena, technical devices, battles, and duels are described. Greater praise, however, is reserved for the love stories. Psychologically plausible, as well as aesthetically pleasing, are in his view the sultan's infatuation for Aranit's daughter, the adulterous passion between Calidora and Selano in the poem of 1606, and the amorous adventures of Pallante and Flora in the definitive version.[86] Writing between 1893 and 1914 about Galileo's friends and correspondents, Antonio Favaro gathered eighteen pages of biographical data about Margherita, together with excerpts from her letters and those of her friends. He reports Rossi's accounts of gossip as facts and imbues many bits of information with irony, such as the announcement of Birago's death in Valerio's letter to Galileo.[87] With a mixture of prurience and high-minded moralism, Angelo Borzelli, in an article on Marino, constructs a story of Margherita's passionate infatuation for the much younger Giambattista, of his subsequent

---

82. Quadrio, *Della storia e della ragione d'ogni poesia*, 6:684.

83. Girolamo Tiraboschi, *Storia della letteratura italiana*, 8:477.

84. Maria Bandini Buti, ed., *Enciclopedia biografica e bibliografica italiana. Poetesse e scrittrici* (Rome: Istituto Editoriale Italiano B. C. Tosi, 1942), 2:216–17.

85. Tommaso Vallauri, *Storia della poesia in Piemonte* (Turin: Tip. Chirio e Mina, 1841), 400–401.

86. Antonio Belloni, *Gli epigoni della Gerusalemme Liberata* (Padua: Angelo Draghi, 1893), 133–40.

87. In that letter Valerio states that after the death of her husband, Margherita will have more time to dedicate to her philosophical studies ("avra' piu' libero spazio di filosofare"), and Favaro adds the comment that no reproach could certainly have been made against this husband of interfering with his wife's habit of surrounding herself with men. See Favaro, *Amici e corrispondenti di Galileo*, 1:10, 21.

abandonment of her, and of her furious revenge in the form of literary criticism.[88] This melodrama, however, was wisely forgotten in a more considered study Borzelli published about Sarrocchi in 1935. From that time on, except for a short page by Benedetto Croce and a brief appearance in a book on women's education by Gian Ludovico Masetti Zannini and in the anthologies of Natalia Costa-Zalessow and of Giuliana Morandini, the name of Sarrocchi has been absent from literary history.[89]

---

88. Angelo Borzelli, *Il cavalier Giovan Battista Marino 1569–1625* (Naples: G. M. Priore, 1898), 86–87.

89. Benedetto Croce, "Donne letterate del Seicento," in *Nuovi saggi sulla letteratura italiana del Seicento* (Bari: Laterza, 1931), 162–63; Gian Ludovico Masetti Zannini, *Motivi storici della educazione femminile,* 39–45; Natalia Costa-Zalessow, *Scrittici italiane dal XIII al XX secolo* (Ravenna: Longo, 1982),128–34; Giuliana Morandini, *Sospiri e palpiti. Scrittrici italiane del Seicento* (Genoa: Marietti, 2001), 36–50.While this introduction was being written, I learned of a master's thesis and a dissertation on Sarrocchi's *Scanderbeide,* by Luciana Novelletto and by Serena Pezzini, respectively. They are listed in my bibliography.

VOLUME EDITOR'S
BIBLIOGRAPHY

PRIMARY SOURCES

Agrippa, Henricus Cornelius (1486–1535). *Declamation of the Nobility and Preeminence of the Female Sex.* Trans., ed., and introd. Albert Rabil Jr. Chicago: University of Chicago Press, 1996.

Albergati, Fabio (1538–1606). *Il cardinale.* Rome: Dragonelli, 1664 (written in 1591).

Ammirato, Scipione (1531–1601). *Discorsi sopra Cornelio Tacito.* Florence: Giunti, 1594; Galatina, Lecce: Congedo, 2002.

Anonymous of Venice. *I fatti illustri del Signor Giorgio Scanderbëgh.* Venice, 1564.

Antibarensis. *Historia Scanderbegi edita per quemdam albanensem.* Venice, 1480.

Aragona, Tullia d' (1510?–1556). *Dialogue on the Infinity of Love.* Ed. and trans. Rinaldina Russell and Bruce Merry, introd. and notes Rinaldina Russell. Chicago: University of Chicago Press, 1997.

Ariosto, Ludovico (1474–1533). *Orlando Furioso (The Frenzy of Orlando).* 2 vols. Trans. and introd. Barbara Reynolds. London: Penguin Classics, 1975.

———. *Orlando Furioso.* Trans. William Stewart Rose. Ed. Stewart A. Baker and A. Bartlett Giamatti. Indianapolis: Bobbs–Merrill, 1968.

———. *Orlando Furioso.* Ed. Cesare Segre. Milan: Mondadori, 1964.

Barleti, Marin [Barletius, Marinus]. *Historia de vita et gestis Scanderbegi, Ipirotarum principis.* Rome, c.1506–8. Published with the title *De vita, moribus ac rebus praecipue adversus Turcas, gestis, Georgij Castrioti, clarissim Epirotarum principis.* Strasbourg: Apud Cratonum Mylium, 1537. Italian trans., *Historia del magnanimo, et valoroso Signor Georgio Castrioto, detto Scanderbego,* trans. Pietro Rocca. Venice, 1554, 1560, 1568, 1580. French trans., *Histoire de Georges Castriot surnommé Scanderbeg, Roy d'Albanie,* trans. Jacques de Lavardin, with the addition of a few details taken from Demetrio Franco's work. Paris, 1576. English trans. of French ed., *The History of Gjergj Castriot, surnamed Scanderbeg, King of Albanie,* trans. Z. I. Gentleman. London, 1596.

Bembo, Pietro (1470–1547). *Gli Asolani.* Milan: Società tipografica de' classici italiani, 1808.

Bergalli, Luisa (1703–79), ed. *Componimenti poetici delle più illustri rimatrici d'ogni secolo.* Venice: Antonio Mora, 1726.

Biemmi, G. M. *Historia di Giorgio Castrioto, detto Scander-begh.* Brescia, 1742.

Boccaccio, Giovanni (1313?–1375). *Concerning Famous Women.* Trans. Guido A. Guarino. New Brunswick, NJ: Rutgers University Press, 1963.

———. *The Decameron. Trans. with introd. and notes G. H. McWilliam.* London: Penguin Books, 1972.

Boiardo, Matteo Maria (1440–94). *Orlando Innamorato.* Trans. with introd. and notes Charles Stanley Ross. Foreword Allen Mendelbaum. English verse ed. Anne Finnigan. Berkeley: University of California Press, 1989.

———. *Orlando Innamorato. Amorum Libri.* Ed. Aldo Scaglione. Turin: Unione tipografica editrice torinese, 1963.

Botero, Giovanni (1544–1617). *Della ragion di stato.* Venice: Giolito, 1589.

———. *Dell'uffitio del Cardinale,* libri II. Rome: Mutj, 1599.

———. *The Reason of State.* Trans. P. J. and D. P. Waley. Introd. D. P. Waley. London: Routledge and Kegan Paul, 1956.

Bronzini, Cristofano (1580–1640). *Della dignità e nobiltà delle donne.* Florence: Zanobi Pignone, 1622.

Bruni, Leonardo (1370–1444). "On the Study of Literature (1405) to Lady Battista Malatesta of Montefeltro." In *The Humanism of Leonardo Bruni: Selected Texts,* trans. and introd. Gordon Griffiths, James Hankins, and David Thompson, 240–51. Binghamton, NY: Medieval and Renaissance Texts and Studies, 1897.

Caesar (Caius Julius Caesar 100?–43 BCE). *The Gallic War.* Trans. H. J. Edwards. Cambridge: Harvard University Press, 1986.

———. *The Gallic War.* Trans. Carolyn Hammond. Oxford: Oxford University Press. 1996.

Capaccio, Giulio Cesare (1552–1634). *Illustrium mulierum et illustrium litteris virorum elogia.* Naples: apud F. Iacobum Carlinum et Constantinum Vitalem, 1608.

Castiglione, Baldassar (1478–1529). *The Book of the Courtier.* Trans. Charles Singleton. Ed. Daniel Javitch. New York: W. W. Norton, 2002.

Cereta, Laura (1469–99). *Collected Letters of a Renaissance Feminist.* Ed. and trans. Diana Robin. Chicago: University of Chicago Press, 1997.

Chioccarelli, Bartolomeo (1580–1646). *De illustribus scriptoribus qui in civitate et regno Neapolis ab orbe condito ad annum usque 1646 floruerunt.* Ms. XIV. A. 28. Biblioteca Nazionale di Napoli.

Contini, Gianfranco, ed. *Poeti del Duecento.* Vol. 1. Milan: Ricciardi, 1960.

Corso, Rinaldo (1525–1580?). *Tutte le rime della illustris. Et eccellentiss. Signora Vittoria Colonna Marchesana di Pescara, con la esposizione del signor Rinaldo Corso.* Ed. Girolamo Ruscelli. Venice: G. B. e M. Sessa, 1558.

———. *Vita di Giberto terzo di Correggio detto il Difensore, colla vita di Veronica Gàmbara, apologia della casa di Correggio.* Ancona: A. de Grandi, 1566.

Dante (Dante Alighieri, 1265–1321). *La commedia secondo l'antica vulgata.* Ed. G. Petrocchi. Milan: Mondadori, 1967.

———. *La divina commedia. Inferno/Purgatorio/Paradiso.* Italian and English. Trans., ed., and introd. Allen Mandelbaum. Berkeley: University of California Press, 1982.

Della Chiesa, Francesco Agostino. *Theatro delle donne letterate.* Mondovì: G. Gislandi and G. T. Rossi, 1620.

Erythraeus, Janus Nicius [pen name of Gian Vittorio Rossi, usually referred to as Eritreo (1577–1647)]. *Pinacotheca imaginum illustrium doctrinae vel ingenii laude virorum, qui auctore superstite diem suum obierunt.* New ed. Wolfenbüttel: Jo. Christoph. Meisner, 1729.

Fedele, Cassandra (1465–1558). *Letters and Orations.* Ed. and trans. Diana Robin. Chicago: University of Chicago Press, 2000.

Fonte, Moderata (1555–92). *La passione di Christo.* Venice: Guerra, 1581.

———. *La resurrezione di Gesù nostro Signore.* Venice: Imberti, 1592.

———. *Tredici canti del Floridoro.* Ed. Valeria Finucci. Modena: Mucchi, 1995.

———. *The Worth of Women.* Ed. and trans. Virginia Cox. Chicago: University of Chicago Press, 1997.

Franco, Demetrio. *Commentario delle cose dei Turchi e del Signor Giorgio Scanderbeg, Principe di Epiro.* Venice, 1545. Republished in Venice in 1584 and 1591 with the title *Gli illustri e gloriosi gesti, et valorose imprese fatte contra Turchi, dal signor Don Giorgio Castriotto, detto Scanderbeg.*

Galilei, Galileo (1564–1642). *Opere. Edizione nazionale.* 15 vols. Florence: Società editrice fiorentina, 1842–56.

———. *Scritti letterari.* Ed. Alberto Chiari. Florence: Le Monnier, 1970.

——. *Tre lettere di Galileo Galilei.* Ed. Gilberto Govi. Rome: Tipografia delle scienze matematiche e fisiche, 1870.

Giovio, Paolo (1483–1552). *Commentarii delle cose de' Turchi, di Paulo Giovio et Andrea Gambini, con gli fatti et la vita di Scanderbeg.* Venice: Figlioli di Aldo, 1541.

———. *Dialogo dell'imprese militari e amorose.* Ed. Maria Luisa Doglio. Rome: Bulzoni, 1978. Originally published in 1555.

Groto, Luigi (1541–85). *Vita dello Scanderbeq.* Venice, 1630.

Guicciardini, Francesco (1483–1540). *Storia d'Italia.* Ed. Silvana Seidel Menchi. Introd. Felix Gilbert. Turin: Einaudi, 1971.

Heredia, Luigi de. *Rime.* Ed. Salvatore Salomone Marino. Bologna: Gaetano Romagnoli, 1875.

Herodotus (484?–430 BCE). *The Histories.* Trans. George Rawlinson. Ed. E. H. Blakeney. Introd. John Warrington. New York: Dutton, 1964.

Homer. *The Iliad.* Trans. A. T. Murray. 2 vols. Cambridge: Harvard University Press, 1985.

———. *The Odyssey.* Trans. A. T. Murray. Revised by William F. Wyat. 2 vols. Cambridge: Harvard University Press, 1999.

Lettere di uomini illustri scritte a M. Antonio Bonciario perugino. Venice: G. B. Merlo, 1839.

Livy (Titus Livius, 59 BCE–17CE). *Ab urbe condita (History of Rome from its Foundation).* Trans. B. O. Foster. Cambridge: Harvard University Press, 1998.

Lucan (Marcus Annaeus Lucanus, 39–65 CE). *Civil War.* Trans. J. D. Duff. Cambridge: Harvard University Press, 1997.

———. *The Pharsalia.* Trans. H. T. Riley. London: Henry G. Bohn, 1853.

Machiavelli, Niccolò (1469–1527). *The Prince.* Ed. and introd. Peter Bondanella. Trans. Peter Bondanella and Mark Musa. New York: Oxford University Press. 1984.

Manfredi, Muzio. *Per donne romane. Rime di diversi raccolte e dedicate al Signor Giacomo Buoncompagni.* Bologna: Alessandro Benaco, 1575.

Manuzio, Aldo (1547–97). *Lettere volgari . . . al molto ill. Sign. Lodovico Riccio.* Rome: Santi, 1592.

Marinella, Lucrezia (1571–1653). *Arcadia felice.* Ed. Françoise Lavocat. Florence: Olschki, 1998.

———. *La colomba sacra*. Venice: Ciotti, 1595.

———. *Dei gesti heroici e della vita meravigliosa della serafica Santa Caterina da Siena*. Venice: Barezzi, 1624.

———. *L'Enrico, ovvero Bisantio acquistato*. Venice: Ghirardo Imberti, 1635.

———. *Holocausto d'amore della vergine Santa Giustina*. Venice: Leni, 1648.

———. *The Nobility and Excellence of Women*. Ed. and trans. Anne Dunhill. Introd. Letizia Panizza. Chicago: University of Chicago Press, 1999.

———. *Vita del serafico et glorioso San Francesco*. Venice: Bertano, 1597.

———.*La vita di Maria Vergine imperatrice dell'universo*. Venice: Barezzi, 1602.

———. *Vita di Santa Giustina*. Florence, 1606.

———. *Le vittorie di Francesco il serafico. I passi gloriosi della diva Chiara*. Padua: Crivellari, 1647.

Marino, Giambattista (1569–1625). *Adone*. Ed. Marzio Pieri. Rome and Bari: Laterza, 1975–77.

———. *La galeria*. Ed. Marzio Pieri. Padua: Liviana, 1979.

———. *Lettere*. Ed. Marziano Guglielminetti. Turin: Einaudi, 1966.

———. *Rime . . . Amorose, Marittime, Boscherecce, Heroiche, Lugubri, Morali e Sacre. Parte Prima (e Seconda)*. Venice: G. B. Ciotti, 1602.

———. *La Sampogna*. Ed. Vania de Maldé. Padua: Guanda, 1993.

Medici, Lorenzo de' (1449–92). *Opere*. Ed. Tiziano Zanato. Turin: Einaudi, 1992.

———. *Tutte le opere. Scritti d'amore*. Ed. Gigi Cavalli. Milan: Rizzoli, 1958.

New American Standard Bible. Carol Stream, IL: Creation House, 1973.

Nogarola, Isotta (1418–66). *Complete Writings: Letterbook, Dialogue on Adam and Eve, Orations*. Ed. and trans. Margaret L. King and Diana Robin. Chicago: University of Chicago Press, 2004.

Nonnus of Panopolis. *Dionysiaca*. Trans. W. H. D. Rouse. Mythological introd. and notes H. J. Rose. Notes on text criticism L. R. Lind. Cambridge: Harvard University Press, 1940.

Novellino, or, One Hundred Ancient Tales. Ed. and trans. Joseph P. Consoli. New York: Garland, 1997.

Ovid (Publius Ovidius Naso, 43 BCE–17 CE). *Amores*. Trans. and introd. Tom Bishop. New York: Routledge, 2003.

———. *Fasti*. Trans. James George Frazer. Cambridge: Harvard University Press, 1989.

———. *Heroides*. Trans., ed., and introd. Harold Isbell. London: Penguin Books, 1990.

———. *Metamorphoses*. Trans. Frank Justus Miller. Cambridge: Harvard University Press, 1936.

Petrarch (Francesco Petrarca, 1304–74). *Africa*. Trans. and ed. Thomas G. Bergin and Alice S. Wilson. New Haven: Yale University Press, 1977.

———. *Canzoniere*. Ed. Gianfranco Contini. Turin: Einaudi, 1964.

———. *I Trionfi*. Ed. Paolo Lecaldano. Milan: Rizzoli, 1966.

Pius II, 1405–64 (Piccolomini, A. S.). *Commentarii rerum memorabilium—Commentaries of Pius II*. Smith College Studies in History, vols. 22, 25, 30, 35, 43. Northampton, MA, 1937–57.

Pliny the Elder (Caius Plinius Secundus, 23–79 CE). *Naturalis Historia*. Ed. D. Detlefsen. Hildesheim: Georg Olms, 1992.

————. *Natural History*. Ed. and trans. H. Rackham, W. H. S. Jones, and D. E. Eichholz. 10 vols. Cambridge: Harvard University Press, 1942–86.

Plutarch (45?–125 CE). *Lives*. Trans. Bernadotte Perrin. 11 vols. Cambridge: Harvard University Press, 1914–26.

————. *Moralia*. Trans. Frank Cole Babbit et al. 15 vols. Cambridge: Harvard University Press, 1927–1969.

Poesias diversas compuestas en deferentes lenguas en las honras que hizo a Roma la Nacion de los Españoles. A la Magestad Catolica de la Reyna Margarita de Austria nuestra señora. Rome: Iacopo Mascardo, 1612.

Politian (Poliziano, pseudonym of Angelo Ambrogini, 1454–94). *Rime*. Ed. Natalino Sapegno. Rome: Edizioni dell'Ateneo, 1967.

————. *Le stanze per la giostra*. Trans. David Quint. Amherst: University of Massachusetts Press, 1970.

————. *Le stanze per la giostra. L'Orfeo*. Ed. Edmondo Rho. Milan: Signorelli, 1969.

Pontanus, G. B (1429–1503). *Historia G. Castrioti*. Frankfurt, 1609.

Rossi, Gian Vittorio. See Erythraeus, Janus Nicius.

Sansovino, Francesco (1521–83). *Dell' historia universale dell'origine e imperio dei Turchi*. 3 vols. Venice, 1564.

Sarrocchi, Margherita (1560?–1617). *La Scanderbeide poema heroico della signora Margherita Sarrocchi. Dedicato all' ill.ma & ecc.ma sig.ra D. Costanza Colonna Sforza marchesa di Caravaggio*. Rome: Lepido Facij, 1606.

————. *La Scanderbeide poema heroico della sig.ra Margherita Sarrocchi dedicato alla principessa D. Giulia da Este. Dal sig. Giovanni Latini . . . dato alla stampa*. Rome: Andrea Fei, 1623. New printings were brought out in 1623, 1633, 1723.

————. *Scanderbeide*, cantos 7.6–17, 11.49–63, and 14.35–45. In *Antologia delle scrittrici italiane*, ed. Iolanda De Blasi, 286–96. Florence: Nemi, 1931.

Scaramelli, Baldassarre. *Due canti del poema eroico di Scanderbeo*. Carmagnola: March'Antonio Bellone, 1585.

Statius (Publius Papinius Statius, c.50–96 CE). *Thebaid*. Ed. and trans. D. R. Shackleton Bailey. Cambridge: Harvard University Press, 2003.

Stigliani, Tommaso (1573–1651). *Canzoniero*. Rome: Giovanni Mannelli, 1625.

Tasso, Torquato (1544–95). *Aminta*. Ed. Claudio Varese. Milan: Mursia, 1985.

————. *Jerusalem Delivered*. Ed. and trans. Anthony M. Esolen. Baltimore: Johns Hopkins University Press, 2000.

————. *Jerusalem Delivered. A Prose Translation*. Trans. and ed. Ralph Nash. Detroit: Wayne State University Press, 1987.

————. *Lettere*. Vol. 4. Pisa: N. Capurro, 1826.

————. *Prose*. Ed. Ettore Mazzali. Milan-Naples: Ricciardi, 1959.

————. *Le rime*. Ed. Bruno Basile. Rome: Salerno, 1994.

Tassoni, Alessandro (1565–1635). *Considerazioni sopra le rime del Petrarca*. Modena: Giulian Cassani, 1609.

Terracina, Laura (1519?– 1577?). *Discorso sopra il governo di tutti i canti d'Orlando Furioso*. Venice: Giolito, 1559.

Thucydides (460?– 404? BCE). *The History of the Peloponnesian War*. Trans. Charles Forster Smith. 4 vols. Cambridge: Harvard University Press, 1921–30.

Toppi, Nicolò. *Biblioteca napoletana, et apparato a gli huomini illustri in lettere di Napoli . . . Dalle loro origini, per tutto l'anno 1678*. Naples: Antonio Bulifon, 1678.

Valerius Maximus (1st century CE). *Memorable Doings and Sayings*. 2 vols. Ed. and trans. D. R. Shackleton Bailey. Cambridge: Harvard University Press, 2000.

Virgil (Publius Virgilius Maro, 70–19 BCE). *Aeneid*. Trans. H. Rushton Fairclough. Rev. G. P. Goold. Cambridge: Harvard University Press, 2000.

———. *Eclogues*. Ed. Robert Coleman. Cambridge: Cambridge University Press, 1977.

———. *Georgics*. Trans. with introd. and notes by Cristina Chew. Indianapolis: Hackett, 2002.

———. *The Georgics*. Trans. with introd. and notes by L. P. Wilkinson. Harmondsworth: Penguin Books, 1982.

———. *The Works of Virgil*. With Commentary by John Conington. Rev. Henry Nettleship. Hildesheim: Georg Olms, 1963.

Voragine, Jacobus de (1230?–1298). *The Golden Legend*. Trans. William Granger Ryan. Princeton: Princeton University Press, 1993.

SECONDARY SOURCES

Ajmar, Martha. "Exemplary Women in Renaissance Italy: Ambivalent Models of Behaviour?" In *Women in Italian Renaissance Culture and Society*, ed. Letizia Panizza, 244–64. Oxford: European Humanities Research Center, 2000.

Alessandrini, A. "Luca Valerio Linceo." In *La matematizzazione dell'universo. Momenti della cultura matematica tra 500 e 600*. Assisi, 1992.

Allaire, Gloria. "Noble Saracen or Muslim Enemy? The Changing Image of the Saracen in Late Medieval Italian Literature." In *Western Views of Islam in Medieval and Early Modern Europe: Perception of Other*, ed. David R. Blanks and Michael Frassetto, 173–84. New York: St. Martin's Press, 1999.

———. "Tullia d'Aragona's 'Il Meschino altramente detto il Guerino' as Key to a Reappraisal of Her Work." *Quaderni d'italianistica* 16.1 (1995): 33–50.

———. "The Warrior Woman in Late Medieval Prose Epics." *Italian Culture* 12 (1994): 33–43.

Asor Rosa, Alberto. *La cultura della controriforma*. Rome and Bari: Laterza, 1979.

———. "La Nuova Scienza, il Barocco e la crisi della Controriforma." In *La letteratura italiana*, ed. Carlo Muscetta, 3–47. Vol. 5: *Il Seicento*. Rome and Bari: Laterza, 1974.

Babinger, Franz. *Mehmet the Conqueror and His Time*. Ed. William C. Hickman. Trans. Ralph Manheim. Princeton: Princeton University Press, 1992. Original ed., *Mehmed der Eroberer und seine Zeit*. Munich: F. Bruckmann, 1953.

Bandini Buti, Maria, ed. *Enciclopedia biografica e bibliografica italiana. Poetesse e scrittrici*. Rome: Istituto Editoriale Italiano B. C. Tosi, 1942.

Battaglia, Salvatore. *Grande Dizionario della Lingua Italiana*. Turin: UTET, 1961–2002.

Belloni, Antonio. *Gli epigoni della Gerusalemme Liberata*. Padua: Angelo Draghi, 1893.

———. *Il poema epico e mitologico*. Milan: Vallardi, 1912.

———. *Storia della letteratura d'Italia, Il Seicento*. Milan: Vallardi, 1929.

Benson, Pamela Joseph. "A Defense of the Excellence of Bradamante." *Quaderni d'italianistica* 4, no. 2 (1983): 135–53.

———. *The Invention of the Renaissance Woman: The Challenge of Female Independence in the Literature and Thought of Italy and England.* University Park: Pennsylvania State University Press, 1992.

Blakeley, E. H., and John Warrington. *Smaller Classical Dictionary.* Rev. William Smith. New York: Dutton, 1958.

Borzelli, Angelo. *Il cavalier Giovan Battista Marino 1569–1625.* Naples: G. M. Priore, 1898.

———. *Note intorno a Margherita Sarrocchi ed al suo poema La Scanderbeide.* Naples: Tipografia Degli Artigianelli, 1935.

Bracket, John K. *Criminal Justice and Crime in Late Renaissance Florence, 1537–1609.* Cambridge: Cambridge University Press, 1992.

Brand, Peter, and Lino Pertile, eds. *The Cambridge History of Italian Literature.* Cambridge: Cambridge University Press, 1996.

Brizzi, Gian Paolo, ed. *La "ratio studiorum." Modelli culturali e pratiche educative dei Gesuiti in Italia tra Cinque e Seicento.* Rome: Bulzoni, c. 1981.

Caccamo, Domenico. "La diplomazia della Contro Riforma e la crociata: dai piani del Possevino alla lunga guerra di Clemente VIII." *Archivio storico italiano* 128, no. 2 (1970): 255–81.

Canonici Fachini, Ginevra. *Prospetto biografico delle donne italiane rinomate in letteratura.* Venice: Dalla tipografia di Alvisopoli, 1824.

Caretti, Luigi. "Galileo uomo di lettere." In *Studi di letteratura e di storia in memoria di Antonio di Pietro,* 107–23. Milan: Vita e pensiero, 1977.

Chemello, Adriana. "La donna, il modello, l'immaginario: Moderata Fonte e Lucrezia Marinella." In *Nel cerchio della luna. Figure di donna in alcuni testi del XVI secolo,* ed. Marina Zancan, 95–170. Venice: Marsilio, 1983.

Cherchi, Paolo. "Seicento. Poetry, Philosophy and Science." In *The Cambridge History of Italian Literature,* ed. Peter Brand and Lino Pertile. Cambridge: Cambridge University Press, 1996. 301–17.

Ciletti, Elena. "Patriarchal Ideology in the Renaissance Iconography of Judith." In *Refiguring Woman: Perspectives on Gender and the Italian Renaissance,* ed. Marilyn Migiel and Juliana Schiesari. Ithaca, NY: Cornell University Press, 1991.

Colombo, Angelo. "Il principe celebrato. Autografi poetici di Tomaso Stigliani e Margherita Sarrocchi." *Philologica* 1.1 (1992): 7–29.

Conti Odorisio, Ginevra. *Donna e società nel Seicento.* Introd. Ida Magli. Rome: Bulzoni, 1979.

Cosentino, Giuseppe. "Mathematics in the Jesuit Ratio Studiorum." In *Church, Culture and Curriculum: Theology and Mathematics in the Jesuit Ratio Studiorum,* by Laidislaus Lukacs and Giuseppe Cosentino. Trans., ed., and introd. Frederick A. Homann, 47–67. Philadelphia: Saint Joseph's University Press, 1999.

Costa-Zalessow, Natalia. *Scrittrici italiane dal XIII al XX secolo.* Ravenna: Longo, 1982.

Cox, Virginia. "Fiction, 1560–1650." In *A History of Women Writing in Italy,* ed. Letizia Panizza and Sharon Woods, 52–64. Cambridge: Cambridge University Press, 2000.

———. "The Single Self: Feminist Thought and the Marriage Market in Early Modern Venice." *Renaissance Quarterly* 48 (1995): 513–81.

————. "Women as Readers and Writers of Chivalric Poetry in Early Modern Italy." In *Sguardi sull'Italia. Miscellanea dedicata a Francesco Villari*, ed. Gino Bedoni, Sygmunt Barański, Anna Laura Lepschy, and Brian Richardson, 134–45. Leeds: Society for Italian Studies, 1997.

Crescimbeni, Giovanni Mario. *Dell'Istoria della volgar poesia*. Vol. 4. Rome: Cracas, 1730.

————. *De' Commentarii intorno all'Istoria della volgar poesia*. Venice: Lorenzo Basegio, 1730.

Croce, Benedetto. "La Pinacotheca dell'Eritreo" and "Donne letterate del Seicento." In *Nuovi saggi sulla letteratura italiana del Seicento*, 124–33, 154–63. Bari: Laterza, 1931.

————. *Poeti e scrittori del pieno e tardo Rinascimento*. Vol. 2. Bari: Laterza, 1945.

Croce, Benedetto, and Santino Caramella, eds. *Politici e moralisti del Seicento*. Bari: Laterza, 1930.

Cuaz, Marco. *Intellettuali, potere e circolazione delle idee nell'Italia moderna (1500–1700)*. Turin: Loescher, 1982.

Dean, Trevor, and K. J. P. Lowe, eds. *Crime, Society, and the Law in Renaissance Italy*. Cambridge: Cambridge University Press, 1994.

Dejob, Charles. *De l'influence du Concile de Trente sur la littérature et les beaux-arts chez les peuples catholiques*. Paris: E. Thorin, 1884.

Delbrück, Hans. *History of the Art of War*. Trans. Walter J. Renfroe Jr. Westport, CT: Greenwood, 1975.

De Mattei, Rodolfo. *Il pensiero politico italiano della Controriforma*. Naples: Ricciardi, 1982.

————. *Il problema della ragion di stato nell'età della Controriforma*. Milan-Naples: Ricciardi, 1979.

Denzler, Georg. *Kardinal Guglielmo Sirleto (1514–1585): Leben und Werk. Ein Beitrag zur nachtridentinischen Reform*. Munich: M. Hueber, 1964.

Dersofi, Nancy. "Laura Terracina." In *Italian Women Writers*, ed. Rinaldina Russell, 423–50. Westport, CT: Greenwood Press, 1994.

Dionisotti, Carlo. *Geografia e storia della letteratura italiana*. Turin: Einaudi, 1967.

————. "Lepanto nella cultura italiana del tempo." *Lettere italiane* 23, no. 4 (1971): 473–92.

Ducellier, Alain. *La façade maritime de l'Albanie au moyen age*. Thessaloniki: Institute for Balkan Studies, 1981.

Fahy, Conor. "Women and Italian Cinquecento Literary Academies." In *Women in Italian Renaissance Culture and Society*, ed. Letizia Panizza, 438–52. Oxford: European Humanities Research Center, 2000.

Faraglia, Nunzio Federico. "Fabio Colonna Linceo Napolitano." *Archivio per le province napoletane* (1885): 39–40.

Farrell, Allen P. *The Jesuit Code of Liberal Education*. Milwaukee: Bruce, 1938.

Favaro, Antonio. "Margherita Sarrocchi." In *Amici e corrispondenti di Galileo*, 6–31. Vol. 1. Venice: Officine Grafiche C. Ferrari, 1894; Florence: Salimbeni, 1983.

Finucci, Valeria. "La scrittura epico-cavalleresca al femminile: Moderata Fonte e Tredici canti del *Floridoro*." *Annali d'Italianistica* 12 (1994): 203–31.

————. "Undressing the Warrior/Re-dressing the Woman: The Education of Bradamante." In *The Lady Vanishes: Subjectivity and Representation in Castiglione and Ariosto*. Stanford, CA: Stanford University Press, 1992. 227–53.

Gabrieli, Giuseppe. "Accademie romane. Gli Umoristi." *Roma* 12, no. 4 (1935): 173–84.

Gegaj, Athanas. *L'Albanie et l'invasion turque au XVe siècle.* Louvain: Bureaux du Recueil, Bibliothèque de l'Université, 1937.

George Kastriot-Scanderbeg and the Albanian-Turkish War of the XVth Century. State University of Tirana, Institute of History and Linguistics. Tirana: The Institute, 1967.

Gerboni, Luigi. *Un umanista del Seicento, G. N. Eritreo* (Città di Castello, 1899).

Ghisalberti, Alberto M., ed. *Dizionario biografico degli Italiani.* Rome: Istituto della Enciclopedia Italiana Treccani, 1960–.

Giamatti, A. Bartlett. *The Earthly Paradise and the Renaissance Epic.* Princeton, NJ: Princeton University Press, 1966.

Giorello, Giulio. "Gli 'oscuri labirinti': calcolo e geometria nel Cinque e Seicento." In *Storia d'Italia. Annali 3: Scienza e tecnica nella cultura e nella società dal Rinascimento a oggi,* ed. Gianni Micheli, 261–380. Turin: Einaudi 1980.

Gravit, F. W. "The Accademia degli Umoristi and Its French Relationships." *Papers of the Michigan Academy* 29 (1935): 505–21.

Graziosi, Elisabetta. "Arcadia femminile: presenze e modelli." *Filologia e critica* 17, no. 3 (1992): 321–58.

Grendler, Paul F. *Schooling in Renaissance Italy: Literacy and Learning, 1300–1600.* Baltimore: Johns Hopkins University Press, 1989.

———. *The Universities of the Italian Renaissance.* Baltimore: Johns Hopkins University Press, 2002.

Günsberg, Maggie. "'Donna liberata'? The Portrayal of Women in the Italian Renaissance Epic." *Italianist* 7 (1987): 7–35.

Hale, John Richard. "Lepanto 1571." In *Famous Sea Fights from Salamis to Jutland.* London: Methuen, 1931. 67–105.

Hale, John Rigby. *War and Society in Renaissance Europe, 1450–1620.* London: Methuen, 1985.

Hanlon, Gregory. *Early Modern Italy, 1550–1800: Three Seasons in European History.* New York: St. Martin's Press, 2000.

Hodgkinson, Harry. *Skanderbeg.* Ed. Bejtullah Destani and Westrow Cooper. Introd. David Abulafia. London: Center for Albanian Studies, 1999.

İnalcik, Halil. *The Ottoman Empire: The Classical Age, 1300–1600.* Trans. Norman Itzkowitz and Colin Imber. New Rochelle, NY: Aristide D. Caratzas, 1973.

———. Review of *Mehmed der Eroberer und seine Zeit,* by Franz Babinger. *Speculum,* 35.3 (July 1960): 408–27.

Jacques, Edwin E. "Temporary Successes of Skanderbeg (1443–1468)." In *The Albanians: An Ethnic History from Prehistoric Times to the Present.* Jefferson, NC: McFarland, 1995. 178–89.

Javitch, Daniel. *Proclaiming a Classic: The Canonization of "Orlando Furioso."* Princeton: Princeton University Press, 1991.

Jed, Stephanie H. *Chaste Thinking: The Rape of Lucretia and the Birth of Humanism.* Bloomington: Indiana University Press, 1988.

Jordan, Constance. *Renaissance Feminism: Literary Texts and Political Models.* Ithaca, NY: Cornell University Press, 1990.

King, Margaret L. "Book-Lined Cells: Women and Humanism in the Early Italian Renaissance." In *Beyond Their Sex: Learned Women of the European Past,* ed. Patricia H. Labalme, 66–90. New York: New York University Press, 1980.

———. "Thwarted Ambitions: Six Learned Women of the Italian Renaissance." *Soundings* 59 (1976): 280–304.

———. *Women of the Renaissance.* Foreword Catharine R Stimpson. Chicago: University of Chicago Press, 1991.

King, Margaret L., and Albert Rabil Jr., eds. *Her Immaculate Hand: Selected Works by and about the Women Humanists of Quattrocento Italy.* Binghamton, NY: Center for Medieval and Early Renaissance Studies, 1983.

Kolsky, Stephen. "Moderata Fonte's *Tredici Canti del Floridoro:* Women in a Man's Genre." *Rivista di studi italiani* 17 (1999): 165–84.

Kristeller, Paul Oscar. "Learned Women of Early Modern Italy: Humanists and University Scholars." In *Beyond Their Sex: Learned Women of the European Past,* ed. Patricia H. Labalme, 91–116. New York: New York University Press, 1980.

Labalme, Patricia H., ed. *Beyond Their Sex: Learned Women of the European Past.* New York: New York University Press, 1980.

Lazzaro, Claudia. *The Italian Renaissance Garden.* New Haven: Yale University Press, 1990.

Lenzi, Maria Lodovica. *Donne e Madonne. L'educazione femminile nel primo Rinascimento italiano.* Turin: Loescher, 1982.

Levati, Ambrogio. *Dizionario biografico-cronologico.* Vol. 5: *Donne illustri.* Milan: Nicolò Tosi, 1822.

Lombardi, Daniela. "Intervention by Church and State in Marriage Disputes in Sixteenth- and Seventeenth-Century Florence." In *Crime, Society, and the Law in Renaissance Italy,* ed. Trevor Dean and K. J. P. Lowe, 142–56. Cambridge: Cambridge University Press, 1994.

Maclean, Ian. *The Renaissance Notion of Woman: A Study in the Fortunes of Scholasticism and Medical Science in European Intellectual Life.* Cambridge: Cambridge University Press, 1980.

Malpezzi Price, Paola. "Lucrezia Marinella." In *Italian Women Writers,* ed. Rinaldina Russell, 234–42. Westport, CT: Greenwood Press, 1994.

———. *Moderata Fonte: Women and Life in Sixteenth-Century Venice.* Madison: Fairleigh Dickinson University Press, 2003.

———. "Woman Warrior." In *Feminist Encyclopedia of Italian Literature,* ed. Rinaldina Russell, 357–59. Westport, CT: Greenwood Press, 1997.

Marinelli, Peter. "Narrative Poetry." In *The Cambridge History of Italian Literature,* ed. Peter Brand and Lino Pertile, 233–50. Cambridge: Cambridge University Press, 1996.

Martuscelli, Domenico. *Biografia degli uomini illustri del regno di Napoli.* Vol. 5. Naples: Nicola Gervasi, 1818.

Masetti Zannini, Gian Ludovico. *Motivi storici della educazione femminile. Scienza, lavoro, giuochi.* Naples: M. D'Auria, 1981.

Maylender, Michele. *Storia delle Accademie d'Italia.* Preface S. E. Luigi Rava. Bologna: Forni, 1976. Original ed., Florence: Molini, 1930.

McLucas, John C. "Amazon, Sorceress, and Queen: Women and War in the Aristocratic Literature of Sixteenth-Century Italy." *Italianist* 8 (1988): 33–55.

Meinecke, Friedrich. *Machiavelism: The Doctrine of Raison d'État and Its Place in Modern History.* Trans. Douglas Scott, with a general introduction by W. Stark. New Haven: Yale University Press, 1957.

Menghini, Mario. *La vita e le opere di Giambattista Marino.* Rome: A. Manzoni, 1888.

Meoli, Rosa. "Margherita Sarrocchi e la sua Scanderbeide." *Shejzat* 13 (1969): 61–69.

Merolla, Riccardo. "Lo stato della Chiesa." In *Letteratura italiana,* ed. Alberto Asor Rosa, 1019–1109. Vol. 2: *L'Età moderna,* pt. 2. Turin: Einaudi, 1988.

Migiel, Marilyn. "Enchantress" and "Epic." In *Feminist Encyclopedia of Italian Literature,* ed. Rinaldina Russell, 76–77, 82–83. Westport, CT: Greenwood Press, 1997.

———. *Gender and Genealogy in Tasso's "Gerusalemme Liberata."* Lewiston, NY: Edwin Mellen Press, 1992.

Migiel, Marilyn, and Juliana Schiesari, eds. *Refiguring Woman: Perspectives on Gender and the Italian Renaissance.* Ithaca: Cornell University Press, 1991.

Morandini, Giuliana. *Sospiri e palpiti. Scrittrici italiane del Seicento.* Genoa: Marietti, 2001.

Murrin, Michael. *History and Warfare in Renaissance Epic.* Chicago: University of Chicago Press, 1994.

Novelletto, Luciana. "La poesia eroica di Margherita Sarrocchi (1562–1617). Lettura della Scanderbeide." Master's thesis. Università degli studi di Padova, 1999–2000.

O'Connor, J. J., and E. F. Robertson. "Luca Valerio." In *Dictionary of Scientific Biography.* New York, 1970–90.

Oldcorn, Anthony. "Lyric Poetry." In *The Cambridge History of Italian Literature,* ed. Peter Brand and Lino Pertile, 251–76. Cambridge: Cambridge University Press, 1996.

Orbaan, Johannes Albertus Franciscus. *Documenti sul Barocco in Roma.* Rome: Società romana di storia patria, 1920.

Panizza, Letizia, ed. *Women in Italian Renaissance Culture and Society.* Oxford: European Humanities Research Center, 2000.

Panizza, Letizia, and Sharon Woods, eds. *A History of Women Writing in Italy.* Cambridge: Cambridge University Press, 2000.

Petronio, Giuseppe, ed. *Dizionario enciclopedico della letteratura italiana.* Palermo: UNEDI, 1966–70.

Pezzini, Serena. "Il ramo cadetto. Epica secentesca e scrittura di donna. La Scanderbeide di Margherita Sarrocchi." Ph.D. diss. Università di Pisa, 2002–03.

Pintard, René. *Le libertinage érudit dans la première moitié du XVIIe siècle.* Paris: Boisin, 1943; Geneva: Slatkine, 1983.

Quadrio, Francesco Saverio. *Della storia e della ragione d'ogni poesia.* 7 vols. Bologna: Pisarri, 1736–44.

Quint, David. "Political Allegory in the *Gerusalemme liberata.*" In *Epic and Empire: Politics and Generic Form from Virgil to Milton,* 213–247. Princeton: Princeton University Press, 1993.

Quondam, Amedeo. "L'ideologia cortigiana di Giulio Cesare Capaccio." In *La parola nel labirinto. Società e scrittura del Manierismo a Napoli,* 187–225. Rome and Bari: Laterza, 1975.

Rabil, Albert, Jr., ed. *Knowledge, Goodness, and Power: The Debate over Nobility among Quattrocento Italian Humanists.* Binghamton, NY: Medieval and Renaissance Texts and Studies, 1991.

———. *Laura Cereta. Quattrocento Humanist.* Binghamton, NY: Center for Medieval and Early Renaissance Studies, 1981.

———, ed. *Renaissance Humanism: Foundations, Forms, and Legacy.* 3 vols. Philadelphia: University of Pennsylvania Press, 1988.

Rajna, Pio. *Le fonti dell'Orlando Furioso.* Ed. Francesco Mazzoni. Florence: Sansoni, 1975. First published 1876.

Rawson, Edward Kirk. *Twenty Famous Naval Battles: Salamis to Santiago.* New York: Crowel, 1899.

Renazzi, Filippo Maria. *Storia dell'Università degli Studi di Roma detta comunemente "La Sapienza."* Vol 3. Rome: Stamperia Pagliarini, 1805.

Ricci, Corrado. *Beatrice Cenci.* Trans. Morris Bishop and Henry Longan Stuart. New York: Boni and Liveright, 1925.

Richardson, Brian. "'Amore maritale': Advice on Love and Marriage in the Second Half of the Cinquecento." In *Women in Italian Renaissance Culture and Society,* ed. Letizia Panizza, 194–206. Oxford: European Humanities Research Center, 2000.

―――. "Narrative Fiction." In *The Cambridge History of Italian Literature,* ed. Peter Brand and Lino Pertile, 223–32. Cambridge: Cambridge University Press, 1996.

Robin, Diana. "Querelle des femmes: The Renaissance." In *Feminist Encyclopedia of Italian Literature,* ed. Rinaldina Russell, 270–73. Westport, CT: Greenwood Press, 1997.

Robinson, Lilian. *Monstrous Regiment: The Lady Knight in Sixteenth-Century Epic.* New York: Garland, 1985.

Rosa, Mario. "La chiesa e gli stati regionali nell'età dell'assolutismo." In *Letteratura italiana,* ed. Alberto Asor Rosa, 257–89. Vol. 1: *Il letterato e le istituzioni.* Turin: Einaudi, 1982.

―――. "Coscienza di ceto e problema dello Stato negli intellettuali napoletani del Seicento." In *Letteratura italiana,* ed. Alberto Asor Rosa, 359–367. Vol. 1: *Il letterato e le istituzioni.* Turin: Einaudi, 1982.

Russell, Rinaldina, ed. *Feminist Encyclopedia of Italian Literature.* Westport, CT: Greenwood Press, 1997.

―――. *Generi poetici medievali.* Naples: Società Editrice Napoletana, 1982.

―――, ed. *Italian Women Writers.* Westport, CT: Greenwood Press, 1994.

Russo, Piera. "L'Accademia degli Umoristi. Fondazione, struttura, leggi: il primo decennio di attività." *Esperienze letterarie* 4, no. 4 (1979): 47–61.

Santoro, Mario. *Letture ariostesche.* Naples: Liguori, 1973.

Scaglione, Aldo. *Essays on the Arts of Discourse.* Ed. Paolo Cherchi, Allen Mendelbaum, Stephen Murphy, Giuseppe Velli. New York: Peter Lang,1998.

―――. *The Liberal Arts and the Jesuit College System.* Philadelphia: John Benjamins, 1986.

Schwoebel, Robert. *The Shadow of the Crescent: The Renaissance Image of the Turks, 1453–1517.* Nieuwkoop: B. de Graaf, 1967.

Shemek, Deanna. "Gender, Duality, and the Sacrifices of History: Bradamante in the *Orlando Furioso.*" In *Ladies Errant: Wayward Women and Social Order in Early Modern Italy,* 77–125. Durham: Duke University Press, 1998.

―――. "Of Women, Knights, Arms, and Love: The 'Querelle des Femmes' in Ariosto's Poem. " *Modern Language Notes* 104 (1989): 68–97.

Smith, William. *Small Classical Dictionary.* New York: E. P. Dutton, 1968.

Southern, Janet. *Power and Display in the Seventeenth Century: The Arts and Their Patrons in Modena and Ferrara.* Cambridge: Cambridge University Press, 1988.

Tamborra, Angelo. "La lotta contro il turco e l'intervento degli stati italiani alla fine del 500." *Ungheria oggi* 5 (1965): 20–29.

Tiraboschi, Girolamo. *Storia della letteratura italiana.* 9 vols. Florence: Molini Landi, 1805–12.

Toffanin, Giuseppe. *Machiavelli e il tacitismo.* Padua: A. Draghi, 1921.

Tomalin, Margaret. *The Fortunes of the Warrior Heroine in Italian Literature: An Index of Emancipation.* Ravenna: Longo, 1982.

Vallauri, Tommaso. *Storia della poesia in Piemonte.* Turin: Tip. Chirio e Mina, 1841.

Varese, Claudio. "Momenti e implicazioni del romanzo libertino nel Seicento italiano." In *Il libertinismo in Europa,* ed. Sergio Bertelli, 265–70. Milan-Naples: Ricciardi, 1980.

Vitullo, Julian. "Contained Conflict: Wild Men and Warrior Women in the Early Italian Epic." *Annali d'Italianistica* 12 (1994): 39–59.

Weinberg, Bernard. *A History of Literary Criticism in the Italian Renaissance.* Chicago: University of Chicago Press, 1961.

Widmar, Bruno, ed.. *Scritti politici del Cinquecento e del Seicento.* Milan: Rizzoli, 1954.

Wilkins, Ernest Hatch. *A History of Italian Literature.* Cambridge: Harvard University Press, 1954.

NOTE ON TRANSLATION

This translation of the *Scanderbeide* is based on the complete edition of 1623. Obscure lines have been checked against those of the earlier version if it includes them. What is published here is a partial edition of Sarrocchi's long poem, one that reduces the original twenty-three cantos to eighteen and excises a few episodes from some of the latter. The omitted cantos describe the king's preparations for the defense and the alignment of his supporters (canto 4); failed attempts at accord between Albanians and Turks (canto 8); Mauro's second and third betrayals, with the consequent entry of enemy soldiers into Croia and the plundering of the town (cantos 11 and 12); and a third Albanian sortie (canto 16). The episodes omitted from the remaining cantos are a sortie of Albanian men from Croia (5.1–52, 68–81); the second half of a protracted love lament (13.122–33); apparitions and visions that Sarrocchi fails to dramatize plausibly (14.1–60); an inconclusive duel between Driarasso and Benci (17.155); and, finally, an adventurous story of love between Glicera and her royal Persian husband, which remains incidental to the main story line (18.22–88).

In most episodes, Sarrocchi's narrative flows rapidly and is vibrant with suspense. Her need for a space ampler than the one provided by the strictures of versification is shown by the occasional run-on stanzas, in which the period continues from one stanza to the next. These more often occur in the fervor of oration and when speedy and complex military actions are described (see, e.g., 1.41–42, 1.58–59, 3.37–38, 5.11–12, 7.49–50, 10.36–37, 21.73–74, 22.52–53). At times, however, sentences become clumsy and monotonous. This is more noticeable in tracts of the first cantos, when miraculous apparitions and religious ceremonies are described, or when the thematic repertory of Petrarchan love and popular laments is indulged in at length. At these points the narration becomes strenuous, 59 words seem to be thrown together haphazardly, rather than being grammatically related, nouns and adjectives are left without verbs, verbs are not properly connected with nouns, and word endings are changed to fit the metrical requirements but not the syntactical order. These linguistic conglomerations, however, reveal a submerged logic, an elliptical synthetic phrasing running underneath the more analytical Italian, a logic perhaps prompted by Latin, a language in which Sarrocchi was proficient.

In part because of these aspects of Sarrocchi's work, I thought it best to translate the *Scanderbeide* in prose. A prose translation enables the reader to read smoothly and attain as full comprehension of the original text as possible, both literal and contextual, making at times explicit what is implicit or elliptically expressed in verse, without obscuring any figurative expression. My translation, therefore, is not a word-for-word transcription of Sarrocchi's verse lines but rather a translation into English prose in the full sense of the word, one that turns to paraphrasing when necessary rather than forfeiting part of the intended meaning. The task of the translator is here taken to be that of giving the version that is the nearest possible to the cultural context of the author, producing therefore in English an impression similar to the one created in Italian by the original text.

For the above reasons, I have sometimes added single words in order to make transitions and connections understandable. By transposing certain words and sentences, I have tried to avoid some logical inconsistencies that a more literal translation would produce. To guard against obscurity, I have made corrections of grammatical gender and substituted proper names for personal pronouns in instances in which the use of pronouns would have resulted in confusion. I have eliminated the insistent repetitions of words that carry a wide semantic meaning, such as *vendetta*, *generoso*, and *superbo*, and have replaced them with words that better fit their context. The Italian *vendetta*, for instance, may mean "vendetta," "revenge," or "justice," but it stands in the poem more often for the blow inflicted with lance or dagger in return for a blow received. I have eliminated capital letters for most abstractions but have retained them for some virtues, for Love, and for stars and planets when the personification is carried out to the end of the sentence.

Following a tradition well established in the translation of Italian epics into English, I have used English names for some of the non-Italian characters and anglicized names when English ones did not exist. Murad, for instance, is used instead of Amuratte, Musaka in place of Musacchio, Orkhan for Orcano, thus following the example of *Jerusalem Delivered*, where Goffredo becomes Godfrey; Ugone, Hugh; Agricalte, Agricalt; and Vincilao, Wenceslaus. As to titles, while the word *signore* has been translated "lord" everywhere, the title of king—which in the original text is used indifferently for Scanderbeg, for Murad, and for other potentates—is never used in reference to the sultan in order to keep the distinction clear between him and the other characters. Finally, I have corrected the frequent errors in the Italian edition in the numbering of the stanzas and modernized the punctuation.

In this volume, each canto is preceded by a brief summary of its contents, and the gist of all omitted passages is found at the appropriate point in the poem. The notes to this translation, the first ones to be provided by any editor, are explanatory of the text; they give reasons for my translation; they suggest Sarrocchi's probable models and sources; they explain legendary and historical narratives, characters, places, and notions implied or referred to in the text; and they provide cross-references to the same theme or topic found in other sections of the poem. An eminent feature of Renaissance poetry was the abundance of similes and descriptions that had come down in codified form and of which poets created new ingenious variations for the readers' pleasure and in their eagerness to outdo one another. Sarrocchi's descriptions are indeed artful, her comparisons always pleasurable, and most of the time they are deftly employed to underline psychological states. For this reason, my notes frequently point out cliché similes, descriptions, and themes and give cross-references for them. Also for easy reference, places and people, historical or fictional, that are not characters in the narrative and are mentioned in the text directly by name are listed in the Glossary. The cast of main characters lists the principal characters and some of the more remarkable minor ones. For the readers' convenience, this section has been divided into two parts: the Albanian camp and the Ottoman camp. Whenever possible, I have added short notes about the historical personages that may have inspired Sarrocchi's fictional characters. The references to verse lines and prose passages are based on the editions listed in my bibliography; and all translations are mine. Finally, a selection of passages from the Italian original is provided in the appendix and entries pertaining to Sarrocchi's times and cultural context are found in the index.

CAST OF MAIN CHARACTERS

IN THE ALBANIAN CAMP

THE KING (Alexander, "the hero"): based on the historical figure of Scanderbeg, the Castrioti lord who, from 1443 to 1468, led the armed resistance to the Ottoman advance into northern Albania; sends messengers to various European states, and Svarte to Naples 1.5–9; is captain of the army besieging Belgrade 1.21; considers disobeying the sultan's orders 1.36–40; gives explanations to Lagnete 1.41–48; camps the army outside Belgrade 1.49; calls Aranit's daughter to his presence 1.64; remembers his Christian upbringing 1.69–70; keeps his promise to Aranit and advises him to take refuge in Buda 1.72; is poisoned 2.8–21; is restored to health 2.27–28; leaves Belgrade and takes possession of Croia 2.32, 2.46–47; sees Ferratte and some of his Janissaries climb the path to the walls of the citadel 5.2–6; kills Ferratte's men and puts on Ferratte's armor 5.9–10; with his men, enters the Turkish camp 5.11; kills Varadin 5.34–35; fights with Armen, captain of the Spahis 5.39–42; kills many Turks 5.44–45; is saved by the Janissaries who believe him to be Ferratte 5.48; takes off the Agah's armor and exits the Turkish camp 5.50; climbs Mount Tumenishti and remains in hiding 5.53–55, 6.52–63; comes across Aranit just arriving from Presa 6.64–67; attacks the Turkish camp 6.81; is offered another horse by Crater when his horse is killed 6.87–92; is challenged by Driarasso and Agrismeta 6.109–15, 6.122; returns to Croia and is welcomed by the populace 6.129; plans to marry Aranit's daughter 7.79–81; sends to look for Crater who has been taken prisoner 7.82; sends Artecin to the imperial court 7.85; summons his captains and announces God's choice of a champion to fight the duel 9.1–4; orders preparations to be made for the duel 9.9; calls Vaconte to his presence 9.13–17; brings aid to the besieged town of Amantia 10.46–47, 10.50; goes to Pallante's rescue 10.66–68; cannot believe Mauro's betrayal 10.75; sends out scouts to gather news about the newly arrived army 13.48; sends

Oronte and Vaconte to spy in the Turkish camp 13.59–61; outranks all defenders in repulsing the attack on Croia 14.68, 14.92–98; makes a gift of his sword to the Ottoman 15.5–6; hopes for Rosmonda's conversion 18.90; prays for the end of the plague, orders a procession, and has a vision 18.117, 18.120–31; advises the Italians to give battle to the Persian fleet 20.13–19; prepares for the next battle, meditates, and prays 21.42–45; orders wood stumps to be collected and wild boars to be caught 21.46–47; advances toward Presa 21.48–49; disposes the army for battle 21.76, 22.2–4; speaks to his soldiers and prays 22.6–18; leads his men to victory 23.51–55, 23.57.

THE CAPTAINS

ARANIT-PALINURO (for "Palinuro," see glossary): inspired by George Araniti or Gjergj Arjanit Komneni, who became Scanderbeg's father-in-law in 1451 and, after signing a treaty with King Alfonso of Naples, attempted to chase the Turks out of Epirus but lost a decisive battle near Berat; as captain at the defense of Belgrade, surrenders to Alexander 1.24; is called Palinuro because of his loyalty 1.26; has a daughter called Dori 1.27; is to die by the sultan's order 1.35; does not suspect the sultan's intentions 1.50–52; is angered by the kidnapping of Dori 1.56; takes refuge in Buda 1.72; understands that Alexander is being poisoned 2.15; sends Mohamet to Belgrade to cure him 2.16; arrives on Mount Tumenishti and comes across Alexander 6.67; enters the battlefield with his men 6.109; proposes Oronte to infiltrate the Turkish camp 13.60; fights at the defense of Croia 14.81–83; fights in the last battle 23.59.

BORSO D'ESTE: suggested by the historical Borso d'Este (1413–71), marquis of Ferrara and duke of Mantua and Reggio, who, however, did not participate personally in any expedition against the Turks; participates in Pius II's crusade and becomes admiral of the fleet 18.139; orders Antreo to be brought to his presence 19.80; consults with his officers about giving battle to the Persian fleet 20.1–5; decides to attack and reviews the fleet 20.20, 20.26; speaks to his men before battle 20.28–36; his ship runs against Tarconte's 20.76; duels with Tarconte, the Persian commander, and kills him 20.84–88; fights in the last battle 21.43, 22.3, 22.29–32.

CRATER: offers his horse to Scanderbeg who has lost his own charger 6.92–93; runs to catch a runaway horse and is taken prisoner 6.101–2; is wounded by Driarasso 6.105; cannot be found after the battle 7.82; is returned by the sultan 10.3; is sent to Amantia with Mauro 10.14; is ordered to guard the walls of the city on the side of the river 10.32; is betrayed by Mauro 10.43–45; tells his story to the king 10.73–74.

MAURO, a collation of several historical personages who at one time or another changed sides, among them Hamza Castrioti, a nephew of Scanderbeg, and Moïs or Mojsi Golem Komneni Thopia, called Dibra, son of Musaka, a brother of George Arjanit:[1] captures Osman on the battlefield 6.117; is sent to Amantia with Crater 10.14; resents having to return his prisoner and is jealous of Crater 10.15–17; is in charge of defending Amantia 10.17, 10.30; takes his revenge on Crater 10.31–45; exits the town with Pallante 10.61; is surrounded by Serpedon's men 10.63; is left to fight alone by Scanderbeg 10.68; is thought not to be a traitor by the king 10.74.

PALINURO. See Aranit.

THOPIA (father of Musaka and Comin), inspired by some member or other of the Thopia family, whose territory extended from below Scutari to Ochrid, and included Croia and the fortress of Berat: is engaged in combat with Radiar 6.97; is slain 6.99; is found by Musaka and carried to Croia 9.83–84; is buried 9.85.

VACONTE: inspired by Tasso's Rinaldo in *Jerusalem Delivered* but also reminiscent of Scanderbeg's real nephew, Hamza Castrioti, who was married to a Turkish woman, at one point defected to the Turks, and after rejoining his uncle again, was captured by them, sentenced to death, and killed; urges the men of Croia to fight to the death 5.100–105; helps Alexander to disentangle his foot 6.91; fights against Driarasso 6.103–4; takes prisoners 6.117; is chosen to fight Agrismeta in a single duel and is equipped for the fight 9.5–9, 9.13–23; arrives at the enclosure and salutes Agrismeta 9.38–39; fights a duel with Agrismeta 9.44–68; returns to Croia and has his wounds taken care of 9.79–80; volunteers to penetrate the Turkish camp and is stopped by the night guard 13.61–86; is captured by Rosmonda and falls in love with her 13.89–93; believes Rosmonda is wounded and runs out of his tent to look for her 15.59; prays God to favor his love for Rosmonda and marries her 18.99–103; is sent by the king toward Presa to lure the Turkish army into battle 21.53–58; fights in the last battle 22.38–50, 23.40–50.

VRAN: perhaps inspired by the historical Simon Altisferi (in Italian Altafoglia), known as Vrana or Urana, who served in the army of King Alfonso of Naples and received from him the title of count[2] and who was Scanderbeg's most loyal captain and friend; runs to Alexander's side and breaks his fall 2.12; takes Mohamet to Alexander 2.19; is entrusted with the defense of Amantia 4; is told by Nardo about Alexander's presumed death

1. See Hodgkinson, *Skanderbeg*, 136–41, 144.
2. Ibid., 227; Gegaj, *L'Albanie et l'invasion turque*, 119 n. 2.

7.29–30; captures Pallante 7.43–47; asks Pallante to give himself up 7.48; takes Pallante to Amantia and inquires about his melancholy 7.54–61; lets Pallante visit Flora 7.62; asks Pallante's father for ransom money and donates it to the couple 10.4–6; is taken ill and forced to stay in bed throughout the siege of Amantia 10.17–18, 10.27–28, 10.30; recovers 10.70–71; blocks the Turkish supply routes 17.62; is sent to block the advance of the Persian army 18.132–33; intercepts Serpedon's men crossing the river and fights against them 23.14–33.

OTHERS

ALFONSO: based on Alfonso I, king of Naples (reigned 1442–58); is tied by bonds of friendship to Scanderbeg 1.7; is to be told of Alexander's successes by Svarte 1.9; welcomes Svarte 1.18; listens to his story 1.19–2.55; offers aid to Scanderbeg 2.55–56.

ARTECIN: is sent to the imperial court to arrange an exchange of prisoners 7.84–85; speaks with the emperor 7.88–94; has a servant, Romidon, who excites the resentment of the Ottoman soldiers 7.95–109; is killed by the sultan in the final battle 23.42–43.

COMIN: is wounded and withdraws to Croia 6.97; grieves for his father's death 9.85; is captured 22.45; is killed 22.47–48.

DORI (Donica in the 1606 version): a clear reference to Marina Andronika, also called Donika, Arjanit Komneni's daughter and Scanderbeg's wife; is presented as Aranit's daughter 1.27–31; is desired by Murad when he hears of her beauty 1.32–35. is almost kidnapped by Lagnete 1.53–63; tells her side of the story 1.64–69; is desired by Alexander as a wife 7.79–81.

FELIN (Alexander's groom): grieves for his master and decides to find out what happened to him 5.72; exits the city during the night and goes down to the valley 5.73–75; is caught and brought into the sultan's presence 5.76; tells all he knows 5.77–78.

MUSAKA (Thopia's young son): leaves the battlefield to accompany his brother Comin, who is wounded 6.97–98; goes back to the battlefield to look for his father's body 9.83–84; cleans and carries home his father's body 9.84; in the final battle, supervenes where his brother Comin has been killed and fights on with the wish to die 22.50, 22.58; is slain 22.60.

SINAN: is asked by Scanderbeg to ambush Ferratte and kill him 5.7; kills other Janissaries 5.8–9; enters the Turkish camp 5.15; kills Armilla, Varadin's wife 5.26; is killed by Varadin 5.30.

SVARTE: is sent as ambassador to Alfonso, king of Naples, to ask for aid 1.8–9; crosses the Adriatic and Italy 1.10–17; is received by Alfonso 1.18; tells Alfonso how Scanderbeg defected and repossessed his father's territories 1.20–2.55; is offered help by king Alfonso 2.56; is asked to point out the way to the Italian contingent traveling to Croia 2.70.

IN THE OTTOMAN CAMP

THE EMPEROR ("the sultan," "the Thracian," "the Turk," "the Ottoman," "the tyrant," Murad [Amuratte, in the Italian text]): loosely based on the historical figure of Murad II, who reigned from 1421 to 1451, died in Adrianople, modern Edirne, and was buried in Brusa, Asia Minor; sends Alexander to the siege of Belgrade 1.21; promises the people of Belgrade they will not be harmed 1.24; hears about Dori's beauty and covets her 1.32; orders Lagnete to kill Palinuro and kidnap the young woman 1.35; is angered by Lagnete's failure 1.74; assents to Baizet's advice to poison Scanderbeg 1.96; arrives at the mosque and listens to Filena 3.19–24; is angered by Alexander's betrayal and decides to head the army against Scanderbeg 3.28; reviews its various national contingents 3.37–102; makes his daughter Rosmonda regent 3.103–4; is informed about the fight between Janissaries and Spahis 5.58–61; sends men to reconnoiter the grounds around the camp 5.67; questions Scanderbeg's groom, Felin 5.76–79; decides to set up Ferratte's body as that of Alexander 5.80–81; enters the fray at the head of his Janissaries 6.94; gives orders to withdraw 6.118; orders Attravante to carry out a strategic maneuver 6.119; fortifies Presa and asks Rosmonda to come to his aid 7.75–76; listens to Artecin's proposal for an exchange of prisoners 7.88–94; is angered by Agrismeta's defeat 10.1; orders not to take prisoners 10.2; orders Sabalio and Pallante to be killed and sends Corcutte to lay siege to Amantia 10.7–9; welcomes Rosmonda into Presa 13.48; prepares for war and sends a messenger to ask for Alexander's sword 15.1–3; gives orders for the games 15.8–9; is much taken with Silveria 15.31–32; accedes to her request and distributes prizes 15.34–42; makes advances to Silveria 17.57–73; is crushed by the news of Rosmonda's defection 18.1; courts Hypsipyle 18.12–17; is consoled by his wife Hypsipyle and by the prospect of receiving aid from Persia 18.20–21; turns for help to a sorcerer 19.8–9; believes that the Persian reinforcement has arrived 20.114; calls a meeting of the satraps 21.1–40; disposes the army for battle 21.61–66; speaks to the soldiers 21.67–76; orders the elephants moved forward 22.63; fights in the final battle 23.38–42; sees

Rosmonda fighting for the Christians 23.40; begins to feel ill 23.59–61; is carried from the battlefield 23.70; despairs 23.71–74; dies 23.75–76.

THE CAPTAINS

AGRISMETA (a Janissary): in the military review 3.92; is in love and duels with his beloved's suitors 3.93–97; climbs the walls of Nicaea 3.98; seeks to fight with Alexander 6.112–13; upbraids Scanderbeg for his defection 6.114–15; avoids Alexander's blow and moves on 6.122; is chosen by the sultan to fight a duel with Vaconte 9.10; is told he has been chosen 9.24–26; prepares for the duel 9.28–34; is contemptuous of his young opponent 9.35–38; duels Vaconte 9.44–66; is killed 9.67.

ATTRAVANTE (captain of a Scythian contingent): in the military review 3.71–72; is instructed by the emperor to cut across the battlefield with his carts and carries out the maneuver 6.119–21, 124–28; is at the siege of Amantia 10.52; kills Oronte 13.74; persuades the emperor to engage the rebels in a field battle at a meeting of the satraps 21.27–40; exits Presa to reconnoiter the territory 21.52; reports to the sultan 21.59; is killed in the final battle by Rosmonda 23.67–68.

CORCUTTE: is ordered to prepare the duel between Agrismeta and Vaconte 9.10; leads the Ottoman army at the siege of Amantia 10.9–13, 10.19–25; believes that Alexander will not come to the rescue of the besieged town 10.49; arraigns his fleeing army 10.51–55; is angered by their rout 10.59; orders Serpedon's withdrawal 10.63; is sent by Rosmonda to hold back the Christians 15.55; is made general of the Thracian army after Rosmonda's defection 21.62; is ordered to move his battalions 23.36; looks like lightning 23.45; tries to hold back the army in flight 23.65; remains to fight with a few of his soldiers 23.67; surrenders to Alexander with Driarasso and Orkhan 23.69.

DRIARASSO (Rosmonda's half brother): leads the men from a region on the Black Sea 3.55; his upbringing and fierceness 3.56–60; fights against Vaconte 6.103; wounds Crater and takes him prisoner 6.105–6; kills Berlinguer 6.106–7; fights with Scanderbeg 6.110–12; is angry with Agrismeta for interrupting his fight 6.113; fights at the siege of Amantia 10.52, 10.58, 10.62, 10.67; is made captain of the Janissaries 15.33; is attacked by the officers who resent his promotion 15.47–52; is made head of a section of the army 21.62; fighting in the final battle side by side with Orkhan and others, is ordered to move his battalions 23.36; remains on the battlefield after the emperor is carried out 23.63; surrenders to Scanderbeg with Orkhan and Corcutte 23.69.

FERRATTE (captain of the Janissaries): in the military review 3.89; kills Ishmael of Gaza and is made Agah 3.90–91; is seen by Scanderbeg from the walls of Croia 5.2; is contemptuous of danger and destiny 5.3; begins to climb the mountain slope to the walls of Croia with a group of his Janissaries 5.2–5; is killed by Sinan 5.7; his armor worn by Alexander 5.9; his death mourned by friends 5.57; his corpse looked for by Janissaries 5.62–67; his body flayed and the skin stuffed to look like Scanderbeg's corpse 5.81–83; is given an honorable funeral service 5.84–86.

ORKHAN: leads the contingent from Astacus 3.50; is much loved by his parents 3.51–52; is sent to Croia to ask for surrender 5.89–92, 5.99; fights at the siege of Amantia 10.52; on duty as the night guard, intercepts Vaconte who has penetrated the camp 13.65–66; is at the assault on Croia 14.99; is an arbitrator of the games 15.12; is made captain of the Spahis 15.33; comes to Silveria's rescue 15.52; doubts Attravante's wisdom 21.60; is assigned a section of the army 21.62; fights in the final battle 23.36–51; continues to fight after the emperor is carried off the field 23.63; surrenders to the Christians with Driarasso and Corcutte 23.69.

ROSMONDA: appears at the military review at the head of the Thracian army 3.79; her emblem and character 3.79–82; is loyal and loves her father 3.83; has recently saved her father's life 3.84–87; is made regent of the empire 3.103–5; is ordered to Presa 7.76; leads an army to Presa and is asked to avenge the murder of two men 13.1–10; meets Silveria and is taken around the mountain by her 13.13–38; persuades Silveria to follow her 13.39–45; pitches camp 13.47; is welcomed by the emperor in Presa 13.48; captures the scouts from Croia 13.54–55; faces up to Vaconte and obtains his surrender 13.77–95; leads the assault on Croia 14.62–104; is told that the officers are fighting among themselves 15.55; is rumored to be near death 15.58; begins to fall in love with Vaconte 15.67–70; is sent to contest Vran blocking the passes 17.62; converts to Christianity and marries Vaconte 18.102–3; is positioned to fight in the final battle next to her husband 22.4; avenges Musaka's death by killing his killer 22.60–61; grieves for Silveria 22.97–98; is seen fighting alongside her husband 23.40; advances against her father's army 23.56; kills Attravante 23.67–68.

SERPEDON (captain of a Scythian contingent): in the military review 3.74; is sent for by Corcutte to fight at the siege of Amantia 10.13; is given the order to cross the river 10.20–22; swims across the river with his men 10.40–43; is ordered to withdraw 10.63; faces Pallante and strikes him 10.65–66; withdraws at the king's arrival 10.67; is told to swim across the river and perform a double maneuver 21.66.

OTHERS

BAIZET: advises the sultan to kill Scanderbeg 1.74–92; arrives in Belgrade 2.1; corrupts Crifier with gold and persuades him to poison Alexander 2.4–7; is killed with Crifier by Scanderbeg's followers 2.35.

FILENA (Selim's wife) : receives Polidor's visit 3.11–12; goes to the mosque to wait for the emperor 3.13–19; begs the sultan to avenge her husband's death 3.20–26.

FLORA (Liprando's daughter): is raised with Pallante 7.5–6; falls in love with him 7.7–10, 7.16–17; asks Pallante to come to her 7.26; eagerly waits for him 7.64–65; spends the night with him, after which they decide to leave together 7.66–74; goes with Pallante to Amantia 10.4; is given the ransom money and goes back into Ottoman territory 10.6; escapes to Amantia with Pallante and his father, Sabalio 10.8.

HYPSIPYLE: is the emperor's consort 18.3; her upbringing 18.6; her beauty and moral qualities of 18.7–11; is abducted by the sultan 18.12; repulses his advances 18.14–15; becomes his consort 18.16–18; consoles the sultan 18.19–21.

LAGNETE: is described as a Turkish baron 1.33; is ordered to kidnap Dori 1.34; is addressed by Alexander 1.40; tries to kidnap Aranit's daughter 1.47–63; returns to the emperor's court and reports to the emperor 1.73–74.

PALLANTE: is Sabalio's son 7.3; as an infant, is left by his father in Phaestus in Liprando's care 7.4; is brought up with Liprando's baby daughter, Flora 7.5; is called by his father to Adrianople 7.5–6; has grown up with Flora and has fallen in love with her 7.7–18; confides his love to Nardo 7.20; is eager to join Flora 7.31–37; gets on the road 7.38; is captured by Vran's scouts and surrenders to Vran 7.43–54; is taken to Amantia, where he aches for Flora 7.56–57; is allowed to go and visit his beloved 7.62–64; arrives in Phaestus and spends the night with her 7.65–72; returns to Amantia with Flora 10.4; is allowed to return with Flora to Thrace 10.6; escapes with Flora and his father, Sabalio, to Amantia 10.8; sees Alexander among the fighting men 10.60; exits Amantia to fight below the walls 10.61; is surrounded by Serpedon's men and is rescued by the king 10.63–68; plans with Vran to intercept the men crossing the river 23.17; tries to stop the fleeing soldiers 23.27; fights against Raimondo and kills him 23.30–33.

POLIDOR: is a Thracian merchant living in Croia 3.2–3; has a friendship with Selim 3.4; feigns being a devout Christian 3.5; leaves Croia for the capital 3.6–9; goes to see Filena, Selim's wife 3.11–12; meets her at the mosque and plans with her how to approach the sultan 3.14; is summoned by the emperor 3.27.

SABALIO (warrior born in Phoestus): is summoned by the sultan to Adrianople 7.2; leaves his baby son, Pallante, with his friend Liprando 7.4; calls Pallante to the imperial army 7.17; offers Vran a rich ransom 10.5; escapes with Pallante and Flora to Amantia 10.8; with Vran, tries to block the passage of the Turkish supply routes 17.62; fights on the banks of the river and then goes to fight in the thick of the battle 23.58.

SELIM (governor of Croia): has the city taken away from him 2.36–37; leaves with his men for the capital 2.38; is killed in the mountain passes while crossing from Albania into Thessaly 2.40–45.

SILVERIA: is described to Rosmonda as a savage woman hiding in the forest 13.4–8; meets Rosmonda and takes her to see her surroundings 13.14–30; is persuaded to join the army 13.42–44; with Rosmonda, intercepts the spies from Croia 13.54; assists Rosmonda in the preparations for the oncoming battle 14.64; fights at the walls of Croia 14.85–91; climbs on the slippery mud 14.105; withdraws from the battle and the soldiers cheer her 14.106; competes in the games against Hamilcar, Altamor, and Battor, and wins 15.14–30; asks the emperor to make Driarasso captain of the Janissaries and Orkhan captain of the Spahis 15.32–33; is upset at the news that the officers are rioting because of her 15.48; enters the fray and kills Hamilcar 15.49–50; is wounded by Battor and kills him 15.52–54; is desired by the sultan 17.56–66; rejects the sultan's advances 17.67–72; runs out of her tent and exits the city 17.74; converts to Christianity 18.104; volunteers to kill the big elephant in the final battle 22.87–95; is squashed by the animal and dies 22.96–99.

VARADIN (standard-bearer of the Spahis): is caught sleeping in bed by the Albanians who have entered the camp 5.16: wakes up and begins to fight against Sinan after Armilla, his wife, is killed 5.27; kills him 5.30; mistakes Scanderbeg for Ferratte, the Agah, and is slain by Scanderbeg 5.33–34.

SCANDERBEIDE

The Heroic Deeds of George Scanderbeg,
King of Epirus

༄

CANTO 1

Invocation to the Muse, dedication to Giulia d'Este, and subject of the epic. As soon as
Scanderbeg has repossessed his family territories in Epirus, which were occupied by the
Ottoman sultan, he sends Svarte to Alfonso, king of Naples, to ask for aid. At the Neapolitan
court, the envoy tells the story of Scanderbeg's defection and of his reentry into his homeland.

1

Sing, O Muse, the king of Epirus;[1] tell how strongly he endured and how
valorously he fought, when the Turkish emperor led Scythian, Persian,
and Arabian armies to Croia to fight against him. Mountains and plains
were covered with dead bodies: many souls went to heaven, many to hell.
The barbarous Ottoman[2] and his troops were slain by the king, on whom
the heavens smiled benignly.

1. This is Alexander Castrioti, or Scanderbeg. During the armed resistance to the Ottoman
advance in northern Albania (1443–68), he was the leader of a number of Albanian chieftains,
but he never took the title of king of Epirus. Epirus was a territory comprehending part of
northern Greece and Albania south of the Apsus River (the Seman of today). That land was
made into a kingdom by Phyrrus (306–272 BCE), was annexed by the Romans in 168 BCE, and
was set up as an independent state in 1204 during the fourth crusade. Reunited to the
Byzantine Empire in 1340, Epirus became part of the Ottoman domain in the following century. Scanderbeg fought for the territories north of the Seman River, not for the land south of
it. Sarrocchi, like her contemporaries, uses the name Epirus to indicate the country claimed by
Scanderbeg's alliance and calls Scanderbeg king of Epirus. The name Macedonia was used
by Italians interchangeably with Epirus (Piccolomini, *Commentaries of Pius II*, 6:460), presumably because the ancient Romans entered the region during their war against the king of
Macedonia.

2. The Italian text applies the epithet of "barbarous," alternatively with "fierce" and "cruel"—
words that are in fact synonymous (*The Cambridge Italian Dictionary*, ed. Barbara Reynolds
[Cambridge: Cambridge University of Press, 1962], s.v. "barbaro")—to the sultan (see 1.24,
1.36–37, 1.50, 3.83, 5.65, 6.67, 15.12, 17.65, 23.76), to his soldiers, and to his captains, especially when describing a pitched battle, as in canto 20 (see 3.39, 3.68, 20.34, 20.43, 20.53). It

2

May you, Giulia,[3] ease with God's favor my heavy task of revealing to the world such famous deeds. The heavens and nature courteously bestowed on you all those graces that now are so pleasing to our souls. This splendidly gifted lady descends from the princely lineage of the Este family, foremost among kings and heroes: the world admires the virtues, all gathered in her, any one of which would make any woman perfect.

3

Happy indeed and fortunate is the man whom Juno has destined to enjoy her many graces, who will become her consort and rest in her bashful embrace.[4] No less happy and content will be the people governed by sovereigns as desirable as these, since to the lady's great beauty such wisdom has been added as to surpass Minerva's merits.[5]

---

is also used to qualify such distant, fabled places as ancient Memphis in 3.32. The ancient Greeks called all the non-Greeks barbarians; the Romans did the same for those who were neither Roman nor Greek. In medieval and Renaissance Christian romances and heroic poems, the quality of barbarity was routinely applied to all infidels. In political rhetoric, the epithet of barbarian was used to excoriate whoever happened to be an enemy at the moment. As Francesco Guicciardini (*Storia d'Italia*, ed. Silvana Seidel Menchi, introd. Felix Gilbert [Turin: Einaudi, 1971], 10) tells us, Pope Julius II Della Rovere regarded the French who had invaded Italy in 1510 as barbarians, and he organized a "Holy League" against them.

3. This is Giulia d'Este (1588–1645), daughter of Don Cesare d'Este (1533–1628), duke of Modena and Reggio, and of Virginia de' Medici, the natural offspring of Cosimo I, grand duke of Tuscany. In *Adone* 11.61.3–6, Marino will call Giulia the "Phoenix of the Po . . . a woman all celestial, always accompanied by Love and by the Graces." When Marino was in Modena around 1605, he eulogized Don Cesare in the madrigal "Non fuggo e non pavento," later included in *La Galeria* (1619). Giulia, described by contemporaries as a woman of singular beauty, was painted by Hans von Hachen and by Sante Peranda. For the art sponsorship of the Este of Modena, see Janet Southern, *Power and Display in the Seventeenth Century: The Arts and Their Patrons in Modena and Ferrara* (Cambridge: Cambridge University Press, 1988). References to Giulia are on pp.10, 13, 16, 29. We do not know what the relationship between Sarrocchi and this aristocratic lady was, if indeed there was one. For writers to find a person of consequence who would accept the dedication of their works was not always an easy task. In a letter Sarrocchi sent to Galileo in 1611, she urges him to find such a personage to whom to dedicate her poem at the Medici court. See Favaro, *Amici e corrispondenti di Galileo*, 1:18.

4. Giulia d'Este seems to have remained single. Rather than being a statement of fact, Sarrocchi's sentence may posit the eventuality of a future husband. The celibacy of this lady, whose name was tied by gossip to that of her uncle, Cardinal Alessandro d'Este, seems to be confirmed by what Giambattista Marino wrote in *Adone* 11.62.3–4: "Until destiny finds a man worthy of her, she will spend her last days unaccompanied." Juno, identified by Romans with the Greek Hera, is the sister and wife of Jupiter, the king of all Olympian gods. She presided over marriages and births and was considered to be the protectress of women. See Ovid, *Fasti* 6.51.

5. Minerva, goddess of wisdom and patroness of arts and crafts, was one of the three major Roman divinities (Ovid, *Fasti* 3.176, 3.815), the other two being Jupiter and Juno. All three gods were worshiped on the Capitol.

4

Courteous and magnanimous lady, do not disdain to welcome under the
wings of the great white eagle[6] my humble Muse. Let her send forth her
song from under their shade, just as the Sun, driving his chariot from Bactria
to Thule,[7] does not disdain to shed his luminous rays on any part of the
world, however humble.

5

When Alexander saw himself in secure possession of the kingdom he had
captured from the Ottoman, and more than one sign made him confident of
the true love and pure faith of the people of Epirus, he ordered several men,
illustrious in lineage and valor, to go as ambassadors to Christian princes
near and far and on his behalf give them an account of his great success.

6

He sent them to you, to whom Jesus destined Rome triumphant, heaven's
abode on earth, and on whose white hair a triple crown bestows divine
powers,[8] and to you, whom all the kings of the world call spouse and queen
of the sea,[9] and to the Bulgarians, to the Swiss, and also to the Neapolitan,
the Spanish, and the French sovereigns.

7

To the Neapolitan king,[10] who was tied to Alexander's father by an enduring
bond of friendship, Alexander sent an ambassador to express his wish to be
as great a friend as his father was; to say that, having escaped from the hands

6. The coat of arms of the Este family showed a white eagle.

7. The cliché expression "from Bactria to Thule" indicates the whole known world. Bactria was
a Persian province (now Bokhara) and Thule was usually identified with one of the Shetland
Islands.

8. The pope referred to here could be any of the four popes—Nicholas V, Callistus III, Pius
II, and Paul II—to whom Scanderbeg sent ambassadors during his campaign. At this point,
however, this being a work of fiction, we may assume this personage to be a collation of the
four pontiffs mentioned above. "Triple crown" indicates the pope's ceremonial hat, made of
three superimposed golden crowns, symbolizing the church militant, penitent, and triumphant. The hat—called tiara or *triregno* and no longer in use since Pope Paul VI Montini
(1963–78)—was probably inspired by the headgear of the ancient Persian kings.

9. This is Venice, whose marriage with the sea is celebrated every year on Ascension Day,
forty days after Easter, with a regatta and the throwing of a wedding ring into the waters of
the Adriatic.

10. Alfonso I had succeeded his father, Ferdinando, to the throne of Aragon, Sardinia, and
Sicily in 1416. Six years later he became the king of Naples as well (1442–58). He continued

of the barbarous enemy, he had now gone back to the true God; and also to
report everything that had occurred and so dispose him to come to his aid.

8

Among Alexander's worthiest followers was Svarte, a man endowed with
such natural eloquence that many an orator often proved far less skilled and
pleasing than he in the art of persuasion.[11] Alexander kept him near him
wherever he went and to him alone entrusted the key to his secrets,[12] so
that Svarte saw and heard all that concerned the conquest of the kingdom.

9

Alexander ordered this very Svarte to be ready in a few hours and then to
go swiftly, while he allowed the other envoys to linger as long as they found
it necessary in order to put on a magnificent display: for it became the
honor of a sovereign to behave like a great king, but where Alfonso was
concerned, friendship demanded love and loyalty far more than pomp.

10

When he was ready to leave, Svarte exited Croia to accomplish what his king
had ordered. He saw Mati go by not far to his right, Lisano to his left, and
Durazzo between himself and Rodoni. From that point he intended to cross
the Adriatic, on whose opposite coast lay Daunia, rich in sweet olives.[13]

11

Intent on a speedy crossing he slid over the wavy plain on a light vessel and
went favored by sea and winds as swift as a falcon flying through the air.[14]

---

his father's policy of intervention in the Balkans. On the long history of the relations of the
monarchies of southern Italy with the Albanian princes, see pp. 21–22 above.

11. Svarte may stand here in place of Paul Kuka, who was sent as ambassador to Naples in
1450, as soon as Scanderbeg learned of the upcoming Turkish invasion (Gegaj, *L'Albanie et l'invasion turque,* 72). Svarte, like many other characters in the poem, proves to be an accomplished
orator. The gift of eloquence is noted repeatedly: see cantos 1.20, 1.55, 7.94.

12. "Io son colui che tenni ambo le chiavi del cor di Federigo, e che le volsi, serrando e dis-
serrando, sì soavi, che del secreto suo quasi ogn'uom tolsi" (I am the man who held both keys
to Frederick's heart, and, locking and unlocking, I turned them with such skill that none but
I knew all his secrets), says Pier della Vigna in Dante's *Inferno* 13.58–61.

13. Mati is the modern River Mat. Lisano and Durazzo are towns, the modern Lëzhë and
Durrës, respectively, which in Scanderbeg's time were Venetian possessions. Rodoni is a
promontory. On the opposite side of the Adriatic is the region of Puglia, called here Daunia,
which is the name that the Greeks gave to a region within it lying on both sides of the Lofante
River. Lofante, now Òfanto, is the river mentioned in stanza 14.

14. The falcon simile, found again at 3.8, has an illustrious provenance: Homer, *Iliad* 15.237–38;
Virgil, *Aeneid* 11.721–24; Dante, *Inferno* 17.127 and *Paradiso* 19.34–36; Petrarch, *Triumphus temporis*
31–32; Ludovico Ariosto, *Orlando Furioso* 2.50.3. The point of Homer's and Sarrocchi's

Suddenly a westerly wind crossed his path and bounced him off course away from the Gargano, on whose lofty majestic top rose rare and salubrious trees.[15]

12

Since the wind opposed his intention to go that way toward Sebeto, he turned to the left and began to navigate close to the Bari coast, a coast abounding in fish and fruit. He landed there, got off his vessel, and, having escaped the storm, he was glad to be able to ride through Puglia on a road that was as easy to ride on as anyone could wish.

13

He touched neither Trani nor Molfetta, but went directly toward Bari. There he needed only to change horses, for sundown was already approaching, and from there he directed his path to Ruo, which once was host to the two great Latin writers, the epic and the lyric poet, at the time when Maecenas dressed the Muses—so unappreciated in our time—in gold and purple.[16]

14

Dawn, the beautiful goddess that gives us the light of day, had hardly begun shedding her splendor on the shores of heaven when Svarte rose from the bed in which he had taken a brief rest and set out again on his speedy journey. He crossed the Lofante River and went by the town of Cannae, where the Roman fought unpropitiously and, in the midst of his ruinous defeat, was assisted by a magnanimous woman.[17]

---

comparisons is the swiftness of the falcon's flight; Virgil uses it to illustrate the rapidity with which the warrior queen Camilla strikes her enemy; Dante, Petrarch, and Ariosto describe the hawk soaring or slowly descending during a hunt. For comparisons with other animals, see canto 1.39n and canto 5.8n.

15. Sarrocchi's "lofty top" would be that section of the Gargano massif where Monte St. Angelo overlooks the Adriatic from a height of 2,755 feet above sea level.

16. Maecenas was a rich Roman *eques* (knight), whose family was from Etruria. He was a minister of Emperor Augustus and great patron of artists and poets. Trani, Molfetta, and Bari are towns on the coast of the Adriatic, in the Puglia region of southern Italy. Ruo, the modern Ruvo di Puglia, is at some distance from the sea. The two Latin poets are Virgil and Horace. In his fifth satire, Horace describes going through this town during a journey made with Virgil in 37 BCE. The two poets were then in the train of Maecenas who, as representative of Augustus, was traveling to Brindisi for a meeting with the envoy of Anthony.

17. Cannae, famous for the battle in which the Romans were defeated by the Carthaginian army of Hannibal in 216 BCE, is now called Canne della Battaglia. It is situated on the Òfanto

15

He sees Cerignola, where the iniquitous Geryon chose to hide his ill-acquired booty; and Ascoli, where he remembered the Tarentine, who here drenched the earth with Roman blood.[18] To the left he saw the town of Bovino and the altar of Janus still rising on a high, ruinous, and barren hill between the Calore and the Tripalto Rivers.[19]

16

He turned his back to Forino and Avellino. Serino and Cardinal were no restraint to his passage. To the right he came upon the Caudine Forks, where Spurius was deceived by enemy cunning and where Pontius, after obstructing their passage, shamed the Romans and forced them to march under the yoke. He then left behind Nola to the left, Acerra to the right, and last he went past Marigliano.[20]

17

On the golden banks of the famous River Sebeto lies a still more famous and noble town, fertile mother of kings and heroes, which takes its name from beautiful Partenope. Here Pomona always smiles delightedly, here

---

River, in the region of Puglia. The Roman generals who fought at Cannae and lost were Paulus Aemilius and Terentius Varro. Fabius Maximus was the general to whom a woman of Tarentum (modern Taranto), conspiring with her lover, captain of the garrison, delivered the town in 209 BCE. The event is recounted by Livy 27.15. 9–19.

18. Cerignola and Ascoli are towns also in the Puglia region. Ascoli, the ancient Asculum Apulum of Apulia Daunia, was the place where Pyrrhus of Epirus—who had gone over to Italy in aid of Tarentum, hence called the Tarentine—defeated the Romans in 279 BCE. See Plutarch, *Lives*, "Pyrrhus" 21.5–7. Geryon was the legendary monster with three bodies who stole Eurytion's oxen and hid them in a land west of Epirus under the setting sun. Sarrocchi identifies this place with Puglia, where Cerignola is situated. Hercules' slaying of Geryon to free the oxen is mentioned by Ovid in *Metamorphoses* 9.186 and by Nonnos in *Dionysiaca* 25.236.

19. Bovino, Calore, and Tripalto are within the area extending from Puglia, on the Adriatic side, to the Tyrrhenian coast, on the opposite side of Italy. Janus was a revered Italian deity, god of beginnings and of ends, of entrances and exits. He was represented with two faces looking in opposite directions. The month of January is named after him. "Iane biceps, anni tacite labentis origo, solus de superis qui tua terga vides" (the two-headed Janus, the starter of the slowly coming year, the only one among the gods who can see his own back) (Ovid, *Fasti* 1.65–66).

20. Marigliano, Acerra, Nola, Avellino, and Forino are towns between Apulia and Naples. Cardinal and Serino have not been traced. The Caudine Forks are a narrow mountain pass near the ancient cities of Caudium, Capua, and Benevento. Here, in 321 BCE, the Romans, led by the consul Spurius Postumus, were ambushed by the Samnites and forced to surrender to their general, Gaius Pontius. Livy 9.1–6

Phoebus descends from the heavens to sing in the company of the Muses;
here gold-clothed Liberality welcomes Virtue with open arms.[21]

18

As soon as he arrived in that noble city, the good Svarte asked for someone
to introduce him to the wise Alfonso. Pleased that Christ's hero had
returned to the true faith, the king welcomed him with signs of friendship
and joy on his regal face and wanted him to sojourn in his spacious residence for the length of his stay.

19

Then he welcomed him to the royal table together with his first barons.
Alfonso sat on a high throne, placed Svarte in front of him, and in his manners and with many gifts he showed his eagerness to honor all those present.
Afterward, the king asked Svarte to tell of Alexander's good and bad fortunes, of how he recaptured his kingdom and returned to the Christian faith.

20

So with a mellifluous outpouring of eloquence, Svarte, whom benign nature
and the heavens had endowed with great intelligence, began to recount the
whole story to his host, the king. But first, as is the custom among us in
Italy, he got up, bowed, sat down again, and, as he knew the Tuscan language, began to speak in Italian.

21

"Alexander was at the walls of Belgrade. The year had hardly gone full circle and reached its close when Murad, now tyrant of Thrace,[22] had sent him
to pitch camp there because, after so many losing battles, and after all his

21. This stanza describes with affection the region around Naples, Sarrocchi's native town.
Naples has the alternative name of Partenope, from the name of the nymph who lived and died
nearby. See Silius Italicus, *Punica* 12.33. The city lies in a valley whose mild climate made it
the favorite resort area of the ancient Romans. Because of its fertility and pleasantness, the
plain is described here as combining abundance (symbolized by Pomona, goddess of fruits and
harvest) and by Liberality, or abundance, with all virtuous pleasures (represented by Virtue
and Phoebus, that is Apollo, the god of the arts and music).

22. This is Murad II, Ottoman emperor (1421–51). Scanderbeg's resistance continued when
Mehmet, Murad's son, took over the scepter. Thrace indicates more precisely the territory that
the Turks had already conquered in Europe. Their major city remained Edirne until 1453,
when Constantinople fell into Turkish hands and became the capital of the Ottoman Empire
with the name of Istanbul.

other captains, who were held high as being very knowledgeable and expert in war, had failed in the attempt to capture the city, he wanted to make use of his last resources.[23]

22

"Alexander, whom neither soldier nor captain ever equaled in either modern or ancient times, soon gave such a performance of military skill that all efforts on the part of the besieged became futile. When they finally realized that whatever they tried by force of brain, heart, or brawn would be for nought, they offered Alexander control of the city, on the condition that the safety of their lives and property be guaranteed.

23

"The magnanimous hero, no less courteous than wise, invincible, courageous, and strong, who had the nobility of his royal ancestors but not their luck, as soon as he heard their offer, stopped the fighting and, in order to save many people from an untimely death, sent off a messenger to the great sire with letters acquainting him with the situation.

24

"The sultan promised that neither the people nor their belongings would be harmed, as Alexander asked, but his words were not consonant with his feelings, while the noble hero believed him to be sincere. Soon a new desire would drive the fierce tyrant to go back on his promise and with more urgency than was customary. But now the messenger returned, the pact was agreed upon, and after Aranit's[24] surrender Alexander took possession of the city.

25

"Fame has it that there was never in Belgrade a captain greater than Aranit. He had seen more cities and more different customs than had the

---

23. The siege of Belgrade described here is reminiscent of the battle between Hungarians and Turks that took place at Kurnovina, near Niš, in Serbia in 1443. The Ottoman army was led by Karambeg, pasha of Rumelia, and it is possible that Scanderbeg, as an Ottoman subject, participated in it under that general (Hodgkinson, *Skanderbeg*, 68; Gegaj, *L'Albanie et l'invasion turque*, 45).

24. The Aranit character is inspired by the historical George Arjanit Komneni. Before Scanderbeg came on the scene, Arjanit Komneni signed a treaty with King Alfonso of Naples, attempted to chase the Turks out of Epirus, and lost a decisive battle near Berat. Sarrocchi may have placed her Aranit character at the siege of Belgrade because Berat, where Arjanit fought against the Turks, was known in Italy by the alternative name Belgrade. He became Scanderbeg's father-in-law in 1451: see canto 7.80–81n. See "Aranit" in the cast of main characters.

sun in its rounds. Once back in his homeland, Epirus, he enjoyed a peaceful and pleasant rest, until one day, asked to go to the help of Belgrade, he became so concerned about the fate of that city that he went with all his men.

26

"From that time on, because he guarded the town with such valor, he was called Palinuro.[25] He was not yet old, but rather more advanced in wisdom than age. He had trained his people to fight so effectively that under their walls the heap of dead enemy soldiers was as high as a mountain, and so many Turks had fallen into the Sava River that they drank its water mixed with their own blood.[26]

27

"Aranit had one only daughter, who was now in Belgrade: her name was Dori.[27] Although she was still young and growing, her limbs were almost fully formed and handsomely shaped. Under the guidance of such a father, she had grown up adorned with every virtue, and she was so beautiful and charming that any other handsome woman paled in comparison with her, just as a worthless piece of glass loses all luster next to a perfect diamond.

28

"Love himself extracted from the veins most deeply hidden inside the earth the fine gold spun into her tresses and gathered in the waves of her blond hair. Select roses and precious frosty snows Love gathered to give color to her lovely cheeks, so that you might well say that a heavenly candor shone in them mixed with a delicate vermilion.

25. I have corrected Polinuro of the Italian text to read Palinuro throughout, because Sarrocchi, as she explains in this sentence, uses it antonomastically to indicate Aranit's steadfast guardianship of Belgrade. In Virgil's *Aeneid*, Palinuro is Aeneas's faithful helmsman. Urged to abandon ship by Sleep, the god who is acting on behalf of Neptune, Palinuro refuses to betray Aeneas. He is put to sleep by the god, falls into the sea still clutching the rudder, and drowns (*Aeneid* 5.835–70 and 6.338–83). Palinuro, from whom the cape in the Cilento region of Campania takes its name, is mentioned throughout European literature as a model of unswerving loyalty. The word "Polinuro," furthermore, may be a misprint in both editions of the poem, neither of which was overseen by the author. See "Sleep" in the glossary.

26. The Sava River runs into the Danube near Belgrade.

27. This character, called Donica in the 1606 draft of the poem, stands for Marina Andronika, the real Arjanit Komneni's daughter, who married Scanderbeg in 1451. See canto 7.79–81.

29

"Her clear forehead was a transparent diamond revealing all the bashful motions of her heart. Her resplendent eyes outshone the sun, when there are no clouds to veil it. No finer rubies, no more precious pearls than those adorning and giving color to her mouth did any mountain ever hide deep in its veins, or the dawn in any oriental valley.[28]

30

"Her throat was milk, her neck made of pure ivory, which straying curls of shiny hair lined with gold. Her young breasts were whiter than snow falling on alpine slopes. Love seemed to delight in throwing burning fire from such icy snow:[29] her feet, her hands, her arms, her whole body could not be praised adequately by human voice.

31

"The heavens all around smiled on her celestial countenance, on her glowing face. The earth seemed to sparkle and the grass to rejoice wherever she turned her glance, for no power was ever seen coming from a more beautiful sun.[30] With the heavenly splendor of her smile she enslaved all minds, stole all hearts away. The Graces, being her handmaidens, gently directed her movements, her gestures, and everything she did.

28. Precious stones from India and from other Asian countries were thought to be of fabulous beauty and size. Dori's comeliness (stanzas 28–30) and that of all handsome women throughout the poem are described in terms of rare and precious stones. See the depictions of Brandoardo's beloved in 3.65; of Flora in 7.12; of Rosmonda in 13.11, 13.79, 13.88; and of Hypsipyle in 18.7–11.

29. The image of unblemished snow resting on alpine slopes, which appears again in 3.80, is the most attractive among the similes, more frequently of pearls, alabaster, and amber, used to heighten the effect of a woman's perfect complexion: see cantos 3.65, 7.12, 13.88, 18.7, and 18.11. It has precedents in *Orlando Furioso* 10.24.4 and Torquato Tasso's *Jerusalem Delivered* 6.26.5 and 9.82.1–2. For the iconography of Love, see 3.64n.

30. A commonplace of courtly love poetry is that the beautiful woman can make nature smile and pay homage to her. Example: "Come 'l candido pie' per l'erba fresca i dolci passi honestamente move, vertù che 'ntorno i fiori apra et rinove, de le tenere piante sue par ch'esca" (As her immaculate foot moves on the new grass with graceful and alluring steps, then a power so extraordinary seems to radiate from her tender soles as to open and bring the flowers to life again) (Petrarch, *Canzoniere* 165.1–4). Similar descriptions are in Politian's *Stanze per la giostra* 1.43–44 and *Orlando Furioso* 1.42. In *Jerusalem Delivered* (18.23) fountains and brooks suddenly appear, plants and trees grow green again, and flowers bloom wherever Rinaldo, the youthful warrior, walks.

32

"Quickly Fame,[31] who flies everywhere murmuring in a thousand tongues, spread out her wings and carried news of her bearing, which was of a beauty no human creature could match. The Thracian heard of it, and feeding his desires day after day upon the imagined image of the beautiful woman,[32] he decided to satisfy his perversely lascivious cravings and at the same time revenge the death of his people.

33

"He quickly summoned one of his barons, one whom he had raised and called Lagnete, a reckless man, cruel beyond reason, accustomed to luxury, gluttony, and sloth. This man not only gloried in his own vices, and often-times encouraged the vicious habits of others, but more than any other served his lord in all debauched and ignoble adventures.

34

"Although he was accustomed to command his subjects most peremptorily, the Thracian set aside his usual arrogant manner and domineering ways now that he had fallen in love. He wished Lagnete to bring him the handsome woman to quench the ardor cramping his heart. And with muted gestures he made more enticing promises of rewards than he could have done with any speech.

35

"By royal decree he sent a heartless order to the people whose safety he had guaranteed. Alexander was to kill Palinuro by the most painful and fero-cious torture, together with those who had defended Belgrade with him or had given him support. All the others were to be deprived of their posses-sions and brought to him as prisoners with their wives and children.[33]

31. The personification of fame is at times interchangeable with that of rumor in this poem (see 1.25, 1.32, 1.46, 1.57, 2.3, 2.15, 3.64, 3.101, 5.87, 10.14, and 15.8) and has many epic antecedents. There are examples in *Aeneid* 3.121 and 4.173, in Ovid's *Metamorphoses* 9.137–40, and in *Jerusalem Delivered* 1.81.1–2 and 20.101.1.

32. People falling in love with someone they have never set eyes on is a topos of medieval courtly literature. The prototype is the *amor de lonh* sung by Jaufré Rudel (c.1130–1179) for the countess of Tripoli, whose beauty the troubadour had heard praised by travelers returning from Antioch by way of coastal Africa. There are two such lovers in *Orlando Furioso*: Alessandra in 20.39 and Alceste in 34.16.

33. The following episode of Murad's reneging on his pledge justifies Alexander's subsequent defection. We, of course, have no way of knowing what exactly Sarrocchi had read or heard about Scanderbeg's campaign. No break of a pledge on the part of Murad ever occurred, as far as I know.

36

"When Alexander heard the reckless command, his great heart was fired with righteous anger, for he knew that breaking one's word brings lasting infamy in the eyes of those who value honor. Then he remembered and mulled over in his mind the offenses and the shame he had suffered by the hand of his cruel lord, who had put his brothers to a miserable death, while he, Alexander, always served him with loyalty.

37

"Now the sultan wanted him to become a new Aegisthus in felony, a new Creon in cruelty,[34] so that never again would he be able to show his face among his people: certainly a fine barter, a well-earned recompense for so many celebrated and glorious deeds! He therefore resolved to deny the wicked tyrant all he asked for and to face whatever wrath and punishment might come.

38

"He carefully thought of a way that would insure the success of his plan. He was fully aware of his strength; he knew his own skill in finding a way out of dangerous situations. He also considered that he could count on the support of his soldiers, of his own countrymen, and of several famous warriors among the infidels of Aranit, should he start a war to their advantage against such an enemy.

39

"The same happens to a lion.[35] When still a cub, he fears the wrath and the rod of his guardian, but if he is beaten when full grown, the innate ferocity

---

In fact, at the siege of Svetigrad, Murad gave his word that people would be safe if the town surrendered, and when his son Mehmet proposed to kill everyone in the fortress, the sultan answered that society can endure only if pledges are respected. See Hodgkinson, *Skanderbeg*, 102.

34. In Aeschylus's *Agamemnon*, Aegisthus seduces Clytemnestra and murders her husband, Agamemnon, who has just returned home from the Trojan War. In Sophocles' *Antigone*, Creon, king of Thebes, forbids the burial of Polynices and sentences Antigone to death for disobeying his order. Creon is also a character in Statius's *Thebaid*. Aegisthus and Creon are frequently used as examples of evildoing and cruelty. Cf. *Orlando Furioso* 21.57.5, 17.2.4, 19.12.2.

35. The comparison of the mighty warrior to a lion, which occurs frequently in heroic literature, is in this poem always different and cleverly adjusted to the specific psychological situation. See 5.43, 7.44, 9.66, 10.62, and 13.53. The image of the two women warriors "looking like lionesses and running as fast as leopards" in canto 13.76, is visually engaging. Cf. *Jerusalem Delivered* 6.30.1. For examples of lion similes in other epic poems, see *Iliad* 16.485–90 and 16.823–26; *Aeneid* 9.339–41, 10.454–55, 10.723–29; *Africa* 4.204–17, 7.1260–61; and *Orlando Furioso* 18.178.

that lingers in his heart is aroused; and as he looks admiringly at the rich mane covering his chest, the abundant hair falling down his back, his hairy paws, his sharp pointed claws, he will indeed make sure that his reaction is going to be harmful to those who beat him.

40

"Alexander considered whether it was possible to remain constant and faithful to the emperor, rather than rebel against him, while denying his request with open and persuasive arguments. He called for Lagnete and in a gentle manner, which nonetheless revealed his high-minded purpose, he said to him:[36] 'I invoke almighty Jupiter[37] to be the witness of my great wish to obey my sovereign.

41

"'Even so, a captain accustomed to war has the obligation judiciously to weigh the advantages and the risks of every campaign, and judge which are greater, without ever allowing himself to be deceived by blind desire. He must consider whether it is reasonable to hope that an uneven and disorganized army of men, with weak leadership and little understanding of warfare, can defeat, by either force or stealth and with hardly any damage,[38]

42

"'an army that is held together with skill and method, led by a competent general, an army in which many are united by a common cause and by a potent bond of passionate loyalty. The instinct of self-love that nature has placed in each one of us is very powerful indeed, and we are urged by our own feelings to give preference to what pleases us most.

36. The following speech by Alexander is the first one delineating policy and strategy in the poem. Baizet's and Artecin's addresses to the emperor, in 1.78–91 and 7.89–93, the speeches of the Italian captains at the war council in 20.2–9, and those of the sultan and the satraps in canto 21.2–40 are similar. The warnings that Alexander gives Lagnete here regarding the evaluation of risks, the competence of generals, the discipline and loyalty of soldiers, and respect for promises given are inspired by the arguments found in Machiavelli's *The Prince* (1513, first published in 1532), in Giovanni Botero's *The Reason of State* (1589), and in Scipione Ammirato's *Discorsi* (1594). Suggestions of possible sources will be given in the following cantos. A general reference to the subject of Machiavelli's work seems to be made by Alexander in the upcoming stanza 47: "this is not the way to enlarge an empire, or to acquire subjects and tributaries."

37. Jupiter, the lord of all gods and protector of Rome, was worshiped in the Capitol. The Romans identified him with the Greek Zeus. In Renaissance epic poems, however, Jupiter often stands for the Christian God, as is the case here.

38. This is a case of a run-on stanza. For more on run-on stanzas, see p. 59 above.

43

"'As our mortal nature prevents us from enjoying air and sun forever, an innate desire seems to take over to perpetuate ourselves in our own off-spring. Consequently we are greatly grieved by the loss of our homeland, our children, and our beloved spouse, and rather than being deprived of them, we would choose to die and lie buried in the very land where we were first brought to life.

44

"'A daughter cannot be taken away from so great a father without risk and huge effort,[39] because many friends, in addition to his own troops, will come to his aid from all around the country. On the other hand, as much as one may deny him this woman, the emperor does not lack comely maidens, for a hundred, a thousand he keeps under key, compared with whose regal beauty this woman is but a humble servant.

45

"'Not only would she be a small reward for such a risky enterprise, but the damage and dishonor would allow very little pleasure. How infamous it would be judged of me and of our great sovereign in every region of the realm! From nearby houses, a fire will often set aflame buildings far removed. Whoever does not keep the promise he has made earlier endangers his possessions, his life, and his honor.

46

"'Not only will he earn ignominy and scorn, which is what all fine spirits abhor, but, as Fame begins to spread the news over the land, more serious damage will be in store for the imperial authority. Many whose loyalty our lord has not yet secured will turn to the Egyptian king; others will be afraid to rely on a master whose word is so untrustworthy.

47

"'This is not the way to enlarge an empire and to hold onto subjects and tributaries. Compassion and love, not cruelty or wrath, will secure and keep them loyal, once they are won over.'[40] Alexander finished, and Lagnete,

39. In *The Prince* 8.17 and 8.19, Machiavelli warns the prince never to seize the property and the women of his subjects, if he does not want to be hated and despised.

40. Machiavelli devotes chapter 17 of *The Prince* to cruelty and mercy. The necessity of establishing ties of mutual affection and trust between sovereign and subjects is discussed by Botero in *The Reason of State* 4.4.

who had made a plan of his own, hid his thoughts as much as he could in his heart, for he was determined to execute the great emperor's orders in whatever manner he could.

48

"He feared an unfavorable outcome and grew weary and confused, considering this and that possible solution. Then he spoke to a shrewd and experienced servant whom he had trusted for a long time. 'My loyal friend, be on the lookout for the moment when we can be certain that the captain of the enemy city is out of his mansion with his men. This is important, but it would take too long to tell you now the reason.'

49

"Alexander was of such a confiding nature, of such magnanimous disposition and exceptional benevolence, that he trusted the Christian people he had defeated and allowed them to go about the city to attend to their business. He camped the army outside the walls while the town gates remained open, because those who were in charge inside trusted him just as much.

50

"Knowing the fierceness of the Thracian, Aranit did not suspect that he could harbor such foolish passion; neither did he think that an enemy woman, moreover a beauty he had never seen, would conquer his heart. The Thracian had a natural tendency to change the object of his desire frequently: still, he had so many women and young maidens in his power, an endless variety of them indeed, and beautiful beyond measure!

51

"These considerations calmed and reassured Aranit, even more than the promise made by Alexander. He therefore did not keep a guard around his house, for he believed the city and his daughter to be safe. But Lagnete's servant, determined to carry out the evil plan, went about it with diligent stealth, and as soon as he saw the captain leave his dwelling, he quickly ran to notify his master.

52

"As his duty required, Aranit had gone to prepare the city for his departure. With gifts and with his presence he consoled the old, the poor, the sick, and the wounded; he made the women who were deprived of either father or

husband feel safe from any possible offense and violence, and sent them to
Buda with a trustworthy escort of holy nuns.[41]

53

"Meanwhile Lagnete rapidly summoned the few men he had brought with
him and quickly ran to kidnap the young virgin from the chaste bosom of
her mother. She cried out for her father, just as a young lamb would that,
caught in the mouth of a greedy wolf, calls out for its shepherd; or like a
young bird that, snatched from the nest, chirps hopelessly trying to escape
from the grip of the rapacious thief.[42]

54

"Her cheeks looked like pale violets, or like a lily cut down by the plow,[43]
or like the dawn overcome by the sun, or like the sun when clouds have
veiled its brilliant red. Her mother was left to wail to the heavens, like a bird
whose little one has been snatched from under her wings by the sharp
talons of a famished hawk.

55

"She beat her breast, she pulled her hair, she struck palm against palm, she
scratched her face and, out of her mind, she called for this and that person
by name, but more often she called for her husband, who could not hear
her. Soon, however—for more than one friendly messenger had run on to
warn him—he was told that his trust had been injuriously betrayed.

56

"I do not know whether grief or anger prevailed in him, for he had both a
ferocious and a fatherly heart; however, his wrath, while restraining him

---

41. This detail of sending women in safety to Buda may have inspired Marinella, who enlarged
upon it in canto 18.58–62 of her *L'Enrico*. There Elessio gives the order for the women to exit
Byzantium under siege: a discussion follows about whether in case of war women and children
should be sent away or remain and be of comfort to the fighters.

42. Dori's kidnapping is not unlike that of Proserpina in Ovid's *Metamorphoses* 5.391–408, who
cries out to her mother while being carried away by Pluto.

43. In epic poetry, lilies and violets are often used to indicate a condition of great danger or
near-death. In *Metamorphoses* 5.392, for instance, Proserpina is picking lilies and violets just
before she is kidnapped by Pluto. The image of the flower ripped by either the plow, lightning, or rain has a famous precedent in *Aeneid* 9.435–37: "purpureus veluti cum flos succisus ara-
tro languescit moriens" (he faded and died, like a red flower cut down by the plow). This
famous simile was imitated by Ariosto in *Orlando Furioso* 18.153, and by Tasso in *Jerusalem
Delivered* 9.85.8, 20.128.5.

from showing pain, urged him to seek revenge recklessly. He ran ahead like an angry tiger of the Hyrcanian forest, or a noble-hearted beast of the Nemean woods that runs after her beloved cub stolen from the den.[44]

57

"The rumor that the captain's daughter had been kidnapped bounced from person to person. At the alarming news, everyone swiftly gathered and started off after the kidnapper. Lagnete was overtaken, a thick crowd surrounded him, and as none of his men were there to defend him, fear counseled him to surrender his prey without contest.

58

"A hunter feels much at a loss if, after catching in his trap a much-sought prey, he sees it run quickly away unbound and free when he least expected it. Similarly Lagnete was stunned with disappointment and shame when the woman was taken away from him. And to avoid disgrace and death, he made up excuses to the people by lying[45]

59

"and saying that he was carrying the woman off only because urged by her, that he had neither broken nor violated their trust. Out of shame the woman blushed and repeatedly denied the allegation when her father inquired about it. But the unscrupulous man dared to insist, so most people believed him. Meanwhile Alexander had heard of the misdeed, and his noble heart flared up in anger and disdain.

60

"Then and there he gathered the best men in his army and picked up his weapons with the intention of recapturing the woman himself. The kidnapper, who saw no other way out, scolded our hero for having little faith in him. 'I have no fear whatever,' he said; 'on the contrary, I boil over with anger. My innocence is my good defense. If the woman gives herself to the emperor of her own accord, why do you raise all this foolish uproar around me?

44. The valley of Nemea, in Greece, was inhabited by an especially ferocious lion, which was eventually killed by Hercules (Heracles for the Greeks) in one of his labors. Ovid, *Metamorphoses* 9.195–97. Hyrcania, a province of the ancient Persian empire, on the south shore of the Caspian Sea, was thought to be full of tigers.

45. On run-on stanzas, see p. 59 above.

61

"'When she heard that the fame of her beauty had inflamed the emperor with amorous passion, she repeatedly sent messengers to beg me to take her away as secretly as possible, because her father is of such a stupid turn of mind that he would never consent to marry her to a Turk. While she, a woman of much higher intelligence, longs for the domain of the powerful Orient.

62

"'A diadem of gems and a golden scepter are more fitting adornments for the gold of her comely hair. A royal name and a royal mantle are more appropriate to her than to any woman who might be found in any place from Boreas to Auster,[46] from the Indian Ocean to the Mauretanian Sea, as truly as an eastern treasure surpasses all others in splendor. The man who reigns over many kingdoms could find no beautiful woman more deserving of his empire and his love than she.'

63

"Lagnete was then silent. Although he had ill-advisedly kidnapped the young woman he should have guarded most, he was so eager to please his great lord that he advanced very cunning reasons to excuse his crime and rebut the captain's words. Alexander, for his part, was amazed and, dubious of the woman's alleged intentions, wanted to learn the truth from her.

64

"He ordered the handsome woman to be brought immediately into his presence, because what he heard seemed improbable in a woman so young and upright. When she was in his presence, Alexander, before everyone and in a very courteous manner, asked her to make the truth known without fear, saying he was her guardian and her knight.

65

"The virgin lowered her luminous eyes while a rosy blush spread over her white cheeks. Then, with a voice that would stop the winds and split asunder any hard surface, she said: 'Making amends for one's own faults by blaming others is a common custom among the pagan people, who do not know of Christ and of how powerfully his right hand descends to punish.

46. That is, from north to south, Boreas and Auster being winds that blow from the north and from the south, respectively.

66

"'Making amends by blaming others is unbecoming, and the wrongdoer's blame increases by it. But if I may be allowed to swear by my true God—although my reverent thought abhors and fears doing so—I never saw this man before, and my mind has not completely understood what he said. I remember that Thracian well enough, for his name has often frightened me.'

67

"After saying these words she stood quietly, and from her beautiful eyes a light of ardent zeal shone forth revealing the purity of her heart, just as pure whiteness shows through a transparent veil, or a purple flower can be seen behind a clear crystal, or a serene sky beyond thin clouds. Although fearless and audacious, Lagnete did not know what to say; flustered, he remained silent.

68

"It pleased merciful God to infuse such grace in those sincere and sweet words that, as surely as gold is further refined by fire, the truth was triumphant and falseness was vanquished. The Roman vestal who carried water from the Tiber in a sieve did not show a greater virginal purity in all her body than this young woman did by the candor of her heart.[47]

69

"At this point, both the pagan and the Christian people knew for certain that the beautiful woman was innocent, and many voices rose around her father rejoicing. At that moment, Alexander felt his mind pierced through by a ray of light sent by the great ruler of the celestial choirs, and he remembered that he was born of Christian ancestors and that all his sins had been washed away in holy water.[48]

70

"From these truthful and persuasive remembrances that hinted at a deep hope in Jesus within him, a secret feeling arose and, intensified by a sense

47. The vestals, Roman priestesses consecrated to Vesta, the goddess of the earth fire, were sworn to chastity for the term of their office. Sarrocchi refers to the story of the vestal Tuccia, who, when accused by the authorities of transgressing on the matter of sexual abstention, was able to carry water from the Tiber in a sieve and, with Vesta's miraculous intervention, prove that she was innocent. Valerius Maximus, *Memorable Doings and Sayings* 8.1, absol. 5.

48. In other words, Alexander now remembers that as a child he was baptized. On the stories about Scanderbeg's conversion and upbringing, see pp. 24–25 above.

of piety, pervaded his soul. Even so, the impression did not linger, because the religious faith to which he had for so long been accustomed chased it away; and, in the end, he believed only the law to which the great sultan had raised him to be truthful.

71

"So he ordered Palinuro to take his daughter away as he wished, and he inflicted no punishment on the other man, although his behavior had pained and shamed him. Very wisely he gave himself the advice not to oppose the emperor's will and to keep the whole truth to himself, for those not so powerful can vie with the more powerful only to their disadvantage.

72

"He would be satisfied only if he could keep the promise to protect the city from offense and damage. So fearing that some new act of treachery might be committed, he ordered everyone to leave. Aranit, wise man that he was, understood perfectly well that he could not contend with the great tyrant and took refuge in Buda with his daughter, his wife, and the most valiant of his men.[49]

73

"Lagnete meanwhile returned to the court with a perturbed face and sadness in his heart. To the Thracian emperor he made his humiliation appear more painful than it really was. To him he said: 'I was surrounded by a great number of men, all very strong and heavily armed. In the end, Alexander took the woman from me and, though a slave, refused to follow your bidding.

74

"'Neither exhortation nor wise warning could persuade him to submit to your awesome command. On the other hand, who can give enough praise to those angelic eyes, to her resplendent mien, and even come close to the truth?' Lagnete was silent, and the emperor, although overflowing with ferocious anger, felt his heart overtaken by desire. Baizet found him in this angry disposition and fed and stirred his anger even more.

---

49. The historical event that may have inspired Sarrocchi here was the decision of the king of Hungary and the ruler of Transylvania to leave the battlefield and return to Budapest after the victory at Niš. In the 1606 edition of the *Scanderbeide*, Alexander too exits Belgrade and takes refuge in Buda, before deciding to return to Croia. See p. 25 above. For the description of Aranit's moral character, see above, canto 1.26n.

75

"Baizet was Alexander's mortal enemy, a man of arrogant and malevolent character. Although his appearance gave a deceiving impression of honesty, he was excessively conceited and indulgent toward himself while envious by inveterate habit of everybody's fame and valor. The greater then was his resentment of Alexander, whose praise for virtue and bravery surpassed everyone else's.

76

"His grudge, feeding upon itself, kept gnawing at him. Inside he boiled and outwardly he was flushed with the color of rage. Long before, Baizet had laid siege to the walls of Belgrade with a large army, and three times he had failed to capture it. Now, resentful beyond measure of Alexander's victory, he was driven on by his own fury and inconsiderately declared the valorous deeds of that strong wise captain to be a gift of blind fortune.

77

"He was blinded by rancor, yet being a master in the art of deceit, he considered which of many insidious ways might bring greater damage to the hero and precipitate him faster toward death. In good time, he proceeded to sharpen the great tyrant's wrath as on a whetstone, so that the web of deceptions he had begun to weave to the hero's harm might come to its completion.

78

"At the opportune moment he was quick to take up the threads he considered useful to his evil web, and lowering his head reverently, he said: 'My lord, whom the entire world loves and worships, whose fame extends to the far west and to the far east, to the south and to the north—what do I say!— nowhere in this wide world of ours and in the world opposed to ours can your valor remain hidden!

79

"'Before your great imperial majesty, the equal of which is not to be found anywhere on earth, my soul trembles and makes my tongue sound every word ever so tremulously! But what is there that the deeply felt loyalty of a faithful servant cannot overcome, when the interest of his lord is at stake? So may this mouth of mine, which cannot remain silent any longer, beg forgiveness for my daring!

80

"'A weak foundation cannot sustain a high and large construction for a long time: a slight wind is sufficient to pull it down, and if the wind does not demolish it, at the very least it shakes it to its foundations. On the other hand, a construction resting on a solid base will stand even when lightning strikes from the sky. In the same fashion, great powers last if they inspire fear and collapse if they do not.

81

"'Empires take their name from *imperare*.[50] Kings are made by fear and respect,[51] and the man who cannot reduce his servants to obedience cannot be called a master. It is fear and whatever impresses the people's minds that make a king divine. Hence the ancient sovereigns very wisely believed that what gave a foundation to their realms was the belief that they were gods.

82

"'Jupiter fended off Capaneus's evil arrogance with his booming thunderbolts. No less fierce was he against the proud and sacrilegious giants who willfully rebelled against the heavens.[52] Juno transformed Callisto's fine features and suppressed Echo's natural power of speech.[53] Numberless minor divinities were no less determined to safeguard their power.

83

"'Emulating the gods, human law has decreed that kings are not to be betrayed by their subjects. Whoever offends those who govern—even in his thoughts—deserves to die, according to ancient custom. We read that David lured his fierce opponent, unarmed, into a solitary and enclosed

---

50. *Imperare* is Latin for "to command" and "to dominate."

51. Machiavelli, in *The Prince*, chapter 17, says that a prince ought to make himself feared and respected at the same time.

52. Capaneus was one of the seven heroes who fought against Thebes, a city of Boeotia. The war against Thebes is the subject of Aeschylus's play *Seven against Thebes* and of Statius's heroic poem *Thebaid*. The giants were a race of aborigines who rebelled against the gods, were defeated by them with the help of Hercules, and were buried in the volcanic region of Sicily. Cf. *Metamorphoses* 9.404.

53. Callisto was a nymph, follower of Artemis, i.e., Diana, and her companion in hunting. She was loved by Jupiter and transformed by his jealous wife, Juno, into a bear. When the bear was killed by Artemis, Jupiter changed his beloved into the constellation of the Bear. The nymph Echo aroused Juno's wrath because, by chattering with her, she distracted the goddess while her husband amused himself with other nymphs. In punishment, Juno made an echo of her. These myths are told by Ovid, *Metamorphoses* 2.409–506, and *Fasti* 2.155–92.

space within his power. But he did not have the daring to kill him, so sacred did he consider the royal state to be.[54]

84

"'There is no need for me to say—as wise as you are, you know it well— how unbecoming it would be to your great valor and to the sublime Ottoman throne that you should be compared with a slave and that he should have no esteem for your sovereignty. At present this slave shares the burdens and honors of war with your best captains. Before him, I too was one of the first generals who laid siege to Belgrade.

85

"'You know that those who fought at that siege, the ones whom you yourself wisely chose, gave in many ventures great proof of their valor and of their ability to select the best men. If they did not conquer the city, they nevertheless reduced it to unbearable straits, and with several horrendous blows shook it and tore it apart with an invincible hand.

86

"'They brought the town to its knees by exhausting it with vigils, hunger, and fatigue, by inflicting many casualties, by wounding and starving many people, while many others suffered in the heat and the cold, by day and by night. As often happens, the foolish populace gave credit not to merit but to fortune's trickery, to someone who, confident that he holds Fortune by the hair, holds you in contempt and in the end rebels against you.

87

"'Following his example, more than one subject will perhaps make a daring move and join him, checked by neither respect nor fear, because an offense that goes unpunished invites another. The desires that a man keeps buried in his heart do not always show on his face, and the loftier the position a sovereign occupies, the higher the number of deceiving faces around him.

88

"'You may have heard the popular saying—a popular dictum is true wisdom—that the injured party always harbors a wish to take revenge against

54. For David refusing to kill Saul, see 1 Samuel 24. David was an important figure in Italian political iconography. Best known are the statues of David by Donatello, Verrocchio, and Michelangelo, all symbolizing republican liberty. Sarrocchi, however, uses the biblical figure to embody the respect for princely powers and rulers in general, very much in the spirit of her time.

the offender. It is then correct to maintain that the perpetrator of the offense ought to think of his own safety and never forgive those he has offended: given the opportunity, it is wise to avert the act of revenge that the injured party plans to exact.[55]

89

"'May the saying teach you then what you must do in this dangerous situation, most high lord. Remember that you sent his brothers to an early and deadly end, that the offense remains in his proud heart,[56] that he grieves, and even though by right the entire world is yours, he is outraged by your taking possession of his kingdom and holding onto it.

90

"'It was your right to put them to death, for the empire must be protected from the merest shade of suspected danger, let alone from an event most disturbing, from which a dangerous effect is likely to issue. I wonder what a strange idea disturbed your tested powers of prophecy when Alexander was not killed with his brothers; but there is still time.

91

"'There is still time, if it pleases you to punish him, for in the future he could harm you, just as now he brings shame on you. One must not forget that many famous Thracians bore arms under his command. Think of that great Roman[57] who longed to be forever king and, with the support of the armies pledged to him, presumed to force the nation under the heavy yoke of dictatorship.'

92

"With these and other very persuasive reasons, Baizet endeavored to bring to fruition his evil plan, with the same great skill with which an expert rider spurs his swift horse and keeps him on the run. He egged on the implaca-

55. Machiavelli advises the new ruler to put to death all those who may plan revenge, for men never forget the offenses they have received. *The Prince* 7–8.

56. On the story of the murder of Scanderbeg's brothers by the sultan, see p. 24 above.

57. Caius Julius Caesar, Roman general and politician (c. 100–44 BCE). He was made dictator of Rome soon after defeating Pompey on the plain of Pharsalus (48 BCE) and was confirmed dictator for life in 44. He was assassinated on March 15—the Ides of March—in a conspiracy headed by Brutus and Cassius. In referring to Caesar as a tyrant, Sarrocchi follows an older, republican political tradition. Her contemporaries, on the other hand, who perhaps were more aware of the times in which they lived, supported an absolute form of government and saw in the Roman dictator the embodiment of royal authority.

ble sovereign, who was in himself very severe, and advised him not to forgive. So, further inflamed by a desire to seek revenge, the sultan accepted Baizet's vicious advice.

93

"'A just concern for my royal state has been worrying me, stirring a persistent desire to do precisely that; a desire that your reasoning now makes even more compelling. But then the consideration of honor held me back, when I pondered the great esteem Alexander enjoyed, just as at times the green leaf of a tree looks better when seen among royal ornaments. So I proposed to put him to death but in a manner that seemed of his own making rather than of mine.[58]

94

"'A magnanimous heart, it is true, does indeed induce a sovereign of clear valor to act in a forgiving manner. It is necessary, however, to abstain from such behavior if one suspects that some danger to the state may follow. Let us then cut off the unhealthy limb that can be dangerous to the whole body. I therefore order you to do it, and I give you full power to see to it in the manner you think best, by use of either sword or venom.'

95

"Baizet considered the matter and then complacently answered with his customary reverence and submissiveness. 'Poison is the best, for a secret death will not entice the people to revolt. Then name me to represent you in Belgrade by firm imperial degree. When in high command, I will be in a position to come up with more than one convenient way to comply with your wishes.'

96

"The Thracian assented to the perverse man's request, and to show how keen he was on the plan, he granted that after Alexander's death Baizet would become general in chief of the army. Comite, a man in whom also the Thracian placed great trust, was made accomplice in this iniquitous and cruel enterprise. Baizet arrived in Belgrade and was welcomed by Alexander with magnanimous heart and pleasing mien.

---

58. Sarrocchi's elliptical sentence means that the sultan could not honorably have ordered Alexander killed earlier, because Alexander, being one of the court favorites, seemed to those around him much worthier than he really was, just as a green leaf is more impressive if seen among royal ornaments.

From CANTO 2

Svarte's report to King Alfonso continues. The king offers to send aid to Alexander and organizes the troops that are to leave under the ambassador's guide. The Italian contingent arrives in Croia and is welcomed by Scanderbeg.

1

"As soon as he arrived, Baizet took command of the territory and did not appear to concern himself with anything else. He feigned with skill and hid his deception so deep in his heart as to seem equal to Alexander in loving disposition. Gold, conquering the heart and dazzling the eye, wins more wars than do metal and fire, and with gold Baizet proceeded to fashion weapons of deception[1] so powerful as to make it impossible for the captain to escape death.

2

"Among the attendants at dinner, no one was a greater favorite of Alexander than Crifier. He served him food with his own hands and thus had the opportunity to kill him unobserved. Baizet set eyes on him and planned to entice him with gold rather than with promises. Crifier coveted honors, was greedy for gold, but he was also diligent in serving his master.

3

"With that intent the shrewd Baizet ordered all his men to please and pay honor to Crifier. He himself treated him with great respect and regarded him as the favorite among his favorites. Fearing, however, that the rumor of

---

1. As these characters are military men, Sarrocchi's metaphor of "weapons" continues the one of "gold wins more wars than do metal and fire" very appropriately.

his preference might go around and make someone suspicious, he pretended to prefer him above all others only because the captain himself held him in great esteem.

4

"Finally, affecting a self-assurance that he did not feel, he took Crifier to a secluded place and there he revealed his plan to him, taking care to do so gradually and agreeably. Crifier listened, turned hot and cold with fear and anger mixed together, and refused to stain his unsullied hand with such an inhuman and horrible crime.

5

"However, when a splendid gift of gold and gems was unfolded before his roving eyes, Crifier was dazzled, unable to resist its splendor. Never had the desired object of a longing lover been so irresistibly alluring; no blond hair, no black eyes, no ivory face had ever taken hold of Crifier's heart so powerfully.

6

"Even so, he turned his eyes away from the evil and resplendent lure and rejected it as he had done before. His craving desire nonetheless increased, nagging and gnawing at his heart. Baizet, not discouraged by Crifier's uprightness, kept on urging, telling him how greatly appreciated his service would be by the emperor, who had promised a kingdom in reward for such a deed.

7

"Ah, arrogant desire of dominion! Ah, human thirst for gold! To what crimes do you not lead men's heart?[2] In the end, as Crifier's greed and ambition prevailed, he set forth to carry out the infamous crime, and disregarding loyalty and casting love and devotion into oblivion, he shamelessly accepted the gift and the poison, preparing to give death to his master.

8

"One day, when the unsuspecting Alexander was comfortably seated at the table among his minor officers, the traitor handed him the food he had secretly tainted with poison. The hidden obnoxiousness did not manifest its

---

2. This is a paraphrase of Virgil's exclamation "Quid non mortalia pectora cogis, auri sacra fames?" (To what do you not force the hearts of mortals, accursed thirst for gold) (*Aeneid* 3.56–57).

deadly power right away, so Alexander ate, for the immediate pleasure of the food was not hampered and the taste gave him no warning.

9

"Once the tables had been cleared and most of the night spent in conversation, Alexander rose to go to bed. Suddenly he felt an aching tug at his heart. The discomfort increased quickly, and then he was shot through by a stabbing pain, the likes of which he had never experienced before. More than once, he was forced to stand still, pale in the face, and motionless in all his body.

10

"By now the beautiful stars in the sky were sending their beams around the heavens, the shadows unfolded their deepest veils, and Night, climbing halfway up the sky in her chariot, gathered the deepest silence around her.[3] As the pain increased unbearably, an ominous cold spread over the good captain's body. Everything around him went dark, and he began to stagger on unsteady feet.

11

"The traitor came forward to help, and his murderous hand propped up the hero's side, as a column would, for he was about to fall down, so much of his great vigor was leaking away. Stupefaction and grief for the unusual happening struck everyone, but the captain very courageously did not complain, and almost as if nothing were bothering him, he asked only that they see to his illness.

12

"Soon his loyal friends rushed to him in a great hurry. The faithful Vran[4] was the first, for he, hearing what had suddenly happened, felt his friend's pain deep in his heart. By now the lethal poison was making its way unobstructed down the hero's veins, and several great experts in the medical arts were hurriedly considering how they might help.

---

3. Sarrocchi's description of the night, which climbs in her chariot on the curve of the sky, spreading silence and veils of darkness, successfully vies with other poets' depictions of nighttime. Cf. Virgil, *Aeneid* 2.268–69, 4.522–28, 8.26–27. Virgil's images are echoed by Ariosto in *Orlando Furioso* 8.79, and by Tasso in *Jerusalem Delivered* 3.71.1–4, 6.52.2.

4. See "Vran" in the cast of main characters.

13

"The more they studied the symptoms, the more certain they became that he had ingested a poison. They did not say so, however, and addressed every effort to curing him. They tried to alleviate with various liquids the aching thirst burning in the hero's chest, but all the while the treacherous hand, by administering new poison, rendered their remedy ineffectual.

14

"In the end every remedy suggested by either the old or the new books turned out to be useless, for the poison that the evil man kept pouring on the food frustrated all attempts on the part of the experts. Nonetheless the illness did not increase as it usually would, because the medical administrations lessened it to a degree. The hero was losing strength but was not in danger of his life, for as much as one potion was harmful, the other proved beneficial.

15

"Spreading her wings on high and untying her tongue into loquacious speech, Fame swiftly reached Palinuro in Buda, striking his heart far more than his ears. The real reason for Alexander's misfortune was clear to him, thanks to signs that remained undecipherable to most: by keeping the promise made to the people of Belgrade, the hero seemed to have sealed his own doom.

16

"Shortly afterward he heard a true and much clearer report from the royal ministers. A pious feeling of gratitude, which is never far from a generous heart, surged in him: 'If I fall down while helping you to safety, you must hold out a hand to help me up.' He summoned the knowledgeable Mohamet and addressed him with these words:

17

" 'My loyal friend, go immediately to the Turkish camp and give high proof of your skills. The hero is near death: see if a timely remedy is still to be found that can save him. His friend Vran will show you the way to him, so look first and only for him. I am certain Vran is weighed down by grief for his friend's misfortune and surely will give you a pass to enter.'

18

"The sun was up and Mohamet had to hurry if he wanted to cross the river. He entered the Hister⁵ and was carried aloft by a ship that seemed to be flying on wings. Aurora rose from her saffron bed,⁶ ushering in the morning light, when Mohamet landed finally near Belgrade, not far from the Turkish camp.

19

"As soon as he arrived, his guide cautiously announced his presence to the loyal Vran, who came forth immediately and led him to where the great warrior lay near death. An oak sprawled on the ground appears darker and stronger after a powerful axe has cut it at its base, because lying on the earth it can fully show how big it is and how rich in branches.⁷

20

"Or perhaps he rather resembles a noble wild animal who, hit on one side by a penetrating arrow and overcome by unbearable pain, hides deep in the forest and can find no help against approaching death. His awesome tail slashes the earth, the big forest trembles, and the air reverberates at each stroke. With his ferocious claws, teeth, and hairy limbs, the animal appears unvanquished even while dying.

21

"The once robust and very vigorous hero now tossed around in bed fighting against the disease. As his strength waned, he drew his last sighs, and a freezing cold spread all over his body. He no longer responded to those

---

5. Hister, in some texts written Ister, is the name of the Danube south of Vienna. The river must be crossed by those who, like Mohamet, travel from Budapest toward Belgrade.

6. Aurora, or Dawn, was the Roman goddess of early morning. Her Greek counterpart is Eos. At sunrise, she rose from the bed of her lover, Tithonus, and ascended the sky upon a chariot. Saffron is the color of the eastern sky at dawn. The description derives from similar ones found in *Odyssey* 5.1 ("Dawn rose from her bed beside old Tithonus to bring light to humans and to gods"), in *Aeneid* 4.584–85 ("already the early Dawn, rising from Tithonus's saffron bed, was spreading a new light over the land"), as well as in Ariosto's *Orlando Furioso* 34.61.5 and Dante's *Purgatorio* 9.1. Cf. below, 2.70 and 3.7.

7. The comparison of a fallen warrior to a felled tree with its branches spread out on the ground ultimately derives from one in *Iliad* 13.177–81: "He fell like an ash tree that on top of a mountain is cut down by the axe and can be seen all around from afar with its young leaves cast on the ground." Tree similes in comparable contexts are also in *Iliad* 13.389–91, 16.485–90, in *Aeneid* 2.626–31, and in *Jerusalem Delivered* 9.39. In canto 3.89 Ferratte is said to stand out among the Janissaries like a pine or a cypress tree among smaller plants.

who addressed him, but even while his outer senses were failing—O unique mystery of God!—he fully understood, for he had kept his judgment whole, as if in perfect health.

22

"By several signs the wise Mohamet understood that life was surrendering to the terrible venom and that the poison had taken such hold of Alexander's heart that only God's hand could save him. A great desire came over him to cure the illness that affected the hero's soul, rather than the one debilitating his body. He asked everyone to leave, as if he were about to apply his medical treatment, and remained alone with Alexander.

23

"Then he said to him: 'O mighty knight, the king of heaven, who reigns over all creation, allows your end to come before its time, according to some unfathomable plan of his. Your royal parents, who had such strong and true faith in God and now enjoy a well-deserved victory in paradise, entreat him to favor your noble soul with eternal life.

24

"'Ah, consider how merciful is the lash with which the celestial hand is flogging you, like that of the wise father who punishes his unruly child who has behaved against his own good! Once your body was robust and healthy, but now where have your great vigor and your extraordinary strength gone? Dispel your blindness, concede that you are nothing but dust and shadow!

25

"'You can find neither shelter nor escape against death, so turn your mind and heart to the Lord! He wants you and looks for you, just as the good shepherd looks for the lamb missing from the herd. If the light has already gone out of your limbs, do not let your soul remain in eternal darkness, for God may well come to the rescue of the body as well, in the same way he has rescued many of his dear people.

26

"'Regolus asked Christ to rescue his son from impending death, and from his dismal funereal bed the young man was able to open eyes that were already sealed in darkness. Lazarus rose from his dark tomb and his soul returned from the gate of Tartarus.'[8] The captain listened to Mohamet and began to feel a zeal descend from heaven into his heart such as he had never felt before.[9]

27

'This was a zeal of charity, of pure faith, a secret zeal that, even though not fully understood on earth, any wise soul can recognize as coming from a high principle, because our health finally rests solely on God. No act, no wish proceeds from us that may be deserving of heaven, if God does not make it worthy. The captain therefore promised that he would return to the holy faith, so that he might enjoy the light of heaven.

28

"A miracle then occurred. As he pronounced those words, words he had uttered more with his heart than with his voice, the Lord, who always listens to heartfelt entreaties, infused a strength in him far greater than he had ever enjoyed before, just as the rays of the sun shine more splendidly after a cloud has by unfortunate chance obscured it. Alexander soon rose feeling quite well, and stretching his arms to the heavens, he gave devout thanks to God.

29

"Evil Baizet, confident that the captain would die or never totally recover, had announced the imperial decree to the camp and had already acceded to the high command. Now he fell back into a sea of worries, between flashes of hope and clouds of fear. He turned his doubting mind this way and that a thousand times, still remaining insecure and undecided.

30

"He kept thinking about the incredible turn of events, and wondering how the hero could possibly have escaped the mortal danger and still enjoy the

8. Regolus has not been traced. Perhaps with this name Sarrocchi refers to the son of the king's officer whom Jesus is asked to cure in John 4.43–54. Lazarus of Bethany is a well-known Gospel character, resuscitated by Jesus after four days in the tomb. See John 2. Tartarus, used by Latin poets synonymously with Hades, stands here for the realm of death.

9. The episode of the doctor Mohamet is a Christian variation of the story of Aeneas being treated by his old doctor, Iapyx, who does not realize that the Trojan hero has already been cured by his mother, the goddess Venus. See *Aeneid* 12.383–429. See also *Jerusalem Delivered* 11.68–75, where Godfrey is confined to bed and cured.

healing air, he suspected an act of deceit or fraud. In the end, however, he
had to be persuaded by the happy news rumored all around, and he decided
to make manifest use of force, since stealthy fraud had been of no avail.

31

"He was certain that all pagan captains and their soldiers would obey his
commanding glance, but he feared that the hero's invincible hand might
counteract his plans. Nonetheless, he was not entirely convinced that
Alexander had suddenly recovered his strength and health. Ah! Doesn't the
stupid man know that God legislates over everything and with a mere sign
of his brow can tear down or hold up the universe?

32

"The hero held the loyalty of the camp and town far more securely than the
Ottoman sultan could rely on his subjects' love. Hence he decided to
retrieve his father's estate and Epirus from the cruel barbarian. He got ready
to fight and no one let Baizet suspect anything about this plan. So we all
rallied to Alexander's side and advanced against the traitor in a rush crying:
'To arms! Revenge! To arms! Revenge!'

33

"His bodyguards answered the call: 'To arms! To arms!' and the people
began to set up a strong defense. Quick to rise, Baizet got hold of his fine
weapons, for he was the first to hear the call. Believing it to be an enemy
assault, he ordered everyone to pick up arms, and having been always on
the lookout, he was astonished by the unexpected attack.

34

"Surrounded by his friends and squadrons, he turned to see where the noise
was coming from, advanced toward it, and as soon as he saw the hero, recognized him, fully armed and stained with blood. Some men were
wounded, others lay dead on the ground. The reason for it was immediately
apparent, but the hero, although angered by this, ordered that only Crifier
and Baizet were to be killed.

35

"But what was the use if common people understood little and if their furor
prevailed over reason? The opposing men, overpowered by a greater force,
put up a weak resistance. The light of life, which so brightly shone and
which all mortals so ardently wish to enjoy, was taken away from all of

them, including Baizet and Crifier, with a thousand penetrating blows on their faces and sides.

36

"The great hero departed from Belgrade more swiftly than one can say. Alan was left on guard. Only a number of his warriors followed him; the others were told to wait in hiding at the point where Thessaly and Albania join.[10] He proceeded to Croia to overtake Selim and take the domain of Epirus away from him.

37

"Either the guards were not sufficiently attentive or they looked favorably on Alexander's daring deed. Had they given the alarm from the fort, Selim might have put up a defense, even though the whole city could not have resisted against so strong a captain. Selim had just entered the council chamber when he saw Alexander arrive wearing full armor.

38

"The first citizens welcomed Alexander with full honor and bestowed on him the government of the city as he demanded. He behaved graciously in conduct and in speech, for he was no less courteous than they were. Selim considered it vain to oppose Alexander, whom he saw armed and befriended by the townspeople, but then, together with his men, he sped away to make everything known to the great tyrant.

39

"The hero disdained to follow him. He had no desire to take revenge on those men, because either he did not care; or with the whole citizenry now glad to be free of a harsh unfair servitude, he promised to defend the town walls against the fierce emperor; or perhaps because, being a strong man of great courage, he wanted to conquer the kingdom by the strength of his valor alone.[11]

10. Thessaly, whose frontiers have changed over time, is roughly the territory between ancient Illyria, Greece, and Epirus. It was included by the Romans in the province of Macedonia and is now part of that country.

11. The alternative in Alexander's mind would supposedly be pursuing Selim and killing him and all his soldiers—which is in any case what will be done in stanza 45. The statement that Alexander wanted "to conquer the kingdom by the strength of his valor alone" is reminiscent, although used in a different sense, of what Machiavelli states in chapter 6 of *The Prince*, namely, that rulers who have conquered territories by their own valor and military skill are more likely to keep them in their domain.

40

"Finally one day, at the time when Phoebus dips his golden curls into the sea and the whole world sinks into darkness, Selim and his men, traveling on land, decided to come out in the open, thinking that now they were less exposed to fickle fortune. They saw in the valleys near their passage something, they did not know what, reflecting the light of the silvery moon.

41

"Selim stared intently in order to discover what it was, and the reflection almost dazzled him. Then he noticed that he had crossed the mountains separating Albania from Thessaly and that below them were found many deep forests frighteningly dangerous for the traveler, not only at night when the shadows spread out their dark veils, but also when the sun casts its brightest glow.

42

"Even so, none of them wanted to retrace his steps: on the contrary, they were eager to go ahead and find out what those reflections were. It looked as if the day were emerging from the bosom of the night, so bright was the light flashing all around. When they were nearer, they realized that they were looking at more than a thousand armed men, whose polished weapons reflected the light of the moon. Further on, they began to distinguish the details: the men were on foot and the horses unmounted.

43

"Their leaders had gathered their weapons and their horses here, where the sun does not penetrate and the light is scarce, and where one can enter only by two paths, one coming from the mountain and the other from a river. Before him, on the side of Thessaly, Selim had forests and valleys; on the side of Epirus he faced a high peak: as he advanced on this difficult road, his eyes were dazzled by the scintillating weaponry.

44

"With trembling hearts and pale faces Selim and his men made full show of their presence, for it seemed to them that this was the best way to avoid harm, imprisonment, and death. But Arioden immediately ordered his men to kill everyone, for he did not wish the evil tyrant to receive any news of his friend's successful progress until he had ascended the royal throne.

45

"Selim was traveling with many men as his escort, men full of courage and well armed, but soon they were surrounded and pressed by the hostile army; the escape route between the mountains and the river was blocked. When the captain's order was heard, a thousand flashing swords were raised, and Selim with all his men were chopped down into a hundred pieces.[12]

46

"Once the country was in his hands, Alexander adopted a royal manner blended with his natural cordiality. His demeanor was at once humanly kind and lofty, for excessive humility is often despised. He exercised his power in a benign way but with a skill that induced his subjects to obedience. After a short time, he gauged correctly that the time had come to let his army enter the city.

47

"He summoned the old and loyal barons of the kingdom and explained the fiendish motivation behind the Ottoman's behavior toward him. He then showed them a prodigious and well-known mark of his hereditary and just right to the kingdom: it was the figure of a sword, a memorable mark indeed, that he had had on his right arm since birth.

48

"The full relief of a drawn sword showed on his arm in proximity to the palm, made of an entanglement of veins and sinews and with more precision than any canny art of man could have produced. When looked at, it inspired amazement and awe, as if it were a veritable weapon of Mars; so eerie was the sign of the superhuman valor allowed him by heaven, the most extraordinary one ever given to man.

49

"With gladness of heart and serene countenance, they all looked at the sign, listened to his story, and gave him praise, enchanted to hear that his valor had overcome all perils. Never did a mother rejoice and delight at the recently regained freedom of her son as much as they did in seeing their legitimate king safe from the cruel tyrant.

12. The slaying of Selim and his soldiers is Sarrocchi's very successful reworking of the episode of Sveno and his troops, who in *Jerusalem Delivered* 8.13–24 are surrounded and killed by Solyman's army when they arrive during the night on the border of Palestine.

50

"All quickly rose to honor him and tried to make themselves known before all others. Everyone demurely bowed and reverently swore to accept him as his rightful king. A light of almost divine splendor seemed to shine forth from his eyes: in majesty and in size he now appeared greater than ever,[13] as if the heavens had infused a new vigor into him.

51

"Several messengers were assigned to go quickly to the people who were still uncertain between hope and fear. These ran to the palace and Alexander came out, for the vast apartments were not large enough for so big a crowd. The throng jostled and pushed forward in order to stare and touch. Many wished to get near and look at him closely, to bow and give him a sign of respect and honor.

52

"He advanced among the people with a pleasant mien and at the same time with royal majesty. Then he began to speak in a manner consonant with his generally serene and dignified countenance. 'Of my numerous and varied misfortuncs, O my dear people, the one that seemed most cruel to me—so much I care for you—was the yoke of servitude that weighed on you.

53

"'I now swear by this scepter and by my head: I shall securely defend you against the Turkish army with my very hand, I shall help you as a son would, I shall love you as a father, I shall keep away from you all dark and horrid nights. I promise you a future serene and tranquil. Be no longer in fear of cruel servitude and be loyal to me, each one of you, as you have always been.' "

54

"He was silent. Then many voices gave a common applause, a popular acclaim similar to the happy military cheer that was heard when Caesar went by on his triumphal chariot.[14] 'Long live, long live the king of Epirus, our native son! May Jesus be blessed, may Alexander reign forever!' The air

13. The physical and moral stature of Alexander is repeatedly remarked on in the poem. Cf. 5.39.

14. Caesar was famously cheered by his soldiers when carried in triumph in the streets of Rome. Other references to him are at 1.91n, 10.47, 19.21n, 20.36n, 20.44, 22.15n, 22.29.

resounded with this jubilation: 'May our good king, whom the true God has revealed to us, dispose of our goods, of our sons, and of our lives as well!' "

55

As Svarte came to the end of his story, all admired his skillful eloquence and praised the hero's extraordinary valor. Would a tie of friendly love compel the wise Alfonso more than any other? As the man of generous heart and great character he was, he took aside the messenger and said: "Tell me if my dear friend is in need of anything in confronting the Ottoman enemy."

56

At this question, the sagacious messenger did not forget to tell him how ill equipped his king was in setting up a defense against so powerful an emperor. The courteous Alfonso then made the decision to send a thousand soldiers to him right away and to provide an even greater support by paying them for the duration of the war.

57–69

Several Neapolitan captains are chosen to lead the soldiers that will go to Alexander's aid. Sarrocchi lists them, celebrating their clans.

70

Aurora had hardly left her old lover[15] when Svarte started on his journey back the same way he had come and pointed out the easy route to the knights and the foot soldiers. In a few days they arrived safely in Croia in the presence of Alexander, who, at the announcement of their arrival, came out to greet the commanders: he embraced them and showed to all the others a friendly face.

---

15. Tithonus, Aurora's mortal lover, is here described as "old", because Aurora obtained immortality for him but forgot to ask Jupiter to grant him youth as well. Cf. stanza 18 and cantos 2.70, 3.7.

CANTO 3

Polidor, a friend of Selim and a devout Muslim, travels to the Ottoman capital and there, with Filena, Selim's wife, plans for the sultan to learn what has happened. Hearing the widow's plea for revenge, Murad orders the army to convene and march against Alexander. The many national contingents of the imperial army are reviewed, and the emperor's warrior daughter, Rosmonda, is made regent of the empire.

1

While the Thracian emperor learned about the occupation of the country carried out by our hero, he, Alexander, as soon as the defense of the city was provided for, turned his attention to divine worship. He had a solemn mass celebrated in honor of Christ in the holy churches, made generous donations, and had the pious priest give thanks to God to the ringing of bells in the bell towers.[1]

2

At that time, in the population of Albania there were many who esteemed the faith in Jesus to be contrary to truth, and who felt deep bitterness when they saw an offense done to Islam go unavenged. Among them was Polidor, who turned over in his mind greater things than anyone else, even though fear kept him silent. The foolish man harbored a zealous attachment to his faith and felt in his heart a great grief for Selim's death.

3

Born in Thrace of not unworthy parents and brought up in the false Turkish faith, he was lucky to augment the possessions he had inherited from his

---

1. Religious observances on the part of the hero, especially before some important enterprise, are underlined in this and in most Christian as well as other histories and epics. See below, 21.44–45.

father by trading and by trusting his great fortune and his own person to the traitorous waters of the sea. And then, for the short span of life left to him, he chose Croia as his permanent residence.

4

He had been tied to Selim by an enduring bond of loyalty and had exchanged with him mutual signs of friendship. Selim had always honored and favored him among the first barons of the kingdom, and he had shown his gratitude with gifts of silver and gold. When he heard of Selim's tragic death, his heart was overwhelmed by grief and anger; furthermore, living under a Christian lord made him feel unprotected.

5

Still, in order to give no cause for suspicion, and for fear of placing his possessions in danger, he put on a face of pious devotion and ran to church ahead of anyone else. He spent there the greater part of the day, apparently embracing the Christian faith and hiding his wish for the king's death. The traitor, still faithful to Islam, had the daring to sit at Alexander's table, where the presence of God is felt.

6

As soon as the frontiers of Epirus were provided with sufficient defenses, the king decided to allow people to go out of the city to trade, as the need for it was great. When Polidor, who was weaving a web of iniquitous deception, had certain knowledge of that decision, he let it be known that he was going out of the city to buy food, so that he might travel to the great sultan in greater safety.

7

One day, as a beautiful dawn was turning into morning, Polidor arose intent on his departure. With her silvery hand Aurora was spreading a shower of dewy pearls over the sky,[2] and a pleasant breeze was making the waves tremble. Soon a favorable wind filled the veils and began to carry the anxious Polidor swiftly aloft.

2. The dewy aspect of the dawn makes this simile a direct derivation of the ones found in *Aeneid* 4.6–7 and in *Fasti* 3.403–4. Its silvery and pearly features are reminiscent of similar precious descriptions of skies and stars, most of which function here as time scansion. See 6.61, 7.36, 7.40, 9.27, 10.20, 19.21, and 19.22. Women's beauty is depicted in similar terms of jewelry and rare materials. Cf. canto 1.29.

8

So speedily did he go on his way that in no time he was out of everyone's sight: never did a peregrine falcon fly on the roads of the sky as swiftly as this man traveled.³ Certain that God's will was being propitious to him, Polidor rejoiced and took courage; but that was stupid of him, for the spirit that stood at the helm of his boat might have been a spirit of hell.

9

In a few days he arrived at the great imperial city. Still, a disturbing doubt made his mind swing one way and the other, just as an unrigged ship sways when it is beaten by gusts of contrary winds:⁴ for he could not decide whether he ought first to make the treason known to the great sultan or go and pay a visit to Selim's wife, this being an obligation of true and constant friendship.

10

Ambition mixed with greed sharply goaded his conscience: he could be remunerated by his high lord and acquire great honor for his loyalty, but at the same time he was afraid of some unthought-of mishap, as occasionally happened to messengers carrying bad news to the great emperor, as to that silly bird whose white feathers were turned black by Apollo.⁵

11

This fear froze his blood, and so, chasing away ambition and greed, he refrained from his first inclination. Now he wanted Selim's inconsolable wife, carrying the burden of her grief, to be the one who would make known to the emperor the great treachery committed against him. So he decided to go, a messenger of cruel news, to the beautiful Filena.

---

3. For a similar falcon simile, see 1.11.

4. Sarrocchi's comparisons are functional rather than just decorative, because they always aim to illustrate the character's psychological condition. Here, the vivid image of a rudderless boat tossing about in a stormy sea contributes most felicitously to the description of Polidor's mind, which is swaying between hope, desire, and fear. This ship is an adaptation of the one found in *Jerusalem Delivered* 7.98.3–8. Tasso, however, employs the simile of the boat defying contrary winds to emphasize the physical strength of the warrior, rather than his mental state.

5. This passage refers to the story told by Ovid in *Metamorphoses* 2.531–95. The "silly bird" was once Coronis, the beautiful daughter of Coroneus, king of Phocis. Pursued by Neptune, she cried out for help, and Pallas came to the rescue by changing her into a bird of shining white plumage. After reporting the gossip that a child without a mother was hidden in a box, Coronis, now a white bird, was changed again, this time into a crow.

12

Whoever could describe her deep and piercing grief, her cries and lamentations, would also be able to count all the flowers that in springtime the sun awakens in the grass with his luminous rays, or all the drops of water the Aegean Sea holds and sprays when contrasting winds swell it. Filena wanted justice to be done right away, for at times revenge makes pain more tolerable.

13

On the day indicated by the star that shines like a flame in the third heaven,[6] at the hour when the Thracian people gathered inside and around the mosque, the emperor set out from his royal mansion to go to reverent and devout worship. On that day, grief-stricken Filena too went to the temple among the solemn crowd.

14

From the moment the terrible news had reached her to this very day, Filena had been going to the mosque where Allah[7] is honored and worshiped, and there she had been comforted by the serene early light of the sun when it merrily makes the world anew. There she had consulted with Polidor, and together they had planned what she would say, how much crying she would do, how she would behave, who would accompany her, what she would say first and what afterward, and how she would be dressed.

15

To give greater credence to her sad condition, and in order to awaken pity in her fierce lord, she wore a simple dress of dark cotton, which came down in ample folds to her heels, and a veil matching the mournful tunic. She tried to hide the beauty of her breasts but they showed even more, for their whiteness shone against the black of the mourning.

---

6. This is Venus, which in the Ptolemaic sky turns around the earth, moving within the third heaven. In the words of Dante, she is the "bella Ciprigna . . . volta nel terzo epiciclo" (the fair Cyprian . . . whirling in the third epicycle") and throwing love-inspiring rays down on mortals. Cf. Dante, *Paradiso* 8.2–3. Politian, *Stanze per le giostra* 1.92.5.

7. In order to render the passage immediately clear to English readers, at the same time keeping faithful to Sarrocchi's meaning, I have translated *Macaon*—or, at times, *Macone*—with "Allah," and not with "Macon," as is done in translations of epics, because it is the divinity that is meant by that name. The Italian *Macone*, commonly found in chivalric narratives, is the translation of Mohammed, who, in analogy to Christianity, was thought to be the Islamic divinity. My rendition does not intend to add to or detract from what might have been Sarrocchi's knowledge of Islam.

16

Her hair fell loosely over her shoulders: gold lost its splendor next to it. No human eye could gaze at her lugubrious garb without marveling. She picked up a great bundle of ashes, all wrapped up in a dark cloth, and as a sign of self-abasement she carried it around in her beautiful hand: and so she went about in that horribly unkempt guise.

17

The great mosque was situated in the most remote and tranquil part of town. At the entrance were a portico and a fountain from which sprang many jets of water. Filena first washed her face, then her hands and feet, for the Turks believe that water gushing from stone not only makes the body clean but also cleanses the soul of all evils and foul sins.

18

Women are never allowed to enter the mosque; they must remain outside to worship Allah, for it is considered sacrilegious and sinful to deem the female sex worthy of such honor. Filena arrived and made a great display of her bereavement at the death of her husband. A great number of women accompanied her, and her little son followed behind alone and naked.

19

As soon as she was inside the portico, she sat down on the ashes she had brought with her, her countenance disfigured by crying and sighing, her voice coming in sobs out of her grieving breast. When the Thracian arrived, the cädi[8] promptly warned him that he could not enter the mosque before hearing out the sorrowful woman who was waiting, and before swearing to avenge her.

20

Filena arose, took one step forward, and prostrated herself before the great emperor. Then, grasping a handful of the ashes on which she was seated, she poured them over herself from head to foot, thus sullying her lovely appearance according to the Turkish custom. Then, recovering her voice from sighs and sobs with some effort, she spoke in this way.

21

"Most high lord, whose fame extends to all lands, from where the sun rises to where it sets: in the name of your unparalleled and incorruptible justice, which surpasses that of the most famous sages of the past, I beg you, bring

---

8. *Cädi* (or *kadi*) is the title given to Islamic magistrates.

some consolation to this disheartened widow, who is wearing these dark veils, although no clothing could ever match in bleakness the much darker grief that oppresses my heart!

22

"We are your servants, and those who offend us offend your royal honor as well. But what am I saying? They have taken possession of Epirus by deceit, and now they are contemptuous of your power and your merits! Do not let the offense and the damage done to you, and my grief with it, go unpunished! Avenge the infamy perpetrated against you and, together with it, avenge this orphan child and my bitter crying!

23

"Maybe Allah wishes the ruin of his children, the destruction and the end of this, his own empire: he is no longer honored and worshiped, for your rule and his divine laws have lost their power." At this point, as her words broke into sobbing, she thrust her hands into her golden hair and with all her strength she tore out as much of it as she could grasp. A great pity for her took hold of the emperor.

24

"Woman, restrain your immense grief. Tell us," he said, "the lamentable reason for it. Place your trust in the word of your emperor, for justice to your injury will be done." As she heard and felt comforted by such a promise, she said: "By treachery they have killed Selim, who held the government of Epirus in your name; and neither does heaven condemn the traitors nor does hell gobble them up!

25

"Do you want to know who is the inhuman, ungodly man capable of such unheard-of cruelty? It is the evil Alexander. Now a Christian, he has contemptuously offended Allah's law by killing the faithful in his population, tearing down the mosques, and desecrating their worship. Does Allah allow this to happen? Is he taking no revenge? Perhaps God wants you, O pious lord, to carry it out!

26

"Bring before your mind's eyes, my lord, the perfect loyalty of my trustworthy consort, the discomforts and the dangers—ah, how many!—he suffered for you! And then consider the brutal manner of his dying!" At this point she said no more, and instead of speaking, she doubled her wailing, beating her breasts and hurting her handsome face with ever more forceful slaps of her hands. The emperor and the people around him were astounded.

27

If bewilderment showed on the sultan's face, a fiercer and more ferocious anger assailed his heart for not having heard anything so far of such happenings. Not to have learned of them seemed to him undignified for a man who held imperial power; so he ordered his first vizier to investigate the details of how such enormous treason could have been committed. The vizier summoned Polidor, heard him out, and then reported the entire plot to the emperor.[9]

28

Having heard the whole story, the sultan went into a rage and disdained counsel from anyone and anything except his own furor. He felt deceived and vilified, his best captains being now in voluntary exile. "Now that he has conquered Epirus"—he shouted—"should we let Alexander come, let him seize Thrace and place me in peril as well?" He cried for revenge, and brimming over with wrath, he planned to recapture that kingdom in person.

29

In a great hurry he ordered the contingents from all nearby nations to assemble with their captains, for he kept these soldiers enlisted in the army in time of war and peace. The bold and proud youths were in a state of agitation; the city resounded with feverish preparations; the deep sound of hammers was heard tirelessly beating into shape, over the anvils, helmets, armor, and shields.

30

The city of Elia sits in the middle of Thrace, in a very beautiful smiling plain.[10] On the western side the Hebrus Aquilonar flows, bringing water

---

9. This episode of the widow and the emperor is modeled on the medieval legend according to which the Roman emperor Trajan (98–117 CE), on his way to war, was delayed by a widow who asked that her husband's death be avenged. The story is told in *Novellino* 69; by Jacobus de Voragine, *The Golden Legend*, 1.178; and by Dante in *Purgatorio* 10.73–93. Another variation of the same story is found here in canto 13.2 ff.

10. Elia is Adrianople (modern Edirne), in Scanderbeg's time the capital of Thrace and of the Ottoman Empire. It remained so until 1453, when Constantinople fell into Turkish hands and became the capital of the empire with the name of Istanbul. The name of Elia may have been chosen by Sarrocchi for metrical reasons, because shorter than Adrianople, and may derive

from the Rhodope Mountains.[11] On the side where the eastern sun shines, the Ardean meadows provide the city with a rich harvest. Not far away, the Aegean Sea often roars in tumultuous waves under the blows of an angry south wind.

31

The imperial seat was moved there, and the emperor ordered the immense army to assemble, line up, and march by, as is the custom in a military review. He viewed it from an edifice of superb construction, raised in the spacious meadow, and from whose height the rolling plains could be seen below stretching out into the distance.[12]

32

In the vast space of that high palace, whose superb facade faces the rising sun, a thousand rooms hide, putting the barbarous Memphis to shame.[13] Inside are many gardens full of flowers and grass, adorned with fountains, grottoes, and theaters. But what can be seen on the outside is of superb and inestimable craftsmanship, surpassing all art and human skill.

33

The walls, where a masterly hand has sculpted various figures in low and high relief, shine with encrusted chrysolite, amber, rubies, and amethyst. Where one first enters the building, there is a door of pure alabaster. Here a row of serpentine columns in Doric style holds up arches of chosen Parian marble.[14]

---

from the name of the Emperor Hadrian, i.e., Publius Aelius—in Italian Elio—Hadrianus (76–138 CE), who founded the city in 125 and after whom Adrianople was named. The Rhodope Mountains (now called Despoto Dagh) are to the west of it, and a valley, here called Ardean, presumably from the river Ardes, is on the south side of the city.

11. The River Hebrus is here called Aquilonar because it flows from the north. Aquilus, or Aquilone, is another name for Boreas, the north wind.

12. This scene of the sultan viewing his army from a high rise is similar to the one in which Xerxes, king of Persia (485–465 BCE), reviews his army and fleet from a high seat of white stone built for the purpose. Herodotus, *The Histories* 7.44.

13. The city of Memphis was the royal residence in the old kingdom of Egypt, c. 2600–2200 BCE. For the use of the word "barbarous," see above, canto 1.1n.

14. The Doric and, in the following stanza, the Corinthian style are classic orders of architecture, of which the first is the simplest and the second the most ornate. Parian marble is from Paros, an island of the Cyclades famous for its quarries.

34

Above it, there is an even more beautiful row of one hundred smaller columns, these in the Corinthian manner, which by the tens form ten verandas, their fronts decorated with gold and their tops with silver. Inside each one, on the walls and on the pavement, fine mosaics are set, showing the illustrious deeds and the glorious ventures of the Thracian kings.

35

In each of them, five windows let in the pure light of the sun. They swing on hinges of bright gold, and ebony shutters close them to create a dark night. The frames are made of porphyry, whose work takes the palm of victory from the sculptors of Samos,[15] for the craftsmanship of the artist here is to be admired more than the quality of the stone.

36

Inside the building are found depictions of figures holding various postures. They are so astonishingly beautiful as to surpass all that Zeuxis, Apelles, or any other famous painter may have created.[16] As soon as one's sight is fixed on them and the mind starts considering that they are depictions and that depictions are not real, then one is even more astonished that those feigned images can resemble reality so much.

37

Richer and most artful is the fine work of pure silver that can be seen in the balcony built above the door, which in size exceeds all the others, five in number, that flank it on each side.[17] Here the proud sultan sits in splendor,

15. The island of Samos, off the coast of Ionia, Turkey, was known throughout the ancient world for its artisans and sculptors. Here Sarrocchi echoes Ovid, who writes of the palace of the Sun: "The craftsmanship is more beautiful than the material" (*Metamorphoses* 2.5). Ovid is echoed also by Politian in *Stanze per la giostra* 1.95.4 and by Tasso in *Jerusalem Delivered* 16.2.6.

16. Zeuxis and Apelles were celebrated Greek painters. Zeuxis was a native of Lucania, Italy, where he flourished c. 424–380 BCE. The anecdote of the birds who mistook his painting for real fruit is famous. Apelles was born in Ionia, Asia Minor. He lived at the time of Alexander the Great, ruler of Macedon (356–323 BCE), and painted his portrait, as well as a painting of Venus Anadyomene.

17. The depiction of the sultan's palace is an ample elaboration of other such descriptions. See the palace of the Sun in Ovid's *Metamorphoses* 2.1–18, the house of Love in Apuleius's *Metamorphoses* 5.1, the palace of Syphax in *Africa* 3.109–328, the palace of Venus in Politian's *Stanze per la giostra* 1.95–119, Alcina's and Logistilla's homes in *Orlando Furioso* 6.70–71, 10.58–60, and Armida's palace in *Jerusalem Delivered* 16.1–8.

adorned with various oriental gems: his head is wrapped in several twisted strips of white veil; a purple robe threaded with silver and gold[18]

38

covers him from shoulder to foot; on the folds are diamonds representing distinct phases of the moon, each one furbished with large oblong pearls, and on the hem are many emeralds and rubies. The majesty of imperial power is displayed in that luxurious pomp, while the haughty and barbarous countenance of the sultan inspires his people with respect and fear.[19]

39

Soon one could hear the sound of the arms carried by the barbaric warriors entering the field. They rushed onto those wide meadows like the waves of turbulent rivers. The mountains reverberated and the valleys echoed.[20] The neighing of horses mingled with the sound of war accouterments and with the dreadful shouts the ferocious youths raised to the sky.

40

The sultan showed himself in all his prowess, for he wanted everyone to base his highest hopes on him. Those who had lived a meek and peaceful existence now wished to show a warlike bravery: they brandished their shining weapons, they flaunted their fierceness by riding on their chargers with a lofty bearing; some shook spears, some unfurled their banners in the wind, others bent their bows almost to the point of release.

41

Thus knights and foot soldiers entered the wide, spacious plain all together, but as soon as they arrived within sight of the great sovereign, their chief sergeant ordered them into ranks. Viewed from afar, under the blazing light of the sun above, that field of resplendent steel and quivering lances looked like a forest bursting into a blaze of flames.

18. For run-on stanzas, see p. 59 above.

19. A ruler ought to inspire his subjects with respect as well as fear, Machiavelli warns in *The Prince* 27. Cf. canto 1.81.

20. The sound of arms and the shout of soldiers reverberating in nearby hills and valleys are a classic topos in the descriptions of pitched battles. "Consonat omne nemus, vocemque inclusa volutant litora, pulsati colles clamore resultant" (the hills rebound with the clamor, the slopes within them resound, and the whole forest echoes), says Virgil in *Aeneid* 5.148–50, and similarly in 7.722, 12.929. "Gli alti monti muggir, muggir le valli" (the high mountains bellowed, the valleys bellowed), writes Tasso in *Jerusalem Delivered* 9.21.5.

42

O Muse![21] You who alone, from the dense obscurity of time and the dark voraciousness of oblivion, can draw out the magnanimous deeds of the past and bring them into the pure, eternal light of day, show me the cities, the people assembled here, the warriors and the arms that went on that great campaign! In spite of many bygone years, you, and you alone, can reveal to me whatever is most hidden.

43

The first to march past in the military review[22] was the army of Bithynia,[23] a land on whose frontiers Claudiopolis[24] stands, and whose northern side dips into the greater sea. Of its three captains, the foremost was Oleander, dearer to the emperor than any other because of his strength, wisdom, and courage, but even more because of his loyalty, thanks to which the emperor could still breathe and see.

44

The leaders of Maronia, a land of bellicose people near the sea, once con-spired to kill the emperor because he had withheld from them some rich and well-deserved spoils of war.[25] Oleander heard about it, and since no one was allowed to travel—both sea and overland passages were closed, and all boat journeys suspended—he daringly spurred his good horse toward the bay.

45

The sky was serene, the sea calm and quiet, and the expanse of the water vast and deep. Oleander directed his way to it and plunged into the liquid vastness. The good horse stumbled under the weight; he sustained the

21. Calliope, the Muse of epic poetry.

22. Reviews of armies are set pieces in military narratives. See *Aeneid* 7.647–817 for the review of the Latin army; *Orlando Innamorato* 2.22.5–33, 23.5–9, 29.3–20 and *Orlando Furioso* 14.11–27 for the assembly of the Saracen troops; and *Jerusalem Delivered* 1.35–64, 17.14–32 for the review of the Christian army and of the Egyptian contingents gathered at Gaza. Sarrocchi's richness of exotic detail and her description of weaponry could have been inspired by Herodotus's depiction of Xerxes' army in *The Histories* 7.61–88.

23. Bithynia was the name of a region of Asia Minor overlooking the Sea of Marmora and the Black Sea. The latter is here called the greater sea, in comparison with the Sea of Marmora, which is smaller. The main cities of Bithynia were Nicomedia (in earlier times called Astacus, and now Izmit), Brusa, and Nicaea (the modern Iznik).

24. I have not been able to trace this town. Perhaps the name of Claudiopolis is used here because Thrace was annexed to the Roman empire in 45 CE, during the reign of Emperor Claudius.

25. Maronia was a Greek colony on the Mediterranean coast of Thrace. The rebellion mentioned by Sarrocchi may have been suggested by historical facts: in 1425, Murad II had to

animal and helped him to swim. With one hand, he held onto the horse's mane, with the other onto the rein that, while swimming, he let loose; and so, O marvel! he went many miles in the vast and dark sea.

46

In that country the imperial palace was far from the seashore. Oleander arrived in time and quickly uncovered the insidious plot planned against the emperor. This very Oleander was now leading the people of Nicaea, a city found on the south side of the sun; there, from the range of the Didamean Mountains, the Sangarius River flows into the valley below.[26]

47

Three thousand of these men wore a scimitar on the side, held a lance in hand, and carried an ironclad cudgel over the saddle. Then six thousand foot soldiers marched past, free of all metal plate and mail. You could well say that heaven flashes and thunders, if thunder can ever equal the noise they make, when from their slings a hail of stones is thrown that goes crashing against armor and helmets.

48

Immediately after them came Osman, leading a crowd more used to fishing than to fighting wars. He was from eastern Nicomedia,[27] whose coastline on the west curves into a bay. This captain exuded charm and beauty; he was more tender of heart than powerful of hand. Golden was his hair, his face was roses and violets, his lips were coral, and his eyes shone with a sunlike splendor.[28]

49

He led two thousand warriors on horseback, armed with sword and lance, but without helmet or hauberk; and six thousand men on foot, with bow and arrows in their hands and a quiver bouncing on their backs. Then came the people of Astacus. Like the Nicomedeans, they also inhabited a land on

---

contend with, and eliminate, some competitors for the throne, among them Moustafa the Duzmeje (İnalcik, *Ottoman Empire,* 19).

26. Oleander comes from Bithynia, where the River Sangarius (the modern Sakarya), the Didomean Mountains, and the town of Nicaea (the modern Iznik) are all situated.

27. Sarrocchi seems to think that Nicomedia is a region and Astacus, mentioned in the next stanza, a town. See canto 3.43n.

28. About Osman's comeliness, which is depicted on the same stereotypical lines used in the description of female beauty, see 9.6.

the sea: on the same seacoast in fact where a balmy shore forms a large bay between two opposite towns.

50

Their heads were protected by a shining cover of steel, their left hands held a long shield; on the other side hung a heavy sword with no sharp point but against whose cutting blow there was no defense. These men had more courage than those who preceded them and deferred to their even more powerful captain, Orkhan. There were four thousand of them on horseback and twelve thousand on foot equipped with swords and spears.

51

Orkhan's father, still living, held the reins of the kingdom of Astacus in place of the emperor and could not come here, although still a vigorous and valiant warrior. The beautiful Dianira had given a noble birth to their son when they were both in their early youth. They were in love with each other then, although he had a wife and she had a husband.

52

She gave birth in secret, and the father, who had no other issue, turned all his affection to this child, who was of such perfect spirit and prowess as to have no equal in all Bithynia. After them marched a select squad from Mysia Major and another from Mysia Minor,[29] excellent fighters with lance, sword, and bow. Both were on foot and on horseback, and two were their captains.

53

The first ones were led by Evander. He did not remember that he had been born a mortal: he had such great confidence in his right hand that he would be ready to face certain death without fear. They inhabited a township near Mount Ida, made fertile by the Xanthus and the Simois Rivers.[30] Both are famous for their resounding waters, and it is impossible to say which of the two is noisier.

54

The soldiers on horseback carried only a lance in hand, and on this side hung large and curved scimitars. They were equipped with light weapons

29. Mysia was the name of a region in the northwest corner of Asia Minor.

30. Simois and Xanthus, or Scamander, are rivers, famous in classic poetry, situated near the city of Troy, not far from Mount Ida. They play leading parts in the plot of book 21 of the *Odyssey*.

so as to be able to fight with agility and strength. Their manner of dress was rich, but not so adorned that the beauty of the workmanship surpassed the value of the material. There were ten thousand of them, and the foot soldiers were as many, clothed and equipped like the knights.

55

Then came Driarasso, born on the banks of the Euxine.[31] His mother was the beautiful and savage Almena, a fierce archer who hunted on the mountains and in the forests of the plain. She taught the young child to spy on the dens of bears and panthers, for she was good at killing them, and she made him wear their bloody skins when he was still too young to hold a weapon.

56

She often told him the terrible story of the Spartan woman who stabbed her son, enraged because he had been the only coward to flee from the Greek army that fought against Xerxes at Thermopylae.[32] Her descendant—she menacingly told him—had the same ideals and would do the same. This way, she bent his native barbaric ferocity toward blood and slaughter.

57

Some time ago, it came to pass that the Thracian gathered all his armies in a spacious plain, for he wished to see a ferocious and dangerous game of bloody fights. There came Driarasso like the fire of lightning bent on the destruction of ripe harvest[33]—the ultimate disaster for all poor farmers— and all present feared his unbeatable might.

58

In the end, when he was surrounded by a group of thirty men, one severe blow hit him on the forehead, but he was such a fighter that the heavier the blows he received, the more courageously and angrily he fought back. So now that he was wounded, he handled the sword and the spear more

---

31. This is the Black Sea, Pontus Euxinus in Latin.

32. Xerxes was the Persian king (485–465 BCE) who crossed the Hellespont, invaded Greece, and after the battle of Thermopylae reached Athens. Here Sarrocchi might have been thinking of the Spartan mother who did away with her son because during the battle he had deserted his post (Plutarch, *Moralia* 3.341.1).

33. This simile of fire burning the harvest has a model in *Aeneid* 2.304–5: "in segetem veluti cum flamma furentibus austris incidit" (as a flame happens to be blown onto the crops by strong winds).

ferociously than before, while blood flowed abundantly out of the wide cut, running down his face and chest in ample measure.

59

With one hand he wiped away the flowing blood and with his lips he sucked it from his hand. This way he became even more ferocious, for that drink restored to him the vigor that, mingled in the blood, was exhaling with his spirit. Some men lay on the ground, others surrendered, still others decided to give up the possibility of a prize. Seeing all this, the Thracian emperor was astounded and asked after his name, his country, and who his parents were.

60

He was not less eager to meet his valiant mother, who was as hardy in warfare as in hunting, and seeing how beautiful and charming in appearance she was, he locked her away with his other royal wives. Then he ordered her son to lead the troops of all his rugged northern lands, which are situated between mountains rich in caves and thick forests, the home of wild mountain beasts.

61

Although they had no armor to wear, his soldiers loved fatigue and disliked peace. Their town was Cyzicus,[34] rich in fine marble and even more in wild bears. They were hunters and loved to handle in war the same weapons they used in the chase. There were a thousand of them on horseback, eleven thousand on foot. The former carried lances and swords, the latter bows and spears.

62

Now came the people from the country called Moesia[35] and sometimes Scythia, a land that extends from the Tomis Mountains down to where the Danube enters the sea. Its waves become so large and powerful that it seems not a river but a sea flowing into another sea; and so distant is one bank from the other that they disappear from sight, just like those of an ocean.

34. Cyzicus was a city on the homonymous island close to the coast of Mysia, in what is now Turkey. The city was famous in antiquity for the temple built by Emperor Hadrian, which was admired as one of the wonders of the world.

35. Moesia, a region that is now divided between Bulgaria and Serbia, was considered to be the European Scythia.

63

The barbaric and ferocious Brandoardo had the care of the people who came forward next. A spotted leopard skin, old and hard, protected their backs. The captain could bend the bow with such a powerful arm and shoot so infallible an arrow as to make it go through an iron vase of more than half a palm in thickness.

64

Fame tells that Brandoardo once fell for the alluring splendor of two beautiful eyes and that the lascivious archer delighted in softening his ferocious heart with sweet lures.[36] But although he tried to lighten the dark horror of his face and soften his roughish and unruly hair, cleaning the mud out of it and making it neat, he still retained his savage appearance.[37]

65

The woman was marvelously provided with comeliness: her hair was a fine gold that tossed and fluttered over roses and lilies, her eyes were stars, her eyelashes ebony, and her lips rubies over hidden pearls. She resembled the goddess Aurora when she first appears on the brightest fields of the sky, but she was also like Galatea,[38] who disdained her uncouth suitor while secretly longing for the sight of her handsome lover.

66

She rejected him, as if he were a frightful and inhuman cyclops, just as Galatea did. So the brutal man tore out her lover's heart with his own hands

---

36. In the Romance phenomenology of love, the woman's eyes are the place from which Cupid, here called the "lascivious archer," most frequently throws the arrows that make the onlooker fall in love. The same imagery is found, for example, in Politian's *Stanze per la giostra* 1.44.1–2; in *Orlando Furioso* 7.12.5–7; and in *Jerusalem Delivered* 3.24.3–4. Other occurrences in this poem are in stanza 93, and cantos 1.30, 13.87, and 18.8.

37. Brandoardo tries to improve his looks just as Polyphemus does when he falls in love with Galatea: "Iamque tibi formae, iamque est tibi cura placendi, iam rigidos pectis rastris, Polypheme, capillos . . ." (Now, Polyphemus, you are careful of your appearance, now you are eager to be liked, now you comb your shaggy hair with a rake . . .) *Metamorphoses* 13.764–65. See next note.

38. Galatea was a sea nymph who loved Acis, described here as her "handsome lover." When the cyclops Polyphemus, jealous of him, crushed Acis under a rock, Galatea changed her beloved into a river flowing from the foot of Mount Etna. Ovid, *Metamorphoses* 13.738–897. The story was a favorite one among Sarrocchi's contemporaries. When in Rome at the beginning of the seventeenth century, Giambattista Marino wrote a small poem that sang the loves of Polyphemus and Galatea (Borzelli, *Il cavalier Giovan Battista Marino*, 80). This work was never published, but twenty-four sonnets treating the same subject were included in his *La Galeria* of 1619.

and forced her to eat it raw.[39] All flowers of beauty faded from her lovely face, as she cried a flood of tears and prayed him to spare her that cruel punishment: in vain, for only feelings can change, not nature.

67

This Brandoardo led fierce soldiers from towns close to one another, full of men with neither loyalty nor laws, men who were accustomed to violence and plunder. Most of these soldiers came from the region where the kindly Roman Muses mourned the sad punishment of the poet of Sulmona.[40] At Naxos they enlisted in the army as mercenaries.

68

These primitive men wore deerskins tied together and treated with an unknown liquid that made them stronger. They shot arrows that had three poisoned points. At the first assault, they scattered and stayed far from one another, for they were used to fighting only as they retreated.[41] All of them were on horseback, and besides the arrows they carried large knives that at times they used for close fighting.

69

Now came the people from frozen Scythia:[42] perhaps no better men than these marched by. These were famous archers and throwers who sat on fast-running carriages. Each carriage was equipped with sharp blades that jutted out large and wide on both sides. The front shaft ended with an iron pike; only the back of the carriage was open to the fight.[43]

39. Sarrocchi's anecdote of Brandoardo's forcing his beloved to eat the heart of her suitor is drawn from the tragic story of *Decameron* 4.9. In Boccaccio's novella, Guiglielmo (*sic*) Rossiglione murders his wife's lover and makes her eat the heart he has just torn out of the dead man's chest.

40. The poet from Sulmona—in the Abruzzi region of Italy—is Ovid (Publius Ovidius Naso). He was banished by the Emperor Augustus to Tomis, on the Black Sea, and died there in 18 CE.

41. The Parthians, people who lived to the southeast of the Caspian Sea, were famous for such military ruses. While fighting on horseback, they pretended to retreat and then suddenly turned around to shoot arrows backward at the pursuing enemy. In *Jerusalem Delivered* 1.50, this fighting tactic is attributed to warriors born in Greece.

42. This is the Asian Scythia, a name that was applied to a land overrun by nomads and that could be used to indicate any region from southeastern Europe to northwestern Asia.

43. Herodotus represents the Scythian tribes as living in carriages and shooting arrows from horseback. *The Histories* 4.47. He does not mention scythed carriages. Scythed carriages are described by Xenophon, *Hellenica* 4.1.19, as belonging to the Persians; by Lucan, *Civil War (Pharsalia)* 1.426, as belonging to the Belgians; and by Francesco Guicciardini, *Storia d'Italia* 10.13, as part of the artillery forces of the Holy League at the battle of Ravenna in 1512.

70

There was more than one driver: they tightened and loosened the bit to six horses, harnessed in two rows, three on each side. They held the horses so skillfully in their course that no one ever fell out of the carriage. A thickly quilted cotton cloth covered men and animals alike. There were two thousand of these carts, full of men armed with spears and poles, all strong and worthy warriors.

71

They were even more valuable because of the supreme daring that had made Attravante, their leader, famous. As it happened, some time ago, when the Persians were overcome by the allied armies of Thrace and Arabia, the Ottoman emperor found himself in mortal danger. At some point, in the hour when all animals are sunk in deep torpor, some cunning Persians surrounded the royal pavilion and were about to kill the emperor while he was lying asleep.

72

The vigilant Scythian rose to his feet, jumped on his carriage with the drivers, and drove it straight to the dangerous spot where the enemies were on the point of attacking the royal tents. He tore into them with such force that he threw both men and horses to the ground, and by the force of his invincible hand, he took the Thracian onto his carriage and brought him out of danger.

73

After these, other Scythians marched in. These were the inhabitants of other settlements and were in no smaller number. Instead of armor, they wore cork bark intertwined with pliable reeds. So equipped, without fear of being carried away by currents, they swam across the rapid waters of the Hister when the warm rays of the sun melted the snows during the months of April and May.

74

Used to swimming, and fierce and daring as they were, they hurtled heavy lances with a firm hand and held massive axes. The horsemen were eleven thousand and the foot soldiers six thousand. Serpedon was their captain: in the water he could overtake the fastest dolphins, and no fish might frisk so swiftly ahead of him that he could not catch it at will with his own hands.

Tacitus tells us that war carriages were also part of the army of the Britons (*Annals* 24.34–35; *Agricola* 35.3).

75

Now one could see the great imperial banner flutter in wide waves in the wind. A horned moon of the finest silver flashed its splendor in a cerulean field. The flag was flanked all around, as by a crown, by hundreds of armed troops, the vigor and flower of the powerful army of the Thracian Empire, on whose eastern shores the Euxine lies.

76

This land is separated and divided from Emathia by Mount Olympus: on the side where Aquilus blows and hisses, it is sheltered by the icy peaks of Mount Haemus, and on the south side the insidious waters of the Aegean hit it with their high rushing tide. It is a country that offers to Ceres the heaviest ears of corn and to Bacchus the most fruitful and the sweetest of vines.[44]

77

The horsemen carried beautiful and powerful weapons: a shield on the arm, a lance in hand, and a sword on the side. They wore overcoats with designs of flowers and grass, sun, moon, and stars, all on a white background. The first ones came from the country where the young man from Abydos lost his strength and perished in the dangerous Hellespont, after praying the gods to let him die on the way back, not on the way out.[45]

78

From Elia and Philipopolis[46] three thousand horsemen, robust and fierce, equipped with lances, could be seen now to enter the field; then

---

44. This stanza describes Thrace. To its west is Mount Olympus, on the other side of which is Emathia, a region of Macedonia; to the north, where Aquilus blows, the country is protected by Mount Haemus; its southern coast is bathed by the Mediterranean Sea. Ceres was the Italian goddess of the fertility of the earth, producer of wheat and corn (Ovid, *Fasti* 1.671–704). Bacchus, or Dionysus, is called by Ovid "genialis consitor uvae" (planter of the joy-giving grape) (*Metamorphoses* 4.14).

45. The young man from Abydos is Leander, who was in love with the priestess Hero of Sestus and swam across the Hellespont every night in order to be with her. Leander would have preferred to drown on his way back, after seeing Hero, not before. The story of the two lovers was told by Musaeus Grammaticus (fifth century CE) in *Hero and Leander*, and was translated from the Greek by Sarrocchi. See p. 8 above. The two lovers are also the sender and the receiver of letters 18 and 19 in Ovid's *Heroides*.

46. Elia and Philipopolis are towns in Thrace, now called Edirne and Plovdiv, respectively. For Elia, see 3.30.

six thousand of the best foot soldiers; after these a double number of soldiers, both on foot and on horseback. And now came the best flower of knighthood from the land where the emperor resided. These were the last to sport themselves in pompous show: as they appeared, the sky took on a new light, flashing hues of purple and gold.

79

The famous arms-bearing daughter of the emperor was the leader of them all, captain and soldier in one. She was born to him of Almena, and in strength and courage she took after her fierce mother. Her beautiful white and pink cheeks showed the spring of her years, her glittering eyes were like bright stars, her limbs slender and strong beyond belief.

80

Her white arms were like unblemished snow or like ermine, white was her dress, richly decorated with more pearls than there are snowflakes over the Apennines in a winter storm.[47] High on her helmet shone a great oriental diamond cut in the shape of a rose; inserted in it there was a stone as blue as a daytime cloudless sky.

81

The color of the diamond signified that her heart harbored a virginal purity with perfectly unsullied chastity; its hardness symbolized a resistance to love's lascivious lures. The gem of the color of the sky meant that in this life she cared for nothing but heaven, while the rose indicated that her name was Rosmonda, for she was as pure as a rose.[48]

82

Only her prowess in war came from her parents, for she was like them in nothing else. She was aflame with a desire for magnanimity, kindness, honor, and virtue. As to charming manners and beauty, neither nature nor the courteous heavens have given any woman qualities equal to what could be admired in her mien and behavior.

47. The Apennines are Italian chains of mountains going from the north to the southernmost tip of Calabria. For the comparison of the woman's skin to the whiteness of snow on alpine slopes, cf. canto 1.30.

48. The Italian word *monda* means "pure." In this poem, chastity—or abhorrence of sexuality—is underlined in all women, not in female warriors exclusively. Cf. 1.29, 7.14, 13.16, 18.10, 18.97.

83

Her wisdom and valor that were above her sex and age, her mind that was innocence clothed in loving countenance, were capable of awakening in the barbarous emperor a far greater benevolence than ordinary fatherly affection. But he is moved even more by her great devotion, a strong attachment that makes her expose herself to a hundred dangers, as a daring warrior becomes a grateful daughter who secures the life of him who gave her life.[49]

84

Not long ago, a powerful and well-equipped army challenged the sultan in an all-out war, and he made ready to fight the decisive battle against the enemy. In the fight the Thracian troops were overcome and lay dead in dark and bloody forests. The enemy advanced and conquered, and neither strength nor counsel could protect the emperor from danger any further.

85

Then the magnanimous daughter appeared, erect on her horse, holding in her hand the sword that never struck in vain. Soon she realized that access to the imperial palace was wide open. Quickly she gathered the camels, tied them together with several chains, and creating a defensive wall against the enemy, stopped their advancing fury.

86

Sometimes, a river overflows its usual banks because of excessive rain or melting snow, and the neighbors, full of fear, hasten to stem the flood with barriers of earth.[50] In the same way Rosmonda was able to hold back the enemy until the golden rays of the sun descended into the ocean waves, and the falling night made it impossible to see with certainty what anyone was doing.

87

She made the victor fall back and quickly rallied her men who had disbanded all over, for she was eager to save as much as possible of at least the

49. Rosmonda's filial love is evocative of the story of Hypsipyle, who saved her father, Thoas, king of Lemnos, when the other women killed all the men on the island. See Ovid, *Metamorphoses* 13.399–400; Nonnos, *Dionysiaca* 30.205.

50. The image of the river overflowing its banks, used in a military context, occurs again, but with different details, in cantos 5.40 and 13.73. It had models in the poems of Boiardo, Ariosto, and Tasso. See *Orlando Innamorato* 1.10.53; *Orlando Furioso* 39.14 and 40.31; *Jerusalem Delivered* 9.22.3–5. They all go back to the river similes of *Iliad* 5.86–92 and *Aeneid* 2.305–7 and 2.496–99.

core of the defeated army. With these men she surrounded the emperor and by an artful maneuver drew him safe and sound out of the perilous situation. At this point of the military review, as the day was almost over, the sultan wished to return to his city.

88

A chosen body of Janissaries[51] on foot—these never abandon the emperor by either night or day—stood forming a circle around him, for now he had mounted his horse. Immortal fame of their exploits resounds as far as the remotest waves of the sea can reach. Each one of them wore a simple coat of mail over his chest, carried a scimitar on his side, and a bow in his hand.

89

As an upright pine or a fully branched cypress tree stands out among smaller plants,[52] so stout-limbed Ferratte stood out among the Janissaries: if he believed in any god, he believed in himself. No doubt he was adept at brandishing his sword, but neither could anyone shoot a feathered dart with more assurance than he. In Gaza he certainly gave an indisputable proof of it, with a feat that was as unusual as it was overwhelming.

90

Gaza is the capital city of Lycia,[53] and the emperor got it into his head to conquer it. "As long as Ishmael is alive, all my efforts will be useless," he said one day when Ferratte could hear it. The latter then took an arrow and on it he wrote: "Ferratte sends you this, Ishmael, O mortal creature." His boast turned out to be truthful, for the arrow hit Ishmael on the back of the neck and passing through his eyes came out in the front.

---

51. The Janissaries were an Ottoman elite corps of foot soldiers, which recruited members among Muslim and Christian hostages and war prisoners converted to Islam. Machiavelli has the Janissaries and the Spahis in mind when he writes that, for his security and the defense of his kingdom, the sultan is always surrounded by 12,000 foot soldiers and 15,000 cavalrymen (*The Prince* 19). In *The Reason of State*, Botero mentions the Janissaries for their loyalty and daring (6.1), as former slaves now faithful to the Turkish cause (8.17), for the great license allowed them on account of their fierceness and devotion (9.14), and in comparison with European soldiers (10.8). Cf. below, canto 3.99n, and canto 5.13.

52. Alexander is likened to a tree in canto 2.19. For Ferratte's contemptuous character, see 5.3.

53. Opinions differ about the location of the ancient town of Gaza, one of the five cities of the Philistines. However, it cannot have been in Lycia, as Sarrocchi says, for Lycia was a region of Asia Minor. Another town by the name of Gaza was in the Persian province of Sogdiana (Lucan, *Civil War* 3.216).

91

The Ottoman emperor was now in possession of that land, because when the local lord died the people turned it over to him. The sultan remunerated Ferratte very handsomely and raised him to the high honor of Agah.[54] Ferratte, a man of proud heart and unshakable loyalties, was once a close friend of our hero, but because of his enduring devotion to his great sire he turned his loving comradery into strong hate.

92

In addition to him there were Xaersis; Radiar, the conqueror of the so-called Lost Islands;[55] Ramassar, famous above all others for setting ambushes and astute snares; Assan; Jafier; Arigazel; Musar, who subdued Syria and Lycia; and you too, fierce Agrismeta, whose fame went as far as the remotest land reached by the sun in its journey.

93

From two black dazzling eyes, two tresses of pure shining gold and a very white hand, Love once set Agrismeta's heart ablaze with more than one burning flame. But he was not the only one smoldering in this happy fire— for Love never allows one to love serenely—and he had many rivals, who were renowned men and made his discomfort greater than his pleasure.

94

Finally, to put an end to his wretchedness, he decided to fight a proper duel with the suitor most pleasing to her and thus gain the reward of victory and the woman or lose his life for her. Had she been guarded by the ferocious Erymanthian boar or by the Lernean Hydra,[56] the daring lover would have gone out alone to win her.

95

So they came to single combat and decided to fight in the presence of their noble prey, so that when strength failed them, they would get it back by

54. Agah was the title given to ministers and governors of the Ottoman Empire.

55. The Lost Islands, usually identified with Iceland, are mentioned in *Orlando Furioso* 32.51–52, 78.

56. The Hydra was a fabulous beast thought to live in the swampy valley of Lerna, in Argolis, Greece. Its nine heads grew back every time they were cut off. The Erymanthian boar roamed on the slopes of Mount Erymanthus in Arcadia. Both animals were slain by Hercules. See Ovid, *Metamorphoses* 9.192. It is interesting to note that Sarrocchi does not confuse the Erymanthian boar, the Hydra of Lerna, and the Nemean lion (1.56). In 1614, a lengthy debate broke out among literati, first in Turin, where Giambattista Marino resided, and then in the rest

looking at the beautiful face of their beloved. Stung by bitter anger and deep regret, the other suitors stood by and looked on to see what the outcome would be, having made a pact to snatch the beautiful woman away from the victor then and there.

96

Agrismeta won, and at that moment one of the suitors was quick to take the woman and run away with her. Agrismeta ran after, overtook him, and with a powerful blow sliced his head in two parts; and he did it with such consideration and skill as to leave the dress of the woman untouched. Then he tucked her under his left arm and turned against the others with undiminished wrath.

97

In that difficult situation, he had to engage in a double type of fencing, one that can be learned only in the schools of Love. He feared not so much for himself as for his darling, on whom his life most dearly depended. Without the protection of a shield before him, he brandished his sword more to defend her than himself; and he was so quick in hitting his adversary that he defended two and wounded many at the same time.

98

He wounded some in the head, some in the chest, others lay dead or dying. So the suitors ran away, abandoning their darling there, for the flame of love did not prove to be as mighty as the sword. This was not his only feat: once, in the presence of the emperor, wearing neither shield nor helmet, Agrismeta climbed the impregnable walls of Nicaea, which its sovereign had encircled with a double moat.

99

Behind the Janissaries now came a second contingent of bodyguards, the Spahis.[57] They were on horseback; none of them had a scimitar, but they were strong of hand and intrepid of heart. Instead of bows, they handled

---

of Italy because, in the sonnet "Obelischi pomposi all'ossa alzaro" (Grandiose obelisks were raised to the bones), Marino had confused the Nemean lion with the hydra of Lerna. See Mario Menghini, *La vita e le opere di Giambattista Marino* (Rome: A. Manzoni, 1888), 118–20.

57. The Spahis (or Sipâhîs) were a mounted army corps of the Ottoman Empire, whose members were drawn only from the Muslim population. They were fierce rivals of the Janissaries. Cf. above, canto 3.88n, and canto 5.13.

huge spears made of oak, and no shield could resist their heavy impact. Instead of short curved daggers, they carried long straight swords. Bearers of death these weapons were, whatever their points touched.

100

The men wore an overcoat made of brown silk, with a beautiful design of many figures. Into the brown were intermingled strands of a flaming purple that flashed out of the darker color and struck terror into the hearts of the onlooker. As at times, in a sky streaked with bloody hues, the incipient darkness of some frightful clouds threateningly forecasts a severe tempest, so their overcoats forecast a tearful destiny and death.

101

Their captain was the courageous and fierce Armen, now on foot but a unique warrior on horseback. Fame has it that he once rode a horse so fast that no footprints were left on the ground;[58] that with his naked hand he pulled off Ghimon's helmet while pressed on all sides by the enemy. Ghimon was a much-feared Persian warrior who later came to the aid of the Thracian emperor as an ally.

102

There were Ortorico, Stilicon, Tridarte, Xantippe, Ramagass, Ali, Renato, and Brandoarte, the great thrower of lances, and Archelor, never surpassed in handling the sword; and many more men famous on the field of Mars, whose names the voracious passage of time has obscured. Happy is the man whom the swan of fame has lifted and borne on its sublime flight above the sun!

103

As soon as the great Thracian was back in his royal palace, he summoned Rosmonda and with spontaneous fatherly love placed his scepter in her hands so that she might govern his people with authority. "You," he said, "upon whom a supreme intellect has bestowed intelligence, wisdom, and courage, will reign and will make your deeds worthy of fame in my name, as you would in your own."

58. In *Aeneid* 7.808–9, it is Camilla, the Volscian woman warrior, who "intactae segetis per summa volaret gramina, nec teneras cursu laesisset aristas" (could fly over uncut ears of corn, leaving in her flight the tender beards untouched). In *Orlando Innamorato* 1.1.69.6–8 and 1.14.4.1–4, the ability to gallop so swiftly as not to touch the ground is attributed to two beloved horses, Baiardo and Rabano

104

The gentle warrior took the imperial scepter with a respectful gesture and said: "I must say that you honor me highly, as is appropriate only to me, because I am your daughter. Still I would prefer that this hand be the avenger of your wrath, because serving in the army, in the midst of battle and death, pleases me more than reigning over lands."

105

Then she fell silent. He embraced her and ordered her to have all the troops ready as soon as the new day began to dawn, for there should be no delay in departure. With great vigilance, that very evening she arranged everything she thought ought to be ready for the appointed hour. Then they all withdrew to their usual bedchambers, for the light of day had been hidden for many hours already.

CANTO 4

The Turkish army sets up camp in the valley of Presa, not far from Croia. In the citadel, those of Alexander's captains who are of the Islamic faith convert to Christianity and make ready to fight at his side.

CANTO 5

The captain of the Janissaries, Ferratte, attempts to climb the steep slope leading up to the walls of Croia, but he and his men are slain by Alexander and his soldiers, who then put on the armor of the Janissaries they have just killed, enter the Turkish camp, and begin to slaughter the sleeping soldiers.

1

When the sun, midway between east and west, began to descend the afternoon sky, casting on earth its most ardent rays, and there was no moisture left in the air, when in the foliage the cicada croaked the loudest, laboring heavily in its chest, at that time the king—since much daylight remained—looked down toward the Turkish camp to see what the enemy was planning and hoping to achieve.

2

And right when the sun started to set, he saw that Ferratte—he recognized his imposing figure, for they had fought together many a war—and his Janissaries were attempting to climb the mountain before the rest of the army. Their movements looked surreptitious: he saw him lie in wait with a chosen few of his men, as if they were about to carry out alone some remarkable exploit.

3

By temperament, Ferratte was reckless of destiny and chance, and he judged it a worthless merit to rein in his recklessness with reason and common sense.[1] He did not consider, or did not care, or was not afraid that the king

---

1. The enemy's violent rush and lack of reason are often stressed in contrast to Alexander and his men's reasonableness and good judgment. Cf. canto 9.8. Ferratte, like Agrismeta in later

might keep men on guard to see what was happening down below, or perhaps he hoped the night would hide his movements.

4

As the valley was at some distance from the upward slope, he did not wait for the sun to go down and disappear into the sea before beginning to climb the steep mountain. Follow what may, he decided to proceed, regardless of whether he was heard or seen, whether he would find a path or would have to make one, and he put all his trust in his sword.

5

The path was so narrow that only one person at a time could walk on it: now it seemed to climb, now to descend, and it was crammed with bushes and rocks. At a certain point, the path led precipitously into a ravine that looked very propitious for an ambush, for it sank so deep that no one waiting at the bottom could be either seen or heard by those walking down into it.[2]

6

From his height Alexander saw these men start on the hard climb and easily guessed that they would attempt to enter the city by some out-of-the-way gate. He thought for a while, then felt certain that down below he would be able kill each one of them. So as soon as it began to grow dark, he exited the town stealthily with some of his chosen men.

7

He gathered around him Dragutte, Arisba, Arioden, and Sinan, men for whom Turkish was the native language, who had followed him out of loyalty and conviction, as many others of the Islamic faith had done. He ordered them to go fully armed to different positions down the escarpment. Sinan went out first and overtook Ferratte: as soon as he saw him, he struck and killed him immediately.

---

cantos, displays the character traits of Turnus and Mezentius in *Aeneid*, of Rodomonte in *Orlando Innamorato* and *Orlando Furioso*, and of Argantes in *Jerusalem Delivered*. Rashness, arrogance, and contemptuousness toward men and gods became mandatory in epic poetry for the depiction of the enemy. Armedonte and Armallo are so described in the less-known poems *Il fidamante*, by Curzio Gonzaga (1582), and *La Croce racquistata*, by Francesco Bracciolini (1605).

2. This ravine is similar to one described in *Aeneid* 11.526–27, where, not far from the Trojan camp, Turnus intends to hide, waiting to ambush Aeneas.

8

The deadly blow caught him unaware on the nape of the neck, a blow so powerful that he crashed to the ground, although he was such a strong and formidable man. A bull staggers about and then collapses in the same way when the nerve center between the horns is hit.[3] Sinan waited for the other men to come down and threw them all dead to the ground.

9

He snuffed the life out of all of them, one by one. The air was already dark around him, and the band of loyal men gathered together, for now the path was free of all Turkish soldiers. Then the king picked up Ferratte's spoils— the surcoat, the cuirass, the shield, and the crested helmet—and put them on. And indeed, being of the same size as Ferratte, with his armor on, he looked quite like him.

10

His men too started putting on the dead men's armor, which was distinct in color and golden ornaments. Each one of them searched for his own size among the many hauberks and surcoats lying around. And because they were more numerous than the dead, our hero saw to it that the best among them got something distinctive to wear, while the men of no outstanding valor were left with outfits as unremarkable as their names.

11

With as quick a step as was allowed them by the darkness and the ruggedness of the path, they walked up out of the ravine and then descended toward the encampment. The Turkish guard saw them, but they continued to approach without hesitation. The guard called out the names of a few or saluted them in some other way, for he believed them to be friends of his. In order not to give themselves away by the sound of their voices, they lifted their hands in response, and passed on[4]

---

3. The image of a bull felled by a stroke on the neck behind the horns, on a ganglion where the sinews come together, has precedents in *Iliad* 17.520–22 and *Aeneid* 5.477–81. Two vivid similes with bulls are also in *Jerusalem Delivered* 3.32.1–4 and 7.55. Numerous are the comparisons of warriors with animals in this poem: see stanzas 43, 47, 51 in this canto, and cantos 1.39, 6.84, 7.44, 9.55, 9.57, 9.66, 10.62, 13.53, and 13.69.

4. About run-on stanzas, see p. 59 above.

12

as if they were in a hurry on some important task, so no one suspected any deception.[5] The men separated and then, hiding in different spots, waited for the moment to attack the Turks. When the food in their warm bodies made the Turkish soldiers heavy, and sleep began to weaken their senses, the king's men rapidly and in unison came out into the open and, wielding their swords, moved toward the crowded tents of the Spahis.[6]

13

Janissaries and Spahis had been vying with each other in bravery for a long time. Knowing this, the king had the idea of taking on the Agah's appearance and making the enemy fall into a trap.[7] Unburdened by all thoughts and fears, the Turks, so superior in number to the Christians, lay down in separate groups here and there and fell deep into sleep, with neither fear nor thoughts, with no weapons, guards, sense of time, order, or warning.

14

The valorous king went ahead of the others and in the darkness deprived many of them of daylight. Some soldiers lay quite dead; others were left dying in rough and hard beds or on soft and decorated couches. It was impossible to distinguish the foot soldiers from the knights. By now, the king had a circle of corpses around him: the pagans[8] were dying deep in sleep; they gasped and moaned in low, broken sounds.

15

The good Sinan cut off Drusus's head, then struck Martasin in the throat: a tepid spring of ill-digested wine more than of blood poured out onto the

5. The Albanian soldiers' disguise is an adaptation of the deceptive exploit of the Trojans, Aeneas among them, who enter the fray after putting on the armor of slain Greeks: *Aeneid* 2.386–430.

6. Scanderbeg was known for his sudden forays against the Turkish army. His tactics are described by Hodgkinson, *Skanderbeg*, 110–13, 201. There were, however, literary precedents for Sarrocchi's episode. In *Jerusalem Delivered* 9.22–24, a similar exploit is carried out by Solyman, who mounts a night attack on the Christian encampment. Tasso asserts the devilish nature of this attack by representing the enemy as being led on by Alecto, a pagan Fury. Other epic characters enter the enemy camp at night and wreak havoc among the sleeping soldiers: Euryalus and Nisus in canto 9.176–449 of *Aeneid*, and Cloridano and Medoro in canto 18 of *Orlando Furioso*. Cf. stanza 37n below.

7. The rivalry between Spahis and Janissaries will soon erupt into a bloody fight, when the Albanians in disguise deceive the Spahis into believing that they are being attacked by their rivals. Cf. above, canto 3.99n, and below, canto 5.33, 36, 48–49.

8. "Pagans" and "Saracens" stand for "Muslims" in this poem, as in all other Italian epic poetry.

ground, for that evening he had transgressed that profane law which the pagans regard as divine.[9] The others too in their turn killed many men, as they moved swiftly from tent to tent.

16

They reached the bed of Varadin, the man who carried the main Turkish flag. Beside him lay a woman of shining beauty, as shining as the sun when it comes up accompanied by golden Dawn. Her hand was resting on her naked white breasts, which were splendid treasures of nature and love, her face gracefully inclining toward them, a face so handsome as to take the boast of beauty away from Spring herself.

17

The other parts of her body, which were slender and relaxed, were covered: she breathed placidly in her sleep, and although her exquisite eyes were closed, a celestial charm seemed to emanate from them. At times it is possible to admire in the same way the shining stars behind a candid cloud, because their splendor comes through the clear density, so bright are they.

18

She was Varadin's wife and her name was Armilla. Ah! where cruel Love had taken her! In her frail hand she had been carrying her lord's spear, far too heavy for her, and had been looking after his horse. Not caring for her golden hair, she cut it: still, her beauty shone no less in her manly attire, for love burned with no less strength in her woman's heart than it ever has in any man's.[10]

19

She derived as much joy from having the object of her love before her eyes in war as she always did in peace, for Mars did not frighten her tender heart,

9. The image of wine spilling out of the body of a slaughtered soldier together with his blood derives from two famous descriptions: Virgil's "cum sanguine mixta vina refert moriens" (in dying, he spits back the wine together with the blood) (*Aeneid* 9.349–50), and Ariosto's "Troncogli il capo il Saracino audace: esce col sangue il vin per uno spillo, di che n'ha in corpo più d'una bigoncia" (the dauntless Saracin cut off his head: from the same spout as the blood spurted the wine, for more than a bucket there was in his body) (*Orlando Furioso* 18.176.6).

10. There are other loyal couples in epic narratives who go to war together and die together. In *Orlando Furioso* (18.179), Medoro kills Labretto and his woman, who are asleep in each other's arms. In *Jerusalem Delivered* (20.93–94), Gildippe and Odoardo are slain one after the other on the battlefield. Lovers who die together were the object of romantic reflection and

even when covered by a hard, blood-stained steel. Hypsicratia once followed her barbarian spouse with the same loyalty and persistence, but with much greater luck than Armilla, for she was slain by her lover's hand.[11]

20

Ah! In those dark and, for her, sad nights, when she held the body of her beloved tight to her breast—the Turkish army had gathered in Elia and was about to leave—how much grace Love lavished on her cheeks, cheeks daubed with pallor and dampened with tears, and how pitiably appealing did Love make her sweet entreaties, so that her consort did not oppose her wish to follow him!

21

Mixing words, sighs, and cries with nectar-sweet kisses and tight embraces, she said: "Where are you going to hide yourself, my lively sun, and thus eclipse my eyes into perpetual darkness? For surely the daylight will be taken from me and my soul will quickly cross over the portal of life if Love allows my soul, which is in you, to go so far away from its natural place![12]

22

"The heavens meant to create me for you alone when they allowed me to be born into the vital air, and soon thereafter Love set my heart aflame with

considered fortunate, as Boccaccio's storyteller declares at the close of the story of Simona and Pasquino, who die within the space of a single day. See *Decameron* 4.7.19. The statement closing this stanza that women can love as much as men is a rebuttal to the old commonplace, traceable to Aristotelian and Galenic physiological theories, according to which women are not capable of loving because of the coldness of their body humors. See Ian Maclean, *The Renaissance Notion of Woman: A Study in the Fortunes of Scholasticism and Medical Science in European Intellectual Life* (Cambridge: Cambridge University Press, 1980, 29–46. The notion of "women's inaptitude for love" is ridiculed by Tullia d'Aragona in her *Dialogue on the Infinity of Love* (ed. and trans. Rinaldina Russell and Bruce Merry, introd. and notes Rinaldina Russell [Chicago: University of Chicago Press, 1997], 69) and is traced back by her to Petrarch's lines "Ond'io so ben ch'un amoroso stato / in cor di donna picciol tempo dura" (I know well that a condition of love lasts but a short time in a woman's heart) (*Canzoniere* 183.13–14).

11. Hypsicratia was the concubine of Mithridates VI, king of Pontus (120–63 BCE). Attired like a man and mounted like a horseman, she followed him in his flight from Pompey, until the king gave her and all his friends a deadly poison, so they would not fall into Roman hands. See Plutarch, "Pompey" 32.7–9; Valerius Maximus, *Memorable Doings and Sayings* 4.6 absol. 2. Hypsicratia and Mithridates are listed as loyal lovers in Petrarch's "Triumphus cupidinis" 3.28–30. See also Giovanni Boccaccio's *Concerning Famous Women*, chap. 6.

12. That the lover's soul goes to live with that of the beloved is a common topos in the phenomenology of love that appears in medieval and Renaissance poetry. See below, canto 7.18.

a consuming passion. Then a noble, equally reciprocated love took possession of me and made me yours: I must, therefore, live with you and die with
you. May Lachesis put out one single thread, so that her pitiless sister will
cut it for both of us.[13]

23

"And you, could you stay separated from your Armilla, who has lived with
you and with you wants to die? These tresses and eyes, this very face and
mouth that once seemed to give you joy and pleasure, conquer your heart
and captivate your soul, have they now perhaps become annoying to you?
Ah! into what doubts these fears of mine are throwing me! how can anyone
be so lacking in trust?

24

"I know that you do not have the power to object to the tyrant's orders and
to his threats. I ask you only to let me come with you in the army, my noble
treasure. You could thus get help from me at any time if I follow close on
your steps; at the very least, my voice will warn you of all impending threats
that might sneak up from behind you."[14]

25

These warm sighs, these honeyed prayers, such kisses, and such agreeable,
though sad, complaints, how could they in the end fail to bend her loving
spouse to her requests? What requests can ever be denied when uttered by
the lips of one's beloved? Ah! her youth is of no avail to her in saving her
life now; neither is her loyalty or her charming looks.

26

Such unusual beauty as hers could certainly make the coldest heart sigh and
fall in love, or at least it could awaken pity in a human soul, but the heartless Sinan had no scruples whatever; or perhaps it was destiny, not cruelty,
if in slaying he did not care whom he slew. He sliced her breasts and her
hand in half: both stood trembling and the arm that had been chopped off
shook.

13. Lachesis is one of three sisters, the Parcae, Roman deities personifying human destiny.
Clotho is the one who spins the thread of life; Lachesis measures the length of the thread,
deciding how long each person is to live; and Atropos breaks it, thus ending life. Ovid,
Metamorphoses 8.452.
14. Armilla's entreaties to Varadin echo those of Giulia to Lelio in Boccaccio's *Filocolo* 1.5 and
those of Doralice to Mandricardo in Ariosto's *Orlando Furioso* 30.32–37.

27

Under the tremor the bed rattled and the woman's blood began to flow in two streams, touching and dampening Varadin, who, shaken and wet, opened his eyes to the light of the fire. Sinan struck again but could not reach him, for Varadin jumped out of bed, got hold of his sword and shield which were near him, and that was sufficient for the courageous man, naked as he was.

28

The situation, which suddenly became dangerous, had him somewhat confused, but his natural valor gave him strength. He saw his beloved cut through and dead, and two opposite feelings, love and hate, took hold of him. Excruciating tears ran down his face, but he did not abate the powerful force of hatred; on the contrary, he added it to the pain, for grief waits for nothing but revenge.

29

As wrath and grief goaded him on, what ferocious animal, what viper did he not resemble? Perhaps he was like an eagle who, returning to her nest after searching for food for her little ones, sees—ah, sorrowful spectacle!— that a hawk has bloodied its claws in them. She flies after the predator in revenge, stung by grief, pain, and fury.

30

Varadin threw himself so quickly against Sinan that it was impossible to see whether he had reached him first or had first hit him on the head. The sword cut him down between tooth and tooth, splitting his throat in half.[15] But Varadin did not let go of his maddening fury, for Sinan's pain seemed slight compared with his own. It did not seem to comfort him, for he wished to inflict in revenge a far more grievous death.

31

Meanwhile the fierce king advanced further into the camp and pierced Argir through. By sheer chance, the King plunged his dagger into the man's

---

15. The original model of this blow on the head is found in *Aeneid* 9.749–52: "Sublatum alte consurgit in ensem et mediam ferro gemina inter tempora frontem dividit" (he raised his sword high in the air, then brought it down and cut the man's forehead between the temples). In turn Varadin will be killed soon, cut in half by Alexander. See stanza 34. In actual fact, Scanderbeg was a man of exceptional strength and was thought, in Botero's words, to have killed two thousand Turks by his own hand. *The Reason of State* 10.4.

side right where that part of the body closed on the lungs—for the air is taken in alternating breaths so as to temper the excessive heat of the heart—and withdrew the dagger before the lungs began to open again: this way the pagan went on to live many more years.

32

The king heard Varadin call for help and believed him to be attacked by his rivals. He ran there and saw his loyal friend lying in his own and in the other soldier's blood. What made him realize that it was his friend was the purloined armor, for his face was unrecognizable, and the cruel barbarian stood over him, not yet satisfied to have maimed and slain him.

33

Varadin's anger grew when he saw the Agah's crested helmet, for he believed he was looking for sure at King Ferratte; so he quickly moved to thrust a powerful blow in his direction. Cuirass and shield, however, were made of a thick, double layer of leather and steel, and remained intact under the blow. At the same time, the king struck him on the left flank with a pointed thrust and the sword came out on the opposite side.

34

He threw Varadin and his shield to the ground, both cut in half. This is not surprising, for it was Alexander's custom to slice in half warrior and armor with a single, powerful blow. Now he had surpassed himself, for anger and grief were added to his native strength. Meanwhile, all the soldiers were awakened by the great noise and ran fully armed shouting "To arms! To arms!"

35

Other Spahis, who were sleeping in nearby tents, came running. There was a light where Varadin lay dead, for he delighted in keeping a fire going. From this fire several others were lit in several other places where Alexander's men were moving, so everyone could recognize the face and the armor of the enemy and of the dead.

36

The surcoat worn by the false Agah led others to the same error Varadin had made. Some picked up their spears, some their swords, others their bows, and soon they were ready to strike. Right away they barred the way of the Christians so that the latter were quickly surrounded. A deadly arrow caught Romer in the ankle; he was the first to hurry out of the circle.

37

Silvan collapsed to the ground pierced through the heart; next to him lay
Tigrin struck in the throat: in vain his sapient father had drawn from the stars
the chart of his cruel destiny.[16] Altamor inadvertently dropped his sword,
and while he was bending over to retrieve it, an arrow shot by his dear friend
Arsace went through his kidney and came out of his belly button.

38

The invincible king then jumped into the midst of the fight and gathered
around him the band of his loyal men. Alcan was the one who came up to
confront him and was caught right on the left side of his face by a right-
handed thrust. Half his skull fell to the ground so violently that the impact
hit Redan in the middle of the head and threw off his helmet; and while Sala
looked astonished at this, the king cut his head in half between the brows
with a single blow.

39

No one could keep up with the king now, neither Arioden, nor Arisba, nor
Dragutte. He alone was able to make the infidel soldiers fall back: they
opened the way before him and turned on their heels. Only you, Armen,
dared oppose the great hero face to face, the hero who brought your soldiers to inescapable death, who towered above the others like a tall mountain,[17] and only you tried your best to hit him right in the face.

40

Just like a mountain, whose slopes a youth tries to hit by throwing stones
with his sling, the king withstood Armen's powerful blow, and all other
lances, all swords and arrows. Just as the confluence of many brooks pro-
duces the waters of a river,[18] many men now pushed together into a thick
mass before him, and the king was unable to give full vent to his consuming fury.

16. The figure of the soothsayer whose prophetic powers fail is taken from the episode of
Cloridano and Medoro in *Orlando Furioso* 18.174, where the augur Alfeo is surprised in bed by
the enemy and quickly slain. Alfeo's end was in turn inspired by that of Virgil's haughty
Rhamnes, whose powers of prophecy also failed, leaving him to die by Euryalus's sword while
deep asleep in the Latin camp. *Aeneid* 9.324–27.

17. By all accounts, Scanderbeg was a very tall man. Epic grandeur, however, required the
hero to tower over all others on the battlefield. See cantos 2.50, 5.46, 6.54, 7.55, and 14.68.
Cf. *Aeneid* 7.783–84, 10.446; Lucan, *Civil War* 7.342; Petrarch, *Africa* 7.999.

18. Other river similes are at 3.86 and 13.73.

41

When he quickly turned to strike, there was neither helmet nor headgear that could remain in place. His agile foot was not stopped, nor was his powerful hand caught by either lance, or arrow, or spear. He penetrated into the thickest of the opposing throng, cutting off one soldier's arm, another's head, while no blow could harm him or fall on target. In the end, among a thousand spears and swords, he came face to face with Armen.

42

What happened was that he hit him on the neck with such fury as to send his helmeted head far off on the ground. Alì looked at the blood gushing out and spilling over, like a liquid pouring out of a shattered vase. The blood squirted him in the eye, right where the visor protects one's vision. He tried to clear up his sight, but then the king darkened it forever.

43

The king wreaked havoc among the enemy, as a bird of prey does among smaller birds and a Caspian lion among lambs.[19] He was like a scourge of heaven that draws reason from just anger, when God's justice punishes the people rebellious to him and his clemency does not forgive. Men fell on top of other men, weighing on one another. While one expired, another gasped, others shouted and moaned.

44

He could see his own armor covered by the blood of his enemy, not his own, and thus made horribly gruesome. Their savage belief seemed to have transmuted into the horror and pain now wrought by the king's hand. But the band of Christians was already all safely out of the danger they were in, for with his valor Alexander had opened a way that gave them an easy escape.

45

The Christians withdrew, thinking they were being followed by their king, while he, still inflamed by the desire to pursue Armen, believed he had several of his soldiers at his side. So, driven by an excess of daring, the king was surrounded and pressed upon by a thousand armed men, and the throng around him increased so that it would take a miracle for him to come out alive in the end.

19. For other comparisons with lions and their precedents, see 1.39.

46

With his big and brawny person the king exceeded all human sizes;[20] he stood so tall above the others that he easily became the aim and target of all eyes and blows, to the point that by now his strength no longer sufficed and all attempts to escape were vain: just as when one head of the Hydra is cut off and many others grow in its place.

47

But although he was as bold and furious as a wild boar surrounded by hunters at a royal hunt—the more the hunters close in, striking the animal with pointed arrows and spears, the more the boar grinds its teeth, rubbing one side against a tree and inflicting deadly wounds on those it manages to reach—still, as the fight continued and became even fiercer, at length the king's strength began to fail.[21]

48

He was fast approaching collapse, so feebly could he now defend himself and so slowly could he strike. But suddenly a rescue party reached him, for a fresh group of armed Janissaries arrived: they were stirred by anger and grief—so persuasive was the king's false appearance—and, upon catching sight of their captain, turned their weapons against their friends and brought help to their enemy.

49

Their help was great, for they were all eminent warriors, famous for strength and courage. New rivulets of blood ran to the ground, brought on by anger, emulation, debt, and honor. As throngs of men died all around, a path was opened for the king's escape: realizing their error, he interpreted that turn of events as a true sign of heavenly aid.

50

As the Spahìs, who were suddenly assailed from behind when they least expected it, turned front to back, and the infighting went on ever more furiously, the king came out of the encirclement but remained still on guard, then withdrew slowly, and as everyone was intent on inflicting

20. See Scanderbeg's imposing stature in stanza 39n of this canto, and in cantos 2.50, 6.54, 7.55 and 14.68.

21. This is a most felicitous elaboration of the wild boar fighting with his attackers in a simile of *Aeneid* 10.707–13 and of *Africa* 7.1245–50. Another boar simile is found in this poem at canto 9.57.

blows and defending himself, he took off the Agah's armor and dropped it to the ground.

51

As a spirited beast comes out of its den compelled by hunger and, with teeth and claws, plays havoc among the animals of the vast forest, and then, sated and observed by no one, hides among the trees, seemingly in fear of being attacked, so the king, when no one was paying attention, made his escape on the open plain.

52

Silently he hurried his long steps, light and free of his deceptive armor. His trusted sword was sufficient defense against all dangerous assaults of beast and man. Steep inclines and precipitous rocks made his way hazardous; now a deep recession, now a swamp was in the way; at other times he had to slash down obstructing branches.

53

He knew the remotest and darkest passes, the most hidden caverns, the most contorted paths.[22] Through these he climbed up to steep and dense forests where the terrain offered greatest advantage and safety. From there, by the best concealed way he could find, he turned his step toward Mount Tumenishti.[23] So long, impracticable, and arduous was his climb that, midway up, he had to rest and hide.

54

Mount Tumenishti looks over the same valley from which the mountain of Croia rises to the sky. The base of one mountain is next to the other, with a narrow space in between. Rocky slopes and deep gorges make for difficult travel up this steep terrain. The king, however, judged it to be his best escape route and stepped up toward it, while the men, fighting below in the dark, could not see him.

22. Scanderbeg's knowledge of the Albanian terrain was considered a decisive factor in his fortunate campaigns. A necessity for all good captains, write both Machiavelli (*The Prince* 14) and Scipione Ammirato (*Discorsi* 13.6–7), is to know their territory and to be able to defend it.

23. This is perhaps the mountain in the northwest of the fortress town, once called Tushemishti, now Mount Scanderbeg, from which in 1450 the Albanian leader launched his sudden attack on the Turkish troops besieging Kruja. He withdrew there again in 1457. See Gegaj, *L'Albanie et l'invasion turque*, 76–77, 117; Hodgkinson, *Skanderbeg*, 99. Alexander's stratagem in the poem has a literary precedent in Virgil's *Aeneid* 11.526–31, where Turnus is briefly described as hiding in ambush on a hill near the Trojan camp. Cf. above, stanza 5.

55

He fed himself with food he could gather in the wild. There was no water to quench his thirst but what fell from the sky and collected in dirty pools on the ground. Now the sun rose and shone splendidly, coloring the sky with a fine pinkish hue. Still there was no reprieve in the fierce fighting below; on the contrary, a new cause was added to its ill-conceived beginning.

56

And that was because, as soon as the morning light was out, the famous armor was found that the king very cunningly had thrown down while making his perilous escape, and the discovery angered them even further, inflaming their hearts to revenge. Ferratte's friends arrived from one side and the other, the fight started up again relentless and ferocious, and many were those who raised their dying voices to the heavens.

57

"Ah, friends! An impious hand, a murderous one has slain Ferratte! Here he lies in pieces on the ground! Ferratte, the great Ferratte, who alone with his great valor could be our worthy leader! After committing such a hideous crime, the infamous men dare to go on enjoying the sun and the sky in our very sight, and after slaying our great chief, they will perhaps have the boldness to kill even us!

58

"Who will be our leader now? Who will defend us now from these vile enemies? Only by plunging our swords into their veins can we safeguard our lives!"[24] The sky was beginning to turn gold and the sun was already shining over the world when—the fight still going on—a new report was brought to the tyrant, warning him about the damage done to his barbaric camp.

59

When the fight had first broken out, more than one messenger had given the emperor the news, but private considerations made him decide that it was unbecoming the imperial majesty to go out to the riot himself. So he

24. Soldiers lamenting the demise of their leaders and swearing vengeance are de rigueur in epic literature. The first such representation is in *Iliad* 18.315–42, where Achilles laments the slaying of his friend Patroclos, and again in *Iliad* 24.713–81, where the death of Hector is mourned by the population of Troy. As is the case with the inhabitants of Croia, those left without a leader are resolute in their determination to go on fighting. See also stanzas 96–98 and 100–105 below.

ordered the very flower of his Janissaries, the ones who were with him, to go instead, but they, deceived by the armor, added to the virulence of the fight that was going on in the night.

60

Now Murad arose from his luxurious bed and stepped out gravely toward the great uproar: the barbarous glow, the severe majesty of his countenance, and his bearded face threw out rays of anger and disdain. All the men were seized by a reverent fear; they held back their hands and withdrew, while the sultan, with menacing eyes and words, inquired after the reason of such great turmoil.

61

Dismayed and totally unaware, the men explained the senseless fight, alternating angry outbursts and reasonable excuses. They condoned the offenses they had given and exaggerated those they had received, for both sides believed they were betrayed. What pained the proud emperor most was to hear of Ferratte's death, and because the man had been the cause of the uproar, he wanted him to pay for it, although he was dead.

62

Several soldiers came across the famous armor and believed they had found Ferratte's great limbs: they saw his surcoat, which they could hardly recognize, so splattered was it with dark red blood; they picked up pieces of his armor, which were scattered in various places, but they were all empty. They were astonished and pained by the strange case; still they continued looking for his trunk, head, foot, or hand, but in vain.

63

Ferratte's limbs, even when sliced into pieces, would be easily recognized, so much did they exceed in size those of any other man. While they looked, scrutinized, turned around, and stared, they found several corpses and discovered that several were of men of the Christian faith. Some faces seemed familiar; they would swear they had seen them somewhere, although they could not remember where.

64

This caused them to suspect, fear, and consider in turn the when and where. In order to make out more clearly the dead men's features, they washed out the blood and dirty dust. Once the memory came back to them, they recognized who those dead men were. Not only did they think they recognized them, they even remembered their names and their countries of origin.

65

Among the dead they found many of those who had followed in the steps of our great hero when he was betrayed by the greedy attendant, and who had joined him against Baizet. So some men went straightaway to the fierce tyrant to tell him what must have happened, while the valiant company that had been deprived of their Agah went to look for him, determined to find him, dead or alive.

66

Then a soldier remembered that at sundown he had seen the awesome knight move around furtively, and that after going around the mountain once, he had begun to climb it, followed by a chosen group of his men. He did not see him come down, unless he managed to do so without being noticed, as he did when he had gone up. The great barbarian turned his thought this way and that and almost refused to believe the obvious.

67

Thinking that a trap had been set by the enemy, he sent men to reconnoiter everywhere. What upset the emperor more than the damage done was the stealthiness with which the deed had been carried out. Obeying his high command, several men went off in search of a better explanation of what had occurred. Some combed this and that slope; others courageously attempted to climb to the top.

68

Meanwhile, as the Christian warriors turned their steps toward the mountain of Croia, leaving the king behind, they lifted the corpses out of the deep gorges and began to throw them down from the slopes into the valley below in order to clear the paths of the horrible stench of death. They still believed that their king was following them, so great were the night shadows and the confusion produced by the battle.

69

While they were going back, nobody realized they had left him among the enemy, but later they became convinced that he alone of many was left behind dead, especially when, after one day had passed, he had not appeared. As this conviction was strengthened, a common grief began spreading in the disheartened city.[25] A moan, an anguished sound of cries, sighs, and sobs rose to the heavens.

70

The fearful and sad old men cried pitifully; so also did the great many armless women and children.[26] They tore out their white hair and their blond locks, because the man who was their hope and protection was dead. The strong of arm, the steady and bold in heart mourned their leader. The captains too were pained and grieved, but they did so somewhere where no one could see or hear them.

71

A rider who has been unexpectedly and fiercely attacked by a group of men waiting in hiding loses heart if he is unarmed and alone, and if the swift horse on which he has placed all hope of escape is killed and collapses under him before he can run from the path of the attack. In the same way, a great fear gripped the frightened city under siege at the news of the redoubtable king's death.

72

More than anyone else in town Felin grieved, who had been the king's groom since his early youth. He loved him more than anyone else, more than his beloved friend Vran who was now away. Felin conceived the idea of leaving the city in secret and entering the Turkish camp under cover of night, for everyone there would be talking about the king's death or about his being taken prisoner.

73

All the pluck was his in this exploit; he neither thought nor cared about danger or a possible disgraceful outcome. He waited to go out the city gates until the sun dipped into the ocean, and then, with a brazen face, he told the guard he was taking some letters of Pyrrhus's to Amantia;[27]

---

25. During a sally on the Turkish troops in 1450, as the Albanians withdrew, Scanderbeg was left behind and believed dead. See Gegaj, *L'Albanie et l'invasion turque,* 78; Hodgkinson, *Skanderbeg,* 110.

26. A cliché description of trembling old men, wailing women, and mourners in general is found in *Iliad* 22.429–30; *Aeneid* 2.486–88, 4.667–68, 11.876–78; Lucan's *Civil War* 2.28–34; Petrarch's *Africa* 4.505–6, 5.80–81; and Tasso's *Jerusalem Delivered* 3.11.1–2, 11.29.7–8.

27. Sarrocchi places this town near Croia. For the situation of Amantia, an ancient city of Epirus, see the glossary.

and the guard, who had known him for a long time, believed him with no hesitation.[28]

74

Felin thought that he could descend the mountain more easily where the bodies of the pagans had been thrown down. He saw that many corpses were caught here and there among stumps and stones: the escarpment was very steep, and furthermore his feet became entangled in bushes full of twisted thorns. As he was on the point of losing his strength and falling precipitously down below, he turned his step back onto the beaten path.

75

He carried a flame in a small copper urn, and the light penetrated the nocturnal air. The sky was obscured by darkness more than usual, for on this night the sun was not sending its light onto the moon. Down below, among those who were sent to look for Ferratte and were now searching in the dark, several saw Felin's light shining up above on the mountain slope.

76

When they saw it, they did not know what it was and were of divided opinion; but when they saw the light descend slowly, they believed it had been lit intentionally. They warned the others about it and waited. So as soon as he set foot in the valley, the king's very incautious friend was captured, tied up, and brought into the great emperor's presence.

77

Looking at him with intent and angry eyes, the sultan inquired about his rank, name, and reason for coming there. Trembling, Felin revealed all: that he had come down into the valley to look for his king, that during the night he and his men had penetrated the camp wearing false coats of arms—the king wearing the Agah's cuirass, the only one that would fit him, and the others those of the Turkish men killed in the ravine.

---

28. The episode of Felin entering Turkish territory in search of news of his master had a famous model in *Orlando Furioso* 18, where two young African soldiers, Cloridano and Medoro, decide to return to the battlefield through the Christian camp by night and look for the body of their slain captain.

78

He ended his story by saying that the only one left behind in the valley was the king and that now the city mourned him for dead. The emperor then clearly saw the reason why his men fought against one another, but he wanted to know far more in the hope that it would offer him the chance to conquer the city. He first considered carefully how that could be done, for he believed the king was away, not dead.

79

He did not believe Alexander to be dead but rather gone some distance from the valley. Still he could not find out for certain. Knowing the terrain so well, he might be hiding in some impassable mountain gorge; his own men, however, were too inexpert about the area to be sent in search of him. "Besides," the sultan reasoned within himself, "if I divulge my suspicion, I will make the people of Croia think for certain that their king is still alive."

80

The wicked devil who always accompanied the sultan soon suggested to him a way to keep the Christian people under pressure, not by force of arms but by sagacious fraud. If the Christian king could look like Ferratte by wearing Ferratte's armor, the sultan hoped that Ferratte could convince the people in the citadel that he was really their king.

81

So he gave orders that Ferratte's body be immediately picked up and— keeping the operation as secret as possible—the skin covering it be flayed off; just as an old woman might peel the dried log of a fir tree of its bark in order to light a fire when, in order to make a living, she gets up early in the morning to spin her wool.

82

They tried their utmost to keep the skin in one piece as they extracted the life-less body from it. With its vital warmth extinguished, every black and putrid vein poured out cold blood, and in the way the pelt of a ferocious and mon-strous beast or snake is sometimes preserved, they kept Ferratte's skin and filled the void inside it with straw, in order to keep the shape of his limbs unaltered.[29]

29. The vicissitudes of Ferratte's body may be a sign of the impression left by the fate encoun-tered in Cyprus by Marcantonio Brigadino, the Venetian governor of Famagusta, when the

83

Then, to hold that shape upright, a long pole was raised in a spot in the valley where it could best be seen from the city above. This was a horribly contrived sight, which shook the Christian souls with a deeply reverberating pain. To make them fall more readily into the trap, those Turks, who knew well how to contrive deceptions, pretended to carry the body to some far deserted wood and expose it to wild animals.

84

After finding Ferratte's body, however, and learning of the tragic failure of his exploit, the emperor did not wish to deprive such an intrepid and loyal warrior of a grand funeral. So he had him honored publicly in a way that did not reveal the truth, for he wanted to avoid any possible suspicion that the skin he had erected was in fact Ferratte's.

85

In order to hide the cunning deception even more shrewdly, he allowed the mourners to wear heavy mourning attire and go unarmed, as became the valor of that great warrior, but only as the time and place permitted. The most prominent captains stood around the big hearse. The funeral pomp was seen from the town above, for in the distance their sight was dazzled by the mantle shining with gold and gems.

86

This mantle covered the hearse all around, so that no one could see the body. It was made of black silk, with sections decorated in gold intertwined with purple silk threads. Many gems reflected the glare of the sun, which, while shedding light on them, seemed less luminous than they were. Then a stone was placed over the corpse without showing it, and the warrior's famous arms were laid on top.[30]

---

island fell into the hands of the Turks. When he was captured in 1571, just before the battle of Lepanto, Brigadino was subjected to prolonged torture and then flayed alive. After he died, his skin was stuffed with straw and was hung in front of his office and in the marketplace. Another detail of Brigadino's horrible end—while alive, he was hoisted by a chain to the mast of the pasha's galley, in view of fleet and army—may have inspired the literary retaliation in canto 20.89–90. See Edward Kirk Rawson, *Twenty Famous Naval Battles: Salamis to Santiago* (New York: Crowel , 1899), 1:71; John Richard Hale, "Lepanto 1571," in *Famous Sea Fights from Salamis to Jutland* (London: Methuen, 1931), 74.

30. Funerals for the slain hero figure prominently in epic poetry. See Hector's funeral in *Iliad* 24.782–804, Pallante's in *Aeneid* 11.29–99; Brandimarte's in *Orlando Furioso* 43.176–79; and Dudon's in *Jerusalem Delivered* 3.67. The pomp of Ferratte's burial conforms to customs in

87

Meanwhile, a varied and confused rumor traveled through the crowd of unsuspecting soldiers. Some of them, as always eager for news, coming from everywhere to see and hear, were deceived by the Agah's skin, and agreed in believing that it was the Christian king's; hair and feet were the same, while the face, being much disfigured, could not be recognized.

88

The emperor was glad that the people believed it and talked about it. He then gave one of his men the task of going up and asking the hostile citadel if they would consent to hear a messenger. Soon a man, after taking off helmet and cuirass, as required by custom, started on his way, as a signal was given from the valley to the people above with the sharp metallic sound of a concave instrument.

89

The town understood that he was coming as a friend and let him get near the ponderous walls. He spoke and then reported to the Thracian emperor that any ambassador of his might go up safely. The man chosen to go was Orkhan, a man young in age but mature in wisdom. After doubling the guards around the walls, the townspeople listened to him without opening the gates.[31]

90

Orkhan did not care whether they opened the gates to him, for he had a shrewd idea well set in mind, and, astute impostor that he was, he hid his intentions under a friendly face and a pleasant manner. And just as if he were presenting an indubitable and unquestionable fact instead of a gross lie, he told them that their king was dead, warned them of imminent danger, and swore that he was giving them heartfelt advice.

91

First he described how their king had been overcome while fighting during the night; how he had left a lasting sign of his valor by killing half the men in the camp; how, when finally he was captured alive, in punishment for his

---

Sarrocchi's times. Funerals had long become the exclusive subject of poetic compositions called *lamenti*, at times more than a thousand lines in length, which eulogized the dead and the personalities participating in the religious rites, and at the same time publicized state policy. See Rinaldina Russell, *Generi poetici medievali* (Naples: Società Editrice Napoletana, 1982), 125–45.

31. A Turkish envoy was in fact sent up to the fortress of Kruja in 1450 to ask for surrender, but his request was rejected. See Gegaj, *L'Albanie et l'invasion turque*, 77; Hodgkinson, *Skanderbeg*, 108.

failure, he was skinned out of the frail cover protecting the limbs of humans; and how they could now see that skin held upright in the field below.

92

He further told them that the oath of loyalty to their king, which they kept unshakably as long as he was alive, was relinquished now that he was dead. Without its leader, the besieged town would hope in vain to hold out much longer. They ought to surrender now, for the emperor promised to forgive all past offenses and be no less clement toward the rebellious captains of the city than he would be to the most innocent people.

93

The highest-ranking chieftains of Croia had come to the wall to hear the grand demand for the city's surrender. The first among them in age, wisdom, and lineage was Pyrrhus. He knew well in what esteem the promises and the leniency of the tyrant could be held; a man who possesses the clear sight of intelligence can wisely learn how to prevent harm to himself by considering how the ruin of others has come about.

94

Whatever danger there may have been dismayed him less than the sight of the skin exposed to view down below. This tormented him and brought great anguish to him and everyone else. They all believed it to be truly the king's skin. Its size, which they could clearly see, allowed no possibility of believing he was not dead, such was the skill that made it look like his very skin, not only to those who were far off, but also to people nearby.

95

The grief felt by the high captains was so deep that although they gave the honor of the first answer to Pyrrhus, they could not help showing on their faces all the anger they felt inside. Meanwhile the crowd, certain that they were in really great danger now, once again raised their cries and laments to the sky, shouting that they would rather suffer torture and death than surrender to the tyrant.

96

Pyrrhus gave his answer to the messenger. "As the free man I am, I shall waste no words with you, for we are accustomed to answer the enemy's requests only by fighting. The shadows will become luminous, the sun will darken, water will harden and marble go soft before our determination changes from what it is, and before the bond that ties us together is undone.[32]

97

"That king, who set us aflame with loving zeal, takes our enduring oath of loyalty with him. May he keep it forever with him in heaven, where neither chance nor destiny avails. You will have your way only here on earth where we wear mortal vestments, not in the other world, which is above time and death. In our souls, in that very best part of us, our loyalty will be forever."

98

As he spoke, Pyrrhus lifted his right hand: "To the last of my strength, as long as this hand can strike, as long as in this town there remains a man breathing, these people, if challenged, will dig a horrible ditch for your corpses. The skin you have raised down below calls for a bloody revenge; it inflames our hearts to retaliation and slaughter."

99

Orkhan was astounded in the face of so much courage and left without giving a reply to Pyrrhus. A burning flame of rightful anger, a holy zeal aroused the Christian people.[33] First it moved from one person into another, then it flared up quickly among the bellicose youths; for at times, against all odds, despair and hopelessness can change fear into steadfast courage.

100

The young Vaconte, accompanied by the honorable band of his Adventurers,[34] ran up to the crowd and shouted: "The only escape remaining to men in hopeless straits is that they have no hope of escaping.[35] Our king was killed in an infamous manner under our own eyes. Soldiers, cap-

---

32. To stress their refusal to surrender, Pyrrhus strings together a series of impossibilities, thus employing the rhetorical figure known as "the world upside down."

33. The religious motivation for the war appears throughout the *Scanderbeide*. Cf. canto 20.82n.

34. The Adventurers were volunteer soldiers, generally reputed to be the most daring in battle. They are a fixture of epic poetry. Cf. Tasso's *Jerusalem Delivered* 1.52.3, 18.73.2, 20.10.5.

35. "Una salus victis, nullam sperare salutem" (One salvation the conquered have: to hope for no salvation), proclaims Aeneas at the fall of Troy, urging a group of Trojans to fight on. *Aeneid* 2.354–55. Aeneas's words may have been a paraphrase of what Lucius Martius said to his troops: "In rebus asperis et tenui spe fortissima quaeque consilia tutissima sunt" (in adverse circumstances when hope is slender, the most daring solution is the safest) (Livy 25.38.18–20). His words are quoted by Botero in *The Reason of State* 9.17, where he strives to demonstrate with historical examples that necessity is a spur to valor. See "Vaconte" in the cast of main characters.

tains, is he to remain unrevenged? Is he to expect from us only a revenge
made of our moans and cries, as if we were women?[36]

101

"That fine reminder that the Spartan soldier tied to his arm before marching to certain death, may you fasten securely to yours, in emulation of that
memorable daring.[37] May as ardent and zealous a wish for revenge melt the
ice of your hearts! Long ago, a small number of men vanquished a large
army: do not let that fine example go unheeded now.

102

"For every one of us killed, a hundred of them shall fall to the ground with
their mortal bodies shattered and drained of blood. They will not laugh at
our grief then, I can assure you! As far as courage, strength, and wisdom are
concerned, they are worthless: their strength and merit consist only in
bragging. They will know the difference between talking and acting, if only
each of us uses all the power he possesses.

103

"What can a helpless people possibly do if they are numerous but living in
servitude, speaking a variety of languages and hardly united at all, against a
people acting under one father and one king, united by a common desire
for revenge?[38] Even if that task were to take from us this fragile life, which
unavoidably will come to an end, let each one of us die for such a beautiful
cause, for a good death bestows honor on an entire lifetime.[39]

104

"We have nothing to fear: from heaven his royal soul, seated in that high
and glorious abode, contemplates our ardent zeal and our desire to avenge

36. For the stereotype of lamenting women, see above, canto 5.70n.

37. I found no reference to this Spartan soldier in any of the classical texts I consulted. Sarrocchi
might have been thinking of an anecdote related by Valerius Maximus (2.7 ext 2) and by Plutarch
(*Moralia* 3.241.16) according to which, before going into battle, Spartan warriors were told by their
women to come back either alive, with their shields on their arms, or dead, on top of them. The
reminder tied to the arm of the soldier, mentioned in this sentence, would, therefore, be the shield.

38. Vaconte's statement echoes Machiavelli's observations about the difficulties faced by a conqueror in holding onto territories occupied by people who do not speak the same language. See
The Prince 3 on mixed principalities. The same idea is repeated here in cantos 14.67 and 17.60.
Botero, on the other hand, maintains the opposite. An army that is not made up of different
people, he says, will prove sluggish, because there will be no spirit of emulation among them.
If the soldiers are of different origins, they will vie with one another and will have a variety of
qualities to contribute. *The Reason of State* 9.14.

39. "Breve et inreparabile tempus omnibus est vitae; sed famam extendere factis, hoc virtutis
opus" (Life is irremediably short for all human beings, but it is the task of the brave to lengthen

him. He sees that his torn and bloody body has been exposed, to the opprobrium of our religion, and from up there he prays that the pagans may suffer by our hand for their cruel deed.

105

"What inflames his heart is not his own death, not his bitter agony; it is the desire to revenge Christ, for up there in heaven he wears a mantle as luminous as his mortal remains down here are gloomy." These words so inflamed the spontaneous enthusiasm of all the youths that they rushed to start the fight without waiting for orders, each one of them stirred to vengeance by his own furor.

106

All the captains and the higher officers tried to hold back the impetuous tumult of the young in gentle but determined ways, at least for a short time. That proved less easy than placating the furor of huge waves in a stormy sea, when Aeolus,[40] giving free rein to violent winds, slashes the Aegean Sea from all directions.

---

it by acquiring fame with glorious deeds), declares Turnus, who is determined to continue the war. *Aeneid* 10.467–69.

40. This was the Roman god of the winds. He ruled them from his abode in the Aeolic Islands, now Isole Lipari, north of Sicily. Ovid, *Metamorphoses* 1.262, 4.663, 14.224.

From **CANTO** 6

The king, who is in hiding on Mount Tumenishti, comes across Palinuro, who arrives bring-
ing a contingent from Buda. Together they go on the attack, joining forces with the Albanian
warriors who meanwhile have sallied forth from Croia. The general melee that follows comes
to an abrupt end when, by the emperor's order, Attravante's war chariots move across the
fighting throng and block the Christian advance.

1—51
While the king is hiding in the nearby mountain, the city warriors decide to attempt a second
sortie.

52

After ascending the path halfway up the mountain all this while, the valiant
king dried the sweat from his brow and at a cool spring quenched the thirst
burning in his throat. Then, standing in suspenseful indecision, he considered
for a while whether to stop there or go down or continue on to a point where
he could most conveniently wait for the night following the day that was
about to begin.

53

He did not consider it safe to descend into the valley now that so little
was left of nighttime. He noticed that the side of the mountain he had just
climbed offered only a few narrow and impracticable caves, and he knew
that on the top of the mountain there was more space, with safer grottoes
inside and a wide plateau outside. So he decided to reach a higher point
and look for a place to rest and think.

54

He hoped to be able to go back to the citadel, but there was a big obstacle to his design: he was afraid he might be seen from the plain below on account of his size, which was far greater than most. Besides, he was in great need of rest, although a short repose was usually enough for him.[1] So he turned his step resolutely up the steep incline, and although he was exhausted, he continued to climb without stopping.

55

As he reached the summit, a luminous dawn arrived, spreading a golden sheen over the mountains. A pleasant moaning murmur was heard: it was the breeze playing among the branches. It sounded like a voice giving vent to pain and renewing the pain of those who heard it. The king listened to that sweet melodious lament and partly wept and partly rejoiced.

56

He planned to rest during the day and then leave as soon as Phoebus withdrew from the sky, relinquishing the way to Cynthia.[2] His amazingly active character disdained lingering idly where only caves, stones, plants, and birds could be seen, and where he had no chance to expose himself to danger for his holy faith.[3] He regretted it, but then wisely changed his mind, for going back involved many risks and certain danger.

57

Then he considered that he had penetrated the camp in a false military attire, that as soon as the enemy general, who well knew the art of war, learned that he was away from the town, he would set up ambushes all around. The best thing, therefore, was to remain there for a few days and then make certain that his reentry into the city was safe.

58

His being away from Croia filled his mind with longing and compassion, for he knew how the people must worry, and how much the captains who were his friends must feel anguish in their hearts. He also knew that if he

---

1. The great Cato too could do with very little rest. Lucan, *Civil War* 9.590.

2. Phoebus is Apollo, the sun god, and Cynthia is Artemis, the moon goddess, called by the Romans Diana. She is called Cynthia from Mount Cynthus in Delos, which, according to legend, is the birthplace of both Artemis and Apollo.

3. About the characters' religious zeal, see canto 20.82.

did not get there soon, they would be afraid he was dead. Loving them, he grieved for their grief, but he had no doubt about their unswerving loyalty.

59

He remained there for two days immersed in thought, but in as good spirits as ever. Fruits and grass provided food and rest, and his vigor did not lessen. As the second night came around, he felt the need of repose and lay down on his side in the meadow. He came out of his sleep at the moment when the night unfolded her richest panoply over the sky.

60

As soon as his senses emerged from slumber, his thoughts fell back on his first worry, for his mind forced him to consider again how he could effect a safe reentry. In the uncertainty of the moment, the bright rays of the stars quivering and scintillating in the pure expanse of the sky delighted his sight, and the pleasure of the eyes brought with it the pleasure of the heart.

61

Those gold and starry heavens took him out of his distressing thoughts, and he said to himself: "Oh, how many beautiful lights were bestowed on the world for its adornment and preservation! The day displays its pure and cheering rays, the night unfolds a star-studded robe! And among them, engaged in gentle rivalry, the moon shines in splendor with silver and the sun with gold.[4]

62

"God's eternal care did show a wonderful skill and commensurate art in creating all this, so that we can see Saturn and Mars rain down an excess of cold or heat, Jupiter and Venus give out their pure temperate splendor together or separately, while, from the fixed and highest stars in the sky, we may draw a variety of sinister or propitious forebodings.

63

"Wise are those human beings who find all the cares of this world to be a bother, who care only to become tenants of the celestial abode, and who, while yet living, still keep rising to the gate leading to it! In the emptiness

---

4. For other descriptions of the night in a sky studded with jewel-like stars, see cantos 3.36, 7.40, and 10.20.

of the air are birds, in the salty waves of the sea are fish, in the distant solitary forests are beasts, and God feeds them all: what then will he not do for man, who was created to acquire knowledge of him?"[5]

64

In this contemplation, as he meditated on God and waited for a rescue that he was certain would come, the king's heart found peace. Suddenly he had the impression of hearing a distant sound of voices and, mixed with it, the noise of trampling feet. He could hear it far away because he had decided to take his rest outside the cave, under the open sky, in order to be able to wake up at once and be prompt and fast to move at the slightest noise.

65

The more he strained to hear, the nearer the sound seemed to be. He arose without delay, grasped his sword, and stood at the ready. Nearby he saw a large clump of shrubs that was hard to penetrate, but from which to walk away and descend to the valley was easier than from any other spot.

66

He quickly turned his step toward it, glancing all around and without making a noise. From there he thought he would be able to see out while remaining hidden, but not because he was afraid of any danger for himself. Soon he saw several men come up the slope and could hear their whispers much closer; then, as the moon dispersed the darkness of the night, the shapes and faces of people could be discerned.

67

He saw Palinuro talking to Ulysses and heard his words distinctly. "Our men can safely hide here from the fierce tyrant. Perhaps, as soon as the sun comes around to shed light into this deep darkness, the celestial heavens will show us the way and means to send a signal to the city."

68–80

Alexander and Palinuro meet, and after considering all possible choices, they agree that the best way back to Croia is by cutting directly across the Turkish camp. At the foot of the mountain, they join the men who meanwhile have come down from the citadel. Together they brace for the attack.

---

5. Alexander's meditation on the beauty of creation is an elaborate variation on the one absorbing Count Orlando during a pause in his duel with Agricane. See *Orlando Innamorato* 1.18.41.

81

Flanked on all sides by his famous soldiers and officers, the king's apparition was like that of ominous Orion when it descends toward the sea from high heaven, tearing apart ropes and masts before the eyes of the unlucky sailors, changing weather and seasons, and bringing about destruction every-where.[6] The king put his fearsome lance to rest, ran ahead at a gallop, and raised his voice to cheer his men.

82

"Come, come, my loyal men! Come on quickly! Dispel the veil of error that blinds your eyes! Your king is safe and sound. Here, look at me! Let no fear linger in your hearts! Now that your king is with you, victory and luck will certainly be yours! Think of the hand of God, how it strikes the guilty with lightning and thunder!"

83

These words, the sight of his well-known appearance, his noble royal presence, his self-assured gaze, his clear forehead, which had never failed to produce fear and awe, had such an effect on these men that the ones among them who were about to retreat to the mountain let go of their mistaken belief in the king's death and stopped in their tracks, raising high shouts of joy to the heavens.

84

When a horrible bear engages a young lion in a cruel and uneven fight, pressing the cub's tender back onto his bristling chest, scratching and rending it with his claws, if the cub sees his courageous mother come to the rescue, his strength and daring are revived.[7] Similarly, as soon as the men saw their king, they became bold fighters again and unbeatable in battle.

85

Soon the Christian king inflicted a deep wound on fierce Araspe and rendered him lifeless. Once he had fallen on the ground, brilliant red blood

---

6. Orion is a constellation that rises in November and is therefore a harbinger of bad weather. This comparison of the king to the ominous Orion is inspired by those in *Iliad* 22.25–29, where Achilles, speeding over the Trojan plain toward Hector, looks like Orion shining among the stars, and in *Aeneid* 10.762–68, where Mezentius is also compared to Orion, but as a giant hunter wading the sea. For other comparisons of warriors with stars, see 13.17 and 23.55.

7. This is a most engaging image among many found in epic poems of animals defending their cubs from predators. Cf. *Iliad* 17.132–34; *Thebaid* 10.414–19; *Orlando Furioso* 19.7.

flowed freely from his wide open heart. He lost all strength and quickly died; his eyes opened once, and then once more, to the pleasant salubrious air; once and again his head lifted from the ground, then fell, and eternal night sealed his sight forever.

86

Then the king threw his massive spear and hit Brandoardo in his left arm, Brandoardo the ruthless Scythian. No steel protected his arm, and so vigorous was the king's blow that the leather over it was pierced through and broke apart. Brandoardo looked at the blood gushing out, and as the spear stung his arm and wrath boiled in his heart, he prepared to strike back ferociously, to revenge the spilled blood that no one had ever drawn from him before.

87

But instead of the enemy who was right in front of him, he forcefully struck the good horse, instantly taking all energy away from the animal. The charger collapsed, and unexpectedly the king's left foot was caught in the stirrup under it. Seeing their advantage, the pagans ran up in numbers, and before the king could get up, they hurried to kill him by sword, lance, spear, battle-axe, and dart.[8]

88

They struck his head, arm, back, chest, and side with as many weapons. Brandoardo too hit him, with a downward stroke so strong that anyone else would have died of it. But the king answered the blows more effectively than before, just as a hard boulder more and more forcibly pushes back the wheel that repeatedly stumbles against it.[9]

89

Brandoardo's anger increased as striking him again and again proved useless, for under so many blows the king remained unharmed. He believed him to be invulnerable to any weapon, and running around him in vain and shouting in vain, he ordered that his bow and arrow be brought to him. But the king kept them at bay and away with his powerful arm as far as the length of his sword.

8. In *Jerusalem Delivered* 3.42, Rinaldo has difficulty rising because his foot is pinned under his horse.

9. In canto 5.40, Alexander was compared to a mountain against which boys throw stones for his ability to withstand the pressure of his assailants; in canto 23.40, he is likened to a rock in a sea of blood for his capacity to slaughter the enemy and resist their attacks.

90

The same sometimes happens when, in a very dark night, a pack of dogs surrounds a passerby: the man, used to such fights, manages to wound or kill one, and when the hounds see that one of them is beaten, they are overcome by fright (so strong is their natural instinct); then, more in fear than because of actual injury, the dogs withdraw and begin to bark at a distance.[10]

91

Virgilio, Vaconte, Piero, and others, realizing the position the king was in, became very worried, for they feared that he might succumb before their very eyes in that sea of enemy soldiers, so they all offered help. This way the king was able to untangle his foot from the stirrup, but seriously hurt by his own heavy weight, he could hardly move or stand.

92

Crater had noticed that daring rescue and had admired their great valor. So, stirred on by a noble concern, he decided to place the great warrior's life before his own. With this worthy plan in mind, he dismounted quickly and offered the reins of his charger to the king. He did it in a hurry because he feared someone might forestall an action so worthy of praise and fame.

93

He feared that someone else might perform that act so worthy of meritorious envy before he could carry it out himself, for a man of great heart places more value in glory than in his own life. Driven by pressing necessity, the strong hero readily got hold of the horse by the gilded halter. He did not believe he was acting unkindly, because Crater was not wounded, while he could hardly stand on his feet.[11]

10. Cf. 7.114, where the scene of a pack of dogs attacking a lonely passerby, and then withdrawing when help for him arrives, is employed to describe the behavior of a cowardly mob.

11. A similar incident occurred in the life of Scanderbeg in 1464. Thrown to the ground during a melee, he was protected by his men until he could mount another horse and start fighting again (Gegaj, *L'Albanie et l'invasion turque,* 139). Always mindful of Roman history, Sarrocchi provides here a justification of Alexander's acceptance of the horse: at Cannae, the Roman general Lucius Aemilius Paulus refused the charger that was offered to him by Gnaeus Lentulus, a tribune of the soldiers, and threw himself back into battle on foot. Plutarch, "Fabius Maximus" 16.6–7; Livy 22.49.6–13. The episode is also mentioned in Petrarch's *Africa* 1.526–55.

94

As soon as he mounted the good steed, his habitual energy came back to him. His left foot hardly hurt him now, and a crowd of loyal soldiers stood around him. Then, expert in the art of war, the king rode to confront the Janissaries. These were now advancing in a formation the shape of a horned moon, and the Thracian emperor was on horseback in their midst.

95

One would be astonished to see the balance of power ever tipping this way or the other; and to observe that at times the captains performed the tasks of soldiers and at other times the knights did the work of foot soldiers. They were also willing to alternate among them the burden of resisting the onslaught or of devising the strategy, so that those who were either too audacious or too slow could be restrained or spurred on.

96

Wherever his soldiers were under greater pressure the mighty king ran quickly to substitute this or that man in some appointed position, ordering and providing what was needed. His shield withstood a storm of arrows and darts, as he covered for others as well as for himself. He used the strength of his arm and his voice, no less a soldier than a captain.

97

In the meantime Thopia came up to face Radiar and they engaged in a dangerous fight. This was a duo not evenly balanced, for in one of them advancing age was draining all strength. Comin and Musaka had gone back to the city: Comin was shedding a great quantity of blood but his valor was undiminished; he had lost his vigor but not his daring.[12]

98

Feeling that both strength and blood were failing his brother, Musaka went with him: he thought he would be lacking consideration if he did not go to take care of him in person. At their young age, neither of them had military obligations, and both were under the care of their father, so you could say they were soldiers of fortune.

---

12. Comin and Musaka are Thopia's sons. In *Jerusalem Delivered* 3.35 there is a brief mention of an old soldier, Ardelio, being slain by Clorinda, who was accompanied in battle by two young sons and was not sufficiently protected by them. See "Thopia" in the cast of main characters.

99

Their proud parent, if one observed him carefully, aimed at victory even now that he had been wounded by the pagan on the shoulder and in the chest. He struck Radiar over the helmet, then stepped aside and moved around him. But the place was too narrow for such fencing, and in the end a single well-aimed blow sliced his head all the way down to his throat.

100

Tiberius, who was fighting not too far from there, saw the danger the old man was in and ran to his aid, but arrived too late. With the speed of a whirlwind, he now struck the killer with a very unusual blow, almost killing him. Radiar seemed uncertain whether or not he should let go of his life: thrown off balance by the weight of his own armor, he wobbled in the saddle for a while, and then fell to the ground.

101

In falling, he caught and threw down under him the pagan Ordorico, who, seeing him fall, had run up to help in friendly concern but in vain. Radiar's excellent charger, free of his rider, ran off into the thick of the enemy. Good Crater saw the animal and moved to catch him, for he was very uncomfortable fighting on foot.

102

As he went in pursuit of the horse—his hope of catching him increased his desire more and more[13]—he turned his back to the men on his own side, and placing his life in dangerous oblivion, he moved into the midst of the Turkish throng. Similarly, in the valley of hell, the sweet water of a brook holds Tantalus in thrall, sometimes lapping his back and at other times, when he is about to reach it, withdrawing quickly away with the speed of a bird in flight.[14]

103

The ferocious Driarasso was fighting against Vaconte, his eternal and fated enemy. When he recognized the well-known features as those of the man

---

13. Crater's desire to capture the horse is not unlike the eagerness of Julio in pursuing a white deer through the forest in Politian's *Stanze per la giostra* 1.35–36.

14. In Greek legend Tantalus is known for the punishment he received for revealing the secrets entrusted to him by Zeus. He was condemned to suffer hunger and thirst in the lower hell, where he was placed within reach of fruit and water that receded when he tried to get hold of them. Ovid, *Metamorphoses* 4.458, 10.41; Politian, *Stanze per la giostra* 1.36.5–8.

who had wounded him before, he attacked him without hesitation. The young man courageously turned to face him, when Occhialì, who wanted to kill him, drew his bow, aimed, let go the string, and the arrow made a small wound in Vaconte's arm.

104

A small quantity of blood began to run out of the cut, and it enraged him enormously. Nessus saw Jupiter's great son in a less menacing and angry mood than the one Vaconte was in now.[15] He moved against the bowman with such haste and with such furor and force as to lop his shoulder off cleanly and send it rolling along the ground. In this manner he took revenge on the man who had struck his arm.

105

Meanwhile Driarasso continued to ride with fury. Further on he saw a speedy horse passing through. It was the horse that Crater had been pursuing for some time without letting him go far out of his reach and sight. By the rich crest on his helmet and the decorated armor, he judged Crater to be a worthy baron, so he lowered his sword quickly and hit the left shoulder in full. Crater was struck by the flat of the sword; even so, he went sprawling to the ground.

106

As soon as he saw the man stretched out on the earth, Driarasso refrained from hitting him again, magnanimous soldier that he was; instead, he ordered his barbarous men to take him prisoner at once. At that moment Berlinguer, who was passing through, bumped his side and touched Driarasso with the point of his sword, pretending with this daring act to be equal to him in strength.

107

Boldness is less powerful than strength, but it can give strength a bigger impact than it would otherwise have. At times good weather dispels a storm only to be overcome later by a tempest. Similarly, venom and anger now raged in Driarasso to such a degree that, lest Berlinguer be left to gloat in

15. Nessus was a centaur who tried to force Deianira, the wife of Hercules (here referred to as Jupiter's great son), and was killed by him. The centaurs were mythological creatures represented as half man and half horse and living in Thessaly. Ovid, *Metamorphoses* 9. 101–33.

his boldness, he plunged his sword into the man's side with a backhand[16] so forcible that no adamant steel could withstand it.

108

He saw the warm blood come out of Berlinguer's wound and streak down the armor, but he made even more blood flow from his head by cutting it down to the shoulders. Now a noise of neighing and of stamping hooves could be heard. The ground reverberated, the air resounded with a frightening sound of different voices and with a cacophony of striking shields, swords, and helmets.

109

The noise moved nearer; nearer it came. It was Aranit's fighting cavalry approaching and then tarrying ominously: with their right hands, they brandished their weapons and struck blows as crushing as thunderbolts, as swift as lightning. Horses and horsemen knocked down and overpowered the harassed throng, confounding the foot soldiers completely. Meanwhile the king scattered death all around him, killing with his dagger and trampling with his horse.

110

Driarasso watched with awe the slaying done all around by that strong arm: wherever the king raised his powerful sword, he brought sure slaughter rather than a fight to his enemy, he awoke fear of certain death rather than anger in their hearts. Although the king was on horseback while he was now on foot, Driarasso yearned to test his valor against the king's.

111

A burning desire of eternal glory now inflamed his heart, which was usually very passionate, for he judged a man wise of mind and great of spirit if he valued honor and showed contempt for life. Against the king, therefore, he brandished his sharp sword, which could cut through any armor made of steel; he did not wound him but left his flank unprotected. Upon receiving that hard blow, the king turned toward him in anger.

---

16. With "backhand" (Brit. "back stroke") I translate *riverso* (also called *rovescio, manrovescio* or *rovescione*). It is the blow thrown by moving the arm from left to right, thus showing the back of one hand to the adversary. It is not to be confused with the *mandritto* or *mandiritto*, which is the blow struck from the right of the offender to the left, and which in English fencing is called "sabre cut." Cf. stanza 112. A *mandritto* is found in stanza 123.

112

In a flash, he struck him with a backhand, but fortunately for Driarasso, the sword only razed the crest of the helmet: the impetus of the blow caught Nardino in his chest instead, making him go flying truncated to the ground. Now came Agrismeta, who, contrary to his custom, today wanted to fight on horseback,[17] and seeing the king's powerful thrust, he was struck in amazement, while his heart filled with envy for his valor.

113

Wishing to test his prowess against that of the king, Agrismeta spurred his horse in that direction. Driarasso shouted at him: "He is fighting with me!"[18] but Agrismeta, eager for glory, did not listen. Blinded by anger and disdain, Driarasso, who saw his chance for a duel taken away from him, dared to attack both knights on horseback, although he was on foot and wounded.

114

Even so, the other man goaded his horse on, but at that moment a great crowd of soldiers crushed onward between them, so that Driarasso was forced to abandon his arduous task, and Agrismeta, now opening his way through the throng, arrived face to face before the king and spoke thus: "Stop chasing these negligible foot soldiers, invincible warrior! You disreputable enemy! For here I come to face your wrath, not your valor!

115

"Once I loved you, now I esteem you only as a soldier, for my heart hurts in seeing that you have rebelled against both God and your sire. Are you that great man, that sage of yore? My mind is incredulous and doubts you to be the one." After this he remained silent, but in that silence he struck a blow as strong and implacable as he was capable of. The king answered benignly to his words, with a blow to his blow.

116

The battle continued unabated. At first, both sides were shedding blood in equal measure, but later it became horribly clear who was the loser in the field. Perforated coats of arms, broken mail, and tattered surcoats could be

---

17. Being a Janissary, Agrismeta ordinarily fights on foot. Cf. 3.88.

18. "This is my fight!" shouts Tancred in protest to Otho, who has already engaged Argantes in combat. *Jerusalem Delivered* 6.30.7.

seen strewn everywhere. Christians and infidels lay dead together, but for every Christian there were a hundred Turks slain.

117

Vaconte took Armeno prisoner with many others, and Mauro[19] captured the beautiful Osman. Osman had escaped from the fray, scrambling up the slope where he believed himself safe. Destiny, however, which is unavoidable, did not allow his friend Orkhan, who was fighting nearby, to come to his aid with all his might, just as it prevented the valiant Ocrin from going to the aid of his friend Armeno.

118

The emperor was amazed and stood disconcerted for a while to see how many of his men were slain, and then he fully recognized that the superhuman valor of a single warrior could put everyone to flight. Although full of rage and grief, he wisely ordered his captains to withdraw all their troops, so that the whole army would not be totally destroyed.

119

At the same time he instructed Attravante to get on the carriages with all his men, ride quickly along the side and up to the front line, and from there to cut across the fighting throng. He should be careful to position each carriage just before the horses of the carriage behind so that the animals would be protected by it, and so that all along the line, the cart in front would shelter the horses of the cart coming after it.[20]

120

The purpose was to restrain the angry impetus of the enemy already on its way to victory, and allow his army, now retreating in confusion, to do so safely. But not all of it, because cutting through the battlefield and forming an unsurpassable wall with his carriages, Attravante was to disregard whatever number of Turks he saw caught between them and the steep incline, who would therefore be abandoned to no uncertain death.

121

When a whirlwind carries hidden within it a heavy quantity of iron, lead, or stone, people run about uncertain of where it will fall and do not know

19. See "Mauro" in the cast of main characters.
20. For the description of these war carriages, see canto 3.69–70.

when to stop. In the same way, the Christian soldiers ran away, scattering about in fear at the onslaught of arrows and spears that bowmen and throwers now rained down from the carts.

122

As the Christian king saw the fearless and bold Agrismeta before him and heard him scold and shame him for rebelling against the Thracian Empire, he angrily thrust a cutting blow toward him, but the good steed moved and saved Agrismeta from the blow. The king was already preparing to strike again when the crush of oncoming soldiers prevented him.

123

So the king went to help his men. First, he drove his sword through Aaron, who was standing on a carriage; then he inflicted a deep wound on Arimon, knocking him down from another carriage; and then, with a right-handed blow, he struck Sorbel, the charioteer, who fell on the sand and into the horse manure. He dove into that muck head first, for his feet were now where his head had been.

124

Now Attravante restored strength to the Ottoman army by forming a wall through the fighting crowd with the carriages, as they often did in battle, and at the same time he cut out and abandoned to certain death a great number of Turkish soldiers: for the fierce tyrant had come to the conclusion that life and death mattered only in relation to victory and to his reign and power, and that the rest of the world might as well perish.

125

The great mover in heaven did not wish to make his beloved people totally free as yet, so by the time the sun approached its abode in the sea, hiding its clear light in it, the Turkish soldiers were given shelter by that unmovable obstacle of mobile carriages, and by the time darkness had folded the world in his nightly mantle, the Christians were robbed of their victory.

126

The poor men who had been separated from their army encountered diverse destinies. More than one was taken prisoner; several were killed; several others defended themselves courageously; others took the sudden decision to run toward the line of carriages and try to escape by hiding under the bellies of the horses, shielded by the carriage in front of them.

127

When the Aegean Sea is tossed about by the northern wind and rises to hit the sky with its big billows, the water is so swollen by the stormy weather that it overflows its banks, now incapable of holding that fury, and the steep coast makes resistance to the big wave by throwing it back. In the same way, finding the carts lined up against them, the Christian soldiers were driven and dashed all the way backward, just like a flooding sea.

128

The Turks withdrew to Presa, raised the bridges, and posted their guards.[21] The Christian king, seeing that the falling night had taken a great victory away from him, returned to the citadel with his men and with those who had come to his aid. Corcutte left the passage open to them and the king withdrew all his troops to safety.

129

He took the prisoners with him and dealt with them mercifully, for he was moved now by a compassion as great as was the merciless determination that urged him on before.[22] As he arrived in the city, no age, no sex, no wisdom or reason, no illustrious ancestry, honesty, or secret beauty could exercise restraint and prevent people from running toward him with great joy, so as to relieve the pain of the death of their fathers, sons, and husbands with the sight of him alive.

21. From this moment Presa is the base of operation for the Turkish army. See "Presa" in the glossary.

22. The Romans were admired for being relentless in war and compassionate when the hostilities were over. They are praised for this policy in Botero's *The Reason of State* 10.9. In Petrarch's *Africa* 4.423–27, Scipio (Publius Cornelius Scipio, the victor over Carthage, 236–183 BCE) is described, like Alexander in this canto, as being fierce in battle and clement in peace.

CANTO 7

Pallante and Flora grow up together, and after discovering that they are not brother and sister, they plan to marry. Pallante is taken prisoner by Vran, who is in charge of the town of Amantia. Vran demands a ransom for Pallante's return and then donates it to the couple. This turn of events enrages the sultan, who decides to punish Vran and lay siege to his town, Amantia. Alexander, meanwhile, sends Artecin to the imperial court to barter for Crater, who was taken prisoner. Artecin's servant, Romidon, insults the Turkish soldiers and barely escapes lynching.

1

Seeing that in the end his fraud turned out in favor of the Christian people, the devil, bellowing in a furious and menacing manner, began to shake the iron chains to which he is tied for eternity. He struck his face blackened by smoke, tore out his bristling hair with redoubled pain, and resolved in mad recklessness to plot henceforth new insidious snares against heaven.

2

A well-known warrior, called Sabalio, had lived for a long time at the Thracian emperor's court. He was born in Epirus and was known as both a courageous fighter in war and a wise man in peace. This twofold merit had made him so famous that the emperor summoned him from his home, where he had sadly and disconsolately been grieving for the untimely death of his wife.

3

In order to allow him some solace, the heavens, which always care for virtue wherever it may be found, while taking his wife from him, gave him a son, who became the only comfort in his deep and unbearable grief. For it often happens that when death unties one vital knot, nature will tie an even stronger one, and the death of one becomes the life of another: thus the stable world stays its unstable course.

4

So the good Sabalio was obliged to place himself under the emperor's orders, which was unwelcome to him beyond measure, for he had to leave his little child behind. Before starting on his journey, however, he chose someone in his hometown of Phaestus,[1] and to this man, who had long proved to be a constant friend, he entrusted the said son Pallante.[2]

5

Liprando was the name of the man in whose care Sabalio left his young son during his difficult exile. The man raised the child at Phaestus as his own son, together with a daughter, his only offspring. Now that the old father was back in Epirus, he decided to call his son to him. Pallante had by this time reached the full flower of youth, when the power of love and nature is felt most strongly.

6

So the beautiful youth Pallante went to live with his father among the Thracian soldiers. And because from that unfortunate and fateful moment when his birth caused his mother's death Liprando had raised him with his own daughter, Flora, he believed her to be his sister and Liprando his father. Flora was slightly younger than he and superior to any other in grace and beauty.

7

The little girl learned to crawl on all fours with him, she stood up on unsteady feet with him; and in his company she would persist in her childish desire to play games and call for her nurse's breast. The children were very gentle toward each other in equal measure, to the delight of those who saw and heard them. They would try to speak, but their mouths, still feeding on milk, could hardly utter their first words.

8

When the April and May of their youth opened the first flowers to the vital air—flowers that on each of their faces bloomed most beautifully under the

---

1. This Phaestus is not the ancient town on the south coast of the island of Crete, but one by the same name in Thessaly, which according to Sarrocchi was within walking distance from the Ottoman army when it camped in Albanian territory.

2. For Pallante's name, see below, canto 7.51n.

luminous gaze of the other—when their minds grew wiser and more mature, they came to share deeply felt secrets and send to their hearts, through sight and sound, feelings ever so warm and sweet.

9

In those childish games and pleasures there was a pure and simple affection, but out of them grew a passion that in time turned maddening beyond measure. It takes longer to kindle fire in a piece of wood that is still green, but afterward the blaze rises higher, because once the wood is dried and ready to feed the flame, the fire engulfs it all at once.

10

The more they looked and listened to each other with pure brotherly and sisterly love, the more they each enjoyed the life-giving splendor of the eyes and the sweet sounds of the words of the other. This way, in their simplicity and longing, they unwittingly played a deceitful game of love, going from happiness to unhappiness, no sooner knowing the meaning of love than being lovers.[3]

11

As they had not been told the truth yet—she believed herself to be his sister and he her brother—the young man would moan all alone, and with tears dampening his handsome cheeks he would lament: "What cruel and relentless destiny, what pitiless fate, what villainous star lets my joy fade when near, and escape when it is beside me?

12

"The diamonds, the rubies, the pearls, the gold, the stars, the sun, and all that shines in her beautiful face were placed by heaven within my reach, but are denied to me.[4] I would be richer if someone else owned that treasure and I could hold it; instead, I am deprived because I have too much, and I am poor for holding too great a prize.

13

"Why am I not happy and satisfied to admire the sweet light of her beautiful eyes, her fine wavy hair, her handsome face, and to listen to her wise and

3. The detail of Pallante and Flora falling in love before knowing the meaning of love is reminiscent of the shepherd in Tasso's *Aminta* 1.2.346–47 and of Florio and Biancifiore in Boccaccio's *Filocolo*. Stories similar to theirs are found also in Franco Bracciolini's *La Croce racquistata* 3.34 (1605), in Scipione Herrico's *Babilonia distrutta* 1.34 (1624), and in Girolamo Graziani's *Il conquisto di Granata* 12 (1650). See Belloni, *Gli epigoni della Gerusalemme Liberata*, 137–38.

4. Compare this description of the woman's beauty with those at 1.27–31, 3.65, 3.80, 13.11, 18.7, and 18.9–10.

sweet words? To what more is this boundless desire urging me? What more does it want? Is there a greater happiness than seeing one's beautiful beloved as much as one desires?

14

"Her beauty is the object of my sight and hearing alone, not the pleasurable goal of some vain and deceitful urge.[5] Still, compelled by love's affection, I long to join my hand to her hand, to quench my insane desire by pressing the snowlike whiteness of her breast to my breast, and alleviate the bitter sighs exhaling from my mouth by kissing her sweet mouth."

15

At night, in bed, separated from his joy, the young man repeated these words and longed for her,[6] not feeling satisfied just to listen to her sweet words and look at her beautiful face. For her part, she sighed just as much in her own reckless way of loving and longing. They both could clearly see the passion hidden in the other's eyes, eyes that ever so often become the mirror of one's heart.

16

They not only perceived the passion hidden in the eyes but could shrewdly hear it in each other's words. The young man, however, was not able to hold her fine hand as frequently as he wished, as he could have done with a sister, for the young woman forbade it; but then he daringly stretched his hand over her flowery cheek as often as possible and from her beautiful mouth would drink kisses far sweeter than those given by any sibling.

17

By this ruse, they kept feeding the flame that they thought they were extinguishing. But now that the father was back in his homeland, he summoned

5. According to the popularized version of Renaissance Platonism, the only moral form of love is one that can be satisfied by hearing and sight alone. These two senses are thought to be "spiritual" because they allow the contemplation of what is beautiful on earth and may lead the soul to meditate on the beauty of the divine essence. The theory was eloquently put forward by the character Bembo in the fourth section of Baldassar Castiglione's *The Book of the Courtier* (1513–28). See also canto 9.2 and 9.4. For an introduction to sixteenth-century treatises on love, see my introduction to Tullia d'Aragona's *Dialogue on the Infinity of Love*, especially 33–35.

6. The best-known case of a lover's sleeplessness is that of Dido in Virgil's *Aeneid* 4.522–32. Other famous cases of lovers' insomnia are found in Ovid's *Amores* 1.2, Boccaccio's *Filostrato* 4.19.1–2, and Ariosto's *Orlando Furioso* 8.79, 32.13, 33.59.

the young man to him. And as the truth was revealed to them, they promised each other that they would become husband and wife, and said it with a joy never experienced by any fortunate lover before or after.

18

The joy was sudden and great, but it did not overcome them; it was partly diminished by the sorrow of the impending separation, because when lovers go their separate ways their souls too are separated, but from their own hearts.[7] But although their utmost wish was denied, they nonetheless took courage from the thought that they would open their hearts to each other by secret letters and with the help of a cautious messenger.

19

Among Sabalio's friends at the imperial court Saladin was the oldest. Each considered the fortunate or unfortunate circumstances befalling the other as his own. They partook of frugal meals together and slept in the same chaste bed, for in them old age had quelled all youthful desires and nature was now satisfied with little.

20

Saladin had a squire called Nardo, a man of strong body and shrewd mind. Pallante confided his burning love to him, and only Nardo was able to console him. Only he, messenger and secretary, brought each lover news of the other, by writing and often by word of mouth: a small comfort to hearts with so ardent a passion.

21

One day, the very morning after the Ferratte incident, Nardo started on his way to Phaestus and arrived where the battle had taken place. Because he had heard Sabalio and Saladin talk and wonder about that event, he stopped at that point and decided to ascertain what had happened on that day and continue the journey the day after.

22

In order to be of help to his master in that moment of danger and defeat, and because spying on other people always seems a wise idea, he looked

---

7. A commonplace of courtly love poetry is that the lover's heart abandons his/her body and follows the beloved everywhere. In the second book of Pietro Bembo's *Gli Asolani* (1505), Gismondo calls this one of the most joyful miracles of love.

around the field where the horrible relentless fight had been going on and heard men talk about the king's demise. The rumor had originated with the satraps and afterward had spread and grown among the soldiers.

23

That shrewd deception had already made great inroads, and the news of the king's death was given for certain; so by now all the camp rejoiced, because it was believed that the fortress would soon surrender without fighting. Nardo heard people talk and watched the funeral; he too believed that the remains of the great Ferratte raised up there were the king's.

24

Stature, hair, and features of the figure convinced everyone that they had belonged to the king, for the two men's ages were about the same, each one surpassing the other by a short span, if at all. After all this, as the Sun began to fall toward the west and Thetis[8] got busy adorning his nightly abode, Nardo took up his intended journey and six miles hence found a hostel.

25

When a new dawn rose in the sky, he diligently started again on his way and traveled so fast that on that very day he arrived and delivered the letter to beautiful Flora. When she saw him appear unexpectedly, her charming face flushed with extraordinary joy, and she wanted him to go back to the camp immediately with a secret message, before anyone could see him.

26

This was because her father was to be away for a few days—on the previous day he had been sent by the Thracian emperor on an important mission to Elia. She therefore begged her dear lover to travel to Phaestus and come to her at the darkest hour of the night, so that, with no one suspecting it, they would be able to bring about an honest consummation to their love.

27

As Nardo started on his return journey, a nasty devil with a wondrous skill let him imagine, in a deceiving vision, the death of so worthy a king in all its details. This made him think about the friendship that tied him to

8. Thetis, a marine divinity, stands here for the sea. She is in the west, preparing the Sun's "nightly abode" in the sea, because seen from Albania, the sunset takes place over the Adriatic. Cf. canto 21.60.

Alexander, a kind of friendship that never lets go of a kind heart, and so if nothing else, he decided to perform the kind act of warning the loyal Vran.

28

Since he had to travel through Vran's territory, he conveniently could take the opportunity to do what he proposed while going his way and still arrive in time with his message. The hours lost in the evening he would recoup on the following morning by getting up early. So he turned his steps toward the fortress, arrived, and the doors were opened to him.

29

From Nardo's Turkish attire, the guard understood him to be from the imperial side; even so, he opened the doors, perhaps because Nardo was alone or because some wicked spirit had made the guard kinder than usual. Nardo told Vran that the king, wearing Turkish clothes and the armor that had belonged to the defunct Ferratte, had come down the valley during the night and had made a surprise attack on the enemy camp.

30

The soldiers in the camp had been caught while lying on the ground heavy with food and drink and had suffered a heavy and merciless onslaught, but in the end Alexander had been captured. Nardo had seen with his own eyes the bloody corpse hung in the camp. At this news Vran was overcome by a fierce pain and could hardly breathe or speak.

31

Then Nardo the messenger brought Pallante news of his woman; the young man felt happy and fortunate, for the hope of a future pleasure now assuaged his pain. Although the road to the town where his beloved lived was short,[9] in his mind he kept counting the miles, because to him, being more impatient than usual, the way to happiness seemed far too long.

32

Every step seemed a league to him, though he would have been ready to go very many miles, not only on harsh and dangerous roads, but also through the horribly dense forests of Hercynia, under darkly cloudy skies, or over the

---

9. For the distance between Flora's home and the camp, see above, canto 7.4n.

deserted sands where Cambyses' armed squads lay buried.[10] The ardent lover would have liked both the road and the time to come to an end in one instant.

33

He wanted to leave by the early light of dawn so that his father could neither see nor hear him. He went to bed but could not sleep; he kept speaking to himself and moaning all night, blaming Dawn for being slow in starting the new day and being lazy beyond her custom. He tirelessly turned this way and that, sighing all the time.

34

Never does a ship loaded with precious merchandise and caught in a storm long for a harbor with the same intensity as when expecting to be stuck on the rocks and then sunk in the violent sea.[11] Never had a prisoner hoped with as much intensity to escape from his dark prison after having been sentenced to die, nor had it ever been so annoying for a tyrant to wait for the royal crown to shine on his head.

35

At times Pallante prayed: "Beautiful goddess, come back, make your blond hair alluring with white and purple violets, induce the sun to come after you!" When he heard the bird announce the day, the bird that also sings at midnight,[12] he believed the day to be about to dawn and called Nardo, so easy is it to be deceived by one's own intense longing.

36

Nardo woke up immediately, arose, opened the window, and looked at the sky: the stars, the jewels that bedeck the dark veil of the night, were shining thick and clear. Realizing that an excess of love and of desire was deceiving the young lover, he laughed and gently made fun of him for being so restless, the more so the more hopeful he had been.

---

10. Hercynia is the Latin name of a mountain range covered by dense forests, now called Black Forest, in southwest Germany. The sands where the soldiers of Cambyses were buried are those of the Arabian desert, which the Persian king crossed in 529–521 BCE on his way to and from Egypt. Herodotus, *The Histories* 3.11–12.

11. As in cantos 3.9 and 23.64, the comparison with a ship in danger of sinking is used to illustrate a psychological situation. See also the pilot simile in stanza 63 of this canto.

12. The nightingale announcing the approach of dawn to secret lovers was a commonplace of many romance narratives, from the medieval *albas* to the various early modern versions of the Romeo and Juliet story.

37

The more confident he became of soon reaching love's joys, the more he lamented the delay and sighed for the desired morning to arrive. Then, afraid of an unpleasant encounter, such as often happens to travelers, he put on a strong and shining coat of armor, even though his body and heart were strong.

38

Nardo carefully helped him fasten his armor. He agreed that it was a good idea to carry a shield, one of steel outside and lined with bone inside; then he hung a sharp sword from his hip. By now, Aurora, leaning her white face out of the red balcony of the east, had made the sky purple with the roses that bedecked her head and gilded it with the gold of her hair.

39

Pallante exited the army quarters and the town, and after leaving some words of excuse with the attentive and wise Nardo in case his father should ask for him, he was soon on his way riding his swift charger. He rode on until the sun, hiding its light in the sea, gave way to the dark and fearful shadows of the night. He never relented his gallop, not even for a moment, and encountered nothing to oppose his progress.

40

As the darkness began to thicken, blackening the air and the countryside all around, and Pallante longingly neared his destination, he got free of his fears and became increasingly happier. The stars were shining. The light of the moon, pouring down a limpid sky, dispelled the shadows, and where it first fell, the treetops seemed to turn their branches into silver.

41

In this moonlight splendor—far too bright for him, for it revealed the smallest objects—the young man turned appealingly toward the moon, and looking straight into the light, "O Cynthia," he says, "don't you remember the love that once warmed you so sweetly? You too poured many painful tears from your beautiful eyes, just as I do now from mine!

42

"You grieved miserably for your lost lover and forgot your bashful coldness. Heedless archer that you were, you were then far too intent on shooting arrows with your strong arm. I will not mention your amorous joys, for forests and trees keep silent about it.[13] Ah! I beg you, hide from me your untimely light!"[14] He wanted to say more, but a band of soldiers was about to come upon him.

43

He kept his eyes fixed on the sky—all his senses were taken up by his longing—and he no sooner heard the noise and the trampling of horses than he found himself surrounded by them. Vran had set up his scouts in this area in order to ascertain the truth about the adverse news he had just received. The road was blocked all around, and the leader himself, dressed in full armor, was not far away.[15]

44

When a lion, molested and bothered by hunger, is about to reach his desired prey, believing he will soon eat it, and then a group of hunters unexpectedly arrives and attacks him—some nearby prick him with lances and spits, while others throw stones and arrows from further away—still hungry and full of anger the lion fights on, for now he tries to fill his empty bowels with their flesh.[16]

45

Similarly Pallante, who was moaning and languishing as the deprived lover that he was, now tried to quench the amorous ardor oppressing his chest in the blood of the attackers who were delaying him so inconveniently. He brandished his sword and with the utmost boldness slew Elmon with a single blow, Elmon who left his beloved new bride sadly crying in Croia.

46

As insults and angry threats began to fly around and swords were menacingly drawn, the scouts told him he ought to consider himself beaten and

13. According to a legend, Artemis (or Selene, the Moon) fell in love with Orion, a beautiful youth whom she saw sleeping on a slope of Mount Latmos, in Caria. She was tricked by Apollo into shooting an arrow at a faraway target, which turned out to be the head of her beloved. William Smith, *Small Classical Dictionary* (New York: E. P. Dutton, 1968), 206.

14. The most famous prayers to the moon raised by warriors on dangerous night errands are found in *Aeneid* 9.403–9, in Statius's *Thebaid* 10.365–70, and in *Orlando Furioso* 18.183–84.

15. Pallante's situation here parallels that of Euryalus and Nisus, who are overtaken by the enemy during their night sortie in *Aeneid* 9.367–85, and that of Cloridano and Medoro, who are blocked by Zerbin's men while trespassing into Christian territory in *Orlando Furioso* 18.188–89 and 19.5–7.

16. For other lion similes see canto 1.39n.

should surrender at once. With great boldness he refused to do so; only afterward did the assailants realize their grievous mistake and how much they had misjudged what valor and power of resistance one single warrior might have.

47

Pallante went on defending himself: with the point of his sword he wounded Arminio; with a backhanded blow he hit the left arm of young Arighetto, whose face went all white while his cuirass turned blood red. Castor, who tried to strike Pallante on the helmet, hit his shield instead and in turn was wounded on his hip. Everyone was amazed, frightened, and angered. All around, the forest resounded with the noise of the fighting.

48

When a sword comes down on another sword, either by the point or by the cutting edge or on the flat, the stroke has such force that the air around trembles and the horrible noise is heard from afar. Vran arrived on a gallop after a short run, and when he saw Pallante defending himself alone against many, he had him encircled by new armed men and ordered him to surrender.[17]

49

Although a warm stream of blood was pouring to the ground from wounds on his right hand, from one arm and a shoulder, Pallante continued to shield himself and to hit with courage and boldness. When he noticed that the valiant Vran was being looked up to and obeyed by all the men who had just arrived, and he realized that he was losing blood in great abundance, with great effort he subdued his sense of dignity.

50

Turning to Vran, he said: "Baron, I will surrender gladly only to you, if you take me prisoner and promise that the harm done to your men will not be

17. Vran is Alexander's closest ally. Throughout the poem he is described as his faithful and beloved friend: 2.12, 2.17, 2.19, 5.72, 7.27. He is in charge of Amantia, but for reasons of plot tactics, during the siege of the town he is confined to bed by a fever. Vran's character seems to be modeled on Vrana (in some texts, Urana) or Simon Altisferi, known in Italy as Altafoglia, who had served in the army of Alfonso of Naples and had received from that king the title of count. During the campaign against the Turks, Altisferi was Scanderbeg's consistently loyal captain and was charged with the defense of Kruja during the siege of 1450 (Hodgkinson, *Skanderbeg*, 103 and 227; Gegaj, *L'Albanie et l'invasion turque*, 11 n. 2). See his name in the cast of main characters.

avenged. Natural law tells me that my defense could not be an offense to
you, for a courageous man must face death with sword in hand, if he cannot escape it."

51

Vran listened with great surprise, realized how courageous the indomitable
young man was, and, judging him from his admirable behavior to be of
noble descent,[18] he said: "Knight, I give you my word of honor that I shall
take you prisoner and protect you from anyone who may want to harm you.
I swear it in the name of my God, who made himself a man.

52

"You defended yourself against the enemy like a warrior of high valor;
therefore I am more moved by admiration for your virtue than I am pained
and angered by the death of my men. Had you offended the beautiful
woman who has my heart in thrall, I still would surrender all desire for
revenge to your valor, and to you alone, such is the sway that virtue can
have over a noble heart."

53

Pallante was reassured by these words; he trusted the captain's promise, and
surrendering to a cruel and unjust fate, he handed him his sword and dismounted from his charger. All the while, however, he warmed the air with
burning sighs of love and went on considering within himself what an insurmountable wall is always to be found between a much-coveted fruit and the
hand that tries to reach it.

54

Vran ordered him to get back in the saddle, although the way to the fortress
from there was short. Except for taking him prisoner, he wished to use all
courtesies toward him. He inquired about the king and was answered with
the truth, for Pallante was well informed, as he himself had seen Alexander
come down the mountain and mount his deadly assault on the enemy camp.

55

He described the dead king's height which was greater than any other person's, the face, the shining eyes, and the regal countenance that inspired in

18. It is worth noticing that Sarrocchi calls her character Pallante (Latin, Pallas) by the name
of the young valorous son of King Evander, who in *Aeneid* 10.474–92, 11.95–99 is slain by
Turnus and tenderly mourned by Aeneas.

all love and respect.[19] As soon as Vran entered his quarters he ordered several people to take care of the young man. His wounds were then opened
and cleaned and he was soon assured of complete recovery.

56

The cuts were not deep but rather large, and gave the impression of being
more severe than they actually were. The young man felt little pain or none
at all from his wounds, but he smarted from a bigger and invisible one.
Hearing him sigh aloud and often, and realizing how spirited this high-
minded youth was, Vran was persuaded that something else must be the
reason for his sorrow, and he kindly encouraged him to reveal it.

57

Pallante replied that there was nothing wrong with him and in saying so
suppressed an even bigger sigh. As the sea waves whipped by the winds are
wont to spill out onto the beach, the ardor constrained in Pallante's heart
tried to escape, and finding the way to sighing and lamenting closed, it
began to come out through the eyes.

58

What the tongue refused to say was revealed by his eyes full of tears. Seeing
clearly his distress and feeling pity for him, Vran asked him again. "The
valor that resides in you—you have shown it!—ties you dearly to me," he
said, "and my heart wishes to know and share at least in part the unhappy
worry that agitates yours.

59

"This imprisonment is small matter, and these wounds are light for someone
of your strength of character, and your noble heart cannot possibly be languishing for such a trivial reason. Do not keep your pain hidden from me,
I beg you. As my prisoner, you may derive comfort, if not remedy, from me
alone, for my desire is to offer you one or the other."

60

He entreated him again and again with very persuasive words, showing a
soul full of passion and well disposed toward him. The prisoner could no

---

19. Sarrocchi's description of Alexander conforms to the epic standards of royal dignity, as well as
to the prescriptions of political treatises regarding the appropriate image to be assumed by a ruler.
Cf. 2.50, 7.55, and 14.68 where Alexander is compared to Jupiter. In *Aeneid* 7.783–84, Virgil writes
of Aeneas: "Splendidly beautiful in his body, he moves fully armed, towering by a whole head over
the other men." In *Africa* 7.999, mighty Scipio towers with his great stature over the legions.

longer hide the truth without being discourteous to the knight; so with abundant tears streaming out of his eyes and down his cheeks, he described his amorous anguish in great detail, and while he was telling his story his words became throttled and choked.

61

Then he added: "I wish I were locked in a dark prison, afflicted by a painful and mortal wound, rather than mocked by my sweet hope of love, for any other misfortune would be a lesser disappointment to me." Vran listened, and being by nature of gentle disposition, he felt pity for him and was reminded at once of how far away was the charming woman who was in possession of his noble heart.

62

A sharp pain began to invade him, as he remembered the bitter passion lingering in his own heart. His face turned pale, and he could not bear Pallante's lamentations and cries. So he turned to the young man and said with great compassion: "I will be glad to let you go if you give me your word of honor that you will come back and be my prisoner again by the new day."

63

The pilot of a ship, when a storm rages dangerously, opposing his journey,[20] and he sees himself wandering aimlessly on the sea, when, his vessel having struck a hard rock, he fears he will be soon sinking in the waves, if a light wind suddenly rises to steady his course and begins to blow him toward the harbor that now appears before him, this pilot can never feel a joy as great as that experienced by our handsome lover.

64

Pallante thanked Vran for the great favor and gave him his word as asked. Meanwhile, his woman awaited him, eagerly counting the minutes, and became very distressed when she saw the appointed time go by. She rejoiced at the slightest noise, believing it to be Pallante, ran to open the door, looked around, and then, regretting his slowness and her own error, she sighed.[21]

---

20. Other similes with ships in peril are in stanza 34 above and in cantos 3.9 and 23.64.

21. Flora is in the same psychological condition as Ruggiero, who at night waits for Alcina in his bedroom, counts mentally her steps toward it, and expectantly opens the door to look outside. *Orlando Furioso* 7.24–25. The same situation was described by Ovid in *Heroides* 19.51–54.

65

Her ears were so alert now that she could hear silence itself. Her lover, no less eager than she, mounted his swift horse, and though he was still ailing, he rode rapidly over the remaining road, more pained by the delay than by his wounds. As soon as he arrived, the ardent lover found someone to take him directly to her presence.

66

She stepped back trembling, remained motionless for some time, and did not say a word. Then she turned pale and rigid like a stone, one moment burning with hope and the next freezing out of fear. She looked at him intently: in her reckless and foolish longing, she believed she was imagining and not seeing what was there, for she had him always so strongly imprinted in her mind that now she believed she was seeing a phantom.

67

Finally she came to her senses, for a vision conjured by intense desire does not last very long, and while she made certain of what was before her, her strong and noble heart beat furiously in her breast. She would have felt less palpitation if an entire army had taken up arms against her. The young man understood how strongly she loved, and he conceived high hopes of reaching love's goal.

68

Although he did not look at her at once, for he had armed himself against the sudden sight of his beloved, his fine pink color ran out of his face and only pallor remained. His luminous eyes became veiled with crying and laughing, for at times after a long delay happiness turns into a sadness that pours out of one's heart in tears.

69

For some time he rested his cheek against hers, which was now wet with his crying. "Time and chance will take away all worries; be reassured, my soul, for in the end heaven will look favorably on us and will make you the beloved wife of your Pallante. When the war is won, my darling," he says, "we shall enjoy each other in happy contentment."

70

Now he looked at her most tenderly and a sunlike splendor shone forth from his eyes. His features changed color and his words were throttled by a mixture of tears and sighs, as happens to a lover who, painfully burning with desire and hope, pleads for his love with increased passion. Pallante did not feign his passionate love; he kissed, embraced, and clasped her tightly to him again and again.

71

Again they promised each other they would be husband and wife, and both saw, with no shadow of a doubt or fear, how strong was the amorous desire in their trusting hearts. Thus, being united as they had hoped, she sweetly received him in her chaste bed. Venus and Mars smiled at them, remembering the sweetness of their past delights.[22]

72

Presently Phoebus brought forth the day, and beautiful Aurora, his harbinger, also arrived. It was then time for Pallante to make his way sadly to the kind knight. Only at this point did the young woman notice the bandages wrapped around Pallante's wounds; she had not seen them before, because her ardent love had immersed her in little else but her pleasure.

73

She asked what had caused them, and he did not answer; he only moaned and sighed from the bottom of his heart. She began to tear out her blond hair, to slap her cheeks and rage against the heavens. She called him ungrateful for trying to hide from her something she could see with her own eyes. "In the future, then, how can you possibly be willing to tell me the truth," she says, "if I will not be able to see it myself?"

74

The beautiful woman cried, slapped herself, moaned, and kept on wailing, until he, unable to hide his unhappiness any longer, was forced to give in. Now she wanted to run away in secret with him, and her young lover did not oppose her wish, for she was ready to face all dangers with him, even death, let alone exile and prison.

75

Meanwhile, considering that his elite soldiers had been defeated in such a famous campaign, the tyrant withdrew to Presa before sunrise, with the favor of darkness and with an escort of carriages. In town, the preparations for the defense went on uninterrupted by either meal or sleep, while

22. The loves of Venus and Mars are told in Ovid's *Metamorphoses* 4.170–89 and in Politian's *Stanze per la giostra* 1.122–23.

soldiers and captains kept guard on the walls. The work continued fervently, and so did the watch.

76

The plan was to fortify the city and render it more defensible than ever before. The emperor wanted to provide it with high walls, double gates, and deep trenches. At the same time, he sent messages to his daughter asking her to gather the flower and vigor of the Ottoman army and come to his aid without delay.

77

He ordered Rosmonda to let her pugnacious mother sit on the throne and govern the empire, and to have the army ready at least before April's air began to melt the ice on the roads. Immediately the warrior princess made her father's high command known to all, called in all debts, and asked of friends and subjects a tribute in support of the war.

78

In the meantime the Christian king had gathered his troops in the city stronghold. All people were thankful to Palinuro, who had taken on the burden of defending the town. They bowed to him, expressing true affection for him in their faces and gestures. On his part, the valiant king proposed to reciprocate with an equal or even greater reward.

79

While the sun traveled over our hemisphere and moved beneath it, pulling the day behind in its train, the king was mulling over a pleasant idea, and now he discussed it with his captains. His loyal people supported him, encouraged, even urged his just desire, reminding him appealingly that it was his duty to give them a legitimate royal heir.

80

They told him that time does not stop but flies away relentlessly, breaking and undoing all the ties made by men, that the city would suffer again as it had in the past, and once more its inhabitants would feel alone and abandoned. They were certain that Aranit's daughter, being so virtuous and beautiful, was well worthy of becoming his wife, that her father would not refuse him the woman in marriage; on the contrary, he would consider it his everlasting glory.[23]

---

23. Aranit's daughter was the object of an attempted abduction in canto 1.27–31, 1.51–63. See also p. 24 above.

81

After long consideration, the king consented to this well-thought-out plan, for that way he would be able to please his loyal followers and at the same time satisfy the strong obligation he had incurred. Palinuro not only assented joyfully and thanked him profusely, but almost pled with him to take her.[24] Before they signed a formal agreement, however, the king wished to free the city from the fierce tyrant's siege.

82

First he wanted to make certain who his prisoners were and who among his soldiers and captains had been captured by the enemy. Several told him that the brave and generous Crater could not be found. Alexander was afraid that Crater, after having given up his horse for him, might have been killed, because once on foot, he remained exposed to mortal danger. A sense of obligation, of courtesy, piety, and love, as well as a painful conscience, caused the king's heart to race.

83

His unfounded fear made the benign and grateful king sigh repeatedly. Thinking that leaving Crater unburied on the battlefield did not become royal honor, he ordered a search. Someone told him that Crater was not dead but taken prisoner. This news pleased the king not a little, for, short of death, all misfortunes can be remedied.

84

Among the Christian king's courtiers was Artecin, a person valued for his courage and knowledge. This man was fond of any doctrine that would teach how men might govern themselves and their families with reason, and what laws might be given to kingdoms, so that good people would not be oppressed by bad ones and everyone, in the common interest and by way of prizes and punishments, could be led to behave virtuously and refrain from crime.[25]

24. In 1451 Scanderbeg did in fact marry Marina Andronika (Dorica, in some chronicles and histories) the daughter of Gjergj Arjanit Komneni Thopia. Contrary to what this text implies, the alliance was of great social and political advantage to Alexander, for the Arjanit Komneni were of very noble descent and enjoyed great prestige abroad.

25. What interests Artecin is the doctrine of statecraft. This stanza in fact gives a good indication of the subjects dealt with in contemporary political tracts. Another appeal to statesmanship is found in canto 1.47, in which Alexander concludes his speech by saying that the conduct he was ordered by the sultan to adopt toward the people of Belgrade is not one that would help a sovereign "to enlarge an empire and to hold onto subjects and tributaries." That statement aptly summarizes Machiavelli's purpose in writing *The Prince*.

85

He was so skilled in pleasing and enchanting his listeners[26]—to a degree comparable to the masters of Athens and Arpino[27]—that when he spoke, the anger and the disdain of all rebellious and stubborn minds melted away and ceased. Our compassionate hero sent Artecin with a message to the great Thracian to ask for a truce, so that the dead might be given a dignified burial. Behind this request a greater plan was hidden.

86

In confidence he told Artecin of his intention to return to the emperor of the Saracens[28] the prisoners he thought were of illustrious ancestry and high military rank, on condition that Crater, and only he, be sent back to him. He told him to put forward this wish at the proper moment, for the pride of the Thracian was known to be dangerous, and forgetting all consideration for his men, the sultan might take revenge even on his friend.

87

He might pretend to ask, out of his own sense of piety, to save that warrior from injury or death, for it was not untoward for a good man to use some guile when dealing with an evil person. Artecin stored away all these instructions in his mind and traveled to the emperor's court, after receiving from him a safe-conduct for himself and others, as he had asked.

88

Once in the emperor's imposing presence, he composed his face, his gestures, and his motions to gravity and attention, and affecting an expression dignified and respectful at the same time, he presented his message in a pleasing manner. The Thracian listened to him benignly, and then without making any promises, and disguising his thoughts under ambiguous words, he replied that reason required him to consider the matter carefully before he could decide.

26. Taking the lead from ancient histories and classic epics, and sharing her contemporaries' interest in oratory, Sarrocchi has made the speeches of lords, ambassadors, and generals a captivating feature of her narrative. Oratorical skills are recommended as very useful to a ruler in Botero's *The Reason of State*, and repeatedly remarked upon in this poem. Cf. above, canto 1.11n.

27. The reference is to Demosthenes and Cicero, the two most famous orators of antiquity, born in Athens and in Arpino, a town near Rome, respectively.

28. In Renaissance chivalric poems, "Saracens" are the Arabs who invaded Europe and against whom Charlemagne and his paladins waged war. In time the term came to indicate Asiatic and African people in general. Cf. 10.39, 13.52, 14.101, 20.13. See above, canto 5.14n.

89

Artecin repeated his request courteously; the emperor did not get angry but listened quietly, recognizing how effective an eloquent speech could be, and how valuable self-assurance and good manners were when used together. "Only good government, Sire, becomes a mind like yours, which is dedicated to governing with reason and justice. You will therefore realize how small a prize this would be compared with what is due to your valorous soldiers.

90

"They have given you the highest proof of devotion, of which a greater one cannot be offered. If you take away from the dead what is due to them, you will also deprive the living of any hope of reward. Those who reign must show compassion and love more often than anger and power; they are not to deny the dead their rightful burial. and when their soldiers are captured, they must free them from the harsh chains of prison.

91

"They also must care in a benign and humane manner for all the wounded[29]—be they servants, relatives, strangers, or prisoners—in the same considerate and humane way my lord behaves toward those men of yours who are his prisoners. I am most confident in his just conduct," Artecin continues, "and that whenever you decide to return his men in your possession, he will return to you all of yours that are now his captives.

92

"People are human and are nurtured, you know, Sire, by humane conditions, not by vicious treatment.[30] All human beings are naturally born free; only force, not reason, makes slaves out of them. So if a king happens to forsake pity, he will destroy his right as well as his power to rule. A ferocious mastiff is made loyal and affectionate more by considered ways than by chains.[31]

93

"A magnanimous soldier can best be controlled and taught to follow orders by a gentle hand, just as a worthy soul can be bent to obedience more readily

---

29. Botero insists that soldiers should be made confident that the state will take care of them if they are wounded or maimed and that a means of livelihood will be provided for them. *The Reason of State* 9.11.

30. This principle too may be traced to Botero: humane laws, he says, make men humane, while cruel regulations and customs make them cruel. *The Reason of State* 1.12, 4.4, 9.11.

31. Cf. the vivid image of a mastiff in action at canto 9.52 below.

by rewards than by punishments. Souls that are full of disinterested courage are lured by the promise of honor and angered by the prospect of shame, and soldiers are more proud and desirous of glory than any other men."

94

While Artecin was thus bending the emperor's indomitable heart toward magnanimity, and with true eloquence was differentiating between violent means and humane and reasonable ones, it so happened that one of his servants started to talk to a large number of Turks gathered around him, among them many ignorant and insolent soldiers with very commonplace judgment.

95

This servant was named Romidon, a man obstinate in his behavior and way of thinking, with a habit of moving about quickly and darting glances here and there, precipitous in his judgment and in talking, and very conceited in his opinions. His body was agile and fast, his hair red, his temples narrow, and his head lean and short.

96

He did not take pleasure in outright deceit, but he could never be quiet; he had to tell right away all he saw and heard, mixing truth and falsehood in all his statements. He so enjoyed his own ingenuity in telling stories that he embroidered, exaggerated, or made up all the facts—to the extent that now he was boasting to be privy to the king's most personal and secret thoughts.

97

Following his instinctual urge, he posed as a great sage before these people. Amused and curious, the crowd stood around him and, pulling his leg, raised praise of him to the heavens. So, full of himself and driven by a foolish zeal for his religion, Romidon began to say that the king in his presence spoke often thus:

98

"In truth, the person who sincerely believes in God is happy on earth now and will be so in heaven later. Those who spread the holy faith in Jesus with piety and zeal eventually will enjoy the beatitude they have been waiting for. All human souls are destined to shed their mortal veil on earth, and no saintly behavior will give it back or allow them to keep it, except the power and word of Christ.

99

"Christ leads all the faithful to good behavior and shows them the way to the truth. The people in whom faith in the good Jesus does not reign are miserable and despicable. The hope of an ignominious gain can easily push these creatures to vile and unjust actions because, out of stupidity, they are incapable of seeing man's real goal, and believe it to be an earthly possession rather than a heavenly one, as it really is.

100

"Jesus warms people's hearts with so much charity as to banish all misleading desires. His earthly and heavenly love affects everyone in the same way, because human minds and hearts, once purified, take on the quality of their divine object and all become endowed with the same great virtue, no matter how different their actions on earth may have been.

101

"Up there they will enjoy that well-deserved and sure reward that makes the soul blissful, and on earth they obtain what they desire, for here too they are awarded an authentic prize of everlasting honor. That mountain that seems to be so difficult to climb may lead us, by the strength of true and holy virtue, to reach a glory that is much desired by all and will last even after death.

102

"So it is that Christ not only gives us heaven but also here on earth makes a steep mountain easy to climb. He instills in us a knowledge that renders vain the power of kings and tyrants, because only reason and justice can invigorate our hand and infuse courage in our hearts. He who does not recognize the true God may never know the art of war and government."[32]

103

At this point Romidon decided to check his speech lest he might incite those people to anger and indignation, except for saying that the zealous king would state this and more in his speeches, which were always about God, and that neither hatred nor envy could poison his pious disposition,

---

32. Romidon's spiel to the Turkish soldiers is certainly the most idiosyncratic among the many speeches scattered throughout this poem. Those delineating a governing policy or a military strategy are listed at 1.40n; others, rallying soldiers in flight, are enumerated at 23.29n. In canto 5.96–98 Pyrrhus rebuts Orkhan's request for surrender, and soon after, at 5.100–105, Vaconte urges the Albanian men to fight to the death.

which always made him regret other people's grief, assist the sick, and give hospitality to the derelict.

104

Although in essence correct, Romidon had expressed the meaning of what the king said with so much distortion and deviation from fact as to turn it into blame of other people. He added much that was near the truth but misleading, and thus he managed to arouse anger in everyone. A generalized insult is most displeasing, such as the one he uttered now by saying that the king called them all stupid and cowardly, good only to subvert both earthly and divine order.

105

People devoid of reasonableness and good faith, who are not up to either obeying or giving orders, place their trust only in violence and weaponry as repositories of justice and truth. Not wanting to believe in anything else, they give way to their impressions and to the power of force, and considering false all laws except their own, they never correct any of their mistakes.

106

Some of the most intelligent soldiers easily recognized Romidon's reckless loquacity for what it was, for in military camps as well as in courts there are people with very capable minds, though they may feed their hopes and desires on false opinions. Everyone tries to win the favor of his lord and master, a favor that evil men never acquire honestly.

107

However, the majority of the less perspicacious men got angry and quickly picked up their weapons. They were exceedingly incensed that a foreigner should dare to insult them in their own country; and without thinking for a moment that they were disrespectful of the emperor's word, they unsheathed their swords, and shouting savagely, all together flung themselves upon Romidon, who now had good reason to fear for his life.

108

In the same way, perhaps, a child unwittingly comes upon a thick swarm of stinging bees, whose rest he has disturbed and whose hive he has broken into, convinced that he was just playing; unexpectedly the bees rush toward him at a great speed, their sharp stings pointed toward his eyes and face. Realizing his error far too late, the child begins to cry and runs away.[33]

109

The insane boaster tried to run from the violent aggression and found escape in flight, for any argument now would have been wrong and useless. At this point, Ormus and Arigazel, who were the captains in charge of the soldiers, came out to see what was happening, and realizing that all sharp orders would be in vain, they tried to placate their men with conciliatory words.[34]

110

Arigazel said to them: "What is the cause of this furor? What drives you to such an error? The sword that strikes and wounds this man is guilty of murdering his own emperor! This man has trusted himself to you on the emperor's word, and whoever betrays his master's sworn promise becomes a much worse murderer than the man who kills him.

111

"Who can accuse of a serious offense a man who is unarmed and can rely only on the strength of his body? A magnanimous man must surely forgive him for any error he may have made. And as far as you are concerned, what punishment for your error must you not expect from the emperor who is as gracious as he is fair toward us? Put your weapons to better use, I pray you! I order you as your friend and captain.

112

"You have the choice of either being forgiven or being punished by your sovereign. What is the point of aggravating and giving him a good reason to get angry with you when he has none at present? Let the imperial court distinguish true from false, let reason alone assign the blame, let the punishment fall on the guilty one with justice, and use your sword only when not doing so proves impossible."

113

The captain advised them so, and in his advice mixed prayers, threats, and promises of punishment and of rewards. He put on an expression imperi-

---

33. The idea of wasps stinging children who have disturbed their hive is borrowed from *Iliad* 16.259–65. For bee similes, see canto 15.56, Virgil's *Georgics* 4.162–69, and *Aeneid* 1.430–34.
34. About the story of Romidon, see pp. 31 and 39 above.

ously wrathful but at the same time severely humane, so that he could hold them back by giving them hope of being pardoned and making them afraid of having aroused the wrath of the great emperor, who expected any hint from him to become a law for all.

114

When bulldogs in a pack are seen to attack in a great rage a passerby who under a dark sky has chanced to come across them inadvertently, if they see their master come to his rescue, not only do they let go of him and withdraw with their heads lowered and their tails between their legs, but they run far off, so great is their fear of their master's anger and threats.

115

In the same way, each man, worried and fearful, certain of error and uncertain of the outcome, now went respectfully before his captain and hid neither fear nor guilt from him. With an air of authority the officers asked them to reveal the cause of what had happened, and the soldiers recounted the event, mixing their story with complaints, increasing Romidon's fault and minimizing their own.

CANTO 8

Angered by Romidon's offensive talk about Christianity and Islam, the sultan demands that faith be championed in single combat. While arrangements are made for it, Alexander has a vision of heaven, in which it is revealed to him that Vaconte is to be the Christian champion.

CANTO 9

Agrismeta is chosen to be the Turkish champion to fight the duel against Vaconte. He loses the fight and dies. The spectators rush into the enclosure and a general melee follows.

1

Full of wonder, the wise leader reopened his eyes to the light of day. All he saw around him seemed dark compared with the splendor of paradise. "If I were in heaven, how did I return to earth again?[1] What new sin has again relegated me here?" he asked, and then, sad and disconsolate, he thought back to where he had been, what he saw and what he heard.

2

But since he had to remain on earth, he curbed the longing burning in his soul, for he knew that those who struggled here would later ascend to heaven to enjoy eternal peace. He knew that immortal justice and immortal love have locked human beings into the prison of the senses, so that they may gain paradise by engaging on earth in a battle that keeps their intellects continuously challenged.[2]

1. Alexander's astonishment at finding himself on earth after his vision echoes very closely Petrarch's lines: "Qui come venn'io, o quando? Credendo esser in ciel, no là dov'era" (I asked myself: "How did I come down here, or when?" believing I was still in heaven, not where I was). From "Clear, fresh, and sweet waters," *Canzoniere* 126.62–63. Similar is Godfrey's surprise after his vision: "Ma poi che si riscote, e che discorre chi venne, chi mandò, che gli fu detto" (But after he woke up and considered who came, who sent, and what was said). *Jerusalem Delivered* 1.17–18.

2. Bedazzled by the phantasmagoria of the sensorial impressions, humankind can no longer perceive the truth it once knew. In the Christian interpretation of this Platonic theory, humankind, by the contemplation of progressively more abstract forms of beauty, may ascend to a purely intellectual contemplation of God. This gradual ascent to the divinity, usually referred to as "the ladder of love," is expounded by Romito in the third book of Bembo's *Gli Asolani* and by the character of Pietro Bembo in the fourth book of Castiglione's *The Courtier.* Cf. canto 7.14 above.

3

Bowing to the will of God, the king prepared himself for toil and travail, because he knew that the more we suffer anguish here, the greater will be our happiness in heaven. Similarly, the snow that is still on the ground at the end of winter forecasts hard work for the farmer; however, the more frozen are the cornfields that begin to thaw in the breezes of spring, the richer and blonder they will become later in the season.

4

He summoned the captains to a private chamber and told them directly what the divine wish was. He let them know what was involved in the choice of the knight and, out of modesty, nothing else. Nonetheless he had them understand that he was told of it when he was in a state in which the confusion of the senses did not veil one's knowledge of the truth,[3] for at times the Sun at his brightest throws his splendor into the most obscure and lowly places.

5

The sun had not gone around its orbit twenty times yet since Vaconte's birth. The flowers of youth bloomed on his face like blond crocuses mingled with white and pink violets. His hair, twisted in lovely ringlets, looked like gold fluttering in waves over snow; and his serene blue eyes gave out flashes of martial fervor.

6

The sparkle of his eyes was enhanced by finely bent eyelashes with a more virile hue of gold; his slightly curved nose showed the majesty of royal blood; his face made an impression of vigor and daring, which turned into graceful handsomeness; and from a mouth made of chosen pearls and rubies came only words that were sparing, truthful, and modest.[4]

7

He had a fair neck, wide shoulders, and full chest. His physique was very well developed for his age. Slender thighs were set against a large chest; the legs were of solid muscle, the foot agile, the knee muscular and well shaped.

---

3. See the previous note.

4. In this and in the preceding stanza, Vaconte—like Osman at 3.48—is described following the same standards of comeliness that in vernacular literature presided over the depiction of female beauty. The images of pearls and rubies may have been suggested by the picture that Virgil gives of young Ascanius, whose fine head framed by blond hair is compared to a gem set in gold (*Aeneid* 10.132–45). Cf. canto 1.29–30 and above, canto 1.29n.

His arms were strong, ending with hands powerful and limber enough to open the bow, throw the spear, and slash the sword around in wide circles.

8

As soon as Alexander announced the preordained choice of the knight, all the captains placed high hopes in Vaconte, feeling confident that he would be the invincible defender of truth, because the eternal knowledge shed light directly into their thoughts and bestowed on them good judgment and reasonableness. So they consented and applauded the choice unanimously, giving praise and thanks to the king in heaven.[5]

9

The wise king ordered old Pyrrhus to make immediate preparations for the martial contest and see to it that the contenders were sheltered both from the Christian and the heathen side. Then he sent word to the emperor that Vaconte had been chosen for such a high purpose. The emperor laughed within himself when he heard that the king had entrusted a boy with so important a task.

10

He thought about all the victories reported by Agrismeta and considered the duel already won. In a happy mood he ordered Corcutte to prepare whatever was necessary for the duel. Corcutte went forthwith out of Presa with many soldiers to whom tasks had been assigned, in order to choose a spot in the countryside that, conforming to military regulations, could be the ground on which the two champions would fight.

11

At the same time Pyrrhus exited Croia with many soldiers: they marched in files and he advanced at their side. The area that was filled with trenches by the Turks was appropriate for the duel, but it was too near the town. So they left it behind, and farther down in the same plain, in its middle, they found a suitable area at equal distance from both Croia and Presa.

12

The provident engineers ordered the site chosen for the duel to be leveled, and they also wanted it free of all encumbrances up to a considerable

---

5. The character of Vaconte may have been suggested by Scanderbeg's favorite nephew, Hamza Castrioti. His traits are also similar to those of Rinaldo, the young romantic hero in Tasso's *Jerusalem Delivered*.

distance, so that everyone could feel secure and protected from any possible enemy ambush. When the field had been carefully cleared, they all began to wait for the day of the great duel.

13

Sitting surrounded by his captains, the king ordered the knight to come to his presence. Just as usually happens when a virgin hears that her parents have given her in marriage to the man she is yearning for, Vaconte listened to the messenger with a premonition of what was going to happen: his face was ablaze with combative enthusiasm that added to the natural air of virility that the simple attire and unkempt hair gave him.

14

He arrived before the king and was received cordially. Even in his benign countenance the king revealed an earnest concern, and as he talked about the event as a predestined one, he showed wisdom and courage far above the human requisite. "Knight, you have been chosen by destiny, and as executor of God's will, not of mine, I place on your shoulders the burden of this grand and responsible task.

15

"I will not remind you of the illustrious lineage that you draw from our oldest ancestors, for you have always despised scepters, diadems, gems, and purple attire as something transitory and fragile. I will not mention the high deeds and the extraordinary proofs of selflessness you have given since childhood, when with an adolescent hand you subdued tigers, bears, and lions.

16

"But what am I saying? Not your youth, not the celebrated deeds carried out by the strength of your arm assure me of victory or make me doubt it; it is that wonderful truth of which I never lost sight in the depth of my being. At Terebinth the giant fell under the first stone thrown by the Hebrew youth, and perhaps God wants to renew that example with you fighting against another evil man.[6]

6. The Hebrew youth is David, who fought against Goliath in the valley of Elah. *Elah* is the Hebrew word for "terebinth," the turpentine tree. See 1 Samuel 17. Terebinth is alluded to also in *Jerusalem Delivered* 7.78.1–2. While Sarrocchi was working on her poem, a fresco of David and Goliath was being painted by Cavalier d'Arpino in the villa called "Il Belvedere" that Cardinal Pietro Aldobrandini, nephew of Clement VIII, had built at Frascati. In 1604 Giambattista Marino, who was the guest and protégé of the cardinal, celebrated the subject of the painting in a poem later included in *La Galeria* (1619).

17

"If God came to the rescue of an unarmed young man who was defending the people dear to him, and helped him to do it, we should not fear defeat, for we are taking on a task entrusted to us by God himself." He said no more than that, and very shrewdly ended his speech rather ambiguously, in order to hide the assurance of victory he had received and not to belittle in Vaconte's eyes his future triumph or his faith in God.

18

Pyrrhus had come back and, hearing what the king had said, announced: "I shall have a part in this victory." And he gave Vaconte a coat of armor and a shining helmet whose power did not seem of man's doing. These weapons had belonged to the powerful and pious Trojan[7] who in antiquity gave origin to the city of Mars; they had been given to the ancient Pyrrhus by that good Roman who saved him from the poison administered by an evil hand.[8]

19

When he saw those famous accouterments, Rodoman said: "If my gifts are not despised, I too wish to join in this illustrious deed by making a military offering. I gained this sword in close contest with strong Torrismondo, and now I give it to you. I then took his sword away as well as his sinful life, which the infinite forgiveness of God condoned, turning it into a better one.

20

"As he was mortally wounded and about to die, he begged to be sprinkled with holy water. At the moment when the grace of the merciful creator of the whole universe penetrated his heart, in that instant he was cleansed of all his old sins and made pure. O high mystery of God! If we understand you well, the same hand that kills may at times give us immortal life.

7. This is Aeneas. He is called "pious" in the Roman sense of *pius*, on account of his devotion to the state, to ancestors, and to the gods. Aeneas's journey from Troy to Latium, where his descendants will found Rome, the city of Mars, is the subject of Virgil's *Aeneid*.

8. The Roman who saved Pyrrhus of Epirus from poisoning—the one called the "Tarentine" in canto 1.15—is the general Caius Fabricius, who refused to kill Pyrrhus, his enemy, as Pyrrhus's physician had offered to do for him, and instead informed the enemy about the intended treason. Plutarch, "Pyrrhus" 21.1–3. By creating the story of the gift—the armor of Aeneas—given by Fabricius to Pyrrhus the Tarentine, Sarrocchi wished to establish a parallel between her poem and the *Aeneid*. In canto 3.463–71 of Virgil's epic, Aeneas, in the land of Epirus, is given the breastplate and the helmet that had belonged to Pyrrhus, son of Achilles, by the son of King Priam of Troy.

21

"Torrismondo was the worst man among the infidels living at the time, but at the moment of losing his mortal life, he was granted an eternal one. He gave me his sword and said: Take this sword, the finest and strongest there is, which has slain so many servants of Jesus. With this sword you must vindicate the unjust deaths of so many, and inflict a similar destiny on as many evil men.

22

" 'No one will be as proud of the spoils he conquers as you should be of mine, because in exchange for a vain and passing glory you have given me a true and eternal triumph in heaven.' " Rodoman was silent, and the king added: "To all the gifts you have received I will add a noble horse, one swifter than the wind and as strong as a bull that is the honor and boast of the Bruttian herd."⁹

23

It was Ferdinand who had sent this horse to the king. He was Appius's brother, and Appius was Vaconte's father. It was a bay horse, well shorn, with hoofs that were dry, thick, and dark; he had ample and well-shaped chest and neck, a small and muscular head; his rump was square, his legs slender, supple, and quick to the gallop. A white star made a fine show on his forehead.

24

On the day preceding the duel the Thracian emperor too summoned his champion, Agrismeta, and said to him: "Invincible knight, the high Prophet destines you to great honor. Had you not been chosen to be the defender of our faith, this duel would be of little glory to your high valor, for these are cowardly people, people afflicted by famine, to whom the heavens have never shown a pleasant face.

25

"So be mindful of Mohammed's honor! For his sake forget everything else! What unworthy infamy would it be for us if you died, what dishonor for God! If I had thought this duel were becoming to an emperor, I would have taken it on myself. But heaven has given me the task of governing the empire, and not of fighting as a soldier."

9. The mountains of Bruttium (modern Calabria in southern Italy) were known for the quality of the cattle.

26

Bowing low before him, the warrior listened to the great Thracian and believed his words to be sincere. And although he was silent out of respect, he made it clear that he would accomplish even more than was asked of him. Then, as the proud and courageous man he was, Agrismeta turned his mind and his steps toward the duel and, once back in his quarters, waited impatiently for the new day to arrive.

27

Dawn opened the high balcony of the sky to the morning light and appeared there, her golden hair adorned with a great diversity of flowers and her limbs wrapped in a bejeweled mantle.[10] The dark horrors that clothed the fearful darkness of Night were torn apart, and she ran away as far as possible into hiding, so ashamed was she of her gloomy pall.

28

As soon as he saw the first light, Agrismeta peremptorily called for his squires to come in a hurry and quickly arose from bed, hardly waiting for the usual services. Around him there were already a larger number of Turks than usual, and more than one friendly hand was ready to help him put on his chosen weapons.

29

Some of them checked minutely to see that they were in order, but he disdainfully took them without even looking and put them on in great haste, impatient of anything that might delay the desired contest. First he covered his legs with leggings of steel that were held in place by buckles of shiny silver; then he concealed his thighs under plates on which a relief of golden stars glittered.

30

He enclosed his chest in a cuirass as hard as adamant and his neck in a very fine throat piece. The very beautiful planet[11] that brings daytime over the earth, with his first rays shines on his sister, the crescent moon, whenever she cannot dispel the dark shadows of the night with her silvery horns: on

---

10. See other natural sights described as studded with precious materials at 3.7, 6.61, 7.36, 7.40, 10.20, and 19.22.

11. The sun. It is clear that Sarrocchi does not endorse the new Copernican theories. These theories, however, began to be widely argued about, and Galileo was condemned for championing them around 1532, well after Sarrocchi's death.

the cuirass their bejeweled faces were made to sparkle in a bright, well-crafted work, she with rubies and he with diamonds.

31

Agrismeta covered his arms with a steel plate divided at the elbow, and what remained unprotected between hauberk and armpits he covered with mail. For safety, as well as for ornament, he shielded his head with a helmet of which there was no equal for craftsmanship and value; the helmet had a crest flashing with emeralds and diamonds and was topped by red feathers waving in the breeze.

32

At one side he hung a sharpened sword closed in a sheath that sent out an agreeable perfume. The pommel glittered with white oriental sapphires, the hilt was etched in resplendent gold, and a flashing decoration of sparkling rubies adorned the gauntlet. Then on the arm he flung a large and thick shield made of three layers of impenetrable whale bone.

33

Thus equipped, Agrismeta walked over to where his charger was waiting, adorned with a superb saddle. The horse was blacker than a black crow, of great stamina, of agile and slender shape. His feet were light and swift in running, three of them white. The head was shaped like a ram's, with a fine white mark on the forehead and nose; his neck was lean and the chest of small proportions.

34

The charger bit the bit and frothed at the mouth, shook his high mane, neighed and spurted; and to show his readiness for battle, he pulled, jerked, and turned this way and that. Soon the knight was addressing the people who stood there, dejected at his departure: "Compose your hearts and your expressions to happiness," he told them, "for in a few hours I will be back victorious."

35

He chose four men to escort him, the closest to him. Behind them came a company led by Talarco, two thousand soldiers in all, as allowed to each side by mutual agreement.[12] Agrismeta mounted his horse and swiftly galloped to

---

12. One thousand is the number of men in *Jerusalem Delivered* who accompany Argantes, the chosen champion of the Muslim faith, to the enclosure where he will fight a duel with a Christian knight, and Agrismeta is as eager to fight here as Argantes is in that poem. See *Jerusalem Delivered* 6.21.1–2.

the enclosure prepared for the combat. When he saw that Vaconte was late, he began to fume with intense resentment and indignation.

36

The more he had to wait for him, the lesser the value he believed his victory would have. He was like a greyhound who sees the wild prey from afar and is prevented from reaching it by thorny and thick hedges; or like a dog taken by an urge to run but held back by his leash. Ah! How mistaken human judgment is! We wait for something we expect to be good, but then it turns out to be something harmful.

37

He galloped all around the field inveighing against the slow passing of time, for he believed that no warrior could escape his great valor. But as quickly as the thunder is heard after a flash of lightning, the other fighter appeared on his charger, in the choicest armor, flanked by his wisest and most trustworthy friends.

38

The count of Arnosa was carrying his fine helmet, which Mars and Phoebus would have said was theirs,[13] a helmet so favored by them that they would wear it even between wars while climbing the sacred mountain. Pyrrhus, who flanked Vaconte on the other side, carried the shield, which had the inner side lined with six layers of well-seasoned cowhide, while the outside was protected by strong steel.

39

Only two massive lances made of old oak had been chosen out of many. Both were thoroughly examined from all sides by two loyal friends, and each of them was given one to carry. And now the courteous Vaconte greeted his enemy with polite words, as a friend is accustomed to do with his friend.

40

Although angry, the pagan warrior looked up and considered the kind gesture, and as he stared at the fresh face of the handsome youth, which sur-

13. Mars and Phoebus had their armor made by Vulcan, the god of forging and smelting, who worked inside Mount Etna. In *Aeneid* 8.424–53, Aeneas's suit of armor is prepared by the cyclopes by order of Vulcan. Virgil's description of that shield is based on Homer's description of Achilles' shield in *Iliad* 18.468–78. Cf. above, stanza 18n.

passed the beauty of snow and roses, and at the radiance of his eyes sparkling in the sun, he was astonished by his youth and comeliness and felt sorry that he would have to kill him.[14]

41

"What mad desire for honor leads you to death at such a tender age?" he asked. "A fate that is benignly inclined toward you arouses in me pity for your age and beauty." On the face of Vaconte, who did not mind dying if he could face death in the service of God, a feeling of piety spread a blush, and a smile appeared that was both friendly and unfriendly.

42

"I thank you for the pity you feel for my dying, which to you seems certain, making you so courteous toward me; but fear of death never prevented me from behaving with honor," he says. And saying so, his beautiful snow-white face was flushed again with an even more attractive red blush, and the bravery of his valiant heart sparkled in his shining eyes.

43

Meanwhile the count placed on his bare head the helmet of the pious Trojan and laced it up. Pyrrhus handed him the shield and urged him to victory for the glory of Jesus. Hearing that the young warrior refused to give up the fight, the haughty pagan became angrier than he was before, when he intended to ask for a different opponent, and without saying another word, he couched his lance, ready for combat.[15]

44

With just as fast a move, the young man turned his charger around and boldly galloped toward him and, with no less boldness and ferocity, aimed his lance at the middle of his opponent's chest, in the attempt to kill him at

14. Agrismeta's pity for Vaconte is suggested by *Aeneid* 10.806–30, where Aeneas kills Lausus and then, looking at his youthful face, is sorry for his untimely death. In *Orlando Furioso* 19.10.7–8, Zerbin is about to kill Medoro but takes pity on him when he sees how beautiful the young man is.

15. In the stanzas that follow, Sarrocchi vies with previous descriptions of single combats. Cf. *Iliad* 22.78–394; *Aeneid* 12.710–952; *Orlando Furioso* 41.68–102, 42.6–17, 46.115–40; *Jerusalem Delivered* 6.40–51, 12.55–63. Sarrocchi's presentation is realistic in many details, plausible at all stages of the action. The beauty and abundance of similes—the mastiff biting the sword, the viper swelling its neck, the wild boar grinding its fangs, the rock contemptuous of the sea crashing against it, the lion roaring in anger, the bull butting in the air, the tower crashing to the ground—give it color and strength. About animal similes see above, canto 1.39n.

the first blow. The metal point remained clean and shiny, because the force of the impact was lessened by the powerful armor: even so, the pagan shook more than once.

45

In the sudden and powerful collision, the knotty wooden lance shattered like glass. The horse was pushed back and was about to fall on his rump, but the good knight, skillfully and measuredly, succeeded, with hands and feet, in pulling the animal up again. Even so, in the violence of the impact, the leather of the saddle broke just under his chest.

46

Now it was the young man who was struck in the visor, exactly where it joined the guard and locked it in; and if the piece had not been perfectly in place, this single blow would have ended the fight. At the same time, the impact unsteadied and weakened Agrismeta's lance, which achieved its aim obliquely and slid off to one side. So the pagan ran his course in vain, while Vaconte gave no sign of faltering.

47

The Turk marveled at seeing the young man still in his saddle after such a terrible blow. His haughty and pitiless mind could not countenance the fact that Vaconte had not fallen; he inveighed against the heavens and, with lance still intact, turned his good steed around to joust again, without considering, in his contemptuous wrath, whether his enemy was in possession of one.[16]

48

Vaconte's good squire, seeing him without a lance, handed over the other, before the opponent could attack him. Now the young knight turned his horse faster than any arrow or whirlwind; and even though the pagan warrior did not stay put where he wanted him, he reached into the mail under the armor, at the point where the arm piece joins the shoulder, and managed to throw him off his horse.

49

At the same moment, his lance could not stand the ponderous impact of the pagan and broke into a hundred pieces. Agrismeta had aimed his at the young man's cheeks but succeeded only in hitting the air and the

---

16. Agrismeta is the prototypical opponent, impatient, relentless, irrational. Cf. above, canto 5.3n.

wind. As soon as his back touched the ground, a terrible anguish came over him: wrath and shame drove him out of his mind, and he went mad with fury.

50

The unusual nature of this fall made the pain, whose sharpness grew steadily, even more anguishing, for he could not explain how it had happened. He did not realize that a buckle was broken and that the saddle could no longer hold him on, and that was why he saw himself slide down the charger's back; but as the saddle still remained half tied on the horse, he could not understand what he had done wrong.

51

He got up and walked toward Vaconte and was so out of his mind with anger that he did not think, nor did he care, about what an unsaddled knight was allowed to do, nor did he consider what his own situation might be. He thought only of plunging his sword into Vaconte's heart and veins and did not look out for his own danger and harm as long as he could inflict a mortal wound on the enemy.[17]

52

With as much rage a mastiff throws himself against a sword or arrow, bites it with its teeth, with no awareness that in its vengeful aggression it is hurting itself even more.[18] Even so, Vaconte waited for him courteously, and seeing him on foot, got off his horse, because he would not allow someone else's incorrect and vile behavior to force him to behave less politely and courageously.

53

"What are you doing? You are my prisoner," he shouted. "Are you forgetting the agreed rules of combat?" The other did not answer and tried to make excuses for his failure with the point of his sword. Seeing that the pagan was ignoring all reason, the young man was offended, and with his shield he fended off the great thrust his opponent's hand had already aimed in his direction.

17. Agrismeta's reluctance to give up the fight reminds us of Ferraguto, who, unsaddled by Argalia, goes on fighting against courtly rules. *Orlando Innamorato* 1.1.73.

18. Here it is the ferociousness of the mastiff that is stressed above all, while at 7.92 the point made was that even fierce animals can be made gentle by gentle treatment. See also canto 14.98 below.

54

Very swiftly, and with all his might, Vaconte hit him on the head with a downward stroke, but the Turk had attentive eyes, alert mind, and two hands quick to respond. With a similar noise clouds pregnant with dark rain clash when Sirius shines; with similar strength Steropes bangs down his hammer when making pointed arrows for Jupiter.[19]

55

The pagan felt the big blow and turned white with anger, but with no fear in his heart. His helmet was intact and he was not wounded, but the terrible stroke stunned him. He was like a viper that becomes bolder when offended: pricking up its scales and swelling its neck, with red eyes flashing, the snake hisses and darts against the man who has thrown a heavy stone at it.[20]

56

He lifted his sword toward Vaconte's left shoulder with such swiftness that the young man had no time to raise his shield to protect it. The sharp blade cut through the steel, found its way into the mail underneath, tearing them both off and onto the ground, and as the shoulder and part of the arm remained naked, it penetrated further, reaching under the breastplate, thus making the blood flow out in a double stream.

57

That terrible thrust affected the pagan and the Christian side of the public in different ways.[21] One side was seized by hope, the other by fear; but both made a wrong forecast, because the danger emboldened the Christian

---

19. Sirius, also called Canis, is the most important star in the constellation of the Great Dog. It appears in July, during the period when summer thunderstorms are the noisiest. Steropes was one of the cyclopes, giants with only one eye on their forehead, who lived inside Mount Etna and helped Vulcan to forge lightning for Jupiter and arrows for heroes. They are written about by Hesiod, Homer, and Ovid.

20. This is an elaboration, very vividly executed, of two well-known precedents: Hector in *Iliad* 22.93–94 and Pyrrhus in *Aeneid* 2.471–72 are compared to snakes ready to strike. The snake similes found in *Orlando Innamorato* 1.8.37.6 and in *Orlando Furioso* 30.56.1, on the other hand, display a comic overtone: Rinaldo and Mandricardo are compared to vipers that have just been stepped on because they are furious at the blows received from their opponents.

21. The reactions of the public during a duel or a competition are recorded in *Aeneid* 5.148–50, 5.181–82; in *Orlando Innamorato* 1.28.27.1–2; in *Orlando Furioso* 30.53.1–4; and in *Jerusalem Delivered* 6.49.

fighter and necessity strengthened his hand, just as a wild boar ruffles up his back and grinds his fangs when pierced by a sharp spear.[22]

58

Like a sturdy rock that stands straight up in the sea and seems contemptuous of the waves that agitate violently around it, Vaconte covered his naked shoulder with his shield and swung his sword around rapidly.[23] The careless pagan now concentrated on hitting him again on the side that remained unprotected and did not think of shielding his own right flank;[24] his heavy hauberk proved unstable and weak.

59

By slashing the metal with a deep cut, Vaconte's sword entered deep in his enemy's side, all the way to the thigh. With the wound now warm with blood and not yet feeling the pain—he would feel it later—Agrismeta did not let his hand fail; on the contrary, he inflicted a very painful injury on the right thigh of his opponent, not far from the knee, but in exchange he received a nasty blow to his left eye.

60

Vaconte had struck his opponent deep inside his body—not in his spirit—and was making him suffer a blow more painful than anything he had ever experienced before. The world twirled around Agrismeta, the light went out of his eyes, and he was barely able to stand on his feet. He gathered all the powers of his courageous heart and from his fleeting vigor drew new strength. The tighter the curve that forcefully bends the bow, the more awesome is the power that shoots the arrow.

61

The anger and the fighting did not abate, and with their blood flowing, both warriors poured out their souls to make their thrusts more dangerous.

22. For this comparison, Sarrocchi seems to have taken hints from other boar similes that occur in military contexts: *Iliad* 13.471–75, *Aeneid* 10.707–18, *Africa* 7.1245–50. Cf. also canto 5.47 above.

23. The image of the rock beaten by winds and by high seas is drawn from *Aeneid* 5.124–28. Other such similes, also used in the context of a battle, recur in *Iliad* 15.618–21, *Aeneid* 10.693, *Orlando Furioso* 45.73.2–4, and *Jerusalem Delivered* 9.31.1–4. It is used again in this poem at 20.84 and 23.40. Ariosto uses another rock simile to express Ruggiero's steadfastness in his love for Bradamante in *Orlando Furioso* 44.61.1–5.

24. At the critical moment Agrismeta becomes so enraged and ashamed of being defeated that he forgets to remain on guard, just as Argante, the losing combatant in *Jerusalem Delivered* 6.43, forgets to cover himself while fighting against Tancred.

They did not seem to feel the blows of the enemy's sword, and blind with angry furor, each tried hard to open a way deep down into the other's bowels, so avid was their lust for inflicting death and reaping vengeance.

62

Finally they gave in to the need for respite, and in order to recover their failing strength, they stepped back. They saw themselves red all over with blood, and almost exhausted, they feared the end and considered in their minds how they might control their furor and use it to greater advantage and lesser damage, and thus avenge their wounds and their shame.

63

Nonetheless, either because his naturally hot temper blinded his intellect, or because he was so upset and angered by the thought of Vaconte's enduring valor, the Saracen started up the fight again with great impatience. The Christian, however, made use of his weapon with great courage and less anger, and aimed and inflicted his blows with intelligence and masterful skill.

64

Vaconte showed his left shoulder bare, and when he leaned forward, one could see the uncovered side of his head. The Turk quickly moved to hit him there and at that moment remained insufficiently protected by the shield. Quickly Vaconte struck him, and as he plunged his weapon into him, he turned on his left side to avoid the oncoming sword, caught it, and threw it back so that it struck in vain.

65

Agrismeta hurt much, but quivered much more with rage, so that both his heart and his face flared up with indignation. Vaconte, alert to his furious violence, dodged him with a quick turnabout; and at the same time he struck a blow with full force that caught him right on the fine helmet, making sparks fly. The excellent quality of the gear protected Agrismeta, but he was nonetheless forced to bow his fearless forehead.

66

So horrendous was the blow that he started to wobble and could hardly stand. He tried to hit his adversary with his sword, but after so much loss of blood his arm was too weak and could no longer strike with its customary force.[25] Then, as he realized that his plan to kill Vaconte had failed, he roared like a lion full of pain and anger.[26]

67

Then, trying in vain to destroy the man who was destroying him, the pagan rushed against Vaconte in a fury, like an enraged bull that runs over the field bellowing and butting aimlessly in the air.[27] Agrismeta collapsed helplessly like a high tower that crashes to the ground after being hit by lightning, like an animal that, even in dying, shakes and hurts the motionless earth with his teeth.

68

The valorous Vaconte considered it an act of cowardice to further stain his sword with a dying man's blood. A happy throng of friends was now running up to praise him to the sky, but the young man bent on his knees in calm devotion, and turning his eyes to the heavens, he gave due and grateful thanks. Then he stood up and welcomed his dear comrades.

69

With a gracious countenance that retained both modesty and regal gravity, he answered them serenely, soothing his mind and dispelling all the anger that had embittered his heart. But as the heat of combat abated, the pain of his wounds increased. He stood erect without moving, suppressed the great discomfort as much as he could, and no matter how strong it became, did not complain.

70

Several men moved out of the throng from the side of victorious Vaconte and advanced toward the dead man to strip him of his famous arms—each was well known to them all—as the military custom allowed. Seeing this and fearing an even greater insult, the Turks, weapons in hand, ran out as well, to make sure that no tear or other damage was done to the body.

71

As no one contested it, the Christians picked up the arms whose enamel was gruesomely stained with blood. The strong captain Clearco took them

---

25. The idea of the defeated warrior too weak to strike his opponent forcefully one last time comes from *Jerusalem Delivered* 19.20, 19.24.

26. For other lion similes see canto 1.39n.

27. This may be a reminiscence of Petrarch's *Africa* 7.599–610, where Scipio and Hannibal are compared to two fighting bulls.

with both hands and lifting them over his head shouted: "Today, these will hang on the high wall of the royal palace, where they will testify to the valor that conquered them and to the superior truth of faith in Jesus."[28]

72

Alardo, who had been struck in his heart by the blow that had killed Agrismeta, whose loyal friend he was, pushed his charger forward and threw his spear with such fury that Clearco was no sooner hit by it than he was instantly killed, before anyone could come to his aid. The young Gorello arrived in time to avenge him and pierced the killer through the chest.

73

He did not stop there, and went on to kill Anchelor who was coming toward him with his lance lowered, because he too wanted to vindicate his religion. The valiant Virginio did not let Gorello fight alone and sent the strong band of his dauntless Adventurers to help, for he now saw many Turks move in block against him.

74

They assaulted each other with such furor, power, and skill that no strength would have been capable of withstanding them. Talarco, well trained in the art of war, divided the Turks into two wings, caught the band of Adventurers in the middle, then closed the sides, bearing on them in force. The Adventurers, who were fewer in number, had neither space nor time to escape.

75

The unfortunate Talarco did not realize that he had caught his own and his men's death in the very center of his company, for the powerful youth not only made a horrible slaughter of the plain soldiers but painted the ground red with the blood of the noble warriors as well, while knights and foot soldiers alike fled in confusion before Carlo and the Lord of Aquino.

76

Talarco, however, had no doubt about his victory, for he saw that the Turks were not slow to strike, while he ran to fight wherever he saw the Christians

---

28. By hanging Agrismeta's armor on the wall of the royal palace in Croia, the Albanians express their renewed determination to win. In many Christian narratives the warrior hangs captured arms on the church wall to signify the sacramental character of the war he is waging. In *Aeneid* 3.287–88, Aeneas fixes the shield of a slain Greek to a doorpost to propitiate good tidings.

about to escape. Then Piero, who saw in what great danger the Adventurers were, moved the soldiers forward at his command, and lopping the fierce Talarco's head off at once, he sent it bouncing to the ground.

77

The infidels no longer had a leader but continued to battle with the Christians to the finish. Arsace killed Brancadoro with a rapier's thrust and inflicted a severe wound on Carlo. With his sword Hirsante cut Paccaron's head down to the chin, which at the time was uncovered, for his helmet had been shattered and thrown to the ground almost at the start of the fray.

78

On both sides many soldiers could be heard moaning and dying, both on foot and on horseback. Some reached their end even without being wounded, for they were trampled by the chargers. Virginio's sword had killed more people than all the other swords together, so broadly did Fortune smile on him. In the end the night brought a stop to the fighting.

79

With the help of his dear friends Vaconte mounted his horse. The motion rattled and worsened his wounds; still, erect in the saddle, he climbed the steep mountain with great fortitude and an undaunted bearing. Then with the pain fiercely worsening, he wanted to have every wound checked, cleaned, and, if necessary, opened and cut.

80

Vessalio opened and cleaned his wounds and then stitched and closed them up again with an expert hand, promising to make him fit again in a short time, so that he could go back into battle. At dawn, many Turks and many Christians came out of their enclosures to take pious care of their dead, burying them as well as one could in time of war.

81

Oh! With what grief and anger the Turks stared at the well-known armor and insignia of friends and comrades that now lay trampled ignominiously on the ground, the very ones who were always the first to go on celebrated and meritorious campaigns! They looked at the many monstrous ways of death, at the various limbs slashed and torn.

82

There was a confusion of corpses: arms and heads thrown far from the bodies, and—horrible sight to behold!—often a face was found on a neck that did not fit. Some turned their faces toward heaven; others, lying face downward, buried them in the earth; some had a cheek missing, some one eye, others half a leg here and the knee over there.

83

Such miserable and gruesome sights stunned their souls with dismay and commiseration. The number of infidels killed appeared to be by far higher than the number of Christians. Musaka now looked for his courageous father and found his body in a pitiable mess, with his head and also his throat cut in the middle, which, however, did not hide his identity.[29]

84

After cleaning off the blood and dust, he joined the two halves of the beloved face. Then the body, grieved over and gathered in Pyrrhus's arms, was carried with loving affection by the soldiers in turns up the narrow and steep road. The king himself, full of sadness and pious feelings, wanted to walk in the funeral procession.

85

Comin, who lay wounded, did not accompany or see his noble father, and he grieved much over it. Meanwhile, the good people of Christ received as good a burial as possible in their assigned single lots. On the other side, the people of Mohammed burned a huge common funeral pyre. Some boastfully exhibited the famous arms of the dead, others stole some of them and hid what they had stolen.

29. His body is found by his son Musaka now, but Thopia was killed by Radiar in the battle of canto 6.99.

CANTO 10

Vran obtains a rich ransom for Pallante and donates it to Flora. This angers the sultan, who in revenge orders Amantia, Vran's town, to be conquered and sends Corcutte to lay siege to it. The siege, however, must be lifted when Scanderbeg arrives in aid of his friend Vran and attacks the besieging army from the rear.

1

Seeing that his rebellious captain had won against Allah's will, the emperor was beside himself, no less furious than Vulcano, Vesuvio, and Mongibello when they burst forth with ardent globules of lava into the sky, and no less angry than Cerberus, when, caught in Alcides' powerful hands, he began to pour a bitter and vicious poison from his many foaming mouths.[1]

2

Even so, he could not vent his ire as he wanted, and forced to hide his bitter disappointment, he planned to take vengeance in good time to come. He considered therefore what had to be decided at the moment. Even so, he showed his arrogant and evil disposition by issuing the cruel order that henceforth no prisoners were to be taken and everyone was to be killed in battle.

3

As soon as he learned that the best captain in his army, his greatest hope, had been slain, and that the king was holding several of his men prisoner—all of

1. Mongibello is another name for Mount Etna. Vulcano is one of the three volcanoes found on an island north of Sicily also named Vulcano, and Vesuvio is the volcano just south of Naples. In Greek mythology, Cerberus was a dog with fifty or a hundred heads, guardian at the gates of Hades, the underworld. In *Hercules Furens* by Euripides, as well as in Seneca's drama by the same title, Alcides (patronymic of Heracles, called Hercules by the Romans) drags the monster up to earth. This story is also told by Ovid in *Metamorphoses* 7.409–15.

them warriors celebrated for their strength and intelligence—the sultan ordered Crater to be returned to him in exchange for all the others. He feigned a pious consideration for his soldiers and, true to his custom, hid his suspicions and fears deep in his heart.

4

In the meantime, the trustworthy Vran had seen Pallante come back to him with his beautiful Flora. As he admired such mature wisdom in one so young, and the faithfulness and constant love they had for each other, when he learned whose son Pallante was, he decided to keep him prisoner in the hope of obtaining a rich ransom of gold and silver in exchange for his worth.

5

So he courteously allowed the young man to send a messenger to the pagan camp. When he was told of what had happened, Pallante's father was angered and much aggravated. Fatherly love, however, burned intensely in him, and he therefore sent a messenger to Vran with an ample reward and repeated entreaties not to refuse such rich ransom for the return of his offspring.

6

The good captain gladly accepted the rich ransom; then he summoned the beautiful Flora and magnanimously made her a present of it, adding no small amount of his own. Then he wanted them to leave at once to console the grieving father and to ask him, in his name, to forgive their youthful error.

7

As soon as the Thracian heard of the generous act toward the woman and the young man, he suspected a deception and flew into a rage, one as great as can possibly be felt in a human breast. Then, after long consideration, he decided—for he distrusted his own officers—to put in jail father and son and prepare a harsh and cruel death for them both.

8

That was not to happen, however, for Saladin soon warned father and son, and they, together with beautiful Flora, set out on the road accompanied by their friend. They traveled quickly and, their destination being so near, soon arrived safe and unobserved. Vran welcomed them in his home and Saladin remained with them.

9

The Thracian's desire to punish them became stronger, for now the offense to his royal honor had become greater, and his heart was torn apart by a hungry lust for revenge. He sent his best captain with a number of warriors, well known for strength and daring, to Amantia, with the order to bring the rebels back to him and burn and tear the city down to its foundations.

10

The place was not far away either by mountain road or through open plain, so that a man who began walking at a quick pace in early morning could reach it before nightfall. As soon as the golden morning dawned, Corcutte started off with footmen and horsemen; he arrived at his destination, but because it was late in the day, he gave orders to pitch camp for the night.

11

Amantia was situated in a low and wide plain, and it could not be seen from afar. Behind the town flowed the River Calinno,[2] which could be crossed by means of a drawbridge when permission to enter was given. On the frontal perimeter of town due protection was provided by human skill expertly imitating nature. So on one side nature made the city secure with a waterway; on the other the ingenuity of men created deep defensive moats.[3]

12

In the company of the most expert engineers, Corcutte surveyed the site thoroughly. The town was so well sheltered by the river and by trenches that he considered it useless to try capturing it by assault. He concluded therefore that it would be better to cross the river and reach the opposite side by way of a deceptive maneuver, well remembering that some of his soldiers, besides being good warriors, were able swimmers and equipped with jackets made of bark.

13

Their leader, Serpedon, however, had not been selected for this campaign, so Corcutte sent a messenger to request the swimmers, for they could come

2. In Sarrocchi's geography the River Calinno flows on one side of Amantia (10.11, 10.19, 10.20, 10.32, 10.48) and on the plain between Croia and Presa (22.14, 23.10, 23.15).

3. Sarrocchi's attention to fortifications throughout her poem reflects the prominent place that military defenses occupy in contemporary political tracts and the advanced state of Italian engineering in that area. Machiavelli discusses the utility of fortified towns in chapter 20 of *The Prince*, and Botero considers the value of fortresses and the way to build them in *The Reason of State*, 6.2, 6.3.

from Presa very quickly. He also informed the emperor of how he intended to conquer and hand over the territory to him. The emperor approved, and keeping the plan secret, he gave only to Serpedon clear orders to depart.

14

The wise king, meanwhile, to whom Fame on her swift wings had borne news of the siege,[4] did not allow his dear friend to be attacked by surprise, as the Ottoman had planned; he sent Mauro[5] with Crater and a squadron of chosen soldiers to Amantia as soon as the sun was beginning to dim its light, so that their arrival would not be known to the enemy.

15

In order to free Crater, the good king had released all the Turks he was holding as prisoners. Mauro, who had captured Osman, became resentful of it beyond reason and measure. Understanding his feelings, the king compensated him in some other way, and fully guessing what had caused his resentment, gave him spoils of great value.

16

This, however, did not assuage Mauro's bitterness, because when, in his usual generous way, the king allowed the captains to keep the spoils they had captured, he hoped for a far larger share. The others courteously gave up their prisoners before the king asked for them, but Mauro renounced Osman only when pressed hard to do so, for he expected to get a rich ransom.

17

The felon gave way to hatred but buried his hate inside, and while hiding his true feelings under a cloak of love, he planned to derive such a reward from this campaign as to make the king regret his decision bitterly. Meanwhile the loyal Vran was forced to remain in bed by a sudden life-threatening illness. Thus a great chance was offered to Mauro, for he was entrusted with the defense of Amantia.

18

An internal burning fever oppressed Vran; it grew stronger and did not abate. Although ill, he always asked news of all engagements and was informed from moment to moment of everything that was going on. He received advice and made decisions whenever needed, for now with

4. About the concept of fame and rumor see above, canto 1.32n.
5. For the Mauro character, see the cast of main characters.

Serpedon's arrival he had more to fear. He had already given the order to raise the bridge at the rear of the town and had decided to mount the main defense on the front walls.

19

Corcutte laid siege to the town as prompted by military practice and was exercising more and more pressure, presuming it would soon be forced to surrender. The Turks could see the Calinno flow through the wide plain not far from where they were and realized they would not be able to advance unless they swam across the river at the point where the bridge could be lowered.

20

Night was already putting on her cloak of dark shadows bejeweled by the heavenly stars[6] when Corcutte ordered Serpedon to cross the Calinno to the opposite side. He was to hide there in the brush with his band of soldiers and remain motionless under cover until the sun rose from Eos's beaches bringing the daylight; then he would be given the signal to move forward.[7]

21

As long as night covered the world in darkness, he remained on the lookout. He took care of various matters in the camp without moving or making a noise, such as those produced by military instruments, until he saw the imperial flag with the silvery moon flutter in his direction. It was agreed that they would give him the signal to move to the assault by waving the banner very high.

22

Only then were he and his men to swim across the river again and then perhaps enter the city, because on the side where the Callino flows the townspeople expected no danger and kept hardly a man on guard. No sooner were Corcutte's orders delivered than they were already swimming over the deep waves like otters; and then, once out of the water, they looked toward the east for the color of the eastern sky to change.

23

In the meantime Corcutte spent the night seeing to it that a great quantity of dry and soft earth, as well as bundles of brushwood, stumps, sods, and

6. About the night sky see 2.10, 6.61, 7.36, and 7.40. Other bejeweled spectacles of nature are at 3.7, 9.27, 10.20, 19.21–22.

7. Eos is the Greek name for Aurora, the goddess of dawn. Eos's beaches indicate the east, where the sun rises.

stones, was carried in and that the town's deep and steep moats were filled. Then, on this side of the town better provided with defenses, he ordered a high mound of earth to be raised.[8] All was supervised by Hamilcar, who was with him and was more skilled in engineering than the Greek of Syracuse.[9]

24

He ordered everyone to work at this construction, for he wanted it to be ready in the morning and fully manned by archers. By the time the sun came out of Ganges, the knoll was furnished with everything necessary. The massive construction rose above the city and could hold an almost infinite number of men. So then, when the dawn came and the reveille had sounded, the young soldiers were called to battle.

25

A sound answered, shouting, "To arms, to arms!" and a thousand men were ready for war. One captain led the soldiers to the front walls, another to the sides. The field general, Corcutte, was in charge of them; surrounded by the archers, he climbed the earth mound, and with the sign of the bright moon painted on the imperial banner, he sent the signal to the men at the river.

26

On hearing the clamorous trumpet, the guard at the wall who was always awake and on the lookout gave the alarm: "Awake! Awake! The camp is about to mount the assault. Hear! Hear! The valley resounds with the clamor of weapons." At this shout all the Christians woke up and got out of bed. Some picked up their bows, others the catapults, still others the spears, and they ran to the defense on the side where the assault was fiercest.

27

On hearing that the great attack had started, Vran, who was sick in bed, was the first to get up, but his legs were not strong enough to support the

---

8. This "mound" of earth is a substitute for any machinery, such as we find in *Jerusalem Delivered* 11.46, used by assailants to approach the walls of the besieged town. It makes Corcutte's assault plausible without preempting heroic action. Cf. 14.86n. In his effort to convince contemporary statesmen to fight against the Ottomans, Botero (*The Reason of State* 10.9) stresses their superior war tactics. Among the many effective Turkish military ruses that impressed him, he mentions their custom of assailing a fortress by shoveling mountains of earth before it and also by scaling its walls over the dead bodies of their own soldiers. This is what Sarrocchi's Turkish assailants are shown doing before the walls of Amantia in stanzas 36–37 below.

9. The Greek of Syracuse is Archimedes, mathematician and natural philosopher, who lived in the Greek colony of Syracuse, Sicily. He built catapults and burning glasses when his city was besieged by the Romans in 212 BCE.

weight of his debilitated body. He felt his knees buckle, and he fell down as soon as he was out of bed. His sight grew dim, the day darkened over him, and everything he saw turned round and round.

28

He felt dejected, but not by a sense of danger, rather because he could not go to the defense of the city. In the same fashion Philip's son lamented during his war, until the Acarnian made him fit to go back fighting.[10] Vran sent Cynthio among the defenders; for in him the knowledge and skill of the old man of Cos had never failed, and what the ancient doctor could accomplish in a few days, this one could do in one hour.[11]

29

So it was that on that day Phoebus bestowed on Cynthio the unique chance to exercise all his knowledge.[12] Thanks to him alone, life and health were seen to return to bodies that were almost dead, and by him their names were taken from the greedy spoils of time, so that his skills could be acknowledged and, at the sound of his fame, every green laurel still unknown would be recognized.

30

Because Vran was totally immobilized and could hardly make his voice heard, Mauro informed him that a company of Scythians and their captain were swiftly swimming across the river and that he himself was not leaving any post unguarded; for what man fears the least often turns into the greatest danger, and no wise captain is ever allowed to say—without great shame to himself—"I had not thought of it."[13]

---

10. Alexander the Great was the son of Philip, king of Macedon (256–323 BCE). When fighting against Darius in Cilicia in 331 BCE, he fell ill and was able to resume fighting after his pedagogue and doctor, the Acarnian, had cured him. Plutarch, "Alexander" 19.2–5.

11. The old man of Cos is Hippocrates (c. 460–377 BCE), the famous physician after whom the Hippocratic oath is named.

12. Phoebus is the epithet of Apollo, the god among whose many attributes was one of protecting the health and life of men. The meaning of the stanza is: During the siege Apollo will give Cynthio, Vran's doctor, the chance to acquire fame through his medical skills and at the same time to make known to the world the valor of the soldiers he will cure.

13. This adage is also found in *Orlando Furioso* 38.38.1–2: "Quantunque io sappia come mal convegna a un capitano dir: non mel pensai" (Although I know how unbecoming it is for a captain to say: I did not think of it). The famous words of Scipio Africanus, who considered his responsibility to gauge correctly the consequences of the actions he was taking, were: "Turpe est in res militari dicere: non putaram" (It is disreputable in military undertakings to say: I did not expect it). Valerius Maximus, *Memorable Doings and Sayings* 7.2.2.

31

Every day he felt the resentment for the loss of the prisoner who had been taken away from him grow and grow, and he became convinced that heaven, understanding his iniquitous idea, had decided to support him. So he made up his mind to act in a way that would make Crater regret having been rescued from capture, for place and time were now giving him the chance to make the man die and appear to have been a coward.

32

Together with his men he ran to the place where the fighting was fiercest; he applied more force here and at the same time sent soldiers to better guard and defend the other sides. But first he ordered Crater to take charge of the side looking over the Calinno River: he wanted him to remain at that site alone, with the few guards that were usually posted there.

33

Burning with fury and already enjoying the evil result, he reasoned within himself: "The king will come to realize, I am sure, how important it is to distinguish between one man and the next, and not rashly give in to passion, as is the fault of all princes." And while he gave vent to his pain and envy, he went on reviewing the defending army.

34

Since for the attack on the city a mound had been raised higher than the wall battlements themselves, Mauro ordered that ingenuity and skill be used in military fashion, that soldiers be disposed behind the crenellated walls to cover that mound, and that wherever their handheld weapons gave sign of failing they were to strike at the enemy from hidden and protected spots with a great quantity of destructive and harmful matter.

35

So from various places they poured down a deadly rain of heavy boulders and fiery missiles, as well as boiling pitch, oil, and lime, all compounded in a rough mixture, so that, although few in number, the defenders were an insurmountable obstacle for the Turks who came boldly up the ladders now leaning against the walls. They were thrown down to their deaths while trying to reach far too high.

36

And all this time, from catapults placed in elevated positions, the enemy threw against them massive stones, sharp arrows, and big logs of wood. Other soldiers labored to fill up the deep trenches; still others, covered overhead by their iron shields, rushed forward:[14] the throng of the enemy arrived swiftly and in tight formation, then withdrew far back, broken up and dispersed,[15]

37

even though they were quick to step back, for they could not escape from the swift hand of the Christians. Stones, arrows, and darts hit them, even when hurled from afar. For each bundle thrown into the moats, hundreds and hundreds of them fell into it, filling the empty space: this way the Christians caused damage to themselves, for the good is never given without the bad.[16]

38

Between the city walls and the high knoll covered with armed warriors, the fighting was the fiercest. On either side pieces of the walls and great chunks of earth could be seen crashing downward. As the dead soldiers plunged to the plain below, those alive pressed into the same place with great bravery. As soon as they arrived they were hit, wounded, burned, and crushed; then they too tumbled down below and filled the ditches.

39

Exposed to that high mound of earth, the Christians felt insecure, because from there the Saracens were able to mount such a strong assault that few of the men defending the walls remained. However, every arrow shot from the battlements reached the pagans without fail and landed so precisely on the mark that the Christians were encouraged to think that the outcome of the battle was not yet decided.

14. Holding their shields over their heads for protection from above and rushing in compact formation toward the walls, these Turkish soldiers formed what the Romans called a *testudo*. This military formation is described by Lucan in *Civil War* 3.474–78. Cf. canto 14.72.

15. For run-on stanzas, see p. 59 above.

16. This passage means that by making the Turkish soldiers fall dead into the ditches, the Christians were helping their enemy, for the corpses that filled the moat facilitated the Turkish advance on the city walls. The Ottoman army generally was—or was thought to be—more numerous than the European ones that fought against it, and the fact that a great many Turkish soldiers died before the fortresses they were laying siege to was seen almost as a calculated tactic.

40

Throughout this combat, Serpedon disposed of the Scythian soldiers in such a way that together they were able to swim again across the river that rendered the city impregnable.[17] Lest they be seen and impeded by those who were on guard on the other side of the river, he selected four of them, the ones he judged to be the best, and sent them to wade the river first.[18]

41

By long tradition these men had learned to swim underwater and were able to remain in it as if they were breathing in the open air. Pantar was one of them, a champion in shooting arrows and hitting his target. In Serpedon's band, and perhaps all the rest in the world, there was no archer more expert than he at the moment, so the captain was rightly confident he would kill the guard at the first attempt.

42

Once the guard was dead, the defenders would be too late to oppose their swimming across the river, for only the first guard would be able to see them from far away and warn his companions inside. And so it came to pass: the infallible hand did not shoot its arrow in vain; it caught the poor Adrasto in the throat, and the other three men came across without opposition.

43

At the moment when Adrasto was killed, the four swimmers were able, without making themselves known, to send a sign to Serpedon, who was waiting in hiding; so the others too were able to swim across and take up their positions. Crater, however, was very much on guard, for a faithful servant rarely makes a mistake: he saw them, gave the alarm with a shout, and immediately sent a messenger to Mauro.

44

From a distance Mauro saw the soldier run toward him white in the face and in great dismay. As soon as he arrived, the messenger described what had

---

17. Corcutte's attempt to capture Amantia from the most inaccessible section of the walls is founded on the advice of military experts. As examples of this stratagem, Botero cites Scipio Africanus, who unexpectedly took Carthage from the lake side, and Antiochus the Great, who entered Sardis from the most unapproachable and, consequently, least defended section of the walls. *The Reason of State* 6.3.

18. Turnus in *Aeneid* 9.812–18 and Rodomonte in *Orlando Furioso* 18.23.7–8 jump into the Tiber and the Seine, respectively, to escape the enemy pressing on them from all sides.

happened in detail, and as he spoke, his voice grew weaker and weaker. The evil Mauro said to him: "You are fearful not without reason: go back, and I will bring you help very soon. Return to defend the wall: I myself will come there to save you, or to die at your side."

45

In making these promises, he lied, for once the messenger had gone, he did not go to their aid. Only when he judged Crater to be dead or fleeing, and the other guard to be dead or running away as well, did he send a good platoon of men. The long delay made a great difference. Crater was wounded and could not resist for long, but he would sooner have given up his life than his guard.

46

But the heavens, who never abandon the innocent, came to Crater's rescue. Upon hearing that the Scythians had left Presa, the king in person hurried to Vran, for he had guessed the reason for their departure, but he did not give any sign of knowing it. He brought the band of Adventurers with him, together with a few more men on foot and on horseback.[19]

47

He was confident in his own strength, so he came with a few devoted friends. He followed carefully in Serpedon's steps and was able to anticipate all his moves. Carthage be silent! and you, Macedon, and you too, Rome: those great men of yours, held in such high esteem, are all surpassed in virtue by these men; only in money and power are these outdone.[20]

48

Lying in wait at night, the king saw the Scythians wade the river and understood how sadly dangerous the situation had become for his friend. He also realized that the unsuspecting Turkish general had not provided his camp with defenses, for he did not imagine that the king, besieged in his own town as he was, would come to engage him in battle on the plain.

19. In *Orlando Furioso* 16.28 too, Paris under siege is saved by the arrival of the English and the Scots, who arrive in the nick of time with Rinaldo at their head. The same situation is found in *Jerusalem Delivered* 9.91.

20. "Carthage," "Macedon," and "Rome" are metonymic references to the three great generals of antiquity: Hannibal, Alexander the Great, and Caesar, i.e., the Carthaginian, the Macedonian, and the Roman general, respectively.

49

Corcutte knew that the king lacked money and people, for his state was totally destitute; and he did not think that he could arrive so quickly, or that he himself would not at least receive a warning in time. All this turned out greatly to favor the plan of the wise and courageous Alexander: he waited for the Turks to go to the assault in a unit, and then he threw himself upon them as fast as lightning.

50

The king entered into the fray with such impact that he threw every squadron into disarray. Never with such force does a big storm destroy a ship or whatever else opposes it on the waves. The Hebrew Samson did not kill as many Philistines with his deadly jaw.[21] These Turks saw their hands, heads, and arms fly before they realized who was causing such bloodshed.

51

When Corcutte turned at that noise and looked behind, he was saddened and dismayed to see his soldiers seized by panic and being routed. He wondered how that mighty king could arrive so quickly and without being noticed. Soon, however, he recovered his courage and presence of mind, and he ran everywhere to retain these and the other men. He came down the knoll, mounted a charger, and began to harangue the soldiers here, a captain there.

52

Orkhan, Driarasso, and Attravante followed him. They all had come on this difficult campaign. In front of them, Corcutte ran all over the battlefield, in the middle and at the sides of it. With his face, voice, and hands he encouraged all those who were afraid and stopped those who were fleeing. "Turn around," he shouted to them, "and look! How is it possible that so many soldiers as you are can run away from one man alone?[22]

21. The biblical Samson found the fresh jawbone of a donkey and killed a thousand Philistines with it. Judges 15.15. He pulled down the temple at Gaza after recovering the strength he had lost when Delilah cut off his hair. Judges 16.19–21. The comparison of the warrior's lethal power to that of Samson is also in *Orlando Furioso* 14.45.5–6.

22. A leader haranguing his fleeing men is a set piece in epic poetry. In *Aeneid* 9.781–87, Mnesthus rebukes the Trojan soldiers who are running away from Turnus; in 11.729–40, Tarcon reduces to shame the cavalry routed by the warrior woman Camilla. In *Orlando Furioso* 17.7–8, King Charles scolds the French troops fleeing from Rodomonte. In *Jerusalem Delivered* 9.47, Godfrey scolds his men fleeing from Solyman. Cf. cantos 13.78–79, 23.28–29, and 23.35 below.

53

"There is only one man there. You have a thousand hands, a thousand arms, a thousand bodies, and a thousand hearts:[23] with a thousand swords you can defend yourselves and strike back. What frightful thing can there be to make you run away? How can strength and courage fail you now, you who have always been victorious, you who have gloriously shed your blood in so many illustrious campaigns?

54

"Will you then let one single moment deprive you of the praise gained by your valor in so many years? Friends! Friends! Keep on fighting! For there is true lasting glory only in fighting. If you do not want to die, turn your faces around, for only your weapons will protect you from your enemy's weapons." So he told them, and the captains who were close behind him said the same.

55

They continued to ride around the field in an attempt to retain the routed army. The men who heard their sharp words soon burned with a shame worthy of praise. They returned to their flag and would now have preferred to die rather than run away. This way Corcutte was able to establish new order in his troops and still hope for victory.

56

Although the dead were many, and many were wounded, Turkish forces were still extensive. The Christians had to fight together without dispersing their strength in too many small groups, so they braced themselves and stood where their captains told them to stand. The Turks came back in a relentless attack that made the earth tremble and the air resound tumultuously.

57

Immense clouds of dust rose to the sky, darkening the clear day with their thickness. The king's contingent was more enveloped and hampered by it, for it was much smaller than the imperial army. Then it could be seen to grow thin and sparse, and the space between the two armies diminished. Now the opponents clashed against each other with a horrendous impact; they fought sword against sword, helmet against helmet, shield against shield.

---

23. "Totidem nobis animaeque manusque" (We have just as many lives, just as many hands), says Pallas appealingly to the Arcadians in rout. *Aeneid* 10.376.

58

Driarasso and all the other valiant captains wished to fight against the great hero one on one, for they would have died a thousand deaths and more rather than behave in a cowardly manner. But they were hampered by place and time, for each of them saw his soldiers scatter and retreat, and considered it the duty of a good captain to save his men above all.

59

Corcutte was bursting with shame and anger that all his people should be so much in fear of one man alone, and he would have sooner died on the spot than go back to his sire with so great a dishonor. But what was the use? In vain he shouted, in vain he rebuked them, for his soldiers were slain as soon as they confronted the king. No sooner did they look at him than they were persuaded that his face and arm were not those of a mortal human being.

60

Pallante saw him from the walls and remembered what he had read: only an angel minister of God, who has been sent to earth holding a wrathful sword in his hand to punish the sins of men, can strike powerful blows and become the dispenser of terrible ills. From his appearance and movements, Pallante would have thought the king to be an angel, except that he knew who he was.

61

The sight awoke such a fighting spirit in the heart of the courageous youth, by nature magnanimous and bold, that he too wanted to compete with the others in the thick of battle. The town suddenly seemed a narrow and unworthy prison for his valor, and so he exited. Quickly Mauro joined him, for he wished to hide his cowardly behavior from the king.

62

They rode on their chargers over the open field where the king threatened and slew. Now the enemies could be certain to be safe, for they ran for their lives and the king was disdainful of striking those who fled. Driarasso followed the routed army at a distance, roaring like an angry lion.[24] He turned around to see if anyone was following him, for no strength was sufficient to oppose the king's invincible sword.

24. About the lion simile, see above, canto 1.39n.

63

Corcutte had already sent word to Serpedon to withdraw. Pallante came up against them as they were coming out of the water for the last time. The Scythian captain had gathered the men around him, according to military procedure, and when he saw Pallante and Mauro alone, he ordered his numerous band to surround them.

64

The courageous young man did not withdraw, although the two had to defend themselves alone from the dangerous attack. Strengthening his arm with a weapon, his heart with resolution, Pallante struck and kept the assailants at bay by skipping lightly on his feet. Meanwhile the Christians on the high walls threw stones, arrows, and darts, but afraid of hitting their own friends, they often let the enemies go unscathed.

65

Pallante struck powerfully and filled the ground with dead and wounded bodies. No firm bark, no swampy cane could resist the vigor of his arm. But the Scythians pressed on and on, and the captain himself joined in. When he saw the ground strewn with corpses, he shouted: "You, you alone will pay for this."

66

"Only you"—he shouted to Pallante—and in so saying he seized the reins of his good charger, rode once around the young man and struck him with a blow to the chest: a stain of blood soon appeared on his white vest. By now the king had moved: at the start he had seen a youth in danger in the enemy camp; now he recognized him and ran to his aid.

67

With his unbeatable sword the king struck the enemy footmen all around him. Serpedon, who had seen Alexander from afar and knew his sword to be worth a thousand others, gave way and withdrew for the safety of his men. He then ran toward the cavalry contingent, led by Driarasso, coming on the gallop to his rescue.

68

The valorous king picked up Pallante, placed him on his horse, and carried him away. With his mind set on saving the wounded young man, he did not notice Mauro, who was left to fight alone. Mauro flew into a rage and remembered the case of Osman and Crater. Then he too withdrew, with his mind set on a bitter vengeance against the king.

69

Meanwhile the Turks rode away at full gallop, abandoning their rich tents full not only of foodstuffs but of much equipment shining with gold and silver. Taking nothing for himself, the generous king made liberal gifts of the spoils and distributed a part of them to the city dwellers according to their merits, to compensate them for the damage they had suffered.[25]

70

When the king reached Vran, he found him on the way to recovery, for the fever had begun to go down at the news that his friend had arrived swiftly and unscathed. In nature what is helpful to the soul is also helpful to the body, just as what is good or bad for the body makes the soul happy or full of pain.

71

When he learned that Vran no longer was in mortal danger, the good king assuaged his fears and grief a good deal, for no brother, father, or son was more dearly loved by him than Vran. For him alone he would give up his kingdom, even the empire of the entire world, his heart and blood, or whatever there is of most value for us mortals.

72

So, thanks to the joy given him by his loyal friend, victorious in this campaign, who never abandoned him and had now saved them from such impending danger, not only did Vran's high fever abate, but, also thanks to the diligence and skill of the king and of more than one excellent doctor, he was able to rise from bed in a very short time.

73

During Vran's illness, however, the king did not fail to provide the others with what they needed. He also remembered the sick and the wounded, and with the piety that tirelessly inflamed his heart he repeatedly cheered both Crater and Pallante, showing a sympathetic attitude, both in words and deeds.

---

25. Fairness in dividing the spoils with soldiers and allies was generally recommended by contemporary political advisors. See Scipione Ammirato in *Discorsi* 17. 2.1–7.

74

Then, after hearing about Crater's sad adventure, he was sorry for him and eager to learn from him, from other people, and from his friend what had happened in all particulars. As he turned the case over in his mind, he almost came to the full realization of the facts. Nonetheless, in his great unparalleled goodness, he did not want to believe that Mauro could be so devilish.

75

The king's mind had the extraordinary capacity of penetrating all the secrets deep in people's hearts. He suspected that something wicked had occurred, but then he was not inclined to ascertain it, because whoever has a pure and unsullied conscience does not wish to judge others quickly and unfavorably. Furthermore, the king trusted his ungrateful servant and did not believe that others could do what he himself would not.

CANTOS 11 AND 12

Mauro first persuades Alexander to welcome some Turkish soldiers who supposedly wish to convert and then, with their help, sets fire to the city granary. Later he induces Alexander's nephew, Ameso, to defect to the Ottomans and opens the doors of the citadel to them. In the carnage and plunder that follow, Alexander kills Tarsius, the Turkish captain.

From CANTO 13

Rosmonda marches with an army toward Presa to her father's aid. On the slopes of Mount Olympus, she meets a woman living in the wild and persuades her to join the army. Vaconte tries to penetrate the Turkish camp, is forced to surrender to Rosmonda, and falls in love with her. The canto ends with him lamenting at length that his passion forces him into a state of listless cowardice.

1

While the valorous Tarsius was approaching his last fateful day, Rosmonda, obedient to the imperial order, carried out the task she had been assigned. Her army, made up partly of foot soldiers and partly of knights in armor, and proceeding in a few long undisturbed marches, arrived at the foot of fabulous Mount Olympus.

2

While the camp was being set up, a woman of advanced age and with an expression of grief on her face approached her. Perhaps this was the way in which the little widow appeared in tears before the Emperor Trajan.[1] As soon as the woman saw Rosmonda, she made her appearance look sadder, her cries sound louder; she began to tear out her hair, to strike her breasts and ask for justice in a high voice.

3

"What happy star, after so much adverse fortune—or should I say 'the just compassion of the great Allah?'—allows me to come forward, O royal maiden, and ask that my injuries be vindicated? Vindicated by you whom

1. This is a reference to the popular medieval legend of Emperor Trajan and the poor widow. Cf. above, canto 3.27n, and below, canto 13.9n.

heaven calls to great deeds," she went on, "not because of your feminine beauty, in comparison with which any other woman's boast is empty, but thanks to your manly valor and virile strength.

4

"On the mountain summit there is a high shady forest, thick with plants and trees. It is possible to ascend to the top only by way of the road you see before you. Human feet scarcely manage to step on it, so narrow and arduous is the path. In that forest hides a fiercely savage woman who in ferocity surpasses all beasts.

5

"A rumor goes that when she was born, her father looked on her hatefully as a bad omen. Confused and saddened beyond all human and fatherly custom, he left her at the source of a spring to be devoured by the wild animals of the mountain: but the animals recognized that her savage nature was similar to their own and gave her life instead of death.[2]

6

"After abandoning her near the spring, the father went back the way he had come. Then a bear (now hear this extraordinary case!) who had heard the little child wail came near her, perhaps because her cubs had recently been taken from her den. The animal, who had breasts full of milk, approached the baby, picked her up, and offered her bosom, as if she were her own baby, and the baby took to it.[3]

7

"Afterward the bear went back into the forest, but every time she felt the weight of her milk, she came back to feed her. The baby was not afraid of the horrible beast; she laughed, played, and bounced contentedly around her. This way one wild animal fed another, until a nasty fate separated them: for a hunter set up an insidious trap and captured the mother, just as he had taken her little ones before.

2. Silveria's upbringing and the description of her in stanzas 14–18 present similarities with those of the nymph Callisto in *Metamorphoses* 2.410–21 and of the warrior Camilla as described in *Aeneid* 11.535–60.

3. The story of Silveria, fed by a bear and then picked up by a hunter, draws some details from the legend of Romulus and Remus, as well. In the Roman legend, the two brothers were fed by a she-wolf and then brought up by Faustulus, the swineherd who found them in the forest. Plutarch, "Romulus" 2.5–6.

8

"The man was astonished when he found the baby girl; he took her with him and had her looked after. Even so, having the heart of a beast, the young woman now avoids all human contact and takes delight only in the company of animals. Although she has no sharp teeth or cutting claws, she now lives without fear among wild beasts in the place where she was abandoned, shooting around arrows and darts. And, poor me! only a while ago, she pitilessly killed my two sons.

9

"I pray you, queen—may you return victorious from this campaign to the kingdom of your great father, with the greatest and worthiest honors you have set your mind on—please vindicate, as only you can, the grievous offense done to me.[4] Uphold my waning strength, since all support has failed me; alleviate my great suffering, for vengeance seems to lessen the damage one receives."

10

The woman redoubled her lamentations; then she was quiet, but looked more pained and sorrowful than before. Rosmonda, who was born as kind as she was beautiful, felt a great compassion in her heart and immediately was seized by a desire to please the woman. So she got off her good horse, turned toward the steep path opening before her, and without hesitation began to climb alone.

11

No helmet hid now her beautiful face,[5] her eyes sparkled with extraordinary brilliance, part of her blond hair was tied up, other locks hung in alluring waves. The path was hard to climb, and a crystalline sweat ran down her rosy cheeks, which, with her beautiful hair undulating at the sides, seemed to be bound in gold, pearls, and rubies.[6]

4. Rosmonda being asked by a woman to avenge the death of her two sons is a reprise of the medieval legend of the Emperor Trajan and the poor widow, as Sarrocchi points out in stanza 2. The story of the sultan delayed by Selim's wife in canto 3.12–28 is the first use of this topical theme, which is not to be confused with a "damsel in distress" case, that is, a knight galloping off to rescue a woman in some sort of distressed condition.

5. Rosmonda having her helmet off is a sure sign of the meaningful scene to come. See pp. 35–36 above.

6. For similar descriptions of female—but at times also of male—beauty, see cantos 1.29–30, 3.65, 7.12, 13.88, 18.7–10. Rosmonda's jewel-like face, set off by the gold of her hair, is modeled after that of Ascanius, Aeneas's young son, whose face "qualis gemma micat, fulvum quae dividit aureum"(shines like a gem set in bright gold). *Aeneid* 10.134.

12

Her shield reflected the light of the shining sun, throwing off a radiant glare. On the shield, in a blue field, a white unicorn could be seen sharpening its metal point on rough bark. On her right side, tied to a chain hung from the shoulder, fell a sword whose hilt and pommel were made of gold adorned with gems, whose value and handicraft were beyond estimation.

13

At the center of the armor plate covering her chest one could see the horrible skull of Medusa: the snakes seemed inflated, their necks erect, and dark poison seemed to seep out of their eyes.[7] While climbing, Rosmonda looked like a new Pallas, inspiring a mixture of dread and delight. As soon as she reached the high slope, she saw the wild huntress and was at the same time seen by her.

14

As she heard a noise, the young woman ran to the pass and turned her eyes defiantly toward whoever might be coming. She carried a bow coarsely made of cornelian cherry, which was hard to draw but could shoot powerful darts. From her shoulder a primitive quiver was slung, inside which many sharp arrows jingled. Her breasts and knees were naked, and her ivory feet were covered by buskins made from the skin of a lynx.

15

Her well-developed and well-shaped limbs, which were slender and more agile than any man's, were covered by the speckled skin of a leopard. Her unkempt hair was golden and curly; her large eyes were beautiful and sparkled with charm and virile boldness. The color of her skin was brown, like the pleasant tan produced by the rays of the sun on a white face.

16

Nature had bestowed on her features good proportions and grace, but also a virile energy. It was impossible to say whether strength or beauty had greater part in her, for they blended together. You might well say that in this maiden Mars had been trained to shoot arrows and Love had learned

7. Rosmonda looks like the warrior goddess Minerva (or Pallas Athena), whose breastplate depicted the face of the Gorgon Medusa. See *Aeneid* 2.615–16, 8.35–37. See Medusa in the glossary.

to strike with a sword.[8] The sight of her did not inspire unchaste feelings; it rather filled the onlooker with awe and respect.

17

She lived unkempt and alone on the mountain and in the forests, always hiding from human sight; and if by chance she was seen, she disappeared immediately, running away as fast as lightning flashing by, or like a falling star plunging from heaven to the lower world in a trail of gold.[9] Harpalyce did not run as swiftly when she outstripped Hebrus in her flight.[10]

18

She ran out only after a straying doe or a slender deer, contending in her swiftness with the winds. The faster she ran, the more beautiful she seemed to become, arousing an ever growing desire to look at her. When all of a sudden she caught sight of Rosmonda's shining armor, she marveled and drew her bow boldly, but then, noticing the golden hair ruffled by the breeze, she stopped and held back her shot.

19

She did not turn around, however, and did not run away bashfully to hide, as was her usual custom, for she saw that the person approaching was a woman. Now the two women looked at each other in amazement, and the beautiful huntress, although shy of company, gently asked the other to say what she was seeking in that place rarely trod by human feet.

20

Rosmonda looked intently at her fine body, which under the uncouth and rough clothing revealed a beauty and boldness that were an unseen blend

8. The meaning here is that the martial traits of Silveria harmonize perfectly with her womanly charms, and it can therefore be said metaphorically that in her person Mars, the god of war, has acquired the requisites of love and that Love has learned the art of war.

9. The comparison to a star falling from the sky in a blaze of gold imitates the simile applied to Pallas Athena in *Iliad* 4.73–78. There the goddess is described plunging from the peaks of Olympus like a star or meteor descending. See a similar comparison at canto 14.64 below. Fighting men, on the other hand, are compared to ominous comets bringing death in their wake. See cantos 6.81 and 23.55.

10. I have not been able to trace the story of Harpalyce. She is said here to be able to outrun the waters of Hebrus (the River Maritza now) perhaps because, brought up as a warrior by her father, the king of Thrace, she became an expert and very swift horsewoman. Alternatively this passage could be explained with another legend: Harpalyce, having killed her father who had raped her, was turned into a bird as punishment for her crime. She has consequently become swifter than the River Hebrus. Harpalyce is mentioned by Nonnos in *Dionysiaca* 12.72.

of feminine charm and manly attractiveness. Then, dropping all severity from her heart, she said to her, who stood in admiration no less than herself: "I wear the glorious scepter of the great emperor, for I am his daughter. I reign in his stead and impart orders anywhere.

21

"Disdaining the delicate inclinations of women, I decided to train for higher endeavors. For that reason I carry a sword, hold a shield, and cover myself with steel. And now—because as a queen I do not tolerate unjust behavior—I have come to ascertain the truth about the brothers killed by your hand, and to hear what good reason you can adduce in excuse for yourself."

22

Hearing that this was the great Thracian regent, the savage virgin, who was an uncouth creature of the woods but intelligent and of noble mind, was not afraid of her; she quickly bowed to her and in a respectful and tame manner said: "To your valor and beauty the heavens have destined the rank they rightly deserve, O high queen.

23

"From me—a coarse woman, used neither to lying nor to the common deceptions of the world—you will hear not an excuse, but the true reason for my behavior and the mad lust of the men I killed. Renouncing the flame of love and marriage, I made up my mind to follow Diana, for I feel no satisfaction or pleasure except in protecting my chaste heart in a shelter of ice.[11]

24

"Aiming at an immoral objective, those vicious men tried to blemish my spotless honor, and very quickly they discovered, and rightly so, how piercing the darts thrown by my hand can be. My heart is not eager to impart a death that is not deserved, for it does not harbor hatred against the just and the innocent; and I do not like to feed on human blood. The animals I slay in the hunt are enough for me."

25

As soon as the royal maiden heard the reason why those two were killed, she said: "Men have never died for a better reason. No, you do not deserve

11. Diana, moon goddess and goddess of the chase, was identified by the Romans with Artemis. In Italian literature she is a virgin huntress, and the nymphs in her retinue are vowed to chastity under pain of death.

punishment, you deserve praise. Stupid people call lovers the men who, in their treacherous behavior, hide hatred under cover of love and deceitfully ensnare the honor of chaste women.[12]

26

"But if your heart is no less gentle than your eyes, hair, and face are beautiful, I pray you tell me your name; show me the safe shelter where you reside, tell me what you eat and how you sleep, how you spend the time after hunting, and how, without any farming, this place can be so beautiful, so pleasing, and so full of flowers and fruit."

27

To Rosmonda Silveria answers: "Where I reside there is no farming done other than by my own hand. I have tended the oaks, the elms, and the laurel trees. I have domesticated the wild grape and other fruits, the fine grass and the flowers. Urged by an unfair anger, my father left me in this mountainous site as soon as I was born. Silveria is my name and so I am called."[13]

28

Without saying any more, she took Rosmonda to her shelter, down where the mountain deepened into a dark valley. No fine marble rose high to the clear sky here, no regal wall encircled it. Her home was located in a solitary and hollow place, enclosed by the shady foliage of trees and of thick ground ivy that twisted and turned like so many snakes.

---

12. Sarrocchi turns Rosmonda's task to administer justice into a plea for more severe legislation in cases of rape. For the profeminist connotations of this episode, see p. 34 above. One cannot help musing whether this episode owes something to Sarrocchi's views on the notorious Cenci case. In 1599, Beatrice Cenci, a young woman from an aristocratic Roman family, was tried and sentenced to die on the scaffold for the murder of her abusive father. Caterina de Sanctis, to whom Cenci had entrusted her baby child, lived at the time in Sarrocchi's household. Presumably on account of her hospitality, Cenci left Sarrocchi a small legacy, as shown by a codicil added by Beatrice to her will just before her execution. Corrado Ricci, *Beatrice Cenci,* trans. Morris Bishop and Henry Longan Stuart (New York: Boni and Liveright, 1925), 185–86. The Cenci case and another famous trial involving a woman—Artemisia Gentileschi (1593–1652), who was raped by fellow painter Agostino Tassi—are indications of a society in transition and of women's desire to change the oppressive laws that were strongly enforced during the Counter-Reformation. For Artemisia Gentileschi, see below, canto 15.39n.

13. Silveria's words are reminiscent of those uttered by the beautiful woman of whom Dante dreams at the threshold of the earthly paradise: "Sappia qualunque il mio nome dimanda ch'i' mi son Lia" (whoever wonders what my name is may know that I am Lia). *Purgatorio* 27.100–101.

29

A small pond and a dried-up swamp blocked the path of anyone who might have wanted to descend there. Nature had dug a deep cave in the rock, and Silveria closed its entrance with a huge stone. There she lit a fire to prepare her food and cooked the raw meat of savage animals. In place of soft linens and feathers, she lay on the rough skins of wild beasts.

30

After showing her everything, she took Rosmonda back by the same way and then led her to another part of the mountain, also hidden, but very spacious and pleasant. Here nature and, to a greater degree, the woman's industry and skill had created such an artful harmony of trees and streams that the place Rosmonda had admired so much before seemed nothing compared with it.

31

Here, the tall spruce and the branchy beech, the glorious palm tree and the green laurel created with their thick and intertwined foliage a shade that was pleasant even under the warm sun of summer. Here the flowery months of April and May smiled, here Autumn crowned his hair with golden fruit, and the twisted vine, leaning on the dear elm, grew high, laden with sweet grapes.

32

Here the roses opened their graceful petals, filling the air with sweet scents. They were beautiful in a variety of ways. Some gathered themselves together so that they were just opening or were already bursting out of the green. Others fully displayed their gorgeous colors: one wrapped in white and another in red petals, they boastfully displayed the milk whiteness of Juno or the blood redness of Venus, the most beautiful goddess of all.[14]

14. Juno is the goddess of wedlock, and the color attributed to her is white, symbolic of womanly chastity; Venus is the goddess of erotic love, symbolized by the color red. For Juno and Venus, the major goddesses of the Olympian heaven, see the glossary. Silveria's habitat has many characteristics of the beautiful orchard that, as Virgil tells us in *Georgics* 4, a Cilician pirate created near Tarentum. Flowery gardens and well-tended groves embellish much Renaissance literature, from Boccaccio's orchard in the introduction to the third day of *Decameron*, to Moderata Fonte's gardens in *Tredici canti del Floridoro* 3.10–15 and 5.10–14. They are the continuation of the medieval topos of *locus amoenus* or "pleasance." This one should be compared with other such descriptions: the garden of Venus in *Stanze per la giostra* 70.92; the garden of Caterina Corner in Pietro Bembo's *Gli Asolani*; Falerina's garden in *Orlando Innamorato* 2.4.20–23; Alcina's and Logistilla's pleasances in *Orlando Furioso* 6.20–22 and 10.61–63; the garden of Nivetta in Bernardo Tasso's *Floridante* 83.54–57; and Armida's voluptuous garden in canto 16 of *Jerusalem Delivered*. For the design of the Renaissance garden, see Claudia Lazzaro's *The Italian Renaissance Garden* (New Haven: Yale University Press, 1990). For gardens and places of

33

It was ordained by heaven that the rose should be queen of all the flowers and should disclose her hair to the morning dew and be crowned with rich gems: a pyrope among the blossoms, a purple splendor in the meadow, one that induced all kind hearts to desire it. Here the rose gently smiled at Zephyr,[15] ornament of the earth, glory of plants.

34

There were graceful myrtle trees arranged in fine order, by far more beautiful than nature and ordinary cultivation could produce. There were narcissi, acanthuses, jasmines, hyacinths, lilies, privets, anemones, crocuses, and violets, all painted a thousand beautiful colors, so that under the rays of the sun the green grass sparkled with the twinkling gold, the emeralds, rubies, pearls, and diamonds seemingly scattered by the breeze.

35

But although such a sight filled, delighted, and charmed the eyes in thousands and thousands of ways, a pleasant mixture of Arabian perfumes floated about, luring the senses even more. Clear brooks, crystalline lakes lingered among the hills and meandered in the groves, making fresh to the touch and sweet to the taste the flowers and fruits in which that beautiful place was rich.

36

Charming birds went in steady flight from branch to branch as they pleased; they had no reason to fear the deceit and damage that a net set by human hands or mistletoe or crooked hook might prepare for them. Here the nightingale did not cry for her stolen children, but rather said in her language, "I burn with love," and made the powerful sound coming from so small a breast resound in the air with a heartfelt song.

---

perfect love and harmony in literature, see A. Bartlett Giamatti, *The Earthly Paradise and the Renaissance Epic* (Princeton: Princeton University Press, 1966).

15. The rose turns to Zephyr very appropriately, for he is the most poetic of winds, the one that brings about springtime, sprinkles the meadows with dew, and makes flowers bloom. See Petrarch's sonnet, *Canzoniere* 310, "Zefiro torna, e 'l bel tempo rimena" (Zephyrus is returning, bringing the good weather with him), and Politian's description of the wind in *Stanze per la giostra* 1.77. The image goes back to Ovid's depiction of the golden age, when spring was eternal, serene Zephyrus blew tepid breezes, and the flowers grew unplanted (ver erat aeternum, placidique tepentibus auris mulcebant zephyri natos sine semine flores). *Metamorphoses* 1.107–8.

37

While the nightingale's lover answered her call, Procne, chirping sadly, renewed her weeping.[16] A pleasant harmony blended many voices together into a more pleasing sound. Schools of fish darted about in the waves and spoke to their lovers in silent language, and their beloveds, although voiceless, could hear them and were consumed by a flame burning in the coolness of the water.

38

Indulging in a pleasant rest in the shade and breeze, Rosmonda looked around in amazement and delight, moved slowly about, and with her white hands picked several flowers. Out of shame the rose turned redder, for Rosmonda kissed its red petals with her beautiful mouth, taking away their first blush.[17] Then, looking at Silveria, she said:

39

"Is it possible that the high virtue that heaven has bestowed on you, the invincible daring and magnanimous heart—which is not only above womanly merit but is in fact superhuman—will be wasted in this solitary place, in this complete wilderness, far away from the sight of human beings, where only wild animals, grass, and mountain slopes can testify to them?

40

"Your proud superior mind ought to disdain humble deeds destined to remain obscure, for that is a valueless reward indeed![18] Those great qual-

16. This sentence and the last one in the previous stanza perhaps simply mean that the nightingale chirps cheerfully while the swallow sings sadly, with no specific connotation added by the reference to the tragic story of Procne and Philomela. According to the story told by Ovid in *Metamorphoses* 6.424–674, when Procne, the daughter of the king of Athens, discovered that her husband, Tereus, had raped her sister Philomela and had cut her tongue out, in revenge she killed her own son Itys and served the child to his father in a tasty sauce. After learning what he had eaten, Tereus ran after the sisters with an axe. They cried for help and were saved by the gods, who changed one into a nightingale and the other into a swallow.

17. Always a metaphor for women's beauty, in fifteenth-century literature the rose became the symbol for the enjoyment of sexual love. A good example can be found in Politian's "Ballad of the roses" (21–24): "Quando la rosa ogni sua foglia spande, quando è più bella, quando è più gradita, allora è buona a mettere in ghirlande, prima che sua bellezza sia fuggita: sicché fanciulle, mentre è più fiorita, cogliam la bella rosa del giardino!" (The rose is most fair and most desired when all the petals are open. Now is the time to place it in a garland, before its beauty fades away. So, young ladies, let us pick the beautiful rose of the garden while it is still in full bloom!).

18. That courageous exploits should be known and admired by all is a principle of the Scottish monks in *Orlando Furioso* 4.56.5–8.

ities were not given to you so that you would just shoot arrows about and cultivate grass.[19] Honor can be defended in crowded cities, in royal palaces too, and in the army, and the fame of chastity is by far more due to the woman who is able to resist when tempted and when she fights for it.

41

"To overpower tigers, lions, bears, and boars, and to be able to shoot darts and arrows a long way, is not a very impressive achievement, only one becoming a country shepherdess. As the invincible warrior you are, if you come away, you will be loved even more than a sister by a royal woman such as myself: only in war can a strong human being attain celebrated victories or a glorious death."

42

So Rosmonda said, and the young woman, after hearing this, remained confused and in doubt for a while, for her mind was undecided about what she ought to do; but in the end she thanked her politely and made apologies for herself: "So then, will you not bear arms above and beyond the custom of the weaker sex?" Rosmonda went on: "The only prize for a fine soul such as yours will be lowly chases and a trophy of wild animals?

43

"Nature made your heart and body as strong and courageous as mine; you could then wear a heavy helmet on your head and a hard steel armor over your limbs!" To Silveria then, in whose heart the sight of the armor had awakened a laudable envy, these last words sounded like a reproach; and shame, brought about by a magnanimous heart, burned inside her.

44

When a peregrine falcon, whose sight has been hindered for a long time by the busy hand of the trainer, is finally allowed to open its eyes, it delights and marvels at the light of the sun shining upon the world; then it opens its flight into the vast field of the sky, happy in pursuit of prey. In the same way, at those words, Silveria's heart warmed at the thought of grand and warlike deeds.

19. Rosmonda's talk to Silveria about manly virtue and glorious deeds shows traces of the speech that Ulysses addresses to his sailors before launching the ship on the treacherous waters of the Atlantic. See Dante, *Inferno* 26.119–20.

45

The two valorous women, equally happy, came rapidly down the mountain into the valley. In a tactful manner Rosmonda asked the bereft mother to quiet her grief and gave her a very generous quantity of gold, because gold can quench a craving thirst for money. The woman's dejected spirits were lifted, for any pain lessens when in the company of riches.

46

At the moment when the great god of Delos,[20] as is his custom, dives into the sea with his golden carriage, leaving the vast fields of the sky scattered with patches of many colors so that the Night may learn how to adorn herself weaving her beautiful veil, the great warrior princess reached the Ematian fields safe and sound with her entire powerful army.

47

It was night. Even so, Rosmonda saw to it that the camp was set up according to military custom. She selected a large section of the countryside and equipped it with tents and trenches in a far more skillful manner than her father had done. In arranging all that, she wanted no one else but herself to be the field marshal, for she had been trained for that art and thereby acquired fame in many illustrious campaigns.

48

The old squadrons came out of Presa to welcome the comrades who had just arrived. The great emperor embraced his daughter joyously and kissed her on the forehead with fatherly love. Meanwhile, as the shadows of the night descended from the mountaintops and enveloped the camp, the good king arranged for a group of loyal men to be sent down the valley to scout and bring back updated news.

49

First among them was Zenoverchio, a man of shrewd intelligence and sagacious mind. He came down the slope with a squad of horsemen as stealthily as he could. The knights rode on swift horses and carried light weapons, so that, if necessary, they would be able to gallop off rapidly. The captain rode next to them and kept the squad close together: bad luck, however, looked upon his assignment.

---

20. Delos, the birthplace of Apollo, the sun god, was the holy place of his worship.

50

As they cautiously went around the camp, circling it first at a distance and then close by, Battor caught sight of them and immediately surmised that the unknown men were enemies. He shouted the alarm, and a whole group of men quickly ran to attack the squad of horsemen. Zenoverchio tried to withdraw with all his men, but the Turks had closed tightly on them.

51

The more compact he saw the circle closing in, the faster Zenoverchio rode on. Then with a great effort he opened his way through the throng of pagans who were on foot, threw more than one to the ground, bumped against them with his horse, or wounded them with his sword. And so he managed to come out of the enemy encirclement; but no one of his men followed him, for now the Turks had caught them in an even tighter circle.

52

Zenoverchio spurred on his good horse and was soon far out of the Saracens' range. But then a selfless thought dawned on him: "Are you escaping alone, you the good captain, alone without your men?" He did not know whether he was feeling more shame or sorrow for the loyal soldiers he had left behind, and like a good shepherd returning to his dear flock, he went back faster than a wave of the sea or the wind in a storm.

53

When a ferocious lioness[21] sees her beloved cubs captured by a hunter, first she languishes in pain, but then, inflamed by fury and hate, she boldly faces the dangerous weapons of the hunters, who are throwing pikes, lances, and darts, and runs up to them ready to stain her claws in their blood. In the same way Zenoverchio was driven by his love for his soldiers, but the infidels closed in on him with far too many men.

54

Hearing the great tumult, several soldiers mounted their horses, the great woman warrior before everyone else. Silveria started on foot, shooting several infallible arrows. They closed all routes of escape. Strength and courage were of no avail to the Christian men: they were thrown off their horses, dead or wounded. Those still alive surrendered to the enemy, now that their captain had been taken prisoner.

21. For other lion similes, see above, canto 1.39n.

55

He had been forcibly captured, for he would not have surrendered, knowing the tyrant's orders well,[22] and he would rather have died sword in hand. His strength was exhausted but his soul was unvanquished. The noble woman warrior, mindful of her father's edict, which had been reported to her by more than one person, allowed, but not without anger and pain, the vital air to be snuffed out of each one of them.

56

To her magnanimous mind, staining one's hand in the blood of prisoners seemed an iniquitous act. Still, the less powerful is always forced to obey the law of the more powerful, even when questionable. She obeyed the order but was repulsed by it, for she could not squelch her habitual innate generosity, and though strong and courageous, she did not like to look upon their death.

57

When a rapacious hawk is seen flying high in the sky, a little bird is bound to fly away to safety, but soon afterward it runs into the grip of a peregrine falcon and is killed. That band of wretched men had hoped to find mercy in the camp of the pagans and trusted them with their lot, and then their lives were slowly extinguished one by one; still, for all the pagans' attention, two of them escaped.

58

Crispo and Ranuccio did not surrender and fled without being noticed toward the citadel. They each rode by a separate and difficult path, but they reunited safely in the valley later on. With their tongues tied by fear and white in the face, they could not speak for quite a while, but then they were able to report in detail the atrocious happening to the king and his captains.

59

Sad and pained for all of them, the Christian king was uncertain about what else to do. He felt greater grief for Zenoverchio, a warrior of outstanding merit among the worthiest. Still he went on considering whether he should try again (for those two could tell him nothing certain) and order others to go down to the camp and, with more luck, find out how numerous the enemy was.

22. The order was given to take no prisoners. See canto 10.2 above.

60

Then his mind was made up: when the sun extinguished all light and the night opened wide its doors to darkness, a few of the strongest and most courageous warriors were to go down to the valley in disguise and bring back an accurate and complete description of the army that had just arrived. The wise Aranit proposed Oronte, who was a clever man and knew the Turkish language.

61

The king approved but remained still in doubt, for it did not seem right to him that Oronte should expose himself to such great risk alone, without another soldier even more courageous and strong to accompany him. As soon as he heard about the dangerous mission, Vaconte, who was again in good health and in possession of his usual fearlessness, immediately volunteered. His uncle was aware of the danger but did not deny him.

62

After taking off his heavy armor, his famous shield, and his shining helmet, lest they arouse suspicion in the enemy, Vaconte put on some unadorned weapons, weapons that were also light, because he thought he would be able to evade the enemy attack by dint of courage and strength alone. So, carefully equipped, the two descended stealthily into the valley during the night.

63

Before they went out, they waited for the sky to get darker but not so late that the infidels were already in bed. Oronte's features and his native language were similar to theirs. There were still many people about; the intruders moved in the midst of the crowd in a confident manner, and people thought they were two of them. They looked on, listened in at several places, and nowhere did they come across anyone who wanted to inquire even about their names.

64

They finally arrived in the city where the sire of the east lived. The gates were not guarded as they had been before, and they could enter and exit as they pleased. Later they went back to the camp and found the soldiers at ease and deep in sleep; and so, having looked at everything at their leisure, they decided to turn their steps toward the exit.

65

Now there remained only the last garrison post to go past, exactly where the clever Orkhan was on duty. The hour was too late to go about with no given assignment, let alone outside the camp, which was very vast. Nicandro, one of Orkhan's officers, looked at Vaconte—by whose invincible hand he had been taken prisoner some time before—and blocked their exit calmly and resolutely, even though he had doubts as to whether he ought to do so.

66

He asked them to give their names and to explain where they were coming from and what they intended to do outside the camp. Oronte, who was quick of speech and even more of mind, answered promptly, while Vaconte, to hide his identity, kept quiet. Nicandro took this as a sign of deception, and staring at his beautiful eyes and face, he asked why he was not talking.

67

Oronte said to him: "This man is from a foreign contingent and has not yet learned the Thracian language." Nicandro, however, who was still looking at that beautiful face, judged this to be an evasive answer. Then he recognized Vaconte, for he had seen him more than once when he was his prisoner. Ah! Marvelous power of the great Allah!—Nicandro thought. The victor was now vanquished and taken prisoner by the very man who had been his captive.

68

When it was clear that he had been discovered and that they could no longer hide among the enemy, Vaconte drew his sword and hit Nicandro with such force as to tear him open from chest to backside. Then, running toward the mountain, he brought out the shield he had kept covered and attempted to climb, turning back to defend himself, with his hand ready to strike.

69

When a fierce horse, famished by a great hunger, has snapped his reins and then suddenly is surprised by his rider in the open field while quelling his craving, he gallops away and, while running, keeps turning around, munching the grass hungrily;[23] so Vaconte, in similar fashion, turned his face and

23. This is a good variation on Virgil's splendid simile of a horse breaking out of the stall and running into the fields neighing and tossing back his head to look behind (*Aeneid* 11.492–97). A comparable simile is in *Iliad* 15.263–68.

his arm backward and fed his craving by slaying this and that soldier following him.

70

He killed more than one man, for the dauntless guards, seeing their captain dead, ran after him. Then Oronte—who was now out of danger and could easily save himself—when he realized that Vaconte was wounded and pressed on all sides, although he himself was securely out of the pursuers' reach, ran to his aid. Oh, rare loyalty! Oh, generous heart!

71

Vaconte struck Dolon, who was coming after him in a great fury, and inflicted on him a deep cut in the left eye. With a huge backhanded blow, he wounded Xerxes right where the thigh was joined to the trunk. Then he hit Androgeo with a slanted slicing thrust, and then Pin, by cutting off his hand from his arm. The hand that held the sword still tried to strike, while falling truncated to the ground.

72

He struck Artemio, who was grieving to see his father fall dead at his feet; his cheeks, his lips, and his words were cut in half by a single blow. While Marfesio was making a loud clamor, Vaconte sliced his head off, and the head fell down still shouting, and the words forming in his throat came out mixed with blood and moans.

73

Swollen by hail, rain, and melting snow, a river rises impetuously and then little by little overflows its banks, flooding the countryside to strange effect: the little birds come down where the fish swam, and the fish rise where the birds sat. In the same way, the throng that surrounded the great warrior was at first small but quickly increased beyond measure.[24]

74

When he saw Oronte fall to the ground, slashed between his eyebrows by Attravante's sword, Vaconte felt an anguish he had never felt before, for Oronte had in vain exposed himself to danger to come to his rescue. So he made a move to strike back and lifted his sword with enormous force in his

---

24. The comparison of the soldiers to a river overrunning its banks is a variant of Virgil's simile in *Aeneid* 2.496–99. Cf. cantos 3.86 and 5.40 above.

arm: the cyclops, when blinded by Ulysses,[25] threw his large stone with far
less power.

75

Angered, he struck in the direction of Attravante and failed to hit him,
for the man nimbly dodged the blow; but it was so heavy and powerful that
it sliced Birio's head sideways. His head jumped high, scattering the brain
in the air, a horrendous sight never seen before. With the same blow he
sliced Olin from the nape of the neck to the chin (a double and far greater
horror).

76

Meanwhile Rosmonda, together with the gentle archer, had chosen her
own spot near Presa to camp. On her breast she was wearing a strong
golden armor, and her head was covered by a rich shining helmet. The
other woman carried a bow in one hand, a quiver on her back, and no shield
covered her tender breast. They both went swiftly, their weapons jingling,
looking like lionesses and running as fast as leopards.[26]

77

The brave woman looked around three, four times to examine her
squadrons and saw many of her captains run off. At this moment the sun
was coming up in the east and the day was dawning. Immediately
Rosmonda's breast was filled with the wrath and scorn that such behavior
deserved. She boiled with shame but in vain tried to hold them back by
shouting and waving her sword at them.

78

"What is the meaning of this flight? Who has robbed you of your courage
all of a sudden?" she shouted at the frightened men. "How can you, as self-
respecting soldiers, choose an infamous life over shining honors, when in
the end death will take whatever is left of any of us? Ah, warriors! Turn your
faces around and be bold, for only in courage and in the strength of arms
can honor, victory, and safety be found.

25. Called Odysseus by the Greeks, Ulysses is the protagonist of Homer's *Odyssey*, which
describes the adventures he encounters during the journey home from the Trojan War. Soon
after landing in Sicily at the foot of Mount Etna, Ulysses is taken prisoner by the cyclops
Polyphemus, but manages to escape from the giant's cave by blinding him with a burning pole.
Odyssey 9.187–542.

26. Cf. canto 1.39 above.

79

"Must we see one man all alone get away free and unhurt, amidst an almost endless throng of men, all strong and armed with powerful weapons? Do you not die of shame?"[27] Then she said no more. A desire for honor reentered the hearts of the dismayed captains, chasing the fear out of them. Soon, after scolding the negligent band of soldiers with disdain, she ran to mount an offense.

80

When she arrived where the young warrior was, she stopped and for a while stared at him. Soon she realized that after Oronte had been surrounded and attacked by many men, he had fought alone, keeping them all at a distance. And now, without a helmet and shield and with the armor hanging in pieces here and there, he went about slashing his tremendous sword fearlessly.

81

The golden hair rose and fell on Vaconte's naked forehead, adding grace to his handsomeness. A pleasant ray of light could be seen coming through the cloud of his wrathful stare. His cheeks were tinged with a fine rosy color mixed with the whiteness of ivory; and a sweat as sweet as dew ran in small rivulets down his spotless skin.

82

Cold pools of water, turned into ice by the sharp wind of winter, eventually thaw in the breeze that blows from the south under the tepid rays of the sun. In the same way, the powerful fury of Rosmonda's martial aggression, which just before had been bent on slaughter and bloodshed, subsided, so intense was the pity aroused in her by his beauty, his valor, his young age, and the danger he faced.

83

Presently the brave woman warrior turned over and over in her mind how she could obey her father's ruling and at the same time save the life of this handsome champion. She knew the irascible character of her parent, whom the enemy's boldness was likely to irritate even more. She quickly decided and, by raising a naked hand, made a sign that the fighting was to stop.

27. Rosmonda's rebuke to the fleeing soldiers is made more compelling than others similar to it by the reminder that no one can escape death. Cf. *Aeneid* 9.781–87; *Orlando Furioso* 17.7–8, 17.14–15; *Jerusalem Delivered* 9.47; and, in this poem, cantos 10.52–54, 23.28–29, and 23.35.

84

Giving way to her obediently, the men in the audacious band lowered their weapons and withdrew. The young man, whom no one now was attacking, also stopped, astonished at what was happening. But the royal woman, who saw him motionless, said: "Noble warrior, lay down your arms and your wrath and allow me to take you prisoner in consideration of your young age.

85

"Forgo your weapons, assuage your anger: I say this out pity for you, to save you from an untimely death. Your valor and your intelligent demeanor make me feel friendlier in my heart than I usually am. Consider the strong throng of armed men pressing on you: even though you have killed many with your powerful hand, still others, as numerous and as strong, are coming up all around you.

86

"Should you refuse to surrender in the name of the law that demands an honorable conduct from all worthy warriors, then I shall be content to make less use of my power and ask you to give yourself up to me as to a woman, so that your gentlemanly act will be justified with cogent reasons by those who will defend your behavior." Here she was silent; then she took off her helmet, and uncovering her charming face, she added a new and more beautiful sun to the sun that was shining that day.[28]

87

Blazing rays were darting from her beautiful eyes: the sky all around became serene; the fields smiled and put out new flowers.[29] Love, who induces us all to love, was seen to throw darts, fling burning shots, and deploy all skills in adding grace to her loveliness and in luring all souls.[30]

88

Lucky indeed were those who were able to see her at that moment, for Love himself loosened her hair with his hand, and the splendor of that pure

28. Here we are at the crucial moment in epic romance when the woman warrior's helmet is off and the hero who sees her falls in love. Cf. *Orlando Innamorato* 3.5.45–46; *Orlando Furioso* 4.41.4; *Jerusalem Delivered* 3.21. On Rosmonda's reprimand to Vaconte at this significant moment in epic poetry, see p. 35 above.

29. For the commonplace of nature brightening in the presence of the beautiful woman, see above, canto 1.31n.

30. On Love throwing darts from the woman's eyes, see above, canto 3.64n.

golden amber dazzled the onlookers. So it was that even though a thorny worry gnawed at the heart of the knight, he forgot all offenses and dangers, his eyes caught in the live splendor of her heavenly charm.

89

Just like a butterfly that some natural beauty lures by its splendor and impels toward death, Vaconte, suddenly enchanted, remained motionless in admiration of her celestial beauty, and his heart succumbed to it. Laying down all his fierceness, which could spread high terror in the entire enemy camp, that very knight, whom a great throng of armed men could not overpower, was vanquished by one single face naked of armor.

90

Looking intently into the dazzling yet serene balmy light issuing from her eyes, whose splendor dispersed all anguish and pain, Vaconte fed his soul with a rare ecstasy. What he saw on her face was an unassuming expression of self-assurance, an unaffected beauty, adorned and enhanced by an honest seriousness, all of which, although not meant to please others, pleased and lured all.

91

He was conquered not by force of arms, only by a face,[31] and so he stood still, caught by that beautiful apparition, and although the wound was imperceptible to the eye, his heart was wounded no less than for being sheathed in solid steel. When the senses are not allowed to come into play,[32] what is seen penetrates the mind with the power of longing: there, a corresponding image is created, and desire increases the longing ever more.

---

31. Orlando in dismay exclaims: "I, [a warrior] who held the whole world in contempt, am vanquished by a woman without weapons!" *Orlando Innamorato* 1.1.30.7–8.

32. This clause means "when one can neither see nor hear one's beloved." The meaning of the whole sentence is: in the absence of the woman, the lover contemplates the image that desire has painted in his heart, and as he does so, his longing deepens. Sarrocchi's somewhat twisted description conforms to Giacomo da Lentini's theorization of love: "Amor è un desio che ven da core / per abondanza di gran piacimento; / e li occhi in prima generan l'amore / e lo core li dà nutricamento . . . ché li occhi rappresentan a lo core / d'ogni cosa che veden . . . e lo cor . . . imagina, / e li piace quel desio" (Love is a desire born in the heart from a great abundance of pleasure; / at first the eyes generate love / and then the heart nourishes it . . . for the eyes are the ones that describe everything they see . . . the heart imagines and takes pleasure from the longing). Quoted from *Poeti del Duecento*, ed. Gianfranco Contini, vol. 1 (Milan: Ricciardi, 1960), 90.

92

The same effect is created by the fervent imagination of a sick man devoured by thirst. Alluring images and longings carry him to hidden valleys, into cold veins of calm and crystalline waves, or perhaps into places where jets of water, falling from shady rocks, irrigate and revive the meadows. In these imaginings, the flame of desire increases, and the greater the flame, the stronger the desire becomes.[33]

93

At the sight of the woman, Vaconte remained speechless and spellbound, overcome by amazement and joy. Rosmonda rested her starlike eyes on him somewhat disturbed, and in an imperious voice spoke again. "I, daughter and captain of the king of kings, I who rule over his powerful army, want to save you, only you out of many men, and you would now disdain the help that has arrived just in time?

94

"I have uncovered my face and shown my hair to prove my consideration for you. If I, who in life have scorned being called a woman, who have concealed and placed no value in feminine beauty, if I, then, who wear arms and with this very hand have conquered bellicose cities and put to flight entire armies, if I now stoop and name myself a woman in order to save you, then I would surely be angered should you contemptuously reject my offer."[34]

95

She said these words in a manner angry and tender at the same time, like a mother who scolds her child threateningly but out of love; and he, Vaconte, who now longed for nothing but her, did not stop to think whether it was done kindly or unkindly. He had entirely forgotten that she was an enemy, and with a respectful and demure expression, just as if he had been defeated, he handed over his powerful sword, a sword still wet and warm with the blood of her people.

96

And so it happened that without using any weapon she conquered a hero of great daring. Oh! How tremendous you are, Love! Who will ever be able

33. This stanza is a reprise of the previous one, with added comparison and elucidation of Giacomo da Lentini's theory of how love is born.

34. For the implications of Rosmonda's upbraiding the listless Vaconte, see p. 35 above.

to escape your tenacious and insidious trap, if in the midst of slaughter and death you can extinguish and humiliate all pride and fury and change the force of long-lasting hatred into a fire that burns ever more with an excess of love?

97—133

Vaconte surrenders, and the canto ends with his lamenting at length that his passion is forcing him into a state of cowardice.

From **CANTO 14**

Rosmonda, at the head of the Ottoman army, mounts an attack on Croia but must withdraw her troops when the rain makes breaching the walls impossible.

1–60
Summoned by God, the angel Michael appears to Marcello Benci and inspires him with the desire to rescue Vaconte from his captivity.

61
The rooster, harbinger of the day, was awake, Dawn was leaving her feathered bed, and the night owl, afraid of the light, was returning to its nest when trumpets and drums sounded a loud military call and awoke the camp, arousing all the troops "to arms, to arms." Soon thereafter many flags were seen unfolding in the wind.

62
Rosmonda allocated her captains to various sites from where they could inflict greater damage and disposed them in combat formation according to the fighting skill that each had trained for and used most effectively. She assigned Rainoldo, Idaspe, and Hamilcar where it was easier to destroy the enemy defenses; she sent Battor and Altamor to climb the high ramparts; the others were told to stand ready to mount a second assault.

63
Rosmonda took off her shiny helmet and wearing her customary armor reviewed the troops: as she ran, the Gorgon painted on her chest plate gave the impression that a whistling sound was coming from the angry

snakes.[1] As she cheered the soldiers and exhorted the captains, her eyes and her whole appearance emanated rays of majesty and of manly boldness that inspired love, fear, and reverence.

64

Silveria followed her everywhere she went: one was on horseback, the other moved briskly on foot. Caring little as usual for other weapons, Silveria carried only a quiver on her back and a bow in her hand.[2] She is like the falling star that at times after lightning can be seen descending from the sphere of fire; or like the constellation of Boötes when, in the heavenly spheres, it is seen flaming in Callisto's wake.[3]

65

Surrounded by the armed men who constituted her royal bodyguard, Rosmonda gave the signal to the squadrons already in position and then moved to one side, away from the ramparts. Soldiers arrived from all directions in great numbers, some bringing long and solid ladders, others heavy loads of earth and tree branches, and with them they started filling the deep moats.

66

One can often see a wave far away in the sea that is tossed by a heavy storm: at one moment it rises high to menace the stars; at another moment it sinks low in the dark center of the ocean. The great army appeared to the Christians above like such a wave; and just like a wave that spills over a beach, the soldiers near the moats could be seen bringing great ruin to the opposite side.

67

All these troops were then engaged in the assault, all in unison, although they were of different minds and customs, originated from different countries, and

---

1. This is Medusa, one of the Gorgons, the mythological monsters provided with claws and wings. Medusa had snakes in place of hair. Her image was depicted on the breastplate of Zeus and on the shield of Pallas Athena. Virgil, *Aeneid* 2.615–16 and 8.438. Ovid, *Metamorphoses* 4.743. Cf. canto 13.13 above.

2. Not unlike the woman warrior Clorinda, of whom we are told that "a costei la faretra e 'l grave incarco de l'acute quadrella al tergo pende" (a quiver and the heavy weight of pointed darts hangs from her back). *Jerusalem Delivered* 11.28.1–2.

3. Callisto is another name for the constellation of the Bear. For the story of Callisto and for Boötes see above, canto 1.82n, and the glossary. Cf. the comparison of Silveria with a falling star at canto 13.17 above.

differed from one another in speech, dress, shields, armor, and weapons.[4] New soldiers were sent forward in battle order, either where they could damage the Christians most, or where it was possible to attempt a less dangerous breach in the wall. All of them remained intent on their assigned tasks.

68

Covered by shining steel and with a long spear in his hand, the Christian king stood before all others. He towered over them in stature and courage, formidable to see even from afar.[5] Such was perhaps the sight of Jupiter when, with a lightning bolt, he dashed down the insanely proud Typhon; for whoever was touched by the king's almost invincible spear was either pushed back or, wounded to death, fell precipitously off the rampart.[6]

69

Virginio was with his men at his right; Pyrrhus, although old and white-haired, stood with his own men on the left (both models of military valor). There was no feeble woman or tired old man in this town unwilling to defend it fighting. They brought stones, boiling water, and pitch, and with them they hit the men below, set them on fire, and blinded them as these substances penetrated the soldiers' helmets.

70

All catapults were charged with heavy stones; the powerful crossbows were armed with winged arrows. Machines rumbled everywhere, their ammunition forcefully cutting open a passage through the air. When one was loaded and another discharged, Fright, Horror, Fear, and Distress flew about with fluttering wings.

---

4. Sarrocchi seems much taken with the variety of people, languages, and cultures that constituted the Turkish Empire, and she often suggests that an army that is not culturally homogeneous cannot be counted on in time of war and in battle. The diversity of peoples encompassed by the Ottoman Empire had been remarked upon, among others, by Machiavelli in *The Prince* 4 and 19, and by Guicciardini in his *Storia d'Italia* 13. In Sarrocchi's time, there were many books in circulation that described the Turkish domains and its many peoples and customs. Among the most popular of these texts was probably *Historia universale dell'origine et imperio dei Turchi* by Francesco Sansovino (1521–83). Cf. cantos 5.103 and 17.60.

5. On Scanderbeg's stature, see above, canto 5.39n.

6. The mythological Typhon, or Typhoeus, was a giant who attempted to vanquish the gods. Jupiter struck him down with a thunderbolt and buried him in Tartarus, under Mount Etna. Ovid, *Metamorphoses* 5.321, 3.303, 5.348, 5.353.

71

Disdain, Revenge, Pride, and Anger surged to hit back, producing a frightening spectacle. Many slashed their swords around because they were forced to defend themselves; but many more, who possessed courage and valor, fought because they were eager for glory, not just to stay alive. Perhaps no one else had ever wished more for life or had ever been more mindful of honor.[7]

72

Soldiers had arrived in great numbers at the foot of the ramparts where the ascent was not so steep and now were intent on climbing. Covered by several shields held close to one another, they stood as if under the shelter of an iron roof.[8] But at the moment when they seemed to be able to climb effortlessly, they became easy targets, for some great weight was about to fall on them: then they were hit by a massive stone pushed from above by a hundred hands, which broke up the clustered shields, shattering them.[9]

73

The bigger, the more massive, the thicker the shields and the armor were, the greater was the damage done by the huge weights crashing on them, shattering weapons, bones, and men's brains into the smallest bits, scattering them further out all mixed together. Still, no fear of fatal blow scared the Turks away from their determined charge, for one could see them climbing up the airy ladders from all sides and showing no fear.

74

The throngs of soldiers attempting to go up these hard-fought routes were sometimes so heavy that the high ladders could not sustain them and broke. The men fell precipitously to the ground and brought down with them others who might be already dead or barely alive. In this way, a confused and varied mound of weapons, pieces of wood, feet, arms, and heads rose to the sky: a horrible sight to behold, one that added to the horror.

7. In the following description of the assault on the walls of Croia, Sarrocchi vies most noticeably with the attacks on the walls of Jerusalem described in *Jerusalem Delivered* 18.64–82.

8. This is the Roman formation known as *testudo*. With their raised shields, the soldiers formed a shed over their heads and, thus protected, advanced toward the enemy. It is described in canto 10.36 above. Cf. *Jerusalem Delivered* 11.37 and 18.74.

9. Throwing an outsized boulder down the walls is a regular feature in the description of assaults on the perimeter of a besieged town. We cannot but appreciate Sarrocchi's inventiveness in emulating her models: cf. *Aeneid* 2.492–93 and *Jerusalem Delivered* 11.38.

75

A long line of agile and dexterous Scythians went rapidly up a very high ladder, and then the Christian soldiers hit it with long poles on the right side: the ladder plunged to the left with a weight that exceeded all measure, bumped into another ladder, and the other knocked down still another, and this another, and so many fell to the ground together.

76

At times something like this happens when workers make ready for construction and erect a great pile of stones with their hands: first one stone, then all the others fall ruinously to the ground. But if the pagans running up those airy tracks repeatedly encountered a terrible death, the Christian warriors did not have any certainty that they too would not fall down from their devastated walls.

77

This mortal conflict shows in how many different tragic ways our lives can end. As they plunged, some men drove their heads into the earth and then tried to disentangle themselves with only their feet sticking out in the air. Others were pierced through and fell outstretched on the earth. Some of those who fell were not killed by enemy blows; rather, as other soldiers fell on top of them, they were crushed by the weight of friendly arms.

78

Battor ran on up one steep ladder and nothing could stop him. He was holding up a large shield made of thick steel to cover head and chest; fearlessly, with this protection alone, he withstood the fury of falling stones, the tempest of boiling water and fiery pitch. Now he was almost at the top of the rampart.

79

With his right hand, which was free of the sword—for he had tied it to his arm with an iron chain—he was about to get hold of the top of the wall when the good king pushed him down with his big spear. It was his good luck that he fell down rolling, so he was not killed by the fall, nor was he wounded by the powerful blow, for the king's spear broke in hitting his sturdy shield.

80

All those who were climbing after him were caught in his precipitous fall and killed; but his own descent was not too ruinous, for the landing ground was made soft by the others. Seeing this happen, the faces of all soldiers blushed for shame, and their breasts were filled with anger and rage. The man who had crashed over the others, however, got up and tried to make up for his failure with hopefully a better try.

81

Darting a disdainful and fierce glance around, he turned his eyes up and saw Rainoldo climbing high above him: the man was already on the last rung of the ladder, about to step on the right side of the breach. Palinuro and with him all his best soldiers bumped and pushed him back, keeping him from coming forward. Rainoldo fought alone in close combat against them all. Seeing this, Battor hurried up behind him.

82

At the very moment when he was about to jump and placed his foot on the remaining rung of the ladder, an arrow was shot from above; it whistled by, scratching his armor plate very lightly. Instead of him, it hit Ramagass in the eye (Ramagass who, competing with him, was coming up very close behind); the impact was so strong that his life was extinguished instantly, at the same time as his eyesight.

83

Meanwhile the fierce King Rainoldo had gained a foothold inside the walls of the fortress, because Palinuro with all his strong and strenuous efforts could not hold him back. With sword securely in hand, he put more than one of Palinuro's men to death, and now he stood face to face with him and held him in close combat. Battor, therefore, could come to his aid with no difficulty.

84

On the left flank Carmentel stood dashingly erect against the sky. Pyrrhus, who did not seem to be hampered by old age, advanced to face him in man-to-man combat. Tiberius, however, stepped in to do battle in his place, fearful that he might in the end collapse. Holding a big shield on his arm and a piercing weapon in his hand, Tiberius put up a barrier and at the same time pushed Carmentel back, so that he could not advance.

85

Meanwhile down below Silveria was fiercely fighting in the thick of battle next to Hamilcar. When they saw that up above Arioden was the only one to offer resistance, preventing Carmentel from jumping inside the rampart, they lifted two big stones from the ground and each threw one with a robust hand. Arioden, all absorbed by the fight, paid no attention to them.

86

The heavy stones flew through the air with the noise of thunder but did not reach the spot aimed at. Hamilcar, who had a hand strong beyond measure, managed to hit Arioden's resilient shield. Silveria stretched out her arm again with great force—no ball would ever be propelled even out of a mortar with such thunder[10]—and her stone, brushing his forehead, fell heavily on his helmet. With that blow, Arioden collapsed and fell onto the path below.

87

Lightly armed, quiver on his back and bow in hand, the great Voivode[11] came up to Silveria and praised her fine hit, his heart full of admiration and envy. Desirous of more praise, the woman then said: "Let us try and see which one of us can open a passage through the enemy with our arrows," and in saying this, she let a dart fly.

88

Her winged bolt flew swift and straight, caught Filandro between the brows, in that very spot of the nose where odors are inhaled in a double pass and the senses can smell them in all their strength. The deadly dart exited from the back of the neck, filling everyone with astonishment. At this point Altamor, who wanted to compete with the woman, aimed an arrow in the direction of Theon.

10. The references to the thunder made by a mortar, in this stanza and at canto 22.68, are the only mentions of firearms in the *Scanderbeide*. In both cases the reference is made in the manner used in canto 16.27.5–6 of *Orlando Furioso*. There Ariosto's readers are reminded of the huge cannonades fired against Padua by Emperor Maximilian of Austria in 1509, when more than fifteen hundred balls were dropped over the besieged city, some more than a hundred pounds in weight. Sarrocchi eschews the new weaponry, just as Boiardo, Ariosto, and Tasso all did before her. Her omission seems to me the more remarkable because, while they were describing wars occurring before the gunpowder revolution, she is dealing with a campaign during which cannons, arquebuses, and muskets were in full use. Michael Murrin explains the omission of firearms in epic poems by the requirement of heroic behavior on the part of the hero, which the description of the new weaponry would curtail. See his *History and Warfare in Renaissance Epic*, 2–14, 23–25. Cf. p.19n and canto 10.23n above.

11. The great Voivode is Altamor, who comes from Valachia, as Sarrocchi tells her readers in canto 12.4, here omitted. *Voivode, voyevoda* in Russian, was a title given to army leaders and to governors of towns and provinces in many Slavic countries.

89

He hit him in the back of the neck where a hard knot of nerves is located
and from where nature communicates vigor to all the limbs in the body. But
Theon was not dead; he only felt an atrocious pain. The beautiful archer
smiled, so proud of herself and so confident of her skill: so she quickly flung
another arrow in the wind and the wind carried this one more rapidly and
forcefully than ever.

90

Her sure hand did not miss the mark; her dart, hitting exactly where the
eye had aimed, went through Tomitan's throat but did not kill him as
she wanted. It caught the neck, leaving untouched the passage that nature
divides in two, one for food, the other for breath, and went straight
through it so cleanly that medical art was able later to restore the man to
health.

91

Angry that it was not going as she had wished, Silveria shot an arrow at
Titio, who was not far from the other: it landed on the hand and the hilt,
exactly where the sword is held, and nailed the man's palm to it. Altamor
was not very careful in his next shot, for his dart hurt Pyrrhus only lightly
on the right flank. At that point, however, a throng of pagans arrived suddenly on the spot and separated the two rivals, putting an end to the competition.

92

Altamor strode off somewhere else, and his heart full of ambitious envy, he
started brooding darkly about being less capable than a woman. Meanwhile
the king, seeing his big spear broken, quickly drew his sword, which was
wide and very long, one that only he could handle, and holding it with both
hands, he defended the breach alone.

93

In the same way the great Roman at the bridge repulsed single-handedly
the united impetus of the Etruscans.[12] The king dealt with the big crowd of
assailants as the farmer does when he gathers the ripe harvest, or when he
thins out with his capable hands the thick branches of poplars on the banks

12. This was Horatius Cocles, the Roman soldier who stood at the entrance to the Sublician
bridge and defended it against the advancing Etruscan army; as soon as the bridge was
destroyed by his friends, he swam to safety to his side, c. 509 BCE (Livy 2.10).

of the Arno River, or when he feeds his famished cattle in the driest days
of summer.

94

By striking with his sword just once, he flung half of Tolon's head—for he
was the nearest—right into the ditch below. An observer of the stars, Tolon
had forecast his fatal blow and had provided himself with a fine helmet, lining it with a steel of extraordinary thickness. But no protection was strong
enough against a force as formidable as that of the king, and one can rarely
escape what the heavens have decreed must happen.

95

The strong-limbed Dalete was six feet tall from head to foot; he wore on
his arm a shield of adamantine strength and held it above his head as a
dependable cover. He ran forward to chase the enemy, and with his ferocious appearance alone, which was that of death itself, he put them all to
flight. Thus protected and bent forward, he now tried to hit the king on a
spot under the belly, where his coat of armor was open.

96

The king stood still; then with his powerful arm he lowered his heavy
sword, and with one cutting blow he shattered Dalete's shield, sending the
pieces flying in the air and, with them, Dalete's arm that held it. As Dalete's
wound cooled, the pain of the cut increased, for all the veins were open to
the flow of blood, and later he would die of pain and weakness, for not
being taken care of in time.

97

The blood poured out from all wounds like a river in flood. By now, the
large and deep ditches were full of corpses, and mixed up with the dead
were many dying soldiers. Around the king there was no longer as great a
throng as there had been before. He heard the sound of the blows and the
shouting of those who were climbing on this and that side: they were
Battor, Rainoldo, and Carmentel followed by their men.

98

Upon hearing far away the barking of mastiffs, the good shepherd, made
vigilant and driven by love, quickly turns to his flock to chase the hungry wolf that he sees entering it, for he fears more for the flock than for

himself.[13] It was the same with the good king: he ran to the aid of his men as soon as he saw the danger in which they found themselves.

99

At the same time the princess warrior ordered Artaban and Orkhan to move up the formations that were waiting way off in the valley. Both were expert captains and great fighters. Now the pagan troops were fresh and the Christians exhausted. One could hear men shout, drums and trumpets sound; the air could be seen darkening with stones and darts.

100

Stirred by the thundering boom of the falling boulders and by the whistling of the flying arrows, the heavens wanted to show the anger of the creator against the pagans. Moved by it, the sky answered with thunder and hid its clarity in a dark haze. Nature perhaps wished to obey the will of divine providence with no aid of miracles.

101

After the thunder, the sky was quiet, but then the rain began to fall slowly from low clouds. The quieter and the thinner it came down, the more bothersome it proved for the Saracens. The rain drenched the surface of the ground, which was made of soft clay, and no foot could maintain a grip on it any longer. The assailants were soon unable to keep a foothold or to advance, because for every step forward they slid one step backward.

102

Meanwhile the king came to the rescue and began slashing his sword around in circles. The powerful Rainoldo came quickly to face him, for he aspired to a glorious victory, but the slippery ground prevented his foot from moving as he wanted, and he was forced to give up his ambitious intent; so was Battor; both were shaken with anger and regret.

103

When the king realized that the right side of the rampart was well protected from attacks, he moved to the left side to help Pyrrhus. The old man was still fighting, and although advanced in age, he fended for himself with

---

13. Cf. canto 9.52 above, where a mastiff comparison is similarly used to describe the impetus of a warrior on the attack.

intelligence and skill; and if he could not go forward, he nonetheless stood firmly on the spot. As the king arrived, Arioden came up the wall.

104

Carmentel, assessing the difficulty of the steep ascent and the inconvenience created by the rainfall, judiciously decided to go back of his own accord and descended with no injuries. Rosmonda, seeing the sunlight disappear and the face of the sky become darker, considered herself robbed of a great victory and ordered the trumpeters to call the army to order.

105

Silveria slackened her hasty pace over the slippery mud and climbed high, and when her foot slipped she was able to lift it and put it down firmly on the ground in a most amazing way. No fire, no dart, no weapon, no stone could stop her, and she kept climbing; nor could the lightning, the thunder, and the arrows raining down on her. She was indifferent to the rain falling from the sky or anything else that might pour over her sturdy vest.

106

All looked at her, astonished and also ashamed of themselves, for she was advancing up the rampart rapidly and nimbly. But when she heard the sound of the retreat, she stopped ready to obey her queen. Rosmonda heard a distinct rumor of admiration go around the camp, a rumor that made increasingly clear how much the beautiful woman archer could and dared to do; she rejoiced for her, just as she would for herself.

From CANTO 15

The sultan is in possession of Alexander's sword and organizes a game in which everyone will compete for it. Silveria wins the competition: she gets the sword and also prevails in having Driarasso made captain of the Janissaries and Orkhan captain of the Spahis. Losing the chance of promotion, as well as the games, many men seethe with resentment. Soon a fight flares up among them during which Silveria is wounded. Vaconte, fearing for his beloved, runs out of his tent to look for her. Rosmonda, after learning the reason for his escape, begins to fall in love.

1

Looking at the rain falling from the sky seemingly to spite him, the cruel tyrant realized that because of the weather his daughter would not be able to give him a victory. He had no fears, however; for he rather believed that the city would not be able to resist much longer and soon the battlements would be scaled. So he decided to give orders for the general attack.

2

With this prospect in mind, he went back to the camp and ordered Hamilcar, whom he judged to surpass all the best engineers who ever existed, to prepare the war machines. He distributed stipends and honors, bestowing them on the formidable captains according to their merits and the support they had given him, while taking from or diminishing his gifts to others.

3

All the while he meditated with a great deal of wonder upon the strength of his opponent. It seemed superhuman to be able, as Alexander did, to slay the enemy with a single blow, were one's weapons made by Vulcan himself.[1] He concluded this to be due to his magic sword, and not to the might of his hand and arm, so he immediately sent a messenger to the hero to ask for that invincible weapon.[2]

4

The king fully realized how formidable his strength appeared to the sultan but was surprised by his foolish arrogance. Then, laughing within himself, wise captain that he was, he nursed the idea of creating serious discord among the enemy, so diverse and of uncertain loyalty, by giving them a reason to vie with each other in valor, a desire never far from a stalwart soldier's heart.

5

So in the hope that a test of valor would arouse a fierce eagerness and bring about a new violent quarrel that would weaken the bellicose and daring troops of his great opponent, the king answered with a shrewd idea in mind: "Go back to your lord and report to him that as he has made this request to us in so chivalrous a manner, we will concede it on a chivalrous condition as well.

6

"Tell him that we are pleased to send him the sword, which in resilience perhaps has no equal, but only on the condition that it goes from this hand to another that will give no less proof of valor in using it. This chance, therefore, should fall on Silveria, who has shown she can surpass the best fighters in valor. The emperor himself will confirm it, if I am not mistaken." And he consigned the sword to the messenger.

7

The messenger returned happily and quickly to his sire. Lest any of his men complain, each believing himself to be the best knight, the sultan intended

---

1. Vulcan was the Roman god of fire who made Jupiter's thunderbolts and Aeneas's armor. Virgil, *Aeneid* 8.416–23, 8.729, 9.148, 11.439; Boiardo, *Orlando Innamorato* 1.16.22; *Orlando Furioso* 2.8.6–8. Cf. above, cantos 9.38n and 9.54n.

2. Magic swords and lances are a common prop in chivalric literature. In *Orlando Innamorato* and *Orlando Furioso* lances and swords work magic for human valor. In heroic epics such weapons are taken seriously. See how much symbolic force is placed in Sven's sword in *Jerusalem Delivered* 8.34–36. Among the many legends in circulation about Scanderbeg, there was one in Sarrocchi's time about the supernatural powers of his sword (Gegaj, *L'Albanie et l'invasion turque*, 32 n. 1). Other seventeenth-century poems in which magic swords play a major role are *Palermo liberato*, by Tommaso Belli (1612); *Amedeide*, by Gabriello Chiabrera (1617); *La Rocella espugnata*, by Francesco Bracciolini (1630); and *Il conquisto di Granata*, by Girolamo Graziani (1650). See Belloni, *Gli epigoni della Gerusalemme Liberata*, 72, 162, 259, 326, 366.

to see a real test of valor and did not consent to give the sword to Silveria. He wanted her to give clear proof of her mettle and to this wise purpose organized a joust right in the camp.

8

Fame had long before spread her wings and loosened her tongue to let everyone know that the young woman had vied with many warriors and had come out best in shooting arrows and hurling stones. The tyrant, who had already begun to long for Silveria because of her unusual beauty, was very pleased to hear her praised and now wished to see her demonstrate her prowess with his own eyes.

9

He summoned his first herald and said to him: "With the commanding authority of your trumpet, announce to all warriors, who have competed honorably with Silveria and twice have been beaten, that she is now throwing a new challenge to them, a challenge carrying no offense, but rather a prize, because whoever proves to be stronger than she is will be given the best sword a knight has ever carried."

10

All the warriors rejoiced. They welcomed the new challenge in the hope of regaining the prestige they had lost and of showing how superior a man is to a woman. They said: "Stupid people call valor anything that has the appearance of bravery, whatever the circumstance leading to victory, without considering whether it is real merit or chance.

11

"In the same way, any manifestation of either strength or intelligence and education appearing in feminine guise is considered a more pleasing and acceptable combination, even when unequal to that of a man." This said, they kept quiet. To show how capable he was, Altamor, a great archer, wished to come forward, and in addition to him the strong Hamilcar offered to compete, and also Battor, the runner.

12

To prepare for these martial games they quickly chose a field perfectly square, which opened and extended on a plain not far from the tents of the besieging Turkish army. On a high balcony and in a separate enclosure sat the great barbaric Thracian; from there he could see and hear everything, and on either side of him were the arbitrators, Orkhan and Carmentel, in full armor.

13

A massive pole was raised in the middle of the field, stuck deep in the ground; it had been the proud mast of a large vessel that waves and storms had shaken to no avail. A disk was placed on top that only a very good shot could reach, and underneath it another target was fixed, as small as the hole of a sieve.[3]

14

Each competitor had to hit the disk while running, and he who failed to hit it this way would accrue more blame than the competitor who did not hit it at all. Here came Silveria, bow in hand and quiver full of darts. She was scantily dressed, her short tunic lifted to one side by a golden girdle adorned with gems.[4] The great Voivode placed himself next to the young woman, for he wanted to compete with her.

15

As soon as Carmentel gave the sign, Silveria fit the notch of the arrow on the string with her fingers, drew the cord back to her shoulder, and as her hand relenting let the arrow fly,[5] she sprang into a nimble and graceful run. The dart whistled through the air and hit the target in the very middle, thus taking away from the others all possibility of victory.

16

Altamor, already seething with anger because the honor of the first draw was given to her, now, after such a magisterial proof of archery, could not hope to make a better shot. A small error might result in a great ignominy, so he stood very firm, stared intently at the target, and with his arrow pierced the smaller target under the high disk in such a way that no place was left for another dart.

---

3. Some details of this archery contest derive from the game described in *Aeneid* 5.485–552.

4. Silveria's appearance here is much like Callisto's in Ovid, *Metamorphoses* 2.411–13. For her too "non erat huius opus lanam mollire trahendo, nec positu variare comas: ubi fibula vestem, vitta coercuerat neglectos alba capillos" (there was no need to spin soft wool or to set her hair in complicated arrangements; a clasp held up her skirt, a white band went around her unkempt locks). See also canto 13.5 above.

5. Similar descriptions of an arrow being notched and then thrown occur in *Stanze per la giostra* 1.40 and in *Jerusalem Delivered* 7.101–2. They have a precedent in the detailed description of an arrow being set up and shot by Pandarus in *Iliad* 4.105–26.

17

Everyone applauded him, for all believed it impossible to equal that hit. So when she picked up a new dart Silveria made them all laugh. Then she shot it, and the arrow remained fixed right on target, for it had caught the notch of Altamor's arrow between its feathers, going straight through it so exactly that her dart remained stuck inside the other.

18

Altamor burned with spite and blushed a purplish red as deep as the shame he harbored inside. The daughter of the great Thracian rejoiced, while all around the camp the soldiers shouted, "Long live Silveria!" No greater was the astonishment of all the people of Latium[6] the day two inexplicable moons appeared, as well as two suns, which vied with the splendor of daylight: a prodigious effect of nature indeed.[7]

19

They also praised the man who had hit the center of the small target so skillfully, for he was a singular archer, but the woman received the first honor, because a shot better than hers had never been seen. Now Silveria must give proof of even greater strength and skill: some great iron poles appeared, and there ran Hamilcar with the air of being very sure of himself.

20

Both were ready for the long-awaited race, and both got hold of the poles with their powerful hands. First bending down, then standing up erect, they lifted it high from the ground and held it there to test its weight. While one raised his pole, the other lowered it. Silveria feigned weakness, by seeming to let it drop at her feet.

21

She deceived her competitor easily once he already believed he held victory in his grasp. Trying to achieve an even greater triumph, he threw his pole as far as he possibly could. But immediately after, the woman, expert

6. In antiquity Latium (Italian: Lazio) was the territory between the Sabine Mountains south of Rome and the sea. Modern Lazio is one of the twenty administrative regions of Italy and comprises a much larger territory.

7. The suns and the moons may be a reference to the Horatii, three Roman brothers, and to the Curiatii, three brothers from Alba Longa, respectively. They fought a duel to determine which city would be supreme in Latium. Livy 1.24–25; *Africa* 1.768–73. The portentous apparition here may have been suggested by the propitious omen that appears at the conclusion of the Trojans' game in *Aeneid* 5.522–28.

master that she was in that Moorish game, flung her pole six palms beyond his, just as swiftly as a light cane goes through water or air.

22

Alban, who was the general referee, marked the distance of the poles on the ground, and Hamilcar, seeing that the woman was ahead, raved against himself and against Allah. No machine could throw a ball made of stone or iron with such power and propel it faster than the long iron pole that he now let fly, surpassing hers by two yards.

23

The valiant woman felt challenged. She bent down to pick up some sand from the ground and rubbed it several times in her hands. Then she stamped one foot firmly on the ground, and lifting the other with her whole power, she threw her pole. The pole surpassed the last mark by ten palms: it thundered through the air and hit Alban right where the foot joined the leg.

24

As the poor man was walking swiftly on the track, marking the reach of each throw on the sand, the pole struck him faster than wind, but not with full impact, although the outcome of it was that his leg would never recover its full strength and he would be unable to stand upright as long as he lived. He did not regret his lack of caution, however, for no hand before had ever reached such distance.

25

Battor wanted to compete with Silveria in the next race,[8] because when he was fighting against the good king, he had slid back and fallen down the steep hill, while she had kept going up very nimbly. A far-reaching fame described her as capable of catching bucks, and of doing so with her own hands, and described him as having overtaken a horse faster than a bird, lighter than a dart.

26

She started off with the speedy runner, and together they dashed toward the goal placed at the end of the long track. They were faster than Boreas blowing at its strongest, and faster than lightning falling precipitously from

---

8. This is going to be a footrace, such as we find in *Odyssey* 8.121–25 and in *Aeneid* 5.286–361. Sarrocchi seems to draw more from the latter, in this and the following stanzas.

the sky. Silveria touched the ground as lightly as if she were flying over ripe wheat without bending its tips, or were skimming weightlessly over the waves of the sea and keeping her feet dry.[9]

27

She ran faster than Battor by as much as he once ran faster than his extraordinarily swift horse. He fully realized that she was going to take the victory away from him if he let her gain ground by the smallest stretch. She pretended to stop, then ran off again; he calculated his time and with a tricky movement tripped her with his foot and knocked her down. She fell on the ground, and he ran past flying over the track.[10]

28

Silveria got up. The dirty trick offended her deeply, and nothing equaled her anger. The farther ahead she saw her competitor and the greater was her fear of defeat, the more prodigious became the vigor that the insult, her sense of self, and the desire to vindicate her honor added to her stride, so that in running she outran herself, and only lightning could be said to resemble her.

29

Very near the end she overtook him, just when he had quieted all fears in his heart and was certain he would be getting the prize. As she went past the finish line, she turned to him with a charming movement of her body and said that she was happy to have fallen down, for the greater the difficulty one overcomes, the more glorious is the victory one derives from it.

30

While she said this, her endearing smile blazed forth, her splendid eyes sparkled brightly, and the effort of the race turned the coloring of her composed face a livelier pink. The race had parted the white veil on her breast,

9. Very much like Camilla, who "vel intactae segetis per summa volared gramina, nec teneras cursu laesisset aristas; vel mare per medium fluctu suspensa tumenti ferret iter, celeris nec aequore plantas" (could fly over the tips of the wheat not yet harvested without harming their tender ears; or could sprint over the swollen waves of the deep sea and never touch the water with her flying feet). *Aeneid* 7.805–6, 7.808–9. See canto 3.101n.

10. In *Aeneid* 5.331–38, Nisus stumbles over the slippery ground and, as he falls down, intentionally trips the upcoming runner, so that his beloved friend, Euryalus, can shoot past and win the race.

revealing her hidden treasure; but the pagan's anger was not assuaged by the lure of love, which entraps only gentle hearts.[11]

31

The beautiful sight of her did not stir him at all, so arrogant was he and so distressed by his defeat; and the terrible pain seething viciously in his heart urged him to a rancorous vengeance. Now the Thracian emperor summoned the woman to him to get the invincible sword and to ask if there was anything else she wished, for his entire great kingdom would be a prize unequal to her merits.

32

He said this while looking at her, and her beautiful figure remained deeply engraved in his mind. For her part, Silveria was fully enjoying her victory and her prize. As amiable and loving as she was, she nourished a brotherly affection for Driarasso and felt an equal and similar feeling for Orkhan, both being valiant and kind warriors.

33

Having heard from many in the camp that Ferratte and Armen had been killed[12] and that the emperor had suspended their high ranks in order to assign them to the warriors who fought most valiantly, Silveria, in a respectful and winning manner, asked that this great reward be bestowed upon her, that the strong Driarasso be made captain of the Janissaries and the wise Orkhan captain of the Spahìs.

34

The great sire conceded the woman's high-minded request and praised her wisdom and intelligence. He then declared openly to all that she had asked for the two excellent knights what was rightly due to them. This request hurt several officers with bitter stings of envy and rancor, for they were not capable of considering objectively other men's merits and now were enraged against her who appreciated them.

11. That true love is found only in gentle hearts is a tenet of "dolce stil novo" poetry. It was first expounded by Guido Guinizzelli (c.1230–1276?) in the song "Al cor gentil rempaira sempre amore" (Love always takes shelter in the gentle heart). Other derivations from lyric poetry can be read at 1.31, 9.1, 13.91, 15.70, 18.8, 18.94, 18.100.

12. Ferratte and Armen were killed in canto 5.7 and 5.42, respectively.

35

Her having won the famous sword annoyed them greatly; that a rumor should circulate that they had proved less capable than a woman displeased them more; that the emperor's esteem for their value should fall further increased their hatred of her; but that she should be the one who assigned them to their rightful rank passed all limits of resentment and anger.

36

So the prize given to the beautiful victor angered the worthiest warriors. Still, the Thracian emperor wished to honor the losers with rich gifts as well, because even if in dexterity and power they were inferior to the woman, who was so strong and skillful in comparison, it did not seem proper to him that he should show less regal magnanimity toward them.[13]

37

On that day, the emperor's splendid royal diadem was adorned with precious black feathers. One might say that nature could ornament only a few rare birds with feathers as beautiful as that. In their midst was a diamond surpassing in splendor all other fine gems, the most valuable that could be found in the entire Indies, a stone that shone among them just like the moon among the stars.

38

The emperor lifted it with his own hands and made a rich present of it to Altamor, who had first entered the courtly race and made his sharp arrow fly so swiftly. With no less courtesy, he ordered that a shield of shining steel be brought to Hamilcar, a shield he kept among the most splendid war trophies he had won from various illustrious kings.

39

It was a shield strongly tempered and surpassing in value any other made in those days. One could see painted on it the head of the Assyrian man who was beheaded by the young Jewish widow.[14] The picture of the man impressed the onlooker with the awesomeness of death, with a suggestion

---

13. Aeneas too awards all those who participated in the races, regardless of whether they were winners or losers. *Aeneid* 5.348–61.

14. The Assyrian man is Holofernes, Nebuchadnezzar's general, who was killed by Judith of Bethulia (Judith 10.13). This story recurred frequently in literature and in the arts. At the

of both Venus and Bacchus; still you might say that the presence of the god was stronger than that of the goddess, so overpowered by sleep did the drunken general appear to be.[15]

40

The emperor also ordered an overcoat to be given to Battor. A stupendous work was embroidered on it. The silk threads gave shape to a thick forest, in the middle of which the handsome Adonis lay dead;[16] the beautiful goddess was bent over him, distraught and pale; around him were many little cupids, some staring with raised eyebrows, seemingly struck with astonishment and grief.

41

But most of them were turned toward the goddess to console her with sweet affection. Some were drying her tender face and gleaming eyes with the

---

beginning of the century, a painting of the biblical heroine was done by Cristoforo Bronzino. Soon Giambattista Marino celebrated it in a madrigal that was later published in *La Galeria* (1619). Like Marino in that collection, Sarrocchi here tries to translate into words the effect produced by a work of art, without implying any of the symbolic meanings conferred on the figure through the ages. In early Christianity the fathers of the church, stressing the notion of Judith's chastity, made her a prefiguration of the Virgin Mary. In Renaissance Florence, she had become the symbol of the city's fierce spirit of independence. According to Scaglione, who refers to Possevino's *Bibliotheca selecta* of 1593, for the Counter-Reformation church the slaying of the Assyrian general represented the defeat of the enemy of Rome at the hands of the Jesuit soldier who fought with the power of knowledge and eloquence. Among the many pictorial representations of Judith, most famous are Botticelli's *Return of Judith to Bethulia*, done in 1470, and Lucas Cranach's painting, completed one century later. In the last few decades, a great deal of interest has been shown in Artemisia Gentileschi, the woman painter who, between 1612 and 1625, executed at least four paintings of Judith and Holofernes. After Sarrocchi's death, the biblical heroine became the protagonist of Bartolomeo Tortoletti's *Giuditta Vittoriosa* (1628) and Giacomo Bianchi's *Giuditta Trionfante* (1642). See Aldo Scaglione, *Essays on the Arts of Discourse*, ed. Paolo Cherchi, Allen Mendelbaum, Stephen Murphy, and Giuseppe Velli (New York: Peter Lang, 1998), 106; Mary Garrard, *Artemisia Gentileschi: The Image of the Female Hero in Italian Baroque Art* (Princeton: Princeton University Press, 1989); Elena Ciletti, "Patriarchal Ideology in the Renaissance Iconography of Judith," in *Refiguring Woman. Perspectives on Gender and the Italian Renaissance*, ed. and introd. Marilyn Migiel and Juliana Schiesari. (Ithaca, NY: Cornell University Press, 1991), 35–70. On Gentileschi, see above, canto 13.25n.

15. Bacchus, the god of wine, and Venus, the goddess of love, are references to Holofernes' intention to possess Judith and to his being drunk and asleep when Judith decapitates him. In this picture, therefore, the general appears to be more taken by sleep than by a desire for love.

16. Adonis was a beautiful Babylonian youth beloved by Aphrodite, i.e., Venus. He died wounded by a boar while hunting. The goddess, inconsolable, made the anemone grow out of his blood. The story is told by Ovid in *Metamorphoses* 10.524–32, 10.708–39. Several poems were written about this legend at the time of Sarrocchi's writing, among them Giambattista Marino's *Adonis*, a reduced version of which circulated among his Roman friends in manuscript form long before it was published in Paris in 1623.

white veil thrown over her chest; others collected her fresh tears into a small urn; some scattered beautiful petals over the young man, while still others fanned him with their wings, trying to revive the vital air in his comely breast.[17]

42

The emperor now summoned the warriors to his high throne and with gracious words told them: "I give these prizes in recognition of your valor, but first of all I give you my love, which I know you hold the dearest." Then he was silent. But the wrath of the men who had lost the race was not assuaged; on the contrary, the scantier their merit, the more painfully their resentment gnawed at them.

43

The night had already folded herself in the luxurious mantle of stars when the warriors went back to their tents. With the new day their hatred had not abated. It fed upon itself while they were asleep; it rose at dawn murmuring secretively in many corners and gaining ever more in strength; finally it made itself known and, seeping into many hearts, burst into furor.

44

Similarly, when the north wind blows among dry branches, a murmur goes around lightly at first; then slowly it begins to gain force, spreading more and more; and soon, as its impetus grows, it howls with seeming anger, the noise of it contending with the noise of the trees. Hearing the hissing sound, the birds flee their nests, the beasts their lairs.

45

The murmur continued with increasing rancor even as the sun was sending down its luminous rays, and a great number of people had gathered in that

---

17. The scene embroidered on the overcoat given to Battor seems to owe much to Politian's depiction of Venus and Mars in *Stanze della giostra* 1.122–23. There, the two gods recline on a bed while some cupids scatter petals over and around them. A similar scene is contained in the third of the three cantos constituting at that time all that Marino had written of *Adonis*. We know this from a letter Giambattista sent to Bernardo Castello in April 1605. Marino, *Lettere*, ed. Marziano Guglielminetti (Turin: Einaudi, 1966), 53. For the definitive version of his poem, Marino expanded the description exponentially. Stanzas 189–92, at the end of it, show the cupids in a variety of activities: depositing bows and arrows, gathering the locks of hair that Venus had torn off in despair, flapping their wings over Adonis to revive him, dipping their wings in the goddess's tears and sprinkling them over his body. Are these parallels a sign of a continuous rivalry between Sarrocchi and her former friend, and could his amplification of the scene be proof of a determination to show his superior inventiveness?

part of the camp where assemblies were usually held. Battor, who was very angry at having been defeated by Silveria, reproved her behavior menacingly in the presence of Arigazel and Musar, who in turn coveted the great honor of Agah more than anyone.

46

Ottorico, Brimarte, Ali, and Renato were also there: they had aspired to the worthy command of the Spahìs. The competitive spirit was so keen among them that they had always vied bitterly with one another. Now that Silveria had obtained that honor for someone else, all these men, who before were full of anger, furor, and envy toward one another, became friends, not out of love, but because they had found a common enemy.

47

Armed with tongues of fire, they threw blazing insults in her direction, and Driarasso, who was not far away, could not help hearing what they said. Inconsiderate of the general regulations that applied to the place, he unsheathed his sword, shouted that they were lying, and forced them to uphold their foolhardy statements or lose their lives.

48

At once a thousand weapons could be seen at the ready, some coming to the help of friends, others intent on separating those who fought. As they struck, the swords at first threw flashes and sparks to the sky, but soon, when they were drawn out of the wounds, they were clearly covered with red blood. Hearing the reason for the scuffle, Silveria grew angry and came running through the thick crowd gathered around, which now parted at the sight of her bow.

49

Seeing her approaching, Hamilcar came from the opposite side. He was troubled by a strong, gnawing rancor, so badly had he failed the test with her. As usual, he held a big shield on one arm and a ponderous two-edged axe on the other. Full of fury, he turned his long step toward Battor and Driarasso, who now faced each other.

50

He touched Driarasso on the right shoulder at the point where the shoulder joins the arm. Silveria let a piercing dart fly from her strong bow and hit him in the chest. The blood spilled out of a double exit, for the dart went through Hamilcar's back and flew further to strike Aribaldan and deprive him of one eye. Hamilcar gasped, went sprawling on the ground, and expired.

51

Giasser, Ernesto, and Arigazel were shocked by their friend's sudden demise. They hurled themselves on Driarasso, one more fiercely than the other, and were not ashamed, as many as they were, to attack a man alone. Battor let go of Driarasso and turned his step, or rather flew like a winged bird against the woman, then raised his hand to strike her; his was a hand accustomed to vicious misdeeds, and a barbaric hand indeed for wanting to harm such beauty.

52

While Silveria was bending her bow again, not expecting Driarasso to let him get away, a heavy blow struck her on her white neck. That whack, however, failed to hit her with full force.[18] Orkhan realized the danger she was in, came quickly to her aid, and gave Battor a double measure of firm blows that did not wound him but made him harmless.

53

Battor paid no attention to the blows, all his attention being directed at harming the beautiful archer. She, meanwhile, had already placed a dart on the string but was standing too near him to be able to shoot it. Orkhan then attacked him ferociously, and Battor, to save himself, was forced to let the woman go. As he did, she stepped back and aimed to strike and make him pay for his blows.

54

As she was about to strike Battor, she took care not to hit her friend who was locked with him in bodily combat. When she saw him opening his mouth and exhaling the heat brought about by the struggle, she released her arrow. The dart made a piercing jab inside the palate and went right

---

18. In *Jerusalem Delivered* 3.30.1–2, Tasso's warrior woman, Clorinda, is caught by a blow that has lost its intended force but still manages to wound her: 'Pur non gì tutto in vano, e ne' confini del bianco collo, il bel capo ferille" (however, the blow fell not in vain, and wounded her head at the point where it joined her white neck).

through the tongue. Battor fell shouting, but deprived of the use of his tongue, he was not able to utter a distinct word.[19]

55

As she looked at him, Silveria said: "So may all tongues be jabbed that enviously jab the innocent with mordacious and vicious words." Meanwhile Rosmonda, who had already heard of the tumult in the camp, had by now received a detailed report; so she sent Corcutte to the ramparts to prevent the Christians from making another sortie at the news of the riot.

56

Just as the ingenious bees, when they have filled their cells with honey and a drone arrives bent on plunder, prepare to fight him and rise one after the other buzzing,[20] so a rumor started in the camp and, carried from one soldier to the next, turned into a riot. The sounds of the fight rumbled on, and soldiers arrived from all sides in droves.

57

The bloody fight spread more and more, with numerous men killed and wounded. The royal maiden came out of her tent, fully armed except for her visor. She alternated prayers, threats, and admonitions; she blamed some here, she upbraided some there, and she gave orders to others. Her beautiful face, her fine eyes were aglow with a light of nobility and majesty.

58

When she arrived where the awful fray began, she saw a miserable and dreadful spectacle. She held back her friend still seething with anger and realized that she was wounded on her left side, neck, and breast. The news, however, was spreading—the crowd mixed facts and gossip—that the princess warrior was languishing near death; some even said they had seen her blood flowing.

19. Cases of life and voice being snatched at the same moment when a soldier's throat is pierced through by a dart are found in *Aeneid* 10.345–47: "rigida Dryopem ferit eminus hasta sub mentum, graviter pressa, pariterque loquentis vocem animamque rapit traiecto gutture" (from afar, the rigid spear lands a heavy blow on Dryops just under his chin, and by going through the throat while he is talking, it takes away both his life and his voice); and in *Orlando Furioso* 9.41.5–7: "alzò un'accetta, e con sì valoroso braccio dietro nel capo lo percosse, che gli levò la vita e la parola" (he lifted an axe and with his strong arm hit him on the back of his head, robbing him of life and words).

20. For another bee simile, see canto 7.108 above.

59

The false news ran through the camp; it reached the emperor, who, being her father, felt for her; it reached Vaconte as well, who was pained no less, for he was bewitched with Rosmonda. As fierce a warrior as he was, he still could not hold the pain in his heart, and he stood there, very pale. But then his senses were revived, and he wanted to make people pay for his grief with their blood.

60–66

Believing Rosmonda to be injured, Vaconte forgets his promise not to leave his tent and runs out to avenge the offense done to her. When they meet, she listens to the explanation for dis-obeying the order, and as she studies him intently, she begins to fall in love.

67

The handsome woman looked at him with great attention, and as she noticed his pallor, his sadness, and his slow movements, she became aware of how much he suffered and how weakened and tortured he must be by his love for her. Seeing this, Love shot an arrow to force some sympathy into her heart; her anger faded, and with the realization of how passionate a lover he was, the ice that had hardened her breast began to melt.

68

While warming and softening the woman's hard and cold heart, Love kept striking the young man relentlessly, so that his face became even paler, his words failed, and he could not reveal to her his hidden desire. His feet were trembling and could no longer sustain the accustomed weight, for the more victorious a man is in war, the more likely it is for him to become pale and tremble and to be vanquished by love.

69

Uncertain between two wishes, she wanted to inquire about him among the soldiers, and when she found out how strong his love was, she rid her heart of all suspicion. Hers was a heart that Love, with his bow at the ready, was about to strike; her heart was already softened by compassion for the pain he suffered, for she had accused him unjustly.

70

Instead of receiving praise and reward, he had been blamed and humiliated. She remembered having seen him sighing and crying. She had the impression of seeing his handsome face everywhere; whatever she looked at showed her that beautiful image of his, making her feel a consuming love everywhere, and whatever she heard seemed to remind her of his sighs, his voice, and his crying.[21]

71

All this while, the fierce tyrant had been very angry about the grave incident, and now he was intent on punishment. He wanted to know who had been so bold and stupid as to dare so much against his royal command. Rosmonda was ordered to investigate. She found that her brother was responsible for what had happened but made excuses for him with her father, for Driarasso had been pushed to it, and so she directed all blame on those who were now dead.

CANTO 16

Scanderbeg's men penetrate the Turkish camp to rescue Vaconte, but the young warrior refuses to escape. Instead, he runs to Rosmonda's tent and helps her to get rid of the Albanians who are about to capture her.

---

21. The idea that a lover sees the image of the beloved everywhere is a direct borrowing from Petrarch's poem "Di pensier in pensier, di monte in monte" (From thought to thought, from mountain to mountain). *Canzoniere* 129.27–39.

From CANTO 17

Silveria, after repulsing the sultan's advances, runs out of the city and meets Rosmonda in the countryside. Together, with the help of Benci, they force their way into the tower where Vaconte lies in chains, liberate him and take refuge at Croia.

1–55

Marcello Benci, just arrived from Italy to help Vaconte, fights a duel with Driarasso and defeats him but spares his life. Even so, the emperor refuses to hand over the young warrior; in fact, he plans to kill him.

56

Following the nighttime attack on the camp, the beautiful archer was in Presa. There she lay hurting in bed, for the movements and the exertion endured during that deadly flight had augmented all her injuries. On her part, she had inflicted on the tyrant a wound far more severe than any she had received, and while her wounds were improving, his were becoming deeper and more troublesome.[1]

57

The handsome woman had been taken to an isolated room of the imperial palace, because the warrior princess wished to have her always near, so great was her affection for her. The Thracian lover was now able to go and

1. Cf. *Orlando Furioso* 19.27.5–28.4: "Quivi a Medoro fu per la donzella / la piaga in breve a sanità ritratta; / ma in minor tempo or sentì maggiore / piaga di questa avere ella nel core. / Assai più larga piaga e più profonda / nel cor sentì da non veduto strale, / che da' begli occhi e da la testa bionda / di Medoro aventò l'arcier c'ha l'ale" (under the maiden's care Medoro's wound closed and healed; but in much shorter time she felt a deeper wound open in her heart. A deeper and wider wound she felt, inflicted by a dart unseen, which the winged archer flung from Medoro's beautiful eyes and golden head).

visit her in person, go back day, morning, and night, and see her and speak to her as he pleased, without giving rise to suspicion.

58

He wanted to know moment by moment what treatment was being administered and how it was being applied. He craved her naked white body but hid his lustful desire very astutely. When she was uncovered, a charming pink virginal blush spread over her face, but soon the lost natural color reemerged like a flower in the sun.

59

The blushes that tinged the beautiful cheek of the chaste goddess were perhaps not so red, when Actaeon saw her bathing naked in the cold waves, and she, angered, tried to put out his amorous fire, splashing him with water.[2] Diana was perhaps less enticing and Actaeon was tied by Love with perhaps weaker chains than was this man, whose fierce heart was captured by the woman's sweet and invigorating beauty.

60

Although he was arrogant and his behavior unrestrained—which came from reigning over so many and such diverse nations[3]—the sweet sight of her, her beautifully composed face, her show of courage and of gentleness made him shy, excited him and restrained him at the same time. Passion had him burning when away from her and freezing when near.[4] Thus the tyrant experienced a love that wore his fiber down with a continuous change of moods.

61

Behind his haughty bearing and kind manners, his soul wavered between hope and fear. This great passion, however, could not chase out of his heart

2. The legend is that Diana, surprised by Actaeon while she was bathing naked at a spring, saw him looking at her in this condition and splashed his face with water, thus turning him into a stag; he was then torn apart by his own hunting dogs. The story is told by Ovid in *Metamorphoses* 3.155–205. Sarrocchi's words echo those of Petrarch's madrigal, in *Canzoniere* 52: "Non al suo amante più Dïana piacque, / quando per tal ventura tutta ignuda / la vide / in mezzo de le gelide acque" (Diana did not appeal more to her lover, when he by chance saw her bathing all naked in the cool waters).

3. For other descriptions of the Ottoman Empire as being made up of many nations, see cantos 5.103 and 14.67 above.

4. Freezing and burning at the same time is what traditionally happens to lovers in the phenomenology of love, in both poetry and prose. Cf. cantos 1.30 and 7.66 above. By taking into consideration the intermittent separation of lover and beloved, here Sarrocchi renders the commonplace oxymoron somewhat more plausible.

the hatred he felt for Rosmonda's prisoner: so all kinds of ideas kept turning in his mind, as he tried to find some cunning way to satisfy both his love and his hatred.

62

Respect for his royal daughter opposed both his wishes; so in order to satisfy one and the other, he, lover and enemy in one, made the shrewd decision of sending Rosmonda to repress the rebellious belligerence of Sabalio, who, together with Vran, was blocking the passes nearby, preventing food supplies from reaching Presa.

63

As soon as the pitiless father had his order delivered to her, Rosmonda selected a group of armed men to go with her, but harboring a deep suspicion in her heart, she asked Silveria to remain with the prisoner. Although not entirely recovered—her wounds had only partly healed and were now less painful—Silveria was strong enough to sit up most of the time and lie in bed only occasionally.

64

When the warrior princess was away, the Thracian waited for Silveria to recuperate. The vicious man wanted to satisfy both his lustful desire and his wish for murder in a single day; so he gave directions to a group of trusted soldiers to capture the baron while he was asleep, while he, appearing in person in Silveria's chamber, blocked her from running to his aid.

65

A great concern for her queen presently troubled Silveria with a deep, heartfelt anxiety. So by cajolery she tried to find out at least what the cruel tyrant's plan was. Her sweet requests gave him hope he might slowly reveal his maddening craving, and in order to win her over, he described in full how he had arranged Vaconte's imprisonment, his death, and his own revenge.

66

Besides the ruse of attempting to stir desire in the woman by revealing his own desire, he, a lover no longer master of himself, could hardly keep any thoughts hidden. Letting down all the guards that the right expression of the face and cautious words might have provided, he disclosed his most intimate secrets to her. When she realized how strong his passion was, she, being chaste and wise, started thinking of how she could escape.

67

The present excitement gave him greater hope and further inflamed his reckless mind. He embraced her, his chest pressed against hers in an unrestrained and frantic manner. Afraid to defile her chaste heart, she pushed him away with her powerful hands. A quiver full of sharp arrows and a bow were available nearby, but she managed to restrain her anger.

68

She attempted to moderate his blind furor and lustful desire with words. She moaned sweetly and regretted that he should want to pick the forbidden fruit against her will: for if the woman did not wish to offer it spontaneously, it did not seem that it ought to be so desirable to a man. She told him that not force, but only accord and pleasure, could induce her heart to acquiesce.

69

"As the wise emperor you are, remember that I was born in the land of the great Allah, and not a servant; remember that the heavens reserve great punishment to the woman who gives in to a man unchastely. So I will be happy to comply only with the wishes of the man who, as he must be, is respectful of the law that forbids satisfying one's amorous urges with a woman who is free and not his wife."

70

Hearing the excellent reasoning of the chaste Silveria, the fierce tyrant, who was in love, conceived the idea of overcoming her objections underhandedly. Pretending to praise her highly, he asked her to accept as an honorable pledge his promise to make her his royal bride at court, and he told her that his word should suffice.

71

He embraced her again, and again she rejected him, even more resolutely than before. A new blush stained the ivory whiteness of her beautiful face, making her even more alluring. Once more she sweetly spoke to him, and to free herself from his embrace she lied and dissembled, for in her heart she was determined to remain chaste, even should she be promised to be made the high queen of the whole world.

72

She said that she believed the generous promise of his royal heart to be sincere; nonetheless, approval ought to be given, she said, by the priest.

Indeed, what she was now asking for was a wedding. At this point he stopped trying to force her; he realized he had embarked on too arduous a campaign, for she was far too strong. So his mind turned to a new plan of deception.

73

Now he intended to wait for dawn to rise in the sky, for he was confident that a wicked priest, a profane worshiper of God, would obey any whim of a formidable sovereign without hesitation. It would be considered a tyrannical act, a profane act against God, to call the priest now, he said, as his impious mind hid his iniquitous intent under a cloak of religious piety.

74

Wishing for the light of the new day to appear soon, he returned to the royal hall, but the clever maiden, not presuming to be strong enough to resist abuse and shame, did not want to remain in bed and wait for daylight. So while everyone lay quietly in the dark, she decided to leave, for she knew of a secret way to exit the city.

75–103

In the countryside Silveria meets Rosmonda on her way back from the expedition against the Christian marauders. They come across Marcello Benci en route to rescue Vaconte. Together, they force their way into the tower where the young knight lies in chains, liberate him, and decide to take refuge together at Croia.

From **CANTO 18**

Crushed by the news of his daughter's defection, the sultan finds comfort in his beautiful wife Hypsipyle. She reminds him of his other daughter, Glicera, who is now queen of Persia and in a position to send him reinforcements. At Croia, meanwhile, Rosmonda and Silveria convert to Christianity, and Rosmonda marries Vaconte. A plague breaks out in the city, killing many people. In Italy, Alexander's envoys obtain the pope's support. An army gathers at Ancona, ready to sail to Epirus.

1

The tyrant learned of Rosmonda's flight, and his mind recoiled in sadness and confusion. His blood rushed to the aid of the sorrow-stricken heart, and the path to his voice was blocked. Of those men who saved the maiden warrior and opened the gates on her orders—orders they were accustomed to obey—several regretted it now, and more than one tried to find an excuse for what he had done.

2

Like a man who, entering a house on fire, is prevented from seeing and breathing by the grimy smoke rising, for his eyes are blinded and his throat is choking, the tyrant, informed of the bad news, could no longer hear, see, or speak one word. He turned his mind in all directions in an attempt to vent his anger, but in vain.

3

His other losses bothered him greatly, but this disturbed and tormented him most of all; and he no longer remembered the handsome face of Silveria, so coveted before. On this grievous occasion, more than any of the many women he sheltered in his quarters, the beautiful

Hypsipyle was prompt to console him with soothing words and winning ways.

4—5

The mention of Hypsipyle becomes here the point of departure for the eulogy of Angela Vitelli, member of a prominent Roman family.

6

Sometimes, in a shady hedge, a pristine rose can be seen blooming in the gentle breeze, under a serene sky, the best thing to admire in the well-tended garden.[1] In a similar way that charming girl had been nurtured like a flower among royal luxuries by the care of a mother who, having lost her beloved spouse, had turned all her affection on her daughter.

7

One looked admiringly at her well-shaped forehead, which surpassed milk and snow in its whiteness, and at the blond wavy hair around it, an adornment richer and more alluring than amber and gold.[2] From that beauty a purity of soul emanated that this world could never soil with its dirt, for God wished to keep her soul unsullied, in harmony with the handsome body that covered it.

8

If one looked into her eyes, oh! then one would believe for sure that Love kept there his main abode; because from them one could see such grace and virtue flowing that no human mind could rise so high as to understand them.[3] One could only say: "Beautiful eyes, Love bestows his full joy on those who look at you, a joy so pleasing that, compared with that perfect pleasure, anything inspired by other beauties would be annoyance and boredom."

1. Sarrocchi's ability to vary traditional similes with measured taste is revealed again in this felicitous comparison between a flower cultivated by an expert gardener and a girl raised by a caring parent. For the topos of the rose, see canto 13.38 above.

2. For the recurring description of female beauty transformed into a precious work of jewelry, see above, canto 13.11n.

3. For the personification of Cupid throwing his darts from the woman's eyes, see canto 3.64 above. The concept that the woman's essence transcends man's capacity to understand it ultimately derives from a sonnet by Guido Cavalcanti (c.1259–1300), "Chi è questa che vèn ch'ogn'om la mira?" (Who is this woman coming, at whom everyone is marveling?) The lines in question are: "non fu sì alta già la mente nostra / e non si pose in noi tanta salute / che propriamente n'aviàm conoscenza" (our mind was never so high and never possessed such power as to acquire an adequate knowledge of her).

9

No less splendid were her star-studded eyelashes, which seemed to be made of pure gold. From them descended a nose well shaped and without blemish. Her cheeks were covered by a hue in which the white and the red of freshly picked roses were blended to perfection, on which candor had spread the thinnest veil to subdue the warm liveliness of the purple.

10

Her heavenly smile opened between ruby-like lips, her gentle voice broke against teeth as fine as pearls. By that radiance and at that sweet sound all hearts were captivated and wanted to languish contentedly. Oftentimes, the roses blooming on her face prevailed over its pure luminous ivory, when bashfulness made her lower her beautiful eyes, spreading a reddish blush over the white dew of her skin.[4]

11

Her lovely limbs seemed to be made of white gleaming alabaster, her breasts were full, her arms roundish, her flanks ample. She looked like Venus come down from heaven. While thinking of her beauty, no one ever tired or grew satiated; on the contrary, before her angelic deportment, all onlookers were inflamed and conquered by love forever.

12

The fame of her exceptional beauty had spread over all the land. Soon fascinated by her, the emperor had her abducted from her home. But her soul would not be enslaved, even if her body could be. By constantly keeping her thoughts chaste, she protected her heart in icy coldness and made it the trusted custodian of her virginal flower.

13

She disliked to dress up her shapely head with ornaments of pearls and gems—golden ties that bind and enslave the soul—and to cover her beautiful body with elegant clothes of purple and gold. She never wavered from her determination to remain modest and chaste, no matter how much they menaced and harassed her. On all occasions, she appeared with her face clear, her hair untouched, and in a simple unadorned garb.

4. Compare the description of Hypsipyle's beauty with that of other female characters in cantos 1.27–31, 3.65, 3.79–80. A point of similarity, besides beauty, between women and some youths is chastity and virtuous mores. Cf. stanzas 97 and 101, and cantos 1.29, 3.81, 7.14, 13.16.

14

Staying with the sultan were many comely women who made up their faces and adorned their hair; they would embrace him passionately and recipro-cate with words and amorous glances. Only Hypsipyle, rebelling against his wishes, spread a red blush over her pale cheeks and lowered her lovely serene eyes, now overflowing with crystalline tears.

15

If he was aroused and wanted to touch her, she moaned and withdrew shyly, but the dewy shine of her eyes became a fire at which Love further sharpened his arrows. She complained to the heavens and to fate. Her pin-ing and her rejecting manner, however, further enticed the Thracian, for tears and pain make a woman more seductive, and a chaste repulse fans the flame of desire.

16

She was called royal consort, but the sultan could select any woman for his pleasure. At the beginning there was no chance that she could be united to him in matrimony according to the law. Even so, he remained tied to her with so strong and tenacious a longing that she was able to guide and influ-ence him first into giving her freedom, and then into celebrating their wed-ding in solemn pomp.

17

So once the ice of her fearful suspicions had thawed, the Thracian emperor satisfied his lascivious desires, for now she was not averse to the sweet love of their matrimonial bed and had become responsive to his passion and feelings. At this moment, then, this wise and beautiful consort arrived in his presence to console him in his bitter sorrow. As soon as he saw her, he was alarmed and asked why she had come.

18

When Jupiter gazes into the shining eyes of his wife and sister, which move around as serenely and calmly as those of a majestic cow,[5] pride of the

---

5. In classical mythology, the god Jupiter, identified by the Romans with the Greek Zeus, and the goddess Juno, identified by the Romans with the Greek Hera, are husband and wife, and also brother and sister, being both children of Cronos and Rhea. "Est aliquid nupsisse Iovi, Iovis esse sororem" (it is something to have married Jupiter and to be his sister as well), exclaims Ovid in *Fasti* 6.27. Zeus is king of heaven and hearth and is armed with thunder and lightning. The Greek epithet for Hera was βοῶπις, i.e., "cow-eyed," hence Sarrocchi's description of Juno's eyes moving around as calmly as those of a cow. Cf. *Iliad* 18.356 and 18.360.

horned herd, then the god's fiery bolts, which he flings to earth most vehe-
mently when irate, easily fall from his grasp. With such eyes Hypsipyle
looked intently at the emperor and sweetly said to him:

19

"Being allowed to come to you any time I wish is a privilege that you
granted to my loyalty. If I dare too much or come at an inconvenient time,
say that you want me to leave." The tyrant smiled, kissed her in a tender
embrace, and soothed his deep sorrow; for much more pleasing thoughts
set in when the senses are aroused by amorous desire.[6]

20

Feeling relieved from the dark cloud of sorrow, the sultan's mind became
clearer, his first impulses were checked, and he tried to think of a remedy
for the impending ruin. Then, as he compared his strength with that of his
enemy, the latter clearly appeared to be inferior or barely comparable to
his own, so rich was he in wealth and domains, in allies and subjects.

21

In his youth the Thracian had had a daughter of such handsome shape and
features as to surpass in beauty, if not in strength, the great princess warrior.
This daughter, who at birth was named Glicera, gave no little hope of coming to his aid and assuaging his fears, because, thanks to her, Erifilio, her
husband and king of Persia, had become an ally.

22–88

A flashback tells us here of how Glicera and Erifilio had fallen in love without ever seeing each
other. As both their parents were against their getting married, the young man decided to travel
to Thrace and woo the princess in person. One day they were caught together in a room of
the royal palace and were condemned to die. His mother, however, intervened in their favor,
and the young lovers were allowed to become husband and wife.

6. Hypsipyle's entrance in this scene, and the effect of her closeness on the sultan, seem to
have been drawn on the model of *Africa* 5.17–222. In Petrarch's poem, Sophonisba approaches
Massinissa who is entering the Numidian capital, Cirta, and appeals to him in an enticing manner. In *Africa* too, after a lengthy description of the woman's charms, we are told of the impression her presence and words make on him: "Immemor armorum iuvenis cui martius ardor
exciderat, gravidumque nove dulcedine forme pectus, et insolitis ardebant viscera flammis"
(setting aside the violence of war to which he was accustomed, the young man's heart began
to weigh under the sweetness of that marvelous beauty and began to burn inside with an
unusual flame).

89

Erifilio sent several squadrons under the command of Ghison, the general of his army. They arrived after the emperor had sent Glicera a messenger. When she learned the actual story of her sister, with a blush reddening her lovely cheeks, she pressured her husband to send a new and larger contingent to seek retribution for what had happened.

90

Meanwhile the king of Epirus rejoiced that so great a princess warrior as Rosmonda had come to him, for it was his ardent zealous wish to augment the flock of those who worshiped the true God. With a reverent expression on his face he gave a clear sign of remembering that she was an empress; at the same time he was determined that she acquire a far greater kingdom in heaven than the one she possessed on earth.

91

He often confided his intention to Vaconte. In hearing of it, the young man was happy beyond all measure, and consumed as he was in flames of love, he already rejoiced in the hope of something still unattained. On her part, the woman was determined to defend her chastity and wanted to make her father realize that it was virtue, not attraction, that made her fall in love.

92

It was virtue. Still, those adored eyes of his seemed to relieve the tight grip in which love held her heart, and his stirring words seemed to assuage the fire burning within. But then, the very respite that prevented the flames of love from consuming her gave them greater strength, just as a log of wood when green keeps down the fire at first but shortly after feeds it quickly.

93

When she was near the object of her desire, she delighted in looking at his vivifying beauty. From his eyes proceeded a warm glow by which Love made ever greater her fondness for him. And she did not mind that his charming eyes showed his ardent passion—entreaties are always imprinted in a lover's eyes—for his passion was enhanced by shyness and respect.

94

"What my tongue cannot say out of fear, Love shows in my eyes, O woman. You can read it there yourself, as my wounded heart repeatedly beseeches you. Why doesn't your gentle heart come to the rescue of someone who is dying for you? One dies this way for certain, when help comes too late; and life is ended because of too much pain.[7]

95

"Can such torture and death come from so worthy and beautiful a cause? Are you not a woman? Will you let this happen? Are you a foe of pity, a rebel to love?" The young man was saying this to her in silent words and with loving eyes. Ah! mysterious and strange skill of lovers, far superior to all other human skills!

96

The virtue that Nature has given one sense often Love confers to another. By natural virtue the eye can only see, but Love gives it also the power to speak, to hear, and to answer. Thus in his eyes Vaconte asked her for relief from his deep and painful anguish; in her eyes Rosmonda showed understanding, and her love was made stronger by his ardor.

97

Even so, the inclination to chastity that dominated in her, the Islamic law in which she had been bred, and also the consideration of her royal father in danger of his life and his domains had an effect on her, no matter how great the power of love; so her virtue came to her rescue, restraining the amorous urge and inciting in her a desire to placate her parent's anger.

98

Several trusted informers close to the sultan gave a reliable report on his feelings: he who had the power of life over her had decided that she should be shown only the pretense of a pardon. Meanwhile by many devout Christians and by the good king himself, a warm prayer was sent up to heaven that a spirit of love might flow into her noble heart from the Father, the Son, and the Holy Ghost.

7. These are topical love themes found throughout early lyric poetry. The contrast between what the lover is too shy to confess and what outward signs clearly proclaim is gracefully treated by Giacomo da Lentini throughout "Meravigliosamente" (Marvelously). In lines 52–54, the lover declares, as a way of concluding: " Sacciatolo per singa / zo ch'eo no dico a linga / quando voi mi vedite" (when you see me, please read in the signs I give what I do not say in words).

99

Love did not prevent the enamored youth from contemplating heaven; on the contrary, at times a pure and holy thought can clear away the confusion caused by too strong a passion. A pious zeal rose from his heart to his eyes and ran down his beautiful cheeks in bitter tears. The mighty warrior was not ashamed of it; in fact he wanted to weep even more.

100

"O king of all the stars, whose divine grace can reach the depth of every heart," he prayed, "look at me, see how easily I burn, how quickly I turn into cinders, for my dear enemy becomes harder than a stone and ever more cruel toward me! Do placate her, as you alone can, do not delay to soften her stony harshness with your holy love. Should you touch her ever so lightly with a spark of your compassion, her eyes would open from darkness to the truth that is yours alone.[8]

101

"You know that now I take pleasure only from a pure kind of love, a love that is no offense to you or to virtue. At times, however, a chaste flame may in time spark a passion not so chaste." He had hardly ended this well-conceived prayer when God brought light into her mind, and spontaneously she asked to be washed and cleansed of all sins in holy water.

102

It was long established in the decrees of heaven that the woman should turn her mind to the holy faith and welcome the divine precepts and rites with the greatest reverence. A warm, soothing flame of love, never felt before, dispelled the icy coldness gripping her heart, and a pure divine fire began to soften her ferocious and unrelenting soul.[9]

8. The Italian clauses "qual dura più la mia nemica impietra" (my enemy becomes harder than a stone and more cruel toward me) and "tu l'ammollisci e spietra," ([you, Love,] do soften her stone-like hardness) bear clear traces of Dante's "petrose" rhymes. These are songs of unrequited love for a woman described as being hard as stone (pietra) in her unresponsiveness to the lover's pleas. The best-known *canzone* in that group of poems is "Così nel mio parlar vogli' esser aspro" (I want to be as harsh in my verse).

9. This is the effect of divine love—*caritas*—which vivifies the shriven soul after repentance and absolution, as catechism instructs Catholics.

103

She offered superb gifts to the church, in the name of God, who is one and distinct in three persons.[10] In the church, the priest's hand besprinkled her with holy water and gave her a vital cleansing. Then Vaconte, who had been a lover, was made a husband, and all his bitter pains were changed to sweet joy. The king, who could not honor Rosmonda as a Thracian queen would deserve,[11] planned her wedding as if she were his own daughter.

104

And because the royal maiden had great affection for Silveria and was loved by her in return, she wished her also to be cleansed and made as pure in her soul as she was in her behavior. Heaven calls on the uncouth shepherd as well as on the great emperor. Silveria was pleased to consent, so Rosmonda and her Vaconte helped her to make herself beautiful at the sacred font.[12]

105

The eternal creator of the universe, whose justice is equal only to his compassion, who often allows the most adverse fate to befall those who are dearest to him, was preparing a new obstacle for his people to overcome. This was perhaps because they were not totally cleansed of their sins, or because he wanted them to earn a greater reward in heaven.[13]

106

In addition to the terrible double misfortune that hunger and the ravages of war had brought them when, in the absence of their strong hero, the citadel came to the brink of destruction, a scourge sent by heaven hit it now with an even greater force, making any other trial seem child's play. A contagious

10. The Trinity.

11. That is to say, Alexander cannot offer her a wedding ceremony as grand and pompous as one fitting a woman of royal blood.

12. Silveria has become beautiful because, after baptism, she is shriven of all sins. The soul whose virtue and purity make it worthy of heavenly beatitude is spiritually beautiful: "di carne a spirto era salita e bellezza e virtù cresciuta m'era" (I had risen from flesh to spirit, and I had grown in virtue and beauty), says Beatrice to Dante, when she reproaches him for his behavior after her death. *Purgatorio* 30.127–28.

13. This period expresses a concept not uncommon in monotheistic religions: God is making his people go through more trials because they have not been sufficiently punished for their sins, or because he wishes to reward them more magnificently in heaven.

plague, repugnant and deadly, began to appear here and there throughout the town.[14]

107

They say that in the citadel, the vapors that the sun extracted from the soil, which had turned into mud by prolonged rains, began to pollute the air, making it more pernicious as they rose higher and higher. Then, as one thing triggers another similar in nature, the pollution was intensified by the poisoned liquid produced by the foul food that the people had been forced to eat during the famine.

108

At the beginning the nasty disease (which kept growing in strength) was not understood by the medical profession. Several doctors concerned about people's health turned and turned the pages of ancient and modern books, but the terrible malady did not spare anyone. The doctors themselves caught it—and more than anyone else—if they went too near the sick or just when they were talking to them.

109

First people began to feel an ache in the head, the like of which no one on earth had ever felt before. Then the eyes began to show a venomous redness. A lurid color covered the tongue and the palate. The face did not turn pale with weakness; it was instead stained with spots of a deep purplish hue and many tumors full of dark pus, with indeed the true imprint of the black death.

110

A bloody liquid leaked out of people's noses. Their breath stank and became thick and heavy; and if sometimes it seemed to the onlooker that the retching brought some relief—for it appeared to unload the heaviness in the chest—it was in fact the dire sign of a worsened condition; because then

---

14. Pestilence—as well as drought—was a frequent occurrence, and many written and oral descriptions circulated in Sarrocchi's time. It is also often mentioned in classical epics: cf. *Aeneid* 3.137–42 and *Civil War* 6.88–105. The plague in Croia is a local infection and not a pandemic, so an explanation must be given of its origin and causes (stanza 107). In the spareness and sequence of details—doctors' preparedness, symptoms of the disease, its effects on the population—Sarrocchi's primary model may have been Thucydides' account in *The History of the Peloponnesian War* 2.47–3.54, rather than the description of the 1348 Florentine epidemic in the introduction to the *Decameron*. Boccaccio's narrative is much richer in details and local color.

the pestilential liquid increased, and the sick began to alternate the putrid
and disgusting vomit with hiccups and belches.

111

Then the voice, affected by the venom, became raucous and sent out a
breath that seemed to burn and set things on fire. People caught the infection in their chest in strange ways, even though they may have taken care
not to become infected. Being in an isolated house would not keep one in
good health, nor would staying in an isolated open field permit anyone to
avoid the horrible contagion.

112

The disease had various effects on people; just as varied was the mixture of
humors in them. Some forgot their names and recognized neither son nor
wife. Some men took their wives by the throat and pulled their hair, convinced that they had caught the deadly disease from them. Others were
persuaded that their own fathers threatened to choke them with a cord or
kill them with a sword.

113

Sometimes a great heat burned in people's blood, drawing from the veins
a warm liquid that slowly turned into sweat and oozed slowly through the
skin, consuming their vital humor. It was just like a wave that first mounts
higher and higher and then, if it continues to swell, spills over. Thus, in
this strange and amazing way the soul would come out with the blood, and
just as red.

114

Those who caught this burning fever suffered a miserable blazing pain.
Their chests became so dry, their thirst so fierce that neither brook nor river
could extinguish it. It seemed to draw strength from its opposite, for it was
increased by the icy water that the sick kept drinking, so intense was the
heat that made them thirsty.

115

It was amazing to see some people look for a deep well or a dark fountain
and then throw themselves in, believing that at the bottom they would
extinguish the fire that excoriated them. Others drank a fetid muddy slush,
for their thirst made them too impatient, and while they expected to be
refreshed, they managed to extinguish their lives instead of their thirst.

116

Not even those rich in gold and silver could find anyone to bring them a drop of clean water. To the others they seemed haunted by fear, as if they were carrying the fury of deep hell in them. They did not lament, nor did they pray to God; they rather dragged themselves about in a fury, and out of their minds they threw themselves out of windows or down a cliff, hoping to escape God's punishment.

117

What could the saintly king do? "The wrath of God scourges your people," he told himself, "and wants to award victory to the brutal Turk, whose mind perhaps is less offensive to heaven than ours is. Ah, no! God is still as benevolent as he always was; he is no less charitable now than he has ever proved to be toward those who, in pure faith, turn to him for grace and redress."

118

So he was thinking, and then he addressed his prayers to God, as he had always done, and in praying he found peace of mind. Soon a warm wave of love filled his heart, clearing away all paralyzing fear.[15] Then he traveled alone over his land and very charitably took care of the people, confident that God would keep him safe in his human progress. And his hopes were not in vain.

119

He had several fires lit inside the city, with logs of juniper and cypress trees, so that the salubrious heat would purify all corners and dry the dampness polluting the air. Those forests had always many such trees, and after the terrible storm benign heaven had made them grow again, and become slender if not big, and great in number.

120

Trusting and hoping in God, the king also ordered a number of devout priests, garbed in sacred green vestments, to go through the city in holy procession and sing the songs of humble prayer that our holy fathers composed in order to appeal to God's compassion when in anger he brandishes his flashing sword against humankind.

15. See *caritas* below, canto 21.44n.

121

The triumphant sign was raised to the sky,[16] and then it marched on, a most frightening ensign to the deep abyss. The clergy followed in two lines, one on the right side, the other on the left. The minor priests went first, and last came the shepherd of souls in a golden robe and shining white miter, carrying Christ in the guise of humble bread.[17] Ah! unsurpassed and most astonishing marvel of all!

122

That precious pledge of the eternal father could be seen in an urn of crystalline marble, which had been carved out of a choice piece of mountain rock. A square canopy of blue silk hung over it, sustained by six staffs. They were held high with loving devotion by as many men, among the first in the kingdom for lineage and domain. Under it, the bishop walked alone; as he passed by, all bowed down to him.

123

The king himself walked in the holy procession. He was barefoot, his head and hands also bare. The captains and the soldiers came after him, dressed in dark clothing and without armor. Sad lamentations rose in the air, and many tears poured down people's faces as they prayed appealingly to heaven, begging for pardon for themselves and for others.

124

The cortege proceeded slowly; their feet moving in synchrony and their voices praying in harmonious concert. Then, going around in a circle and arriving from the opposite side, the procession returned to the major church from which it had set out. And there, renewing the common lamentation, a demonstration of dejected humbleness was given anew before the church doors: they all threw themselves down to the ground and kissed the earth, stretching their arms to heaven.

125

With his eyes full of tears the king began to pray on his knees thus: "For a long time now, O God, you have been venting your wrath on us. I beg you, for pity's sake, refrain your anger. These are still your people! Pray, tell me, how have they offended you? If I am perchance the sole sinner, if

16. The cross. As harbinger of salvation, it is a triumph over evil.
17. A bishop carrying the Eucharistic host.

I deserve a greater punishment than this, then inflict it deservedly on my head alone.

126

"I do not know what wrong I have committed to deserve your disapproval, as unworthy as I am of your divine love. Perhaps there is no man more offensive than I. And you, my lord, who can see the weakness in the most secret recess of my heart, do amend it. If it must be by punishment, then I shall wait for it, but do bestow your pardon on your beloved people.

127

"Look at the grief and the mourning everywhere, look at the dead who are left unburied, for there is no more room for them in the ground. The corpses are everywhere on the earth, heaped together in many stacks. The contagion of this disease is so horrible that even the birds, when famished they turn their beaks on the corpses, encounter the same end and fall dead of the same disease.

128

"Do not inveigh against your people with such anger any longer! If I am the only one to deserve punishment, then punish me alone! Hold back your avenging hand from all the others, do not let a whole people perish because of one sinner." So the king prayed, and while he was praying—oh, amazing sight!—he saw a thick, bloody, dark red cloud being torn open in places by horrible flashes of light and then hovering over and all around the citadel.

129

At that moment, God tore apart the veil that prevents humans from seeing pure spirits, and sharpening the king's weak senses, he let him see an angel[18] fly through the dense air and play cruel and deadly havoc all around. Sheer horror flashed out of the angel's eyes and horror from his face; blood rained from his hair and from his wings; blood dripped down his right hand from the very sword that God had given him: and it was God who now made him go.

130

No earthly face, no human mind could think of a contrivance so rare and powerful that it might oppose or even delay that unassailable divine

18. Cf. *Jerusalem Delivered* 18.92, where the Archangel Michael allows Godfrey to see in the sky the invisible armies that are aiding the assault on Jerusalem.

weapon. Wherever the raging indignation of heaven lowered its timeless sword to deal a lethal blow, there atrocious pains and inescapable death appeared in various and horrifying ways.

131

Whenever the angel struck, then bodily wounds were inflicted, pitiable and horrendous. Tears poured down the king's cheeks more abundantly now, and far more urgent became the prayers he sent up to heaven. But then, oh, king beloved by heaven! he heard God's words ordering the angel to cease: he saw the angel desist and then fly to heaven. And suddenly, the dark veil was cleared from the sky.

132

Meanwhile the news was out that the daughter of the Thracian emperor was sending him aid and that the Persian army was near, a few miles away beyond the Astrean Mountains.[19] The king then made the wise decision to ask Vran to oppose its advance by every possible means, for Vran was nearer the pass by which those contingents would travel. He communicated his intention to a trusted messenger.

133

Ulysses was the messenger, the very man whom Palinuro had assigned to Vran as the scout in that area. He left at once and by a safe route reached the valorous captain, who immediately brought out of the protective wall all the men he could spare and with them made ready to obstruct the passage of the Persians through the dangerous territory they had to traverse.

134

In Italy, meanwhile, the messengers sent by the king arrived first at the Vatican and at the Sacred College,[20] and there all requests presented to the Holy Father were granted. Furthermore, the pope anticipated the messengers in their other missions, and in order to reach consensus, by means of letters and through envoys he not only described the real situation

---

19. Given Sarrocchi's penchant for etymological derivations, Astrean Mountains may simply mean "eastern mountains," from Astreus, a Titan, who in some legends is the husband of Aurora (the dawn, which rises in the east).The daughter sending aid to the sultan is Glicera, the Persian queen mentioned in stanza 21 above, not Rosmonda.

20. The Sacred College is the College of Cardinals.

but tactfully added enticements, distributing offers, encouragements, and suggestions.[21]

135

As zeal and piety awakened in all hearts an admirable desire for religious honors, the first Italian contingent was prepared. Furthermore, the high shepherd and father opened the gates to heaven's treasures, for he blessed all and forgave all sins that may have been committed on earth by the repentant faithful who were embarked on this pious campaign of military aid.

136

In the land of the Picenes, on the coast of the Adriatic Sea, where a steep hill rises, lies a town that takes its name from a mountain in the shape of an elbow. This is a welcoming and sheltering harbor for many ships that come to rest securely in it. Rome, which built the great mausoleum on the Tiber, here built a monument facing the rising sun.[22]

137

The captain gave the order for all the people united in faith and piety to direct their route toward this place, which is almost at the center of Italy. At the hour when the sky sheds its light most abundantly, all the soldiers gathered here. All threatening clouds were now dissolved, and the waves on the cerulean surface of the sea were calm.

138

O Muse! You are like a sun that gives light to all virtuous souls! You can rescue from the dark and stagnant mists of obscurity the eminent deeds diminished or devoured by the preying tooth of time! You Muse, whom Apollo honors and cherishes the most, do shed your light on my darkened intellect, so that I may reveal the number and names of all those squadrons and captains!

21. This is clearly Pope Pius II (1458–64), to the world Enea Silvio Piccolomini, celebrated author and humanist scholar. He called for a crusade against the Turks when he was already old and in bad health. At Ancona, where he waited for the support he had succeeded in obtaining from Italian and foreign princes, he died suddenly in 1464, and his expedition aborted. Pius's attitude toward the Turks and his desire for "holy war" are succinctly explained by Robert Schwoebel in his *The Shadow of the Crescent: The Renaissance Image of the Turks, 1453–1517* (Nieuwkoop: B. de Graaf, 1967), 64–67. For Pius II and other historical characters, see pp. 23 and 29 above.

22. The town is Ancona, situated on the northern border of the Piceni region, on a bay shaped like an elbow (hence Ankon, in Greek, for the town was founded by the Greeks of Syracuse, Sicily). The Arch of Trajan, which faces the sun in the city harbor, was built in 115 CE, while the mausoleum on the Tiber—later changed into the Castel St. Angelo—was erected later by Emperor Hadrian (117–138 CE).

139

Borso[23] was elected general of that invincible army by unanimous vote. It is hard to say whether his eloquent pen or his strong army honored him more and made him more illustrious. He was looked on as the first man in Ferrara, one who was to pass a ducal title on to his descendants. He added such glory to Azzo's lineage that Azzo could be said to shine thanks to him, not he thanks to Azzo.[24]

140

Among the senators in the Vatican who assisted the Vicar of God in sustaining Peter's burden, Giuliano Cesarini[25] was foremost. Pius, who reigned over all Christian souls, admired and valued his virtues greatly and sent him now as his nuncio with the army sailing toward the Croian hero.

141

He led a group of noble and erudite men, of great and rare intelligence, some of whom followed a military career while others attended the academy. Some Barbadori were there, and some of the Sacramosi; there were some from the Giusti family, the Sareghi and the Lomellini, some of the Magalotti, Casa, Guidiccioni, Guerenghi, Aleandri, and Tassoni.

142

As his loyal companion, to be consulted during all dangerous campaigns, he chose Maffeo Barberini, to whom Flora, a generous and courteous mother, had given a home. The fame of his goodness and virtue reached beyond the Hister, the Don, and the Nile, just as the Maffeo living now shines, shedding gold on our age of iron.

23. This character was inspired by Borso d'Este (1413–71), marquis of Ferrara and duke of Mantua and Reggio. See p. 30 above.

24. Alberto Azzo II (d. 1097) was the ancestor of the dukes of Ferrara. He took a new name after the castle he owned at Este, near Padua. One of his sons, Guelfo IV, having inherited the property of his uncle, became the first Guelph duke of Bavaria. From 1180, his descendants were known as Brunswick-Lünenburg, and in 1714 they ascended to the throne of England with the name of Hanover.

25. Giuliano Cesarini was a classical scholar and a diplomat. As a legate of Pope Eugenius IV, he went to Budapest to organize a campaign of eastern European states against the Turks. He died in the battle of Varna, where in 1444 King Ladislaus of Hungary was defeated by Murad II. This character's presence in the poem is a reminder of the more recent mission and death of the nephew of Pope Clement VIII, Gian Francesco Aldobrandini, who led the papal contingent in the war against the Ottomans in 1595, 1597, and 1601. For Cesarini and Aldobrandini, see their entries in *Dizionario biografico degli Italiani*, vol.24 (1980), 188–95; and vol. 2 (1960), 105–6. About the expedition organized by Clement VIII, see pp. 21 and 30 above.

143

This Maffeo, clad in purple robes, an important member of the holy consistory, has the muses and the virtues always close, and they bow to him as to a god. Ah! May the heavens allow us to see Peter's golden keys in his hands! How happy and content we all would be, free to enjoy the return of the beautiful fortunate age of those bygone years![26]

144

We would then see white pure days as foretold by infallible Fate: sheep and wolves would then walk together, feeding on the same meadow in freedom and safety; oaks would ooze honey; ripe grapes would hang from thorny branches; gratifying fountains would feed milk to happy young shepherds. And the world would no longer be in need of laws.

26. The golden age. At the time of Sarrocchi's writing, Maffeo Barberini—descendant of the man present in this poem as a participant in Pius II's crusade—was an influential member of the College of Cardinals (here "holy consistory"). He became pope with the name of Urban VIII in 1623.

From CANTO 19

Following an order from the sultan to destroy the papal fleet, the sorcerer Zebad calls forth the spirits of hell and a huge gale disperses the Italian ships far and wide. When the storm subsides, several vessels come together again and begin to sail along the coast of Asia Minor. As they turn west, they come across a small boat. The owner of the boat, a Persian, claims to know nothing of military doings, but under torture he confesses that an army from all parts of the Persian Empire has gathered at Smyrna and is now ready to set sail in aid of the sultan. He lists the Persian contingents and their captains.

1

In the land of Phoenicia and in the region that can be seen directly opposite the island of Cyprus,[1] separated from it by a stretch of the sea, was born a sorcerer called Zebad, expert in all magic and divinatory art, the likes of whom no other age ever saw. His birthplace was the only place where he liked to live.[2]

2

Not far from the soft and sea-lapped beach, a stony path led to his home, and there two big rocks turned their backs to the sun and with their height took away the light of day. On a straight line opposite them, two mountains rose to the sky no less menacingly. They were clad in greenery and gave way to a valley that stretched out between them.

---

1. Phoenicia was a region of the Middle East, roughly corresponding to Jordan, Lebanon, and part of modern Israel. Off its shores is Cyprus.
2. Sarrocchi's Zebad is an offshoot of Tasso's Ismen in *Jerusalem Delivered*. See how closely these two sorcerers resemble each other as described in stanza 6 and in Tasso's poem, canto 2.1.

3

A narrow path made it possible to walk from down below up to the steep ridge, and once the flowery top was reached, a pleasant restful plain appeared to the tired climber. Several rocks and many trees growing close together offered shelter from the sunlight and provided grateful comfort with their thick shade, creating an impression of pleasantness and dread at the same time.

4

Tree branches just as dense and green bedecked the backs of the rocks, a robe of greenery clad both mountains too, and the peaks all around declined toward the plain. The light of the sun was dimmed by an entanglement of branches and shone weakly over the valley even at the height of day, because the trees created a greater shade at the time of the year when the sunlight was stronger.

5

In the middle of the valley was a square table made of marble, and of marble also were the seats around it. During the warm season the wizard took his meals here, and here he spent most of the day. From far away, his home, hidden deep among the rocks, appeared always covered by a dense dark cloud. Here the godless sorcerer shook the mountains and restrained the winds with the sound of his cursed words.

6

By his extraordinary power he could tear tombs apart, draw souls out of hell, and make decayed bodies and naked bones come out of their cold graves. Then the air could be heard to resound with moaning, and horrendous ghosts could be seen escaping from the infernal fire or receding obediently at his command.

7

He could dissolve thick dark clouds and restore the sky to its original pure splendor, and then again cover its beautifully clear face with a thick smudge of black vapor. Let us then cease the great praise given to the sorcerer who lived at the time of King Arthur and his famous knights,[3] for this magician was greater by far, and the tyrant had heard of his powers.

---

3. The sorcerer living at the time of King Arthur and the knights of the Round Table is Merlin. Cf. *Orlando Furioso* 3.9–14, 33.4, 33.7.

8

The sorcerer's custom was to call forth the infernal host from deserted and dark caves to sunny peaks and also to observe the motions and the rays of the stars in remote and untrodden places. Neither pardons nor promises could induce him to leave his abode, not even for a short journey. The emperor, therefore, sent him a note written by his own hand to communicate what he wished.

9

The demands he made on paper were the following: "You who can force nature and the elements, I ask to stir up clouds, storms, lightning in the sky, and winds on the sea, so that the fleet of our enemy will be immersed, and the life of their soldiers extinguished. May waves and rocks break up the fleet and submerge it, may a hurricane divide and disperse it."

10

Besides being moved by the royal command, the sorcerer was very eager to do something for his faith,[4] especially because the certain news of the Christian reinforcements had brought fear to all infidels. After deciding which kind of infernal power he should use to agitate the Aegean Sea, the sorcerer swiftly came out of his cave and flew over the waters, so strong was his desire to obey his great master.

11–19

Called forth by Zabed, the spirits of hell rush out of their hiding places, intent on bringing about a huge gale.

20

Every ship in the Christian fleet had already sailed way from that pleasant coast, when Dawn looked at herself in the enchanting expanse of the blue waters, happily smiling in her white splendor. The sea reflected the image of the sky, and the sky, in emulation of it, sent back the image of the sea, so that the earth appeared adorned by a double sea, a double sky, and a double dawn.

21

Imitating the dew falling from heaven, the waves broke and lifted their foam, and Dawn let down her gem-studded hair, filling the sky with crystalline rays. The sea rippled placidly under the gentle early morning breezes

---

4. The sorcerer too is fired by religious zeal. Cf. below, canto 20.82n.

as lightly as the Saône does when its waves are so slow and calm that no eye can discern in which direction the river runs.[5]

22

It was also the same as when, in early spring, at the point where the Adige runs into the immense plain, Zephyr can be seen making the new grass quiver, and the tranquil sea seems to float beautiful white and blue flowers on its wide expanse. You might even have said, as you looked at it from afar, that the waves and the foam were sapphires and pearls.[6]

23

The ships sailed on the foaming waves and, under the command of expert pilots, advanced into the high sea on well-known routes. As the sun, sitting on the horizon, began to shoot out its rays, the ships in a harmonious motion of breeze and wave sailed by Brindisi, with Valona on the other side, as the Adriatic, sitting in the middle, holds those opposite lands apart.[7]

24

Now, an endless host of wicked demons rushed out of the Stygian night.[8] The sea was stirred up from its deepest sands, and the waves rose up and fell down shuddering. The tenebrous prison holding the atmosphere in its furthermost grottoes also broke open, and the whirlwinds held inside it came shrieking from that center of darkness.

25

As soon as the gates suddenly opened, they could be seen to escape from those deepest recesses and then rise wrapped in stormy clouds while the air filled with darkness. They came on one after another so rapidly that no part of the sky remained uncovered. Then they fell precipitously over the sea and turned its waters upside down.

---

5. In *Commentarii de bello gallico* 1.12, Julius Caesar writes that the River Saône moves so slowly that "the eye cannot determine in which direction it flows." This description is repeated by Ariosto in *Orlando Furioso* 14.64.4.

6. For similar descriptions of natural sights resplendent with precious materials, see 3.7, 6.61, 7.36, 7.40, 9.27, and 10.20.

7. Brindisi is a town in the region of Puglia, on the Italian side of the Strait of Otranto, in the lower Adriatic Sea. Valona, now Vlore, is on the Albanian side.

8. It is the darkness of the netherworld, from Styx, one of the four rivers of hell. Ovid, *Metamorphoses* 4.432–45.

26

From the Nabathaean regions,[9] the east wind, angered toward Favonius, started off against the west. All around, fearful clouds let fall a humor hardened and pressed into marble-like ice. On the opposite side, Aquilus clad in horror rushed forward against Notus even more stridently, and Notus threw against that northern freeze a tempestuous sea with waves that rose menacingly into the sky.[10]

27

Different voices were heard shouting at the same time, with much discordant scraping of wheels and lines. Lightning flashed in the air, and the vast portals of heaven boomed with thunder. From the thick clouds, which had suddenly appeared all around, a darkness of almost hellish hue stole the light of day, hiding the sky away from all eyes, while a deep night hovered over the waters.

28

Every time a horrendous flash of light crossed the darkness, the good pilot shouted an order to save the ship, but his voice was hardly heard, for all over, in the air and in the wavy sea, there floated a discordant sound of different voices. The sky above thundered, and the sea below moaned, and in the middle the wind howled horrendously.

29

Fearing extreme ruin, each man tried his best for the common safety. Some took the oars out of the water; others repaired the damaged sides of the ship and reinforced them; others pulled down the sails from the high mast and rigged up the small ones; still others rushed to empty the water coming into the vessel and returned the sea to the sea.[11]

9. Nabathae was the Roman designation for the section of Arabia on the Red Sea. Here "Nabathaean" stands for "eastern."

10. Favonius is the Latin name for Zephyrus, the west wind; Aquilus is the north wind; Notus is the south wind. Sarrocchi's description of contrary winds clashing over land and sea is likely an elaboration of *Aeneid* 2.416–19, although the comparison has several precedents in epic poetry. "Adversi rupto ceu quondam turbine venti confligunt, Zephyrusque Notusque et laetus Eois Aurus equis: stridunt silvae, saevitque tridenti spumeus atque imo Nereus ciet aequora fundo (as when a gale breaks out, contrary winds, Zephyr, Notus, and Aurus riding high out of the east, will clash; forests will hiss harshly, and Nereus, foaming fiercely, with his trident will churn the sea from the farthest deep). Cf. other such similes in *Iliad* 13.338–41, *Aeneid* 10.356–57, *Jerusalem Delivered* 9.52.1–4, and again in this poem, in stanza 35 below, and cantos 5.106 and 23.37.

11. Ships flung about the expanse of the sea and hurled on rocks and into shallows are a frequent motif in classical literature: see, for instance, *Aeneid* 1.102–23 and Lucan's *Civil War*

30

Every effort, every attempt was in vain, so fiercely were the sea, the winds, and the heavens fighting against one another. The wind held the sea in contempt, the rain swelled it. For the proud wizard, to have brought this about was not enough. Now, melting into rain, the sky mixed with the sea; the waves rose high, and a path was forcefully opened in the waters: as one fell down, the other rose; the sea seemed changed into the sky, the sky into the sea.

31

Time and again an awesome wall of water reared the ships into the air and pitched them against the sky. Over the horizon the masts seemed to scrape the heavens with their tops. It looked as if the murky waters of Acheron[12] were plunging headlong to the bottom of the sea, while the waves threw the white foam very high and the sands of the deep agitated turbulently.

32

Amerigo was there, the man who later went around the wider circle of the earth on a light ship.[13] Powerless was his skill now, and so great all around were danger and confusion that he could not see where the nasty upheaval was taking him. A raging vortex pulled away the good Giacinto: although he was tied to the mast with ropes,[14] he was torn off the stern head down and quickly disappeared from sight.

5.597–653. Of captains' commands that cannot be heard, and of sailors pouring back water into the sea, there are instances in Ovid's *Metamorphoses* 11.484–85; in Boiardo's *Orlando Innamorato* 2.6.13.8, 3.4.5.7; and in Ariosto's *Orlando Furioso* 41.11. A mention of orders not heard is also in Lucrezia Marinella's *L'Enrico* 5.10.

12. Acheron is the name of a river in the netherworld, on whose banks the shades of the dead gather.

13. Amerigo Vespucci (1454–1512), working for Spain and Portugal, sailed twice along the coast of South America and in one journey arrived at the estuary of Rio de la Plata. He was the first to realize that the lands reached by Columbus were a new continent, and from then on the new continent was named after him. See p. 30 above. The geographic discoveries are mentioned, or indirectly referred to, in several epic poems. See for example the circumnavigation of Africa and Columbus's journey to the new world in *Orlando Furioso* 15.18. 21–22 and in *Jerusalem Delivered* 15.30–32.

14. Giacinto fastened with ropes reminds us of Homer's Ulysses. Sailing near the island of the Sirens, generally understood to be Capri, and fearing he would not be able to resist their call, Ulysses filled the ears of his companions with wax and had himself tied to the mast of the ship. *Odyssey* 12.261–77.

33

Giacinto was his pilot, for intelligence and skill more dear to him than any other. With him he had hoped to journey into the interior of the mistaken continent[15] and sail a great deal around the earthly sphere. With penetrating flashes of light, he sent out the order for the ships to move away from one another, so that the unmanageable gale might not scatter and bang them together, out of control of those who held the rudder.

34

Even though they prepared at once to obey his command, the wind and the sea did not allow it, for the swollen water increased its throbbing and the gale slashed the ships with increasing force and vehemence. Giving up all resistance, oars and masts shattered, bows broke off into the waves (frightfully lugubrious sight!); a huge mountain of water then crashed on the vessels.

35

From high above, Notus kept blowing menacingly, and in its great violence it pulled eight minor ships out of the fleet, blew them away with fury, and hurled them violently toward Zante.[16] Amerigo could not do enough for his craft, nor could Bondelmonti, nor Strozzi, nor Nori. Africus[17] angrily pushed Dino toward Naxos, and Eurus sank Corsi's ship into the sand.

36

Cosimo, the great Tuscan,[18] in vain attempted to move slowly over the watery way, so that the bulging waves and darkened air might not send him smashing against reefs and sandbanks. All effort was impossible for his vessel, because as weakened as it was already, it now slackened even further and opened all its joints. He barely managed not to be swept as far as the Cyclades Islands, as Barberini and Cassino had been.

15. "The mistaken realm" is America, because it was mistaken for India.

16. Italian name for Zákynthos, an island in the Ionian Sea then under Venetian control.

17. Africus is a wind blowing from the south, in Italy called *libeccio*.

18. Cosimo, also spelled Cosmo, is presumably Cosimo de' Medici (1389–1464). Politian (Angelo Poliziano, 1454–94), a poet-scholar in the generation following Cosimo, wrote of him: "Who does not know the old glory and the celebrated honor of the great Cosimo, splendor of Italy, whose homeland called itself his daughter?" *Stanze per la giostra* 2.3.13. This elder Cosimo was a great supporter of Pius II. His descendant and namesake, Cosimo I, grand duke of Tuscany, contributed twelve galleys to the papal fleet that fought at Lepanto. See p. 30 above.

37

Doria, Fieschi, and Centurione were pushed toward Ithaca (Ulysses' kingdom). The good leader Pernone was thrown into the Lyncean Sea[19] and his ship driven into a sandbank. Neither reason nor wisdom nor skill could prevent this disaster, or save Adorno and Fregoso from ending up at Rhodes, and Marino from taking a separate route toward Crete.

38–65

After gathering some men around him, Giuliano, the holy vicar, prays for everybody's safety and promises that they all will make amends for their sins. The storm subsides, and ten ships land in a quiet bay near the town of Paphos, on the island of Cyprus; other vessels arrive later. The local king welcomes them in a friendly manner, but in order to preserve the peace he has established with the sultan, he refuses to give them military aid.

66

They rested safely here, and now there was nothing to prevent them from repairing what the sea had destroyed, from buying sails and rigging, cutting down pines and fir trees—all of which grew abundantly in this place—or from wandering leisurely and safely in the royal residence and around the beautiful and gay city. And anything they asked of the king he graciously conceded.

67

Once they were rested and a diligent repair of the ships was completed, the clear waves, the tranquil breeze, the serene sky, and the shining sun invited them to start again on their way. At departure time, they were joined by Isarco, who, failing to obtain help from the king and being an expert master in devising deceptions against the enemy, declared himself willing to help in any way he could.

68

God, who can inflame the coldest minds with amorous fire, keeps infusing into the earth and exhaling into the sky burning vapors capable of adding strength to the loving instinct. In this way throngs of snakes are produced in the warm humor of the earth. With these, Isarco planned to bring irreparable damage to the camp of the fierce tyrant.

69

He collected some snakes on whose skin the poison had made darker blotches, others whose dangerous tongue vibrated ever so menacingly, and

---

19. I have not been able to trace a Lyncean Sea. Sarrocchi may have so named the tract of the Aegean that faces Argos, the city of which Lynceus was once the king.

also some whose eyes flashed out most fiercely. He put them into vases one by one. Afterward, he fed them bitter leaves of aconite and hellebore, and no other food, so that the hunger and the imprisonment would increase their rage and poisoning power.[20]

70

Thus furnished, the Christian fleet set sail out of the harbor in military order. Just then a southeasterly wind rose to swell the sails and pushed them along gently. The good helmsmen broke the motions of the sea with expert timing, adding their skill to the speed produced by the breeze, and very soon the ships overtook the coast of Caria to starboard.[21]

71–75

They pass by Caria and, Rhodes and proceed westward toward the Cyclades.

76

On the sixth day, just as Dawn began to spread her golden robe on the blue paths of the sky flooding them with light, the Cyclades came into view nearby. As they arrived where the body of water expanded to form a wide gulf, in the stretch where the sea flows most rapidly between Crete and Milos, they saw a small boat sailing out toward them.

77

The boat advanced full sail and, without realizing it, came all of a sudden right up against the enemy fleet, which was hidden behind the island of Crete and could not be seen from a distance. The pilot sitting at the helm could therefore be excused if his small boat was quickly surrounded by several ships and everyone on board tied up with ropes.

78

In a similar manner, the fish that frisked about in the salty waters of the sea are surrounded by many nets and taken out of the water, as the incautious prisoners they have suddenly become. Among those who were on the boat, a man came forward declaring himself to be the leader, and with an unperturbed face he asked to be led to the captain.

20. See the description of the snakes in Pliny's *Naturalis Historia* 8.32–37 and in Lucan's *Civil War* 9.607–837. Unlike Dante, who, in *Inferno* 24.97–117, in a spirit of poetic rivalry uses Lucan's descriptions as the starting point of some nature-defying metamorphoses, Sarrocchi provides her emulation of the Latin text with scientific explanations. See cantos 20.62–65, 20.94–106 below and related footnotes.

21. Caria is the ancient name of a region in Asia Minor, now Turkey.

79

Many bands of purple silk were twisted around his head in a manner that was at once rich and artfully disarrayed; a simple but superb vest covered his body. To Isarco, who was Greek, the man's clothes, his head cover, as well as his features and speech said that he was from Persia and going as a messenger to the enemy camp.

80

Borso ordered the Persian to be brought into his presence and asked him what news he was carrying to the great Thracian and how the Persian king was planning to come to his aid. The man answered in a shrewdly couched speech: "I never inquire about other people's business, for there is no hint of curiosity in my mind. Nor am I accustomed to linger in a single place, but only as long as it is required by the art and convenience of my profession.

81

"I trade in cinnamon and saffron, or whatever goods I am lucky to come by. I try to increase my father's business, which is far too scanty to earn me a life free of want, a life that I often expose to the risks of unequal fortune on land and sea. After selling a great quantity of merchandise, I am now going to Crete to buy more.

82

"One of my ships is in Crete with a trusted crew waiting for my arrival and for a supply of gold sufficient to reload the vessel with merchandise. And because they have been expecting me for quite a time, I am traveling on this light skiff in a great hurry, as you can see." The man, whose name was Antreo, spoke thus, with an expression of sincerity on his face, as if he were actually telling the truth.

83

The Christian men were silent, almost believing his explanation, as he intended. But the shrewd Isarco, who was always mistrustful, had questioned the crew in Antreo's absence. At his questioning, his servants had shown confusion, so he realized that Antreo was lying. Once the deception was discovered, Amerigo ordered him to be placed under torture.

84

In the flower of youth, Amerigo was a hothead, always ready to fly into a temper. Furthermore he believed that anger, when addressed toward God's enemy, became a tool of reason. While Antreo was being tortured, Isarco feigned compassion and friendship toward the Persian. The man was of slender frame and of little endurance, and he could not stand the terrible suffering for long.

85

Although he was of sharp and shrewd mind, his bodily pain betrayed him in the end, for the tie that joins the soul to this mortal shell of ours is so strong and tenacious that the senses themselves are led astray and the power to resist fails. The unfortunate man said all to Isarco, to whom the Persian language was well known.

86

Isarco comforted him and asked him again in his language to tell the truth, and to this end he used courteous manners and shrewdly alluring flattery. Antreo then related how the Persian king, in order to come to the aid of the Turkish emperor, had gathered a great army, calling up people from every town with men of able minds and bodies.

87

"Sir," he began, "I come from Smyrna,[22] and I travel to the Thracian emperor to inform him that there is an army in the Persian realm ready to come to his aid. When my boat set out to sea, every floating vessel had already been loaded, for the Thracian himself had communicated in writing with my king about the ships that should travel to him.

88

"We all have come to Smyrna by land, and it is there that the Thracian emperor has sent his ships. Tarconte is our captain: he is our foremost warrior, whether he is wanted in council or fully armed on horseback . . ."

88–101

Antreo gives a catalogue of the Persian contingent and in the end specifies that his king is contributing war machines and a great number of war elephants. These animals carry on their backs wooden turrets from which arrows, spears, and stones can be hurled against the enemy.

---

22. Smyrna (the Turkish Ismir) is a town on the Mediterranean coast of Turkey, then Asia Minor.

From CANTO 20

The Persian fleet is approaching. Borso and Scanderbeg, to whom an envoy has been sent for his opinion, are in favor of attacking it at once. The battle begins: the Italians are overwhelmed and their ships are almost all destroyed. Convinced that he will soon die, Borso faces up to Tarconte and kills him. Tarconte's head is fixed on top of the mast, in view of all the Persians. The Persians lose courage and the battle. Those Italians who survive manage to reach Croia.

1

Antreo swore that in every way he had told them all he knew. Borso made careful note of it, although he did not believe it entirely and wished to have it confirmed by other prisoners. Even after he had become persuaded that he had been told the truth, he did not free Antreo of his chains; he only reassured him of no more torture and danger. Then he called a meeting of the chief captains.

2

"If we consider when the enemy fleet left the harbor, we must infer that now it is near us," he said, "so there is no doubt that it will appear soon if we remain here waiting. It would be unwise to think that we can escape, because our speed will depend on the winds. We will not be able to repel the enemy attack by turning our backs to it, but only by launching a frontal assault.

3

"We did not expose ourselves to the risks of war and sea, we did not leave our beloved children and cherished wives, urged on by an ambitious desire of possession or because we expected to return to our country laden with enviable and rich spoils, but because we were inspired by holy zeal and hoped in time to come to exchange this earthly life for one in heaven.

4

"Let us not be dismayed by the huge army of the enemy, which makes the Thracian so powerful and daring, or by the small forces of the Christian king, to whose aid we are going. Even so, it will be twice as difficult for us to win when the Persian contingent has joined the Turkish army. It is not a foolish decision to face up to danger that cannot be avoided; it is the wise thing to do."

5

Borso stopped here, and in the sudden silence, a murmur of approval wafted in the air from all sides, like the sound made occasionally by Boreas when it blows among tree branches, or by the water of a brook breaking over stones and pebbles. Only Ascanio Catamur did not agree. He was afraid and reluctant. "It is indeed a rash decision," he declared, "for a few people to go against an almost endless number of enemies.

6

"Let us not give in, by God, to such foolish thought and expose ourselves to the risk of death to no advantage. Even if the Persians join the Turks, our victory will not necessarily be impossible. The unvanquished valor of the glorious king and the impregnable fortifications of his citadel will give us strength, while they will take strength from us, so that, in reciprocal support, we will advance on the difficult path.

7

"Although the Persian fleet is near, there is still such a long stretch of sea between us that we can arrive much earlier than they can, should every ship of theirs take on wings; as long, that is, as we do not delay any further and do not let their fleet advance on its course. We must abandon all hesitation if we do not want our shame to become greater than our damage."

8

These words were uttered by Ascanio, who until then was reputed a military man of great valor and wisdom, but his reputation changed in people's estimation, so many were the signs he gave of cowardly fear. At that moment, however, he was able to hide it under the appearance of truth, and the minds and hearts of those soldiers remained undecided, not because fear did away with their courage, rather because their consideration and daring became more temperate and cautious.[1]

9

Their hesitation was resolved by Isarco the Greek. "Let us go immediately to warn the devout king. The serenity of this cloudless sky is gently inviting us to set sail. The distance between Crete and Epirus is not so great: it is possible to navigate keeping close to land and avoid being caught suddenly by strong winds."

10

They chose the Italian Fausto to be the messenger. He was the captain of the contingent from Picenum and such an accomplished sailor that no one could perhaps be found better than he. In less time than it takes to think of one word, he descended into a boat with a deep sinking hull, and thus hidden from everyone's sight, he began to navigate as swiftly as a bird in flight, in the company of a single expert and trusted navigator.

11

He arrived in Epirus just at the time of day when the sun falls precipitously into the sea. The tyrant had long withdrawn into the city of Presa, so the way was wide open to this messenger. By night he climbed up to the citadel and imparted information to the king about all that had happened. The hero was not perturbed; he rejoiced at the news that the fleet of his allies was now safe.

12

The spies he had in the enemy camp had told him that reinforcements were coming to the Turks. He also knew how the blast of contrary winds had almost sunk the allied fleet into the sea, but he did not know at all that after being thrown and scattered all around, it had safely arrived in Cyprus. So hearing that the fleet was out of danger, he felt by far more pleasure now than he had felt dismay before.

---

1. It is reasonable to suppose that in describing this exchange of opinions Sarrocchi was influenced by what was known of the war council called before the battle of Lepanto. A speech similar to this in considering the suitability of giving battle, but couched in more general terms, can be found in Marinella's *L'Enrico*, 19.14–18.

13

The Italian knight informed him of everything, even about the snakes kept in the vases, which the Greek intended to use as a covert weapon to bring damage and shame on the Saracens. He told him that the allied ships were now poised to fight the enemy fleet, which was quickly heading toward them. After turning his mind this way and that to assess all possible choices—for he was in doubt as to what to do—the king finally reached a decision.

14

He was aware of how dangerous it would be for him if the Persian army joined the Turkish camp. He could defeat both if they were still separate—he thought—but if they united, he could no longer be certain. He had a firm trust in Roman capabilities, whose lasting fame resounded far and wide; so he could be confident that one Christian soldier was worth ten of the infidels.

15

Furthermore, the Persians were neither accustomed to nor skilled at fighting on the sea, as the Italians were; neither did he place his trust in war machines to bring about a victory. After considering all this, the king replied to the knight in this manner: "Oftentimes, when one leader surpasses the other in experience, it is possible for a few to overcome a great many enemies by just using some common sense.

16

"The working of a good mind and efficient execution can do much more than bodily strength; the Christians can undoubtedly be successful if they carry out their intention as planned. A few men, if carefully trained, have nothing to fear from a great number of unskilled people if they fight with powerful weapons that cannot be countered, and if they use torches that are inextinguishable and penetrate deeply.

17

"If the Italians throw at the enemy sulfuric torches capable of starting fires that cannot be put out, the ships will burn in the middle of the sea, for sea water cannot snuff the blazes out.[2] So if the Christians can be expected to

2. Before the invention of cannons and firearms, throwing flaming torches on the enemy was common practice and often described in Greek and Roman epics. In *Iliad* 15.716–75, Hector tries to set fire to the Greek fleet; in *Aeneid* 9.69–76, Turnus and his men throw torches on the Trojan vessels; in Lucan's *Civil War* 3.680–96, the Massilian ships, fighting for Pompey, go up in flames when combustible arrows are shot over them from Brutus Albinus's fleet, fighting for Caesar.

win because they are accustomed to naval battles, when we add intelligence and skill to military might, against whom will we not be able to fight?

18

"Should all skill be in vain, and should the Persians prove stronger on the sea than on land, then you can throw the vases at them, thus letting the snakes come out and renew the fight. As soon as their prisons are open, as famished as they have become, the snakes will immediately go after food, and they will bring fear and confusion with both their frightening appearance and their poisonous teeth.

19

"I feel much regret in my heart for being detained here in the besieged city, because perhaps our sword would not be useless in this great battle, and then there would be no need of tricky means." He said no more. This extraordinarily strong warrior disdained to praise himself even when speaking the truth, for invincible valor is proved by indubitable actions, not by obstreperous boasts.

20

The knight set everything down in his mind and in addition obtained from the king a written communication. He untied the rope of his shallow vessel and went his way, and upon joining the fleet he went aboard the flagship. He gave the written message to the commander-in-chief, who also wished to hear everything the knight had heard. Then Borso gathered all the captains again and made known to them the opinion of the king.

21

He reassured them that it would be a good and wise decision to follow the advice of such a hero. There was a bay on the south coast of Crete where the fleet could remain hidden, out of danger of being detected. So they moved their ships out of the route they had come into this area in order not to be detected from afar. On the morning following that very night, the enemy fleet made its appearance close by.

22

A man of very sharp eyesight, perched on the high mast of a forward vessel, began to shout: "What a great number of sails I see unfurling in the wind! They are advancing toward us! I can see the sun already shining on them, its splendid, scintillating beams reverberate, and the sea, seemingly vying with the sky, throws those rays back, one thousand for every one of them."

23

All captains immediately ordered a sailor, chosen for his sharp vision, to climb up to the crow's nest and gaze all around to a great distance. What they saw was a huge fleet being pushed along by so favorable a wind that it seemed to glide over the water. It was advancing so fast into attacking range that a courageous defense had to be set up immediately.

24

All the ships of the Christian fleet exited the bay into the open sea as fast as arrows, or as swift as the wind. The commander disposed them in a long even row and placed himself in the middle. Soon after, two more straight lines, like two big wings, were formed on both sides; their front tips joined the first row at an obtuse angle, and then their armed points were pushed forward.

25

On one of these ships, to the left, the admiral of the fleet placed Isarco, a captain unsurpassed in naval warfare; to the right he stationed Pernone, whose reputation for wisdom and strength excelled no less than that of the other. Behind the main line he wanted the Tuscan warrior,[3] so that he could be ready to repulse the enemy, should they plan to attack from the rear.

26

On a boat so swift and light as to leave—you might say—the wind behind, Borso reviewed the men and spurred them on with his determined composure and encouraging words. The nuncio of the great first priest was with him, clad in a golden mantle, with covered front and side slits that showed a vest of pure white underneath.[4]

27

His head and hands were bare; in one he held the image of the divine man on the holy cross, the Christ who, in his justice and love, wanted to atone for our unworthy sins. In the other hand he held a white sheet of paper, a promise of pardon and grace of which all those who had come on this high

3. Supposedly, Cosimo de' Medici. See above, canto 19.36.

4. This is the papal nuncio, Giuliano Cesarini, who was a cardinal, hence the description of his vestments (cf. canto 18.140 above). The first priest is the pope, who is the bishop of Rome. In the following stanza, the nuncio, holding the pope's letter in his hand, will remind soldiers and captains of the absolution granted them by the holy father. Cf. canto 18.135.

crusade had been made worthy by the great shepherd, who is the only one allowed to open the gates of heaven.

28

When most of them had heard it well, for it had been read in their midst, Borso realized that their holy faith had impressed a pious and devout feeling in their souls. "Soldiers, how fortunate you are, for a great God, against whom nothing can and has ever been able to endure, chose and sent you here to vindicate the many injuries done to him. He will protect you.

29

"Each one of you must then remind himself that he has taken up arms for that God who has always made his determined champions powerfully victorious in the most risky enterprises. The sun stood still in obedience to his nod, the fire tempered its burning flames. He is God, the lord of hosts, the one who bestows victories and everlasting glory.

30

"Your pious deeds are guided by God, against whom no contrary fate can prevail. It would indeed be extraordinary if you disgraced yourselves, you who were once the masters of the entire world! Romans! Those people gathered there are the cowardly successors of the Persian people who were once courageous and strong, but unsuccessfully opposed your valor.[5]

31

"You weakened the strength of their kings by making them your tributaries for a long time indeed.[6] If you are defeated by them now, consider what shame would perpetually obscure your fine lineage! Let us not be afraid! Today your name will begin to shine brightly forever, you will prevail over this cowardly horde, for against them goes Rome, and Borso, and Christ.

5. The allusion is to the Parthians of Roman times, with whom the army of Rome often clashed. *Persae* was the name used by the Romans to indicate all the people east of the Caspian Sea.

6. This and the preceding statement refer to the diplomatic victories reported by Augustus after the battle of Actium in 31 BCE. They are alluded to as military victories by Virgil (*Aeneid* 7.604–6). By returning to Phraates IV of Persia the son who had been abducted by his enemy, the Emperor Augustus obtained the return of the Roman standards that had been captured by the Parthians in a battle fought against Anthony and Crassus in 36 BCE. Phraates also sent his four sons to Augustus as hostages in recognition of Roman authority. See *Fasti* 5.579–86.

32

"But why am I trying to prove with words arguments that you yourselves can read in the works of God? You had the proof of how much he is capable of doing, how ready he is to comply with your smallest requests. Didn't he just now once again bestow light upon the sun? Didn't he calm and placate billows and storms? When you were dispersed and scattered on enemy soil, he liberated and saved you and gathered you together again.

33

"God has not allowed these wicked people to come forward against you without a very good reason; he did it to your greater glory, so that you may now open the path to a worthier victory.[7] So remember: the tyrant is to be overcome and defeated—it will be easy—and the world will bow to you, honor you, and call you new masters of the East.

34

"You, defenders of a good and just king, whom the heavens have made superior to all others in virtue, you in whose character and action the ancient daring has not yet languished, you who still prove how the entire world seemed a narrow space for Roman valor, you who vanquished the world, will you be afraid now of a barbaric people, with neither skill nor strength?

35

"Of these who seem such a big army to you, one hundred men are hardly worth one of you, for they are accustomed to fight only on land. On land they can scare enemies who have no courage, but on the unstable sea, at the mercy of winds and waves, they hardly know how to handle their weapons. I can already see them defeated at the first assault and you laden with trophies and rich spoils.

36

"But why am I exhorting you thus? Speaking about your past glories may even be offensive to you, and with good reason, because your hearts draw their gallant daring from your virtues alone."[8] Here he fell silent, and soon in all of

7. This sentence echoes Machiavelli's arguments and phrasing when, urging the prince to attempt a daring enterprise in seemingly desperate conditions, he cites two examples from Persian and Jewish history to clinch his argument: for the leadership of Moses to shine, it was necessary that the people of Israel be enslaved in Egypt; for the courage of Cyrus to show, it was necessary that the Persians be oppressed by the Medes. *The Prince* 26.

8. We have here the first of four captivating speeches delivered in turn by Borso, Tarconte, the sultan, and Alexander to their troops. See the others in stanzas 42–47 below and in cantos

them a fine desire for an honorable victory began to grow. "Hurrah! Hurrah!" the young warriors shouted. "We shall win! Christ will win! Christ will reign!"

37

As soon as he became fully aware of the Latin reinforcements, the crude Tarconte, to whom all this had been reported by several who had seen the fleet from above, immediately guessed what had in fact happened. Then, after calling his top leaders into council, he told them what he had learned; they concluded that their numbers, all counted, gave no uncertain hope of victory.

38

He gave orders for the ships to space out and take position in a circle. Then he reinforced the middle without closing the circle, for he wanted it to open with two points directed toward the Christians, just as Cynthia, the moon, appears in the sky when she is still crescent and her two horns are not quite filled in; and this is because their enemy was so reduced in number that they planned to entrap them by opening a way in their midst.

39

He then stationed the rearguard in a straight line—they were neither scarce in numbers nor without strength—one indeed so thick and strong that there was no danger of its being outflanked. Very carefully he saw to it that no industry of war or high state of alertness was forgotten, and he ordered Tumombel to move to the front with his archers and hold the enemy ships in place with arrows.

40

To insure safety, where the circling line took a sharper turn and grew thicker, he placed a good number of his best warriors, so that when the enemy came to the attack they would not let them open a way in. He placed Arunte and Gelon in charge, for they both showed intelligence, as well as daring and strength, in the way they fought. On the horns of this

---

21.70–75 and 22.7–17. Sarrocchi may have taken hints from the addresses made to the troops by Scipio and Hannibal before the battle of Zama (Livy 30.32.6–11; *Africa* 7.1034–1103, 7.1149–1215), and from the speeches of Caesar and Pompey before Pharsalus (Lucan, *Civil War* 7.250–329, 7.342–382). Similar to Sarrocchi's descriptions are those Marinella's of Venier and Alessio placing their troops in position and talking to them before battle. See *L'Enrico* 3.1–8, 3.9–13, 3.16–17. About Lucrezia Marinella's probable emulation of this poem, see pp. 40–41 above.

deployment he placed the fierce Circassians,[9] Ratisba to the right and King Galeasso to the left.

41

To the same side he ordered the good Cireno and on the opposite flank the strong Roceldo, so that where the circle ended its curvature, there would be courageous warriors capable of offering resistance. Finally he stationed himself in the middle, right where the circle grew thicker and more round, as the Christian captain had done. After giving his orders, he reviewed the whole, overseeing and taking care of everything.

42

With his presence and words, he too inspired in his men a desire of great, immortal glory. "People born to be raised aloft by the wings of fame with a clearly resounding acclaim," he told them, "in all of Asia there has never been a people as ferocious and bellicose as you. I know you are disdainful of fighting against men used only to comforts, riches, and luxuries.

43

"These are not the people who conquered the Indians, the Persians, and the Africans; these are different, far distant from them in their lineage, of mixed blood, made of a thousand filthy races, for a long time spread out and mixed with that of barbarians, for that noble blood of old has never been seen since. No warlike spirit will give valor to sons descended from such parents.[10]

44

"Even if they descended from them, no vestige is left of their ancient valor, for debased by cowardly serfdom, they are made slaves in a narrow, closed corner of the world. But even if every one of them were so zealous as to prove himself a Caesar, or were like the great strong Cursor,[11] even if these people were indeed what they once were, what could they do, being so few, against so many of us?

9. The Circassians, people from Circassia, a region south of the Don River and east of the Sea of Azov, are part of the Persian contingent.

10. Tarconte's description of the Italians owes much to the reprimands that Pompeo Colonna and Antimo Savello hurled at the citizens of Rome when—according to Francesco Guicciardini's *Storia d'Italia* published 1537–40—they tried to stir them up against the rule of Pope Julius II. See *Storia d'Italia* 10.1–3

11. Cursor is Papirius Cursor, who repeatedly defeated the Samnites in 325–309 BCE and is ranked in generalship with Alexander the Great by Livy (9.16.19).

45

"And even if they were greater in number than all of us put together, and strong and courageous besides, their leader is far too young and dares to attempt more than he is capable of. From the maternal breast not too long ago[12] he sucked a tempestuously driving ambition, but if he is not obeyed, what could he possibly do, even if he were to give orders to a numerous and daring army?

46

"The providence of great Allah, who takes good care of his people, the high fortune of having the protection of heaven, all this for sure destines them to be prey to your valor and makes you certain of victory. The enemy king placed all his hopes in them, but they were dispersed by the winds, and hardly one of them is left to fight against one hundred of us.

47

"By winning, each one of you will become worthy of a great triumph and high glory, if you indeed will subjugate the people into whose hands your ancient kingdom once fell, as even today is widely reported." After saying this, he fell silent. All the ships let their sails loose in the wind, ready for the upcoming battle. A gentle breeze made the great royal flag flap; the sky above was clear, the sea below tranquil.

48

The heads of the Persians, wrapped in purple bands, rose high under the white sails lightly fluttering. Such is the sight of cotton in the fields of Egypt when it opens up into white soft puffs. Their ships now advanced in a row like high hills whose treetops are covered with snow: at their feet are blue flowers, in the middle are roses, the sails are like veils, and the sea is smiling placidly.

49

The sight of them going forth to battle was an object of delight, not of fear, to the onlooker.[13] It could be said that the Christian fleet offered an equally

12. The real Borso, who was born in 1413, was not that young in 1464, when Pope Pius II's expedition was to have taken place. In mentioning her character's youth, Sarrocchi may have been influenced by a speech that Hannibal made during a parley with Scipio, in which he declared himself to be apprehensive about his opponent's young age. Livy, 30.30.11. Petrarch, *Africa* 7.305.

13. The apparition of the Persian ships in this canto has the same effect on Cosimo's men as the one the highly decorated Turkish vessels, with their arrays of flags and streamers, were said to have had on the Christians at the battle of Lepanto. The order of battle in Sarrocchi's poem also corresponds to that of the Lepanto encounter. See Rawson, *Twenty Famous Naval Battles*, 76, 79.

impressive sight, except that their ships rose up to cover the pure rays of the sun. From their black shapes the weapons threw such flashes of dazzling light as to resemble the sky when thunder and lightning tear through the dark clouds and close in all around.

50

Turning its speedy wheels, the sun had so advanced into the expanse of the sky that it could now hurl its rays down onto the Christian warriors in a direct line: reflected by lances, by shining shields, coats of armor, and helmets, the light set the air ablaze with glowing fires, dazzling the sight of the Persians and striking terror into them.

51

On both sides, a great number of masts rose like antennae toward the sky, making it look like a forest on a short and cold day, a forest marvelously rich in tall trees, one that the northern wind had undressed of all branches and deprived of all green decoration. Now, at a short distance from each other, the armadas sent out a prolonged sound of martial trumpets.

52

Drums and kettledrums accompanied the sound of bronze bells; on both sides dark clouds of sharp arrows and heavy stones were hurled into the air; they swirled around swiftly from the barbarian and the Christian side, thrown by bows, catapults, and by hand, and by whatever means might propel them afar very rapidly.

53

The shouts of the barbarians hit the air and rose so high into the sky that nothing else could be heard. The din of trumpets and drums weighed oppressively on the ears, like the sound made by cows when they moo and run aimlessly about in forests, valleys, or on steep hills, if rapacious hands have stolen their beloved little ones.

54

The Persian vessels were slender and light, so each pilot could steer his ship as he pleased. He could let go and send it very speedily toward the enemy or restrain it from the run; he could move it straight ahead, or transversely, or draw it back when it was too far advanced. So if their ships were inferior in massive power, they were superior in their ability to move about and attack any other vessel in full safety.

55

The Roman ships were higher and heavier, capable of steadier flight but not of one as agile, because on moving water they were almost as stable as if they were on motionless land. However, they could smash very heavily against enemy vessels, and they could take hold of them so tenaciously that all defense and any attempt of escape were afterward in vain. By now, several Christian ships had let their rudders loose and were running precipitously to clash against the Persians.

56

Now the sea opened a large path to the fleets. The sun, the eternal planet, darkened behind the flying arrows, and all the infernal horrors seemed to pour forth from the valley of hell. A confused clamor rose to the sky; the air reverberated with it, and in that howling sound the heavens seemed in fear of being overcome by the thundering sea.

57

The impact was horrible and varied: what happened to each ship was also different. Some had turned upside down into the sea; some had their stern, others their bows under water; some were still erect but so far deep down that only the top of the mast could be seen. Some vessels had lost all their oars, others bounced about without a pilot.[14]

58

Many of them could be seen leaning ominously toward the water on the right or on the left, just like scales that vacillate in suspense, going down one moment, coming up the next. A vessel that could be seen a little while ago now was totally hidden, for the sea had swallowed it whole; meanwhile, an immense number of axes, hammers, and swords were flying here and there.

14. Several details of this battle—hurling missiles from bulwarks, the clashing of ships, mangled bodies floating on the sea, the waves reddened by blood—are taken from Lucan's description of a naval encounter between Caesar's fleet and the allies of Pompey off the coast of Massilia (modern Marseille) in *Civil War* 3.538–751. Cf. above, canto 20.17n. Another subtext of the battle in this canto could have been the description of what had occurred at Lepanto, as found in many texts in circulation at the time. In turn, Sarrocchi's description may have been the model for Marinella's battle at sea in canto 8.10–30 of *L'Enrico*. To her description of the sea fight the Venetian poet adds a component of magic with the story of the sorcerer Esone, whose idea is to burn the Venetian fleet with the fire of hell.

59

It could be said that the sea was sending out flashes, as if competing with
a sky in which Jupiter throws down his lightning bolts in great anger.
Weapons, broken by other weapons and met by still others, sent around
flares and sparks. Men fell into the cerulean fields by the thousands: some
were dead, others wounded, and often, in a variety of strange ways, the
killers were killed and fell down on the heels of those they had killed.

60

Christians and pagans jumped from their vessels to other vessels in deadly
rivalry, filling the wavy plains of the sea with severed trunks, sliced heads, legs,
feet, arms, and hands: a miserable sorrowful sight. You could not say what was
more frightful, the great number of the dead or the variety of the dying.

61

Bodies fell down in such great quantity that the expanse of the sea seemed
too small. Some appeared to have their legs under water, their busts above
it but with no arms. Others were kept afloat by their shields, which could
not sink; they had lost thighs and hands and had only their miserable trunks
left. Others had lost one leg or had had an arm sliced; others were missing
their hands and now swam with their maimed limbs.

62

The Christians were now reduced to very small numbers, and seeing that their
power was not sufficient to win, they decided to employ different means, for
they knew that arrows and lances would be of little use. They had various materials that could start a fire, and they had those fiercely deadly snakes, which the
shrewd Greek had carried in earthen vases and distributed among them.

63

They moved to an appropriate distance from the enemy ships so that they
could hit them more efficiently, and then they threw substances that could
immediately ignite strong and inextinguishable fires. Afterward, they hurled
the vases over—in them Isarco had enclosed different but all very voracious
serpents—for using such expedient means brings no demerit to a captain
when sheer force fails.

64

As the snakes were thrown, astonishment and fear suddenly got hold of the
Persian hearts. At first they were confused and upset by a natural horror

more than by any hurt, but soon the serpents, escaping from the vases in which they were imprisoned and searching for food in those narrow spaces, began to cling to the men in various ways. They hissed and whistled and had fire in their eyes.

65

How could anyone describe the terrible ways the snakes clung to different parts of their bodies? In an attempt to defend themselves, the Persians pulled the snakes away from their arms, necks, and legs and threw them overboard. Others flung them down, pierced them through, and chopped them with their swords, axes, and pikes, thus taking revenge on them for their own harsh destiny.

66

Meanwhile a horrible fire went up into the sky in one thousand serpentine flames. Such weaponry, hitherto unknown to the Persians, filled them with amazement and fright. It was astonishing indeed to see how the fire could burn on water. One could not believe one's eyes, because, as the flames multiplied and jumped from one to the next vessel, it looked as if the fire brought war to the water, and the water to the fire.

67

Christians and infidels were drowned, killed, burned, and wounded, were mixed together by chance. You could see the waves carry enemies in one group over here, friends far from each other over there. You could see some men float together for a while and then be pulled apart by some obstacle hidden in the water, water that was covered with broken planks and human bodies.

68

Ferocious Mars had spread his bloody mantle all over. Antreso was running from stern to bow to escape the atrocious fire, but finding that the flames were burning everywhere, he jumped. He could not, however, reach Artomin's boat, which was passing swiftly by, and (mirabile dictu) the poor man was lanced through between the beaks of the two ships.[15]

69

When the man who was piloting his ship was killed, Polion tried to swim to safety, and when he thought he had reached his friends' protection, he

---

15. Antreso's death is not unlike that of Lucan's Gyareus, who is hit by a missile while trying to jump into a passing ship and is left dangling in the air. *Civil War* 3.592–602.

took hold of Gelon, who was among them, but then a globe of burning fire struck his right shoulder and stuck to it, consuming his nerves, his veins, and his bones; and so he died by fire while trying to escape from water.

70

Galeano fled the fire that had already caught up with him, and finding no better place to run to, he climbed up the mast to take refuge on the top. When he was halfway up, an arrow hit him in the middle and went through his body in such a way that he remained hanging there, with useless hands and feet, for they could not take him any higher; and he died in the air, while he was on fire and sailing on water.

71

With Fortune looking unfavorably on his intentions, the Roman Zenon daringly turned his ship around. For a long time, by studying the horned moon and the directions in which the sun shot off his fiery rays, he was accustomed to forecasting whether the following day was going to be a bright or a dark one. It seemed that only to him were the heavens willing to reveal the right time to set sail and plow the sea.

72

Now he tried in vain to send his ship, which was bulky and heavy, clashing against Creso's vessel, for another man's skill, just as great as the threatening power of the waves, restrained his insane pride. A pike arrived quivering in the air and went through his heart. As he died, he relinquished the rudder: Anselmo took over the helm, and the sea recognized the change of pilot.

73

Ploteo, a great swimmer, had also come with the fleet to fight against the Persians. He carried no weapons in his hands, no sword, no lance, no bow or arrows, no axe, battleaxe, or hammer. Of slender body and agile limbs, he could see the smallest things in the secret lap of the sea and could bring them up from the lowest depths.

74

Trying to bring victory to his side in a manner perhaps never heard of before, he embraced this and the other of his enemies as they tried to escape from weapons or fire, and as they swam he pushed them down below the waves and drowned them, while he remained unharmed. This went on until he rose from underwater too quickly, and his death, albeit of one man alone, atoned for many other deaths.

75

This occurred because after swimming and drowning a poor man mercilessly, he darted upward like a fish, head first, thinking that he would come out in the open, but, instead, he went banging against the hull of a ship. His eyes faltered and lost sight, his neck snapped, and his feet, hands, and breath lost strength, like glass in the fire, and soon his body filled with water.[16]

76

Now Tarconte and Borso were face to face. Their ships were running against each other and were about to clash with enormous impact, each vessel provided with irons ready to grapple the other so firmly that later it would be difficult to separate them. In the same way two fierce lions rush against each other, or two falcons launch themselves in opposite flight: each vessel seemed to take on a lion's mane, or the wings, the beak, and the claws of a bird.

77

Perhaps (if we may compare a human event to another) the powerful Hector and the fierce Achilles ran against each other in their last fatal duel with the same impetuous rush; then Mount Ida could scarcely see who was winning, for their chariots leaned so much on one side.[17] The impact bent both ships tremendously, with a greater force than any wave or stormy gale could have produced, blowing either leeward or windward.

78

Fear did not daunt the courage of the Persian warriors; they did not give way in face of enemy swords, for daring protected their hearts and bodies with solid armor and adamantine shields. You could see them rally and go on the attack with redoubled valor; they jumped onto the enemy ships, trying, in competition with one another, to become worthy of great glory.

---

16. Ploteo's manner of killing his foes, and the way he finally dies, are a close variation of what happens to a Phocaean sailor in Lucan's *Civil War* 3.696–708.

17. Hector, the valorous defender of Troy, and Achilles, the most powerful fighter among the Greeks besieging the town, fight a decisive duel in Homer's *Iliad* 22.246–336.

79

The Christian troops were thinning out, for in a short time they were assaulted with axes, lances, spears, arrows, and swords from all sides. Most of them received several deadly blows; most fell down stabbed to death; many drank their own blood mixed with sea water. Now Bimarte himself and other Persians were able to board the Christian vessels from many broken sides.

80

The pagans could step inside with ease, and they made such inroads that those on board were compelled to give way. Borso could no longer force anyone to put up any resistance. In the confusion and mixture of soldiers, friends were wounded instead of enemies. It was little use trying to recognize who was who by the armor, so thick was the crowd and so tight the space.

81

With a heart aflame with pious zeal and eyes full of devout tears, Giuliano prayed to the great divine Motor not to disdain to look on his faithful people. He had not lost trust in God; he only feared that his men might not be worthy of God's grace. He was confident that God might want, in that battle, to pardon them charitably or, reserving his right to do so, inflict punishment on them.

82

Certain of defeat, he was resolved to die but wanted to do it as a great warrior, embracing a common destiny. He did not believe it a sin to hold a weapon in his holy hands, hands that held Christ; because spoils and trophies, when obtained in a bloody battle against God's rebels, were gratifying to heaven, and waging war is not unbecoming to those who must defend their lives and their faith.[18]

83

The courageous Borso realized that his men and all effort and hope were vain now that his ship was full of victorious barbarians. So with his heart full of daring valor, he wanted to die an honorable death, at least a death

18. At this climactic moment of her narrative, Sarrocchi seems to feel the need to justify a war waged by the church of Rome, here represented by the papal nuncio. Invocations to God and religious motivations for the conflict are underscored in the poem in stanzas 3, 28, and 36 of this canto, and in cantos 5.99, 5.104, 6.56, 9.24, 9.43, 19.10, 21.71.

such as was needed for the enemy to keep a sad memory of this day, and for
no enemy near him to be able to boast about a victory.

84

He went toward Tarconte, whose identity was made obvious by his rich and
valuable armor. He struck a direct blow and caught him on the forehead.
The gold and the enamel of his beautiful helmet fell in many shiny shards,
but the matchless steel withstood the blow as strongly as a mountain would.
Raging with anger, Tarconte charged against him, while remaining shielded
by more than a hundred hands.

85

Still, the deadly duel could not be stopped, for the two men were too taken
up with each other. With so many men poised against Borso, Tarconte, in
violation of the respected rules of war, pressed upon him and struck. Borso
moved round and round, fearing nothing, now raising his shield, now dealing a blow. He hit first someone behind him, then someone else on his side,
and then went back to face Tarconte.

86

Ottavio Adami and some men who had survived the terrible onslaught
came forward, and cutting through the thick circle of men, they brought
timely support to their captain, whom the ferocious barbarian had already
wounded in the chest. From a deep wound blood ran down Borso's armor,
but the young man gave no sign of fear; on the contrary, he put his intelligence and skill to use with even greater daring.

87

Seeing that now he had a great deal of help, and certain that his rear was
covered, he stabbed Tarconte in the throat and left him with a big, gaping
wound. Tarconte would have liked to respond, but his hand faltered as he
tried to do so, and he began to stagger. Timing his move carefully, Borso
raised his sword and struck him again in the same spot.

88

Tarconte fell with arms outstretched to the bottom of the ship, filling it with
blood. His limbs were covered with the sweat that exuded from the heat and
cold that now contended in his body. Finally his spirit wafted into the air,
and his limbs remained stiff on the ground. Meanwhile Cosimo, the great
Tuscan, seeing the danger in which Borso found himself, ran to his aid.

89

The throng of infidels who saw their leader fall dead did not wait. Some jumped back on their ships, others dove into the sea. Cosimo whirled his sword around, wounded, killed. Then he ordered the head of the dead Persian captain impaled on the top of the mast (one of them had cut it from the body), so that everyone could see it.[19]

90

By raising the big skull, they also raised fear and terror in all the pagans. Courage and strength failed also in those who had dared and had boasted the most, especially because on every side many ships could be seen in Christian hands, for they had been defended so badly by the pagans that one Christian ship had taken hold of three or four of theirs.

91

The valor of the infidels waned and their fear grew at seeing the danger they were in, while the courage and power of the Christians revived and increased, and they became sure of themselves. The added strength of the fearless Tuscan was an encouragement to the Roman soldiers, who were now fighting a bloody and still uncertain battle on the left flank.

92

They might have fallen into the hands of the enemy had they not followed Isarco's sound advice. Isarco, meanwhile, to make his orders heard distinctly, had often taken his visor away from his face, and when a soldier shouted at him that he would be killed if he kept exposing his bare features, he answered that it would be better for him to die than to let his voice go unheard by his men.

93

But while he was saying so, an arrow went through his right eye and came out at the nape of the neck.[20] Oh, unique wisdom of Mars and Minerva! You two conjoin valor and wisdom and teach us that a captain meets a good and

---

19. Parading the head of the slain enemy in front of his army in order to discourage the soldiers was common practice in war. A similar occurrence is described by Herodotus in *The Histories* 7.238, in *Aeneid* 9.465–67, by Livy 27.51.11, and in Lucan's *Civil War* 8.436–37, where headless bodies are paraded before the enemy. Cf. canto 5.82 above.

20. At the battle of Lepanto, the Venetian admiral, Agostino Barbarigo, fought with his visor open and was killed by an arrow piercing his face. Hale, "Lepanto 1571," 94.

glorious death if he dies in order to let his soldiers live.[21] For that side of the fleet maintained its order and was not defeated: in fact, it survived intact.

94

The victory was also made certain by another event, which was the effect of something that had been put in motion earlier. The snakes that had come out of the vases had scattered in the midst of the Persian men. Several of them had been bitten and left infected with different poisons, because the many kinds of snakes carried a variety of venom, thus causing a variety of poisonous deaths.[22]

95

The smallest among them was called jacol.[23] This kind caused by itself more hurt than all the others. This viper darts around so quickly that in comparison the arrows of a Scythian hand move much slower. Many men received a very painful wound; many others were killed quickly. One of them is Capusco, a mere soldier, but a rather well deserving and distinguished leader.

96

The vase that contained the snake smashed against the mast and shattered into many pieces. The deadly snake remained wound up there, positioned almost as if it were ready to strike; then, falling from above, it came down with a great impact as if falling from the top of the mast. Then the snake flung itself off, flew, and passed from the man's left temple into his brain, leaving him dead.

97

The snake called dipsas is smaller but much more dangerous, for it can inflict a profound and painful wound.[24] This snake bit Gemin in the heel very lightly, and he did not feel the puncture. But he certainly felt the pain

21. That is to say, Mars and Minerva, who are gods of war and wisdom, respectively, teach us that a glorious death is the reward of a captain who sacrifices himself for his soldiers' lives.

22. The description of the snakes and of the kind of deaths brought about by their bites emulates the one given by Lucan in *Civil War* 9.607–838.

23. The name comes from the Latin *iacolum*, that is, "javelin," because this snake was thought to dart at its victim from a tree or a pole. It is mentioned by Lucan in *Civil War* 9.720. The manner in which Capusco is poisoned by the viper in the next stanza is patterned on the death of Paulus, who is shot through the head from temple to temple by a jacol darting from the trunk of an oak (*Civil War* 9.822–927).

24. This snake, also called dispa, was said to be found in Syria and in the Libyan desert. According to the ancients, its bite brought about an unquenchable thirst. *Civil War* 9.718.

of the fearful poison later, for it began to burn inside his bowels as his blood and vital spirits were being destroyed, his humor drained, and his life snuffed out slowly.[25]

98

He was not relieved by the exudation of a single drop of sweat from his body; he could not make a sound, nor could his dried-up heart put forth a humid tear. In such a state of burning, his parched tongue stuck to his parched palate. Never under Sirius was a sick person oppressed by such a burning fever or made to suffer a thirst comparable to his.[26]

99

The largest vein of crystalline water, running ever so swiftly through a field, pouring forth and precipitating from a stony hill into a thousand rivulets, did not seem to be sufficient to satisfy his need and quench his thirst. What perhaps could have done it was the River Don if it were added to the Nile, when the latter comes gurgling down in flood from several sources.

100

Still he went ahead to meet all dangers; he did not care about dying because all risks seemed negligible compared with his condition. Now an arrow flew whizzing through the air. Poor Glauco received it in the throat, and as a big spurt of blood came out of it, Gemin applied his mouth to it, started drinking it, and so voraciously sucked the blood from the wound that he left the man far more bloodless than he would have been by the wound alone.[27]

101

Finally, in order to quench the terrible thirst that had increased while he was drinking that strange liquor, he voluntarily threw himself in the water, and his thirst and life ended at the same time. He died because now he had too much of what he wanted. What hope can human beings place in anything mortal? Life hides a trap under each beautiful flower, for something

25. In *Civil War* 9.736–60, Aulus, Cato's standard bearer, does not feel the viper's bite, but the venom meanwhile creeps silently through his body, consuming marrow and entrails and preventing perspiration.

26. It was a common belief that the diseases occurring in the hot days of summer were brought on by Sirius, the dog star, which is in ascendancy at that time of year. Cf. canto 9.54 above.

27. In *Civil War* 9.758–60, Aulus, again, is made so thirsty by the poison that he begins to drink the blood oozing from his own body.

harmful will derive from anything that is denied, and a worse evil will ensue if it is obtained.

102

Ah, viper! with your tooth you injected Orino with an ardor no less pernicious. As the nasty poison spread through his veins, his skin began to swell with a force that filled his body and tensed it with a putrid humor, deforming all human shape. And as the man took on the appearance of a big beam with the same thickness all around, he was unable to hold up his own weight any longer.

103

He tried in vain to lift his foot, now heavier and bigger than its natural shape. The helmet and the cuirass that before covered him with ease could no longer contain him. When Boreas blows most fiercely in the air, it never fills a flying sail as much. Orino burst, and down he went to frighten the monsters of the deep, with a weight more monstrous than theirs.[28]

104

Haemorrhois, another horrible serpent, added Tullo to the great number of the dead, and did so in an amazing manner.[29] He plunged his tooth in the man's throat and injected a terrible poison into his veins: fleeing the extraneous venom, the blood began to come out in a thousand rivulets from whatever hole it could find most quickly, and thus emptied the veins of all their liquid.

105

The blood came out in thick rivulets from everywhere, also from the nose and ears, and it was of a color one would think similar to that of the crocus when it is crushed by Corinthian stones. Blood as red as fire ran down his sad face; his tears were blood, and the blood flooded the whole body, which had become one single big wound.

---

28. Orino's death is like that of Nasidius, whose body, swollen beyond all possible human growth, is no longer contained by his coat of mail. *Civil War* 9.790–804.

29. Haemorrhois is the first snake mentioned by Lucan in canto 9.709 of his poem. Tullus, the Roman soldier bitten by it, is described as losing blood from mouth, nostrils, and skin. Cf. *haemorrhois* in Salvatore Battaglia, *Grande Dizionario della Lingua Italiana* (Turin: UTET, 1961–2002), 5:135.

106

Running away from death with a happier outcome, Arban showed how effective willpower can be, for a wise man may sometimes mitigate an evil fate, if not avoid it outright. As soon as he was bitten by a viper, he very courageously and without hesitation cut his own hand, and in this way he closed the veins to the obnoxious poison. Thus he providently drew a good result from a bad beginning.[30]

107

Meanwhile the burning torches that had been flung beforehand had set aflame a hundred and more ships. The unfortunate men did not know which one of the two deadly dangers they should flee more. Still the pestilential infection brought about by the horrible poison frightened them less than the relentless fire, for the voracious mouths of the flames burned and devoured, while the venom still conceded some delay.

108

Some ran from the water into the burning flames; then from the fire they ran again toward the water, for they estimated that pain of approaching death less fierce than the other. Poor wretches, for they changed their minds about both; their dear lives were being destroyed either way; and so they tried to escape from the very death of which they had already begun to die.

109

The distress and the fear of the Persians spread all over the fleet, affording a horrible spectacle. Some, ever so intent to escape one type of death, ran into another, or into two; sometimes even into three, and often into an even greater torture; at other times, even four, each one of which was horrendous: they were burnt by the fire, stung by the poison, then drowned in water, and also pierced by spears.

110

What a miserable spectacle that was! One could also notice that everyone loved himself above all others. It might happen, it is true, that a man offered a hand to his friend or to a compatriot in order to rescue him from the sea or from the fire; but as soon as he became aware of the risk he himself was running, he quickly gave up, for it was too dangerous. For love of self, he might even let go of his brother, his father, or his own son.

30. For the same reason, in *Civil War* 9.828–33, a poisoned soldier cuts off his arm at the shoulder with a swift stroke of his sword.

111

This way the smaller number prevailed over the superior one. The Persians could no longer put up a resistance, and those who, totally shaken and exhausted, did not die fell into the hands of the enemy. The white of the foam and the blue of the waves were obliterated by the blood, by weapons strewn all over, by torn sails, by burning planks fallen from the smashed and burned-out ships.

112

The chariot that carries the golden light of day had already disappeared beyond the western sky. In its place, fires burned here and there most frighteningly, tearing across the smoke-filled air and throwing blazes into the sky. Then in the gloomy shadow an extraordinary vision appeared that filled every heart with terrifying horror: in the darkness, in the midst of fire and smoke, bodies were seen drifting on the water, like damned souls floating in the rivers of hell.[31]

113

Later on in the day, when the sun, encircled by blazing rays, had completed half of its swift journey, reaching the highest point in the sky, and from there begun to send down more luminously its salubrious splendor, at that time of day when the heat is so great and dry that no earthly vapor can diminish it, at that moment the victors came in sight of Albania and pointed out its beaches with a happy shout.

114

There they landed and happily set their feet on firm soil. Then on the following day at sundown they reached Croia by the only path leading to it. As soon as the seacoast filled with the Christian throng, news of it was brought to the great Thracian, who mistakenly believed it to be the Persian reinforcement.

115–20

Meanwhile the Persian army is approaching, and Vran, who was sent to obstruct its arrival, is forced to withdraw.

31. This terrible scene is not unlike that of the site of the battle of Lepanto at the end of the hostilities: a mention of that scene is found in all the reports that reached Europe afterward and is present in many poems celebrating that famous victory. The following stanza from the poem *L'Austria* (1573), by Ferrante Carafa, is an example: "Acrebbe il mar, l'acque divenner rosse / da fiume che non vien da colle o monte / ma da vene, da spoglie umane conte / e da piaghe larghissime si mosse" (the sea swelled, the waves were turned red by rivers that were not coming from mountains or hills, they were coming from very large wounds and from human remains exposed to view). Quoted by Quondam, *La parola nel labirinto*, 76.

CANTO 21

The sultan calls together an assembly of the satraps, and after listening to their views, he decides to fight the enemy in an open field battle. The king too is ready for war. A few Albanian horsemen are sent to the vicinity of Presa to lure the enemy into attacking. Before the fighting begins, the emperor delivers a speech to the various national contingents in his army.

1

Now that all the Persian army had passed over to this side of the mountains, the Ottoman emperor hoped to defeat the enemy, even though their fleet was unfortunately lost. Upon hearing, however, that the Italian troops had reached Croia safely, he called together a council of high satraps in order to face the upcoming danger with all possible safeguards.

2

He sat on the high imperial throne and the others sat on silk carpets, which were kept, as we know, for such great occasions. The emperor honored them more magnificently than usual and invited the opinion of everyone graciously, so they all might say openly what they thought, putting fear and obeisance aside, for what mattered most now was the interest of the empire.[1]

3

"We have seen the strength of the adversary," the emperor told them; "we have experienced his military prowess: what may we expect from the

1. The sultan's war council is reminiscent, especially in its structure, of the assembly held by Xerxes before his invasion of Greece. At that meeting, Artabanus speaks against the projected expedition, while Mardonius declares himself strongly in favor of fighting. Herodotus, *The Histories* 7.8–11. Similarities are also to be found between this convocation and the assembly of the Latins in *Aeneid* 11.376–444, in which Turnus stirs the men's spirits in favor of the war.

enemy army now that it is reinforced and braced by new arrivals? The situation to consider is this: is it advisable to take our chances in the open field, or is it preferable to wear the enemy down with a long siege, taking into account that the citadel will not be able to avert a shortage of food?

4

"Now that the powerful Persian army has joined us, it may not be futile to strive for victory, even though the Ausonian[2] daring has deprived us of the support that the fleet would have provided." Here the sultan sighed. Then he fell into a solemn silence, first turning his eyes toward Artaban and then toward Ramassar. As he held his gaze steadily on the latter, he, Ramassar, got up quickly and spoke before anyone else could do so.

5

He began to speak but not before bowing deeply once or twice before the high throne. "My lord, Epirus is a country of dense mountainous terrain. The hope of conquering it in battle is unfounded. Furthermore, as you have discovered both in war and in peacetime, this land creates shrewd and well-trained men, and their leader has great strength and a very sagacious mind.

6

"Guided by a man of such valor, they have defeated us. If you consider carefully, it is not the number of men that gives one victory, it is rather the prudence and skill of the soldiers. We may also add the consideration that those fighters of yours who were defeated are not to be considered cowards and fools, and toward you, their lord, they have been of constant dedication and incorruptible loyalty."[3]

7

He wanted to say more, but the great tyrant turned his eyes again toward Artaban, as if the burden of giving advice fell more heavily on him as a man endowed with better judgment than the other. Artaban rose, bent his knees humbly, lowered his head, and placed one hand over his heart. "I shall tell you sincerely, my lord, if you permit, all that my mind and experience have taught me.

2. *Ausonia* is another name for Italy, hence the adjective *Ausonian* for Italian.

3. Ramassar's speech makes some of the points stressed by Machiavelli when he points out what a ruler must secure if he wants to maintain and defend his state, namely, the loyalty of his subjects, their attachment to freedom, a well-trained army, and a good knowledge of the terrain over which he must fight. *The Prince 5*, 14.

8

"When your interest requires it, we must say nothing but the simple truth, so I will start where Ramassar ended, from the capacity and character of the enemy. The people of Epirus are loyally attached to their king, and as he said, they hold in great esteem their freedom and glory, and furthermore they are proud and ferocious toward foreigners.

9

'They are passionate and eager to show Alexander how ready they are to disregard their safety in his interest. They consider it a great virtue to be hostile to the glorious name of the Ottomans: it is esteemed by them a glory for a noble warrior to shake off the humiliating burden of servitude, for they think there is no more just war than one waged to escape a cruel and unbearable serfdom.

10

'They think that a sovereign who puts down the criminal is a tyrant, so easy is it for men to go astray in their judgment. You saw yourself what the outcome of past wars was like, from the first to the last; what is more, you will have against you many other new great fighters, all of high and well-known ability. A just and sincere man must not hide the truth about the enemy.

11

"You know that hatred is born out of fear; hatred, that is, against the person who causes fear in us. With hate, a desire rises in people's heart to get rid of fear by killing the person who brings it about. This is why the people of Epirus have joined your enemy: in order to get rid of their frightening suspicion that they might fall into a brutal servitude, to say nothing of the fact that they are united to their rightful king by ties of love.[4]

12

'Thus, united in love, steady, constant, they become strong and courageous in war. If armies were made only of people who loved one another, they would always be victorious. So, if a few men defeated us before, when we were great in number, now that your army has lost so many soldiers and they are joined by many famous warriors, we have a weak hope of victory indeed.

4. In *The Prince* 3 and 5, Machiavelli insists that subjects are kept loyal to a hereditary prince by ties of affection and that if they are used to liberty, they will never forgive its loss.

13

"But we will fight again against these daring warriors who have already overcome and defeated us, and also against those strong soldiers who have joined them and have destroyed so many of our allies across the seas. Men who have good intellect are less likely to make mistakes than those who are led on by lack of judgment. Men who are wise and prudent wait for the right time and place to counterattack and do it with a minimum of damage to themselves.

14

"So now that more than one of our most reputed warriors has been killed by that daring army and the appalling news has come of the aid being lost, which was beyond all reasonable expectation, you can see whether any courage still remains in our soldiers by just looking into their faces. Those who in war harbor fear often turn their backs where their faces ought to be.

15

"When sudden and unexpected turns of events take place during various stages of a battle, the simple soldiers, the ones who are not very intelligent, are more likely to be seized by terror. In such a case, greater damage may be caused by a single fearful man trying to run away than by a thousand enemy soldiers who, facing up to our naked weapons, are capable of buttressing their breasts with a shield of courage.

16

"Experience has shown to us more than once that when a captain leads his army with intelligence, the enemy is more easily dismayed and defeated than by either weaponry, a lengthy war, or hardships. In these circumstances, one is able to win without danger, without bloodshed, even without any fighting. A wise man must not fail to consider this possibility, when he sees no advantage in behaving otherwise.

17

"Those who allow themselves to be carried away by furious anger cause ruin and shame to themselves and give proof of being stupid rather than strong. In such cases, when the damage is greater than the reason that led them to fight, it becomes clear that in trying to get something of scanty import, a great deal more is lost.

18

"The glorious victories and the great trophies that you obtained vanquishing kings and countries, which allowed you to extend your domain (you must remember it) beyond the Hister and the Ganges, all this will make you see clearly that if you are defeated now, your great name will surely lose prestige: for people of gallant heart value glory more than any kingdom.

19

"A captain does not deserve to be considered a valuable leader if he exposes himself and others to useless risks, when reason and military experience demonstrate that the loss of his army is certain. Human intelligence can rarely be confident of victory in war, but if one behaves according to good military practice, one can always have a proper justification for one's losses.[5]

20

"There is, however, something more to fear than just your enemy and the support he has recently received, and it is this: if you lose the war, the shame of it may be followed by a greater and more devastating damage, for your authority may be seriously disputed; your subjects may revolt and take up arms against you. For it happens at times that the people, by joining their efforts, become strong enough to overthrow their sovereign.

21

"May I be allowed, my lord, to speak the truth in all sincerity, for your interest is at stake. The Thracian people are friendly only in appearance; in fact they are perpetually desirous of change, with no sense of honor to hold them in check. They are fickle, disloyal—a fact that also other leaders have experienced—they hate your rule, and what keeps them down is only the force of fear, not a bond of love.[6]

5. Reasonableness, caution about taking unnecessary risks, the expedients of diplomacy, and the advantages of embarking only on defensive wars were questions considered at length by political treatises in Sarrocchi's time. In *The Reason of State* (1589), Botero recommended careful consideration of risks before embarking on military campaigns and advised never to attempt anything that is not likely to succeed, reasonableness and prudence being the major part of men's intelligence. See *The Reason of State* 2.1–2, 2.2, 3.4, 10.5, and 10.9.

6. Being hated by one's subjects makes the position of a ruler precarious, Machiavelli and Botero agree. Both consider ways in which a balance might be struck between severity and fear on one side, and indulgence and disobedience on the other. The problem for a ruler is to be determined and severe and at the same time avoid being hated and despised for it. He should not be so merciful, however, as to let discipline and respect be forgotten. *The Prince* 10, 17, and 19; *The Reason of State* 1.8, 1.11, 1.18, 4.4.

22

"It is then not out of cowardice that I advise you to abandon your great campaign, for it would be reckless of you now to expose yourself to the danger of an all-out battle. I advise you instead to lay protracted siege to the city and close all roadways around it to any transportation of victuals, so that the enemy will die of starvation and you will win without fighting and without bloodshed.[7]

23

"I also advise you not to stay here, but to return within the frontiers of your empire, and from there to carry out raids on the hostile forces by land and sea. When you leave, those famous foreign soldiers will go back to their country, for they will no longer have any reason to remain here, and you will face fewer enemies.

24

"Should they remain, the inhabitants of Epirus, although loyal to their king, will fail him, because the food they have saved is not sufficient to feed the new soldiers and knights; and lacking gold, these rebels will not be able to buy enough victuals for them all. Even if gold grew as easily for Alexander as it did for Midas,[8] what use would it be if no food can be found?

25

"Facing the terrible affliction of starvation, your enemy will not be able to endure for long, and when there are only a few of them left and in a weakened condition, they will not be able to defend themselves from enemy attack. In this manner they will wear themselves out slowly, like the sick who hide a consuming fever inside their bones, and with small effort and damage to you, your hopes will be fulfilled."

26

He then was silent. The great sovereign did not seem to be happy with what he had just heard and had been seething with anger from the start,

7. Scipione Ammirato was peremptory in maintaining that the skill and wisdom of a general are shown in his ability to overcome the enemy by starving the population rather than by fighting a bloody open battle. *Discorsi* 13.5. The advice given by Artaban in stanza 23 to withdraw into Thrace reflects another of Ammirato's considerations: whether it is good military practice to wait for the enemy on one's territory or to advance into his territory and embark on a preventive campaign. See also Machiavelli, *Discourses* 18.1–7.

8. Midas was king of Phrygia. He prayed to Dionysus that everything he touched would turn into gold. His wish was granted to the letter. Ovid, *Metamorphoses* 11.85–126.

because Ramassar had dared to speak of matters so far beyond the scope of his experience. He believed that good advice could not come from someone who did not possess great quantities of gems and gold, and that an important person should take advice from his inferiors only if it concerned a skill they had acquired in their profession, out of need.

27

The emperor did not believe it possible to find intelligence among the poor and did not realize that the man had correctly forecast the future. What infuriated him even more was the fact that a king in his speech had agreed with a lower-class person. So in a rather angry fashion the sultan nodded to others. Attravante rose from the floor and, although showing consideration and deference toward the sultan, began to speak with a great deal of impatience and boldness.

28

"Magnanimous lord, I do not know how you could be patient for so long and not get angry, letting this man show his cowardice, a man who has the reputation of being wise and intrepid. I too praise the desire to preserve the glory of the lands you have conquered and subjugated, something for which people far away respect you and those who are near fear you—but only as an invincible conqueror should be feared.

29

"He cannot be a warrior of great valor who is at any time afraid of danger and death. Only men of base and cowardly nature worry about it, not those who are courageous and valorous. There is no better way of life, nor one more secure, than the way of self-reliance; for to acquire glory with some illustrious deed is never possible without running a degree of danger.[9]

30

"I too concur that your very high fame should not be diminished but should rather expand further and further in perpetual growth, but it ought to do so by the strength of an invincible sword and a dauntless heart, not with blame and shame. You should go forward to face the enemy and not withdraw like

---

9. At the war council convened by Xerxes, Mardonius, who is in favor of invading Greece, maintains that no enterprise can be embarked upon without danger, and that everything men may acquire can be obtained only with a struggle. Herodotus, *The Histories* 7.9. Botero warns rulers that no action can be taken without bringing about some damage or disadvantage, because there no good without evil. *The Reason of State* 2.6.

a coward back to your lands. It is impossible—do take my advice—to escape danger without running any risk whatsoever.

31

"Some of your best warriors—I do not deny it—were robbed of their lives and of their day of glory; but was there ever a case when Fortune kept her face smiling on the same soldiers throughout an entire long war? If we consult the history of the Greek and the Roman heroes, we can see that there never was a warrior among them who rose to the high pinnacle of glory without great struggle and danger.

32

"This is required of your high valor, which has already seen the Hungarians, the Greeks, and the great people of Poland crawl vanquished at your feet:[10] so can we put this victory in doubt? Will your famous name be brought down into the mud by some obscure slave of yours, when you have conquered in battle kings and kingdoms?

33

"The expert archer who wants to hit his target must aim very carefully before he releases the arrow. A wise warrior, who is about to go on a campaign, must consider wisely what are the chances of victory and of defeat. Prudent men must disregard any probable losses, or, if possible, inflict the same on the enemy; if they do not reciprocate in kind, their loss will double and their shameful defeat will appear obvious to everyone.

34

"If ordinary men burning with rightful indignation wish to vindicate their humiliations and, to achieve that goal, place their lives and reputations frequently on the line, then what will a man both powerful and wise do if he is urged on by his high position and by the offense he has received? A strong leader, an illustrious emperor, is never allowed to skirt a necessary danger.

35

"Add the fact that there is nothing in the world on which human judgment—often so wrong—is likely to give a more uncertain verdict than in the case of unpredictable events of war. But the consideration that a high and glorious

10. The Hungarians and the Poles were defeated by the Turks at Varna in 1444 and at Kosovo in 1448. Salonika (modern Thessaloniki) was taken from the Greeks in 1430.

enterprise might have an unfavorable outcome should never prevent a good leader from expecting victory, because being undecided about whether to embark on a worthy and glorious action is in itself an unworthy act.

36

"Even if, against all expectations, you did lose several of your famously daring men, you can still dispose of that outstanding battalion of Janissaries that you, as the great captain you are, have organized. You still have the best of these soldiers at your disposal, and do you not expect to be supported by them?[11] I do not consider Driarasso equal to them, for he is a feckless soldier, but they certainly are not.

37

"Besides, just now you have received the most timely help of many strong Persian knights, each one of whom will surely remain devoted and loyal, since their king is joined to you by family ties. Do not be discouraged by the many men lost and killed on the seas, for the Persians were not born to fight on water and so were easily overcome and defeated.

38

"But if, contrary to your customary daring, your heart gives in to fear, I cannot reasonably promise that you will be able to withdraw by a secure route. In that case, whether you remain in Thrace or in Macedonia, you will not be able to take care and prevent your enemy from getting supplies of food by land and sea and from attacking you in your rear.

39

"You can wisely foresee that wherever you go into safe territory, the ordinary soldiers will become exceedingly fond of inactivity, reluctant to exert themselves, and too inclined to rest. Perhaps then you will be defeated (may God forbid it!), just as the Carthaginian army was defeated by the Romans on the Iberian plains.[12] May such misfortune fall on my head first!

11. The discipline and effectiveness of the Janissaries were well known in Europe. According to Botero, the Janissaries had made Murad master of a large part of his domain, were employed wherever loyalty and courage were required, and were allowed great freedom in consideration of their bravery and fierceness. *The Reason of State* 5.1, 8.18, 9.14.

12. Machiavelli and Botero recommend that military discipline be kept up at all times, for leisure is pernicious to the effectiveness of the army. *The Prince* 14; *The Reason of State* 9.10. The Roman consul Lucius Marcius defeated the Carthaginians in Spain in 212 BCE. The comparison is apt because the Carthaginians after many victories had lulled themselves into inactivity. Livy 25.37–39.

40

"A good captain knows well that the greater advantage is on the side that begins the battle, on the side of those who lead the events rather than being led by them, and on the side of those who inflict injuries rather than of those who receive them. And if losses must occur, the loss will be smaller for the side fighting on enemy territory."[13] At these words the great Thracian lifted his eyes like one who had just heard something that pleased him.

41

Hearing this, the young soldiers sent up a happy shout, for they were reckless and eager to fight. The men mature in age and wisdom did not dare to contradict and remained quiet and thoughtful.[14] Thus, they all prepared themselves and their weaponry for war. The Thracian, however, being an expert and wise leader, saw to it that the soldiers who had just arrived took a rest and recovered from the battle they had fought and from the hardship of travel.

42

In his besieged land, the Christian king, who had victory engraved in his heart, fed and refreshed the men who had come to his aid, so that they might soon be ready to fight again. The fear that the food he had in store would last for a much shorter time than he intended greatly preoccupied him, and besides he worried that his enemy would triumph if he did not defeat them with the help of the men who had just joined him.

43

Although he had done his best to cure them, many were the soldiers among the wounded and the dying who had in fact died, and several captains had as well. When the strength of those alive was fully restored, Borso asked the king to dispose of the foreign warriors, who were now invigorated, as he pleased and as his wisdom best advised.

44

For he was not only a king but also a skilled and wise military man; he knew his territory well, and thanks to his extensive knowledge of it, he could

13. Fittingly for this fiction, Attravante's speech is a long list of wrong reasons for going to war. Conspicuously misconceived is his suggestion that the Turks ought to attack, for common military wisdom in Sarrocchi's time was that the side that started the war would lose in the end (Murrin, *History and Warfare in Renaissance Epic*, 29).

14. After Mardonius's speech in favor of the war, the Persians too did not dare to utter an opinion contrary to his. Herodotus, *The Histories* 7.10.

easily guess what ambush the enemy might prepare. Soon, the wise king turned his mind to God and started his operations with a religious ceremony: he ordered all his soldiers to unload the weight of their sins and replenish their hearts with Christian charity.[15]

45

As an example to all the people in the city, he was the first to enter the sacred doors of the cathedral, and in that stony temple of Peter, he met with his first captains.[16] Here Giuliano loosened the chains with which evil Satan tied and pulled human souls to himself;[17] it was the power that the great shepherd had bestowed exclusively on him to pass on to lesser priests.

46

Other people, both local citizens and foreigners, did the same, so effective was the example set by the elders. Then, when the holy, life-giving sacraments had been administered, the king, whose aim was directed entirely toward victory, gave the order to search the nearest wooded mountains, catch alive all the wild boars they could find, and in addition cut down those thick branches—that countryside was full of them—that could easily be set ablaze and kept burning.

47

Out of those branches he wanted torches to be made that, smeared with pitch and sulfur, would be flung like great smoking and hissing missiles among the enemy. They would deliver fires that no strong wind would be able to extinguish. He knew well that by nature elephants are afraid both of fire and of wild boars. The Persians had many such big animals; on their backs they carried turrets in which many armed soldiers could hide.[18]

15. Sarrocchi is alluding to the Catholic sacraments of confession and communion and to the feeling of benevolence and generosity toward all (charity) that fills the shriven soul.

16. Main enterprises, such as expeditions and battles, were always preceded by religious ceremonies, either pagan or Christian. And the leaders who respected religious customs and participated in them were usually commended. See, for instance, Plutarch, "Fabius Maximus" 4.3; Machiavelli, *The Prince* 2; Botero, *The Reason of State* 2.15.

17. They are now free of Satan because, after confession and repentance, Giuliano has given them absolution.

18. The Romans were first surprised by an attack of elephants during the battle of Heraclea, which they fought against Pyrrhus of Epirus in 280 BCE. By the time they faced the Carthaginians at Zama, in 202 BCE, they had learned how to defend themselves from the elephants with javelins and torches. Livy 30.33.14–16. Pliny the Elder (23–79 CE) writes of elephants trained for war in *Naturalis Historia* 8.1–39. Cf. canto 22.18 and 22.69 below.

48

After giving these instructions in view of a general battle, at dawn the king marched out of the city ramparts. At the rear of his army he placed squads of knights and foot soldiers, should a stealthy attack come from that side; then he ordered other squads, similar in number and strength, to advance in front at short intervals, so that should the enemy appear suddenly, they would be ready to give warning.

49

When he reached a secure spot, he stopped and sent the knights to a position facing the city of Presa. A high mountain sheltered him to the right, the River Calinno ran impetuously to the left, and in the field opening to the rear he positioned his footmen: so all the surrounding countryside was safe and he was everywhere strongly protected.

50

Foodstuffs were brought here, tents raised, trenches dug; and so they settled in, for the king hoped to lure the Turk into an open battle in this area. Then he sent Ulysses across the river—for he was well acquainted with the roads and byways of the region—with an urgent message to Vran, telling him that the king had arrived and that he must stand ready to give support when necessary.

51

He now wanted Cosimo to take charge of his men. Cosimo alone was to be their captain, and together with Piero he was to go up the mountain and there keep an eye on faraway roadways. From the top of the plain, he was to send signs of any new movements he saw, thus leaving the Turk no chance to mount a surprise attack.

52

The area where the Albanians had stopped was a few miles nearer to Croia than it was to Presa. The Thracian wanted to know their intention: why they had stopped there and gone no further. Attravante took on himself the audacious task of scouting and satisfying the sultan's desire to know, and Tuvigon, a famous warrior, together with many of his Persian soldiers, set out on the road with him.

53

The guards that had been positioned on the mountaintop saw them and sent warning to the camp below. Vaconte galloped swiftly against the Turks to give them no opportunity to approach the camp, and Camillo and his men followed him. They did not come face to face with the enemy, however; they rather remained standing at the sides, because the reflections of the weaponry struck them in the eyes. Some placed their lances at rest, others gripped their swords ready to fight.

54

According to orders received, Vaconte held his men back because it was his intention to obey his king's wise decision. He saw that the pagans were not many, as he looked at them from a distance. Then, on purpose, he turned around and ran off with Camillo, both looking as if they were fleeing from a great danger. The other captains ran too, for they knew the plan, and after the officers the simple soldiers followed.

55

Salomon was standing in the middle of the road with his men ready to give support. Many of them were so near the Turks that it was too late for them to turn back. With no presentiment of his own destiny, Mario, a Roman warrior, brandishing a knotty pole, ran toward Tuvigon and hit him so hard that he seemed to be about to fall.

56

The big pole shattered, and the Persian, unhurt by the big blow, boiling with anger, ran forward and struck Mario on the head with such force that Mario fell, dying, between the legs of Tuvigon's horse. While the formidable Persian was turning his horse around unaware, Osmeno, a great warrior dear to Vaconte, struck him with a right-hand blow and believed he had slashed him across the back.

57

Although the blow was heavy, the Persian remained steady and strong, for his coat of mail was of adamantine resistance. Seeing that he was shedding no blood, Osmeno turned his back and ran away. But the Persian hit him in turn with such force that his soul was about ready to leave its sweet abode by many exits. He fell to the ground, and in his death rattle he drank his own blood with the dust that enveloped him.

58

Still the strength of the Latin warriors revived, although there was no captain to encourage them on, and several pagans stained the earth with the color of their blood. Finally the Christians turned their backs, the Persian squadron moved to pursue them, and Salomon created disturbances on their path. In the end the Persians withdrew, although they could have prevailed and seen their enemy run away.

59

With great self-confidence Attravante went back to Presa and related all to the Ottoman emperor: that on land the Italian valor was good for nothing, that he was furthermore convinced—he had had experience of it just now—that they would run away at the very start of military action. The emperor was happy to hear it and ordered his captains to get all their men ready for battle at sunrise.

60

Orkhan and other men of sound mind thought Attravante's opinion might be wrong and that rhetoric was oftentimes a persuasive means to raise expectations too high. They knew the truth; still they were afraid and kept quiet. The sun was not yet out of Thetis's lap, where it rests during the night[19] before mounting high in the sky, when all the captains very quietly led out the army and positioned it in the spacious plain.

61

The tyrant too came out on the field, and there he divided the army into three sections. The first one was made of the valorous contingent of the Persians, and their leader was Tornon. In the second section he placed Prince Artaban, Oleander, and the great Voivoide—to whom he gave the high command held by the fierce Driarasso before he was elected Agah.

62

He assigned the third section to Driarasso, for he was in command of the Janissaries, whose ferocious manner of fighting created a terror that spread among the enemies now as much as it had before. With him, and vying with him in intelligence and courage, he positioned Orkhan and his Spahìs, then Rainoldo with Elin, while Corcutte was the captain leading the Thracian army.

63

He placed Hannibal, who now headed the battalion that was before under Battor's command, with his own men, and next to him Giafier, who used to

19. For Thetis see canto 7.24 above and the glossary.

be in charge of Hamilcar's contingent. They were all assigned to the royal battalion, in the midst of which he himself was going to fight. He had great trust in their valor, for he saw their number still intact.

64

The army, thus displayed in three distinct positions, had taken the shape of a half-moon, empty in the middle, full all around, but not so pointed at the end of each horn. He placed the footmen between the horsemen, so that they would not be trampled should the knights turn on themselves, and out in front he positioned the elephants.

65

He placed the animals of greater size and power right up front facing the enemy, for he assumed that once positioned there, they would not turn back. Then he sent Arigazel with the Ethiopian king toward the mountain in order to strike the enemy from behind, because they were very skilled in turning around their horses while fighting and in striking and quickly withdrawing at the opportune moment.

66

Serpedon was captain of the Scythian warriors who were free of armor and wore a light protective garment. He had a double charge, for he led Brandovardo's contingent as well. The emperor ordered him to wade the Calinno River a first time and then once more, so as to attack the enemy from the rear with a sudden double maneuver.

67

Being emperor of many different countries, the sultan was accustomed to hear various tongues and manners of speech, and he had learned to speak many languages.[20] Upright on his horse, he went in person at a speedy gallop to exhort the troops to the fight, because he had no need of interpreters and wanted to be heard and understood clearly by all.

68

He rode quickly around the camp, stopping here and there, so that all foreigners might hear him; he made his clever speech in various tongues, appealing to the soldiers' sense of loyalty. He reminded the strong, the

20. Similarly in Livy 30.33.12, Hannibal exhorts the Carthaginians before battle mainly through interpreters, because his army includes many cultures and tongues; and so does Hannibal in *Africa* 7.1141–42.

courageous, and the ferocious ones of their points of strength and pride; he told the lowly soldiers how they could ennoble their lineage with valor, and the noble ones how to add luster to theirs.

69

He reminded the Persians of their allegiance to their king, of their honor, of the possible humiliation of their country, of the great reward they would receive from himself, a great emperor, and how loudly the fame of their deeds would resound in the world. He spoke of the valor by which several of them would make their poor families rich, for they would take home valuable spoils; the lean old days would come to an end and the discomforting hardships would be over forever.

70

Then suddenly the emperor paused, and putting on a very grave expression, he came to rest where he could best be heard by his soldiers. "My loyal men," he said to them, "today the great Prophet has answered your prayers. Complying with your insistent desire, he has, deservedly and with justice, furnished you with invincible swords; with them God wants to attain victory, for they are his, not yours, nor mine.

71

"Your wish was to be able to show our great Prophet that your valor is worthy of real praise, and that you are able to win courageously in the light of day, and that you are not made bold by darkness and deceit. This cowardly enemy, the one you are facing now, is capable of attaining victory only by deception, for he lacks courage; he hides behind ramparts, or in the mountains, and fights with the help of darkness and fire.

72

"The Christians have fought against you only when you did not expect to be attacked, under cover of night or, if during the day, making use of ambushes and other deceptions. But today, in the light of the sun, in the open field, where it will be easy to detect their deceits, who will surpass you in virtue, valor, and power, as well as in courage, determination, and bodily strength?[21]

---

21. The use of stratagems and subterfuges in war was the object of moral considerations. Botero justifies the use of deceptions in war and gives examples of ruses employed by Lysander the Spartan and by Hannibal the Carthaginian. *The Reason of State* 9.22.

73

"Even if all of them were perfect warriors and your equal in valor, still they do not dispose of more than two hands and more than one heart.[22] Even if they are courageous and strong, they have but one breast, while your number is by far superior to theirs and no fear can hide in your heart. They are a few, we are many. The only possible reason to doubt our victory might be

74

"the Italian soldiers who arrived not long ago. They have killed our valorous allies with artifice and deception; they have traded honor with poisonous monsters and with fiery weapons never seen before. But now we are on land and in a place clearly lit, where each soldier can show his real worth. Tuvigon and Attravante, as you know, have had the opportunity to test their valor here not long ago.

75

"Remember all those illustrious and glorious deeds of yours that I myself have witnessed, not just heard of. And you, my loyal and dear Janissaries— who are my power, the ones I have nourished, the equal of whom the heavens cannot see anywhere in their rounds from India to the African shores—show today that you are always equal to yourselves, for nothing new is asked of you, but only what you have been always and everywhere."

76

He ended his speech thus, hoping to bring about a fierce and unexpected assault on the enemies and throw them into a rout. But the king was happy to hear the news, for he had already received many warnings from the camp above that the great Thracian was about to give battle. And as his troops were always ready, and there were few of them, while the sky was still dark and the Turks far away, he began to march out his army at an easy pace.

22. A similar image is used to describe the army's strength in canto 10.53 above.

CANTO 22

The big frontal battle begins. The elephants go on the attack, but soon, frightened, they turn around, causing great damage to their own side. One huge elephant, however, is wreaking havoc among the Christians. Silveria volunteers to kill the animal but is crushed to death when the elephant collapses over her.

1

A light breeze murmured among the leaves and branches, the valleys sent back the echo, and the birds alternated the murmur with sweet sounds. The dew and the luminous rays of Dawn were spreading out of the eastern balcony, and her blond white treasure dabbed the grass with silver, the sea with gold.

2

In the early light, when all the troops were out in the open plain, the king ordered them into ranks, and because he knew that the Persians and the Scythians were accustomed to fight turning about, he divided them into six squadrons, positioning them toward the mountain and toward the river, and for the Latin and the Greek knights[1] he selected a location near them.

3

In order to protect the fighting army all around, he wanted the Italians on the left, with Borso in command. On the right he placed the Albanians, including his nephew. The former were to reach as far as the mountain, and the latter were to spread out as far as the river. In the middle he arranged

---

1. "Latin" stands for Italian, "Greek" for Albanian. This is because, with the division of the Roman Empire by Emperor Constantine, Epirus became a region of the eastern section, which was henceforth called the Greek Byzantine Empire.

the foot soldiers in a formation shaped like a square and larger than any other.

4

He then allocated Rosmonda to a spot where she could provide support to her husband, assigned Arioden to a squadron of cavalrymen as an added reinforcement, and Marcello to some other group. Behind the foot soldiers was still another strong platoon, and Rodoman was made their captain. He then ordered all of them to move in square formation so as to be able to give battle on four sides.[2]

5

Surrounded by the corps of Adventurers—each one of them chosen from among the best in the army—the king advanced mounted on a high steed, his head and chest protected by impenetrable steel armor. He rode to all sections of the army with his face uncovered, his regal countenance giving an impression of dignity and honor, inspiring glorious virtue and sweet affection, and compelling all souls to respect and love.

6

The people of ancient times fooled themselves if they thought that Mars rode like this, for certainly he did not do it in such a martial manner. When he reached a spot in the vast plain where the number of soldiers arranged in files was greater, the king stopped. His voice then rose, and sounding divine rather than human, he began to encourage them to fight: his eyes shone, his whole appearance was more impressive than ever.

7

"Brave warriors, whose valor I have seen victorious and unsurpassed in all campaigns, the time has now come to earn, through effort and danger, great glory in heaven and great honor on earth: let that be for the glory of Christ! Now the time has come to acquire fame and greater spoils, in the certainty of fighting face to face with a people not as strong as you.

8

"These are the same people, the same Turks that you have routed and beaten so often. When you fought wars at their side, your valor was well

2. Preliminaries of battle with detailed disposition of troops are commonly described in poems as well as in histories: see, for instance, Livy 30.32–33 and *Africa* 7.987–98, 7.1111–38, both for the battle of Zama.

known, but when you turned your arms against them, your name became even more famous while theirs fell into obscurity, because without you that strength, which only you gave them, failed.

9

"Likewise, that very Turk, who remained undefeated and victorious when he was with me, that same Turk is now broken and defeated because I no longer fight for him. I do not make heedless claims, I do not appeal to people who might perchance have seen what I describe. I call on you as my witnesses, on your very selves. When we were fighting in the enemy army, I was not only a friend but a son and a father to you.

10

"Do not let their number dismay you, for they are very diverse and confused. Be reminded of Lucullus and Tigranes, and of those few Greeks who once fought against so many Persians.[3] And remember how many were killed a while ago by our allies, how many you have routed and disbanded. As cowardly as they are, they will not look into your faces, they will not return your glances.

11

"Neither the presence of their lord among them, nor his obdurate resolve, will save the empire, that is certain; for he himself will be the first to flee, solicitous of his realm and his life. And then will any strong warriors be left in the field? Soldiers often imitate their captain, and a single coward running away has often brought fear to a large number of strong men.

12

"I, on the other hand, shall remain with you in all turns of fortune; I shall change neither heart, nor face, nor place; I shall be undaunted by danger and death. Minister of your good fortune and caring little or not at all about mine, I shall expose my chest naked to weapons and fire. Today, my warriors, you shall acquire spoils and trophies greater than anyone in the world has ever captured in the past.

13

"All the gold and the gems that the vast rich eastern countries ever produced, all that the great emperor ever took from a thousand great kings and

3. Tigranes was the king of Armenia who was defeated by the Roman general Lucullus in 69 BCE. The Greeks fought against the Persians when Xerxes, king of Persia, invaded Greece, c. 480 BCE.

in a thousand campaigns, all that bounty God in heaven has reserved for you, entirely for you. God has always bestowed his protection on you, by whose hands he has already planned to punish those who rebel against him.

14

"May Calinno, more than any other river, carry in its noisy way the fame of this day, a day memorable more than any other. May it spread the news with its everlasting sound, with its indefatigable motion. Now look at the sun rising, adorned with rays; see how unusually luminous is its golden mane. This is a presage that the memory of our victory will shine as splendidly as the sun itself.

15

"So my valorous soldiers, go, all of you, to certain glory and high rewards, strike your lances and swords tirelessly over the enemies of our holy faith. You are delayed and held back now only by me, I know.[4] There you can already see the enemy army! Here I can see your unsurpassed valor shine forth from your eyes!"

16

At this point he stood in silence. Then he rode to all sections of the army, one by one, stopping wherever he considered it expedient. He spurred on the courageous and encouraged the fearful, arousing their most dormant feelings. Like a great storm blowing over the grass and beating down the harvest, his wise speech either lessened fear or drove it from the soldiers' hearts.

17

Then, turning to the select soldiers that accompanied him everywhere, he said: "May my choice of you give me a fame as worthy of boasting and as becoming of your high valor as you can make it." And looking up at the sky and arming himself with the holy and revered sign, he made a cross over his forehead and breast: "May this sign be a shield against the enemy squadrons: to the omnipotent Father, to the Son, and to the Holy Ghost."

18

He prayed. Then he saw a multitude of armed men move forward in waves all around the plain. Immediately he turned to one of his men and asked

---

4. "Ah, you want to get at the enemy and I detain you with my speeches!" says Caesar rallying his troops on the fields of Pharsalus. Lucan, *Civil War* 7.295–96.

for Tanugio, a captain and an old assistant of much bravery, perhaps of more intelligence than strength; and to him he assigned the task of confronting the elephants that were now coming forward in front of the foot soldiers.

19

In addition to wild boars and incendiary torches, which he had already prepared, he wanted him to bring long and sharp iron pikes with which to goad the beasts and prick them in the eyes and on the flanks. By now the Persian swords were throwing out lightning and thunder; between the two armies the space narrowed, and the ranks of the Christian footmen could see at close quarters the positions assigned to the opposite ranks.[5]

20

The armor and clothes of the Italian warriors filled the Persians with wonder. They looked astonished at the great crests rising over the helmets, at the enamel decorated in different colors and reflecting the light from helmets and shields. They marveled at the shining horses, protected by steel just like the men who rode them, at the different types of plumage rising from their heads and fluttering in the sun.

21

They looked at the various emblems, decorations, and surcoats, stupendous in their highly artistic decorations, at the unfurled flags that seemed to wave like the sea, but above all, at the great royal two-headed eagle, red in a field of gold, which seemed a portent of blood and dominance over the silver moon of hostile Thrace.[6]

22

As the sun rose from the horizon, sending its rays over the army, you might have thought that several suns were rising together from the side of the mountain and from the side of the river, because many reflections were flashed by the steel, the silver, and the gold. When the two armies were near enough for each to be heard by the other, the pagans sounded their clamorous and husky instruments to intimidate the enemy.

---

5. The detail of the narrow space remaining between the two armies just before they clash is found in *Civil War* 7.461–64.

6. These are the Castrioti banner and the Ottoman flag, respectively. With respect to the former, Sarrocchi has substituted gold for red and red for black. Cf. canto 10.21 above.

23

The riverbanks and the mountain peaks reverberated with the sound of timpani and kettledrums.[7] The Christians responded immediately with their own trumpets and played so skillfully that they overpowered with their merry sound the noise of the men shouting and of the horses neighing. With their bellicose sound, the instruments lifted all their spirits and sent joy and merriment from ear to heart.

24

As soon as the sound was heard, consternation went through the heart of every barbarian soldier. Now, many men were bending the strings of their bows; with their slings some hurled stones; others waited for the enemy with swords lifted; others lowered the points of their pikes; still others couched their lances and sat tight on horseback: everyone in various ferocious attitudes made ready for battle.

25

As flashes of lightning are often seen to open their way through dense clouds and fall precipitously to earth, in the same way all these arrows could be seen flying through the air on their way to strike one and the other side. In the same way the man who tilled the soil at Alba saw a frightening shower of stones rain from the sky, killing not only lambs, bulls, and oxen, but also peasants and shepherds.[8]

26

If at the first assault deadly blows were struck from afar on both sides, what can we say the second, more impetuous and ferocious encounter was like, when many powerful spears were shattered into hundreds of pieces? Some men were lying on the ground pierced through and slain; others were unharmed, but barely able to stand; others could be seen dragged around by their horses, for they could not free their foot from the stirrup.

27

The Persian soldiers could not resist the hostile impact as much as their enemies did, because they were not protected by armor and because they

7. Nearby hills and valleys echo the sounds of armies colliding, and the din of battle reverberates in the sky: *Iliad* 21.9–11; *Aeneid* 12.722, 12.724, and 12.757.

8. Tullus Hostilius, the third king of Rome, destroyed Alba Longa and had it plowed under. According to legend, he died (about 640 BCE) when the gods, angered by his cruel behavior, showered stones on him. Livy 1.29. 5.

were mounted on less powerful horses, and so they were overpowered, killed, and thrown to the ground by their opponents who wore armor. When the lances were broken, both sides drew out different weapons for fighting, and different and terrifying ways of killing could be seen on both sides, and with comparable results.

28

The heavy sledgehammers killed by crushing; the short and curved scimitars could often cut shields and breastplates crosswise and inflict deep wounds on men. Some were at the same time hit and cut up by battleaxes; others received heavy blows from hammers; others, slashed in half by swords, collapsed to the ground; still others were run through by rapiers and spears.

29

Who could describe and adequately extol the merits of the great Latin valor? Rome could not more greatly praise Caesar in Thessaly, Claudius at Urbino, or Scipio at Carthage,[9] either for the majesty of their horses or for the strength and beauty of their helmets and coats of mail shining with gold. Borso flashed a glowing light from his eyes that could be seen coming through the visor.

30

He threw over Olin, slashing his head in half, and then Rutan, struck where the neck joins the bust, and Rigaffan, who was running daringly toward him with much impetus and vigor, though advanced in age. He wounded him on the thigh with such a backhanded blow that he, a good and just man in his religion, would go back home safe and sound and would be looked on by those people as a miracle of Allah.

31

Whoever was struck first, died first, for no one could last long battling with him. No iron shield could resist him, no double plate, not even the strongest mail ever made. It was not the single soldier alone who ran away from Borso's right hand, it was the whole great army that fled, rank by rank, as when grain is threshed in the farmyard in the warm days of summer and the wind spreads the dry chaff around.

9. This is a reference to the decisive battle between Caesar and Pompey at Pharsalus (Thessaly) in 48 BCE; to the victory of the general Claudius Nero over Hasdrubal at the Metauro River, near Urbino (Italy), in 207 BCE; and to Scipio Africanus's rout of Hannibal's army, at Zama near Carthage (North Africa), in 202 BCE.

32

When Feranec, who was fighting nearby, saw his standard turning around in flight, he began to menace and hit a soldier here, reproach another one there, while running into the thickest entanglement of warriors. Borso measured his time to strike him and caught him full on the face with the flat of the sword. Collapsing under the blow, the man hit the rump of his horse; the animal kicked back and bounced him far off.

33

It often happens on a beach that a whistling blast of wind swirls the light sand round and round, and the sand that has just been moved is quickly replaced by some new sand. In the same way, the man had hardly been thrown off his mount when a whole heap of horses, warriors, and arms crashed on him, and he remained on the ground buried under that heavy weight, killed in war without being slain by a weapon.

34

The helmet was not yet excessively heavy over Cromio's white hair, for he was still robust and bold. He carried a long shield in the shape of a half circle and mounted a frisky Numidian charger. The shield covered him completely; he rode his horse with agility and speed. While he was harassing all and no one could hold him back, Pompiglio saw him and stopped almost in spite of himself.

35

He struck him with a quick downward blow on the head, and then he made a deep cut on his chest, first lowering then raising his hand so rapidly that both moves had their effect. The sword was powerful; it pierced and cut but came out clean and shiny, and the African escaped all further blows by shifting and by protecting himself with his shield.

36

Now Cromio circled the good Latin, struck and feigned to strike, withdrew to duck, hit him and then swung out in a large circle, so that a certain distance always remained between the two. The Roman was vexed, and since he could not catch the rider, he decided to aim at the horse; and after a thousand attempts, he hit the animal on the sinewy spot in the middle of the mane.

37

Feeling great pain in the muscles and in the nerves where life was flowing, the charger reared and pawed in the air with his hoofs, with teeth ready to bite. The animal shook his back furiously because the reins, rubbing over the wound, exacerbated it further; so the Saracen dismounted, but as soon as he touched ground the Roman threw him over, and once he was lying down, his own horse trampled over his chest.

38

Vaconte was not too far away. His troops were waiting impatiently for him to give the sign of battle. They were all shouting, boasting that they were going to rout the Muslims, throw down their flags, raise the great holy ensign of Christ, and slaughter all God's rebels in a way that would not leave any remembrance of their names in the world.

39

But face to face against Vaconte now advanced Oleander, Artaban, and Carmentel. A shower of stones and arrows rained down in circling waves, slaying this group of men and the other. Once the lances were broken in the second assault, they began to fight at close quarters in single combat, colliding against each other with shields, helmets, swords, and arms— breast to breast, face to face.

40

If one of them displayed greater courage, the resolution and determination of the others grew. Any offending blow aggravated anger and furor, and the furor in turn increased wrath and fury. So you might say that the sun did not see anyone equal or superior to these fighting men, but weapons cut down their number and power, so that in the end courage began to struggle against fear.

41

As crops in a field are lashed down by Boreas and begin to sway this way and that like sea waves, so these armies could be seen to win ground on one side and lose it on the other. Then, in the place where some troops retreated and gave way, others resisted, still others went forward, shoved, increased the impetus and the uproar, struck, and forced their enemy to strike.

42

It seems that against the furor and unleashed madness cruelty raged all over most violently. Oleander swirled around an iron sledgehammer with both hands, for he did not think it sufficient to handle a sword. No shield, no cuirass, no helmet or plate was safe, for all fell to the ground in many pieces. Vaconte saw him, admired his great fury, and although enraged, remained almost in adoring awe of him.

43

Seeing that the more he lingered, the greater became the number of casualties among his fighting men, Vaconte moved forward to meet Oleander, necessarily stepping on the numberless bodies that lay on the ground. That fierce warrior went into a rage, for he could hardly stand that any mortal man should dare to face him alone. He began to lift his sledgehammer to strike a downward blow: Vaconte's thin sharp sword met it in midair.

44

Oleander could not lift his hammer any further, for Vaconte had stopped it as it was beginning to strike, and his sword had fallen on the hammer with such force as to cut clearly through where it struck. At that moment an unusual sound was heard by both of them; they turned, the fierce pagan looking astonished and still holding in his hand the weapon broken in half.

45

Vaconte was of such gallant prowess that now, seeing his enemy unarmed, he refrained from striking again, almost as if he were concerned about him. Then he saw that Comin had been made a prisoner. He saw him without a sword in hand and without a helmet on his head. Several people were on either side, in front, behind; they were poking him with their lances, while he was not trying to strike anyone. These men were all under the lead of Oleander, who was the captain-in-chief of many other captains.

46

That mixed group of fiendish soldiers had captured him after his horse collapsed, unsaddling him. Now they took him away, for the emperor had given orders to take prisoners, because he wanted to capture Rosmonda alive, and even more because he had heard that the Italian contingent was rich in all kinds of treasure, and he planned to get a handsome ransom from Rome and other cities.

47

All these soldiers, therefore, were keen on their great prey, and each one was claiming him as his prisoner. They had come to the point of trading insults and were about to fight over him when one Aegisthus came up before them and said: "Friends, let us get rid of the cause that makes us quarrel!" As he spoke, being a brutal man, he stabbed the youth most viciously in the chest.

48

Like a red flower trampled over by a wheel or damaged by the heat of a summer day, the young man fell dying to the ground, already covered by a mortal pallor and with an expression so appealingly woeful as to move even the angered heart of these barbarians, who were his enemies. All of them raised an indignant voice at that villainous man, calling his misdeed ferocious and barbaric.[10]

49

Merit, sense of duty, love, piety, and disdain all were found in Vaconte. They caused so much chagrin in him that he now considered it unworthy of a knight to hold his own safety dearer than revenge. The strongest and rarest steel would have been a weak obstacle to his anger, and Aegisthus had no armor, so what was there to restrain him? Vaconte cut him in half, from the head all the way down to his kidneys.

50

Then he went on against Alen, who was nearby and wore nothing on his head, while his breast was also naked and unarmed. Vaconte hit him with a forward thrust so powerful as to drive pieces of his big shield inside his chest. But here came Musaka, Comin's brother, who had heard the cruel and tragic case. He did not wish to outlive his great grief; he wanted to die, not just take revenge.

51

Meanwhile Oleander, who suddenly found himself deprived of a fight, turned around to retaliate for the loss of his sledgehammer and the presumptuous impudence of the man who had dared attack him. Striking with his sword repeatedly, he sliced legs, heads, hands, arms, and shoulders, opening up a bloody path before him, and all the while he looked for the knight and called to him in a high voice.

---

10. A situation comparable to this one develops in *Orlando Furioso* 19.13–14. There Zerbin is angered by the cowardly act of one of his men who has just wounded Medoro in the chest. A soldier felled by the enemy and compared to a flower cut by the plow or by a storm is found in *Orlando Furioso* 18.153. Ariosto's model is in Virgil's *Aeneid* 9. 435–37 and in Ovid's story of Hyacinthus in *Metamorphoses* 10.190–95. Cf. stanza 60 below.

52

At that slaughter, at that shouting, Virginio, who was not far away, turned his eyes in anger, lifted his sword, and struck a big blow on his shield, breaking it in half. This made the pagan angrier than before, for he thought a great deal of his shield, which was round and made of a triple layer of bone, leather, and steel. With his heart brimming with rage at that offense, Oleander plunged toward the opponent with a strong downward blow and

53

in return hit the warrior in the chest. The adamantine hauberk, however, protected Virginio, and the blow did not reach his body, while he managed to hit the other on the right shoulder with a powerful downstroke. All the men around them had turned to look at that valiant contest, when a blow caught the pagan with full force and his hand could barely hold onto the sword.

54

Now that he could no longer defend himself with his shield, he hurled the half still left to him against Virginio's visor with the left hand that was still undamaged. The impact opened the visor, leaving his face exposed, and almost killed him. More than once Virginio seemed to be about to fall over, but then a superhuman effort steadied him in the saddle.

55

Oleander's right hand was no longer functioning, while Virginio's horse was still in perfect order. Several Christians arrived to aid him and surrounded the Saracen in a tight circle. Virginio, as soon as his energy revived, felt his heart burning with shame and anger: so he confronted the pagan and after a long and dangerous fight managed to finish him off.

56

He then cut Smirin in that part of the neck where nature makes the voice stronger, so that he was denied, while being killed, the usual comforting relief that comes with moaning, no matter how briefly. On the other hand, Criton shouted and yelled, for an arrow had flown into his chest and another had run into his back, inflicting a second corresponding wound and closing the exit to the blood.

57

The metal of one arrow had run up against the other, and the power of one had blunted the power of the other. For a while his blood did not know by which wound to come out; then it began to gurgle out of both in great abundance, while an icy cold spread over the dying body and his soul divided in half and came out on both sides.[11]

58

Meanwhile Musaka was crying that he wanted to die like his brother, so distraught with grief was he. He killed one and then another man, all the while complaining that he happened to encounter only men who could be easily overpowered by his strong arm. But soon some among the best enemy captains formed a tight and dangerous circle around him; even so, still intent on revenge, he pierced Michael through the heart, unsaddling him.

59

Michael had been caught by surprise by Musaka's powerful blow, for he was a warrior of uncommon strength, but at that moment he had his eyes fixed on Marcello, who was coming forward wounding everyone around him. Michael was struck on the face and on the side of his body; he seemed to have rapidly lost all his strength, and soon he died. Carmentel, the first to become aware of this, ran to his side and killed his killer.

60

Carmentel smashed Musaka's adamantine helmet and with it the bony box that contained the brain. The young man bent his head toward one shoulder with the same wilting movement that a poppy full of seed makes keeling over its stem when hit by a rainstorm.[12] Rosmonda looked at him and hurriedly came to vindicate his death, for it was too late to help.

61

She hit the young man's killer with a powerful blow and hurled him dead to the ground. Such was her speed that Carmentel's hands could not react; even his eyes could not see, and he fell down almost at the same time as the man he had killed. Many men who had been intrepid up to that moment were struck with amazement and fear as soon as they witnessed that blow and ran away; but the Christians gave them no chance to flee and soaked the ground with their blood.

11. Criton's death is a variation of what happens to Catus, the soldier who is pierced in the back and in the breast at the same time. As the two weapons meet in his body, the blood does not know at first which cut to flow out of, but then its force casts both javelins out, thus letting Catus die of two wounds. Lucan, *Civil War* 3.585–91.

12. Cf. above, canto 22.48n.

62

On the Christian side all field captains had been warned by the king that as soon as the Persian leader came on the attack with the ferocious towering beasts, they must regroup all the soldiers in long rows facing one another and at such intervals as to leave enough space between them for the elephants to advance with ease.

63

So now that the fierce tyrant of the Thracian people had ordered the big beasts moved forward, the Christian ranks quickly opened up and disposed themselves in many rows facing one another. They stood in such order so as to allow the animals to enter and go by for some distance: similarly the lawns of a beautiful garden are arranged to allow easy paths in their midst.

64

In order to make use of many elephants, the Persians had gathered some from the swampy lowlands and some from the mountains. The former were as stupid and beastly as the latter were intelligent and obedient; the first as fond of food and rest as the second of glory and illustrious deeds. There were some intelligent and docile animals to be found in the countryside too, but they had far less strength and endurance.

65

Their clever tamer had tied some very sharp swords to the trunks of the strong and intelligent elephants, and the animals, just as if they had human minds, turned and pushed the weapons forward to hit and slash, so that many warriors among the most powerful and famous were cut up and killed. Furthermore, all the elephants carried turrets on their backs full of warriors and weapons.

66

The men who were up there hurled down lances, spears, arrows, and stones, which could kill with great ease because they were thrown from a height onto soldiers below who were crowded together. The Christian king placed himself in front to sustain and drive back that first attack; he commanded and disposed, ordered and executed as fitting the place, the time, the need.

67

A thousand hands could be seen all together throwing lances, a thousand more throwing pointed spears against the sides of the elephants and on their big heads, and a thousand lively flames flashed, for the provident man had distributed them all around, to be ready when needed. At the same time one could see the natural enemies of the elephant advance: they were the wild boars grunting and grinding their teeth.

68

The elephants then began to trumpet, and their sound made the countryside echo and reverberate. Never had Boreas hissed and screeched this way, when trapped in a forest; never had an iron ball, when hurled from a mortar, thundered this way through the air;[13] and never had the sea churned and bellowed so, when struck by contrary winds at the same time.

69

The animals holding the swinging swords with their trunks whirled around with a fury that surpassed all imagination, and all the horses and horsemen caught by them were trampled to death. Still the ruse of opening some paths in front of them reduced their ability to hurt. Even so, many of the soldiers who had first confronted those horrible beasts perished.[14]

70

The men who could wave the torches around now moved more securely, so great was the terror that the fire struck in the wild beasts when it appeared before their eyes unexpectedly. Who could deny the enormous power of nature or the influence of the celestial spheres? One single grunt, one small flame could overcome the courage of those animals who were so undaunted in the face of death.

71

As the inner faculties of the animals were in commotion, their large limbs began to tremble, and the chambers in the towers above shuddered and shook with a frightful noise. At the strong motion of men and weapons inside, the joints of the turrets started to open, not only at the base and around the sides but also on top, thus revealing their most hidden and enclosed spaces.

13. The comparison with a mortar, the use of which is projected into the future and not present in the story, is suggested by a similar one in *Orlando Furioso* 16.27 (see also here at canto 14.86). Rodomonte in Paris makes walls fall down with a crash greater than any that will be produced by the mortars at the siege of Padua in 1509. For the use of guns in this and in other sixteenth-century sieges, see Hale, *War and Society*, 216. See also above, canto 14.86n.

14. At the battle of Zama, to avoid being trampled by the elephants, the Romans sprang back to make way for them and then counterattacked with javelins and flaming torches. Livy 30.33.12–16. See also the elephant stampede at Zama in *Africa* 7.1216–25.

72

A thick shower of darts, pikes, and heavy stones began to come down, for all the men above, persuaded that the turret would not stand the furious assault, were determined to make the enemy pay for it. And then, finally, with their flanks stabbed by sharp spears, harassed by the fierce sound of the boars, frightened by the flaming torches waving before their eyes, the elephants began to turn back.

73

With this the Persians began to encounter their worst defeat, a fatal ruin without repair, for those beasts that had not turned their backs to flee, the ones that courage held fast in their places, could now be easily approached. Now that the beasts were paralyzed by terror, the Christian soldiers started quickly to cut off their feet with scimitars and battleaxes.

74

Every time one of those heavy animals fell down, all the mountains around trembled, all the valleys seemed to bellow ominously, because the tower also fell. And the beasts, which had turned their backs to run away, brought unexpected damage to their own side. With their swords they opened a bloody path before them; they bumped footmen and mounted warriors and threw them to the ground; and with their trunks they sent them flying.

75

The good tamer very quickly managed to stop more than one beast, for he was there for that purpose, ready to beat them on the head with a hard blow of a sharp pike; he thus saved many men with the loss of a few animals. Even so, a horrendously deadly disaster and some terrifying scenes unfolded, when several towers fell to the ground and many Persian soldiers died.

76

Over here a turret leaned on one side and kept going down, while another that was swaying menacingly before suddenly steadied itself. Over there one that showed signs of coming down very slowly collapsed faster than the others. The people enclosed within moved away from the side toward which the turret was pitching, ran to the opposite side, and tried with their chests and strong firm hands to press, push, counterbalance, and steady the structure.

77

Some warriors scrambled out to safety and held on fast to several towers already fallen to the ground, but then other towers came tumbling down on top of the first, and the wretched men were crushed in between. Some had jumped earlier from up above, only to be smashed by their own turret falling after them.

78

Some men were quick to jump out first; others, also trying to escape, threw themselves out soon after without waiting; still others jumped on top of these, so the ones smashed the others. The soldiers who hung from the tottering towers on the outside were pierced by spears or by well-aimed darts and remained affixed to the wooden structures: an unusual and pitiful spectacle to behold!

79

Amer too resolved to escape in this manner and threw himself down from his tower, but he jumped such a short distance that he fell over the elephant's head. The beast, incensed, flung him into the air so amazingly high that not even a bird could fly so far. On the way down he caught the Roman Fulvio on the back of the neck and instantly snuffed the daylight out of him.

80

He survived the fall, however, landing on the enemy side safe and sound. He felt beaten and broken all over his body, but his spirits remained undaunted and his will supreme. As soon as his strength revived he rose quickly and, brandishing a sword, handled it so cautiously and adroitly that he opened a way through the enemy and withdrew safely to his side.

81

The most valiant warrior of them all was the Christian king, for he spread terror in the Persian army. A huge tower tottered about, still sustained by the strength of a thousand hands: when the powerful arm of the king threw a sharp knotty lance against it, the massive, thundering weapon cleaved the air, then drove into the tower with great impact, and remained there quivering.

82

Soon, under that force that exceeded all forces, the tower crashed swiftly and relentlessly to the ground, like a poor hut struck by lightning. The

Persians tried in vain to hold it up. Several of their soldiers bent their bows and aimed their catapults at him; several pressed on with sword in hand or tried to strike and cut him down with their lances. He was never reached, did not feel or take notice of the blows, almost as if he were a celestial being, not a mortal man.

83

Tuvigon, reduced to the last resort, hoped to find safety in height, for he was riding on the back of a fierce elephant that had no equal in size. In his resplendent steel armor he glittered like the sun; the air itself was in awe of him. With his robust arm he held his lance aloft, and then he hurled it down with a tremendous throw.

84

Noticing that Tuvigon was entering the thick of the melee, the hero threw a heavy lance at him, but he found it quite impossible to reach him. As soon as he saw the king's lance coming, the man pulled out his sword and knocked it down. Then with his left hand he took up his own lance, but courage did not fail the good king.

85

He circled him without using his sword and tried with great care to pull him to the ground with his spear; but now unavoidably, while the man's hand was quick to follow his mind, the elephant was slow to move. And so as Tuvigon drove the beast forward and then attempted to turn it around quickly, he fell headlong to the ground, and there the beast trampled the rider to death, a man who had been robust and vigorous.

86

Now the animal was free, without a weight and without a rider, and nobody could hold back his defiant fury. Torches advanced against him unavailingly; the boars could not frighten him. Several Christians hit the hard skin with spears and lances, but in vain. The animal crashed through the rows of men crosswise and opened his way through them, bumping, lifting them up, and throwing everyone over.

87

The beautiful woman archer was looking attentively at the belligerent beast. When she saw that no one had the courage to go near, a valiant anger filled her heart; so politely she asked the warrior princess to let her go alone on that dangerous errand, for she was used to killing such animals and had come across many of them on the mountains and in the forests.[15]

88

Rosmonda did not at all like letting her go alone on such a mission and had some misgivings about her safety, for nothing seemed to resist the beast's violence; but realizing how critical the situation was, she let her have the honor of such a splendid challenge, for she was partly reassured by the young woman's past manner of life and her expertise in hunting.

89

Over her fine silvery cuirass Silveria was wearing a vest decorated with an artful work of gold embroidery and with beautiful gems the likes of which neither the Indus nor the Tagus had ever produced.[16] On her head she wore a strong and superb helmet—a rich and beautiful gift from her queen—and a short dagger at one side; her arms were free of all weapons, except for bow and arrows.

90

Her face was bare, and a shimmering splendor radiated from her luminous eyes; for now they shone more and revealed her combative spirit more fearlessly than ever. The helmet could not hide her hair completely; some strands blew charmingly in the wind, others fell down in light waves over her forehead, like a golden frame encasing a diamond.

91

Her hand, which was armed, vowed war; her beautiful eyes promised peace. The dense crowd now gave way, opening a passage to her as she desired. This test of valor pleased the king, because it pleased and delighted Rosmonda; and so he refrained from hurting the elephant and moved to where the Turks offered most resistance.

92

Now that they had to look out for their own safety, the Persian soldiers were routed and reduced to so helpless a state as to be no longer danger-

---

15. In the *Aeneid* 11.498–830, the Volscian woman warrior, Camilla, offers to confront the enemy cavalry at close quarters; after many forays against the enemy, she is pierced through by an arrow shot by the Trojan Arruns, as her Volscian troops to a man stare at her in alarm.

16. The Indus and Tagus (today Tajo) Rivers stand metonymically for India and Spain.

ous. The king, surrounded by his men, caused fierce and horrible damage in the enemy ranks. In the meantime, Silveria released her bow; the dart flew rapidly through the air and brought a partial night on the huge elephant, for it struck its right eye and blinded it.

93

An intense pain made the animal shake and thrash, and his trumpeting resounded against the mountains and in the plain. Then he began to run toward the side where the hostile hand had thrown the arrow. When the beast saw the woman, it started charging, but it was still far away. For her part the young woman, being of valiant heart, considered it cowardly to take protection against the oncoming danger.

94

So she decided to renew the attack close by, and setting aside the bow, she made ready to strike the animal with another weapon. She seemed to have taken on wings as she dodged the beast, which was now lowering its trunk toward her; then, before it could reach her, she, being alert to it, ran nimbly under it, escaping in time. You might have thought she was in total control of timing and of motion.

95

Now that she had managed to get where she wanted and considered herself out of danger, she was careful to direct her next blow exactly where the animal's skin was softest. There, at the end of the ribs, she plunged her dagger into the heart and wounded it. The animal shrieked and fell, and as it fell, it crushed the unfortunate woman's limbs and together they died.

96

She had full confidence that after striking the deadly blow, she would be able to escape easily and swiftly from under the huge animal, as she had always done before. But she stumbled over a big stone lying on the ground and hurt her delicate foot: so she remained squashed from the stomach down to her feet, while the rest of her body lay languishing supine in the open.

97

As she fell, a confused sound of many murmuring voices was heard to rise. The royal damsel, her face tinged by pity, descended from her horse and gave orders to raise the dead elephant from the body. Then, loosening the cuirass on Silveria's chest, and pulling the helmet off her golden hair, she called her name repeatedly.

98

"Silveria, my Silveria," she repeated, "how cruel is the destiny that now separates and tears us apart! What grievous sin of mine now prevents me from accompanying you to heaven, for you are going there for sure!" Saying these words, Rosmonda dampened the young woman's face and breasts with the tears that now flowed abundantly from her eyes, and she became so oppressed by grief that she could no longer speak, but only cry.

99

With this rain of love falling over her, the gentle archer seemed to revive: she lifted her hand, opened her beautiful eyes, and murmured something, I do not know what, something that could not be heard. Then her hand fell; she was silent and could only keep her eyes fixed on her who could read in them "O my empress, your servant does not forget you even while dying."[17]

100

A dark cloud took the sun away from Silveria's fine eyes, and a white pallor spread over her beautiful face, as sometimes lilies and violets fade when they are cut,[18] or as a hyacinth begins to languish slowly when picked by a virgin's hand. Her beautiful alluring color did not disappear, for now death, having become a killer of gods, was triumphant and smiled on her face.

17. At the point of death Camilla too turns to a woman friend with a message and a last farewell. *Aeneid* 11.820–24.

18. When Clorinda dies, "a lovely pallor spreads over her face, like violets mingled with lilies." *Jerusalem Delivered* 12.69.1–2.

CANTO 23

The battle continues until it becomes clear that the Albanians and their allies are winning. The sultan, aggrieved by the turn of events, loses consciousness and is carried away from the battlefield. Soon after, he dies.

1

Fully engaged in battle was also the squadron of Christians who had taken position on the mountaintop. The king did not send anyone else up there, thinking there was no longer need. Those soldiers had walked across the mountain to the side the Turks were likely to climb, had obstructed the path with tree trunks, dug a trench, and taken shelter in it.

2

Sinolfo and Arigazel found that they were not able to cross to the other side because the entrenchment was much better defended than they had expected; but neither they nor their soldiers were at all dismayed. For their part, the Christian men, exhibiting the same daring and armed with better weapons, resisted them, for they were positioned in a very good spot and were arranged so skillfully as to be able to keep the enemy at bay by shoving them back and throwing them down.

3

Here as much as elsewhere the terrible fight went on, its fury, killing, and slaughter ever increasing. The ground was strewn with weapons, truncated heads, arms and hands, and blood mixed with dust. Often, falling down, a man brought down the enemy with him, and in this manner the killer too lost his life. Several men, hit by the enemy, dragged down with them the friends to whom they were clinging for safety.

4

In the midst of all this, Ridolfo went out on the path; he wanted to catch Arigazel by surprise and confront him at close quarters. The man had neither armor plate nor mail; but though not powerfully armed, he was agile and fast. The Turk stepped back in time, bent his bow, and sent a deadly arrow through Ridolfo's heart. With both breath and soul failing, Ridolfo fell to the ground deadly pale.

5

As that great warrior died, so died hope for the Christians: they looked at him and lost heart. The more fearful they became and the more they withdrew, the more daringly the pagans came forward, trying to jump together over the obstacles gathered to impede their advance. Then, after the death of that first captain, Cosimo too was hit by a fierce blow on the helmet.

6

A round heavy stone had caught him right on the forehead where the skull is hardest. He did not die but fell shaking to the ground, while a dismally dark cloud suddenly obscured his eyesight. Made more audacious and freer than before, the pagans tried to use their brains in addition to their strength, and with two-edged axes and other heavy objects they began to smash the interposed beams.

7

The strongest among them were chosen to do it, and they were soon poised to carry out the order. Around them, however, there was such a thick crowd that they found it impossible even to raise their arms. When they saw that their work was impeded, they began to shout to the others—for they wanted to be heard by everyone—to clear out and step back; they did not realize that by shouting they frightened the soldiers.

8

As they kept repeating with stentorian voices for all to withdraw, the soldiers heard the noise and believed that a great number of fresh reinforcements had arrived to give support to the Christians. They turned their backs and started running as fast as they could, as if they could see no other escape from death. At that moment, the wise Cosimo, now aware of their mistake, rose from the ground.

9

Although stunned and still giddy from the horrible blow he had received, he rose and, convinced he could now win, ran quickly in pursuit of them with his men. So much good and so much bad had come from that deceptive shout, indeed, from one single mistaken voice. Fortune has great power on earth in any sort of situation. Is there anything in war that luck cannot do?

10

Finally, he who holds the heavens and the universe in his power, who tramples fortune and fate under his foot, turned a pitiful glance toward the faithful in distress. While on this side the infidels were routed and dispersed, on the side of the Calinno River a fearful and deadly battle was taking place, leaving dead bodies scattered in the water and along the riverbanks.

11

As a strong sun thawed the ice of winter, several brooks carried the water to the river, raising its level high; the water then inundated the ford, as it had done oftentimes before. Now the river was turning stones rapidly around, as well as heaps of wood, which the waters, raging like the sea when stirred by a severe storm, had uprooted from mountains and forests.

12

Then the waves, turning onto themselves and coming swiftly one after the other, created a vortex that twisted around deeply in the sands, then pulled, uprooted, and swallowed trees and stones. The river now was turbulent and full of whirlpools, and the ford had become very dangerous for those who tried to wade it, as the feet that stepped over the uneven depth of the riverbed vacillated and failed.

13

No less dangerous was it to walk on the ravaged banks for those who tried to enter or exit the river. The banks were too precipitous for anyone to climb down and were also too steep for climbing up, for they were made slippery by clay and uneven by clods, and they were strewn with so many and such thick thorny shrubs that even the eye could not find a clear spot. Still, once they got as far as the river, the pagans tried to enter by a few paths that did not seem so dangerous.

14

In order to cross safely they had prepared some light and slender boats. But now Vran had reached the opposite bank ready to wade the river from the other side. As the distance was not great, he could see the other bank and the enemies coming over the water across the river. Being a good captain and very expert in the technique of war, he immediately understood what the enemy was attempting to do.

15

If he crossed the river at the point he had reached, he would come directly up against the great tyrant, for whose territory the river served as boundary. On the other hand, the Saracens, before they could wade the Calinno, had to come along the bank by a long roundabout way in order to attack the Christians' flank and rear.

16

The good Vran thought: "O blind reasoning of men! In looking recklessly for your advantage, you often act against common sense!" In order to be of greater help to his friend and protect him and his men from this oncoming danger, he proceeded to prevent the enemy from attacking and thought of a way not entirely unwise, because even though he would have to pay a very high price for it, he would acquire clear recognition as a valorous man.

17

He turned to Cir, Pallante, and Ottavio and acquainted them with his plan. Together they selected a stretch of the bank covered with trees that seemed very good for hiding and attacking the enemy. Then they distributed their men in various covered positions and waited for the pagans to come across. As the enemy landed on the bank, completely exhausted from wading the river, they were wounded, killed, and thrown back into the water.

18

Sometimes a great number of locusts ruin crops that are not yet ready to harvest and, singed by fire, fall wingless into the valley. That band of pagans fell into the river in the same way: the waters were soon stained with blood and strewn with helmets, shields, bows, darts, lances, and swords. Metal could be seen sinking, wood floating and moving round and round.

19

Running for shelter, some men began to climb trees and hide in the thickness of branches. Some held their swords high with their hands and tried to save themselves every way they could. Others, whose feet had been cut off, hung miserably from the branches they managed to seize with their arms; some of them fell down, overcome by their weight or by pain. Some lost their hands, others were slain.

20

Perched on a plane tree, Ader saw nearby the tree very dear to Hercules,[1] and thinking he could hide much better there, he conceived the idea of jumping over. While he was making the jump, he was wounded: one foot remained caught on a tree branch, while his head fell into the water. In dying he was wronged by three ills: he was hung in midair, he was wounded, and he was drowned.

21

Savino lifted his powerful arms brandishing a big battleaxe, and with it he chopped down and threw into the river the trees in whose branches the enemy soldiers were hiding. He pushed those men backward, keeping the pressure on to prevent them from coming forward. Then he took up a knotty spear and began hitting them from a distance.

22

Those who died by the sword or were killed by arrows were indeed lucky in their misfortune, because they were not caught in that man-to-man clash and did not die of drowning or of a cause even worse than that. As they were pushed backward by heavy spears and their horses bumped against the boats, many knights were thrown off their saddles, fell into the water headfirst, were crushed in between, and so they drowned.

23

The difficulty as well as the pain increased when a stone or trunk was carried around by the eddy—either floating on the wave or just under it—for it hit and sank the men who had fallen into the water. No longer could boats loaded with men be seen leaving the opposite bank, for most enemy soldiers had been routed or killed. Vran therefore believed that he had won the battle.

1. The tree sacred to Hercules, called Heracles by the Greeks, was the poplar.

24

But he was mistaken, for the higher captains had not sent their best soldiers to wade the river; they had sent ahead the very worst. After that, they stopped to consider in which way they could try to defend themselves from the assailants. Vran, who did not see and did not think of this, began to reorder his troops into ranks.

25

Then a servant came up to him and said: "A second large contingent of the enemy is coming, covered with bark. They swim like fish in the sea and go faster than birds in flight. They have reached the riverbank and are crowding in. Alas! They are all everywhere already! And they are not here alone; behind them, to make the crossing safer, horses in great number are wading the river.

26

"In addition to the footmen clothed in bark, who have already crossed the river, there is a stronger contingent of men on horseback. These are more numerous and are fitted with tougher armor." While Osir made this report, the tumult grew and the noise increased all around: now Vran saw that his people were being routed and dispersed in all directions.

27

Adami, Benci, and Pallante, and all the others in high command, tried to check the frightened crowd on the run. They begged and threatened, but all in vain. Vran did not forget, as he had not forgotten before, that a captain must have courage: he buckled up his helmet, picked up a great lance, and swiftly ran to where the shouting was loudest.

28

He reproached as cowards all the soldiers he encountered on his way. "If you do not care about your king," he told them, "who is so just and compassionate toward you, how can you forget the duty, the love, and the pity due to your fathers, your sons, and your wives? What hope will be left for you, what refuge, and what land to inhabit, if you lose this land?

29

"Is there someone here who believes he can be safe from the tyrant after rebelling against him? There is no escape, believe me, but in our swords, in our right hands, in our breasts. Even if we could go back into our mother's womb, that would not be a secure refuge for us, because the merciless tyrant would be happier to pull us out of that belly more than any mother would be."[2]

30

Meanwhile Vran reached the tract of the bank where Rainaldo was fighting along with his men. Pallante held him back and resisted him without conceding any ground. He stopped his own soldiers from fleeing by either reproaching or praising them. He urged on this man and that man, and if many of them ran away, still he was not left alone to fight against such a crowd.

31

Vran moved up there raging with violent anger and hit Orin in the hollow of the neck. He fell; then Vran gave a blow to Franchin, also in the throat, right where the cheeks come to an end. Ormuss turned his horse around to get out of the way and made a wide turn touching the extreme point of the bank; the bank gave way and he fell into the river.

32

Then the captain struck Osmeno in the middle of the chest, Gruman on his side, Arrigo between his eyebrows. The Christian men who had fled before were now coming back, picking up courage and strength. Rainaldo saw the strong leader on foot frightening everybody into a rout; he turned his reins and with his horse gave him a big shove that threw him to the ground headfirst.

33

Then he threw his knotty spear at him, right where the cuirass joins the thigh piece. Although he did not succeed in killing him, the blow spread a deadly pallor over his cheeks. Pallante saw this and flung himself against Rainaldo, for if Vran suffered bodily, he, Pallante, was very chagrined. So he hit Rainaldo in the belly button with force and threw him dead to the ground before his friend could do it.

34

All this while, Tarnon, who had seen the Persian men defeated and on the run, burning with shame and indignation, began to assemble those who were

2. The captains' appeal to fleeing soldiers is ingeniously varied. Corcutte urges them to use their strength and courage (10.52–54). Rosmonda appeals to their sense of honor, for there is no escape from death (13.78–79). Here Vran warns his men that there is safety only in fighting the enemy. In stanza 35, Tarnon, furious, pursues them with threats.

still around. Then he ran impetuously in a crosswise direction, for the dead elephants were an obstacle to his moving in a straight line; but soon, seeing that all the ranks were depleted, he lost all hope of victory and wanted to die.

35

As he saw the Persian standards fold and fall, he moved resolutely toward them and managed to hold his ground thanks to his own great courage and presence of mind rather than the courage of his men. "This is not the way to safety, this is not that chance of bounty that you had hoped for, you wretched people," he shouted at them. "Where are you running? Go, go back to offer resistance! Go to your death!"[3]

36

With words such as these, and a face that showed no fear, he revived the failing daring of his men. With the arrival of Arioden, however, the great tyrant had decided to relocate his squadrons. Artaban, Driarasso, Orkhan, and Corcutte now moved all their battalions with a speed not unlike that of a torrent when the waters rush down after the sun has melted the ice on the mountains.

37

The Christian foot soldiers did not give them time to strike many blows. Similarly, at times, Eurus and Notus run precipitously against each other in warlike mood from the top down to the bottom of the mountains, ruining the thickest forests and vying in uprooting and breaking them down. Trees that have stood like ancient rustic fortresses collapse, their branches and bark torn away.

38

The great tyrant shone splendidly in his steel armor, superbly upright on his powerful charger. He was surrounded by his loyal soldiers, but now and then he could be seen darting rapidly away from them. He plunged his sharp sword into Crito's left side and lopped Bruno's head off with great force, throwing him from the saddle to the ground; and there the man remained, shedding his brains mixed with his blood.

39

Then the tyrant turned his gaze to where the battle was most ferocious and impenetrable, showing outwardly a thirst for blood as burning and deep as

3. Cf. above, canto 23.29n.

the one that fed his heart. Now, on three sides of him, he saw his soldiers either totally destroyed or routed and on the run, and he could see that the Adventurers—the king was fighting among them—brought about not single deaths, but general slaughter.

40

He saw Rosmonda and Vaconte encircled by the bodies of the many soldiers they had wounded and killed; and he noticed that the Christian king had slain a throng of people and drained the blood out of the entire pagan camp. In that storm of blows and injuries, he looked like an iron rock in a sea of blood.[4] He could clearly see where he was fighting, for the ground all around him was covered with severed limbs.

41

The cruel tyrant was now choked by an even greater fit of anger, if that was possible. With intrepid daring and strength of hand, he pushed on, scattering people all around, killed, and ran wherever the Thracian blood was shed most abundantly. Then he threw a pointed spear against Vaconte, who was the nearest of all those courageous men, and would easily have hit him in his breast if the strong cuirass had not protected the young warrior.

42

The spear went through the leather and the bone of the lining, but not through the metal layer. The barbaric emperor was ferocious and very bold, a warrior of great endurance and strength. He escaped the countermove by shifting quickly to the side of his adversary and throwing a new blow at him, and by chance he caught Artecin who was passing by and snuffed his vital breath right then and there.

43

The sharp point caught such a spot in the neck that both his windpipe and his gullet were pierced through. Artecin, who had a sweet and sonorous voice, now fell down making a faint and hoarse sound. A new flame of contemptuous anger flared up in Vaconte's face and heart, for the young man felt for Artecin a more affectionate love than he did for his own father.

44

Who can describe the squadron of warriors that defended and provided support to the emperor? What a scourge they were to the Christian troops!

4. Cf. similar comparisons at cantos 6.88n and 9.58 above.

What terror they inspired when they went on the attack! Impossible to say whether one man was fiercer than the next, for they all scattered death around them with their swords, and each competed in showing the enemy that he was a far mightier warrior than any of his comrades.

45

Orkhan advanced into the thickest of the battle in front of all the others, and soon he was seen to slay a great number of Latins. He plunged his sword into Zaccaria's chest, right through the heart that sat kinglike in its middle; then he lopped off Mario's right arm, while incautiously he was trying to strike a blow over his helmet. Behind him the fierce Corcutte, the highest captain in the field, looked like the lightning that comes after thunder.

46

In these horrifying and diverse moments of the battle, it was impossible to discern which side was prevailing, for they were killed in alternating waves, and those who seemed on the point of losing suddenly appeared to be winning—just as in a storm of contrary winds one does not know which one will prevail with its fury. Certainly here each man seemed to be determined to bring about victory by his own hands alone.

47

Elin had lifted his arm to bring down a powerful cutting blow over Vaconte, who was the enemy nearest him. Vaconte's shining helmet sent out fiery sparks, his head was bent over by the blow, but the bold youth, who was of daring heart as well as of powerful hand, was quick to respond to that offending blow and tried to hit the other man's right side with his pointed sword. The man, however, was able to dodge it, for he was alert and able to react instantly.

48

Then, wishing to pierce him through, he turned around to hit him in the same crude and heartless way in which he had killed Ormen. Vaconte's armor, which once was Aeneas's, on which both Brontes and Vulcan intensely labored,[5] was not even scratched, and the blow came up empty, which made Elin rage against the heavens, for he had not been able to penetrate either armor or shield. Meanwhile Albin, wanting to vindicate Ormen, flung a deadly arrow at him.

---

5. Vulcan, the god of fire, forging, and smelting, forged the armor for gods and heroes. Brontes was the cyclops who made Jupiter's thunderbolts. Ovid, *Metamorphoses* 2.5, 2.106, 12.614, 13.289; and *Fasti* 4.287–88; Nonnos, *Dionysiaca* 14.59, 27.91, 28.195.

49

The cruel barbarian found no escape, for the inescapable dart traveled directly and swiftly towards its mark. It resembled lightning that falls with an ominous flash from a stormy sky on the high sea or on the grassy fields, while an icy fear fills the hearts of peasants, shepherds, or sailors floating about on the tempestuous sea in total exhaustion.

50

But Vaconte was angry and resentful, for he wanted to strike that deadly blow himself, especially because the death of the terrible pagan had struck high terror into the infidels' ranks. Even so, the Christian soldiers too languished under the enemy attack, either beaten or dead; and all the flags could now be seen folding and falling down and leaving free passage to the enemy.

51

Neither force, nor advice, nor skill, nor reason could hold the faithful in place any longer (so frightened were they). They trembled before Driarasso, Orkhan, and their men, who seemed to strike and kill everyone. Only the Christian king put up a resistance with his squadron, urging the last of his men to continue to fight. It could be said that he alone was beating them back, because as many as twelve of their best men were now dead.

52

The strong king struck Giron between the nape and the neck with such force that a very strange thing happened. His head was seen flying up high and then coming down on the front of Ascanio's saddle. When he saw this, Ascanio believed it to be his own head, fear had so much increased his cowardice. He cried: "Alas! He has cut off my head!" and with this outcry he made all the others laugh.

53

Not even the king's superhuman valor could call back each standard-bearer to his place, but he succeeded in stirring courage in his men's hearts with words and with his intrepid and combative presence. He brought back into the ranks those who had run out, stopped those who had fled, and assembled them again. "Are you ready then to behave so ignominiously," he asked them, "as to leave your king to fight alone?"

54

With his sublime and formidable voice he held back soldiers and captains. He gave help with both his actions and his bearing, wherever he estimated the need to be greater. He was an omnipresent hero, running from the first ranks to the last ones, on this side and the other, disappearing into them and coming out of them, like a star in the sky that hides in the clouds one moment and reappears the next.

55

He truly shone like a comet in the sky, bringing life to some and death to others.[6] In the soldiers the will to fight was revived, and now they all followed his valorous example. A torrent swollen by the rain falls precipitously from a high mountain, pulling down stones and tree trunks. In similar fashion the king pulled behind him a throng of men wherever he went.

56

Everywhere the ground was wet and stained by blood and with a horrible cover of limbs and corpses over it. It looked like the dining tables of the fierce centaurs when they were bloodied by Hercules' hand.[7] The valiant daughter advanced with a band of soldiers to hold back her father, now an enemy; at the same time Rodoman moved and came to her side, ready to provide support.

57

No matter how great a warrior one was, no one was safe from the king's invincible hand. Not so many snowy flakes can be seen falling on the Apennines thrown down by icy Arthur;[8] not as much hail, hard and condensed like marble, ever comes down over the Syrtes,[9] when the sea rages during a winter storm: so many were the men that he was pulling down to their death from their saddles.

58

The Christian warriors went forth wherever their comrades before them, with tremendous impact, had come into collision with the enemy, so that

6. In *Iliad* 22.25–29, Achilles running toward Hector looks like Orion shining balefully in the sky. In Dante's *Paradiso* 24.12, the souls of the blessed in heaven sparkle like glowing comets. In *Africa* 7.1117–18, the great Scipio, fighting on the fields of Zama, resembles a comet hurling through space and bearing a sad omen to the universe. In *Jerusalem Delivered* 7.52.6, Argantes is like a comet spreading its bloody, streaming locks in the dry air. Cf. cantos 13.17 and 6.81 above.

7. The reference is to the legend according to which Hercules killed the centaurs while on an expedition against the Erymanthian boar. Ovid, *Metamorphoses* 9.191.

8. Arthur, or Arctos, is the constellation of the Great Bear. It is called "icy" here because it appears in the northern sky, near the pole.

9. The Syrtes were two stretches of the coast of North Africa made perilous by sandbanks and quicksands.

those who before were bold now were afraid, and those who were frightened now picked up courage. The soldiers who had fled were coming back, forcing into a rout those who had made them flee. Sabalio, after repelling the enemy on the riverbank, arrived to give aid to the Christians on the left side.

59

Aranit too was here with the ferocious Bulgarian contingent in pursuit of the Turkish army. He provided no small help to the good king in annihilating the enemy who were dispersed and disunited. In seeing so many of his people vanquished, although many could still go on fighting, the emperor lost heart and turned pale; then a deep despair froze his senses.

60

And this was either because a divine fury urged him to free his beloved people; or because, against the nature of his stalwart heart, an unusual terror gripped him; or because, as the perfect general he was, he realized that with that valorous captain the Christians would be victorious in the field; or just because man, who is similar to God, can see when he has finally reached the end of his life.

61

Even so, he restored his natural courage to his heart, for he was born a strong and valiant warrior, and although the enemy was fierce, he decided to try a last resort. Still, that a former slave of his should be able to boast of defeating so great an emperor filled him with a rage so pernicious that he suddenly lost his senses right on the spot.

62

The Janissaries formed a solid and powerful shield all around him, and all the Spahìs who saw him ran quickly to his side. But the ailing emperor was not aware of the danger of his impetuous and unwise wrath. With their weapons his men opened a way for him; then they lifted him up like dead weight and carried him away.

63

Seeing him go, Orkhan and Driarasso took it as a bad omen, for they greatly feared his last day had come, but they did not give any outward sign of apprehension. Since the emperor could not run any danger while he was being carried way, they decided to let him go without them so as not to let the soldiers become aware of it, for they tended to be affected by their lord's absence.

64

On a ship tossing without defenses on a sea that rises high all around, when the man at the rudder has been pulled into the water and the waves gurgle, foam, and seem about to cover the mast, the people, who do not know how to pilot the boat and have little expertise with navigation, are overcome by fear because no defense is left to them against certain death.[10] Deprived of their lord, the pagans were afraid no less in this war than they would have been in such a deadly sea storm.

65

Neither skill nor wisdom nor strength was of any avail, for all men took flight when the sultan was gone. After that first fear a new terror seized them, and they did not dare to look straight at the enemy. Corcutte attempted to hold them back: he begged, reproached, and threatened; he lamented and tried to cheer them up and persuade them that honor is always bought at high price.

66

He told them they could save themselves only by building up a shield against the enemy with their own lives. This last advice encouraged a few to remain firm and strong in place; but (as the majority is always weak and unstable) a small number of the most courageous remained, for only a desire for honor kept these few there, to die not to win.

67

They remained, certain to die, and they defended themselves with such daring and strength that one would have doubted the final outcome except that they were so few and the men around so many. The right reward was certainly meted to Attravante, who was slain by Rosmonda's single blow: for he despised the Latins and the Greeks, and his advice had been reckless and foolish.[11]

68

Rosmonda killed him before her brother's very eyes (whom she would not want to harm, so much did she love him), and also—appropriately so—in Sinolfo's presence, for Attravante had voiced such doubts about her brother

10. In *Jerusalem Delivered* 7.98.3–8, Tasso compares a warrior's resistance under the blows of his enemy to the strength of a ship caught in a storm. "Argante . . . is like a high rudderless ship on a stormy sea, with sails torn and spars shattered" (Argante . . . par senza governo in mar turbato, rotte vele ed antenne, eccelsa nave). Here Sarrocchi successfully adapts the simile to express the psychological situation of the soldiers who learn that their captain is no longer with them in battle. A similar adaptation is in canto 3.9 above.

11. This refers to the speech that Attravante made at the meeting of the satraps in canto 21.28–40. He also called Driarasso a "feckless soldier" (21.36).

and she wanted to take revenge on him.[12] But perhaps God, who calls souls to himself in various ways, had decided beforehand to save him, for the man now repented having helped the Thracian against his own true faith.

69

Together with Hannibal, he gave himself up to the king in a humble and suppliant fashion. When they saw the pagan army defeated and in flight, Corcutte, Driarasso, and Orkhan, considering surrender more dignified than death, placed themselves in the hands of the woman, who entreated them to do so, as a friend to two of them and as a sister to the other.

70

Meanwhile, the powerful and loyal group of men carried away the distraught emperor, and pushing through a bloodied path, took him out of the raging battle. The pitiable man quickly came to himself, and at the same time his anger returned. He looked around in astonishment, and when he realized that he was off the battlefield, he was overpowered by anger.

71

It seemed to him that he had fled, and his heart burned with heroic outrage. He would rather have lived his last day than to be pointed out as a coward. "Let us go, let us go," he said, "let us go back, for Murad may be defeated, but he can never be made a coward. My kingdom may be taken away by an unjust Fate, but the merit of being worthy of one is mine alone."

72

He could hardly suppress his fury and refrain from striking those who held him down. He heard cries of fear and pain and a great noise of trampling rise behind them. So against his will, he was forced to quell the reckless daring that urged him to go back and die, for now he realized that the Turkish army had been routed and everyone was either dead, or running way, or taken prisoner.

73

In a great hurry, the emperor was taken to Elia, for no other place among the faraway towns seemed as secure, not because he was afraid of dying, but to prevent him from falling into the hands of his enemy. As soon as he

---

12. The Italian stanza remains obscure. My rendering, with *consorte* translated as "brother"—both the Italian word and the corresponding English term *consort* mean "brother," "relative," and "associate" as well as "spouse"—gives reason to Attravante's disparagement of Driarasso, Rosmonda's half-brother, in canto 21.36, and consequently to her wish to kill him in front of both Driarasso and Sinolfo. The reference, in fact, seems to be also to canto 17.43 and 17.57—stanzas that have been omitted—where Sinolfo insistently defends Driarasso's merits as a valorous warrior.

arrived, he rushed with great fury headfirst against a wall, because in his insane grief, dying in this fashion seemed to him faster.

74

Now he called out to his defeated army: "Hope and comfort of my empire! You were its strength and its power! I see now that your bright fame has fallen; and Murad, the great emperor, wants to die! Your greatness competed with the sun; it extended from east to west. Now I see your power lowered and tamed, while wreaths of laurel will crown the heads of our enemy for eternity.

75

"But something even worse I see, for my awesome empire, which was once unbeaten, now is being destroyed by the hand of a serf!" At this point the sultan became silent. His men tried to calm his fiery anger and force their help on him. In the end he collapsed and, fixing his eyes on the heavens, lost all color. As his soul was unable to linger any longer, the emperor silently died, and by dying he himself bestowed a full victory on his adversary.

76

Thus the emperor's soul fell precipitately into the Stygian swamp, to the realm beyond, where the fire rages on with the greatest intensity. Charon, the merciless boatman, was gloatingly waiting for him in his floating vessel:[13] but no dark master of the infernal deep will ever be able to inflict on the proud man a pain harsher than the one he himself suffered, remembering that he had died defeated by one of his slaves.[14]

---

13. Stygian swamp stands for Styx, the river of the underworld (cf. canto 19.24 above), and Charon is the old ferryman who carries the newly arrived souls across the waters of death. Virgil, *Aeneid* 6.296–316, 6.369; Ovid, *Metamorphoses* 10.70–73; Dante, *Inferno* 3.82 ff.

14. The sultan's death parallels that of other famous literary characters. In *Aeneid* 12.951–52, Turnus falls mortally wounded and his living spirit flies disdainfully into the dark. In Petrarch's *Africa* 5.1011, Sophonisba dies and "her fierce soul descends into hell." In *Orlando Furioso* 46.140, Rodomonte is killed by Ruggiero and his soul runs swearing to the banks of Acheron. In *Jerusalem Delivered* 19.26.5–6, Argante dies while still threatening, furious to the last. It is also noteworthy that the sultan's spirit remains untamed even in the underworld, very much like Farinata's in Dante's *Inferno* 10.77–78. And, as in the case again of the Florentine leader, what torments him more than the pains of hell is the thought of his political defeat. Of course, the best-known villain who in death precipitates himself headlong into hell is Don Giovanni, as in the libretto Lorenzo da Ponte wrote for Mozart in 1787. Sarrocchi's ending follows the account given by Barletius. In real life, Murad II lifted the siege of Kruja in November 1450 and died, probably of apoplexy, in 1451 in Edirne.

APPENDIX: EXCERPTS FROM CANTOS 5, 6, 13, AND 22 IN ITALIAN

Canto 5.11–34. During their first sortie the Albanians, disguised as Janissaries, penetrate the enemy camp and bring slaughter among the sleeping solders. Death of Varadin and Armilla.

A gran passo all'insù muovono il piede
quanto dal buio e 'l calle è lor concesso;
indi scendono al campo; ecco li vede
il Turco, e pur lor va sicuro appresso.
A caso appella alcun ch'amico il crede
or per diverso or per lo nome istesso.
Quei, se notizia dar teme alla voce,
tace e alza la mano, e va veloce

per importante affar mostrando fretta,
e così alcun d'inganno alcun non pave.
Lo stuol diviso in varie parti aspetta
l'ora ch'a dar l'assalto al Turco s'have:
tosto che 'l primo sonno i sensi alletta,
e avvien che 'l cibo col vapor n'aggrave,
degli Spaghì sen viene unito e ratto
ai folti alberghi, il ferro ignudo tratto.

Gianizzeri e Spaghì per lunga usanza
contendenti fra lor son di valore;
onde 'l Re si pensò con la sembianza
de l'Agà far ch'ognun prendesse errore.
Il Tracio stuol, che tanto il fido avanza,
giace senza pensier, senza timore
nel sonno immerso, e in là e in qua diviso,
senz'arme, guardia, tempo, ordine, avviso.

Passa il Re valoroso e gli altri avante,
e invola a molti nella notte il giorno.
Chi giace affatto estinto e chi spirante
in rozzo e duro letto, in molle adorno,
non si distingue il cavalier dal fante.
Ha già d'uccisi un ampio cerchio intorno,
moribondo il pagan dal sonno oppresso
singhiozza e geme in suon tronco e sommesso.

Parte la testa a Druso il buon Sinano,
la gola indi trafigge a Martasino:
con tepido ruscel sparge egli al piano
via più che 'l sangue il mal digesto vino,
per cui la sera trasgredì profano
il precetto che 'l Turco ha per divino.
Uccidon gl' altri, gl' altri anco a vicenda,
e trascorrendo van di tenda in tenda.

Son giunti ormai di Varadino al letto,
che il vessillo maggior porta di loro.
Gli è donna a lato di lucente aspetto,
qual sol ne l'alba incoronato d'oro.
Pos'ella ignuda in sù l'eburneo petto,
di natura e d'amor pompa e tesoro,
la man, ver cui piega soave il volto,
che 'l più bel pregio a Primavera ha tolto.

L'altre membra coperte ha sciolte e snelle,
e in dolce sonno placida respira;
e benché chiuse sian le luci belle,
la celeste beltà pur da lor spira.
Così talor in ciel lucenti stelle
sotto candida nube altri rimira,
dalla cui densità tanto son chiare
lo splendor scintillante ancor traspare.

Consorte a Varadin, costei si noma
Armilla: ahi dove il crudo Amor l'adduce!
L'asta a la debil man soverchia soma
porta e 'l corsiero al suo signor conduce;
sprezza e accorcia la dorata chioma,
ma in abito viril non men riluce,
ché non men arde in sua virtute amore
qual pria d'ogni uomo or d'ogni donna il core.

Tal gioia trae d'aver l'amato obietto
in guerra e in pace agl'occhi suoi davante,

ché Marte non spaventa il molle petto,
benché sanguigno e crudo acciar l'ammante.
Tale il barbaro sposo a lei diletto
Ipsicratea seguì fida e costante,
ma ben d'Armilla ella più fortunata,
ché morte a lei sol diè la mano amata.

O come allor ch'eran le Turche squadre
raccolte in Elia al dipartirsi accinte,
in quelle notti a lei funebri e atre,
tenendo il sen all'amate menbra avvinte,
rendesti Amor le guance sue leggiadre
di pianto asperse e di pallor dipinte,
e infondesti pietà ne' dolci preghi
che 'l consorte il seguirlo a lei non neghi.

Mescendo con sospir pianti e parole,
nettarei baci, amplessi stretti, disse:
"Dove a celar ten vai, vivo mio sole,
per far agli occhi miei perpetua ecclisse?
Ben avverrà che 'l giorno a me s'invole,
ché, s'Amore fé che l'alma mia ne gisse
in te, così dal natural suo loco
lunge, al varco mortal sarà tra poco.

"Per te solo a crearmi il cielo intese
et a l'aura vital mi fece uscire,
dove, subito uscita, Amor mi accese
il petto d'ardentissimo desire.
Pari affetto gentil per tua mi prese:
viver teco debb'io dunque e morire.
Stenda Lachesi un filo ond' in un'ora
lo tronchi poi l'inesorabil suora.

"E tu star puoi d'Armilla tua diviso,
che teco visse e teco ancor non moia?
Queste chiome, quest'occhi e questo viso,
questa mia bocca a te dolcezza e gioia,
ond' aver l'alma e 'l cor arso e conquiso
mostrasti un tempo, or ti son forse a noia?
Ahi, che dubbio il dolor mi pone innanzi?
Non so come di fé ciascuno avanzi!

"Io so che contrastar non hai potere
ov'il Tiranno impera, ove minaccia.
Ch'io segua te sol ne l'armate schiere,
o mio nobil tesor, prego ti piaccia.

Potrai soccorso in ogni tempo avere
da me che seguirò di te la traccia;
una mia voce almen da tergo intesa
t'avvertirà di traditrice offesa."

Sospir sì caldi e sì melati prieghi,
baci e querele sì soavi e meste,
come far non potran ch'al fin non pieghi
l'innamorato sposo a sue richieste?
Che grazia sarà mai ch'amante neghi
che dall'amata bocca a lui sien chieste?
Ahi, ch'età fresca or non le giova, o fede,
o vago volto, ad impetrar mercede.

E ben far può la singolar beltate
ch'ogni più freddo cor sospiri e arda,
o in uman petto almen destar pietate,
ma spietato Sinan punto non tarda,
e forse fu destin, non crudeltate,
ch'egli a chi fere al ferir non guarda:
gli have il petto e la man per mezzo tronco,
tremano ambe le parti e sbatte il monco.

Il letto ancor nel gran tremor si scote
e corre il sangue in dipartito fiume,
e quinci Varadin bagna e percote;
percosso e molle egli apre i lumi al lume.
Sinano il colpo addoppia allor, né puote
giungerlo a pien, che salta ei dalle piume,
la spada ch'ha vicin prende e lo scudo,
e tanto basta al coraggioso ignudo.

Ben il confuse il caso aspro improvviso,
ma forza diegli il natural valore;
vede il diletto suo morto e reciso;
l'assaglion due contrari, odio e amore;
bagna di pioggia dolorosa il viso,
ma de l'ira ammorza il fiero ardore,
anzi s'unisce al duol, che non aspetta
altro rimedio, il duol, che la vendetta.

A l'ira dunque, al duol ch'il cor gli punge,
qual fera o serpe fia ch'unque assomigli?
Aquila è forse tal che, andando lunge
per trovar esca a' pargoletti figli,
misera! vede allor ch'al nido giunge
falcon, ch' in essi insanguinò gli artigli.

Gli move dietro a la vendetta il volo
da pietà spinta e da disdegno e duolo.

Tal sen corre costui velocemente,
né sai se prima il giunga o 'l fere in testa.
Scende il ferro a Sinan fra dente e dente,
e in due parti ferito il collo resta;
né ammorza Varadin la sete ardente,
poca pena a la sua gli sembra questa.
Non gli sembra ch'a pien questo il conforte,
che vendetta maggior vorria di morte.

Ma intanto il Re feroce oltra inandando
trafisse Argir da l'uno a l'altro lato:
gran ventura di lui, gli passò il brando
nel petto a punto in quella parte a lato
ch'il soverchio calor del cor temprando
ministra l'aura a l'alternar del fiato;
chiudeva l'ali, e pria ch'ella l'aprisse,
trasse il ferro, e il pagan più lustri visse.

Ode il Re Varadin ch'aita chiede,
ché degli emoli suoi lo crede insulto;
ve accorre e morto il fido amico vede
nel proprio sangue e ne l'altrui sepulto.
Ch'egli quel desso sia gli fan sol fede
l'arme mentite, sì gli è il volto occulto
e 'l barbaro crudel sopra gl' ha scorto,
non sazio averlo lacerato e morto.

Divenne in Varadin l'ira più accensa
de l'elmo de l'Agà scorto il cimiero,
che il Re Ferrate sia sicuro pensa
e va ratto a trovar d'un colpo fiero.
La coperta e lo scudo ha doppia e densa
d'acciaio e cuoio, e resta al colpo intiero;
il Re lui fere a la sinistra costa
di punta, e 'l ferro uscì da l'altra opposta.

Lo scudo e lui manda in due parti al suolo,
né meraviglia fu, ch'ebbe in usanza
a traverso tagliar a un colpo solo
l'arme e 'l guerrier con singolar possanza.
Ora al natio valor di sdegno e duolo
aggiunti in lor virtú se stesso avanza.
Al gran tumulto intanto ognun destato
arme! arme! grida, e là sen' corre armato.

Canto 6.110–28. Alexander, Driarasso, and Agrismeta meet on the field of battle. Realizing that he is losing the fight, Murad orders a tactical maneuver that will force the Albanians to withdraw.

Driarasso pien di meraviglia mira
l'uccision di quella destra forte,
ch'ovunque il ferro impetuoso gira
strage al nemico e non battaglia porte,
onde spavento sol desta, non ira,
in tutti i cor d'inevitabil morte.
E benché 'l Re a cavallo, egli pedone,
brana di quel valor far paragone.

D'eterna gloria un bel desire ardente
gl'infiamma l'alma ad avamparne avvezza,
onde di saggia e generosa mente
stima chi per onor vita disprezza.
Vibrasi contra lui la sua possente
spada, ch'ogni arma adamantina spezza;
piaga non fa, ma lascia il fianco ignudo,
il Re si volge irato al colpo crudo.

Fulminando un riverso a lui rivolse,
ma sua ventura sol rase il cimiero;
portò l'empito il brando e al petto colse
Nardino, e lo mandò tronco al sentiero.
Ecco Agrismeta, il qual fuor d'uso volse
in quel giorno pugnar sovra il destriero,
l'ingonbra al colpo fier d'alto stupore,
punto d'invidia generosa il core.

E venir desiando a prova seco
ratto sprona il destriero a la sua volta.
Driarasso grida a lui: "Pugna egli meco!"
Vago d'onor, nulla colui l'ascolta;
d'ira e di sdegno Driarasso cieco,
la battaglia di man vistasi tolta,
sì come egli era a piè stanco e ferito
d'assalir ambi duo fora anco ardito.

Ma sì il corsier quegli veloce sprona
e tanta calca in mezzo a lor si mette
che l'alta impresa al fin l'uno abbandona;
l'altro apre co'l destrier le turbe strette
e giunto a fronte al Re, così ragiona:
"Più le turbe fugar basse e neglette

lascia, invitto guerrier, nemico indegno!
Io forse all'ira, al tuo valor non vegno.

"T'amai, or sol ti pregio e 'l cor mi fiede
a Dio vederti e al tuo Signor rubello.
Tu quel grande, e quel saggio? Ahi, che nol crede
la mente, e dubia è pur se tu sia quello."
Tacque, e se non che nel tacer gli diede
colpo qual puote mai spietato e fello;
rispondea il Re benigno a quanto espose,
ma pur co 'l ferro al feritor rispose.

Durava ancor la general battaglia
dov' ognun parimente il sangue sparse;
prima, ma poi nel fin chi manco vaglia
ne le campagne orribilmente apparse.
Gl'usberghi rotti e la spezzata maglia
e le forate sopraveste e sparse
vedeansi, e 'l fido appo l'infido spento;
ma per ogni Cristian di Turchi cento.

Vaconte in carcer preso Armeno trasse
con altri molti, e Mauro il vago Osmano,
che dal piano sorto in parte si ritrasse
ove sicuro esser credea, ma invano.
Nel tuo fatal destin fu che vietasse
con ogni suo poter l'amico Orcano,
ch'era a quel luogo a guerreggiar vicino,
né quel d'Armeno il valoroso Acrino.

Pien di stupor alquanto in se ristette
che tanti vinti sian l'Imperatore,
e vede ben che tutti in fuga mette
d'un sol nemico il sovruman valore.
Pur saggio, al fine ai capitan commette,
sebben colmo di rabbia e di dolore,
che, perché affatto il campo omai non pera,
raccolgano a ritrarsi ogni lor schiera.

Nel tempo istesso impera ad Attravante
ch'egli con tutti i suoi sul carro ascenda,
e, correndo per fianco in un istante,
verso la fronte la battaglia fenda.
Posto un carro a' destrier de l'altro avante,
perché i destrier de l'un l'altro difenda,
e così sempre il carro antecedente
schermo faccia ai destrier ch'have il seguente.

E si sforza frenar l'impeto e l'ira
del campo ostil già vincitor sicuro;
e perché gir lo stuol, che se ritira
confuso, puote mal tutto in sicuro,
non curi mentr' il campo ei fende e gira
per far de' carri inespugnabil muro,
sebben, tra carri e 'l monte, a manifesta
strage di Turchi alcuna schiera resta.

Ma qual da turbo, che in sen ampio serra
nembo grave di ferro o piombo o pietre,
la turba, incerta ove quel cada a terra,
fugge, né però sa dove s'arretre:
tal il volgo fedel sen' fugge ed erra
pavido dal votar da le faretre
e da le lance che, dai carri fuori,
tempestan giù gl'arcieri e i lanciatori.

Ma il Re fedel, come si vide a fronte
Agrismeta venir sì ardito e fero,
e si sentì rimproverar con onte
d'esser stato rubello al Tracio impero,
gl'alzò grave fendente irato in fronte,
ma lo sottrasse al colpo il buon destriero;
e ben tentava il Re miglior vendetta,
ma turba l'impedì calcata e stretta.

Il Re dunque dei suoi corre in aita
ed ha prima sul carro Aron trafitto,
abbattuto Arimon d'aspra ferita
e l'auriga Sorbel d'aspro mandritto,
che ne lo sterco e ne la rena trita
del piano e de cavalli ha il capo fitto,
traboccando dal capo entro a quel loto
sbatte, ove tenne il capo i piedi a voto.

Ora Attravante avea di guerra a l'uso
l'esercito Ottoman renduto forte
con trincea di carri, e fuora escluso
gran stuol di Turchi a manifesta morte:
ché 'l fier Tiranno avea tra sè conchiuso
ch'il vincer e 'l morir d'altrui gl'importe
sol tanto quanto vincitor impera,
purch'ei regni e trionfi, e il mondo pera.

Ma perché il gran Motor del Ciel non vuole
liberar anco a pieno suo popol caro,

quella di mobil carri immobil mole
al Turco intanto far poteo riparo,
ch'a l'albergo marin vicino il sole
giunse e poi chiuse dentro il lume chiaro;
la notte allor la gran vittoria tolse,
che nel suo manto oscuro il mondo involse.

Ebbe il misero stuol che fu diviso
dall'esercito suo varia ventura.
Più d'un fatto è prigion, più d'un ucciso,
si difende più d'un senza paura;
altri partito prende all'improvviso,
ricovra ai carri e di scampar procura
sotto a le pance de' destrier nascosto,
ch' ha per ischermo un altro carro opposto.

Qual, se da l'Aquilon l'Egeo percosso
s'innalza e fere il ciel con l'onda vasta,
e sì dal flutto procelloso grosso
divien ch'il letto al suo furor non basta,
e avendo per uscir l'impeto mosso,
l'alto lito il respinge e a lui contrasta;
tal, trovando de carri opposta sponda,
respinto il fido stuol a dietro inonda.

Il Turco intanto si rinchiude in Presa
alzando i ponti con le guardie intorno.
Ma poi ch'il fido Re vide contesa
tanta vittoria dal cadente giorno,
con la gente venuta in sua difesa
e gl'altri suoi, fé alla città ritorno.
Lasciò libero passo allor Corcutte
e salve ritirò le schiere tutte.

Canto 13.11–44. *Rosmonda climbs Mount Olympus, meets Silveria, and persuades her to join the army.*

Con l'elmo ella il bel viso or non asconde,
scintillan gli occhi un più ch'uman splendore;
parte annodate son le chiome bionde
e parte in preda ad un lascivo errore.
Malagevole è il calle a poggiar, onde
l'irriga l'ostro un cristallin sudore,
cui ondeggaindo intorno i vaghi crini
paion legati in or, perle, e rubini.

Vibra lampi e fulgor lo scudo intorno
al sol che, ripercosso, il ripercote,

ch'in azzurro color bianco unicorno
serba, che 'l ferro aguzza ad aspra cote.
Con l'elsa e 'l pomo d'or di gemme adorno,
cui mal stimar l'opra e 'l valor si puote,
di catena al destro omero ligato
sen' va 'l brando a cader nel manco lato.

Ne l'usbergo, onde s'arma, in mezzo al petto
l'orribil teschio di Medusa appare;
sembran gonfie le serpi, il collo eretto,
per gli occhi fuore atro venen spirare,
tale in vista d'orrore e di diletto
qual Pallante novella altrui compare.
Del giogo altero già, già tanto acquista,
vide la cruda arciera e insieme è vista.

Che sentendo il rumor sen' corse al varco
drizzando fiera a chi venia lo sguardo;
di cornio ha mal tagliato e ruvid'arco,
al tender duro, all'allentar gagliardo;
ha di rozza faretra il tergo carco,
cui dentro più d'un suona acuto dardo;
nudo ha il petto e 'l ginocchio, e sol coturno
veste di lincea pelle il piede eburneo.

E di leopardo maculata pelle
copre le membra ancor grandi e formate,
sopra ogn'uso viril disciolte e snelle;
le chiome inculte son crespe ed aurate;
le luci grandi, rilucenti e belle,
di maschio ardir ripiene e venustate;
bruno ha 'l color, ma par dal solar raggio
in un candido volto un dolce oltraggio.

Giusta e vaga natura in lei comparte,
ma robusta e virile ogni fattezza;
né sai ben dir qual abbia in lor più parte
mista insieme la forza o la bellezza.
Dirai ben ch'avventar gli strali Marte
o col brando a ferir Amor s'avvezza;
né vista accende unque impudico affetto,
ma desta a tema, a riverenza il petto.

Abita monti e boschi inculta e sola,
agli occhi altrui sempre celata stassi
e, vista a caso mai, tosto s'invola

qual fulgor che lampeggia e ratto passi,
o qual stella dal ciel cadente vola
con aurea striscia a gl'elementi bassi;
né Arpalice unqua sì veloce corse
qualor fugace più l'Ebro percorse.

Sol dietro a vaga damma o cerva snella,
qualor co' venti in correr suo contende,
si mostra e più fugace appar più bella,
onde il desio più di vederla accende.
All'improvvise e lucid'arme or ella
si maraviglia e l'arco ardita tende,
si ferma e lo ritien, visto poi come
l'aura increspa a colei l'aurate chiome.

Né come suol ritrosa e fuggitiva
per celarsi da lei rivolge il piede,
ché donna esser la scorge; or quella arriva,
e l'una e l'altra con stupor si vede;
la bella cacciatrice, ancorché schiva
sia di compagna, lei dolce richiede
che dice, che ricerca, ivi che vuole,
dove raro e non mai poggiar uom suole.

Ma colei fiso il bel sembiante mira
che sotto l'aspro vestimento incolto
bellezza, ardir non più veduto spira
con venustà viril donnesco volto:
onde a lei, che non meno ancor l'ammira,
dice, dal core ogni disdegno tolto:
"Del sommo Imperator lo scettro altero
reggo io sua figlia, e d'ogni intorno impero.

"Sdegnando il molle femminil ingegno,
a miglior studi ho gl'usi miei conversi;
spada cingo però, però sostegno
scudo, però d'acciar mi ricopersi:
et or a te sol per intender vegno,
ch'ingiusto oprar regina io mai soffersi,
di quei german per la tua man già morti
qual cagion degna or per tua scusa apporti."

La vergine selvaggia allor che sente
costei de la gran Tracia Imperatrice,
nata d'accorta e generosa mente,
benché rozza di boschi abitatrice,

non paventa, non già, ma riverente
s'inchina tosto e mansueta dice:
"A tal bellezza, a tal valor destina
stato qual deve il cielo, alta Reina.

"Or da me rozza e a mentir non usa,
e d'ogni frode popolar lontana,
saprai vera cagion, non falsa scusa,
degli uccisi ver me la voglia insana.
Io d'Imeneo, d'Amor la face esclusa,
rivolsi i passi a seguir Diana,
ch'altro piacer non provo, altro diletto
ch'armarmi sol di gel pudico il petto.

A disonesto fin questi empi intenti,
il mio candido onor macchiar tentaro,
onde a ragion poi quanto sian pungenti
gli strali miei per questa man provaro.
Non ch'odio contra a giusti e innocenti
m'ingombri il cor d'ingiusta morte avaro,
non ché di sangue uman nutrir mi piaccia:
bastan le fere a me ch'uccido in caccia."

La donzella real l'alta cagione
de gli estinti da lei subito ch'ode,
"Morte unqua altra non fu con più ragione,
dice; non pena, no, merti, ma lode.
Nome d'amante il cieco volgo impone
così ad un cor che con inganno e frode
l'odio ricopre sotto il vel d'amore,
del chiaro onor donnesco insidiatore.

"Ma se non men de le tue belle chiome,
de' tuoi bell'occhi e del bel viso adorno
hai cor gentil, pregh'io dimmi 'l tuo nome,
mostrami il chiuso tuo fido soggiorno,
come ti cibi e dormi, e poscia come,
dopo le caccie tue, dispensi il giorno,
come senza cultor sì vago e ameno
sia questo loco, e d'erbe e frutti pieno."

A Rosmonda Silveria: "Altri cultori
non v'ha dove stanz'io, che la mia destra;
le querce io coltivai, gli orni e gli allori;
domestica rendei l'uva silvestra,
e gl'altri frutti e l'erbe vaghe e i fiori.
Nata appena lasciommi in parte alpestra

il genitor mosso da ingiusto sdegno.
Silveria è il mio nome ond'io chiamata vegno."

Tace, e la guida al suo ricetto prima,
là dove cupo il monte in giù profonda.
Non fino marmo al ciel chiaro il sublima,
non muraglia regal largo il circonda,
ma giace in parte solitaria ed ima,
d'arbori cinto con ombrosa fronda,
ch'edere intorno spesse in più ritorte
avvincono carpon serpenti e torte.

Più d'un mentre ch'al chino il piè discende
breve stagno rattien, secca palude.
Natura un cavo tufo a l'imo fende;
Silveria il varco con gran sasso chiude.
Al suo vitto ella qui le fiamme accende,
le carni coce qui selvagge e crude;
qui giace in dorsi e ruvidi e ferini,
che sono in vece a lei di piume e lini.

Mostratole a pien ciò quindi si parte
e lei per la via stessa indietro mena,
e la guida del monte in altra parte
profonda pur, ma spaziosa amena.
Questa ha natura e più l'industria e l'arte
d'arbori e d'acque vagamente piena,
onde il loco primier tanto lodato
da lei nulla rassembra a questo a lato.

Qui l'alto abete e 'l ramoruto faggio,
la gloriosa palma, e 'l verde alloro
tesson grat'ombra al caldo estivo raggio
con intrecciate e folte chiome loro;
ride fiorito qui l'aprile e 'l maggio,
si cinge autunno il crin di pomi d'oro,
la torta vite al caro olmo s'appoggia,
grave de le dolci uve, e in alto poggia.

Qua la rosa apre le vezzose foglie,
empiendo l'aere di soavi odori;
varia e vaga colà stretta l'accoglie
che spunta a pena, o già del verde è fuori;
l'una in vermiglie e l'altra in bianche spoglie
involta a prova mostra i bei colori,
questa co' latte di Giunone e quella
splende col sangue de la dea più bella.

E s'era ai fior dal cielo imperio dato
di lor la rosa esser dovea regina,
e ben di ricche gemme incoronato,
apre il crin d'oro a la celeste brina
ch'è piropo de' fiori, ostro del prato,
onde a bramarla i cor gentili inchina;
lieve a zefiro ride, amor spirante,
ornamento al terren, gloria e le piante.

Vaghi mirteti in bell'ordin distinti,
sovra ciò che natura e 'l culto suole,
narcisi, acanti, gelsomin, giacinti,
gigli, ligustri, adon, croco e viole,
di color mille in un vaghi e dipinti,
col bel verde de l'erbe a' rai del sole,
sembran da l'aura sparsi e ventillanti
smeraldi, oro, rubin, perle e diamanti.

Ma benché in mille, in mille guise vaghi
gli occhi tal vista renda, empia e diletti,
mista d'odor Sabei spiranti e vaghi,
soavità par che più 'l senso alletti;
limpidi rivi e cristallini laghi
stagnan fra colli ed erran fra boschetti,
e rendon freschi al tatto e dolci al gusto
quel luogo de' fior vago e frutti onusto.

Vezzosi augelli con securo volo
vanno a diletto lor di ramo in ramo,
né temon che lor porti inganno o duolo,
la tesa rete, il vischio e l'adunc'amo.
Non plora i tolti figli il rusignolo,
ma dice in suo latino: "io ardo, io amo,"
fa l'aere intorno d'amoroso affetto
gran voce risonar da picciol petto.

Mentre l'amata al suo chiamar risponde,
garrisce Progne e rinovella il pianto,
e molte varie voci in un confonde
grata armonia di più soave canto.
Guizzano a schiera i pesci in grembo a l'onde,
muti a l'amica lor parlando intanto,
che lei, che gl'ode ancorché senza voce,
ne le fredde acque il foco ardente coce.

Rosmonda con diletto e maraviglia
guardando, il passo lentamente scioglie;

ristoro in tanto a l'aura, a l'ombra piglia,
e con la bianca man più fiori coglie;
per vergogna divien più allor vermiglia
la rosa, ché l'onor premier le toglie
coi purpurei color la bocca bella;
Silveria guarda e poi così favella.

"Dunque fia ver che quel sovran valore
che largo il ciel comparte a la tua mano,
l'ardir invitto e'l generoso core
più di donna non pur, ma più ch'umano,
in loco solitario, e pien d'orrore,
da le viste de gl'uomini lontano
s'impieghi e solo fian fere selvagge
testimonio di lui, l'erbe e le piagge?

"D'umili imprese omai (vil premio oscuro)
sdegni l'altera tua mente superba.
Tante eccellenze a te date non furo
per fere saettar, coltivar erba.
In città popolose, in regio muro,
e fra l'arme onestate ancor si serba;
più si deve a colei nome di casta
che, tentata, via più pugna e contrasta.

"Vincer tigre e leone e orso e cinghiale,
avventando lontan dardi e quadrella,
di paventoso rischio è gloria frale,
sol dovuta di boschi a pastorella.
Guerriera invitta tu, donna reale
meco amata sarai più che sorella.
Solo in guerra acquistar puote l'uom forte
gloriosa vittoria o illustre morte."

Sì l'una dice e l'altra, avendo inteso,
buona pezza riman dubia e confusa,
l'animo a quel che deggia far sospeso;
grazie le rende al fin dolce e si scusa.
"Dunque non sosterrai de l'arme il peso
tu sopra quel che 'l sesso debil usa—
replica quella—e fia di tua bell'alma
di fere e caccie sol bassa e vil palma?

"Ti fe' natura la persona e 'l petto
ben del mio forte e coraggioso al paro;
puoi la chioma coprir co'l grave elmetto,
premer le membra puoi co'l duro acciaro."

Silveria allor cui generoso affetto
l'arme vedute al cor prima destaro,
quest'ultimo parlar quasi rampogna
accese di magnanima vergogna.

Qual falcon pellegrin, se mano industre
il veder lungo tempo a lui contende,
s'apre al fin gl'occhi e, come il mondo illustre
il sol diletto e meraviglia prende
e del ciel vasto per lo campo illustre
dietro alla preda allegro il vol distende;
cotal Silveria a quel parlare accese
l'animo a grandi e bellicose imprese.

Canto 22.65–100. During the conclusive open-field battle, the elephants are launched to the assault. Silveria volunteers and is killed.

L'accorto mastro a le gran man avvinti
dei forti e saggi avea brandi pungenti,
al pungere, al tagliar l'han volti e spinti
questi, quasi ch'umane avesser menti,
onde furon da lor trafitti, estinti
molti guerrieri de' chiari e de' possenti.
Ben tutti al dorso ordigni han smisurati,
i quali gravidi son d'arme e d'armati.

Avventando venian questi sublimi
lance, pili nel pian, pietre e saette,
che con più forza uccidean più ne gl'imi
luoghi giù tratti e ne le turbe strette.
A sostener, a rintuzzar quei primi
empiti il fido Re primier si mette,
apparecchia, eseguisce, ordina, impera
secondo il luogo, il tempo, il bisogn'era.

Vedi di mille e mille man congionte
lance e spiedi vibrar punture mille
de le belve a gran fianchi, a la gran fronte,
e mille lampeggiar vive faville:
così ratto curò d'averle pronte
il provvid'uomo a l'uso e compartille.
E già il nemico natural presente
ecco cinghial grugnisce, arrota il dente.

Urlano allor le belve all'ululato,
quel campo intorno trema e ne rintrona.

Né fra le selve mai Borea serrato
stridente più così sibila e suona;
anzi non da bombarda unque cacciato
ferreo globo così per l'aria tuona,
non da gli avversi venti uniti insieme
percosso il mar mai così mugghia o freme.

Quei ch'a le nari han le pungenti spade
l'aggiron con furor sì violento
ch'ogni pensiero eccede, e giunto cade
cavallo e cavalier di vita spento.
Pur manda l'arte de le aperte strade
irrito il più di lor gran colpi al vento.
De' guerrier nondimen molti periro,
ch'incontrar pria l'orrende belve ardiro.

Pur quella parte d'essi è più sicura
che le faci vibrar più vicin puote,
sì le belve a terror move l'arsura
ch'insolita le viste a lor percote.
Possanza or chi ti nega o di natura
o influsso pur de le celesti rote?
Vince quel cor, che sprezzò morte ardito,
una lieve facella, un vil grugnito.

Le gran membra di fuor treman commosse
le naturali lor virtute interne,
e de le torri dier crollanti e scosse
a dentro orribil suon l'ampie caverne.
De l'arme e de' guerriei a gli urti smosse
le congionture s'allargar superne,
non pur le basse d'ogni intorno ai lati,
scoprendo i luoghi più chiusi e celati.

Nembo maggior di strali allor si vede
di lassù trar di pili e pietre dure,
che vendicar più ognun se vuol, se crede
che l'alta mole a quel furor non dure.
Al fin ciascuna belva indietro riede,
sentendo ai fianchi pur l'aspre punture,
udendo il fier cinghiale e le vibranti
faci vedendo fiammeggiarsi avanti.

Quinci il danno maggior del Perso venne,
la ruina fatal senza riparo,
ch'a quelle belve, che l'ardir pur tenne
ferme e 'l tergo a fuggir non rivoltaro,

con scimitarra i fidi e con bipenne
correndo immantinente i piè tagliaro:
puonno ad esse appressarsi a lor talento
sì quelle ingombra natural spavento.

Trema al cader di sì gran pondo a terra
ogni monte vicin, mugghia ogni valle,
ch'ogni lor torre ancor con lor s'atterra,
ma quelle ch'al fuggir volgon le spalle
ai propri amici inopinata guerra
fanno e co' brandi apron sanguigno calle,
pedoni e cavalier sossopra al suolo
mandan con gli urti e con le nari a volo.

Più d'una tosto il buon rettor n'arresta,
che preparato ad uopo tal là siede,
con ferro acuto a gran percossa in testa
e con danno di pochi a' più provvede.
Ma la strage non di men cruda e funesta
in orribil sembianze allor si vede,
con le torri le genti e l'arme Perse
precipitar, perir varie e diverse.

Ecco una torre appar cadente e china,
altra ecco cade, ecco il cader rattiene;
e tal che minacciò tarda ruina
più ratta al pian precipitando viene.
Ma lasciando la parte ove dechina
a l'opposta di lei lo stuol s'attiene,
e, con petto e con man possente e ferma,
l'urta, la spinge, contrappesa e ferma.

Salvo alcun de' guerrieri alcun drappello
al lato che restò sovra s'attacca
di più d'un già caduto al pian castello
quando un altro improvviso ecco si stacca,
e sopra dà precipitando a quello,
e colti in mezzo gl'infelici ammacca.
Fuor d'altro altri saltò, ma da l'istesso
che dietro gli ruina è in terra messo.

Altri anco fuor saltar primier s'affretta;
altri, che 'l proprio scampo anco procaccia,
senza aspettar dietro a colui si getta;
altri a lui sopra, e sì l'un l'altro schiaccia.
Trafigge in aria alcun aspra saetta

più d'un ch'al non cader la torre abbraccia,
resta da lancia o strale al legno affiso,
spettacol miserando ed improvviso.

Scampare in guisa tal pur si consiglia
Amero, e dalla torre ei salta in giuso,
ma spazio così corto al salto piglia
ch'a l'elefante fier cade sul muso,
che l'alza verso il ciel con maraviglia
tanto, che poco augel vola più suso;
e in cadendo su'l tergo a Fulvio coglie
romano, e 'l giorno allor allor gli toglie.

Rattenne intanto lui l'alta percossa
che vivo cadde tra' nemici al piano;
la persona sent'ei franta e percossa,
ma, d'alma invitta e di voler sovrano,
racquistar può sì la perduta possa
che forge e arma contra a lor la mano,
e così cauto e destro il ferro gira
che si fa strada e salvo a' suoi ritira.

Ma sovra tutti feritor possente
il Re fedele il Perso stuol paventa.
Smisurato castello e già cadente
di mille mani il gran poter sostenta.
Quando la nodoruta asta pungente
con poderosa mano il Re gli avventa,
fende l'aer massiccia ella e tonante,
indi si ficca in quel dura e tremante.

Facile e ratto allor nel pian trabocca
da quel poter ch'ogni potere eccede,
com'umil casa suol da fulmin tocca,
e in darno il Perso sostentarlo crede.
Rota più d'un la fromba e l'arco scocca,
più d'un con spada o lancia il punge e fiede:
non è giunto, o non sente, o non glien cale,
quasi celeste sia, non uom mortale.

Tuvignon ecco a le miserie estreme
alta speranza viene, alto riparo:
ad un fiero elefante il dorso preme
ch'ivi in grandezza altro non ebbe paro.
Par che scintilli il sol, l'aria più teme
a quel che l'arma rilucente acciaro,

a l'asta che con man robusta libra,
e dura e ponderosa a tempo vibra.

Avvistosi l'eroe subito d'esso
ch'or nel denso entra quel della battaglia,
nuova trave gli avventa in guisa appresso
che 'l nemico colpir mal è che vaglia;
anzi, avvisato quel nel punto stesso,
trae fuor la spada e al Re la lancia taglia,
la sua ratto prendendo ei con la manca,
ma non l'ardir per questo al buon Re manca.

Gli gira al fianco e sdegna oprar la spada,
ma corlo al piè col tronco ha buon riguardo;
forz'è che secondar la mente vada
la man veloce e l'elefante tardo,
e al piano colui precipitanto cada,
ancor che sì robusto e sì gagliardo,
a punto nel voltar, che volea presta
la belva, e belva il suo signor calpesta.

Ben nessun la sua furia frenar puote,
senza peso e rettor sciolta e sicura;
van le faci ver lei d'effetto vote,
non ha feroce de' cinghiai paura;
con lance e spiedi in van pur la percote
più d'un fedel sovra la pelle dura;
gli ordini, le fila in un rompe a traverso,
urta, apre, alza, ognun getta al pian riverso.

A riguardar la bellicosa fera,
cui d'appressar nessun par ch'abbia ardire,
sen stava intenta allor la bella arciera
svegliando dentro al cor le nobil ire.
Dolce indi prega la regal guerriera
che sola a tanto impresa or la lass'ire,
in uccider esperta ella tai belve
che più ne vide e vinse in monte e in selve.

Quantunque soffra mal la donna forte
ch'a tanta impresa senza lei si muova
ed abbia alcun timor de la sua morte,
ché nulla a quel furor resiste o giova,
pur, pensando al gran caso or quanto importe
al grand'onor di così bella prova
concede, ch'assicura il cor in parte
nel cacciar di colei l'usanza e l'arte.

Sovra a fina corazza argentea vesta
distinta con lavor di sottil ago,
la copre d'oro e di più gemme intesta,
a cui simil non diè l'Indo né 'l Tago.
Di tempra e pregio elmo superbo in testa
de la Reina sua don ricco e vago,
di stocco arma il bel fianco e 'l braccio, scarco
d'altr'arme, ha in vece lor lo stral e l'arco.

Ignudo ha il viso, e da le luci chiare
vibra splendor più scintillante fuore
che da lor più splendenti or più traspare
più dell'usanza sua guerriero il core.
Non può la chioma sì l'elmo celare
che ne reprima affatto il dolce errore,
ma in su la fronte lieve e ondeggiante
n'esce quasi oro a circondar diamante.

Tal da' begl'occhi e da la man saetta
guerra n'indice e in un promette pace.
S'apre la turba allor calcata e stretta
et a lei qual desia l'adito face:
ma sì la prova al Re fedel diletta,
poi che a Rosmonda sì diletta e piace,
che non vuole a la belva ei far offesa,
e corre u'l Turco fa maggior difesa.

Che lo stuol Perso è tanto oppresso e vinto
che intento a sua salute altrui non noce.
Strage fa il Re da' suoi guerrier sol cinto
de l'inimico orribile e feroce.
Ma, Silveria lo stral da l'arco spinto,
fendendo quei sen va l'aria veloce,
e notte in parte a la gran belva arreca,
ché 'l destro occhio trafigge e insieme acceca.

Per gran dolor si scosse e si contorse
e d'urlo rimbombar fé il monte e 'l piano,
e a vendicarsi in ver la parte corse
ch'aventò il colpo la nemica mano.
L' andò contro a colei, come ciò scorse,
sebben gran spazio era da lei lontano,
ma di cor generoso atto codardo
stimò di rischio in caso tal riguardo.

E si risolve onde vicin l'assale
con altr'arme ferirla, e l'arco lassa:

par che pronte a schivar ella abbia l'ale,
la belva che ver lei le nari abbassa,
avvisata colei pria, che le cale
di sotto a lor pur una volta passa,
in tal guisa leggiera e così a tempo
che dirai ch'ella imperi al moto, al tempo.

Si stima or ben d'ogni periglio fuore,
quel conseguito a pien ch'a l'oprar volle;
cerca nel colpo sol non far errore
dove ha la belva più la pelle molle,
ché nel fin delle coste ed indi al core
lo stocco caccia, ch'a ferirla tolle:
urla e cade, e le membra a cader preme
de l'infelice, e muoiono ambo insieme.

Nel volersi ritrar, quando a la fera
sì smisurata il mortal colpo diede,
che di sottrarsi a lei snella e leggera,
come soleva ebbe sicura fede.
Sdrucciolando cadeo nel piano, ov'era
gran sasso, in cui percosse il molle piede:
restò schiacciata da le gambe fino
al ventre, il resto langue al ciel supino.

Subito al suo cader suon indistinto
e flebil di più voci alzar s'intese,
ma con sembiante di pietà dipinto
la donzella real dal destrier scese,
torle di sopra l'elefante estinto
fece e al sen le rallentò l'arnese,
le trasse l'elmo da l'aurate chiome,
e di lei chiamò più volte il nome.

"Silveria mia, Silveria—a dir riprende—
qual destin empio or ne divide e parte?
Qual mio grave fallir or mi contende
su nel cielo, ove poggi, accompagnarte?
Così dicendo, il volto e 'l sen le rende
molle de l'onde de' begli occhi sparte,
e sì fatto dolor l'opprime intanto
che più parlar non può, se non col pianto.

Parve al nembo d'amor, che sì l'asperse,
che l'arciera gentil si risentisse;
alzò la man, le vaghe luci aperse,

e non so che, che non s'intese, disse:
la man le cadde, tacque, e le coverse
luci in colei sol tener puote fisse,
che in lor pur lesse: "O Imperatrice mia,
te non per morte la tua serva oblia."

Nube atra involve de' begl'occhi il sole,
e un candido pallor tinge il bel volto,
qual recisi talor gigli e viole
e da vergine man giacinto colto,
quando languir in sul principio suole;
né affatto il vago o 'l bel color gli è tolto:
par che qual de gli Dei fatta omicida
morte trionfi e nel bel volto rida.

GLOSSARY

Abydos (3.77), ancient city of the Troad, on the Hellespont. It was the home of Leander, who swam across the Hellespont every night to meet with Hero, a priestess living at Sestus, on the Thracian side.

Acerra (1.16), town near Naples.

Acheron (19.31, 23.76n), river of Hades, i.e., the underworld.

Actaeon (17.59), a hunter who surprised Artemis (Diana) while she was bathing naked and who was turned by her into a stag and torn to pieces by his own hounds.

Adige (19.22), river of northern Italy, flowing from the Alps to the Po Valley.

Adonis (15.40, 15.41), a Babylonian youth beloved by Aphrodite. He died of a wound received from a boar while hunting.

Adventurers (5.100, 9.73, 9.74, 9.76, 10.46, 22.5, 23.39), soldiers not in permanent service and reputed to be always the fiercest in battle.

Aegisthus (1.37), seducer of Clytemnestra and murderer of her husband, Agamemnon, when he returned home from the Trojan War.

Aeneas (1.26n, 2.26n, 5.5n, 5.12n, 5.100n, 7.51n, 7.55n, 9.18nn, 9.38n, 9.40n, 9.71n, 10, 11n, 15.3n, 15.36n, 23.48), the protagonist of Virgil's *Aeneid*.

Aeolus (5.106), Roman god of the winds. According to legend, he lived in the Aeolian Islands (also called Lipari Islands) off the north coast of Sicily, hence his name.

Africus (19.35), Latin name for the southwest wind that blows in Italy from Africa, today called "libeccio."

Agah (3.91, 5.13, 5.33, 5.36, 5.50, 5.65, 5.77, 5.87, 15.45, 21.61), title usually given to the state administrators of the Ottoman Empire.

Alba Longa (15.18n, 22.25), city of Latium that competed with Rome for supremacy in that region.

Alcides (10.1, 23.50), name given to Hercules, who was the grandson of Alcaeus. He was called Heracles by the Greeks. See Hercules.

Amantia (5.73, 7.48n, 10.9, 10.11, 10.14, 10.17, 10.23n), ancient city of the Amantes, native people of Epirus, known to the Romans as Amantini. It was situated on the heights between the Vjosa and the Shushica Rivers, not far from Vlora.[1] Sarrocchi, however, situates her Amantia in the plain six kilometers from Croia, perhaps after Barletius's geography: "Diximus enim jam Croiam Epiri urbem esse, in campis Aematiae," where "Aematia" is in fact the Mati River.[2]

Apelles (3.36), Greek painter, born in Ionia, Asia Minor. He lived at the time of Alexander the Great and painted his portrait, as well as a famous painting of Venus Anadyomene.

Apennines (3.80, 23.57), the chain of mountains extending from the north to the very south of the Italian peninsula.

Aquilus (3.30n, 3.76, 19.26), Roman name for Boreas, the north wind.

Arpino (7.85), a town in Latium, region around Rome, and the birthplace of Cicero.

Arthur (23.57), the main star in the constellation of the Great Bear, in the northern hemisphere.

Arthur (19.7), legendary king, head of the Roman-British resistance to the Saxon invasion of England. He is the main character in the stories of the Round Table, which are called Arthurian romances.

Ascoli (1.15), town in the region of Puglia, the ancient Apulia region. See Tarentine.

Astacus (3.43n, 3.48n, 3.49, 3.51), older name of Nicomedia, the capital of Bithynia, on the Sea of Marmora. See Nicomedia.

Astrean Mountains (18.132), possibly "eastern mountains," from Astreus, a Titan who, in some mythological stories, is the husband of Aurora or Dawn, which rises in the east.

Aurora (1.18, 2.70, 3.7, 3.65, 7.38, 7.72, 10.20n, 18.132n), or Dawn, Roman goddess of the early morning. In mythology, she is the concubine of Tithonus, son of the king of Troy, whom she made immortal when he was already old.

Ausonian (21.4), Italian, from "Ausonia," ancient Greek name for Italy.

Auster (1.62), Greek name of one of the south winds, called Notus by the Romans and Scirocco by the Italians.

---

1. Alain Ducellier, *La façade maritime de l'Albanie au moyen age* (Thessaloniki: Institute for Balkan Studies, 1981), 25.

2. Gegaj, *L'Albanie et l'invasion turque*, 33.

Avellino (1.16), town in southern Italy, northeast of Naples.

Bacchus (3.76, 15.39), god of wine and merriment.

Bactria (1.4), or Bactriana, a province of Persia, the modern Bokhara.

Bari (1.12, 1.13), town in Puglia, region of southern Italy.

Bithynia (3.43, 3.52), region of Asia Minor, lying on the Sea of Marmora and the Black Sea.

Boötes (14.64), a star in the constellation of the Great Bear.

Boreas (1.62, 3.30n, 15.26, 20.5, 20.103, 22.41, 22.68), north wind. In mythology, Boreas was the brother of Eurus, Zephyrus, and Notus, southeast, west, and southwest winds, respectively. He lived in a cave of Mount Haemus, in Thrace.

Bovino (1.15), the Roman Bovinum, capital of Samnium and now Pietrabbondante. Several other nearby towns and rivers are mentioned in 1.15–16. They are all found between Naples and the region of Puglia.

Brindisi (1.13n, 19.23), Italian town in the region of Puglia.

Brontes (23.48), a cyclops who forged the thunderbolts for Jupiter (Zeus) and worked on the armor of Aeneas. See Cyclops.

Bruttium (9.22), the most southern part of Italy, what is now southern Calabria.

Buda (1.52, 1.72, 2.15, 18.140n), Budapest.

Cädi (3.19), or kadi, an Islamic magistrate delegated by the sovereign to administer justice according to Islamic law.

Caesar (1.91n, 2.54, 10.47n, 10.48, 19.21n, 20.17n, 20.36n, 20.44, 20.57, 22.15n, 22.29), Caius Julius Caesar, the Roman general and writer, who was famously cheered by his soldiers when carried in triumph in the streets of Rome.

Calinno (10.11, 10.19, 10.20, 10.32, 10.49, 21.66, 22.14, 23.10, 23.15), in Sarrocchi's geography, a river near Amantia and in the plain between Croia and Presa.

Callisto (1.82, 13.5n, 14.64, 15.14n), a nymph, companion of Artemis in hunting, who was ravished by Zeus, persecuted by his wife, Juno, and metamorphosed into the constellation of the Bear.

Calore (1.15), small river north of Naples.

Cambyses (7.32), ancient king of Persia who crossed the hot sands of Arabia and conquered Egypt in 529–521 BCE.

Cannae (1.14), the modern Canne della battaglia, on the Òfanto River, in the region of Puglia, famous for the battle in which the Romans were defeated by the Carthaginian army of Hannibal in 216 BCE.

Capaneus (1.82), one of the seven heroes who fought against Thebes; he was struck by Zeus's thunderbolt while scaling the walls of that town (Statius, *Thebaid* 10.845; Dante, *Inferno* 14.46–48, 14.63–72).

Caria (7.42n, 19.70), region on the southwest coast of Asia Minor, in what is now Turkey.

Carthage (6.129n, 10.40n, 10.47, 22.29), Phrygian city northeast of Tunis, against which the Romans fought the Punic Wars; it was destroyed by them in 146 BCE, was rebuilt by Caesar in 44 BCE, later became a flourishing Christian center, and was finally destroyed by the Arabs in 697 CE.

Caudine Forks (1.16), narrow mountain pass near the ancient city of Caudium, in southern Italy, between Capua and Benevento, where in 321 BCE the Romans, trapped by the Samnites and forced to surrender, suffered the infamy of marching under the yoke.

Centaurs (6.104n, 23.56), fabulous creatures, half horse and half man, who lived in the mountains of Thessaly. Hercules killed some of them while he was pursuing the Erymanthian boar. See Nessus.

Cerberus (10.1), mythological dog with many heads, guardian at the doors of Hades, the underworld. In one of his labors, Hercules carried the monster up to earth.

Ceres (3.76), early Italian goddess of the harvest.

Cerignola (1.15), town in the region of Puglia.

Charon (23.76), the ferryman of the underworld, who carried the newly arrived dead across the river of Hades.

Claudiopolis (3.43), a town that Sarrocchi places in Thrace, on the frontier with Bithynia. The town is perhaps called by this name because Thrace was annexed to the Roman Empire in 45 CE, during the reign of Emperor Claudius.

Claudius (22.29), Roman consul who defeated Hasdrubal at the Metauro, a river near Urbino, in 207 BCE.

Cos (10.28), one of the Sporades Islands, birthplace of the physician Hippocrates (born c. 460 BCE), after whom the Hippocratic oath is named.

Creon (1.37), ancient king of Thebes who forbade the burial of Polynices and sentenced Antigone to death for disobeying his order.

Croia (1.1, 1.10, 1.72n, 2.36, 2.70, 3.3, 5.54, 5.58n, 5.68, 5.73n, 5.79, 5.93, 6.58, 7.45, 9.11, 9.71, 10.11n, 14.71, 18.106, 18.140, 20.114, 21.1, 21.52), modern Kruja, town north of Tirana, known in Roman times as Acrium, in the province of Illyricum. The town fortress, perched on a rocky spur of the Arbëni Mountains, was practically impregnable.

Cursor (20.44), possibly Cursor L. Papirius, a Roman general who repeatedly defeated the Samnites in the Samnite Wars, 325–309 BCE.

Cyclades (3.33n, 19.36, 19.76,), a group of islands between Crete and mainland Greece. Milos and Naxos are the best known of them.

Cyclops (3.65n, 3.66, 9.38n, 9.54n, 13.74, 23.48n), in Greek and Roman mythology, a race of gigantic one-eyed shepherds, living on the slopes of Mount Etna, in Sicily. The most famous of the Cyclopes is Polyphemus, who loved the nymph Galatea and was blinded by Ulysses. (Homer, *Odyssey* 9.105–566.) See Ulysses.

Cynthia (6.56, 7.41, 20.38), goddess of the moon and the chase, called Artemis by the Greeks and Diana by the Romans.

Cyzicus (3.61), ancient town on the Sea of Marmora, in northwest Turkey.

Daunia (1.10, 1.15n), or Dannia, ancient Greek name for the Italian land on both sides of the Òfanto river, in the Puglia region.

Delos (6.56n, 13.46), island of the Cyclades in the Aegean Sea, birthplace of Apollo and place of his worship.

Diana (1.82n, 6.56n, 13.23, 17.59), Roman goddess of the chase, identified with the Greek Artemis. See Actaeon and Cynthia.

Didamean Mountains (3.46), mountains of Bithynia.

Dipsas (20.97), a snake also called dispola.

Durazzo (1.10), town in northern Albania, the Roman Dyrrachium and modern Durrës, which in Scanderbeg's time was under Venetian domination.

Echo (1.82), a nymph who with her chattering distracted Juno, while Juno's husband, Jupiter, amused himself with the other nymphs. In punishment for it, Juno changed her into an echo.

Elia (3.30, 3.78, 5.20, 7.26, 23.73), Adrianople (the modern Edirne), then the capital of Thrace and of the Ottoman Empire. In 1453 Constantinople fell into Turkish hands and became the capital of the Ottoman Empire. See Thrace.

Emathia (3.76), region of Macedonia separated from Thrace by Mount Olympus.

Emathian fields (13.46), the countryside below Croia. Sarrocchi may have named them after the Mati River (modern Mat), which flows through it.

Eos (2.18n, 10.20), Greek goddess of the dawn, Aurora for the Romans. See Aurora.

Epirus (1.1, 1.5, 1.15n, 1.24n, 1.25, 1.32, 2.36n, 2.43, 2.54, 3.6, 3.22, 3.24, 3.28, 5.73n, 7.2, 7.5, 9.18n, 18.90, 20.9, 20.11, 21.5, 21.8, 21.11, 21.24, 22.2), a territory between the Ionian Sea and the Pindhos Mountains, now divided between Albania and Greece. It was unified into a kingdom by Pyrrhus (306–272 BCE) and annexed by the Romans after his death.

Erymanthian boar (3.94, 23.56n), famous boar that roamed on the slopes of Mount Erymanthus, in Arcadia, and was slain by Hercules in one of his labors.

Eurus (19.35, 23.37), southeast wind.

Euxine (3.55, 3.75), the Roman Pontus Euxinus and modern Black Sea.

Favonius (19.26), another name for Zephyr, the west wind.

Forino (1.16), town southwest of Avellino in the Italian region of Campania.

Galatea (3.34n, 3.65, 3.66), a sea nymph who rejected the cyclops Polyphemus and changed her lover Acis into a river, whom the cyclops then crushed under Mount Etna.

Gargano (1.11), mountainous promontory projecting into the Adriatic from southern Italy.

Gaza (3.43n, 3.89, 3.90, 10.50n), garrison town of Egypt and then one of the cities of the Philistines. It was besieged by Alexander the Great and by the crusaders. Sarrocchi seems to think that Gaza is in Lycia, a region in southwest Asia Minor.

Geryon (1.15), three-bodied monster who stole Eurytion's oxen and hid them in the land of Erythia, near the setting sun. Heracles was ordered to fetch the oxen and bring them to Eurystheus; he did so, after slaying Geryon. This is the subject of Heracles' tenth labor.

Gorgon (13.13n, 14.63), one of three sisters who could turn the beholder into stone. They were represented as monsters with claws and wings. The most famous of them is Medusa. She is represented with snakes in place of hair.

Haemorrhois (20.104), a legendary African snake whose bite poisoned the victim's blood and made it ooze off the skin.

Haemus (3.76), mountain range of Thessaly, now called the Great Balkans.

Harpalyce (13.17), mythical Thracian maiden, was raped by her father, Clymenos. After killing the child she had by him, she served it to Clymenos as a meal. In punishment of her crime, she was turned into a night bird.

Hebrus (3.30, 13.17), river of Thrace, now called Maritza.

Hector (5.58n, 5.86n, 6.81n, 9.55n, 20.17n, 20.77, 23.55n), Trojan hero in Homer's *Iliad*. He was killed by Achilles.

Hercules (1.56n, 1.82n, 3.94n, 10.1n, 23.20, 23.56n), called Heracles by the Greeks, and also Alcides because he was the son of Alcaeus. In one of his labors, he brought up Cerberus from the lower world. During his expedition against the Erymanthian boar, he killed the centaurs who had attacked him while he was dining in his cave.

Hercynia (7.32), German mountain range covered by dense forests.

Hister (2.18, 3.73, 18.142, 21.18), another name for the Danube River.

Hydra (3.94, 5.46), an imaginary animal described at times as a lion with three heads, at other times as a dragon. It lived in Lerna (a swampy valley in Argolis, Greece) and was eventually killed by Hercules in one of his labors.

Hypsicratia (5.19), concubine and follower of King Mithridate of Pontus during his military campaigns. She willingly died of the poison provided by him so that she would not fall into enemy hands.

Hyrcania (1.56), region on the south shore of the Caspian Sea, part of the ancient Persian empire.

Ida (3.53, 20.77), mountain in Asia Minor, near Troy.

Jacol (20.95), a snake, called Iaculus by the Romans.

Janissaries (2.19n, 3.12n, 3.88, 3.89, 3.99, 5.2, 5.13, 5.48, 5.59, 5.94, 15.33, 21.36, 21.62, 21.75, 23.62), Ottoman elite corps of foot soldiers, which included Muslims as well as Christians converted to Islam. See Spahis.

Janus (1.15), Roman god of gates and doorways, generally represented with two opposing faces.

Juno (1.3, 1.82, 13.32, 18.18n), Roman goddess of matrimony and protector of the female sex.

Jupiter (1.3n, 1.40, 1.82, 3.70n, 6.62, 6.104, 7.55n, 9.54, 14.68, 15.3n, 18.18, 20.59), Roman god, identified with the Greek Zeus.

Lachesis (5.22), one of the three Parcae, goddesses of the night and destiny. Lachesis is the one who decides how long each human life is to be.

Latium (9.18n, 15.18), modern Lazio, is the central administrative region of Italy where Rome is situated. In antiquity the name indicated the territory between the Sabine Mountains and the sea.

Lazarus (2.26), a character from the Gospels, resuscitated by Jesus after four days in the tomb.

Lernean Hydra (3.94). See Hydra.

Lisano (1.10), town in northern Albania, now Lëzhë, at that time a Venetian possession called Alessio.

Lofante (1.14), modern Òfanto, a river in the region of Puglia, in southern Italy.

Lucullus (22.10), Roman general who defeated Tigranes, king of Armenia, in 69 BCE. See Tigranes.

Lycia (3.90, 3.92), region on the south side of Asia Minor, now Turkey.

Lyncean Sea (19.37), possibly the sea off Argos, where the legendary King Lynceus once reigned.

Maecenas (1.13), minister of Emperor Augustus, famous for his patronage of Virgil and Horace.

Marcius (21.39) Roman general who defeated the Carthaginians in Spain in 212 BCE.

Marigliano (1.16), small town northeast of Naples.

Maronia (3.44), a Greek colony on the Mediterranean coast of Thrace.

Mars (2.48, 3.102, 6.62, 7.19, 7.71, 9.18, 9.38, 13.16, 20. 68, 20. 93, 22. 6), Roman god of war, lover of Venus. He is mentioned here also as the star.

Mati (1.10), a river in northern Albania, the modern Mat, in the Italian text called Mattin.

Mauretanian Sea (1.62), sea of Mauretania, a Roman colony of northern Africa, corresponding to part of Algeria and Morocco.

Medusa (13.13, 14.63n). See Gorgon.

Memphis (3.32), old city of Egypt, circa 2600–2200 BCE.

Midas (21.24), king of Phrygia. His prayer to Dionysus that everything he touched would turn into gold was granted.

Milos (19.76), island of the Cyclades, archipelago between Crete and mainland Greece.

Minerva (1.3, 13.13n, 20.93), Roman goddess of intelligence, patroness of inventions and crafts, including spinning and weaving.

Moesia (3.62), country corresponding to Bulgaria and part of Serbia.

Molfetta (1.13), a town in Puglia, the ancient Apulia.

Mongibello (1.10), old name of Mount Etna, in Sicily.

Mysia (3.52, 3.61n, 3.62), region in the northwest corner of Asia Minor, now Turkey.

Nabathae (19.26), the section of Arabia on the Red Sea.

Naxos (3.67, 19.35), the major island of the Cyclades, archipelago in the Aegean Sea.

Nemea (1.56, 3.94n), valley in Argolis, Greece, where Heracles killed the Nemean lion.

Nessus (6.104), a centaur who tried to force the wife of Hercules (here Jupiter's son), Deianira, and was killed by him.

Nicaea (3.43n, 3.46, 3.98), then an important town of Bithynia, the modern Isnik, in Turkey.

Nicomedia (3.43n, 3.48), city of Bithynia, originally called Astacus, in northwest Turkey. Sarrocchi calls Nicomedia a region and Astacus a town.

Nola (1.16), town north of Naples.

Notus (19.26, 19.35, 23.37), south wind. See Auster.

Olympus (3.76, 13.1, 13.17n), mountain of Thessaly, traditionally the abode of the Greek gods.

Orion (6.81, 7.42n, 23.55n), constellation that rises in November bringing cold and rain.

Palinuro (1.26n), in Virgil's *Aeneid*, Aeneas's faithful ship pilot.

Pallas (3.10n, 7.51n, 10.53n, 13.13), other name of Athena, Greek goddess of war and guardian of the state.

Parian (3.33), fine marble from Paros, one of the Cyclades Islands in the Aegean Sea.

Partenope (1.17), legendary name of a siren who lived and was buried in the territory of the future Naples and subsequently gave her name to the town.

Philipopolis (3.78), town founded by Philip of Macedon, capital of Thrace under the Romans, now called Plovdiv.

Philistines (3.90n, 10.50), people living in the Gaza region, rivals of the people of ancient Israel. See Samson.

Phoebus (1.17, 2.40, 6.56, 7.72, 9.38, 10.29), another name for Apollo, the sun god.

Phoenicia (19.1), region of the Middle East, roughly corresponding to Jordan, Lebanon, and part of modern Israel.

Picenes (18.136), Italic people living in the region called Picenum, which is along the Adriatic and roughly corresponds to the southern half of the modern region of Marche. On the northern border of this area is the city of Ancona.

Picenum (20.10). See Picenes.

Pomona (1.17), Roman goddess of fruit trees, particularly abundant in Campania, the region around Naples.

Pontius (1.16). Samnite general who in 321 BCE forced the Romans to surrender and pass under the yoke. See Caudine Forks.

Presa (6.128, 7.75, 9.10, 9.12, 10.11n, 10.13, 10.46, 13.48, 13.76, 17.56, 17.62, 20.11, 21.49, 21.52, 21.59), in Sarrocchi's geography, the base of military operation for the Turkish army. The place that linguistically suggested this name to Sarrocchi could have been Pritzren, or Preza, the latter a citadel situated on a hill facing Kruja, on the side of Cape Rodoni.[3] In the poem, however, Presa is given the strategic importance of Elbasan, a Turkish fortress on the Shkumbin River, much further to the south. In Roman times Elbasan, then known as Scampa, flourished because of its position on the Via Egnatia, a continuation of the Via Appia, leading from Italy to Greece. Destroyed during a Serbian-Bulgarian invasion around 1355, Elbasan was rebuilt by Mehmet II in 1466 and became his base of operations against

---

3. Ducellier, *La façade maritime*, 15.

Scanderbeg.[4] Barletius writes: "He [Mehmet] fitted it in every particular and made it an inhabited town, just as it had been many years
before, abounding in every needful and desirable thing."[5]

Procne (13.37), daughter of the Athenian king Pandion. She was changed
into a bird by the gods as she cried for help while being run after with
an axe by her husband, Tereus.

Puglia (1.10n, 1.12, 1.13n, 1.14n, 1.15n, 1.18n, 19.23n), or Puglie, region
of southern Italy. See Daunia.

Pyrrhus (1.15n, 9.18, 21.47n), king of Epirus and, for two short periods,
king of Macedon, who lived from 319 to 273 BCE. In 280 he crossed
the Adriatic and went to the aid of the Tarentines who were fighting
against Rome. He defeated the Romans at Asculum (Asculi), in
Apulia, in 279. His forces, however, were almost exhausted in that
battle, and from that time on, a victory with heavy losses has been
called a Pyrrhic victory.

Pyrrhus (9.18n, 9.55n), also called Neoptolemus, son of Achilles. In Virgil's
Aeneid he appears among the Greeks at the fall of Troy in canto
2.469–91and 2.526–47 and is mentioned as the founder of the kingdom of Epirus in canto 3.296 and 3.319.

Rhodes (19.37), island off the coast of Turkey.

Rhodope (3.30), a mountain in Thrace.

Rodoni (1.10), promontory on the northern coast of Albania, now Rodonit.

Ruo (1.13), the modern Ruvo di Puglia, in southern Italy.

Samos (3.35), island off the coast of modern Turkey. In antiquity, it was
famous for its school of statuary.

Samson (10.50), biblical judge (twelfth century BCE) who revealed to a
Philistine woman, Delilah, that the secret of his strength lay in his
long curls. She cut off his hair and consigned him to the Philistines.
After recovering his strength, Samson pulled down the temple at
Gaza, killing many of his enemies. (Judges 13.16.).

Sangarius (3.46), a river in Bythinia (Turkey), tributary of the Simois and
now called Sakarya.

Sava (1.26), river that runs into the Danube at Belgrade.

Scipio (6.129n, 7.55n, 9.67n, 10.30n, 10.40n, 20.36n, 20.45n, 22.29,
23.55n), Roman general, surnamed Africanus, who defeated Hannibal
at Zama, near Carthage, in 202 BCE.

4. Hodgkinson, *Skanderbeg*, 30–31.

5. Quoted in ibid., 212.

Scythia (3.62, 3.69), name alternatively given to a region comprising what is now Ukraine, Georgia, part of Rumania, and southwestern Russia, or to a territory east of the Don River and reaching as far as China. Sarrocchi gives Scythia the alternative name of Mysia, which, however, was all included in what is now Rumania.

Sebeto (1.12, 1.17), the Roman Sebethus, modern Sàbato, a small river running near Naples in Campania .

Simois (3.53), one of the two rivers near Troy made famous by Homer, the other being the Scamander.

Sirius (9.54, 20.98), the Dog Star.

Sleep (1.26n), or Somnus in Latin, son of Night and the brother of Death. He dwells in the Cimmerian Caves, on the farthest side of the Ocean. Sleep's sons, Ikelos and Morpheus, lingered at the foot of their father's bed and changed themselves into dreamlike figures, Ikelos into various human figures and Morpheus into animal ones.

Smyrna (19.87, 19.88), city of the Aegean coast of Turkey, Ismir in Turkish.

Spahis (3.88n, 3.99, 5.12, 5.35), mounted army corps of the Ottoman Empire, whose members were drawn from the Moslem population. They vied in valor with the Janissaries. See Janissaries.

Spurius (1.16), Roman general ambushed by the Samnites in the Caudine Forks in 321 BCE. See Caudine Forks.

Steropes (9.54), one of the Cyclopes who lived inside Mount Etna and helped Vulcan to forge lightning for Jupiter and arrows for heroes. See Cyclops.

Stygian night (19.24), dark night, from Styx, a river in the world of the dead.

Stygian swamp (23.76), swamp formed by the River Styx in the netherworld. See Dante, *Inferno* 7.106.

Sulmona (3.67), town in the Abbruzzi region, in central Italy, birthplace of Ovid. See Tomis.

Syracuse (10.23, 18.136n), Greek colony of Sicily, where Archimedes, mathematician and natural philosopher, lived in the third century BCE.

Syrtes (23.57), stretches of the North African shore where hidden rocks, quicksands, and variable tides make for perilous landings.

Tagus (22.89), river in central Spain, the modern Tajo.

Tantalus (6.102), legendary king of Lydia who, in punishment for having betrayed the trust of Zeus, suffers in hell the pain of never being able to get hold of the food and the water that seem to be within his reach.

Tarentine (1.15, 9.18n), Pyrrhus of Epirus, who defeated the Roman army near Asculum (Ascoli), in Apulia, in 279 BCE.

Tartarus (2.26, 14.68n), synonym of Hades, the underworld.

Terebinth (9.16), Valley of Elah, where David fought Goliath.

Thermopylae (3.56), a mountain pass in Thessaly where one thousand Greeks died in 480 BCE fighting the Persian army.

Thessaly (2.36, 2.41, 2.43, 6.104n), region sharing the frontiers with Epirus on its eastern side.

Thetis (7.24, 21.60), a marine divinity, whose name often stands for the sea.

Thrace (1.21, 3.3, 3.28, 3.30, 3.43n, 3.44n, 3.71, 3.76n, 3.78n, 13.17n, 21.22n, 21.38, 22.21), name used to refer to the European territory that in Scanderbeg's times was occupied by the Turks.

Thule (1.4), an island regarded by the ancients as the furthest northern point in Europe, at times identified with one of the Shetland Islands, at other times with Iceland, as in Virgil's augury to Augustus: "Tibi serviat ultima Tule" (*Georgics* 1.30).

Tigranes (22.10), king of Armenia (94–55 BCE), defeated by the Roman general Lucullus, submitted to Pompey, and was left by him in possession of Armenia with the title of king.

Tomis (3.62, 3.67n), town on the west side of the Black Sea, now Constantsa in Rumania. The poet Ovid was exiled there by Emperor Augustus. The region is surrounded by mountains, here called Tomis Mountains.

Trajan (3.27n, 13.2, 13.9n, 18.136n), Roman emperor (98–117 CE). According to a medieval legend, he stopped to do justice for a wronged widow before proceeding to the battlefield.

Trani (1.13), town on the Adriatic coast, in the Puglia region.

Tripalto (1.15), small river north of Naples.

Tumenishti (5.53, 5.54), a mountain next to the one on which the fortress of Croia is perched. Sarrocchi calls it Toministo. She is probably referring to the mountain at the northwest side of the city, which was once called Tushemishti, and now is called Mount Scanderbeg.

Typhon (14.68), one of the giants who fought against the gods. He was struck by Jupiter's thunderbolt and buried under Mount Etna, in Sicily.

Ulysses (13.40n, 13.74, 19.32n, 19.37), Greek hero of the Trojan War and protagonist of Homer's *Odyssey*. He wandered throughout the Mediterranean before being able to reach the island of Ithaca, his birthplace and kingdom. In Sicily he escaped from the cyclops Polyphemus by blinding him in his only eye. He is also a character in Dante's *Inferno* 26.119–20. See Cyclops.

Urbino (22.29), a town in the Marche region of Italy.

Valona (19.23), Albanian town and harbor, modern Vlore.

Venus (2.26n, 3.36n, 3.37n, 7.71, 13.32, 15.39, 15.40n, 15.41n, 18.11), the goddess Venus or Aphrodite, lover of Mars; (3.13n, 6.62), a star.

Vesuvio (10.1), volcano on the eastern shore of the Bay of Naples, Italy.

Vizier (3.27), title given in the Ottoman Empire to a man in the position of a high minister of state.

Voivode (14.87, 15.14), or *voyevoda* in Russian, title given to army leaders and to governors of towns and provinces in many Slavic countries; here it is used in reference to Walachia.

Vulcan (9.38n, 9.54n, 15.3, 23.48), Roman god of fire who made Jupiter's thunderbolts and the armor for gods and heroes.

Vulcano (10.1), name of a volcano on the homonymous island of the Lipari archipelago (the Aeolian islands of old), north of Sicily.

Xanthus (3.53), river god of the Scamander River. It stands here for the river itself. Scamander and Simois are the two celebrated rivers of the Troad, running west and north of Troy, respectively..

Xerxes (3.31n, 3.43n, 3.56, 21.2n, 21.29n, 22.10n), king of Persia who defeated the Greeks at Thermopylae in 480 BCE.

Zante (19.35), Venetian name for Zákynthos, an island in the Ionian Sea, off the coast of Greece.

Zephyr (13.33, 19.22, 19.26n), or Zephyrus, a west wind.

Zeuxis (3.36), Greek painter, native of Lucania, Italy, who flourished c. 424–380 BCE. The anecdote of the birds who mistook his painting for real fruit is famous.

SERIES EDITORS'
BIBLIOGRAPHY

PRIMARY SOURCES

Alberti, Leon Battista (1404–72). *The Family in Renaissance Florence*. Translated by Renée Neu Watkins. Columbia: University of South Carolina Press, 1969.

Arenal, Electa and Stacey Schlau, eds. *Untold Sisters: Hispanic Nuns in Their Own Works*. Translated by Amanda Powell. Albuquerque: University of New Mexico Press, 1989.

Astell, Mary (1666–1731). *The First English Feminist: Reflections on Marriage and Other Writings*. Edited and introduction by Bridget Hill. New York: St. Martin's Press, 1986.

Atherton, Margaret, ed. *Women Philosophers of the Early Modern Period*. Indianapolis, IN: Hackett, 1994.

Aughterson, Kate, ed. *Renaissance Woman: Constructions of Femininity in England: A Source Book*. London: Routledge, 1995.

Barbaro, Francesco (1390–1454). *On Wifely Duties* (preface and book 2). Translated by Benjamin Kohl in Kohl and R. G. Witt, eds., *The Earthly Republic*. Philadelphia: University of Pennsylvania Press, 1978, 179–228.

Behn, Aphra. *The Works of Aphra Behn*. 7 vols. Edited by Janet Todd. Columbus: Ohio State University Press, 1992–96.

Boccaccio, Giovanni (1313–75). *Famous Women*. Edited and translated by Virginia Brown. The I Tatti Renaissance Library. Cambridge, MA: Harvard University Press, 2001.

———. *Corbaccio or the Labyrinth of Love*. Translated by Anthony K. Cassell. 2nd rev. ed. Binghamton, NY: Medieval and Renaissance Texts and Studies, 1993.

Brown, Sylvia. *Women's Writing in Stuart England: The Mother's Legacies of Dorothy Leigh, Elizabeth Joscelin and Elizabeth Richardson*. Thrupp, Stroud, Gloucestershire: Sutton, 1999.

Bruni, Leonardo (1370–1444). "On the Study of Literature (1405) to Lady Battista Malatesta of Moltefeltro." In *The Humanism of Leonardo Bruni: Selected Texts*. Translated and introduction by Gordon Griffiths, James Hankins, and David Thompson. Binghamton, NY: Medieval and Renaissance Studies and Texts, 1987, 240–51.

Castiglione, Baldassare (1478–1529). *The Book of the Courtier*. Translated by George Bull. New York: Penguin, 1967. *The Book of the Courtier*. Edited by Daniel Javitch. New York: W. W. Norton, 2002.

Christine de Pizan (1365–1431). *The Book of the City of Ladies*. Translated by Earl Jeffrey Richards. Foreword by Marina Warner. New York: Persea, 1982.

––––––. *The Treasure of the City of Ladies*. Translated by Sarah Lawson. New York: Viking Penguin, 1985. Also translated and introduction by Charity Cannon Willard. Edited and introduction by Madeleine P. Cosman. New York: Persea, 1989.

Clarke, Danielle, ed. *Isabella Whitney, Mary Sidney and Aemilia Lanyer: Renaissance Women Poets*. New York: Penguin, 2000.

Crawford, Patricia, and Laura Gowing, eds. *Women's Worlds in Seventeenth-Century England: A Source Book*. London: Routledge, 2000.

Daybell, James, ed. *Early Modern Women's Letter Writing, 1450–1700*. Houndmills, England:: Palgrave, 2001.

Elizabeth I: Collected Works. Edited by Leah S. Marcus, Janel Mueller, and Mary Beth Rose. Chicago: University of Chicago Press, 2000.

Elyot, Thomas (1490–1546). *Defence of Good Women: The Feminist Controversy of the Renaissance*. Facsimile Reproductions. Edited by Diane Bornstein. New York: Delmar, 1980.

Erasmus, Desiderius (1467–1536). *Erasmus on Women*. Edited by Erika Rummel. Toronto: University of Toronto Press, 1996.

Female and Male Voices in Early Modern England: An Anthology of Renaissance Writing. Edited by Betty S. Travitsky and Anne Lake Prescott. New York: Columbia University Press, 2000.

Ferguson, Moira, ed. *First Feminists: British Women Writers 1578–1799*. Bloomington: Indiana University Press, 1985.

Galilei, Maria Celeste. *Sister Maria Celeste's Letters to Her Father, Galileo*. Edited by and Translated by Rinaldina Russell. Lincoln, NE: Writers Club Press of Universe.com, 2000. Also published as *To Father: The Letters of Sister Maria Celeste to Galileo, 1623–1633*. Translated by Dava Sobel. London: Fourth Estate, 2001.

Gethner, Perry, ed. *The Lunatic Lover and Other Plays by French Women of the 17th and 18th Centuries*. Portsmouth, NH: Heinemann, 1994.

Glückel of Hameln (1646–1724). *The Memoirs of Glückel of Hameln*. Translated by Marvin Lowenthal. New introduction by Robert Rosen. New York: Schocken Books, 1977.

Henderson, Katherine Usher, and Barbara F. McManus, eds. *Half Humankind: Contexts and Texts of the Controversy about Women in England, 1540–1640*. Urbana: Illinois University Press, 1985.

Hoby, Margaret. *The Private Life of an Elizabethan Lady: The Diary of Lady Margaret Hoby 1599–1605*. Thrupp, Stroud, Gloucestershire: Sutton, 1998.

Humanist Educational Treatises. Edited and translated by Craig W. Kallendorf. The I Tatti Renaissance Library. Cambridge, MA: Harvard University Press, 2002.

Joscelin, Elizabeth. *The Mothers Legacy to Her Unborn Childe*. Edited by Jean leDrew Metcalfe. Toronto: University of Toronto Press, 2000.

Kaminsky, Amy Katz, ed. *Water Lilies, Flores del agua: An Anthology of Spanish Women Writers from the Fifteenth Through the Nineteenth Century*. Minneapolis: University of Minnesota Press, 1996.

Kempe, Margery (1373–1439). *The Book of Margery Kempe.* Translated by and edited by Lynn Staley. A Norton Critical Edition. New York: W. W. Norton, 2001.

King, Margaret L., and Albert Rabil, Jr., eds. *Her Immaculate Hand: Selected Works by and about the Women Humanists of Quattrocento Italy.* Binghamton, NY: Medieval and Renaissance Texts and Studies, 1983; second revised paperback edition, 1991.

Klein, Joan Larsen, ed. *Daughters, Wives, and Widows: Writings by Men about Women and Marriage in England, 1500–1640.* Urbana: University of Illinois Press, 1992.

Knox, John (1505–72). *The Political Writings of John Knox: The First Blast of the Trumpet against the Monstrous Regiment of Women and Other Selected Works.* Edited by Marvin A. Breslow. Washington, DC: Folger Shakespeare Library, 1985.

Kors, Alan C., and Edward Peters, eds. *Witchcraft in Europe, 400–1700: A Documentary History.* Philadelphia: University of Pennsylvania Press, 2000.

Krämer, Heinrich, and Jacob Sprenger. *Malleus Maleficarum* (ca. 1487). Translated by Montague Summers. London: Pushkin Press, 1928. Reprint, New York: Dover, 1971.

Larsen, Anne R., and Colette H. Winn, eds. *Writings by Pre-Revolutionary French Women: From Marie de France to Elizabeth Vigée-Le Brun.* New York: Garland, 2000.

de Lorris, William, and Jean de Meun. *The Romance of the Rose.* Translated by Charles Dahlbert. Princeton, NJ: Princeton University Press, 1971. Reprint, University Press of New England, 1983.

Marguerite d'Angoulême, Queen of Navarre (1492–1549). *The Heptameron.* Translated by P. A. Chilton. New York: Viking Penguin, 1984.

Mary of Agreda. *The Divine Life of the Most Holy Virgin.* Abridgment of *The Mystical City of God.* Abridged by Fr. Bonaventure Amedeo de Caesarea, M.C. Translated from the French by Abbé Joseph A. Boullan. Rockford, IL: Tan Books, 1997.

Myers, Kathleen A., and Amanda Powell, eds. *A Wild Country Out in the Garden: The Spiritual Journals of a Colonial Mexican Nun.* Bloomington: Indiana University Press, 1999.

Russell, Rinaldina, ed. *Sister Maria Celeste's Letters to Her Father, Galileo.* San Jose: Writers Club Press, 2000.

Teresa of Avila, Saint (1515–82). *The Life of Saint Teresa of Avila by Herself.* Translated by J. M. Cohen. New York: Viking Penguin, 1957.

Weyer, Johann (1515–88). *Witches, Devils, and Doctors in the Renaissance: Johann Weyer, De praestigiis daemonum.* Edited by George Mora with Benjamin G. Kohl, Erik Midelfort, and Helen Bacon. Translated by John Shea. Binghamton, NY: Medieval and Renaissance Texts and Studies, 1991.

Wilson, Katharina M., ed. *Medieval Women Writers.* Athens: University of Georgia Press, 1984.

———, ed. *Women Writers of the Renaissance and Reformation.* Athens: University of Georgia Press, 1987.

Wilson, Katharina M., and Frank J. Warnke, eds. *Women Writers of the Seventeenth Century.* Athens: University of Georgia Press, 1989.

Wollstonecraft, Mary. *A Vindication of the Rights of Men and a Vindication of the Rights of Women.* Edited by Sylvana Tomaselli. Cambridge: Cambridge University Press, 1995. Also *The Vindications of the Rights of Men, The Rights of Women.* Edited by D. L. Macdonald and Kathleen Scherf. Peterborough, Ontario, Canada: Broadview Press, 1997.

Women Critics 1660–1820: An Anthology. Edited by the Folger Collective on Early Women Critics. Bloomington: Indiana University Press, 1995.

Women Writers in English, 1350–1850. 15 vols. published through 1999 (projected 30-volume series suspended). Oxford University Press.

Wroth, Lady Mary. *The Countess of Montgomery's Urania.* 2 parts. Edited by Josephine A. Roberts. Tempe, AZ: MRTS, 1995, 1999.

————. *Lady Mary Wroth's "Love's Victory": The Penshurst Manuscript.* Edited by Michael G. Brennan. London: The Roxburghe Club, 1988.

————. *The Poems of Lady Mary Wroth.* Edited by Josephine A. Roberts. Baton Rouge: Louisiana State University Press, 1983.

de Zayas, Maria. *The Disenchantments of Love.* Translated by H. Patsy Boyer. Albany: State University of New York Press, 1997.

————. *The Enchantments of Love: Amorous and Exemplary Novels.* Translated by H. Patsy Boyer. Berkeley and Los Angeles: University of California Press, 1990.

SECONDARY SOURCES

Ahlgren, Gillian. *Teresa of Avila and the Politics of Sanctity.* Ithaca, NY: Cornell University Press, 1996.

Akkerman, Tjitske, and Siep Sturman, eds. *Feminist Thought in European History, 1400–2000.* London: Routledge, 1997.

Allen, Sister Prudence, R.S.M. *The Concept of Woman: The Aristotelian Revolution, 750 B.C. – A.D. 1250.* Grand Rapids, MI: William B. Eerdmans, 1997.

————. *The Concept of Woman.* Vol. 2, *The Early Humanist Reformation, 1250–1500.* Grand Rapids, MI: William B. Eerdmans, 2002.

Andreadis, Harriette. *Sappho in Early Modern England: Female Same-Sex Literary Erotics 1550–1714.* Chicago: University of Chicago Press, 2001.

Armon, Shifra. *Picking Wedlock: Women and the Courtship Novel in Spain.* New York: Rowman & Littlefield Publishers, Inc., 2002.

Backer, Anne Liot Backer. *Precious Women.* New York: Basic Books, 1974.

Ballaster, Ros. *Seductive Forms.* New York: Oxford University Press, 1992.

Barash, Carol. *English Women's Poetry, 1649–1714: Politics, Community, and Linguistic Authority.* New York: Oxford University Press, 1996.

Battigelli, Anna. *Margaret Cavendish and the Exiles of the Mind.* Lexington, KY: University of Kentucky Press, 1998.

Beasley, Faith. *Revising Memory: Women's Fiction and Memoirs in Seventeenth-Century France.* New Brunswick: Rutgers University Press, 1990.

Beilin, Elaine V. *Redeeming Eve: Women Writers of the English Renaissance.* Princeton, NJ: Princeton University Press, 1987.

Benson, Pamela Joseph. *The Invention of Renaissance Woman: The Challenge of Female Independence in the Literature and Thought of Italy and England.* University Park, PA: Pennsylvania State University Press, 1992.

Benson, Pamela Joseph, and Victoria Kirkham, eds. *Strong Voices, Weak History? Medieval and Renaissance Women in their Literary Canons: England, France, Italy.* Ann Arbor: University of Michigan Press, 2003.

Bilinkoff, Jodi. *The Avila of Saint Teresa: Religious Reform in a Sixteenth-Century City.* Ithaca: Cornell University Press, 1989.

Bissell, R. Ward. *Artemisia Gentileschi and the Authority of Art.* University Park: Pennsylvania State University Press, 2000.

Blain, Virginia, Isobel Grundy, AND Patricia Clements, eds. *The Feminist Companion to Literature in English: Women Writers from the Middle Ages to the Present.* New Haven, CT: Yale University Press, 1990.

Bloch, R. Howard. *Medieval Misogyny and the Invention of Western Romantic Love.* Chicago: University of Chicago Press, 1991.

Bornstein, Daniel and Roberto Rusconi, eds. *Women and Religion in Medieval and Renaissance Italy.* Translated by Margery J. Schneider. Chicago: University of Chicago Press, 1996.

Brant, Clare, and Diane Purkiss, eds. *Women, Texts and Histories, 1575–1760.* London: Routledge, 1992.

Briggs, Robin. *Witches and Neighbours: The Social and Cultural Context of European Witchcraft.* New York: HarperCollins, 1995; Viking Penguin, 1996.

Brink, Jean R., ed. *Female Scholars: A Tradition of Learned Women before 1800.* Montréal: Eden Press Women's Publications, 1980.

Broude, Norma, and Mary D. Garrard, eds. *The Expanding Discourse: Feminism and Art History.* New York: HarperCollins, 1992.

Brown, Judith C. *Immodest Acts: The Life of a Lesbian Nun in Renaissance Italy.* New York: Oxford University Press, 1986.

Brown, Judith C. , and Robert C. Davis, eds. *Gender and Society in Renaissance Italy.* London: Addison Wesley Longman, 1998.

Bynum, Carolyn Walker. *Fragmentation and Redemption: Essays on Gender and the Human Body in Medieval Religion.* New York: Zone Books, 1992.

———. *Holy Feast and Holy Fast: The Religious Significance of Food to Medieval Women.* Berkeley: University of California Press, 1987.

Cambridge Guide to Women's Writing in English. Edited by Lorna Sage. Cambridge: University Press, 1999.

Cavanagh, Sheila T. *Cherished Torment: The Emotional Geography of Lady Mary Wroth's Urania.* Pittsburgh: Duquesne University Press, 2001.

Cerasano, S. P. and Marion Wynne-Davies, eds. *Readings in Renaissance Women's Drama: Criticism, History, and Performance 1594–1998.* London: Routledge, 1998.

Cervigni, Dino S., ed. *Women Mystic Writers. Annali d'Italianistica* 13 (1995) (entire issue).

Cervigni, Dino S., and Rebecca West, eds. *Women's Voices in Italian Literature. Annali d'Italianistica* 7 (1989) (entire issue).

Charlton, Kenneth. *Women, Religion and Education in Early Modern England.* London: Routledge, 1999.

Chojnacka, Monica. *Working Women in Early Modern Venice.* Baltimore: Johns Hopkins University Press, 2001.

Chojnacki, Stanley. *Women and Men in Renaissance Venice: Twelve Essays on Patrician Society.* Baltimore: Johns Hopkins University Press, 2000.

Cholakian, Patricia Francis. *Rape and Writing in the "Heptameron" of Marguerite de Navarre.* Carbondale: Southern Illinois University Press, 1991.

———. *Women and the Politics of Self-Representation in Seventeenth-Century France.* Newark: University of Delaware Press, 2000.

Christine de Pizan: A Casebook. Edited by Barbara K. Altmann and Deborah L. McGrady. New York: Routledge, 2003.

Clogan, Paul Maruice, ed. *Medievali et Humanistica: Literacy and the Lay Reader.* Lanham, MD: Rowman & Littlefield, 2000.

Clubb, Louise George (1989). *Italian Drama in Shakespeare's Time.* New Haven, CT: Yale University Press.

Conley, John J., S.J. *The Suspicion of Virtue: Women Philosophers in Neoclassical France.* Ithaca, NY: Cornell University Press, 2002.

Crabb, Ann. *The Strozzi of Florence: Widowhood and Family Solidarity in the Renaissance.* Ann Arbor: University of Michigan Press, 2000.

Cruz, Anne J., and Mary Elizabeth Perry, eds. *Culture and Control in Counter-Reformation Spain.* Minneapolis: University of Minnesota Press, 1992.

Davis, Natalie Zemon. *Society and Culture in Early Modern France.* Stanford: Stanford University Press, 1975. Especially chapters 3 and 5.

———. *Women on the Margins: Three Seventeenth-Century Lives.* Cambridge, MA: Harvard University Press, 1995.

DeJean, Joan. *Ancients Against Moderns: Culture Wars and the Making of a Fin de Siècle.* Chicago: University of Chicago Press, 1997.

———. *Fictions of Sappho, 1546–1937.* Chicago: University of Chicago Press, 1989.

———. *The Reinvention of Obscenity: Sex, Lies, and Tabloids in Early Modern France.* Chicago: University of Chicago Press, 2002.

———. *Tender Geographies: Women and the Origins of the Novel in France.* New York: Columbia University Press, 1991.

Dictionary of Russian Women Writers. Edited by Marina Ledkovsky, Charlotte Rosenthal, and Mary Zirin. Westport, CT: Greenwood Press, 1994.

Dixon, Laurinda S. *Perilous Chastity: Women and Illness in Pre-Enlightenment Art and Medicine.* Ithaca: Cornell Universitiy Press, 1995.

Dolan, Frances, E. *Whores of Babylon: Catholicism, Gender and Seventeenth-Century Print Culture.* Ithaca: Cornell University Press, 1999.

Donovan, Josephine. *Women and the Rise of the Novel, 1405–1726.* New York: St. Martin's Press, 1999.

De Erauso, Catalina. *Lieutenant Nun: Memoir of a Basque Transvestite in the New World.* Translated by Michele Ttepto and Gabriel Stepto; foreword by Marjorie Garber. Boston: Beacon Press, 1995.

Encyclopedia of Continental Women Writers. 2 vols. Edited by Katharina Wilson. New York: Garland, 1991.

Erdmann, Axel. *My Gracious Silence: Women in the Mirror of Sixteenth-Century Printing in Western Europe.* Luzern: Gilhofer and Rauschberg, 1999.

Erickson, Amy Louise. *Women and Property in Early Modern England.* London: Routledge, 1993.

Ezell, Margaret J. M. *The Patriarch's Wife: Literary Evidence and the History of the Family.* Chapel Hill: University of North Carolina Press, 1987.

———. *Social Authorship and the Advent of Print.* Baltimore: Johns Hopkins University Press, 1999.

———. *Writing Women's Literary History.* Baltimore: Johns Hopkins University Press, 1993.

Farrell, Michèle Longino. *Performing Motherhood: The Sévigné Correspondence.* Hanover, NH: University Press of New England, 1991.

The Feminist Companion to Literature in English: Women Writers from the Middle Ages to the Present. Edited by Virginia Blain, Isobel Grundy, and Patricia Clements. New Haven, CT: Yale University Press, 1990.

The Feminist Encyclopedia of German Literature. Edited by Friederike Eigler and Susanne Kord. Westport, CT: Greenwood Press, 1997.

Feminist Encyclopedia of Italian Literature. Edited by Rinaldina Russell. Westport, CT: Greenwood Press, 1997.

Ferguson, Margaret W. *Dido's Daughters: Literacy, Gender, and Empire in Early Modern England and France.* Chicago: University of Chicago Press, 2003.

Ferguson, Margaret W., Maureen Quilligan, and Nancy J. Vickers, eds. *Rewriting the Renaissance: The Discourses of Sexual Difference in Early Modern Europe.* Chicago: University of Chicago Press, 1987.

Ferraro, Joanne M. *Marriage Wars in Late Renaissance Venice.* Oxford: Oxford University Press, 2001.

Fletcher, Anthony. *Gender, Sex and Subordination in England 1500–1800.* New Haven, CT: Yale University Press, 1995.

French Women Writers: A Bio-Bibliographical Source Book. Edited by Eva Martin Sartori and Dorothy Wynne Zimmerman. Westport, CT: Greenwood Press, 1991.

Frye, Susan and Karen Robertson, eds. *Maids and Mistresses, Cousins and Queens: Women's Alliances in Early Modern England.* Oxford: Oxford University Press, 1999.

Gallagher, Catherine. *Nobody's Story: The Vanishing Acts of Women Writers in the Marketplace, 1670–1820.* Berkeley: University of California Press, 1994.

Garrard, Mary D. *Artemisia Gentileschi: The Image of the Female Hero in Italian Baroque Art.* Princeton, NJ: Princeton University Press, 1989.

Gelbart, Nina Rattner. *The King's Midwife: A History and Mystery of Madame du Coudray.* Berkeley: University of California Press, 1998.

Glenn, Cheryl. *Rhetoric Retold: Regendering the Tradition from Antiquity through the Renaissance.* Carbondale: Southern Illinois University Press, 1997.

Goffen, Rona. *Titian's Women.* New Haven, CT: Yale University Press, 1997.

Goldberg, Jonathan. *Desiring Women Writing: English Renaissance Examples.* Stanford: Stanford University Press, 1997.

Goldsmith, Elizabeth C. *Exclusive Conversations: The Art of Interaction in Seventeenth-Century France.* Philadelphia: University of Pennsylvania Press, 1988.

———, ed. *Writing the Female Voice.* Boston: Northeastern University Press, 1989.

Goldsmith, Elizabeth C., and Dena Goodman, eds. *Going Public: Women and Publishing in Early Modern France.* Ithaca: Cornell University Press, 1995.

Grafton, Anthony, and Lisa Jardine. *From Humanism to the Humanities: Education and the Liberal Arts in Fifteenth-and Sixteenth-Century Europe.* London: Duckworth, 1986.

Greer, Margaret Rich. *Maria de Zayas Tells Baroque Tales of Love and the Cruelty of Men.* University Park: Pennsylvania State University Press, 2000.

Hackett, Helen. *Women and Romance Fiction in the English Renaissance.* Cambridge: Cambridge University Press, 2000.

Hall, Kim F. *Things of Darkness: Economies of Race and Gender in Early Modern England.* Ithaca, NY: Cornell University Press, 1995.

Hampton, Timothy. *Literature and the Nation in the Sixteenth Century: Inventing Renaissance France*. Ithaca, NY: Cornell University Press, 2001.

Hannay, Margaret, ed. *Silent But for the Word*. Kent, OH: Kent State University Press, 1985.

Hardwick, Julie. *The Practice of Patriarchy: Gender and the Politics of Household Authority in Early Modern France*. University Park: Pennsylvania State University Press, 1998.

Harris, Barbara J. *English Aristocratic Women, 1450–1550: Marriage and Family, Property and Careers*. New York: Oxford University Press, 2002.

Harth, Erica. *Ideology and Culture in Seventeenth-Century France*. Ithaca: Cornell University Press, 1983.

————. *Cartesian Women: Versions and Subversions of Rational Discourse in the Old Regime*. Ithaca: Cornell University Press, 1992.

Harvey, Elizabeth D. *Ventriloquized Voices: Feminist Theory and English Renaissance Texts*. London: Routledge, 1992.

Haselkorn, Anne M., and Betty Travitsky, eds. *The Renaissance Englishwoman in Print: Counterbalancing the Canon*. Amherst: University of Massachusetts Press, 1990.

Herlihy, David. "Did Women Have a Renaissance? A Reconsideration." *Medievalia et Humanistica*, NS 13 (1985): 1–22.

Hill, Bridget. *The Republican Virago: The Life and Times of Catharine Macaulay, Historian*. New York: Oxford University Press, 1992.

A History of Central European Women's Writing. Edited by Celia Hawkesworth. New York: Palgrave Press, 2001.

A History of Women in the West.
>   Volume 1: *From Ancient Goddesses to Christian Saints*. Edited by Pauline Schmitt Pantel. Cambridge, MA: Harvard University Press, 1992.
>   Volume 2: *Silences of the Middle Ages*. Edited by Christiane Klapisch-Zuber. Cambridge, MA: Harvard University Press, 1992.
>   Volume 3: *Renaissance and Enlightenment Paradoxes*. Edited by Natalie Zemon Davis and Arlette Farge. Cambridge, MA: Harvard University Press, 1993.

A History of Women Philosophers. Edited by Mary Ellen Waithe. 3 vols. Dordrecht: Martinus Nijhoff, 1987.

A History of Women's Writing in France. Edited by Sonya Stephens. Cambridge: Cambridge University Press, 2000.

A History of Women's Writing in Germany, Austria and Switzerland. Edited by Jo Catling. Cambridge: Cambridge University Press, 2000.

A History of Women's Writing in Italy. Edited by Letizia Panizza and Sharon Wood. Cambridge: University Press, 2000.

A History of Women's Writing in Russia. Edited by Alele Marie Barker and Jehanne M. Gheith. Cambridge: Cambridge University Press, 2002.

Hobby, Elaine. *Virtue of Necessity: English Women's Writing 1646–1688*. London: Virago Press, 1988.

Horowitz, Maryanne Cline. "Aristotle and Women." *Journal of the History of Biology* 9 (1976): 183–213.

Howell, Martha. *The Marriage Exchange: Property, Social Place, and Gender in Cities of the Low Countries, 1300–1550*. Chicago: University of Chicago Press, 1998.

Hufton, Olwen H. *The Prospect Before Her: A History of Women in Western Europe, 1: 1500–1800*. New York: HarperCollins, 1996.

Hull, Suzanne W. *Chaste, Silent, and Obedient: English Books for Women, 1475–1640.* San Marino, CA: The Huntington Library, 1982.

Hunt, Lynn, ed. *The Invention of Pornography: Obscenity and the Origins of Modernity, 1500–1800.* New York: Zone Books, 1996.

Hutner, Heidi, ed. *Rereading Aphra Behn: History, Theory, and Criticism.* Charlottesville: University Press of Virginia, 1993.

Hutson, Lorna, ed. *Feminism and Renaissance Studies.* New York: Oxford University Press, 1999.

Italian Women Writers: A Bio-Bibliographical Sourcebook. Edited by Rinaldina Russell. Westport, CT: Greenwood Press, 1994.

Jaffe, Irma B., with Gernando Colombardo. *Shining Eyes, Cruel Fortune: The Lives and Loves of Italian Renaissance Women Poets.* New York: Fordham University Press, 2002.

James, Susan E. *Kateryn Parr: The Making of a Queen.* Aldershot: Ashgate, 1999.

Jankowski, Theodora A. *Women in Power in the Early Modern Drama.* Urbana: University of Illinois Press, 1992.

Jansen, Katherine Ludwig. *The Making of the Magdalen: Preaching and Popular Devotion in the Later Middle Ages.* Princeton, NJ: Princeton University Press, 2000.

Jed, Stephanie H. *Chaste Thinking: The Rape of Lucretia and the Birth of Humanism.* Bloomington: Indiana University Press, 1989.

Jordan, Constance. *Renaissance Feminism: Literary Texts and Political Models.* Ithaca: Cornell University Press, 1990.

Kagan, Richard L. *Lucrecia's Dreams: Politics and Prophecy in Sixteenth-Century Spain.* Berkeley: University of California Press, 1990.

Kehler, Dorothea and Laurel Amtower, eds. *The Single Woman in Medieval and Early Modern England: Her Life and Representation.* Tempe, AZ: MRTS, 2002.

Kelly, Joan. "Did Women Have a Renaissance?" In her *Women, History, and Theory.* Chicago: University of Chicago Press, 1984. Also in Renate Bridenthal, Claudia Koonz, and Susan M. Stuard, eds., *Becoming Visible: Women in European History.* 3rd ed. Boston: Houghton Mifflin, 1998.

———. "Early Feminist Theory and the *Querelle des Femmes.*" In *Women, History, and Theory.*

Kelso, Ruth. *Doctrine for the Lady of the Renaissance.* Foreword by Katharine M. Rogers. Urbana: University of Illinois Press, 1956, 1978.

King, Catherine E. *Renaissance Women Patrons: Wives and Widows in Italy, c. 1300–1550.* Manchester: Manchester University Press (distributed in the U.S. by St. Martin's Press), 1998.

King, Margaret L. *Women of the Renaissance.* Foreword by Catharine R. Stimpson. Chicago: University of Chicago Press, 1991.

Krontiris, Tina. *Oppositional Voices: Women as Writers and Translators of Literature in the English Renaissance.* London: Routledge, 1992.

Kuehn, Thomas. *Law, Family, and Women: Toward a Legal Anthropology of Renaissance Italy.* Chicago: University of Chicago Press, 1991.

Kunze, Bonnelyn Young. *Margaret Fell and the Rise of Quakerism.* Stanford: Stanford University Press, 1994.

Labalme, Patricia A., ed. *Beyond Their Sex: Learned Women of the European Past.* New York: New York University Press, 1980.

Laqueur, Thomas. *Making Sex: Body and Gender from the Greeks to Freud.* Cambridge, MA: Harvard University Press, 1990.

Larsen, Anne R. and Colette H. Winn, eds. *Renaissance Women Writers: French Texts/American Contexts.* Detroit, MI: Wayne State University Press, 1994.

Lerner, Gerda. *The Creation of Patriarchy* and *Creation of Feminist Consciousness, 1000–1870.* 2 vols. New York: Oxford University Press, 1986, 1994.

Levin, Carole, and Jeanie Watson, eds. *Ambiguous Realities: Women in the Middle Ages and Renaissance.* Detroit: Wayne State University Press, 1987.

Levin, Carole, et al. *Extraordinary Women of the Medieval and Renaissance World: A Biographical Dictionary.* Westport, CT: Greenwood Press, 2000.

Lewalsky, Barbara Kiefer. *Writing Women in Jacobean England.* Cambridge, MA: Harvard University Press, 1993.

Lewis, Jayne Elizabeth. *Mary Queen of Scots: Romance and Nation.* London: Routledge, 1998.

Lindsey, Karen. *Divorced Beheaded Survived: A Feminist Reinterpretation of the Wives of Henry VIII.* Reading, MA: Addison-Wesley, 1995.

Lochrie, Karma. *Margery Kempe and Translations of the Flesh.* Philadelphia: University of Pennsylvania Press, 1992.

Lougee, Carolyn C. *Le Paradis des Femmes: Women, Salons, and Social Stratification in Seventeenth-Century France.* Princeton, NJ: Princeton University Press, 1976.

Love, Harold. *The Culture and Commerce of Texts: Scribal Publication in Seventeenth-Century England.* Amherst: University of Massachusetts Press, 1993.

MacCarthy, Bridget G. *The Female Pen: Women Writers and Novelists, 1621–1818.* Preface by Janet Todd. New York: New York University Press, 1994. Originally published 1946–47 by Cork University Press.

Maclean, Ian. *Woman Triumphant: Feminism in French Literature, 1610–1652.* Oxford: Clarendon Press, 1977.

———. *The Renaissance Notion of Woman: A Study of the Fortunes of Scholasticism and Medical Science in European Intellectual Life.* Cambridge: Cambridge University Press, 1980.

MacNeil, Anne. *Music and Women of the Commedia dell'Arte in the Late Sixteenth Century.* New York: Oxford University Press, 2003.

Maggi, Armando. *Uttering the Word: The Mystical Performances of Maria Maddalena de' Pazzi, a Renaissance Visionary.* Albany: State University of New York Press, 1998.

Marshall, Sherrin. *Women in Reformation and Counter-Reformation Europe: Public and Private Worlds.* Bloomington: Indiana University Press, 1989.

Masten, Jeffrey. *Textual Intercourse: Collaboration, Authorship, and Sexualities in Renaissance Drama.* Cambridge: Cambridge University Press, 1997.

Matter, E. Ann, and John Coakley, eds. *Creative Women in Medieval and Early Modern Italy.* Philadelphia: University of Pennsylvania Press, 1994. (Sequel to the Monson collection, below.)

McLeod, Glenda. *Virtue and Venom: Catalogs of Women from Antiquity to the Renaissance.* Ann Arbor: University of Michigan Press, 1991.

Medwick, Cathleen. *Teresa of Avila: The Progress of a Soul.* New York: Knopf, 2000.

Meek, Christine, ed. *Women in Renaissance and Early Modern Europe.* Dublin-Portland: Four Courts Press, 2000.

Mendelson, Sara and Patricia Crawford. *Women in Early Modern England, 1550–1720.* Oxford: Clarendon Press, 1998.

Merchant, Carolyn. *The Death of Nature: Women, Ecology, and the Scientific Revolution.* New York: HarperCollins, 1980.

Merrim, Stephanie. *Early Modern Women's Writing and Sor Juana Inés de la Cruz.* Nashville, TN: Vanderbilt University Press, 1999.

Messbarger, Rebecca. *The Century of Women: The Representations of Women in Eighteenth-Century Italian Public Discourse.* Toronto: University of Toronto Press, 2002.

Miller, Nancy K. *The Heroine's Text: Readings in the French and English Novel, 1722–1782.* New York: Columbia University Press, 1980.

Miller, Naomi J. *Changing the Subject: Mary Wroth and Figurations of Gender in Early Modern England.* Lexington: University Press of Kentucky, 1996.

Miller, Naomi J., and Gary Waller, eds. *Reading Mary Wroth: Representing Alternatives in Early Modern England.* Knoxville: University of Tennessee Press, 1991.

Monson, Craig A., ed. *The Crannied Wall: Women, Religion, and the Arts in Early Modern Europe.* Ann Arbor: University of Michigan Press, 1992.

Musacchio, Jacqueline Marie. *The Art and Ritual of Childbirth in Renaissance Italy.* New Haven, CT: Yale University Press, 1999.

Newman, Barbara. *God and the Goddesses: Vision, Poetry, and Belief in the Middle Ages.* Philadelphia: University of Pennsylvania Press, 2003.

Newman, Karen. *Fashioning Femininity and English Renaissance Drama.* Chicago: University of Chicago Press, 1991.

Okin, Susan Moller. *Women in Western Political Thought.* Princeton, NJ: Princeton University Press, 1979.

Ozment, Steven. *The Bürgermeister's Daughter: Scandal in a Sixteenth-Century German Town.* New York: St. Martin's Press, 1995.

Pacheco, Anita, ed. *Early [English] Women Writers: 1600–1720.* New York: Longman, 1998.

Pagels, Elaine. *Adam, Eve, and the Serpent.* New York: HarperCollins, 1988.

Panizza, Letizia, ed. *Women in Italian Renaissance Culture and Society.* Oxford: European Humanities Research Centre, 2000.

Parker, Patricia. *Literary Fat Ladies: Rhetoric, Gender, and Property.* London: Methuen, 1987.

Pernoud, Regine, and Marie-Veronique Clin. *Joan of Arc: Her Story.* Revised and translated by Jeremy DuQuesnay Adams. New York: St. Martin's Press, 1998 (French original, 1986).

Perry, Mary Elizabeth. *Crime and Society in Early Modern Seville.* Hanover, NH: University Press of New England, 1980.

———. *Gender and Disorder in Early Modern Seville.* Princeton, NJ: Princeton University Press, 1990.

Perry, Ruth. *The Celebrated Mary Astell: An Early English Feminist.* Chicago: University of Chicago Press, 1986.

Petroff, Elizabeth Alvilda, ed. *Medieval Women's Visionary Literature.* New York: Oxford University Press, 1986.

Rabil, Albert. *Laura Cereta: Quattrocento Humanist.* Binghamton, NY: MRTS, 1981.

Ranft, Patricia. *Women in Western Intellectual Culture, 600–1500.* New York: Palgrave, 2002.

Rapley, Elizabeth. *A Social History of the Cloister: Daily Life in the Teaching Monasteries of the Old Regime*. Montreal: McGill-Queen's University Press, 2001.

Raven, James, Helen Small, and Naomi Tadmor, eds. *The Practice and Representation of Reading in England*. Cambridge: University Press, 1996.

Reardon, Colleen. *Holy Concord within Sacred Walls: Nuns and Music in Siena, 1575–1700*. Oxford: Oxford University Press, 2001.

Reiss, Sheryl E., and David G. Wilkins, ed. *Beyond Isabella: Secular Women Patrons of Art in Renaissance Italy*. Kirksville, MO: Truman State University Press, 2001.

Rheubottom, David. *Age, Marriage, and Politics in Fifteenth-Century Ragusa*. Oxford: Oxford University Press, 2000.

Richardson, Brian. *Printing, Writers and Readers in Renaissance Italy*. Cambridge: University Press, 1999.

Riddle, John M. *Contraception and Abortion from the Ancient World to the Renaissance*. Cambridge, MA: Harvard University Press, 1992.

———. *Eve's Herbs: A History of Contraception and Abortion in the West*. Cambridge, MA: Harvard University Press, 1997.

Rose, Mary Beth. *The Expense of Spirit: Love and Sexuality in English Renaissance Drama*. Ithaca, NY: Cornell University Press, 1988.

———. *Gender and Heroism in Early Modern English Literature*. Chicago: University of Chicago Press, 2002.

———, ed. *Women in the Middle Ages and the Renaissance: Literary and Historical Perspectives*. Syracuse: Syracuse University Press, 1986.

Rosenthal, Margaret F. *The Honest Courtesan: Veronica Franco, Citizen and Writer in Sixteenth-Century Venice*. Foreword by Catharine R. Stimpson. Chicago: University of Chicago Press, 1992.

Sackville-West, Vita. *Daughter of France: The Life of La Grande Mademoiselle*. Garden City, NY: Doubleday, 1959.

Sánchez, Magdalena S. *The Empress, the Queen, and the Nun: Women and Power at the Court of Philip III of Spain*. Baltimore: Johns Hopkins University Press, 1998.

Schiebinger, Londa. *The Mind Has No Sex? Women in the Origins of Modern Science*. Cambridge, MA: Harvard University Press, 1991.

———. *Nature's Body: Gender in the Making of Modern Science*. Boston: Beacon Press, 1993.

Schutte, Anne Jacobson, Thomas Kuehn, and Silvana Seidel Menchi, eds. *Time, Space, and Women's Lives in Early Modern Europe*. Kirksville, MO: Truman State University Press, 2001.

Schofield, Mary Anne, and Cecilia Macheski, eds. *Fetter'd or Free? British Women Novelists, 1670–1815*. Athens: Ohio University Press, 1986.

Shannon, Laurie. *Sovereign Amity: Figures of Friendship in Shakespearean Contexts*. Chicago: University of Chicago Press, 2002.

Shemek, Deanna. *Ladies Errant: Wayward Women and Social Order in Early Modern Italy*. Durham, NC: Duke University Press, 1998.

Smith, Hilda L. *Reason's Disciples: Seventeenth-Century English Feminists*. Urbana: University of Illinois Press, 1982.

———. *Women Writers and the Early Modern British Political Tradition*. Cambridge: Cambridge University Press, 1998.

Sobel, Dava. *Galileo's Daughter: A Historical Memoir of Science, Faith, and Love*. New York: Penguin, 2000.

Sommerville, Margaret R. *Sex and Subjection: Attitudes to Women in Early-Modern Society*. London: Arnold, 1995.

Soufas, Teresa Scott. *Dramas of Distinction: A Study of Plays by Golden Age Women*. Lexington: The University Press of Kentucky, 1997.

Spencer, Jane. *The Rise of the Woman Novelist: From Aphra Behn to Jane Austen*. Oxford: Basil Blackwell, 1986.

Spender, Dale. *Mothers of the Novel: 100 Good Women Writers Before Jane Austen*. London: Routledge, 1986.

Sperling, Jutta Gisela. *Convents and the Body Politic in Late Renaissance Venice*. Foreword by Catharine R. Stimpson. Chicago: University of Chicago Press, 1999.

Steinbrügge, Lieselotte. *The Moral Sex: Woman's Nature in the French Enlightenment*. Translated by Pamela E. Selwyn. New York: Oxford University Press, 1995.

Stocker, Margarita. *Judith, Sexual Warrior: Women and Power in Western Culture*. New Haven, CT: Yale University Press, 1998.

Stretton, Timothy. *Women Waging Law in Elizabethan England*. Cambridge: Cambridge University Press, 1998.

Stuard, Susan M. "The Dominion of Gender: Women's Fortunes in the High Middle Ages." In *Becoming Visible: Women in European History*, edited by Renate Bridenthal, Claudia Koonz, and Susan M. Stuard. 3rd ed. Boston: Houghton Mifflin, 1998.

Summit, Jennifer. *Lost Property: The Woman Writer and English Literary History, 1380–1589*. Chicago: University of Chicago Press, 2000.

Surtz, Ronald E. *The Guitar of God: Gender, Power, and Authority in the Visionary World of Mother Juana de la Cruz (1481–1534)*. Philadelphia: University of Pennsylvania Press, 1991.

———. *Writing Women in Late Medieval and Early Modern Spain: The Mothers of Saint Teresa of Avila*. Philadelphia: University of Pennsylvania Press, 1995.

Teague, Frances. *Bathsua Makin, Woman of Learning*. Lewisburg, PA: Bucknell University Press, 1999.

Tinagli, Paola. *Women in Italian Renaissance Art: Gender, Representation, Identity*. Manchester: Manchester University Press, 1997.

Todd, Janet. *The Secret Life of Aphra Behn*. London: Pandora, 2000.

———. *The Sign of Angelica: Women, Writing and Fiction, 1660–1800*. New York: Columbia University Press, 1989.

Valenze, Deborah. *The First Industrial Woman*. New York: Oxford University Press, 1995.

Van Dijk, Susan, Lia van Gemert, and Sheila Ottway, eds. *Writing the History of Women's Writing: Toward an International Approach*. Proceedings of the Colloquium, Amsterdam, 9–11 September. Amsterdam: Royal Netherlands Academy of Arts and Sciences, 2001.

Vickery, Amanda. *The Gentleman's Daughter: Women's Lives in Georgian England*. New Haven, CT: Yale University Press, 1998.

Vollendorf, Lisa, ed. *Recovering Spain's Feminist Tradition*. New York: MLA, 2001.

Walker, Claire. *Gender and Politics in Early Modern Europe: English Convents in France and the Low Countries*. New York: Palgrave, 2003.

Wall, Wendy. *The Imprint of Gender: Authorship and Publication in the English Renaissance.* Ithaca, NY: Cornell University Press, 1993.

Walsh, William T. *St. Teresa of Avila: A Biography.* Rockford, IL: TAN, 1987.

Warner, Marina. *Alone of All Her Sex: The Myth and Cult of the Virgin Mary.* New York: Knopf, 1976.

Warnicke, Retha M. *The Marrying of Anne of Cleves: Royal Protocol in Tudor England.* Cambridge: Cambridge University Press, 2000.

Watt, Diane. *Secretaries of God: Women Prophets in Late Medieval and Early Modern England.* Cambridge: D. S. Brewer, 1997.

Weber, Alison. *Teresa of Avila and the Rhetoric of Femininity.* Princeton, NJ: Princeton University Press, 1990.

Welles, Marcia L. *Persephone's Girdle: Narratives of Rape in Seventeenth-Century Spanish Literature.* Nashville: Vanderbilt University Press, 2000.

Whitehead, Barbara J., ed. *Women's Education in Early Modern Europe: A History, 1500–1800.* New York: Garland, 1999.

Wiesner, Merry E. *Women and Gender in Early Modern Europe.* Cambridge: Cambridge University Press, 1993.

———. *Working Women in Renaissance Germany.* New Brunswick, NJ: Rutgers University Press, 1986.

Willard, Charity Cannon. *Christine de Pizan: Her Life and Works.* New York: Persea Books, 1984.

Winn, Colette and Donna Kuizenga, eds. *Women Writers in Pre-Revolutionary France.* New York: Garland, 1997.

Woodbridge, Linda. *Women and the English Renaissance: Literature and the Nature of Womankind, 1540–1620.* Urbana: University of Illinois Press, 1984.

Woods, Susanne. *Lanyer: A Renaissance Woman Poet.* New York: Oxford University Press, 1999.

Woods, Susanne, and Margaret P. Hannay, eds. *Teaching Tudor and Stuart Women Writers.* New York: MLA, 2000.

INDEX